HISTORY OF THE JEWS

HISTORY OF THE JEWS

BY
HEINRICH GRAETZ

VOL. V

From the Chmielnicki Persecution of the Jews in
Poland (1648 C. E.) to the Period of Emancipation in Central Europe (c. 1870 C. E.)

PHILADELPHIA
The Jewish Publication Society of America
5717–1956

CONTENTS.

CHAPTER I.

CHMIELNICKI AND THE PERSECUTION OF THE JEWS OF POLAND BY THE COSSACKS.

CHAPTER II.

SETTLEMENT OF THE JEWS IN ENGLAND AND MANASSEH BEN ISRAEL.

CHAPTER VI.

GENERAL DEMORALIZATION OF JUDAISM.

CHAPTER VII.

THE AGE OF LUZZATTO, EIBESCHÜTZ, AND FRANK.

CHAPTER VIII.

THE MENDELSSOHN EPOCH.

CHAPTER IX.

THE NEW CHASSIDISM.

CHAPTER X.

THE MEASFIM AND THE JUDÆO-CHRISTIAN SALON.

CHAPTER XI.

THE FRENCH REVOLUTION AND THE EMANCIPATION OF THE JEWS.

CHAPTER XII.

THE JEWISH-FRENCH SYNHEDRION AND THE JEWISH CONSISTORIES.

CHAPTER XIII.

THE REACTION AND TEUTOMANIA.

CHAPTER XIV.

BÖRNE AND HEINE.

CHAPTER XV.

REFORM AND YOUNG ISRAEL.

CHAPTER XVI.

AWAKENING OF INDEPENDENCE AND THE SCIENCE OF JUDAISM.

CHAPTER XVII.

THE YEAR 1840 AND THE BLOOD ACCUSATION AT DAMASCUS.

CHAPTER XVIII.

EVENTS PRECEDING THE REVOLUTIONS OF FEBRUARY AND MARCH, 1848, AND THE SUBSEQUENT SOCIAL ADVANCE OF THE JEWS.

HISTORY OF THE JEWS

HISTORY OF THE JEWS.

CHAPTER I.

CHMIELNICKI AND THE PERSECUTION OF THE JEWS OF POLAND BY THE COSSACKS.

Condition of the Jews in Poland before the Outbreak of Persecution— Influence of the Jesuits—Characteristics of Poles and Jews—The Home of the Cossacks—Repression of the Cossacks by the Government—Jews appointed as Tax Farmers—Jurisdiction of the Synods—The Study of the Talmud in Poland—Hebrew Literature in that Country becomes entirely Rabbinical—Character of Polish Judaism—Jews and Cossacks—Chmielnicki—Sufferings of the Jews in consequence of his Successes—The Tartar Haidamaks—Fearful Massacres in Nemirov, Tulczyn, and Homel—Prince Vishnioviecki—Massacres at Polonnoie, Lemberg, Narol, and in other Towns—John Casimir—Lipmann Heller and Sabbataï Cohen—Renewal of the War between Cossacks and Poles—Russians join Cossacks in attacking the Jews— Charles X of Sweden—The Polish Fugitives—"Polonization" of Judaism.

1648—1656 C. E.

POLAND ceased to be a haven for the sons of Judah, when its short-sighted kings summoned the Jesuits to supervise the training of the young nobles and the clergy and crush the spirit of the Polish dissidents. These originators of disunion, to whom the frequent partition of Poland must be attributed, sought to undermine the unobtrusive power which the Jews, through their money and prudence, exercised over the nobles, and they combined with their other foes, German workmen and tradespeople, members of the guilds, to restrict and oppress them. After that time there were repeated persecutions of Jews in Poland; sometimes the German guild members, sometimes the disciples of the Jesuits, raised a hue and cry against them. Still, in the calamities of the Thirty Years' War, fugitive Jews sought Poland, because the canonical laws against Jews were not applied there with strictness. The high nobility continued to be dependent on Jews, who in a measure counterbalanced the national defects. Polish flightiness, levity, unsteadiness, extravagance, and recklessness were compensated for by Jewish prudence, sagacity, economy, and cautiousness. The Jew was more than a financier to the Polish nobleman ; he was his help in embarrassment, his prudent adviser, his all-in-all. Especially did the nobility make use of Jews in developing recently established colonies, for which they had neither the necessary perseverance nor the ability. Colonies had gradually been formed on the lower Dnieper and the northern shore of the Black Sea, by runaway Polish serfs, criminals, adventurers from every province, peasants, and nobles, who felt themselves cramped and endangered in their homes. These outcasts formed the root of the Cossack race at the waterfalls of the Dnieper (Za-Porogi), whence the Cossacks obtained the name of Zaporogians. To maintain themselves, they took to plundering the neighboring Tartars. They became inured to war, and with every success their courage and independent spirit increased.

The kings, who needed the Cossacks in military undertakings and to ward off the inroads of Tartars and Turks, granted them some independence in the Ukraine and Little Russia, and appointed a chieftain over them from their own midst, an Attaman, or Hetman, with special marks of dignity. But the bigoted temper of King Sigismund III and the Jesuits made the Cossacks, who might have become an element of strength for Poland, the source of endless discontent and rebellion. The Zaporogians for the most part were adherents of the Greek Church, the Greek Catholic confession being predominant in southern Poland. After the popes by means of the Jesuits had weakened and oppressed the Polish dissidents, they labored to unite the Greek Catholics with the Romish Church or to extirpate them. With the warlike spirit of the Cossacks this change was not easy; hence a regular system of enslavement was employed against them. Three noble houses, the Koniecpolski, Vishnioviecki, and Potocki, had control of colonization in the Ukraine and Little Russia, and they transferred to their Jewish business agents the farming of the oppressive imposts falling on the Cossacks. Thus Jewish communities gradually spread in the Ukraine, Little Russia, and even beyond these provinces. The Cossacks, for instance, had to pay a tax at the birth of a child and on every marriage. That there might be no evasion, the Jewish revenue farmers had the keys of the Greek churches, and when the clergyman wished to perform a baptism or a marriage, he was obliged to ask them for the key. In general, the position of the Jews in districts where none but Poles dwelt was better than in those which besides Polish inhabitants contained a German population, as was the case in the large cities, Posen, Cracow, Lublin, and Lemberg.

By reason of their great number, their importance, and their compact union, the Jews in Poland formed a state within a state. The general synod, which assembled twice a year at Lublin and Jaroslaw, formed a legislative and judicial parliament from which there was no appeal. At first called the Synod of the Three Countries, it became in the first quarter of the seventeenth century the Synod of the Four Countries (Vaad Arba Arazoth). An elective president (Parnes di Arba Arazoth) was at the head, and conducted public affairs. The communities and rabbis had civil, and, to a certain extent, criminal, jurisdiction, at least against informers and traitors. Hence no Jew ventured to bring an accusation against one of his race before the authorities of the country, fearing to expose himself to disgrace and contempt from public opinion, which would have embittered his life, or even entailed death. Almost every community had its college of judges, a rabbi with two assessors, before whom every complaint was brought, but the final decision rested with the synod. The synod also concerned itself about honesty in dealing and conduct, and in weight and measure, wherever Jews were affected.

The study of the Talmud in Poland, established by Shachna, Solomon Lurya, and Moses Isserles, reached a pitch attained at no previous time, nor in any other country. The demand for copies of the Talmud was so great that in less than twenty years three editions had to be printed, no doubt in thousands of copies. The study of the Talmud was a greater necessity in Poland than in the rest of Europe. The rabbis, as has been already said, had jurisdiction of their own, and decided according to Talmudical and Rabbinical laws. The great number of Jews in Poland, and their fondness for litigation, gave occasion to intricate law cases. The rabbi-judges were obliged to go back to the source of law, the Talmud, to seek points of support for such cases. The contending parties being themselves well informed and acute, the reasoning of the rabbis had to be flawless to escape criticism. Hence Rabbinical civil law in Poland met with extraordinary cultivation and extension, to adapt it to all cases and make it available for the learned litigants. Thus the ever-growing subtlety of the method of Talmud study depended on current conditions and wants, and on the circumstance that each Talmudist wished to surpass all others in ingenuity.

It would be tedious to enumerate the Rabbinical authors of Poland in the first half of the seventeenth century. The cultivation of a single faculty, that of hair-splitting judgment, at the cost of the rest, narrowed the imagination, hence not a single literary product appeared in Poland deserving the name of poetry. All the productions of the Polish school bore the Talmudical stamp, as the school regarded everything from the Talmudical point of view. The disciples of this school looked down almost with contempt on Scripture and its simple grandeur, or rather it did not exist for them. How, indeed, could they have found time to occupy themselves with it? And what could they do with these children's stories, which did not admit the application of intellectual subtlety? They knew something of the Bible from the extracts read in the synagogues, and those occasionally quoted in the Talmud. The faculty for appreciating the sublimity of biblical doctrines and characters, as well as simplicity and elevation in general, was denied them. A love of twisting, distorting, ingenious quibbling, and a foregone antipathy to what did not lie within their field of vision, constituted the character of the Polish Jews. Pride in their knowledge of the Talmud and a spirit of dogmatism attached even to the best rabbis, and undermined their moral sense. The Polish Jews of course were extraordinarily pious, but even their piety rested on sophistry and boastfulness. Each wished to surpass the other in knowledge of what the Code prescribed for one case or another. Thus religion sank, not merely, as among Jews of other countries, to a mechanical, unintelligent ceremonial, but to a subtle art of interpretation. To know better was everything to them; but to act according to acknowledged principles of religious purity, and exemplify them in a moral life, occurred to but few. Integrity and right-mindedness they had lost as completely as simplicity and the sense of truth. The vulgar acquired the quibbling method of the schools, and employed it to outwit the less cunning. They found pleasure and a sort of triumphant delight in deception and cheating. Against members of their own race cunning could not well be employed, because they were sharp-witted ; but the non-Jewish world with which they came into contact experienced to its disadvantage the superiority of the Talmudical spirit of the Polish Jews. The Polish sons of the Talmud paid little attention to the fact, that the Talmud and the great teachers of Judaism object even more strongly to taking advantage of members of a different faith than of those of their own race.

The corruption of the Polish Jews was avenged upon them in a terrible way, and the result was, that the rest of the Jews in Europe were for a time infected with it. With fatal blindness Polish Jews offered the nobility and the Jesuits a helping hand in oppressing the Zaporogian Cossacks in the Ukraine and Little Russia. The magnates wished to make profitable serfs of the Cossacks, the Jesuits hoped to convert the Greek heretics into Roman Catholics, the Jews settled in the district expected to enrich themselves and play the lord over these pariahs. They advised the possessors of the Cossack colonies how most completely to humiliate, oppress, torment, and ill-use them ; they usurped the office of judges over them, and vexed them in their ecclesiastical affairs. No wonder that the enslaved Cossacks hated the Jews, with whom their relations were closest, almost more than their noble and clerical foes. The Jews were not without warning what would be their lot, if these embittered enemies once got the upper hand. In an insurrection of the Zaporogians under their Hetman in about 1638, despite its brief duration, they slew 200 Jews, and destroyed several synagogues. Nevertheless, Jews lent a hand, when in consequence of the insurrection the further enslavement of the sufferers was determined upon. In the year 1648, fixed by that lying book, the Zohar, they expected the coming of

the Messiah and the time of redemption, when they
would be in power, and, therefore, they were more
reckless and careless than was their custom at other
times.   Bloody retribution was not long delayed,
and struck the innocent with the guilty, perhaps the
former more severely than the latter.

It proceeded from a man who understood how to
make use of the increasing hatred of the Cossacks
for his purposes, and who was regarded by his
countrymen as their ideal. Bogdan Chmielnicki
(Russian Chmel), born about 1595, died 1657, before whom all Poland trembled for several years,
gave Russia the first opportunity of interfering in
the Polish republic, and was a frightful scourge for
the Jews. Chmielnicki, brave in war and artful in
the execution of his plans, impenetrable in his
schemes, at once cruel and hypocritical, had been
vexed by Jews, when he held the subordinate position of camp secretary (Pisar) of the Cossacks subject to the house of Koniecpolski. A Jew, Zachariah Sabilenki, had played him a trick, by which he
was robbed of his wife and property. Another had
betrayed him when he had come to an understanding with the Tartars. Besides injuries which his
race had sustained from Jewish tax farmers in the
Ukraine, he, therefore, had personal wrongs to
avenge. His remark to the Cossacks, "The Poles
have delivered us as slaves to the cursed breed
of Jews," was enough to excite them. Vengeance-
breathing Zaporogians and booty-loving Tartars
in a short time put the Polish troops to flight
by successful manœuvres (May 18, 1648). Potocki,
the lieutenant-general, and 8,000 Poles, according
to agreement, were delivered to the Tartars. After
the victory the wild troops went eastward from the
Dnieper, between Kiev and Pultava, plundering
and murdering, especially the Jews who had not
taken flight ; the number of the murdered reached
several thousand. Hundreds underwent baptism

in the Greek Church, and pretended to be Christians, in order to save themselves. Fortunate were those who fell into captivity with the Tartars; they were transported to the Crimea, and ransomed by Turkish Jews. Four Jewish communities (Porobischa and others) of about 3,000 souls resolved to escape massacre by surrendering to the Tartars with all their property. They were well treated, and sold into Turkey, where they were ransomed in a brotherly manner by those of their own race. The Constantinople community sent a deputy to Holland to collect money from the rich communities for the ransom of captives.

Unfortunately for the Poles and Jews, King Vladislav, for whom Chmielnicki had shown some respect, was removed by death. During the interregnum of several months, from May to October, 1648, the usual Polish dissension occurred, which crippled every attempt at resistance. At first Chmielnicki drew back, apparently inclined to negotiate with the crown, but he gave his creatures full power to ravage the Polish provinces. R gular troops of murderers, called Haidamaks (the Tartar word for partisans), were formed under brutal leaders who cared not a straw for human life, and who reveled in the death-struggles of their Polish and Jewish foes. In the name of religion they were urged by the Greek popes to murder Catholics and Jews. The commander of each troop had his own method of exercising cruelty. One had thongs slung round the necks of Catholic and Jewish women, by which they were dragged along; this he called "presenting them with a red ribbon." A few weeks after the first victory of the Cossacks, a troop under another of these chiefs advanced against the stronghold of Nemirov, where 6,000 Jews, inhabitants and fugitives from the neighborhood, had assembled; they were in possession of the fortress, and closed the gates. But the Cossacks had an understanding with the Greek Christians in the town, and put on Polish uniforms in order to be taken for Poles. The Christian inhabitants urged the Jews to open the gates for their friends. They did so, and were suddenly attacked by the Cossacks and the inhabitants of the town, and almost entirely cut down amid frightful tortures (Siwan 20—June 10, 1648).

Another Haidamak troop under Kryvonoss attacked the town of Tulczyn, where about 600 Christians and 2,000 Jews had taken refuge in the fortress. There were brave Jews among them, or necessity had made them brave, and they would not die without resistance. Nobles and Jews swore to defend the town and fortress to the last man. As the Cossack peasants understood nothing of the art of siege, and had repeatedly suffered severely from the sorties of Jews and Poles, they resorted to a trick. They assured the nobles that their rage was directed only against the Jews, their deadly foes; if these were delivered up, they would withdraw. The infatuated nobles, forgetful of their oath, proposed that the Jews should deliver up their arms to them. The Jews at first thought of turning on the Poles for their treachery, as they exceeded them in numbers. But the rabbi of Tulczyn warned them against attacking the Poles, who would inflict bloody vengeance, and all Poland would be excited against the Jews, who would be exterminated. He implored them to sacrifice themselves for their brethren in the whole country; perhaps the Cossacks would accept their property as ransom. The Jews consented, and delivered up their arms, the Poles thereupon admitting the troops into the town. After the latter had taken everything from the Jews, they set before them the choice of death or baptism. Not one of them would purchase life at that price; about 1,500 were tortured and executed before the eyes of the Polish nobles (Tamuz 4—June 24). The

Cossacks left ten rabbis alive, in order to extort large sums from the communities. The Poles were immediately punished for their treachery. Deprived of the assistance of the Jews, they were attacked by the Cossacks and slain, proving that violators of their word cannot reckon on fidelity towards themselves. This sad event had the good effect that the Poles always sided with the Jews, and were not opposed to them in the course of the long war.

At the same time another Haidamak troop, under a leader named Hodki, had penetrated into Little Russia, and caused dreadful slaughter in the communities of Homel, Starodub, Czernigov, and other places east and north of Kiev. The Jews of Homel are said to have suffered martyrdom most firmly, on the same day on which the Tulczyn community was annihilated. The leader of the troop had all the Jews of Homel, inhabitants as well as fugitives, stripped outside the town, and surrounded by Cossacks, and called upon them to be baptized or to expect a most frightful death. They all, men, women, and children, to the number of about 1,500, preferred death.

Prince Vishnioviecki, the only heroic figure amongst the Poles at that time, a man of penetration, intrepid courage, and strategic ability, defended the cause of the persecuted Jews with devoted zeal. He took the fugitives under the protecting wings of his small, but brave force, with which he everywhere pursued the Cossack bands to destruction. But, because of his limited power, he could accomplish nothing of lasting import. Through petty jealousy, he was passed over at the election of the commander-in-chief against the Cossack insurrection, and instead of him three were chosen, of a character calculated to help on Chmielnicki to further victories.

Annoyed at the pitiful policy of the regent, the primate of Gnesen, Vishnioviecki followed his own course, but was compelled to retreat before the overpowering number of the roving troops and the Greek Catholic population in sympathy with them, and so destruction was brought on the Jews, who had reckoned on his heroic courage. In the fortress of Polonnoie, between Zaslav and Zytomir, 10,000 Jews, partly inhabitants, partly fugitives from the neighborhood, are said to have perished at the hand of the besieging Haidamaks and the traitorous inhabitants (Ab 13—July 22).

The unfortunate issue of the second war between Poles and Cossacks (September, 1648), when the Polish army, more through dread of the Tartars under Tugaï Bey and the incapacity of its generals, than through Chmielnicki's bravery, was scattered in wild flight, and collected only behind the walls of Lemberg, prepared a bloody fate even for Jews who thought themselves safe at a distance from the field of battle. There was no escape from the wild assaults of the Zaporogians, unless they could reach the Wallachian borders. The blood of slaughtered and maltreated Jews marked the vast tract from the southern part of the Ukraine to Lemberg by way of Dubno and Brody; in the town of Bar alone from two to three thousand perished. It scarcely need be said that the brutal cruelty of the regular Cossacks, as well as of the wild Haidamaks, made no distinction between Rabbanites and Karaites. The important community of Lemberg lost many of its members through hunger and pestilence, and its property besides, which it had to pay to the Cossacks as ransom.

In the town of Narol the Zaporogians caused a revolting butchery. It is said that in the beginning of November 45,000 persons, among them 12,000 Jews, were slain there with the cruellest tortures. Among the corpses remained living women and children, who for several days had to feed on human flesh. Meanwhile the Haidamaks roamed about in Volhynia, Podolia, and West Russia, and slaked their revenge in the blood of nobles, Catholics, clergy, and Jews, to thousands and tens of thousands. In Crzemieniec an inhuman monster slew hundreds of Jewish children, scornfully examined the corpses as Jews do with cattle, and threw them to the dogs. In many towns Jews, as well as Catholics, armed themselves, and drove the bloodthirsty Cossacks away.

The election of a king, which finally was effected— and, though the Polish state was on the brink of an abyss, it took place amidst fights and commotions— put an end to bloodshed for the moment. Although for the most part in a drunken condition, Chmielnicki retained sobriety enough to dictate, among his conditions of peace, that no Catholic church should be tolerated, nor any Jew live, in the Cossack provinces. The commission, unable to accept the conditions, departed without settling the business (February 16, 1649). The Jews, who had reckoned upon a settlement, and returned to their home, paid for their confidence with death, for the Cossacks surrounded the towns with death-cries. Thus, a second time, many Jews and nobles perished at Ostrog (March 4, 1649).

The breaking off of the negotiation with Chmielnicki led to a third encounter. Although the Polish army this time appeared better armed on the field of battle, it had as little success as before. In the battle at Sbaráz it would have been completely destroyed by the Zaporogians and Tartars, if the king had not wisely come to an understanding with the Tartar chief. Thereupon followed the peace (August, 1649), which confirmed Chmielnicki's programme, among other points that concerning the Jews. In the chief seats of the Cossacks (*i. e.*, in the Ukraine, West Russia, in the district of Kiev, and a part of Podolia) they could neither own or rent landed estates, nor live there.

In consequence of this convention, the Poles and

Jews were unmolested for about a year and a half, although on both sides schemes were harbored to break the agreement at the first opportunity. As far as residence was allowed them, the fugitive Jews returned to their homes. King John Casimir allowed the Jews baptized according to the Greek confession openly to profess Judaism. In consequence, the baptized Jews fled from the Catholic districts to Poland to be free from compulsory Christianity. This permission was especially used by Jewish women whom the rude Zaporogians had married. The Jews brought back into Judaism many hundreds of children, who had lost their parents and relatives, and had been brought up in Christianity, investigated their descent, and hung the indication of it in a small roll round their necks, that they might not marry blood relations of forbidden degrees. The general synod of rabbis and leaders which assembled at Lublin in 1650 occupied itself entirely with the attempt to heal, at least partially, the wounds of Judaism. Many hundreds, even thousands, of Jewish women did not know whether their husbands lay in the grave, or were begging in the East or West, in Turkey or Germany, whether they were widows or wives, or they found themselves in other perplexities created by the Rabbinical law. The synod of Lublin is said to have hit upon excellent arrangements. Most probably the lenient Lipmann Heller, then rabbi of Cracow, strove to effect a mild interpretation of the law relating to supposed death. At the instigation of the young, genial rabbi Sabbataï Cohen (Shach), the day of the first massacre at Nemirov (Siwan 20) was appointed as a general fast day for the remnant of the Polish community. The hoary Lipmann Heller, at Cracow, Sabbataï Hurwitz, at Posen, and the young Sabbataï Cohen drew up penitential prayers (Selichoth), mostly selected from older pieces, for this sad memorial day.

After a pause of a year and a half, the war between Cossacks and Poles broke out in the early part of the year 1651, the first victims again being Jews, as Chmielnicki and the wild Zaporogians now fell upon the Polish territory where Jewish communities had again settled. The massacre, however, could not be so extensive as before; there no longer were thousands of Jews to slaughter. Moreover the evil days had inspired the Jews with courage; they armed a troop of Jewish soldiers, and enlisted them in the king's service. The fortune of war turned against the Cossacks, and they were obliged to accept the peace dictated by the king (November 11, 1651). John Casimir and his ministers did not forget to guard the rights of the Jews in the treaty. They were to be permitted to settle anywhere in the Ukraine, and to hold property on lease.

This treaty also was concluded and ratified only to be broken. Chmielnicki had accepted it to strengthen himself and restore his reputation with the Cossacks. As soon as he had gained his first object, he began hostilities against the Poles, from which Jews always suffered most severely. In two years after the first insurrection of the Zaporogians, more than 300 communities were completely destroyed by death or flight, and the end of their suffering had not yet arrived. The Polish troops could not withstand the violent attacks or skillful policy of Chmielnicki. When he could no longer hope for help from the Tartars, he combined with the Russians, and incited them to a war against unhappy Poland, divided against itself. In consequence of the Russian war in the early part of 1654 and 1655, those communities suffered which had been spared by the Cossack swarms, *i. e.*, the western districts and Lithuania. The community of Wilna, one of the largest, was completely depopulated (July, 1655) by slaughter on the part of the Russians and

by migration. As if fate were then determining
upon the partition of Poland, a new enemy was
added to the Cossacks and Russians in Charles X
of Sweden, who used Poland as the first available
pretext to slake his thirst for war. Through the
Swedish war, the communities of Great and Little
Poland, from Posen to Cracow, were reduced to
want and despair. The Jews of Poland had to drink
the cup of poison to the dregs. The Polish general,
Czarnicki, who hated the Jews, ill-used those spared
by Cossacks, Russians, and the wild Swedes of the
Thirty Years' War, under the pretense that they
had a traitorous understanding with the Swedes. The
Poles also behaved barbarously to the Jews, destroyed
the synagogues, and tore up the holy scriptures.
All Poland was like a bloody field of battle, on which
Cossacks, Russians, Prussians, Swedes, and the
troops of Prince Ragoczi of Transylvania wrestled ;
the Jews were ill-used or slain by all. Only the
Great Elector of Brandenburg behaved leniently towards them. The number of Jewish families said to
have perished in ten years of this war (600,000) is
certainly exaggerated, but the slaughtered Jews of
Poland may well be rated at a quarter of a million.
With the decline of Poland as a power of the first
rank, the importance of Polish Judaism diminished.
The remnant were impoverished, depressed, and
could not recover their former position. Their
need was so great, that those who drifted to the
neighborhood of Prussia hired themselves to Christians as day laborers for field work.

As at the time of the expulsion of the Jews from
Spain and Portugal every place was filled with
fugitive Sephardic Jews, so during the Cossack-
Polish war fugitive Polish Jews, wretched in appearance, with hollow eyes, who had escaped the sword,
the flames, hunger, and pestilence ; or who,
dragged by the Tartars into captivity, had
been ransomed by their brethren, were seek-

ing shelter everywhere. Westwards, by way of
Dantzic and through the Vistula district, Jewish-
Polish fugitives wandered to Amsterdam, and were
forwarded thence to Frankfort-on-the-Main and
other Rhenish cities. Three thousand Lithuanian
Jews came to Texel in the Netherlands, and were hos-
pitably received. Southwards many fled to Moravia, Bohemia, Austria, and Hungary, and wandered from those places to Italy. The prisoners
in the armies of the Tartars came to the Turkish provinces, and some of them drifted to
Barbary. Everywhere they were received by their
brethren with great cordiality and love, cared for,
clothed, and supported. The Italian Jews ransomed
and supported them at great sacrifice. Thus, the
community of Leghorn at this time formed a resolution to collect and spend a quarter of their income
for the liberation and maintenance of the unfortunate
Polish Jews. The German and Austrian communities, also, although they had suffered under the
calamities of the Thirty Years' War, exercised that
brotherly feeling which they rarely professed with
their lips, but cherished the more deeply in their
hearts.

The number and misery of those escaped from
Poland were so great, that the German communities
and probably others were obliged to devote the
money intended for Jerusalem to the maintenance
of Polish Jews. The Jews of Jerusalem dependent
on alms, who were drained by the pasha and his
subordinates, felt the want of their regular support
from Europe. They soon fell into such distress,
that of the 700 widows and a smaller number of
men living there nearly 400 are said to have died
of hunger.

The Cossack persecution of the Jews, in a sense,
remodeled Judaism. It became Polonized, so to
speak. The Polish-Rabbinical method of study had
long dominated the Talmudical schools of Germany

and Italy through the abundant literature by Polish authors. Now, through the fugitives, most of whom were Talmudical scholars, it became authoritative. Rabbinical appointments were mostly conferred on Polish Talmudists, as in Moravia, Amsterdam, Fürth, Frankfort, and Metz. On account of their superiority in their department, these Polish Talmudists were as proud as the Spanish and Portuguese fugitives had been, and looked down with contempt on the rabbis who spoke German, Portuguese, and Italian. Far from giving up their own method in a foreign country, they demanded that all the world should be regulated by them, and they gained their point. People joked about the "Polacks," but nevertheless became subordinate to them. Whoever wished to acquire thorough Talmudic and Rabbinical knowledge was obliged to sit at the feet of Polish rabbis; every father of a family who wished to educate his children in the Talmud sought a Polish rabbi for them. These Polish rabbis gradually forced their sophistical piety upon the German, and partly on the Portuguese, and Italian, communities. Through their influence, scientific knowledge and the study of the Bible declined still more than previously. In the century of Descartes and Spinoza, when the three Christian nations, the French, English, and Dutch, gave the death-blow to the Middle Ages, Jewish-Polish emigrants, baited by Chmielnicki's bands, brought a new middle age over European Judaism, which maintained itself in full vigor for more than a century, to some extent lasting to our time.

CHAPTER II.

SETTLEMENT OF THE JEWS IN ENGLAND AND MANASSEH BEN ISRAEL.

Obstacles to the Resettlement of Jews in England—Manasseh ben Israel—His Character and Attainments—Christian Students of Jewish Literature: Scaliger, the Buxtorfs, Selden, and Vossius—Women devote themselves to Hebrew—The Fifth-Monarchy Men: Expectation of the Millennium—Enthusiastic Friends of the Jews—The Puritans—Cromwell and Holmes—Nicholas' Protection of the Jews—"The Hope of Israel"—Fresh Victims of the Inquisition—Manasseh ben Israel's Negotiations with the English Parliament—He journeys to London, and is graciously received by Cromwell—A Council sits at Whitehall to decide the Question of the Re-admission of the Jews—Prynne's anti-Jewish Work—Controversial Pamphlets—Manasseh's "Vindication"—The Re-admission of the Jews connived at.

1655—1657 C. E.

AT the very time when the Jews of Poland were trodden down, slaughtered, or driven through Europe like terrified wild beasts, a land of freedom was opened, from which the Jews had been banished for more than three centuries and a half. England, which the wise queen Elizabeth and the brave Cromwell had raised to be the first power in Europe, a position very different from that of crumbling Poland, again admitted Jews, not indeed through the great portal, yet through the back door. But this admission was so bruited abroad, that it was like a triumph for Judaism. The Jews of Amsterdam and Hamburg looked with longing to this island, to which they were so near, with whose merchants, shipowners, and scholars they were in connection, and which promised wide scope for the exercise of their varied abilities. But settlement there seemed beset with insuperable obstacles. The English episcopal church, which exercised sway over the English conscience, was even more intolerant than the popery which it persecuted.   Not granting freedom to Catholics and Dissenters, would it tolerate the descendants of those aspersed in the New Testament?   The English people, who for centuries had seen no Jew, shared to the full the antipathy of the clergy.   To them every Jew was a Shylock, who, with hearty goodwill, would cut a Christian to pieces—a monster in human form, bearing the mark of Cain.   Who would undertake to banish this strong prejudice in order to render people and rulers favorable to the descendants of Israel?

The man who undertook and executed this difficult task did not belong to the first rank of intellectual men, but possessed the right measure of insight and narrowness, strength of will and flexibility, knowledge and imagination, self-denial and vanity, required for so arduous an undertaking. Manasseh ben Israel, second or third rabbi at Amsterdam, who at home played only a subordinate part, the poor preacher who, to support his family, was obliged to resort to printing, but obtained so little profit from it, that he wished to exchange pulpit oratory for mercantile speculation, and was near settling in Brazil ; he it was who won England for Judaism, and, if he did not banish, diminished the prejudice against his race.   To him belongs the credit for a service not to be lightly estimated, for there were but few to help him.   The release of the Jews from their thousand years' contempt and depreciation in European society, or rather the struggle for civil equality, begins with Manasseh ben Israel.   He was the Riesser of the seventeenth century.   As has been stated, he was not in the true sense great, and can only be reckoned a man of mediocrity.   He belonged to the happily constituted class of persons, who do not perceive the harsh contrasts and shrill discords in

the world around, hence are confiding and enterprising. His heart was deeper than his mind. His
power rested in his easy eloquence, his facility in
explaining and working out ideas which lay within
his narrow field of vision, and which he had acquired
rather than produced. Manasseh ben Israel had
complete grasp of Jewish literature, and knew the
Christian theology of his time, and what was to be
said on each point, *i. e.*, what had been said by his
predecessors. On the other hand, he had only a
superficial knowledge of those branches of learning
which require keenness of intellect, such as philosophy and the Talmud. His strength was in one
respect his weakness. His facility in speaking and
writing encouraged a verbose style and excessive
productiveness. He left more than 400 sermons in
Portuguese, and a mass of writings that fill a
catalogue, but discuss their subjects only superficially. Manasseh's contemporaries looked upon
his writings with different eyes. The learning
amassed therein from all literatures and languages,
and the smoothness of form riveted their attention,
and excited their admiration. Among Jews he was
extraordinarily celebrated; whoever could produce
Latin, Portuguese, or Spanish verse, made known
his praise. But even Christian scholars of his time
over-estimated him.

In Holland, which, by the concurrence of many
circumstances, and especially through the powerful
impulse of Joseph Scaliger, the prince of philologists,
had become in a sense the school of Europe, the
foundation was laid in the seventeenth century for
the wonderful learning contained in voluminous
folios. At no time had there been so many philologists with early-matured learning, iron memory, and
wonderful devotion to the science of language, as in
the first half of the seventeenth century, which
seems to have been specially appointed to revive
what had so long been neglected. All the literary

treasures of antiquity were collected and utilized; statesmen vied with professional scholars. In this gigantic collection there was little critical search for truth; the chief consideration was the number of scientific facts gathered. The ambition of many was spurred on to understand the three favored languages of antiquity—Greek, Latin, and Hebrew—and their literatures. Hebrew, the language of religion, enjoyed special preference, and whoever understood it as well as the other two tongues was sure of distinction. Joseph Scaliger, the oracle of Dutch and Protestant theology, had given to Rabbinical literature, so-called, a place in the republic of letters beside the Hebrew language, and even the Talmud he treated with a certain amount of respect. His Dutch, French, and English disciples followed his example, and devoted themselves with zeal to this branch of knowledge, formerly regarded with contempt or even aversion.

John Buxtorf, senior (born 1564, died 1639), of Basle, may be said to have been master of Hebrew and Rabbinical literature, and he rendered them accessible to Christian circles. He carried on a lively correspondence in Hebrew with Jewish scholars in Amsterdam, Germany, and Constantinople. Even ladies devoted themselves to Hebrew language and literature. That prodigy, Anna Maria Schurmann, of Utrecht, who knew almost all European languages and their literature, corresponded in Hebrew with scholars, and also with an English lady, Dorothea Moore, and quoted Rashi and Ibn Ezra with a scholar's accuracy. The eccentric queen Christina of Sweden, the learned daughter of Gustavus Adolphus, understood Hebrew. Statesmen, such as Hugo Grotius, and the Englishman John Selden, seriously and deeply engaged in its pursuit for their theological or historical studies.

But Christian scholars, with all their zeal, had not yet acquired independence in Rabbinical literature;

without a Jewish guide, they could not move, or felt unsafe. To Christian inquirers, therefore, Manasseh ben Israel's treatises, which presented many Rabbinical passages and new points of view, were highly welcome. Much of the Talmudic literature became accessible through his clear exposition. Hence, Dutch scholars sought out Manasseh, courted his friendship, fairly hung upon his lips, and gradually discarded prejudice against Jews, which even the most liberal-minded men in the most tolerant country of Europe had not laid aside. Manasseh was joined particularly by those eager inquirers who were persecuted or declared heretics by the ruling church. The learned Vossius family, even John Gerard Vossius, senior, although filled with strong hatred against Jews, was affable to Manasseh. His son, Dionysius Vossius, a prodigy of learning, snatched away by death in his eighteenth year, on his death-bed translated into Latin Manasseh's "Reconciler" (Conciliador) shortly after its appearance. Isaac Vossius, the youngest son, who filled an honorable office under the queen of Sweden, recommended Manasseh ben Israel to her. By this family he was made acquainted with the learned statesman Hugo Grotius, who also received instruction from him. The chief of the Arminians, Simon Episcopius, sought intercourse with Manasseh, as did Caspar Barlæus, who as a Socinian, *i. e.*, a denier of the Trinity, was avoided by orthodox Christians. He attached himself to Manasseh, and sang his praise in Latin verses, on which account he was attacked yet more violently, because he had put the Jewish faith on an equality with the Christian. The learned Jesuit Peter Daniel Huet also cultivated his friendship. Gradually the Chacham and preacher of Amsterdam acquired such a reputation among Christians, that every scholar traveling through that city sought him out as an extraordinary personage. Foreigners exchanged letters with him, and obtained from him explanations on difficult points. Manasseh had an interview with Queen Christina of Sweden, which stimulated her kindness for the Jews, and her liking for Jewish literature. So highly did many Christians rate Manasseh ben Israel, that they could not suppress the wish to see so learned and excellent a rabbi won over to Christianity.

Most of all Christian visionaries, who dreamt of the coming of the Fifth Monarchy, the reign of the saints (in the language of Daniel), crowded round Manasseh ben Israel. The Thirty Years' War which had delivered property and life over to wild soldiers, the tyrannical oppression of believers struggling for inward freedom and morality—in England by the bishops and the secular government, in France by the despotic Richelieu—awakened in visionaries the idea that the Messianic millennium, announced in the book of Daniel and the Apocalypse, was near, and that their sufferings were only the forerunners of the time of grace. These fantastic visionaries showed themselves favorable to the Jews; they wished this great change to be effected with the participation of those to whom the announcement had first been made. They conceded that the Jews must first take possession of the Holy Land, which could not easily be accomplished, even by a miracle. For, the lost Ten Tribes must first be found, and gathered together, if the prophetic words were not to fall to the ground. The tribes assembled to take possession of the Holy Land must have their Messiah, a shoot out of the stem of Jesse. But what would become of Jesus, the Christ, *i. e.*, Messiah, in whom Jews could not be made to believe? Some of the Fifth Monarchy visionaries conceded to Jews a Messiah of their own, in the expectation that the struggle for precedence between the Jewish and the Christian saviour would decide itself.

Such apocalyptic dreams struck a responsive chord in Manasseh ben Israel's heart. He also expected, not the reign of the saints, but, according to Kabbalistic reckoning, the speedy advent of the Messianic time. The Zohar, the book revered by him as divine, announced in unambiguous terms, that Israel's time of grace would begin with the year 5408 of the world (1648). Manasseh in his innermost being was a mystic, his classical and literary education being only external varnish, not diminishing his belief in miracles. Hence he was pleased with the letter of a Christian visionary of Dantzic, expressing belief in the restoration of the glory of the Jews. John Mochinger, of the old Tyrolese nobility, who had fallen into the whirlpool of mysticism, wrote to Manasseh ben Israel in the midst of an eulogium on his learning: "Know and be convinced that I duly honor your doctrines, and together with some of my brethren in the faith, earnestly desire that Israel may be enlightened with the true light, and enjoy its ancient renown and happiness." At a later period another German mystic of Dantzic established relations with the Kabbalistic Chacham of Amsterdam—viz., Abraham von Frankenberg, a nobleman, and a disciple of Jacob Böhme. He openly said: "The true light will come from the Jews; their time is not far off. From day to day news will be heard from different places of wonderful things come to pass in their favor, and all the islands shall rejoice with them." In daily intercourse with Manasseh were two Christian friends, Henry Jesse and Peter Serrarius, who were enthusiasts in the cause of Israel's restoration. In France, in the service of the great Condé, there was a peculiar visionary, Isaac La Peyrère of Bordeaux, a Huguenot, perhaps of Jewish-Marrano blood. He had the strange notion that there were men before Adam (pre-Adamites), from whom all men except the Jews were descended. In a book on the subject, which brought him to the dungeon of the Inquisition, he attached great importance to the Jews. In another work on " The Return of the Jews," he maintained that the Jews ought to be re-called from their dispersion in all parts of the world, to effect a speedy return to the Holy Land. The king of France, the eldest son of the Church, has the duty to bring about this return of the eldest son of God. He, too, entered into communication with Manasseh.

The greatest number of ardent admirers " God's people" found in England, precisely among those who had powerful influence in the council and the camp. At the time when the Germans were fight-ing each other on account of difference of creed, invoking the interference of foreigners, and impair-ing their own freedom and power, England was gaining what could never be taken away, religious and, at the same time, political freedom, and this made it a most powerful and prosperous country. In Germany the religious parties, Catholics, Luth-erans, and Calvinists, in selfish blindness demanded religious freedom each for itself alone, reserving oppression and persecution for the others. These internecine quarrels of the Germans were utilized by the princes to confirm their own despotic power. In England, the same selfishness prevailed among the Episcopalians, Presbyterians, and Catholics, but a fourth party arose whose motto was religious freedom for all. The senseless despotism of Charles I and the narrow-mindedness of the Long Parliament had played into the hands of this intelli-gent and powerful party. England, like Germany, resembled a great blood-stained battle-field, but it had produced men who knew what they wanted, who staked their lives for it, and effected the rejuven-escence of the nation. Oliver Cromwell was at once the head which devised, and the arm which executed sound ideas. By the sword he and his army ob-

tained religious freedom, not only for themselves,
but also for others.   He and his officers were not
revengeful freebooters or blood-thirsty soldiers, but
high-minded, inspired warriors of God, who waged
war against wickedness and falseness, and hoped
for, and undertook to establish a moral system of
government, the kingdom of God.   Like the Maccabees of old, the Puritan warriors fought " sword in
hand, and praise of God in their mouth."   Cromwell
and his soldiers read the Bible as often as they
fought.   But not out of the New Testament could
the Roundheads derive inspiration and warlike courage.   The Christian Bible, with its monkish figures,
its exorcists, its praying brethren, and pietistic saints,
supplied no models for warriors contending with a
faithless king, a false aristocracy, and unholy priests.
Only the great heroes of the Old Testament, with
fear of God in their hearts and the sword in their
hands, at once religious and national champions,
could serve as models for the Puritans : the Judges,
freeing the oppressed people from the yoke of foreign domination ; Saul, David, and Joab, routing the
foes of their country; and Jehu, making an end of
an idolatrous and blasphemous royal house—these
were favorite characters with Puritan warriors.   In
every verse of the books of Joshua, Judges, Samuel,
and Kings, they saw their own condition reflected ;
every psalm seemed composed for them, to teach
them that, though surrounded on every side by un-
godly foes, they need not fear while they trusted in
God.   Oliver Cromwell compared himself to the
judge Gideon, who first obeyed the voice of God
hesitatingly, but afterwards courageously scattered
the attacking heathens ; or to Judas Maccabæus,
who out of a handful of martyrs formed a host of
victorious warriors.

To bury oneself in the history, prophecy, and
poetry of the Old Testament, to revere them
as divine inspiration, to live in them with every

emotion, yet not to consider the people who had originated all this glory and greatness as preferred and chosen, was impossible. Among the Puritans, therefore, were many earnest admirers of " God's people," and Cromwell was one of them. It seemed a marvel that the people, or a remnant of the people, whom God had distinguished by great favor and stern discipline, should still exist. A desire was excited in the hearts of the Puritans to see this living wonder, the Jewish people, with their own eyes, to bring Jews to England, and, by making them part of the theocratic community about to be established, stamp it with the seal of completion. The sentiments of the Puritans towards the Jews were expressed in Oliver Cromwell's observation, " Great is my sympathy with this poor people, whom God chose, and to whom He gave His law; it rejects Jesus, because it does not recognize him as the Messiah." Cromwell dreamt of a reconciliation of the Old and the New Testament, of an intimate connection between the Jewish people of God and the English Puritan theocracy. But other Puritans were so absorbed in the Old Testament that the New Testament was of no importance. Especially the visionaries in Cromwell's army and among the members of Parliament, who were hoping for the Fifth Monarchy, or the reign of the saints, assigned to the Jewish people a glorious position in the expected millennium. A Puritan preacher, Nathaniel Holmes (Holmesius), wished, according to the letter of many prophetic verses, to become the servant of Israel, and serve him on bended knees. The more the tension in England increased through the imprisonment of the king, the dissensions between the Presbyterian Long Parliament and the Puritan army, the civil war, the execution of King Charles, and the establishment of a republic in England, the more public life and religious thought assumed Jewish coloring. The only thing wanting to make one think

himself in Judæa was for the orators in Parliament
to speak Hebrew. One author proposed the
seventh day as the day of rest, and in a work showed
the holiness of this day, and the duty of the English
people to honor it. This was in the beginning of
1649. Parliament, it is true, condemned this work
to be burnt as heretical, scandalous, and profane,
and sentenced the printer and author to punishment.
But the Israelite spirit among the Puritans, especially
among the Levelers, or ultra-republicans, was not
suppressed by these means. Many wished the
government to declare the Torah to be the code for
England.

These proceedings in the British islands, which
promised the exaltation of Israel at no distant period,
were followed by Manasseh with beating heart.
Did these voices not announce the coming of the
Messianic kingdom? He hoped so, and put forth
feverish activity to help to bring about the desired
time. He entertained a visionary train of thought.
The Messiah could not appear till the punishment of
Israel, to be scattered from one end of the earth to
the other, had been fulfilled. There were no Jews
then living in England. Exertions must be made
to obtain permission for Jews to dwell in England,
that this hindrance to the advent of the Messiah
might be removed. Manasseh therefore put himself
into communication with some important persons,
who assured him that "the minds of men were
favorable to the Jews, and that they would be acceptable and welcome to Englishmen." What especially justified his hopes was the "Apology" by
Edward Nicholas, former secretary to Parliament,
"for the honorable nation of the Jews." In this
work, which the author dedicated to the Long
Parliament, the Jews were treated, as the chosen
people of God, with a tenderness to which they were
not accustomed. Hence the author felt it necessary
to affirm at the end, that he wrote it, not at the

instigation of Jews, but out of love to God and his country. The opinion of the apologist was, that the great sufferings brought upon England by the religious and civil war were a just punishment for English persecution of the saints and favorites of God, *i. e.*, the Jews, and an urgent admonition to atone for this great sin by admitting them and showing them brotherly treatment. The author proved the preference and selection of Israel by many biblical quotations. He referred to a preacher who had said in Parliament in connection with the verse : " Touch not mine anointed, and do my prophets no harm," that the weal or woe of the world depended upon the good or bad treatment of God's people. God in His secret counsel had sustained this people to the present day, and a glorious future was reserved for them. Hence it was the duty of Englishmen to endeavor to comfort them, if possible give them satisfaction for their innocent blood shed in this kingdom, and enter into friendly intercourse with them. This work also defends the Jews against the accusation of having crucified Jesus. The death of Jesus took place at the instigation of the Synhedrion, not of the people. In most impressive terms it urges the English to comfort the afflicted and unhappy Jews. The pope and his adherents, he said, would be enraged at the kind treatment of the Jews, for they still inflicted cruelty and humiliation upon the people of God, the popes compelling the Jews to wear opprobrious badges, and Catholics avoiding all contact with them, because they abhorred idols and heathen worship.

This work, which, more than friendly, absolutely glorified the Jews, excited the greatest attention in England and Holland. Manasseh ben Israel was delighted with it, thinking that he was near his object, especially as his friend Holmes at once communicated with him on the subject, saying that he himself was about to prepare a work on the millen-

nium, in which he would emphasize the importance
of the Jews in the molding of the future.   Manasseh
ben Israel immediately set to work to do his share
towards the realization of his object.   He, however,
as well as the Christian mystics in England, had
one anxiety; what had become of the lost Ten
Tribes banished by the Assyrian king Shalmanassar?
A restoration of the Jewish kingdom without these
Ten Tribes seemed impossible, nay, their discovery
was the guarantee of the truth of the prophetic promises. The union of Judah and Israel which some of the
prophets had impressively announced would remain
unfulfilled if the Ten Tribes had ceased to exist.
Manasseh, therefore, laid great stress upon being
able to prove their existence somewhere.   Fortunately he was in a position to specify the situation
of the Ten Tribes.   Some years before, a Jewish
traveler, named Montezinos, had affirmed on oath
that he had seen native Jews of the tribe of Reuben,
in South America, and had held communication
with them.   The circumstantiality of his tale excited
curiosity, and inclined his contemporaries to belief.
Antonio de Montezinos was a Marrano, whom business or love of travel had led to America.   There
he had stumbled upon a Mestizo (Indian), who had
excited in him a suspicion that members of his race
were living in America, persecuted and oppressed
by the Indians, as the Indians had been by the
Spaniards, and later experiences confirmed the
suspicion.

    Antonio de Montezinos, or Aaron Levi, had
brought the surprising news to Amsterdam, and
had related it under oath to a number of persons,
among them Manasseh ben Israel (about 1644).
Afterwards he went to Brazil, and there died.   On
his deathbed he repeatedly asserted the truth of
the existence of some Israelite tribes in America.
Manasseh ben Israel was firmly convinced by the
statement of this man, and made it the foundation

of a work, entitled "Israel's Hope," composed to pave the way for the Messianic time. The Ten Tribes, according to his assumption, had been dispersed to Tartary and China, and some might have gone thence to the American continent. Some indications and certain manners and customs of the Indians, resembling those of the Jews, seemed to him to favor this idea. The prophetic announcement of the perpetuity of the Israelite people had accordingly been confirmed; moreover there were signs that the tribes were ready to come forth from their hiding-places and unite with the others. The time of redemption, which, it was true, could not be foretold, and in the calculation of which many had erred, appeared at last to be approaching. The prophets' threats of punishment to the Jews had been fulfilled in a terrible manner; why should not their hope-awakening promises be verified? What unspeakable cruelty the monster of the Inquisition had inflicted, and still continued to inflict, on the poor innocents of the Jewish race, on adults and children of every age and either sex! For what reason? Because they would not depart from the Law of Moses, revealed to them amidst so many miracles. For it numberless victims had perished wherever the tyrannical rule of the Inquisition was exercised. And martyrs continued to show incredible firmness, permitting themselves to be burnt alive to honor the name of God.

Manasseh enumerated all the autos-da-fé of Marranos and other Jewish martyrs which had taken place in his time.

Great excitement was caused among Dutch Portuguese Jews by the burning of a young Marrano, twenty-five years old, well read in Latin and Greek literature. Isaac de Castro-Tartas, born at Tartas, a small town in Gascony, had come with his parents to Amsterdam. Glowing with zeal and a desire to bring back to Judaism those Marranos who con-

tinued Christians, he prepared to travel to Brazil
In vain his parents and friends warned him against
this mad step. In Bahia he was arrested by the
Portuguese, recognized as a Jew, sent to Lisbon,
and handed over to the Inquisition. This body had
no formal right over Isaac de Castro, for when
arrested he was a Dutch citizen. The tribunal in
vain tried to induce him to abjure Judaism. Young
De Castro-Tartas was determined manfully to endure a martyr's death in honor of his faith. His
death was attended with the *éclat* he had longed
for. In Lisbon the funeral pile was kindled for him
and several others, on December 22d, 1647. He
cried out of the flames, " Hear, O Israel, God is
one," in so impressive a tone that the witnesses of
the dreadful spectacle were greatly moved. For
several days nothing else was talked of in the
capital but the dreadful voice of the martyr Isaac de
Castro-Tartas and the "Shema," uttered with his
last breath. People spoke of it shudderingly. The
Inquisition was obliged to forbid the uttering of the
word "Shema" with a threat of heavy punishment.
It is said, too, that at that time it was determined to
burn no more Jewish heretics alive in Lisbon.

The Amsterdam community was stunned by the
news of successive executions of youthful sufferers.
De Castro-Tartas had parents, relatives, and friends
in Amsterdam, and was beloved on account of his
knowledge and character. The rabbi, Saul Morteira, delivered a memorial address on his death.
Poets deplored and honored him in Hebrew and
Spanish verses, and, horrified by the new atrocities
of the Inquisition against Jews, Manasseh ben Israel
wrote "Israel's Hope." Even the reader of to-day
can feel grief trembling in every word. Indeed, if
martyrs could prove the truth and tenability of the
cause for which they bleed, Judaism needs no further
proof ; for no people and no religion on earth have
produced such numerous and firm martyrs. Ma-

nasseh used this proof to draw the conclusion that, as promised sufferings had been inflicted, so the promised redemption and regeneration of God's people would be fulfilled. He sent this Latin treatise on the existence of the Ten Tribes and their hopes to a prominent and learned personage in England, to be read before Parliament, which was under Cromwell's influence, and before the Council of State. In an accompanying letter Manasseh explained to Parliament his favorite idea, that the return of the Jews to their native land—the time for which was so near—must be preceded by their complete dispersion. The dispersion, according to the words of Scripture, was to be from one end of the earth to the other, naturally including the island of England, in the extreme north of the inhabited world. But for more than 300 years no Jews had lived in England; therefore, he added the request that the Council and Parliament grant Jews permission to settle in England, to have the free exercise of their religion, and to build synagogues there (1650). Manasseh made no secret of his Messianic hopes, because he could and did reckon upon the fact that the saints or Puritans themselves wished for the "assembling of God's people" in their ancestral home, and were inclined to help and promote it. He also intimated in his letter, that he was resolved to go to England, to arrange for the settlement of the Jews.

Manasseh ben Israel had not reckoned amiss. His request and dedication were favorably received by Parliament. Lord Middlesex, probably the mediator, sent him a letter of thanks with the superscription, "To my dear brother, the Hebrew philosopher, Manasseh ben Israel." A passport to England was also sent to him. The English ambassador in Holland, Lord Oliver St. John, a relative of Cromwell, told him that he wished to go to the Amsterdam synagogue, and gave him to understand,

probably according to Cromwell's instructions, that
England was inclined to gratify the long-cherished
wish of the Jews. Manasseh took care that he be
received in the house of prayer with music and
hymns (about August, 1651). However, the goal
to which he seemed so near was removed by political complications. England and Holland entered
into a fierce war, which broke off the connection between Amsterdam and London. Manasseh's relations to his elder colleague, Saul Morteira (1652),
and the president, Joseph da Costa—it is not known
on what account—became strained, and in an angry
mood he formed the resolution to leave Amsterdam. The directors of the community succeeded
in establishing a tolerable understanding between
the two chachams, but Manasseh had neither the
cheerfulness required nor a favorable opportunity
to resume his adventurous scheme.

But when Oliver Cromwell, by the illegal but
necessary dissolution of the Long Parliament, assumed the chief power in April, 1653, and showed
an inclination to conclude peace with the States
General, Manasseh again took up his project.
Cromwell had called together a new parliament, the
so-called Short, or Barebones, Parliament, which
was composed wholly of saints, *i. e.*, Puritan preachers, officers with a biblical bias, and millennium visionaries. The partiality of Cromwell's officers for the
old Jewish system is shown by the serious proposition that the Council of State should consist of
seventy members, after the number of the Jewish
synhedrion. In Parliament sat General Harrison, a
Baptist, who, with his party, wished to see the
Mosaic law introduced into England. When Parliament met (July 5, 1653), Manasseh hastened to repeat his request, that Jews be granted permission
to reside in England. The question of the Jews
was immediately put on the programme of business.
Parliament sent Manasseh a safe conduct to Lon-

don, that he might conduct the business in person. As the war between England and Holland still continued, his relatives and friends urged him not to expose himself to the danger of a daily change of affairs, and he again put off his voyage to a more favorable time. The Short Parliament was soon dissolved (December 12, 1653), and Cromwell obtained kingly power under the title of Protector of the Realm. When he concluded peace with Holland (April, 1654), Manasseh thought the time well suited for effecting his wishes for the redemption of Israel. He was encouraged by the fact that three admirals of the English fleet had drawn up a petition in October, 1654, to admit Jews into England. Manasseh presented his petition for their admission to Cromwell's second, still shorter Parliament, and, probably at his instigation, David Abrabanel Dormido, one of the leading men at Amsterdam, at the same time presented one to the same effect, which Cromwell urgently recommended to the Council for speedy decision (November 3, 1654).

Manasseh reveled in intoxicating dreams of the approaching glorious time for Israel. He regarded himself as the instrument of Providence to bring about its fulfillment. In these dreams he was upheld and confirmed by Christian mystics, who were eagerly awaiting the millennium. The Dutchman, Henry Jesse, had shortly before published a work, "On the Speedy Glory of Judah and Israel," in the Dutch language. The Bohemian physician, mystic, and alchemist, Paul Felgenhauer, went beyond the bounds of reason. Disgusted with the formal creed of the Evangelical Church, and the idolatrous tendency of Catholicism, he wrote during the Thirty Years' War against the corruption of the Church and the Protestant clergy, and wished for a spiritual, mystical religion. By a peculiar calculation, Felgenhauer was led to believe that the year six thousand and the advent of the Messiah connected with it

were not far off.   Persecuted in Germany by Catholics and Protestants, he sought an asylum in Amsterdam, and there formed the acquaintance of
Manasseh ben Israel.   Between these men and a
third visionary, Peter Serrarius, the speedy coming
of the Messianic time was often the subject of conversation.   Felgenhauer then composed an original
work (December, 1654) entitled "Good News of
the Messiah for Israel!   The redemption of Israel
from all his sufferings, his deliverance from captivity, and the glorious advent of the Messiah are nigh
for the comfort of Israel.   Taken from the Holy
Scriptures of the Old and New Testament, by a
Christian who is expecting him with the Jews."
Felgenhauer places the Jewish people very high, as
the seed of Abraham, and considers true believers
of all nations the spiritual seed of Abraham.   Hence
Jews and Christians should love, not despise, one
another.   They should unite in God.   This union
is near at hand.   The bloody wars of nation against
nation by sea and land in the whole world, which
had not happened before to anything like the same
extent, are signs thereof.   As further signs he accounted the comets which appeared in 1618, 1648,
and 1652, and the furious Polish war kindled by the
Cossacks.   Verses from the Bible, especially from
Daniel and the Apocalypse, with daring interpretations, served him as proofs.   Felgenhauer denied
an earthly Messiah, nor did he allow the claim of
Jesus to the title.

As this half-insane work was dedicated to Manasseh, he was obliged to answer it, which he did with
great prudence (February 1, 1655), gladly welcom-
ing the pages favorable to Jews, and passing over
the rest in silence.   The good news concerning the
near future was the more welcome to his heart, he
said, as he himself, in spite of the afflictions of many
centuries, did not cease ardently to hope for better
times.

" How gladly would I believe you, that the time is near when God, who has so long been angry with us, will again comfort His people, and deliver it from more than Babylonian captivity, and more than Egyptian bondage! Your sign of the commencement of the Messianic age, the announcement of the exaltation of Israel throughout the whole world, appears to me not only probable, but plain and clear. A not inconsiderable number of these announcements (on the Christian side) for the consolation of Zion have been sent to me from Frankenberg and Mochinger, from France and Hungary. And from England alone how many voices! They are like that small cloud in the time of the prophet Elijah, which suddenly extended so that it covered the whole of the heavens."

Manasseh ben Israel had the courage to express without ambiguity Jewish expectations in opposition to the opinions held by Christian enthusiasts. They, for the most part, imagined the fifth monarchy, which they alleged was about to commence, as the millennium, when Jesus would again appear and hand over the sovereign power to the saints. The Jews would have a share in it; they would assemble from the ends of the earth, return to their ancestral home, and again build Jerusalem and the Temple. But this would be only an intermediate state, the means to enable the whole Twelve Tribes to acknowledge Jesus as Messiah, so that there be but one flock under one shepherd. Against this Manasseh ben Israel composed a treatise, ended April 25, 1655, on the fifth kingdom of the prophecy of Daniel, interpreting it to mean the independence of Israel. In this work, called "The Glorious Stone, or the Image of Nebuchadnezzar," and dedicated to Isaac Vossius, then in the service of the queen of Sweden, he put forth all his learning to show that the visions of the "four beasts," or great kingdoms, had been verified in the successive sway of the Babylonians, Persians, Greeks, and Romans, and therefore the coming of the fifth kingdom also was certain. This was shown in Daniel plainly enough to be the kingdom of Israel, the people of God. In this Messianic kingdom all nations of the earth will have part, and they will be treated with kindness, but the authority will ever rest with Israel. Manasseh disfigured this simple thought by Kabbalistic triviality and sophistry. It is singular that not only did a learned Christian accept the dedication of this essentially Jewish work, but the celebrated painter Rembrandt supplied four artistic engravings representing Nebuchadnezzar's, or Manasseh's vision.

Manasseh had received a friendly invitation from the second Parliament assembled by Cromwell; but as it had meanwhile been dissolved, he could not begin his journey until invited by the Protector himself. He seems to have sent on in advance his son, Samuel ben Israel, who was presented by the University of Oxford, in consideration of his knowledge and natural gifts, with the degree of doctor of philosophy and medicine, and according to custom, received the gold ring, the biretta, and the kiss of peace. It was no insignificant circumstance that this honor should be conferred upon a Jew by a university strictly Christian in its conduct. Cromwell's will appears to have been decisive in the matter. He sent an invitation to Manasseh, but the journey was delayed till autumn. Not till the end of the Tishri festivals (October 25-31, 1655) did Manasseh undertake the important voyage to London, in his view, of the utmost consequence to the world. He was received in a friendly manner by Cromwell, and had a residence granted him. Among his companions was Jacob Sasportas, a learned man, accustomed to intercourse with persons of high rank, who had been rabbi in African cities. Other Jews accompanied him in the hope that the admission of Jews would meet with no difficulty. Some secret Jews from Spain and Portugal were already domiciled in London, among them being the rich and respected Fernandez Carvajal. But the matter did not admit of such speedy settlement. At an audience, Manasseh delivered to the Protector a carefully composed petition, or address. He had obtained the authorization of the Jews of the different countries of Europe to act as their representative, so that the admission of Jews into England might be urged not in his own name alone, but in that of the whole Jewish nation.   In his petition he skillfully developed the argument, by means of passages from the Bible and the Talmud, that power and authority are conferred by God according to his will; that God rewards and punishes even the rulers of the earth, and that this had been verified in Jewish history; that great monarchs who had troubled Israel had met with an unhappy end, as Pharaoh, Nebuchadnezzar, Antiochus Epiphanes, Pompey, and others.   On the other hand, benefactors of the Jewish nation had enjoyed happiness even here below, so that the word of God to Abraham had been literally fulfilled :—

" ' I will bless them that bless thee, and curse them that curse thee.' Hence I, one of the least among the Hebrews, since by experienc, I have found, that through God's great bounty towards us, many considerable and eminent persons both of piety and power are moved with sincere and inward pity and compassion towards us, and do comfort us concerning the approaching Deliverance of Israel, could not but for myself, and in the behalf of my countrymen, make this my humble Address to your Highness, and beseech you for God's sake that ye would, according to that piety and power wherein you are eminent beyond others, vouchsafe to grant that the great and glorious name of the Lord our God may be extolled, and solemnly worshiped and praised by us through all the bounds of this Commonwealth ; and to grant us place in your country, that we may have our Synagogues, and free exercise of our religion.   Pagans have of old . . . . granted free liberty even to apostate Jews: . . . . how much more then may we, that are not Apostate or runagate Jews, hope it from your Highness and your Christian Council, since you have so great knowledge of, and adore the same one only God of Israel, together with us. . . . For our people did . . . . presage that . . . . the ancient hatred towards them would also be changed into goodwill: that those rigorous laws , . . . against so innocent a people would happily be repealed."

At the same time Manasseh ben Israel circulated through the press a " Declaration " which served to explain the reasons for admitting Jews, and to meet objections and allay prejudices against their admission.   All his reasons can be reduced to two—one mystical and one of trade policy.   The mystical reason has been repeatedly explained. His opinion coincided with that of many Christians, that the return of the Israelites to their home was near at hand. According to his view the general dispersion of the Jews must precede this event :—

" Now we know how our nation is spread all about, and has its seat and dwelling in the most flourishing countries of the world, as well in America as in the other three parts thereof, except only in this considerable and mighty island. And therefore, before the Messiah come . . . . first we must have our seat here likewise."

The other reason was put in this form : that through the Jews the trade of England would greatly increase in exports and imports from all parts of the world. He developed this point of the advantage which the Jews might bestow at great length, showing that on account of their fidelity and attachment to the countries hospitable and friendly to them they deserved to be treated with consideration. Besides, they ought to be esteemed, on account of their ancient nobility and purity of blood, among a people which attached importance to such distinctions.

Manasseh ben Israel considered the commerce to which Jews were for the most part devoted from a higher point of view. He had in mind the wholesale trade of the Portuguese Jews of Holland in the coin of various nations (exchange business), in diamonds, cochineal, indigo, wine, and oil. Their money transactions were not based on usury, on which the Jews of Germany and Poland relied. The Amsterdam Jews deposited their capital in banks, and satisfied themselves with five per cent interest. The capital of the Portuguese Jews in Holland and Italy was very considerable, because Marranos in Spain and Portugal invested their money with them, to evade the avarice of the Inquisition. Hence Manasseh laid great weight on the advantages which England might expect from his enterprising countrymen. He thought that trading,

the chief occupation, and, to a certain extent, the
natural inclination, of the Jews of all countries since
their dispersion, was the work of Providence, a mark
of divine favor towards them, that by accumulated
treasures they might find grace in the eyes of rulers
and nations.   They were forced to occupy themselves with commerce, because, owing to the insecu-
rity of their existence, they could not possess landed
estates.   Accordingly, they were obliged to pursue
trade till their return to their land, for then "there
shall be no more any trader in the house of the
Lord," as a prophet declares.

Manasseh ben Israel then took a survey over all
the countries where Jews, in his time, or shortly
before, by means of trade, had attained to importance, and enumerated the persons who had risen to
high positions by their services to states or rulers.
However, much that he adduced, when closely considered, is not very brilliant, with the exception of
the esteemed and secure position which the Jews
occupied in Holland.   Then he quoted examples of
the fidelity and devotedness of Jews in ancient and
modern times towards their protectors.   He forcibly
refuted the calumny that the Jews had been banished
from Spain and Portugal for treachery and faithlessness.   It was easy for him to show from Christian
authors that the expulsion of the Jews, and their
cruel treatment by Portugal, were at once criminal
and foolish, and most emphatically condemned by
wise rulers.   He took occasion to defend his brethren against three other charges : usury, child murder, and proselytism.   To wipe off the stain of
usury, he made use of the justification employed by
Simone Luzzatto, a contemporary Jewish Italian
author, that usury was objectionable not in itself, but
in its excess.   Of great weight was the fact which
he adduced, that the Portuguese Jews, for whom he
was pleading, abhorred usury as much as many
Christians, and that their large capital had not been

obtained from it.   Manasseh could repudiate with
more vehemence the charge of murdering Christian
children.   Christians made the accusation,he thought,
pretty much from the motives that influenced the
negroes of Guinea and Brazil, who tormented those
just escaped from shipwreck, or visited by misfortune in general, by assuming that such persons
were accursed of God.

"We live not amongst the Black-moors and wild-men, but amongst
the white and civilized people of the world, yet we find this an ordinary course, that men are very prone to hate and despise him that
hath ill fortune ; and on the other side, to make much of those whom
fortune doth favor."

Manasseh reminded the Christians that there had
been a time when they, too, had been charged by
heathens with being murderers of children, sorcerers,
and conjurers, and had been punished by heathen
emperors and officials.   He was able to refer to a
case of his own time, that of Isaac Jeshurun, of
Ragusa, a Jew repeatedly tortured for child murder,
whose innocence had come to light, and filled the
judges with remorse.   Manasseh denied the accusation of the conversion of Christians to Judaism,
and referred to the injunction of the Jewish law to
dissuade rather than attract proselytes.

"Now, because I believe, that with a good conscience I have discharged our nation of the Jews of those three slanders. . . .   I may
from these two qualities, of Profitableness and Fidelity, conclude,
that such a nation ought to be well entertained, and also beloved and
protected generally of all.   The more, considering they are called in
the Sacred Scriptures the sons of God. . . . .   I could add a
third (point), viz., of the Nobility of the Jews, but because that point
is enough known amongst all Christians, as lately it has been shown
. . . .   by that worthy Christian minister, Mr. Henry Jessey . . .
and by Mr. Edw. Nicholas, Gentleman.   Therefore I will here forbear
and rest on the saying of Solomon . . . .   'Let another man's mouth
praise thee, and not thine own.'"

Cromwell was decidedly inclined to the admission
of the Jews.   He may have had in view the probability that the extensive trade and capital of the
Spanish and Portuguese Jews, those professing Juda-

ism openly as well as secretly, might be brought to England, which at that time could not yet compete with Holland. He was also animated by the great idea of the unconditional toleration of all religions, and even thought of granting religious freedom to the intensely hated, feared, hence persecuted Catholics. Therefore, he acceded to the wish of the Jews to open an asylum to them in England. But he was most influenced by the religious desire to win over the Jews to Christianity by friendly treatment. He thought that Christianity, as preached in England by the Independents, without idolatry and superstition, would captivate the Jews, hitherto deterred from Christianity.

Cromwell and Manasseh ben Israel agreed in an unexpressed, visionary, Messianic reason for the admission of Jews into England. The Kabbalistic rabbi thought that in consequence of the settlement of Jews in the British island, the Messianic redemption would commence, and the Puritan Protector believed that Jews in great numbers would accept Christianity, and then would come the time of one shepherd and one flock. To dispose the people favorably towards the Jews, Cromwell employed two most zealous Independents, his secretary, the clergyman Hugh Peters, and Harry Marten, the fiery member of the Council, to labor at the task.

At last the time came to consider the question of the admission of Jews seriously. They had been banished in the year 1290 in pursuance of a decree enacting that they should never return, and it was questionable whether the decree was not still in force. Therefore, Cromwell assembled a commission at Whitehall (December 4, 1655), to discuss every aspect of the matter. The commission was composed of Lord Chief Justice Glynn, Lord Chief Baron Steel, and seven citizens, including the Lord Mayor, the two sheriffs of London, an alderman, and the recorder of the city, and fourteen eminent cler-

gymen of different towns.   Cromwell mentioned two
subjects for discussion : whether it was lawful to
admit Jews into England, and, in case it was not
opposed to the law, under what conditions the
admission should take place.   Manasseh had formulated his proposal under seven heads : that they
should be admitted and protected against violence ;
that they should be granted synagogues, the free
exercise of religion, and places of burial ; that they
should enjoy freedom of trade ; and that their disputes should be settled by their own rabbis and
directors ; and that all former laws hostile to
Jews should be repealed for their greater security.
On admission, every Jew should take the oath of
fidelity to the realm.

There was great excitement in London during the
discussion on the admission of the Jews, and popular feeling was much divided.   Blind hatred against
the crucifiers of the Son of God, and blind love for
the people of God ; fear of the competition of Jews
in trade, and hope of gaining the precedence from
the Dutch and Spaniards by their means, prejudiced
ideas that they crucified Christian children, clipped
coin, or wished to make all the English people Jews—
these conflicting feelings disturbed the judgment
for and against them.   Cromwell's followers, and
the Republicans in general, were for their admission ; Royalists and Papists, secretly or openly his
enemies, were opposed to the proposal.   The people
crowded to the hall where the Jewish question was
publicly discussed.   At the very beginning the legal
representatives declared that no ancient law excluded the Jews from England, for their banishment
had been enacted by the king, without the consent
of Parliament.   The city representatives remained
silent ; the most violent were the clergy, who could
not rid themselves of their hatred against Jews,
derived from the gospels and their theological literature.   Cromwell, who most earnestly wished to see

them admitted, therefore added three clergymen,
among them Hugh Peters, from whom he expected
a vote favorable to the Jews.   The question was not
brought to a decision in three sittings.   Cromwell
therefore ordered a final discussion (December 18,
1655), at which he presided.   The majority of the
clergy on this day, too, were against the admission
of Jews, even the minority favoring it only with due
precautions.   Cromwell, dissatisfied with the course
of the discussion, first had the theological objections
refuted by Manasseh ben Israel, then expressed himself with much warmth, and reprimanded the clergy.
He said that he had hoped to receive enlightenment for his conscience; instead, they had made
the question more obscure.   The main strength of
his arguments was : The pure (Puritan) gospel must
be preached to the Jews, to win them to the church.
"But can we preach to them, if we will not tolerate
them among us ? "   Cromwell thereupon closed the
discussion, and resolved to decide the matter according to his own judgment.

He had not only the opposition of the fanatical
clergy to contend against, but also that of the multitude, who shared their prejudiced feeling.   The
enemies of the Jews made every effort to win over
the people against their admission.   They spread
the report that the Jews intended to buy the library
of the University of Oxford, and, if possible, turn St.
Paul's into a synagogue.   They sought to bring
Cromwell's friendship for the Jews under suspicion,
and circulated the report that an embassy had come
to England from Asia and Prague to find out
whether Cromwell was not the expected Messiah of
the Jews.   A clerical pamphleteer, named William
Prynne, stirred up a most fanatical excitement
against the Jews.   He composed a venomous work,
"A Short Demurrer," in which he raked up all false
accusations against them of counterfeit coining, and
the crucifixion of Christian children, and briefly

summarized the anti-Jewish decrees of the thirteenth century, so as to make the name of Jew hated. From other quarters, also, various publications appeared against them. John Hoornbeek, a Dutchman, composed a book on the conversion of the Jews, in which he pretended to be their friend, but actually sought to asperse them. John Dury, an Englishman residing at the time at Cassel, was also resolved to make his voice heard about the Jews ; he weighed arguments for and against their admission, and at last inclined to the view that it was a serious matter to permit Jews to enter England. His work was printed and distributed. Probably at Cromwell's suggestion, Thomas Collier wrote a refutation of Prynne's charges, dedicating it to the Protector. He even justified the crucifixion of Jesus by the Jews, and concluded his work with a passage in the taste of that time :

" Oh, let us respect them; let us wait for that glorious day which will make them the head of the nations. Oh, the time is at hand when every one shall think himself happy that can but lay hold on the skirt of a Jew. Our salvation came from them! Our Jesus was of them! We are gotten into their promises and privileges! The natural branches were cut off, that we might be grafted on! Oh, let us not be high-minded, but fear. Let us not, for God's sake, be unmerciful to them! No! let it be enough if we have all their [spiritual] riches."

While the admission of Jews met with so many difficulties in England, the Dutch Government was by no means pleased with Manasseh ben Israel's efforts to bring it to pass, fearing, doubtless, that the Amsterdam Jews would remove to England, with all their capital. Manasseh was obliged to pacify the Dutch ambassador in an interview, and to assure him that his exertions concerned not Dutch Jews, but the Marranos, watched with Argus eyes in Spain and Portugal, for whom he wished to provide an asylum. Manasseh waited six months in London to obtain from Cromwell a favorable decision, but without success. The Protector found no leisure to attend to the Jewish question, his energies were devoted to obtaining the funds necessary for the government and foreign wars, refused by one Parliament after another, and to frustrating the royalist conspiracy against his life. Manasseh's companions, who had given up all hopes of success, left London; others who, having fled from the Pyrenean peninsula, were on their way thither, turned back, and settled in Italy or Geneva.

But the friends of the Jews were unwearied, and hoped to produce a change of mind in the people. One of "the saints" published a small work (April, 1656), in which he briefly summarized the proceedings at the discussion on the admission of Jews, and then added:

"What shall be the issue of this, the most high God knoweth; Rabbi Manasseh ben Israel still remains in London, desiring a favorable answer to his proposals; and not receiving it he hath desired, that if they may not be granted, he may have a favorable dismission, and return home. But other great affairs being now in hand, and this being business of very great concernment, no absolute answer is yet returned to him."

To elicit a thorough refutation of all the charges advanced by the enemies of the Jews and the opponents of toleration, a person of high rank, in close relation with the government, induced Manasseh ben Israel to publish a brief but comprehensive work, in defense of the Jews. In the form of a letter he stated all the grounds of accusation. These included the current slanders: the use of the blood of Christians at the Passover, curses upon Christians and blasphemy against the God of the Christians in Jewish prayers, and the idolatrous reverence alleged to be shown the Torah-scrolls. The defense of the Jews, which Manasseh ben Israel composed in reply (April 10), and which was soon afterwards circulated through the press, is perhaps the best work from his pen. It is written with deep feeling, and is, therefore, convincing; learned matter is not wanting, but the learning is subordinate to the main object. In the composition of this defense Manasseh must have had peculiar feelings. He had come to England the interpreter or representative of the people of God, expecting speedily to conquer the sympathy of Christians, and pave the way for the lordship of Israel over the world, and now his people was placed at the bar, and he had to defend it. Hence the tone of this work is not aggressive and triumphant, but plaintive. He affirmed that nothing had ever produced a deeper impression on his mind than the letter addressed to him with the list of anti-Jewish charges.

"It reflects upon the credit of a nation, which amongst so many calumnies, so manifest (and therefore shameful), I dare to pronounce innocent. And in the first place, I cannot but weep bitterly, and with much anguish of soul lament, that strange and horrid accusation of some Christians against the dispersed and afflicted Jews that dwell among them, when they say (what I tremble to write) that the Jews are wont to celebrate the Feast of Unleavened Bread, fermenting it with the blood of some Christians whom they have for that purpose killed."

To this false charge so often made, among others by Prynne, the greatest part of his defense is devoted, and it is indeed striking. He traced the accusation to false witnesses or the confession of accused persons under torture. The innocence of the accused was often brought to light, but too late, when they had been executed. Manasseh confirmed this by an entertaining story. The physician of a Portuguese count had been charged by the Inquisition as a Judaizing Christian. In vain the count pledged himself for his orthodoxy, he was nevertheless tortured, and himself confessed that he was a Judaizing sinner. Subsequently the count, pretending serious illness, sent for the inquisitor, and in his house, with doors closed, he commanded him in a threatening tone to confess in writing that he was a Jew. The inquisitor refused ; then a servant brought in a red-hot helmet to put upon his head. Thereupon the inquisitor confessed everything demanded by the

count, who took this opportunity to reproach him
with his cruelty and inhumanity.

Manasseh ben Israel besides affirmed with a solemn oath the absolute falsehood of the oft-repeated
charges as to the use of Christian blood.

After meeting the other accusations against the
Jews, he concludes his defense with a fine prayer and
an address to England :

> " And to the highly honored nation of England I make my most
> humble request, that they would read over my arguments impartially,
> without prejudice and devoid of all passion, effectually recommending
> me to their grace and favor, and earnestly beseeching God that He
> would be pleased to hasten the time promised by Zephaniah, wherein
> we shall all serve him with one consent, after the same manner, and
> shall be all of the same judgment ; that as his name is one, so his fear
> may be also one, and that we may all see the goodness of the Lord
> (blessed for ever !) and the consolations of Zion."

This last work of Manasseh ben Israel produced
in England the favorable effect desired. Though
Cromwell, amidst the increasing difficulties of his
government, could not fully carry out the admission
of the Jews, he made a beginning towards it. He
dismissed Manasseh with honorable distinctions, and
granted him a yearly allowance of one hundred
pounds (February 20, 1657) out of the public treasury. The Jews were not admitted in triumph
through the great portal, but they were let in by
Cromwell through a back door, yet they established
themselves firmly. This was in consequence of an
indictment brought against an immigrant Marrano
merchant, Antonio Robles, that he, a Portuguese
Papist, had illegally engaged in business pursuits in
England, but he was acquitted by the Protector on
the ground that he was not a Catholic, but a Jew.
Thus the residence of such Jews was suffered ; they
could therefore drop the mask of Catholicism. Two
respected Marranos, Simon de Caceres and Fernandez (Isaac) Carvajal, in fact received Cromwell's
permission to open a special burial-ground for the
Sephardic Jews settled in London (1657). In con-

sequence of this permission it was no longer necessary to make a show of attending church or of
having their newly-born children baptized. But they
occupied an anomalous position. Being strangers,
and on account of their insignificant numbers, they
lived not exactly on sufferance, but were ignored.
Thus Manasseh ben Israel's endeavors were not
entirely vain. He did not draw the pension
awarded him, nor did he live to witness the coming
up of the seed scattered by him, for on the way
home he died, at Middelburg, probably broken down
by his exertions and the disappointment of his hopes,
even before he reached his family (November, 1657).
His body was afterwards brought to Amsterdam,
and an honorable epitaph was put over his grave.
But his zealous activity, outcome though it was of
Messianic delusions, bore fruit, because it was sincere. Before he had been dead ten years, Jews
were gradually admitted into England by the monarchy which succeeded the republic. A community
was assembled which soon became organized, a
room was fitted up in King street as a synagogue,
and Jacob Sasportas, the wanderer from Africa,
Manasseh ben Israel's companion, was chosen rabbi.
The branch community of London took as its model
that of Amsterdam. From this second stronghold,
occupied by Portuguese Jews, afterwards proceeded
the agitation for popular freedom and the liberation
of the Jews.

CHAPTER III.

THE SCEPTICS.

Condition of Judaism—Complete Triumph of the Kabbala—The Disciples of Isaac Lurya—Vital Calabrese, Abraham de Herrera, and Isaiah Hurwitz—Immanuel Aboab—Uriel da Costa ; his Career and Death—Leo Modena; his Character and his Writings —Deborah Ascarelli and Sarah Copia Sullam, Jewish Authoresses—Leo Modena's veiled Scepticism—The Travels and Influence of Joseph Delmedigo—The Writings of Simone Luzzatto.

1620—1660 C. E.

JUDAISM, then in its three thousandth year, was like a rich kernel, covered and concealed by crusts deposited one upon another, and by extraneous matter, so that only very few could recognize its true character. The Sinaitic and prophetic kernel of thought had long been covered over with the three-fold layer of Sopheric, Mishnic, and Talmudical explanations and restrictions. Over these, in the course of centuries, new layers had been formed by the Gaonic, Spanish, French, German, and Polish schools, and these layers and strata were enclosed by an unsightly growth of fungus forms, the mouldy coating of the Kabbala, which, settling in the gaps and chinks, grew and ramified. All these new forms had already the authority of age in their favor, and were considered inviolable. People no longer asked what was taught in the fundamental Sinaitic law, or what was considered of importance by the prophets ; they scarcely regarded what the Talmud decided to be essential or non-essential ; the Rabbinical writers alone, Joseph Karo and Moses Isserles being the highest authorities, decided what was Judaism. Besides, there were superadditions from the Polish schools, and lastly the Kabbalistic dreams of Isaac

Lurya. The parasitic Kabbala choked the whole religious life of the Jews. Almost all rabbis and leaders of Jewish communities, whether in small Polish towns or in cultivated Amsterdam, the Chacham Isaac Aboab de Fonseca, as well as Isaiah Hurwitz, the emigrant to Palestine, were ensnared by the Kabbala. Gaining influence in the fourteenth century, contemporaneously with the ban against science, it had made such giant strides since Isaac Lurya's death, or rather committed such gigantic ravages, that nothing could keep it in check. Lurya's wild notions of the origin, transmigration, and union of souls, of redemption, and wonderworking, after his death attracted more and more adherents into his magic circle, clouding their minds and narrowing their sympathies.

Lurya's disciples, the lion's whelps, as they boastfully called themselves, made systematic efforts to effect conversions, circulated most absurd stories about Lurya's miracles, gave out that their master's spirit had come upon them, and shrouded themselves in mystery, in order to attract greater attention. Chayim Vital Calabrese had been most prominent, and with his juggleries deluded the credulous in Palestine and the neighboring countries (1572-1620) till his death. He claimed to be the Ephraimitic Messiah, and therefore assumed a sort of authority over his fellowdisciples. In Jerusalem, where he resided for several years, Vital preached, and had visions, but did not meet with the recognition he expected. Only women said that they had seen a pillar of fire or the prophet Elijah hovering over Vital while he preached.

In Safet, Vital, imitating his master, visited graves, carried on exorcism of spirits, and other mystic follies, but not living on good terms with his colleagues, especially his brother-in-law, Gedaliah Levi, of whom he was jealous, he settled at Damascus (1594-1620), continued his mystifications, affected great personal importance, as if the salva-

tion of the world rested on his shoulders, and
preached the speedy appearance of the Messiah,
and his mission to hasten it. Jesus and Mahomet, repenting their errors, would lay their crowns at
his feet. Ridiculed on account of his wild proceedings, and declared to be a false prophet, he took
vengeance on his detractors by gross slanders.

In old age he continued his mystical nonsense,
saying that he had been forbidden to reveal his visions, but this prohibition having been withdrawn, he
could now announce that certain souls living in
human bodies would be united to him—of course, in
a subordinate capacity—to bring about the redemption, one of the souls destined for this mission being
in a foreign country. This was a bait to attract
Kabbala enthusiasts, and thus secure a following.
And enthusiasts hastened from Italy, Germany,
Poland, and other countries to play a Messianic part.
The manuscript notes left by Lurya gave rise to
further frauds. Vital asserted that he alone was in
possession of them, and obtained a decree from the
college at Safet, declaring that no one was authorized to publish information about Lurya's Kabbala
elsewhere. Kabbalists became the more anxious
to possess this incomparable treasure. Chayim
Vital's brother, Moses Vital, took advantage of their
eagerness to make a good business of it. During
an illness of his brother's, he caused the writings
found at his house to be copied, and sold them at a
high price. After his recovery, Chayim Vital
affirmed that the writings stolen were not the genuine ones ; these he would never publish. He is
said in his will to have directed them to be laid in his
grave. Nevertheless, after his death, his son, Samuel Vital, sold Luryan Kabbalistic revelations, and
published his father's dreams and visions in a
separate work. An immigrant Marrano from Portugal, a devotee of the Kabbala, asserted that he had
found the best collection in Vital's grave.

After this time a regular search was made after the Kabbala of Lurya and Vital. Whoever was in possession of copies, and offered them for sale or publication, found ready purchasers. Messengers were employed to give this fraud currency in the Jewish communities. Israel Saruk, or Sarug, a German, one of Lurya's disciples, introduced the Luryan Kabbala into Italy, gained many adherents for it, and much money for himself. His account of his master's miracles offended the taste of very few. From Italy he betook himself to Holland, and there gained a disciple who knew how to give the Kabbalistic frenzy a philosophic complexion. Alonzo, or Abraham, de Herrera (died 1639), a descendant of the Great Captain, the viceroy of Naples, was introduced by Saruk into the mysteries of the Luryan Kabbala. Having lived a Christian during the greatest part of his life, he was more familiar with non-Jewish philosophy than with Jewish literature ; therefore it was easy to deceive him into taking dross for gold. He felt clearly that Lurya's Kabbala betrayed resemblances to Neoplatonic philosophy, but this disturbed De Herrera little, or rather, it confirmed the Kabbalistic teaching, and he endeavored to explain one by the other. Finding it impossible to reconcile the two systems, he, too, fell into idle talk and rambling expressions. Abraham de Herrera, who, as has been stated, became a Jew at a ripe age, could not learn Hebrew, and hence had his two Kabbalistic works, the " House of God " and the " Gate of Heaven," translated by the Amsterdam preacher Isaac Aboab from Spanish into Hebrew, and in his will set apart a considerable sum of money for their publication. The author and translator doubtless thought that they had rendered an inexpressibly great service to Judaism. But by the meretricious splendor which these works imparted to the Kabbala, they blinded the superficial minds of the average Portuguese Jews, who, in spite of their knowledge of classical literature and European culture, abandoned themselves to the delusions of the Kabbala. Manasseh ben Israel and all his older and younger contemporaries in Holland paid homage to mysticism, and had no doubt of its truth and divinity.

In Germany and Poland two men, half Polish and half German, brought Lurya's Kabbala into high estimation : Isaiah Hurwitz (Sheloh), called the Holy, and Naphtali Frankfurter, to whom we may perhaps add the credulous Solomon, or Shlomel, of Moravia, who glorified the silliest stories of wonders performed by Isaac Lurya, Vital, and their circle, in letters sent to Germany and Poland, which were eagerly read and circulated.

However, in this thick unsightly crust overspreading the Kabbala, some rifts and chinks appeared, which indicated disintegration. Here and there were found unprejudiced men, who felt and expressed doubts as to the truth of Judaism in its later Rabbinical and Kabbalistic form. Many went further, and included Talmudical interpretation. Others advanced from doubt to certainty, and proceeded more or less openly against the existing form of Judaism. Such inquirers, of course, were not to be met with among German and Polish, nor among Asiatic Jews ; these considered every letter in the Talmud and Zohar, every law in the code (Shulchan Aruch) as the inviolable word of God. The doubters were only in Italian and Portuguese communities, which had relations with educated circles. A pious adherent of tradition, Immanuel Aboab, of Portuguese origin, who had long resided in Italy, felt called upon to compose a defense of the Judaism of the Talmud and the rabbis (Nomologia, composed 1616-1625), showing an unbroken chain of exponents of true tradition down to his own time, a well-meant, but not very convincing work. The confused Kabbalist

Naphtali Frankfurter complained of his comtempo-
raries who ridiculed the Talmud. Three or four
gifted investigators more or less frankly revealed
the scepticism working beneath the surface. These
three men, differing in character, mode of life, and
position, were Uriel Acosta, Judah Leo Modena, and
Joseph Delmedigo ; we may perhaps add Simone
Luzzatto to the list. They endeavored to lay bare
the disadvantages and weaknesses of existing Judaism ; but not one of them was able to suggest or
apply a remedy.

Uriel da Costa (Gabriel Acosta, born about 1590,
died April, 1640) was an original character, whose
inward unrest and external course of life could not
but bring him into conflict with Judaism. He was
descended from a Portuguese Marrano family at
Oporto, whose members had been made sincere
believers in Christ by the terrors of the Inquisition.
His father, at least, who belonged to the higher
classes in Portugal, had become a strict Catholic.
Young Gabriel learnt ecclesiasticism and the accom-
plishments of a cavalier from his father, was, like
him, a good rider, and entered upon a course of
education, limited, indeed, but sufficient for that time.
He adopted the only career open to young Portuguese of the upper middle class, by means of which
the gifted could rise to distinction, and to a certain
equality with the nobility. He was prepared for the
law, a study which might pave the way to the second
rank, the clerical. In his youth the Jesuits had
already obtained powerful influence over men's
minds, and their methods of exciting the imagination
and subduing the intellect by depicting everlasting
damnation and the punishments of hell had proved
effectual. Nothing but punctilious, mechanical worship and continual confession could overcome the
terrors of hell.

Gabriel da Costa, in spite of his punctilious
ecclesiasticism, did not feel quieted in his conscience.

Daily mechanical exercises failed to influence his mind, and continual confession to obtain absolution from the lips of the priest pleased him less as he became more mature. Somewhat of the subtle Jewish spirit remained in his nature, and shook the strongly built Catholic system of belief to its foundations. The more deeply he plunged into the Catholic Jesuitic teaching, the more did doubts trouble him, and disturb his conscience. However, he accepted a semi-ecclesiastical office as chief treasurer to an abbey about 1615. To end his doubts, he investigated the oldest records of Holy Scripture. The prophets were to solve the riddles which the Roman Catholic Church doctrines daily presented to him. The fresh spirit which breathed from out of the Old Testament, disfigured though it was in its Latin guise, brought repose to his mind. The doctrines of Judaism appeared the more certain, as they were recognized by the New Testament and the Church, while those of Catholicism were rejected by Judaism; in the one case there was unanimity, in the other, contradiction. Da Costa formed the resolution to forsake Catholicism and return to Judaism. Of an impulsive, passionate temperament, he sought to carry his resolution into effect quickly. With great caution he communicated his intention to his mother and brothers—his father was already dead—and they also resolved to expose themselves to the danger of secret emigration, to leave their hearth and home, give up a respected position in society, and exchange the certain present for an uncertain future. In spite of the Argus-eyed espionage of Marranos by the Inquisition and the secular authorities, the Da Costa family succeeded in gaining a vessel and escaping to Amsterdam (about 1617-18). Gabriel da Costa and his brothers were admitted to the covenant of Abraham, and Gabriel changed his name to Uriel.

Of a hot-blooded nature, an enthusiast whose

imagination overpowered his judgment, Uriel da Costa had formed for himself an ideal of Judaism which he expected to meet with in Amsterdam, but which had never been realized. He thought to see biblical conditions, supported by pure Pentateuchal laws, realized in the young Amsterdam community, and to find an elevation of mind which would at once clear up the puzzles that the Catholic Church could not solve. What the Catholic confessors could not offer, he thought that he would be able to obtain from the rabbis of Amsterdam. Da Costa had built religious and dogmatic castles in the air, and was annoyed not to meet with them in the world of reality. He soon found that the religious life of the Amsterdam community and its established laws did not agree with Mosaic or Pentateuchal precepts, but were often opposed to them. As he had made great sacrifices for his convictions, he thought that he had the right to express his opinion freely, and point to the gap which existed between biblical and Rabbinical Judaism. He was deeply wounded, embittered, and irritated, and allowed himself to be completely overpowered by his feelings. He did not stop at mere words, but regulated his conduct accordingly, openly disregarded religious usages, and thought that in opposing the ordinances of the "Pharisees" (as, in the language of the Church, he called the rabbis), he was recommending himself to the favor of God. He thereby brought upon himself unpleasantnesses destined to end tragically. Were the Amsterdam Jews, who had suffered so much for their religion, quietly to see one of their members openly assail and ridicule Judaism, become so dear to them? Those born and brought up in the land of the Inquisition had no idea of toleration and indulgence for the conviction of others. The rabbis, perhaps Isaac Uziel and Joseph Pardo, threatened Da Costa with excommunication, *i. e.*, expulsion from the religious community and severance of all relations with it, if he persisted in transgressing the religious ordinances of Judaism. This opposition only served to increase Da Costa's passion ; he was ill-content to have purchased new fetters by the sacrifices he had made. He continued to disregard the laws in force, and was eventually excommunicated. Uriel's relatives, who had more easily adapted themselves to the new faith, avoided him, and spoke not a word to him. Thus Da Costa stood alone in the midst of a great city. Separated from his race, friends, and relatives, a stranger amongst the Christian inhabitants of Amsterdam, whose language he had not yet learnt, and thrown upon himself, he fell more and more into subtle speculation. Acting under excessive irritation, he resolved to publish a work hostile to the Judaism of the day, and bring out particularly the glaring contrast between it and the Bible. As irrefragable proof, he intended to emphasize that the former recognized only bodily punishments and rewards, and taught nothing as to the immortality of the soul. But he discovered that the Bible itself observes silence about a purely spiritual future life, and does not bring within the circle of religion the idea of a soul separated from the body. In short, his investigations led him away not only from Catholicism and Rabbinical Judaism, but from the Bible itself. It is not known how it was circulated that the excommunicated Da Costa intended to give public offense, but he was anticipated. Samuel da Silva, a Jewish physician, in 1623 published a work in the Portuguese language, entitled " A Treatise on the Immortality of the Soul, in order to confute the Ignorance of a certain Opponent, who in Delusion affirms many Errors." In the course of the work the author plainly named Uriel, and described him as " blind and incapable." Da Costa thought his opponents, especially the rabbis, had hired Da Silva's pen to attack him. Hence he hastened to publish his work, also in Portuguese (1624-1625), entitled

"An Examination of the Pharisaic Traditions, compared with the written Laws, and Reply to the Slanderer Samuel da Silva." The fact of his calling his
opponent a slanderer shows his confusion, for he
actually asserted what Da Silva had reproached him
with, that the soul is not immortal. As he now had
unequivocally declared his breach with Judaism, he
had to take the consequences. Before, he had been
openly scorned by young people in the street as an
excommunicant, a heretic, an Epicurean (in the Talmudical sense); he had been pelted with stones, disturbed and annoyed in his own house (as he thought,
at the instigation of the rabbis). Now, after the
appearance of his work, the official representatives
of the Amsterdam community complained to the
magistrates that by denying the immortality of the
soul, he had attacked not only the teaching of Judaism, but also of Christianity, and had published
errors. Da Costa was arrested, kept for several
days in prison, at last fined 300 gulden, and his work
condemned to the flames. The freest state of that
time believed that it had the right to keep watch over
and limit freedom of thought and writing; its distinction was merely that it kindled no funeral piles for human beings. Da Costa's brethren in race could not
have persecuted him very severely, for he was able to
bear excommunication during the long space of fifteen years. Only his isolation was a heavy burden;
he could not endure to be avoided by his family as
one infected with the plague. Da Costa was not a
strong-minded man, a thinker of the first order, who
could live happily in his world of ideas as in boundless space, unconcerned about the outer world, and
glad of his solitary freedom; he could not do without
the world. He had invested his capital with one of
his brothers, and he thought that it would be endangered if he continued the war against the community.
He thought of taking a wife, which was impossible
so long as he was excommunicated. Hence he at

last yielded to the urgency of his relatives to become
reconciled with the community. He was willing, as
he said, " to be an ape among apes."   He confessed
Judaism with his lips at the very time when he had in
his heart thoroughly fallen away from it.

Da Costa, in his philosophical inquiries, had come
upon a new discovery. Judaism, even in its pure
biblical form, could not have been of divine origin,
because it contradicts nature in many points, and
God, the Creator of nature, can not contradict Himself in revelation. He cannot command a principle
in the Law, if He has implanted in nature an opposing principle. This was the first step to the deistic
tendency then appearing in France and the Netherlands, which acknowledged God only in nature, not
in the moral law, and in religious and political development. Da Costa's theory supposed a religion of
nature inborn in man, which produced and built
up the moral law, and culminated in the love of
members of a family to one another. The best in
Judaism and other revealed religions is borrowed
from the religion of nature. The latter knows only
love and union ; the others, on the contrary, arm
parents and children against one another on account
of the faith. This theory was the suggestion of his
bitterness, because his relatives avoided him, and
showed him but little consideration. Da Costa appears to have put forward as the religion of nature
what the Talmud calls the Noachian commandments.

In spite of his complete falling away from Judaism, he resolved, as he himself states, on the intervention of his nephew, and after passing fifteen
years in excommunication (about 1618-1633), to
alter his course of life and actions, make a confession, or rather put his signature to such a document,
an act of what he himself describes as thorough-
going hypocrisy, designed to purchase repose and
comfort, at the cost of conviction. But his passion-

ate nature robbed him of both. He could not impose renunciation upon himself to conform to the religious usages of Judaism, but transgressed them immediately after his penitent confession. He was detected by one of his relatives, and they all, especially the nephew who had brought about the reconciliation, were so embittered that they persecuted him even more relentlessly than those less nearly connected with him. They again renounced intercourse with him, prevented his marriage, and are said to have injured him in his property. Through his passionate hatred of Judaism, which he had confessed with his lips, he committed an act of folly which exposed his true sentiments. Two Christians, an Italian and a Spaniard, had come from London to Amsterdam to attach themselves to Judaism. When they consulted Uriel da Costa on the subject, he gave a frightful picture of the Jewish form of religion, warned them against laying a heavy yoke on their necks, and advised them to continue in their own faith. Contrary to promise, the two Christians betrayed Da Costa's remarks on Judaism to the leaders of the community. The war between them and him broke out afresh. The rabbis summoned him a second time before their tribunal, set before him his religious transgressions, and declared that he could escape a second severe excommunication only by submitting to a solemn penance in public. More from a sense of honor than from conviction he refused this penance, and so was a second time laid under the ban, much more severe than the first, in which condition he continued for seven years. During this time he was treated by the members of the community with contempt, and even spat upon. His brothers and nephews behaved with the greatest severity towards him, because they thought by that means to force him to repentance. They reckoned on his helplessness and weakness, and they did not reckon amiss.

Da Costa meanwhile had reached middle age, had been made submissive by conflicts and excitement, and longed for repose. By process of law, which he had instituted against the Amsterdam authorities, he could obtain nothing, because he could not put his complaints into a tangible form; he consented, therefore, to everything demanded for his humiliation. His public penance was to be very severe. There was no definite prescription on the subject in the religious Code, which, in fact, is opposed in spirit to public penance; the sinner is not to confess aloud his transgressions against religion, but in silence to God. Judaism, from its origin, objected to confession and the mechanical avowal of sins. For this reason it remained for the college of rabbis to appoint a form of penance. The Amsterdam rabbis and the communal council, consisting of Marranos, adopted as a model the gloomy form of the tribunal of the Inquisition.

As soon as Da Costa had consented to his humiliation, he was led into one of the synagogues, which was full of men and women. There was to be a sort of auto-da-fé, and the greatest possible publicity was given to his penance because the scandal had been public. He had to ascend a stage and read out his confession of sins: that he had desecrated the Sabbath, violated the dietary laws, denied articles of faith, and advised persons not to adopt Judaism. He solemnly declared that he resolved to be no longer guilty of such offenses, but to live as a true Jew. On a whisper from the first rabbi, probably Saul Morteira, he went to a corner of the synagogue, stripped as far as the girdle, and received thirty-nine stripes with a scourge. Then he was obliged to sit on the ground, after which the ban was removed. Not yet having satisfied the authorities, he had to stretch himself out on the threshold of the synagogue, that those present might step over him. It was certainly an excessive penance which was imposed upon him, not from a desire of persecution or vengeance, but from religious scrupulousness and mimicry of Catholic forms. No wonder that the disgrace and humiliation deeply wounded Da Costa, who had consented to the punishment, not from inward repentance, but from exhaustion. The public disgrace had shaken his whole being, and suggested thoughts of revenge. Instead of pitying the rabbis as the creatures of historical conditions, he hated them with a glowing feeling of revenge as the refuse of mankind, and as if they thought of nothing but deception, lying, and wickedness. His wounded sense of honor and heated imagination saw in the Jews of the Amsterdam community, perhaps in all the Jews on the earth's surface, his personal, venomous foes, and in Judaism an institution to stir up men to hatred and persecution. Thinking that he was surrounded by bitter enemies, and feeling too weak for a fresh conflict, he resolved to die, but at the same time to take vengeance on his chief persecutor, his brother (or cousin). To excite the sympathy of his contemporaries and posterity, he wrote his autobiography and confession, which, however, contain no new thoughts, only bitterness and furious attacks against the Jews, intermingled with fresh aspersions of them in the eyes of Christians: that even at this time they would have crucified Jesus, and that the state ought not to grant them freedom of religious profession. This document, drawn up amidst preparations for death, breathed nothing but revenge against his enemies. After he had finished his impassioned testament, he loaded two pistols, and fired one at his relative, who was passing his house. He missed his aim, so he shut the door of his room, and killed himself with the other weapon (April, 1640)

On opening his residence after the report of the shot, they found on the table his autobiography, "An Example of Human Life," in which he brought

Jews and Judaism to the bar, and with pathetic sentences described them as his excited imagination in the last hour suggested. By this act and legacy Da Costa showed that he suffered himself to be overpowered by his feelings rather than guided by reason. He was neither a thinker nor a wise man, nor was his a manly character. As his system of thought was not well balanced, leading him to oppose what existed as false and bad, because it was in his way, he left no lasting impression. His Jewish contemporaries persisted in stubborn silence about him, as if they wished his memory to fall into oblivion. He acted like a boy who breaks the windows in an old decaying building, and thus creates a draught.

The second seditious thinker of this time, Leo (Judah) ben Isaac Modena (born 1571, died 1649), was of another stamp, and was reared in different surroundings. Leo Modena was descended from a cultivated family which migrated to Modena, in Italy, on the expulsion of the Jews from France, and whose ancestors, from lack of intellectual clearness, despite their education, fostered every kind of superstition and fanciful idea.

Leo Modena possessed this family peculiarity in a high degree. He was a marvelous child. In his third year he could read a portion from the prophets ; in his tenth, he delivered a sort of sermon ; in his thirteenth, he wrote a clever dialogue on the question of the lawfulness of playing with cards and dice, and composed an elegy on the death of the teacher of his youth, Moses Basula, in Hebrew and Italian verses having the same sound—a mere trifle, to be sure, but which at a riper age pleased him so well that he had it printed. But the marvelous child did not develop into a marvelous man, into a personage of prominence or distinction. Modena became, however, the possessor of astonishingly varied knowledge. As he pursued all sorts of occupations to support himself, viz., those of preacher, teacher of Jews and Christians, reader of prayers, interpreter, writer, proof-reader, bookseller, broker, merchant, rabbi, musician, matchmaker, and manufacturer of amulets, without ever attaining to a fixed position, so he studied many departments of knowledge without specially distinguishing himself in any. He grasped the whole of biblical, Talmudic, and Rabbinic literature, was well read in Christian theological works, understood something of philosophy and physics, was able to write Hebrew and Italian verses—in short, he had read everything accessible through the medium of three languages, Hebrew, Latin, and Italian. He remembered what he read, for he possessed an excellent memory, invented a method of sharpening it still more, and wrote a book on this subject. But Leo Modena had no delight either in knowledge or poetry; neither had value for him except so far as they brought bread. He preached, wrote books and verses, translated and commented, all to earn money, which he wasted in card-playing, a passion which he theoretically considered most culpable, but in practice could not overcome. At the age of sixty he acquired property, but lost it more quickly than he had acquired it, squandering 100 ducats in scarcely a month, and twice as much in the following year. Knowledge had not enlightened and elevated him, had had no influence on his principles. Leo Modena possessed neither genius nor character. Dissatisfied with himself and his lot, in constant disquiet on account of his fondness for gaming, and battling with need, he became a prey to doubt. Religion had no power over his heart; he preached to others, but not to himself. Unbelief and superstition waged continual war within him. He envied naïve believers, who, in their simplicity, are undisturbed by doubt, expect, and, as Leo added, obtain happiness from scrupulously observing the ceremon-

ies. Inquirers, on the other hand, are obliged to
struggle for their faith and the happiness dependent
upon it, and are tortured incessantly by pangs of
doubt. He had no real earnestness nor true conviction, or rather, according to his humor and mood,
he had a different one every day, without being a
hypocrite. Hence he could say of himself, " I do
not belong to the class of painted people, my outward conduct always corresponds with my feelings."

Leo Modena was sincere at each moment. On
one day he broke a lance for the Talmud and Rabbinical Judaism, on the next, condemned them
utterly. He disapproved of gaming, and grieved
that the stars had given him this unfortunate propensity, for he believed also in astrology; yet he
prepared a Talmudical decision defending it.
When the Venetian college of rabbis pronounced
the ban on cards and dice, he pointed out that gaming was permissible by Rabbinical principles, and
that the ban had no justification. His disciple,
Joseph Chamiz, a physician and mystic, once asked
him his opinion on the Kabbalistic transmigration of
souls. Modena replied that as a rule he would profess belief in the doctrine even though convinced of
its folly, in order not to be pronounced a heretic and
a fool, but to him he was willing to express his sincere and true views. Thereupon Leo Modena prepared a work to expose the absurdity and incon-
sistency with Judaism of the belief in transmigration
of souls. But so feebly was this conviction rooted
in his nature that, having had an extraordinary experience, he again, at least for a time, believed in
the transmigration of souls, a favorite theory of the
Kabbala.

The Ghetto of Venice must have been a totally
different place from that of Frankfort, or Prague, or
from the Polish-Jewish quarters, since it was possible for men like Leo Modena, with his peculiar
principles, and Simone Luzzatto, as little of a gen-

uine rabbi, to be members of the rabbinate. In the largest Italian community next to that of Rome, consisting of 6,000 souls, there were cultivated Jews interested in Italian and general European culture, and enjoying not only social, but also literary intercourse with Christian society. The walls of the Ghetto formed no partition between the Jewish and the Christian population. At this time, in the age of Shakespeare, there was no Shylock, certainly not in Venice, who would have stipulated as payment for his loan a pound of flesh from his Christian debtor. The people properly so called, workmen, sailors, and porters, precisely in Venice, were milder and more friendly towards Jews than in other Christian cities. Jewish manufacturers employed 4,000 Christian workmen in the lagoon city, so that their existence depended on their Jewish employers alone. At the time of a devastating pestilence, when, even in this well policed city, the reins of government became slacker and looser, and threatened to fall from the hands of those in power, Jewish capitalists voluntarily offered their money to the state to prevent embarrassment. There were not a few among them who vied with the cultivated classes among the Christians in the elegant use of the Italian language in speaking and writing, and in making good verses. Besides the two rabbis, Leo Modena and Simone Luzzatto, two Jewish poetesses, Deborah Ascarelli and Sarah Copia Sullam, are illustrations thereof. The first, the wife of Joseph Ascarelli, a respected Venetian, translated Hebrew hymns into elegant Italian strophes, and also composed original verses. A Jewish-Italian poet addressed her in verses thus : " Others may sing of great trophies, thou glorifiest thy people."

The graceful and spiritual Sarah Copia (born about 1600, died 1641) excited a certain amount of attention in her time. She was an original poetess and thinker, and her gifts, as well as her grace,

brought her temptations and dangers. The only
child of a wealthy father, Simon Copia (Coppio) in
Venice, who loved her tenderly, she yielded to her
inclination for instruction, and devoted herself to
science and literature. To this inclination she
remained true even after her marriage with Jacob
Sullam. Sarah Copia Sullam surpassed her sex and
even men of her age in knowledge. She delighted
in beauty, and breathed out her inspirations in
rhythmic, elegant verses. Young, attractive, with a
noble heart and a penetrating understanding, striving
after high ideals, and a favorite of the muses, Sarah
Sullam fascinated the old as well as the young.
Her musical, well-trained voice excited admiration.
When an elderly Italian priest, Ansaldo Ceba, at
Genoa, published an heroic poem in Italian strophes,
of which the scriptural Esther was the heroine, Sarah
was so delighted, that she addressed an enthusiastic
anonymous letter full of praise to the author (1618).
It pleased her to see a Jewish heroine, her ideal,
celebrated in verses, and the attention of the cultivated public directed to Jewish antiquity. She
hoped that thereby the prejudice against the Jews
of the day would vanish. Sarah did not conceal
from the poet that she always carried his poetical
creations about with her, and at night put his book
under her pillow. Instead of finding satisfaction in
the sincere homage of a pure woman's soul, Ceba,
in his zeal for conversion, thought only of bringing
her over to Christianity. When he heard Sarah's
beauty extolled by the servant whom he sent with
presents and verses, love for her awoke in him.
This was increased by her sending him her portrait,
accompanied by enthusiastic verses in the exaggerated style of that time, in which she said: "I carry
my idol in my heart, and I wish everyone to worship
him." But the beautiful Venetian Jewess did not
allow herself to be entrapped. She held firmly to
her Jewish beliefs, and unfolded to her priestly friend

the reasons that induced her to prefer Judaism. In vain did Ceba, by tenderness, reproofs, and sentimental languishing, with intimations of his speedy end, and his longing to be united with her in heaven, endeavor to make her waver in her conviction. When he begged permission to pray for her salvation, she granted his request on condition that she might pray for his conversion to Judaism.

Her exceptional position as poetess, and her connection with Christians of high rank, brought her renown, not unattended by annoyances. Slanderous fellow-believers spread the report, that she esteemed the principles of Judaism but lightly, and did not fully believe in their divinity. An unprincipled Christian priest, Balthasar Bonifaccio, who later occupied the position of bishop, published a work accusing the Jewess Sarah Sullam of denying the immortality of the soul. Such a charge might in Catholic Venice have had other effects than that against Uriel da Costa in free-thinking, Protestant Amsterdam. Not merely fine and imprisonment might have been inflicted, but the Inquisition might have sentenced her to the dungeon, to torture, and perhaps even the stake. Hardly recovered from illness, she wrote (1621) a manifesto on the immortality of the soul, full of ripe dialectics, noble courage, and crushing force, against her slanderous accuser. The dedication to her deceased father is touching, and still more touching is her fervent psalm-like prayer in melodious Italian verses. The consciousness that she, a woman and Jewess, could not rely on her own strength, but only on help from above, spreads a halo about her memory. The end of this affair is not known. Ceba's epic "Esther" probably induced Leo Modena to translate Solomon Usque's tragedy on the same subject from Spanish into Italian verse ; he dedicated it to Sarah Copia, whose epitaph he composed in melodious Hebrew verses.

Leo Modena also had frequent intercourse with Christians. His peculiar nature, his communicative disposition, and great learning, as also his wit and his fondness for gaming, opened the doors of Christian circles to the volatile rabbi. Christian disciples sat at his feet. The French bishop Jacob Plantavicius, and the half-crazed Christian Kabbalist Jacob Gaffarelli, were his pupils. Nobles and learned men corresponded with him, and permitted him to inscribe his works to them with flattering dedications. Leo Modena held in Italy nearly the same position as Manasseh ben Israel in Holland. In the conversation of serious men and in the merry circle of gamesters, he often heard the ceremonies of Judaism ridiculed as childish nonsense (Lex Judæorum lex puerorum). At first he defended his religion, but gradually was forced to admit one thing and another in Judaism to be defective and ridiculous ; he was ashamed to be so thoroughly a Jew as to justify all consequences. His necessities led him, on pressure from Christian friends, to render single portions, and at last the whole, of the Jewish code accessible to the Christian public in the Italian language. An English lord paid him for the work, with the intention of giving it to King James I, who made pretensions to extensive learning. Afterwards his Christian disciple Gaffarelli had this work, entitled "The Hebrew Rites," printed in Paris, and dedicated it to the French ambassador at Venice. In this work, eagerly read by Christians, Leo Modena, like Ham, uncovered his father's nakedness, exposed the inner sanctuary of the Jews to prying and mocking eyes. To the uninitiated, that which within the Jewish circle was a matter for reverence could not but appear petty, silly, and absurd. Leo Modena explained what ceremonies and statutes Jews employ in connection with their dwellings, clothing, household furniture, up-rising and lying down, physical functions, and in the synagogues and

schools.   Involuntarily the author associated himself
with the despisers of Judaism, which he as rabbi had
practiced and taught.   He showed that he was conscious of this :

> "While writing I in fact forgot that I am a Jew, and considered
> myself a simple, impartial narrator.   However, I do not deny that I
> have taken pains to avoid ridicule on account of the numerous cere-
> monies, but I had no intention to defend and palliate, because I wished
> only to communicate, not convince."

However, it would be an error to infer from this
that Leo Modena had at heart completely broken
with Rabbinical Judaism.   He was, as has been
stated, not a man of firm and lasting convictions.
Almost at the same time when he exposed the rites
of Judaism to the Christian public, he composed a
defense of them and oral teaching in general against
attacks from the Jewish side.   A Hamburg Jew of
Marrano descent had raised eleven points to show
the falsehood of Talmudic tradition.   Of these
arguments some are important, others frivolous.
The Hamburg sceptic laid chief stress on the point
that Talmudic and Rabbinic ordinances are additions to Pentateuchal Judaism, and the Pentateuch
had expressly forbidden additions of this sort.   At
the wish of certain Portuguese Jews, Leo Modena
confuted these objections, raised by a sciolist.   His
confutation was a feeble performance, and contains
nothing new.   With Leo Modena one never knew
whether he was earnest in his belief or his unbelief.
As in youth he had brought forward reasons for and
against games of chance, had finally condemned
them, and nevertheless freely engaged in them, so
he behaved with regard to Talmudical Judaism.
He attacked it, defended it, made it appear ridiculous, and yet practiced it with a certain degree of
honesty.
Some years after his vindication of Talmudical
Judaism against the Hamburg sceptic he composed
the best work (1624) that issued from his active

pen.   On the one side it was a weighty attack on Rabbinical Judaism, such as had hardly been made even by Christians and Karaites, on the other side, an impressive defense of it.   He did not venture to put his own name to the heavy charges against Judaism, but used a fictitious name.   The part which contains the attacks he called "The Fool's Voice" (Kol Sachal), and the defense, "The Roaring of the Lion" (Shaagath Aryeh).   Leo Modena allotted to two characters his own duplex nature, his varying convictions.   He makes the opponent of Judaism express himself with a boldness such as Uriel da Costa might have envied.   Not only did he undermine the Rabbinical Judaism of the Talmud, but also biblical Judaism, the Sinaitic revelation, and the Torah.   But the blows which Leo Modena, under the name of Ibn-Raz of Alkala, in an attack of unbelief, inflicted on oral teaching, or Talmudical Judaism, were most telling.

He premises that no form of religion maintains itself in its original state and purity according to the views of its founder.   Judaism, also, although the lawgiver expressly warned his followers against adding anything, had many additions thrust upon it. Interpretation and comment had altered many things in it.   Ibn-Raz (or Leo Modena in his unbelieving mood) examines with a critical eye Jacob Asheri's code, and at each point marks the additions made by the rabbis to the original code, and where they had weakened and distorted it.   He goes so far as to make proposals how to clear Judaism of excrescences, in order to restore genuine, ancient, biblical, spiritual Judaism.   This was the first attempt at reform : a simplification of the prayers and synagogue service, abolition of rites, omission of the second day of the festivals, relaxation of Sabbath, festival, Passover, and even Day of Atonement laws. Every one was to fast only according to his bodily and spiritual powers.   He wished to see the ritual for slaughtering animals and the laws as to food set aside, or simplified. The prohibition to drink wine with those of other creeds made Jews ridiculous, as also did the strictness against alleged idolatry. All this, observed Ibn-Raz, or Leo Modena, at the close, does not exhaust the subject ; it is only a specimen of the evil of Rabbinical Judaism. He knew well that he would be pronounced a heretic, and persecuted on account of his frank criticism, but if he could open the eyes of a single reader, he would consider himself amply rewarded.

Had Leo Modena been in earnest with this bold view, which would have revolutionized the Judaism of his day, had he uttered it to the world with deep conviction, he would no doubt have produced great commotion in Judaism. But criticism of the Talmud was only mental amusement for him ; he did not intend to engage in an actual conflict. He composed a reply with as little sincerity, and let both attack and defense slumber among his papers.

Leo Modena was more in earnest with the attack on the Kabbala, which had become burdensome and repulsive to him. He felt impelled to discharge destructive arrows against it, and this he did with masterly skill. He called the anti-Kabbalistic work, which he dedicated to his disciple Joseph Chamiz, a Luryan enthusiast, "The Roaring Lion" (Ari Noham). From many sides he threw light on the deceptions, the absurdity, and the falsehood of the Kabbala and its fundamental source, the Zohar. Neither this work nor his attacks on Talmudical Judaism were published by him : the author was not anxious to labor in either direction. To a late age he continued his irregular life, without striving after real improvement. Leo Modena died, weary of the conflict, not with gods (*i. e.*, ideas) and men, but with himself, and of the troubles which he had brought upon himself.

Apparently similar, yet differing fundamentally

from him, was the third burrower of this period:
Joseph Solomon Delmedigo (born 1591, died 1655).
Scion of an old and noble family, in whose midst
science and the Talmud were cultivated, and great-
grandson on the female side of the clear thinker
Elias del Medigo, he but slightly resembled the
other members of his house.   His father, a rabbi in
Candia, had not only initiated him into Talmudic
literature, but also made him learn Greek.   Later
Delmedigo acquired the literary languages of the
time, Italian and Spanish in addition to Latin.   The
knowledge of languages, however, was only a means
to an end.   At the University of Padua he obtained
his scientific education; he showed decided inclination for mathematics and astronomy, and could
boast of having as his tutor the great Galileo, the
discoverer of the laws of the heavens, the martyr to
natural science.   By him he was made acquainted
with the Copernican system of the sun and the
planets.   Neither Delmedigo nor any believing Jew
labored under the delusion that the stability of the
sun and the motion of the earth were in contradiction to the Bible, and therefore heretical.   Delmedigo also studied medicine, but only as a profession ; his favorite subject continued to be mathematics.   He enriched his mind with all the treasures of knowledge, more varied even than that of
Leo Modena, to whom during his residence in Italy
he clung as a disciple to his master.   In the circle
of Jewish-Italian semi-freethinkers he lost the simple
faith which he had brought from home, and doubts
as to the truth of tradition stole upon him, but he
was not sufficiently animated by a desire for truth
either to overcome these doubts and become settled
in the early belief to which he had been brought up,
or unsparingly to expose the false elements in Jewish tradition.   Joseph Delmedigo was as little
formed to be a martyr to his convictions as Leo
Modena, the latter by reason of fickleness, the
former, of insincerity.

With doubt in his heart he returned to his home in Candia, and gave offense by his free mode of thought, especially by his preference for secular knowledge. He made enemies, who are said to have persecuted him, and was obliged to leave his native land. Then began a migratory life, which drove him from city to city, like his model Ibn-Ezra. Like him, he made friends with the Karaites wherever he met them, and they thronged to his presence. At Cairo Delmedigo celebrated a complete triumph with his mathematical knowledge, when an old Mahometan teacher of mathematics, Ali Ibn-Rahmadan, challenged him, a youth, to a public combat, in which Ali was beaten. The victorious combatant was magnanimous enough to show honor to Ali before the world. Instead of betaking himself to Palestine as he had intended, Delmedigo traveled to Constantinople; here also he attached himself to the circle of the Karaites, and at last passed through Wallachia and Moldavia to Poland. There, mathematics procuring him no bread, he practiced medicine, of which, however, he had learnt more from books than by the bedside of patients. In Poland he passed for a great physician, and was taken into the service of Prince Radziwill, in Wilna (about 1619-1620). Here, through the excessive attention given to the Talmud, general culture was forsaken, but youths and men eager for learning, especially Karaites, thronged to Delmedigo to slake their thirst for knowledge. A half-crazed Karaite, Serach ben Nathan of Trok, who had an inclination to Rabbinical Judaism, in order to show his extensive knowledge, with mock humility laid before him a number of important questions, which Delmedigo was to answer offhand, and sent him a sable fur for the Polish winter.

Delmedigo found it to his advantage, in order to give himself the appearance of a distinguished character in Poland, to shroud himself in silence and seclusion. He at first answered Serach's questions not personally, but through one of his companions, an assistant and follower, Moses Metz. This man described his teacher as a choice intellect, a demi-god, who carried in his brain all human and divine knowledge. He sketched his appearance and character, his occupation and behavior, regulated, as he said, by higher wisdom, gave information about his descent from a learned and distinguished family on his father's and his mother's side, and, as his teacher's mouth-piece, imposed upon the credulous Karaite by saying that he had composed works on all branches of knowledge, at which the world would be astonished, if they came to light. Metz also communicated to Serach some of his teacher's theories in mathematics, religion, and philosophy, and thus still more confused Serach's mind. In his communications on Judaism, which Delmedigo either made himself or through Moses Metz, he was very cautious ; here and there, it is true, he allowed a suggestion of unbelief to glimmer through, but quickly covered it over with a haze of orthodoxy. Only where he could do so without danger Delmedigo expressed his real opinion.

When he at last sent the Karaite an answer to a letter with his own hand (about 1621), he did not conceal his true views, but declared his preference for Karaism and its ancient teachers, loaded them undeservedly with praise, exalted science, and ridiculed the delusions of the Kabbala and its adherents. In the same letter to Serach, Delmedigo indulged in scoffs against the Talmud, and thought the Karaites fortunate that they were able to dispense with it. He had nothing to fear when he unburdened his heart before his Karaite admirer.

Delmedigo does not seem, on the whole, to have been at ease in Poland. He could not carouse with the nobles whom he attended professionally for fear of the Jews, and it was not possible to earn money

in so poor a country.   So he betook himself by way
of Dantzic to Hamburg, where a Portuguese community had been lately permitted to settle.   His
knowledge of medicine seems to have met with little
esteem in the city on the Elbe.   What was his skill
in comparison with that of the De Castros, father
and son?   He was compelled, in order to subsist,
to undertake a certain amount of rabbinical duty, if
only as preacher.   For the sake of bread he had
to play the hypocrite, and speak in favor of Rabbinical Judaism.   Nay, in order to dissipate the rumor
from Poland, which represented him as a heretic, he
was not ashamed to praise the Kabbala, which he
had shortly before condemned, as the highest wisdom, before which philosophy and all sciences must
be dumb.   For this purpose he prepared his defense
of the secret doctrine, in refutation of the crushing
arguments against it by one of his ancestors, Elias
Del Medigo.   His work was of the kind to throw
dust in the eyes of the ignorant multitude; it displayed a smattering of learning on all sorts of subjects, but no trace of logic.   He was too clever to
maintain the sheepish style of dull, stupid credulity,
and could not refrain from satire.   He defended the
genuineness of the Zohar as an ancient work by
Simon bar Yochaï, or at least by his school.   He
argued that one must not be shocked by its many
incongruities and absurdities; the Talmud also contains not a few, and is yet a sacred book.   To save
his reputation with the more intelligent, Delmedigo
intimated that he had defended the Kabbala only
from necessity.   We must not, he says, superficially
judge the character of an author by his words.   He,
for instance, was writing this defense of the Kabbala
at the desire of a patron of high position, who was
enamored of it.   Should this friend come to be of
another mind, and require an attack upon the Kabbala, he would not refuse him.   In conclusion, he
observes that philosophical students would no doubt

ridicule him for having turned his back on wisdom, and betaken himself to folly ; but he would rather be called a fool all his life than for a single hour transgress against piety.

This work, commenced in Hamburg, Delmedigo could not finish there. A pestilence broke out, and drove him, physician though he was, to Glückstadt. In this small community, where, as he said, there was neither town (Stadt) nor luck (Glück), he could find no means of subsistence, and he traveled on to Amsterdam about 1629. He could not attempt to practice medicine in a city where physicians lived of even higher eminence than at Hamburg, and so was obliged a second time to apply himself to the functions of rabbi. To show his importance, he printed his scientific replies to the questions of his Polish admirers, with the fulsome eulogies, clouds of incense, and foolish homage which the young Karaite Serach had offered him. It is a work of truly Polish disorder, in which mathematical theorems and scientific problems are discussed by the side of philosophical and theological questions, in a confused way. Delmedigo took care not to print his attacks upon the Kabbala and the Talmud, and his preference for the Karaites—in short, all that he had written to please the rich Serach. Instead of publishing an encyclopædic work which he boastfully said he had composed in his earliest youth, and which embraced all sciences and solved all questions, he produced a mere medley.

The Amsterdam community was then full of suspicion against philosophy and culture owing to the reckless behavior of Da Costa, and therefore Delmedigo thought it advisable to ward off every suspicion of unbelief, and get a reputation for strictest orthodoxy. This transparent hypocrisy did not answer well. He was, it is true, appointed preacher, and partially rabbi, in or near Amsterdam, but he could remain in Holland only a few years. Poor

and unstable as he was, he went with his wife to
Frankfort-on-the-Main about 1630 to seek means
of subsistence.   But here, in a German community,
where Rabbinical learning was diffused, he could
not obtain a rabbinical office ; but he could turn his
medical knowledge, scanty as it was, to account.
As he felt no vocation for the office of rabbi, nor for
medical practice, it was a matter of indifference if
he changed the preacher's gown for the doctor's
mantle.   He was engaged, under irksome conditions, as communal doctor (February 14, 1631).
How long he remained at Frankfort is not known ;
his position cannot have been favorable, for he removed to Prague (about 1648-1650), and in this
most neglected community he settled.   Later (1652)
he was at Worms, probably only temporarily, and
ended his life, which had promised so much, and
realized so little, at Prague.   Nor did he publish
any part of his great work, which he had announced
with so much pomposity.

In a measure Simone (Simcha) Luzzatto (born
about 1590, died 1663) may be reckoned among the
sceptics of this time.   He was, at the same time as
Leo Modena, rabbi in Venice.   Luzzatto was not
an eminent personage ; but he had more solidity
than his colleague Modena, or than Delmedigo.
By the latter, who knew him personally, he was
praised as a distinguished mathematician.   He was
also well read in ancient and modern literature.
His uprightness and love of truth, which he never
belied, distinguished him more than his knowledge
and learning.   A parable which Luzzatto wrote in
Italian in his youth shows his views, as also his
maturity of thought, and that he had reflected early
on the relation of faith to science.   He puts his
thoughts into the mouth of Socrates, the father of
Greek wisdom.   At Delphi an academy had been
formed to rectify the errors of human knowledge.
Reason immediately presented a petition from the

dungeon, where she had been so long kept by orthodox authority, to be set at liberty. Although the
chief representatives of knowledge, Pythagoras and
Aristotle, spoke against this request, and uttered a
warning against her liberation, because, when free,
she would produce and spread abroad most frightful
errors, yet the academy set her at liberty; for by
that means alone could knowledge be promoted.
But the newly liberated minds caused great mischief; and the academicians were at a loss what to
do. Then Socrates rose, and in a long speech
explained that reason and authority, if allowed to
reign alone, would produce only errors and mischief;
but if mutually limited, reason by revelation, and
revelation by reason, they mingle in the right proportion, and produce beautiful harmony, whereby
man may attain his goal here below and hereafter.
This thought, that reason and faith must regulate
and keep watch over each other, which, in Maimuni's
time had passed into a commonplace, was at this
period, under the rule of Lurya's Kabbala, considered in Jewish circles a bold innovation.

Simone Luzzatto did not suffer himself to be ensnared by Kabbalistic delusions; he did not cast
reason behind him; he was a believer, but withal
sober-minded. He did not share the delusion of
Manasseh ben Israel and others that the lost tribes
of Israel were existing in some part of the world
enjoying independence as a military power. With
sober Jewish inquirers of former times, he assumed
that Daniel's revelation does not point to a future
Messiah, but only reflects historical events. He
composed a work on the manners and beliefs of the
Jews, which he proposed to exhibit "faithfully to
truth, without zeal and passion." It was probably
designed to form a counterpart to Leo Modena's
representation, which cast a shadow on Judaism.

Luzzatto's defense of Judaism and the Jews,
under the title "A Treatise on the Position of the

Hebrews," is masterly. It speaks eloquently for his practical, sober sense, for his love of truth, his attachment to Judaism, and his solid knowledge. He did not wish to dedicate it to any individual patron out of flattery, but to the friends of truth in general. He conjured these friends not to esteem the remnant of the ancient Hebrew nation, even if disfigured by sufferings, and saddened by long oppression, more lightly than a mutilated work of art by Phidias or Lysippus, since all men were agreed that this nation was once animated and led by the greatest of Masters. It is astonishing what thorough knowledge the rabbi had of the commerce of that time, and the influence upon it of the political position of European and neighboring Asiatic states. The object of his defense was primarily to disarm the ill-will of certain Venetian patricians against the Jews in that strictly governed state. The common people had little antipathy to the Jews; they lived to some extent on them. But among those who had a share in the government there were fanatical religious zealots and envious opponents, who advocated further restrictions, or even banishment. It did not suit them that the Venetian Jews, who, shut up in the Ghetto, possessed neither land nor the right to carry on a handicraft, competed with them in finance and trade. The commercial city of Venice, far surpassed by the new naval powers, Holland and England, which had gradually obtained control of the trade with the Levant, saw many of its great houses of business in splendid misery, while new Jewish capitalists stepped into their place, and seized the Levantine business. With artful turns and delicate hints, Luzzatto gave the politicians of Venice to understand that exhaustion was hastening the downfall of the republic. The prosperous cared only to keep what they had acquired and for enjoyment, and former Venetian commerce seemed to be falling into the hands of foreigners. Hence the

Jews had become a blessing to the state. It was more advisable to leave its extensive trade, especially that of the East, to native Jews, and to protect them, than to see it diverted to neighboring towns, or to strangers, who formed a state within the state, were not always obedient to the laws, and gradually carried the ready money out of the country. Luzzatto calculated from statistics that the Jews contributed more than 250,000 ducats to the republic every year, that they gave bread to 4,000 workpeople, supplied home manufactures at a cheap rate, and obtained goods from distant countries. It was reserved for a rabbi to bring this political-economical consideration, of vital importance for the island republic, to the notice of wise councilors. Luzzatto also called attention to the important advantage which the capital of the Jews had recently been, when, during the pestilence and the dissolution of political government, the Jews had spontaneously offered money to the state to prevent embarrassment.

Luzzatto also defended the Jews against attacks on the religious side, but on this point his exposition is not original. If he brought out the bright traits of his Jewish contemporaries, he by no means passed over their dark ones in silence, and that redounds to his credit. Luzzatto depicted them in the following manner. However different may be the manner of Venetian Jews from their brethren in Constantinople, Damascus, Germany, or Poland, they all have something in common :—

"It is a nation of timid and unmanly disposition, at present incapable of political government, occupied only with its separate interests, and caring little about the public welfare. The economy of the Jews borders on avarice ; they are admirers of antiquity, and have no eye for the present course of things. Many are uneducated, without taste for learning or the knowledge of languages, and, in following the laws of their religion, they exaggerate to the most painful degree. But they have also noteworthy peculiarities—firmness and endurance in their religion, uniformity of doctrinal teaching in the long course of more than fifteen centuries since the dispersion ; wonderful steadfastness, which leads them, if not to go into dangers, yet to endure the severest suffering. They possess knowledge of Holy Scripture and its exposition, gentleness and hospitality to the members of their race—the Persian Jew in some degree suffers the wrongs of the Italian—strict abstinence from carnal offenses, extraordinary carefulness to keep the family unspotted, and skill in managing difficult matters. They are submissive and yielding to everyone, only not to their brethren in religion. The failings of the Jews have rather the character of cowardice and meanness than of cruelty and atrocity."

What Luzzatto's position was with regard to the Talmud he did not distinctly state, but only explained generally that there are three or four classes of Jews : Talmudists or Rabbanites, who hold the oral law of equal authority with the Bible ; secondly, a philosophical and cultured class ; and, lastly, Kabbalists, and Karaites. Yet he intimated that he held the Talmudical tradition to be true ; whilst he considered the Kabbala as not of Jewish, but of Platonic, Pythagorean, and Gnostic origin. One of his disciples relates of him that he ridiculed the Kabbalists, and thought their theory had no claim to the title of tradition ; it was wanting in the Holy Spirit.

These four thinkers, more or less dissatisfied with the Judaism of the day, who were furnished with so much intellect, knowledge, and eloquence, yet exerted very little influence over their Jewish contemporaries, and thus did not break through the prevailing obscurity in the smallest degree. Luzzatto wrote for only a limited class of readers, and did not inflict, or wish to inflict, heavy blows on Judaism. Uriel da Costa missed his mark on account of his violent, impatient disposition ; Leo Modena was himself too wavering, driven hither and thither by the wind of conflicting opinions, to acquire serious convictions and do battle for them. His attacks on the weak side of Judaism, as has been stated, were made in private. Joseph Delmedigo did more harm than good through his insincerity and hypocrisy. Lacking character, he sank so low as to speak in favor of the confused doctrines of the Kabbala, and by the weight of his knowledge confirmed and increased the delusion of the multi-

tude.   But from two other quarters, by two quite
opposite characters, weighty blows against Judaism
were delivered, threatening completely to shatter it.
Reason incorporated, as it were, in one Jew, and
unreason incarnate in another, joined hands to treat
Judaism as abolished and dissolved, and, so to
speak, to dethrone the God of Israel.

CHAPTER IV.

SPINOZA AND SABBATAÏ ZEVI

Spinoza's Youth and Education—His Intellectual Breach with Juda-
ism—Fresh Martyrs of the Inquisition—The Rabbis and Spinoza
—Excommunication—Spinoza's "Tractate" and "Ethics"—
Spinoza's Writings Concerning Judaism—Spinoza's Contem-
poraries in Amsterdam—De Paz and Penso—The Mystical
Character of the Years 1648 and 1666—Sabbataï Zevi's early
Career—The Jerusalem Community—Sabbataï's Travels—
Nathan Ghazati—Sabbataï announced in Smyrna as the Mes-
siah—Spread of Enthusiastic Belief in the pseudo-Messiah—
Manoel Texeira—Ritual Changes introduced by the Sab-
batians—Sabbataï proceeds to Constantinople—Nehemiah Cohen
—Sabbataï Zevi's Apostasy to Islam and its Consequences—Con-
tinuation of the Sabbatian Movement—Death of Sabbataï and
Spinoza—Results of the Sabbatian Imposture.

1656—1677 C.E.

WHILST Manasseh ben Israel was zealously laboring
to complete the fabric of Judaism by hastening on
the Messianic era, one of his disciples was applying
an intellectual lever to destroy this edifice to its
foundation and convert it into a shapeless dust
heap. He was earnest about what was only amusement for Leo Modena. The Jewish race once
more brought a deep thinker into the world, one
who was radically to heal the human mind of its
rooted perversities and errors, and to prescribe a
new direction for it, that it might better comprehend
the connection between heaven and earth, between
mind and matter. Like his ancestor Abraham, this
Jewish thinker desired to break to pieces all idols
and vain images, before which men had hitherto
bowed down through fear, custom, and indolence,
and to reveal to them a new God, not enthroned in
heaven's height beyond their reach, but living and
moving within them, whose temple they themselves
should be. His influence was like that of the storm,

deafening and crushing down, but also purifying and refreshing.

The lightning flashes of this great philosophical genius did greatest injury to Judaism which was nearest to him. In the degradation of the religion of his day and its professors, even his searching gaze could not recognize the fair form concealed beneath a loathsome exterior.

This great thinker, the most famous philosopher of his time, who brought about a new redemption, was Baruch Spinoza (really Espinosa, born in Spain 1632, died 1677). He belonged to a family eminent for neither intellect nor wealth. No sign at his birth portended that he would reign for more than two centuries a king in the realm of thought. With many other boys, he attended the Jewish school, consisting of seven classes, recently established in Amsterdam, whither his parents had migrated. With his extraordinary talents he surely kept pace with the requirements of the school, if he did not exceed them. In his thirteenth or fourteenth year he was probably introduced by Manasseh ben Israel to the study of the Talmud, and initiated into Hebrew grammar, rhetoric, and poetry. He received final instruction in Rabbinical lore from Saul Morteira, the greatest Talmudist of his time in Amsterdam. Together with Spinoza Morteira taught others who later had more or less influence on Jewish history, but were of quite another stamp.

Moses Zacut (1630–1697), a descendant of the famous family of that name, was held to be Morteira's first disciple. From his youth upwards, with his predilection for mysticism and poetry, he formed a direct contrast to Spinoza. He loved what was inexact and obscure, Spinoza the clear and definite. Two incidents may serve to portray Moses Zacut. He was asked when young what he thought of the fabulous narratives of Rabba Bar-Bar-Chana in the Talmud, which are like those of Münchhausen, and he replied that he regarded them as historical. When young he learned Latin like most Portuguese youths in Amsterdam. Later, he so regretted having learned that language, that he fasted forty days in order to forget it, because, as he thought, this tongue of the devil was not compatible with Kabbalistic truth. Another fellow-disciple of Spinoza was Isaac Naar (Nahar), likewise a mystic, and of a spiteful and not over-scrupulous nature.

Thirst for knowledge stimulated Spinoza to venture beyond the limited circle of studies pursued in Morteira's lecture-room. He plunged into the writings of older Jewish thinkers, three of whom alike attracted and repelled him : Ibn-Ezra with his free-thinking and his reticence, Moses Maimuni with his artificial system, aiming at the reconciliation of faith and science, of Judaism and philosophy, and Chasdaï Crescas with his hostility to traditional philosophy. Spinoza was also at home in the Kabbala, the main doctrines of which had been rendered accessible through Abraham de Herrera and Isaac Aboab. These various elements heaved and fermented in his mind, which strove for insight, and excited in his breast tormenting doubts, to which Ibn-Ezra's covert unbelief mainly contributed. A youth of fifteen, Spinoza is said to have expressed his doubts in the form of questions to his master Morteira, which may have not a little perplexed a rabbi accustomed to beaten tracks. To these elements of scepticism, conveyed to him from Jewish literature, others were added from without. Spinoza learned Latin, in itself nothing remarkable, since, as has been remarked, nearly all the Jewish youths of Amsterdam, as well as Christians of the educated classes of Holland, regarded that language as a means of culture. But he was not contented with superficial knowledge ; he desired to drink deep of classical literature. He sought the instruction of an eminent philologist of his time, Dr. Franz van den

Enden, who lectured in Amsterdam to noble youths, native and foreign. Here he learned, in contact with educated Christian youths, to adopt a different point of view from that which obtained in Morteira's lecture-room and in Jewish circles. Van den Enden also strongly influenced his mind. Though not an atheist, he was a man of sceptical and satirical vein, who turned religious customs and prejudices to ridicule, and exposed their weaknesses. But what with him was the object of humor and wit, excited Spinoza's susceptible and analytical mind to deep reflection and meditation. The natural sciences, mathematics, and physics, which he pursued with devotion, and the new-born, imposing philosophy of Descartes (Cartesius), for which his mind had special affinity, extended his circle of vision and enlightened his judgment. The more he imbibed ideas from various sources, assimilating them with those innate in him, and the more his logical understanding developed, the more did he become alienated from Judaism, in its Rabbinical and Kabbalistic trappings, and love of Van den Enden's learned daughter was not needed to make him a pervert from Jewish belief.

Independent, judicial reason, which disregards what is traditional or hallowed by time, and follows its own laws, was his mistress. To her he dedicated pure, undivided worship, and she led him to break with inherited views. All that cannot be justified before the inexorable tribunal of clear human vision, passed with him for superstition and clouded thought, if not actual frenzy. His ardent desire for truth, pure truth and certainty, led him to a complete breach with the religion endeared to him from childhood ; he not only rejected Talmudical Judaism, but also regarded the Bible as the work of man. The apparent contradictions in the books of Holy Scripture appear to have first raised his doubts as to their inspiration. It must have cost him a hard struggle to give up the customs and opinions endeared to him through manifold ties, and to become, to a certain extent, a new man. For Spinoza was quite as much a moral character as a deep thinker. To hold anything as false in theory, and yet from fear, custom, or advantage to adopt it in practice was impossible for him. He was differently constituted to his revered master Descartes, who kept away from the church the torch of truth which he had kindled, made a gap between theory and practice to avoid offending that church, and, for example, vowed a pilgrimage to our Lady of Loretto for the success of his system and its destructive tendency. According to Spinoza's idea every action ought to be a true reflection of reason. When he could no longer find truth in Judaism, he could not bring himself to follow its ritual precepts. He ceased to attend the synagogue, cared no longer for the Sabbath and the festivals, and broke the laws concerning diet. He did not confine himself to the renunciation of Judaism, but imparted his convictions to young men who sought his instruction.

The representatives of the community of Amsterdam were the more concerned at the daily increasing report of Spinoza's estrangement from, and hostility to Judaism, as they had in a measure looked upon the gifted youth as their exponent, and as a firm support to the jeopardized religion of their fathers. Now it was to be feared that he would abandon it, go over to Christianity, and devote his intellectual gifts to doing battle against his mother-faith. Could the representatives of that faith, the college of rabbis and the secular heads of the community, behold with indifference this systematic neglect of Judaism in their midst? Fugitives were ever coming from Spain and Portugal, who forfeited their high position, and staked life and property, to remain true to Judaism. Others with unbending attachment to the faith of their fathers, let them·

selves be dragged to the dark prisons of the Inquisition, or with cheerful courage mounted the funeral pile. A contemporary writer, an eye-witness, reports:

"In Spain and Portugal there are monasteries and convents full of Jews. Not a few conceal Judaism in their heart and feign Christianity on account of worldly goods. Some of these feel the stings of conscience and escape, if they are able. In this city (Amsterdam) and in several other places, we have monks, Augustinians, Franciscans, Jesuits, Dominicans, who have rejected idolatry. There are bishops in Spain and grave monks, whose parents, brothers, or sisters, dwell here (in Amsterdam) and in other cities in order to be able to profess Judaism."

At the very time when Spinoza became estranged from Judaism, the smoke and flames of the funeral piles of Jewish martyrs rose in several cities of Spain and Portugal, in Cuenca, Granada, Santiago de Compostela, Cordova, and Lisbon.

In the last-named city a distinguished Marrano, Manuel Fernando de Villa-Real, statesman, political writer, and poet, who conducted the consular affairs of the Portuguese court at Paris, returned to Lisbon on business, was seized by the Inquisition, gagged, and led to execution (December 1, 1652). In Cuenca on one day (June 29, 1654) fifty-seven Christian proselytes to Judaism were dragged to the auto-da-fé. Most of them only received corporal chastisement with loss of property, but ten were burned to death. Amongst them was a distinguished man, the court-saddler Balthasar Lopez, from Valladolid, who had amassed a fortune of 100,000 ducats. He had migrated to Bayonne, where a small community of former Marranos was tolerated, and had returned to Spain only to persuade a nephew to come back to Judaism. He was seized by the Inquisition, tortured, and condemned to death by the halter and the stake. On his way to the scaffold, Balthasar Lopez ridiculed the Inquisition and Christianity. He exclaimed to the executioner about to bind him, "I do not believe in your Christ, even if you bind me," and threw the cross which had been forced upon him to the ground. Five months later twelve Marranos were burnt in Granada. Again, some months later (March, 1655), a promising youth of twenty, Marcos da Almeyda Bernal, whose Jewish name was Isaac, died at the stake; and two months afterwards (May 3d) Abraham Nuñes Bernal was burnt at Cordova.

Whoever in the community of Amsterdam could compose verses in Spanish, Portuguese, or Latin, sang or bewailed the martyrdom of the two Bernals. Was Spinoza's view correct that all these martyrs, and the thousands of Jewish victims still hounded by the Inquisition, pursued a delusion? Could the representatives of Judaism allow unreproved, in their immediate neighborhood, the promulgation of the idea that Judaism is merely an antiquated error?

The college of rabbis, in which sat the two chief Chachams, Saul Morteira and Isaac Aboab—Manasseh ben Israel was then living in London—had ascertained the fact of Spinoza's change of opinion, and had collected evidence. It was not easy to accuse him of apostasy, as he did not proclaim his thoughts aloud in the market-place, as Uriel da Costa had announced his breach with Judaism. Besides, he led a quiet, self-contained life, and associated little with men. His avoidance of the synagogue, the first thing probably to attract notice, could not form the subject of a Rabbinical accusation. It is possible that, as is related, two of his fellow-students (one, perhaps, the sly Isaac Naar) thrust themselves upon him, drew him out, and accused him of unbelief, and contempt for Judaism. Spinoza was summoned, tried, and admonished to return to his former course of life. The court of rabbis did not at first proceed with severity against him, for he was a favorite of his teacher, and beloved in the community on account of his modest bearing and moral behavior. By virtue of the firmness of his character Spinoza probably made no sort of conces-

sion, but insisted upon freedom of thought and conduct. Without doubt he was, in consequence, laid
under the lesser excommunication, that is, close intercourse with him was forbidden for thirty days. This
probably caused less pain to Spinoza, who, self-
centred, found sufficient resource in his rich world
of thought, than to the superficial Da Costa. Also,
he was not without Christian friends, and he, therefore, made no alteration in his manner of life. This
firmness was naturally construed as obstinacy
and defiance. But the rabbinate, as well as the
secular authorities of the community did not wish
to exert the rigor of the Rabbinical law against him,
in order not to drive him to an extreme measure,
i. e., into the arms of the Church. What harm might
not the conversion to Christianity of so remarkable
a youth entail in a newly-founded community, consisting of Jews with Christian reminiscences ! What
impression would it make on the Marranos in Spain
and Portugal? Perhaps the scandal caused by Da
Costa's excommunication, still fresh in men's memories, may have rendered a repetition impracticable.
The rabbis, therefore, privately offered Spinoza,
through his friends, a yearly pension of a thousand
gulden on condition that he take no hostile step
against Judaism, and show himself from time to time
in the synagogue. But Spinoza, though young, was
of so determined a character, that money could not
entice him to abandon his convictions or to act the
hypocrite. He insisted that he would not give up
freedom of inquiry and thought. He continued to
impart to Jewish youths doctrines undermining
Judaism. So the tension between him and the representatives of Judaism became daily greater ; both
sides were right, or imagined they were. A fanatic
in Amsterdam thought that he could put an end to
this breach by a dagger-stroke aimed at the dangerous apostate. He waylaid Spinoza at the exit
from the theatre, and struck at the philosopher with

his murderous weapon. But the latter observed the hostile movement in time, and avoided the blow, so that only his coat was damaged. Spinoza left Amsterdam to avoid the danger of assassination, and betook himself to the house of a friend, likewise persecuted by the dominant Calvinistic Church, an adherent of the sect of the Rhynsburgians, or Collectants, who dwelt in a village between Amsterdam and Ouderkerk. Reconciliation between Spinoza and the synagogue was no longer to be thought of. The rabbis and the secular authorities of the community pronounced the greater excommunication upon him, proclaiming it in the Portuguese language on a Thursday, Ab 6th (July 24th), 1656, shortly before the fast in memory of the destruction of Jerusalem. The sentence was pronounced solemnly in the synagogue from the pulpit before the open Ark. The sentence was as follows:

"The council has long had notice of the evil opinions and actions of Baruch d'Espinosa, and these are daily increasing in spite of efforts to reclaim him. In particular, he teaches and proclaims dreadful heresy, of which credible witnesses are present, who have made their depositions in presence of the accused."

All this, they continued, had been proved in the presence of the elders, and the council had resolved to place him under the ban, and excommunicate him.

The usual curses were pronounced upon him in presence of scrolls of the Law, and finally the council forbade anyone to have intercourse with him, verbally or by writing, to do him any service, to abide under the same roof with him, or to come within the space of four cubits' distance from him, or to read his writings. Contrary to wont, the ban against Spinoza was stringently enforced, to keep young people from his heresies.

Spinoza was away from Amsterdam, when the ban was hurled against him. He is said to have received the news with indifference, and to have remarked that he was now compelled to do what he would otherwise have done without compulsion. His philosophic nature, which loved solitude, could easily dispense with intercourse with relatives and former friends.   Yet the matter did not end for him there.   The representative body of the Portuguese community appealed to the municipal authorities to effect his perpetual banishment from Amsterdam. The magistrates referred the question, really a theological one, to the clergy, and the latter are said to have proposed his withdrawal from Amsterdam for some months.   Most probably this procedure prompted him to elaborate a justificatory pamphlet to show the civil authorities that he was no violator or transgressor of the laws of the state, but that he had exercised his just rights, when he reflected on the religion of his forefathers and religion generally, and thought out new views.   The chain of reasoning suggested to Spinoza in the preparation of his defense caused him doubtless to give wider extension and bearing to this question.   It gave him the opportunity to treat of freedom of thought and inquiry generally, and so to lay the foundation of the first of his suggestive writings, which have conferred upon him literary immortality.   In the village to which he had withdrawn, 1656-60, and later in Rhynsburg, where he also spent several years, 1660-64, Spinoza occupied himself (while polishing lenses, which handicraft he had learned to secure his moderate subsistence) with the Cartesian philosophy and the elaboration of the work entitled "The Theologico-Political Treatise."   His prime object was to spread the conviction that freedom of thought can be permitted without prejudice to religion and the peace of the state; furthermore, that it must be permitted, for if it were forbidden, religion and peace could not exist in the state.

The apology for freedom of thought had been rendered harder rather than easier for Spinoza, by the subsidiary ideas with which he crossed the main lines of his system. He could not philosophically find the source of law, and transferred its origin to might. Neither God, nor man's conscience, according to Spinoza, is the fountain of the eternal law which rules and civilizes mankind; it springs from the whole lower natural world. He made men to a certain extent "like the fishes of the sea, like creeping things, which have no master." Large fish have the right, not only to drink water, but also to devour smaller fish, because they have the power to do so; the sphere of right of the individual man extends as far as his sphere of might. This natural right does not recognize the difference between good and evil, virtue and vice, submission and force. But because such unlimited assertion on the part of each must lead to a perpetual state of war of all against all, men have tacitly, from fear, or hope, or reason, given up their unlimited privileges to a collective body, the state. Out of two evils—on the one hand, the full possession of their sphere of right and might, tending to mutual destruction, and its alienation, on the other—men have chosen the latter as the lesser evil. The state, whether represented by a supreme authority elected for the purpose, such as the Dutch States General, or by a despot, is the full possessor of the rights of all, because of the power of all. Every one is bound by his own interest to unconditional obedience, even if he should be commanded to deprive others of life; resistance is not only punishable, but contrary to reason. This supreme power is not controlled by any law. Whether exercised by an individual, as in a monarchy, or by several, as in a republic, it is justified in doing everything, and can do no wrong. But the state has supreme right not merely over actions of a civil nature, but also over spiritual and religious views; it could not exist, if everyone were at liberty to attack it under the pretext of religion. The government alone has the right to control religious affairs, and to define belief, unbelief, orthodoxy, and heresy. What a tyrannical conclusion ! As this theory of Spinoza fails to recognize moral law, so it ignores steadfast fidelity. As soon as the government grows weak, it no longer has claim to obedience ; everyone may renounce and resist it, to submit himself to the incoming power. According to this theory of civil and religious despotism, no one may have an opinion about the laws of the state, otherwise he is a rebel. Spinoza's theory almost does away with freedom, even of thought and opinion. Whoever speaks against a state ordinance in a fault-finding spirit, or to throw odium upon the government, or seeks to repeal a law against its express wish, should be regarded as a disturber of the public peace. Only through a sophistical quibble was Spinoza able to save freedom of thought and free expression of opinion. Every man has this right by nature, the only one which he has not transferred to the state, because it is essentially inalienable. It must be conceded to everyone to think and judge in opposition to the opinion of the government, even to speak and teach, provided this be done with reason and reflection, without fraud, anger, or malice, and without the intention of causing a revolution.

On this weak basis, supported by a few other secondary considerations, Spinoza justified his conflict with Judaism and his philosophical attacks upon the sacred writings recognized by the Dutch States. He thought that he had succeeded in justifying himself before the magistrates sufficiently by his defense of freedom of thought. In the formulation of this apology it was apparent that he was not indifferent to the treatment which he had experienced from the college of rabbis. Spinoza was so filled with displeasure, if not with hatred, of Jews and Judaism, that his otherwise clear judgment was biased. He, like Da Costa, called the rabbis nothing but Pharisees, and imputed to them ambitious and degraded motives, while they wished only to secure their treasured beliefs against attacks. Prouder even than his contemporaries, the French and English philosophers, of freedom of thought, for centuries repressed by the church, and now soaring aloft the more powerfully, Spinoza summoned theology, in particular, ancient Judaism before the throne of reason, examined its dogmas and archives, and pronounced sentence of condemnation upon his mother-faith. He had erected a tower of thought in his brain from which, as it were, he wished to storm heaven. Spinoza's philosophy is like a fine net, laid before our eyes, mesh by mesh, by which the human understanding is unexpectedly ensnared, so that half voluntarily, half compulsorily, it surrenders. Spinoza recognized, as no thinker before, those universal laws, immutable as iron, which are apparent in the development of the most insignificant grain of seed no less than in the revolution of the heavenly bodies, in the precision of mathematical thought as in the apparent irregularity of human passions. Whilst these laws work with constant uniformity, and produce the same causes and the same phenomena in endless succession, the instruments of law are perishable things, creatures of a day, which rise, and vanish to give place to others: here eternity, there temporality; on the one side necessity, on the other chance; here reality, there delusive appearances. These and other enigmas Spinoza sought to solve with the penetration that betrays the son of the Talmud, and with logical consecutiveness and masterly arrangement, for which Aristotle might have envied him.

The whole universe, all individual things, and their active powers are, according to Spinoza, not merely from God, but of God; they constitute the infinite succession of forms in which God reveals Himself, through which He eternally works accord-

ing to His eternal nature—the soul, as it were, of
thinking bodies, the body of the soul extended in
space.   God is the indwelling, not the external
efficient cause of all things ; all is in God and moves
in God.   God as creator and generator of all things
is generative or self-producing nature.   The whole
of nature is animate, and ideas, as bodies, move in
eternity on lines running parallel to or intersecting
one another.   Though the fullness of things which
have proceeded from God and which exist in Him
are not of an eternal, but of a perishable nature, yet
they are not limited or defined by chance, but by the
necessity of the divine nature, each in its own way
existing or acting within its smaller or larger sphere.
The eternal and constant nature of God works in
them through the eternal laws communicated to
them.   Things could, therefore, not be constituted
otherwise than they are ; for they are the manifestations, entering into existence in an eternal stream,
of God in the intimate connection of thought and
extension.

What is man's place in this logical system ?   How
is he to act and work?   Even he, with all his greatness and littleness, his strength and weakness, his
heaven-aspiring mind, and his body subject to the
need of sustenance, is nothing more than a form of
existence (Modus) of God.   Man after man, generation after generation, springs up and perishes, flows
away like a drop in a perpetual stream, but his
nature, the laws by which he moves bodily and mentally in the peculiar connection of mind and matter,
reflect the Divine Being.   Especially the human
mind, or rather the various modes of thought, the
feelings and conceptions of all men, form the eternal
reason of God.   But man is as little free as things,
as the stone which rolls down from the mountain ;
he has to obey the causes which influence him from
within and without.   Each of his actions is the product of an infinite series of causes and effects, which

he can scarcely discern, much less control and alter at will. The good man and the bad, the martyr who sacrifices himself for a noble object, as well as the execrable villain and the murderer, are all like clay in the hands of God; they act, the one well, the other ill, compelled by their inner nature. They all act from rigid necessity. No man can reproach God for having given him a weak nature or a clouded intellect, as it would be irrational if a circle should complain that God has not given it the nature and properties of the sphere. It is not the lot of every man to be strong-minded, and it lies as little in his power to have a sound mind as a sound body.

On one side man is, to a certain extent, free, or rather some men of special mental endowments can free themselves a little from the pressure exercised upon them. Man is a slave chiefly through his passions. Love, hate, anger, thirst for glory, avarice, make him the slave of the external world. These passions spring from the perplexity of the soul, which thinks it can control things, but wears itself out, so to speak, against their obstinate resistance, and suffers pain thereby. The better the soul succeeds in comprehending the succession of causes and effects and the necessity of phenomena in the plan of the universe, the better able is it to change pain into a sense of comfort. Through higher insight, man, if he allows himself to be led by reason, can acquire strength of soul, and feel increased love to God, that is, to the eternal whole. On the one hand, this secures nobility of mind to aid men and to win them by mildness and benevolence; and creates, on the other, satisfaction, joy, and happiness. He who is gifted with highest knowledge lives in God, and God in him. Knowledge is virtue, as ignorance is, to a certain extent, vice. Whilst the wise man, or strictly speaking, the philosopher, thanks to his higher insight and his love of God, enjoys tranquillity of soul, the man of clouded intellect, who abandons himself to the madness of his passions, must dispense with this joyousness, and often perishes in consequence. The highest virtue, according to Spinoza's system, is self-renunciation through knowledge, keeping in a state of passiveness, coming as little as possible in contact with the crushing machinery of forces—avoiding them if they come near, or submitting to them if their wild career overthrows the individual. But as he who is beset by desires deserves no blame, so no praise is due the wise man who practices self-renunciation; both follow the law of their nature. Higher knowledge and wisdom cannot be attained if the conditions are wanting, namely, a mind susceptible of knowledge and truth, which one can neither give himself, nor throw off. Man has thus no final aim, any more than the eternal substance.

Spinoza's moral doctrines—ethics in the narrower sense—are just as unfruitful as his political theories. In either case, he recognizes submission as the only rational course.

With this conception of God and moral action, it cannot surprise us that Judaism found no favor in Spinoza's eyes. Judaism lays down directly opposite principles—beckons man to a high, self-reliant task, and proclaims aloud the progress of mankind in simple service of God, holiness, and victory over violence, the sword, and degrading war. This progress has been furthered in many ways by Judaism in the course of ages. Wanting, as Spinoza was, in apprehension of historical events, more wonderful than the phenomena of nature, and unable as he therefore was to accord to Judaism special importance, he misconceived it still further through his bitterness against the Amsterdam college of rabbis, who pardonably enough, had excommunicated him. Spinoza transferred his bitterness against the community to the whole Jewish race and to Judaism. As has been already said, he called the rabbis

Pharisees in his "Theologico-Political Treatise" and in letters to his friends, and gave the most invidious meaning to this word. To Christianity, on the contrary, Spinoza conceded great excellencies; he regarded Judaism with displeasure, therefore, detected deficiencies and absurdities everywhere, while he cast a benevolent eye upon Christianity, and overlooked its weaknesses. Spinoza, therefore, with all the instinct for truth which characterized him, formed a conception of Judaism which, in some degree just, was, in many points, perverse and defective. Clear as his mind was in metaphysical inquiries, it was dark and confused on historical ground. To depreciate Judaism, Spinoza declared that the books of Holy Scripture contain scribes' errors, interpolations, and disfigurements, and are not, as a rule, the work of the authors to whom they are ascribed—not even the Pentateuch, the original source of Judaism. Ezra, perhaps, first collected and arranged it after the Babylonian exile. The genuine writings of Moses are no longer extant, not even the Ten Commandments being in their original form. Nevertheless, Spinoza accepted every word in the Bible as a kind of revelation, and designated all persons who figure in it as prophets. He conceded, on the ground of Scripture, that the revelation of the prophets was authenticated by visible signs. Nevertheless, he very much underrated this revelation. Moses, the prophets, and all the higher personages of the Bible had only a confused notion of God, nature, and living beings; they were not philosophers, they did not avail themselves of the natural light of reason. Jesus stood higher; he taught not only a nation, but the whole of mankind on rational grounds. The Apostles, too, were to be set higher than the prophets, since they introduced a natural method of instruction, and worked not merely through signs, but also through rational conviction. As though the main effort of the Apostles, to which their whole zeal was devoted, viz., to reach belief in the miraculous resurrection of Jesus, were consistent with reason !   It was only Spinoza's bitterness against Jews which caused him to depreciate their spiritual property and overrate Christianity.   His sober intellect, penetrating to the eternal connection of things and events, could not accept miracles, but those of the New Testament he judged mildly.

In spite of his condemnatory verdict on Judaism, he was struck by two phenomena, which he did not fully understand, and which, therefore, he judged only superficially according to his system.   These were the moral greatness of the prophets, and the superiority of the Israelite state, which in a measure depend on each other.   Without understanding the political organization, in which natural and moral laws, necessity and freedom work together, Spinoza explains the origin of the Jewish state, that is, of Judaism, in the following manner :   When the Israelites, after deliverance from slavery in Egypt, were free from all political bondage, and restored to their natural rights, they willingly chose God as their Lord, and transferred their rights to Him alone by formal contract and alliance.   That there be no appearance of fraud on the divine side, God permitted them to recognize His marvelous power, by virtue of which He had hitherto preserved, and promised in future to preserve them, that is, He revealed Himself to them in His glory on Sinai ; thus God became the King of Israel and the state a theocracy.   Religious opinions and truths, therefore, had a legal character in this state, religion and civic right coincided.   Whoever revolted from religion forfeited his rights as a citizen, and whoever died for religion was a patriot.   Pure democratic equality, the right of all to entreat God and interpret the laws, prevailed among the Israelites.   But when, in the overpowering bewilderment of the revelation from Sinai, they voluntarily asked Moses to receive the laws from God and to interpret them, they renounced their equality, and transferred their rights to Moses. Moses from that time became God's representative. Hence, he promulgated laws suited to the condition of the people at that time, and introduced ceremonies to remind them always of the Law and keep them from willfulness, so that in accordance with a definite precept they should plough, sow, eat, clothe themselves, in a word, do everything according to the precepts of the Law. Above all, he provided that they might not act from childish or slavish fear, but from reverence for God. He bound them by benefits, and promised them earthly prosperity—all through the power and by the command of God. Moses was vested with spiritual and civil power, and authorized to transmit both. He preferred to transfer the civil power to his disciple Joshua in full, but not as a heritage, and the spiritual power to his brother Aaron as a heritage, but limited by the civil ruler, and not accompanied by a grant of territory. After the death of Moses the Jewish state was neither a monarchy, nor an aristocracy, nor a democracy; it remained a theocracy. The family of the high-priest was God's interpreter, and the civil power, after Joshua's death, fell to single tribes or their chiefs.

This constitution offered many advantages. The civil rulers could not turn the law to their own advantage, nor oppress the people, for the Law was the province of the sacerdotal order—the sons of Aaron and the Levites. Besides, the people were made acquainted with the Law through the prescribed reading at the close of the Sabbatical year, and would not have passed over with indifference any willful transgression of the law of the state. The army was composed of native militia, while foreigners, that is, mercenaries, were excluded. Thus the rulers were prevented from oppressing the people or waging war arbitrarily. The tribes were united by religion, and the oppression of one tribe by its ruler would have been punished by the rest. The princes were not placed at the head through rank or privilege of blood, but through capacity and merit. Finally, the institution of prophets proved very wholesome. Since the constitution was theocratical, every one of blameless life was able through certain signs to represent himself as a prophet like Moses, draw the oppressed people to him in the name of God, and oppose the tyranny of the rulers. This peculiar constitution produced in the heart of the Israelites an especial patriotism, which was at the same time a religion, so that no one would betray it, leave God's kingdom, or swear allegiance to a foreigner. This love, coupled with hatred against other nations, and fostered by daily worship of God, became second nature to the Israelites. It strengthened them to endure everything for their country with steadfastness and courage. This constitution offered a further advantage, because the land was equally divided, and no one could be permanently deprived of his portion through poverty, as restitution had to be made in the year of jubilee.

Hence, there was little poverty, or such only as was endurable, for the love of one's neighbor had to be exercised with the greatest conscientiousness to keep the favor of God, the King. Finally, a large space was accorded to gladness. Thrice a year and on other occasions the people were to assemble at festivals, not to revel in sensual enjoyments, but to accustom themselves to follow God gladly; for there is no more effectual means of guiding the hearts of men than the joy which arises from love and admiration.

After Spinoza had depicted Israel's theocracy quite as a pattern for all states, he was apparently startled at having imparted so much light to the

picture, and he looked around for shade. Instead
of answering in a purely historical manner the questions, whence it came that the Hebrews were so
often subdued, and why their state was entirely destroyed; instead of indicating that these wholesome
laws remained a never realized ideal, Spinoza suggests a sophistic solution. Because God did not
wish to make Israel's dominion lasting, he gave bad
laws and statutes. Spinoza supports this view by a
verse which he misunderstood. These bad laws,
rebellion against the sacerdotal state, coupled with
bad morals, produced discontent, revolt, and insurrection. At last matters went so far, that instead
of the Divine King, the Israelites chose a human
one, and instead of the temple, a court. Monarchy,
however, only increased the disorder; it could not
endure the state within the state, the high-priest-
hood, and lowered the dignity of the latter by the
introduction of strange worship. The prophets
could avail nothing, because they only declaimed
against the tyrants, but could not remove the cause
of the evils. All things combined brought on the
destruction of the divine state. With its destruction by the Babylonian king, the natural rights of
the Israelites were transferred to the conqueror, and
they were bound to obey him and his successors, as
they had obeyed God. All the laws of Judaism,
nay, the whole of Judaism, was thereby abolished,
and no longer had any significance. This was the
result of Spinoza's inquiry in his "Theologico-
Political Treatise." Judaism had a brilliant past,
God concluded an alliance with the people, showed
to them His exalted power, and gave them excellent laws; but He did not intend Israel's preëminence to be permanent, therefore He also gave bad
laws. Consequently, Judaism reached its end more
than two thousand years ago, and yet it continued
its existence! Wonderful! Spinoza found the
history of Israel and the constitution of the state

excellent during the barbarism of the period of the Judges, while the brilliant epochs of David and Solomon and of King Uzziah remained inexplicable to him.   And, above all, the era of the second Temple, the Maccabean epoch, when the Jewish nation rose from shameful degradation to a brilliant height, and brought the heathen world itself to worship the one God and adopt a moral life, remained to Spinoza an insoluble riddle.   This shows that his whole demonstration and his analysis (schematism) cannot stand the test of criticism, but rests on false assumptions.

Spinoza might have brought Judaism into extreme peril; for he not only furnished its opponents with the weapons of reason to combat Judaism more effectually, but also conceded to every state and magistrate the right to suppress it and use force against its followers, to which they ought meekly to submit. The funeral piles of the Inquisition for Marranos were, according to Spinoza's system, doubly justified; citizens have no right on rational grounds to resist the recognized religion of the state, and it is folly to profess Judaism and to sacrifice oneself for it.   But a peculiar trait of Spinoza's character stood Judaism in good stead.   He loved peace and quiet too well to become a propagandist for his critical principles. "To be peaceable and peaceful" was his ideal; avoidance of conflict and opposition was at once his strength and his weakness.   To his life's end he led an ideally-philosophical life; for food, clothing, and shelter, he needed only so much as he could earn with his handicraft of polishing lenses, which his friends disposed of.   He struggled against accepting a pension, customarily bestowed on learned men at that time, even from his sincere and rich admirers, Simon de Vries and the grand pensionary De Witt, that he might not fall into dependence, constraint, and disquiet.   By reason of this invincible desire for philosophic calm and freedom from care, he would not decide in favor of either of the political parties, then setting the States General in feverish agitation. Not even the exciting murder of his friend John de Witt was able to hurry him into partisanship. Spinoza bewailed his high and noble friend, but did not defend his honor, to clear it of suspicion. When the most highly cultivated German prince of his time, Count-Palatine Karl Ludwig, who cherished a certain affection for Jews, offered him, "the Protestant Jew," as he was still called, the chair of philosophy in the University of Heidelberg under very favorable conditions, Spinoza declined the offer. He did not conceal his reason: he would not surrender his quietude. From this predominant tendency, or, rather, from fear of disturbance and inconveniences and from apprehension of calling enemies down upon him, or of coming into collision with the state, he refused to publish his speculations for a long time. When at last he resolved, on the pressure of friends, to send "The Theologico-Political Treatise" to press, he did not put his name to the work, which made an epoch in literature, and even caused a false place of publication, viz., Hamburg, to be printed on the title-page, in order to obliterate every trace of its real authorship. He almost denied his offspring, to avoid being disturbed.

As might have been foreseen, the appearance of "The Theologico-Political Treatise" (1670), made an extraordinary stir. No one had written so distinctly and incisively concerning the relation of religion to philosophy and the power of the state, and, above all, had so sharply condemned the clergy. The ministers of all denominations were extraordinarily excited against this "godless" book, as it was called, which disparaged revealed religion. Spinoza's influential friends were not able to protect it; it was condemned by a decree of the States General, and forbidden to be sold—which only caused it to be read more eagerly. But Spinoza was the more

reluctant to publish his other writings, especially his
philosophical system. With all his strength of
character, he did not belong to those bold spirits,
who undertake to be the pioneers of truth, who usher
it into the world with loud voice, and win it adherents, unconcerned as to whether they may have to
endure bloody or bloodless martyrdom. In the unselfishness of Spinoza's character and system there
lurked an element of selfishness, namely, the desire
to be disturbed as little as possible in the attainment of knowledge, in the happiness of contempla-
tion, and in reflection upon the universe and the
chain of causes and effects which prevail in it. A
challenge to action, effort, and resistance to opposition lay neither in Spinoza's temper, nor in his
philosophy.

In this apparently harmless feature lay also the
reason that his most powerful and vehemently conducted attacks upon Judaism made no deep impression, and called forth no great commotion in the
Jewish world. At the time when Spinoza threw
down the challenge to Judaism, a degree of culture
and science prevailed in the Jewish-Portuguese
circle, unkown either before or after; there reigned
in the community of Amsterdam and its colonies a
literary activity and fecundity, which might be called
classical, if the merit of the literary productions had
corresponded with their compass. The authors
were chiefly cultivated Marranos, who had escaped
from the Spanish or Portuguese prisons of the Inquisition to devote themselves in free Holland to their
faith. and free inquiry. There were philosophers,
physicians, mathematicians, philologists, poets, even
poetesses. Many of these Marranos who escaped
to Amsterdam had gone through peculiar vicissitudes.
A monk of Valencia, Fray Vincent de Rocamora
(1601-1684), had been eminent in Catholic theology. He had been made confessor to the Infanta
Maria, afterwards empress of Germany and a per-

secutor of the Jews. One day the confessor fled
from Spain, reached Amsterdam, declared himself
as Isaac de Rocamora, studied medicine at the age
of forty, and became the happy father of a family
and president of Jewish benevolent institutions.
The quondam monk, afterwards Parnass (president
of the community), was also a good poet, and wrote
admirable Spanish and Latin verses.

Enrique Enriquez de Paz of Segovia (1600-1660),
the Jewish Calderon, had a very different career.
Having entered the army while young, he behaved
so gallantly that he won the order of San Miguel,
and was made captain. Besides the sword, he
wielded the pen, with which he described comic figures and situations. Enriquez de Paz, or, as he
was styled in his poetical capacity, Antonio Enriquez de Gomez, composed more than two and
twenty comedies, some of which were put upon the
stage at Madrid, and, being taken for Calderon's productions, were received with much applause. Neither
Mars nor the Muses succeeded in protecting him
against the Inquisition ; he could escape its clutches
only by rapid flight. He lived a long time in France.
His prolific muse celebrated Louis XIV, the queen
of France, the powerful statesman Richelieu, and
other high personages of the court. He bewailed
in elegies his misfortunes and the loss of his country,
which he loved like a son, step-mother though she
had been to him. Although blessed by fortune,
Enriquez de Paz felt himself unhappy in the rude
north, far from the blue mountains and mild air of
Spain. He lamented:

"I have won for myself wealth and traveled over many seas, and
heaped up ever fresh treasures by thousands ; now my hair is
bleached, my beard as snowy white as my silver bars, the reward of
my labors."

He lived in France, too, as a Christian, but proclaimed his sympathy with Judaism by mourning in
elegiac verses the martyrdom of Lope de Vera y

Alarcon.   Finally he settled down in the asylum of
the Marranos, whilst his effigy was burnt on the funeral pile at Seville.   There had been again a great
auto-da-fé (1660) of sixty Marranos, of whom four
were first strangled and then burned, whilst three
were burned alive.   Effigies of escaped Marranos
were borne along in procession, and thrown into
the flames—amongst them that of the knight of
San Miguel, the writer of comedies.   A new-
Christian, who was present at this horrible sight,
and soon after escaped to Amsterdam, met Gomez
in the street, and exclaimed excitedly: "Ah!
Señor Gomez! I saw your effigy burn on the
funeral pile at Seville!"   "Well," he replied, "they
are welcome to it."   Along with his numerous secular poems, Enriquez Gomez left one of Jewish
national interest in celebration of the hero-judge
Samson.   The laurels which the older Spanish
poet Miguel Silveyra, also a Marrano, whom he
admired, had won by his epic, "The Maccabee,"
haunted him until he had brought out a companion
piece.   To the blind hero who avenged himself on
the Philistines by his very death, Gomez assigned
verses which expressed his own heart :

> " I die for Thy holy word, for Thy religion,
> For Thy doctrine, Thy hallowed commandments,
> For the nation adopted by Thy choice,
> For Thy sublime ordinance I die."

Another point of view is presented by two emigrant Marranos of this period, father and son, the
two Pensos, the one rich in possessions and charity,
the other in poetical gifts.   They probably sprang
from Espejo, in the province of Cordova, escaped
from the fury of the Inquisition, and at last settled,
after many changes of residence, as Jews in Amsterdam.   Isaac Penso (died 1683) the elder, a
banker, was a father to the poor.   He spent a tithe
of the income from his property on the poor, and
distributed, up to his death, 40,000 gulden.   His

decease aroused deep regret in the community of
Amsterdam. His son (Felice) Joseph Penso, also
called De la Vega from his mother's family (1650-
1703), was a rich merchant, and turned his attention to poetry. A youth of seventeen, he awoke
the long-slumbering echo of neo-Hebraic poesy,
and caused it to strike its highest note. Joseph
Penso boldly undertook a most difficult task; he
composed a Hebrew drama. Since Immanuel
Romi had written his witty tales in verse, the neo-
Hebraic muse had been stricken with sterility, for
which the increasing troubles of the times were not
alone to blame. Moses da Rieti and the poetic
school of Salonica composed verses, but did not
write poetry. Even the greatest of Jewish poets,
Gebirol and Jehuda Halevi, had produced only lyric
and didactic poetry, and had not thought of the
drama. Joseph Penso, inspired by the poetical air
of Spain, the land of his birth, where Lope de
Vega's and Calderon's melodious verses were
heard beside the litany of the monks and the cry of
the sacrificial victims, transferred Spanish art
forms to neo-Hebraic poetry. Penso happily imitated the various kinds of metre and strophe of
European poetry in the language of David and
Isaiah.

One may not, indeed, apply a severe standard to
Joseph Penso's drama, but should endeavor to forget that long before him Shakespeare had created
life-like forms and interests, For, measured by
these, Penso's dramatic monologue and dialogue
seem puerile. However free from blame his versification is, the invention is poor, the ideas commonplace. A king who takes a serious view of his responsibilities as ruler is led astray, now by his own
impulses (Yezer), now by a coquette (Isha), now by
Satan. Three other opposing forces endeavor to
lead him in the right way—his own judgment
(Sechel), divine inspiration (Hashgacha), and an

angel.   These are the characters in Penso's drama
" The Captives of Hope " (Asiré ha-Tikwah).   But
if one takes into consideration the object which
Penso had in view, viz., to hold up a mirror to Marrano youths settled at Amsterdam, who had been
used to Spanish licentiousness, and to picture to
them the high value of a virtuous life, the performance of the youthful poet is not to be despised.
Joseph Penso de la Vega composed a large number
of verses in Spanish, occasional poetry, moral and
philosophical reflections, and eulogies on princes.
His novels, entitled " The Dangerous Courses "
(los Rumbos peligrosos), were popular.

Marrano poets of mediocre ability were so numerous at this time in Amsterdam, that one of them,
the Spanish resident in the Netherlands, Manuel
Belmonte (Isaac Nuñes), appointed count-palatine,
founded an academy of poetry.   Poetical works
were to be handed in, and as judges he appointed
the former confessor, De Rocamora, and another
Marrano, who composed Latin verses, Isaac Gomez
de Sosa.   The latter was so much enraptured of
Penso's Hebrew drama, that he triumphantly proclaimed, in Latin verse :

" Now is it at length attained !   The Hebrew Muse strides along on
high-heeled buskin safe and sound.   With the measured step of
poetry she is conducted auspiciously by Joseph—sprung from that
race which still is mostly in captivity.   Lo ! a clear beam of hope
shines afresh, that now even the stage may be opened to sacred song.
Yet why do I praise him ?   The poet is celebrated by his own poetry,
and his own work proclaims the praise of the master."

Another of the friends of the Jewish dramatist
was Nicolas de Oliver y Fullana (Daniel Jehuda),
poet, and colonel in the Spanish service ; he was
knighted, entered the service of Holland, and was
an accurate cartographer and cosmographer.   There
was also Joseph Szemach (Sameh) Arias, a man of
high military rank, who translated into Spanish the
work of the historian Josephus against Apion, which
controverted the old prejudices and falsehoods

against Jews. This polemic was not superfluous even at this time. Of the Jewish Marrano poetesses, it will suffice to name the fair and gifted Isabel Correa (Rebecca), who twined a wreath of various poems, and translated the Italian popular drama, "The True Shepherd" (Pastor Fido, by Guarini) into beautiful Spanish verse. Isabel was the second wife of the poet-warrior, De Oliver y Fullana.

Of a far different stamp was the Marrano Thomas de Pinedo (Isaac, 1614-1679) of Portugal, educated in a Jesuit college at Madrid. He was more at home in classical than in Jewish antiquity, and applied himself to a branch of study little cultivated in Spain in his time, that of ancient geography. He, too, was driven out of Spain by the Inquisition, and deemed himself fortunate to have escaped unhurt. The philologist De Pinedo dwelt later on in Amsterdam, where he printed his comprehensive work. He composed his own epitaph in Latin.

We must not leave unmentioned a personage celebrated at that time perhaps beyond his deserts, Jacob Jehuda Leon (Templo, 1603-1671). If not a Marrano, he was of Marrano descent, and resided first at Middelburg, then at Amsterdam, and was more an artist than a man of science. Leon devoted himself to the reproduction of the first Temple and its vessels, as they are described in the Bible and the Talmud. He executed a model of the Temple on a reduced scale (3 yards square, 1½ in height), and added a concise, clear description in Spanish and Hebrew. Work of so unusual a character attracted extraordinary notice at a time when every kind of antiquarian learning, especially biblical, was highly prized. The government of Holland and Zealand gave the author the copyright privilege. Duke August of Brunswick, and his wife Elizabeth, wished to possess a German translation of Leon's description, and commissioned Professor John Saubert, of Helmstädt, to undertake it. While corresponding with the author so as to ensure thoroughness, he was anticipated by another man who brought out a German translation at Hanover. This circumstance caused great annoyance to Professor Saubert. Templo, as Leon and his posterity were surnamed from his work in connection with the Temple, engaged in controversies with Christian ecclesiastics on Judaism and Christianity, and published a translation of the Psalms in Spanish.

In this cultivated circle of Spinoza's contemporaries were two men who lived alternately at Hamburg and Amsterdam, David Coen de Lara and Dionysius Musaphia, both distinguished as philologists, but not for much besides. With their knowledge of Latin and Greek they explained the dialect of the Talmud, and corrected errors which had crept into the earlier Talmudical lexicons. David de Lara (1610-1674) was also a preacher and writer on morals ; but his efforts in that direction are of small value. He associated too much with the Hamburg preacher, Esdras Edzardus, who was bent on the conversion of the Jews. The latter spread the false report that De Lara was almost a Christian before he died. Dionysius (Benjamin) Musaphia (born about 1616, died at Amsterdam, 1676), a physician and student of natural science, was up to the date of the monarch's death in the service of the Danish king Christian IV. He was also a philosopher, and allowed himself to question various things in the Talmud and the Bible. Nevertheless he held the office of rabbi at Amsterdam in his old age.

Much more important than the whole of this circle was Balthasar Orobio de Castro (1620-1687). He also sprang from Marrano parents, who secretly continued to cling to Judaism, in that they abstained from food and drink on the Day of Atonement. In this meager conception of Judaism, Orobio was brought up. Endowed with clear intellect, he studied the decayed and antiquated philosophy still taught in Spanish academies, and became professor of metaphysics in the University of Salamanca. This fossilized philosophy appears neither to have satisfied him nor to have brought him sufficient means of subsistence, for he applied himself in riper years to the study of medicine. In this pursuit Orobio was more successful; he gained a reputation at Seville, was physician to the duke of Medina-Celi, and to a family in high favor with the court, and amassed considerable wealth. He was a happy husband and father, when the Inquisition cast its baleful glance upon him. A servant, whom he had punished for theft, had informed against him. Orobio was seized, accused of Judaism, and thrown into a narrow, gloomy dungeon, where he had not room to move, and where he spent three years (about 1655-1658).

At first he filled up his time with philosophical subtleties, as pursued at the Spanish universities. He undertook to defend a thesis, acting at the same time in imagination as the opponent, who interposes objections, and as the judge, who sums up and sifts the arguments. By degrees his mind grew so perplexed that he often asked himself, "Am I really Don Balthasar Orobio, who went about in the streets of Seville, and lived in comfort with his family?" His past seemed a dream, and he believed that he had been born in prison, and must die there. But the tribunal of the Inquisition brought a change into his empty dream-life. He was ushered into a dark vault, lighted only by a dull lamp. He could hardly distinguish the judge, the secretary, and the executioner, who were about to deal with his case. Having been again admonished to confess his heresy, and having again denied it, the hangman undressed him, bound him with cords, which were fastened to hooks in the wall, brought his body into a swinging

movement between the ceiling and the floor, and
drew the cords so tight, that the blood spurted from
his nails.   His feet, moreover, were strongly bound
to a small ladder, the steps of which were studded
with spikes. Whilst being tortured, he was frequently admonished to make confession, and was
threatened, in case he persisted in denial, with the
infliction of still more horrible pains, for which,
though they caused his death, he would have to
thank his own obstinacy, not the tribunal.   However,
he survived the torture, was taken back to prison
to allow his wounds to heal, then condemned to
wear the garb of shame (San Benito), and was finally
banished from Spain. He betook himself to Tou-
louse, where he became professor of medicine in the
university.   Although respected in his new position,
Orobio could not long endure the hypocrisy.   He
went to Amsterdam, publicly professed the Jewish
religion, and assumed the name of Isaac (about
1666). No wonder that he became a bitter opponent of Christianity, which he had learnt to know
thoroughly. He became an adherent of Judaism
from conviction, proved himself a courageous and
able champion of the religion of his fathers, and
dealt such powerful blows to Christianity as few
before him, so that a distinguished Protestant theologian (Van Limborch) felt compelled to reply to
Orobio's attacks.

All these cultivated youths and men, the soldier-
poets Enriquez Gomez, Nicholas de Oliver y
Fullana, and Joseph Arias, and the writers Joseph
Penso, Thomas de Pinedo, Jacob Leon, David de
Lara, and Dionysius Musaphia, knew of Spinoza's
attacks upon Judaism, and undoubtedly read his
"Theologico-Political Treatise." Isaac Orobio associated with Spinoza. Yet the blows by which
the latter strove to shake Judaism did not cause
the former to waver in their convictions. This is
the more remarkable, as simultaneously, from

another side, Judaism was covered with shame, or,
what comes to the same thing, its followers everywhere in the East and West, with few exceptions,
became slaves to a delusion which exposed them to
the ridicule of the world, and enveloped them for
the first time in the darkness of the Middle Ages.

Without suspecting it, Spinoza possessed in the
East an ally, diametrically his opposite, who labored
to disintegrate Judaism, and succeeded in throwing
the whole Jewish race into a turmoil, which long
interfered with its progress. Sabbataï Zevi was at
once Spinoza's opposite and his ally. He possessed
many more admirers than the philosopher of Amsterdam, became for a space the idol of the Jewish race,
and has secret adherents even to the present time.
Sabbataï Zevi (born Ab 9, 1626, died 1676), of
Smyrna, in Asia Minor, was of Spanish descent, and
became the originator of a new Messianic frenzy,
the founder of a new sect. He owed the attachment which he inspired even as a youth, not to his
qualities of mind, but to his external appearance and
attractive manner. He was tall, well formed, had
fine dark hair, a fine beard, and a pleasant voice,
which won hearts by speech and still more by song.
But his mind was befogged by reason of the pre-
dominance of fancy; he had an enthusiastic temperament and an inclination to what was strange,
especially to solitude. In boyhood Sabbataï Zevi
avoided the company and games of playmates,
sought solitary places, and what usually has charms
for the young did not attract him. He was educated
by the current method. In early youth he studied
the Talmud in the school of the veteran Joseph
Eskapha, a staunch Talmudist of Smyrna, but did
not attain to great proficiency. The more was
he attracted by the confused jumble of the Kabbala. Once introduced into the labyrinth of the
Zohar, he felt himself at home therein, guided by
Lurya's interpretation. Sabbataï Zevi shared the

prevailing opinion that the Kabbala can be acquired only by means of asceticism.   He mortified his body, and bathed very frequently in the sea, day and night, winter and summer.   Perhaps it was from sea-bathing that his body derived the peculiar fragrance which his worshipers strongly maintained that it possessed.   In early manhood he presented a contrast to his companions because he felt no attraction to the female sex.   According to custom Sabbataï Zevi married early, but avoided his young, good-looking wife so pertinaciously, that she applied for divorce, which he willingly granted her.   The same thing happened with a second wife.

This aversion to marriage, rare in the warm climate of the East, his assiduous study of the Kabbala, and his ascetic life, attracted attention. Disciples sought him, and were introduced by him to the Kabbala.   Twenty years old he was the master of a small circle.   He attached disciples to himself partly by his earnest and retiring manner, which precluded familiarity, partly by his musical voice, with which he sang in Spanish the Kabbalistic verses composed by Lurya or himself.   Another circumstance must be added.   When Sultan Ibrahim ascended the throne, a violent war broke out between Turkey and Venice, which made the trade of the Levant unsafe in the capital.   Several European, that is, Dutch and English, mercantile houses in consequence transferred their offices to Smyrna. This hitherto insignificant city thereby acquired importance as a mart.   The Jews of Smyrna, who had been poor, profited by this commercial development, and amassed great riches, first as agents of large houses, afterwards as independent firms. Mordecai Zevi, Sabbataï's father, from the Morea, originally poor, became the Smyrna agent of an English house, executed its commissions with strict honesty, enjoyed the confidence of the principals, and became a wealthy man.   His increasing prosperity was attributed by the blind father to the merit of his Kabbala-loving son, to whom he paid such great reverence, that it was communicated to strangers. Sabbataï was regarded as a young saint. The more discreet, on account of his folly, declared him to be mad. In the house of his English principal, Mordecai Zevi often heard the approach of the millennium discussed, either he himself or some of his people being enthusiastic believers in the apocalypse of the Fifth Monarchy. The year 1666 was designated by these enthusiasts as the Messianic year, which was to bring renewed splendor to the Jews and see their return to Jerusalem. The expectations heard in the English counting house were communicated by Mordecai Zevi to the members of his family, none of whom listened more attentively than Sabbataï, already entangled in the maze of the Luryan Kabbala, and inclined to mistake enthusiastic hopes for prosaic fact. What if he himself were called upon to usher in this time of redemption? Had he not, at an earlier age than any one before, penetrated to the heart of the Kabbala? And who could be more worthy of this call than one deeply immersed in its mysteries?

The central point of the later Kabbala was most intense expectation of the Messiah; Lurya, Vital, and their disciples and followers proclaimed anew, "The kingdom of heaven is at hand." A peculiar redemption was to precede and accompany it—the redemption of the scattered elements of the original soul (Nizuzoth) from the fetters of original evil, the demon nature (Kelifoth), which, taking a hold on men through the fall of the angels or divine elements, held them in captivity, impeded their upward flight, and necessitated the perpetual transmigration of souls from body to body. As soon as the evil spirit was either consumed, annihilated, rendered powerless, or at least existed by itself without admixture of the divine, then the Kabbalistic order (Olam ha-Tikkun) would prevail, streams of mercy would pour forth without let or hindrance upon the lower world through the channels of the Sefiroth, and fructify and miraculously quicken it. This work of redemption can be accomplished by every truly pious man (Zaddik), who having an enlightened soul, and being initiated into the Kabbala, stands in close union with the world of spirits, comprehends the connection between the upper and lower world, and fulfills all religious exercises (Kewanoth) with concentrated devotion and with due regard to their influence upon the higher powers. Still more effectually the Messiah, the son of David, will accomplish the annihilation of demoniacal powers and the restoration of lost souls, or rather the collection of the scattered elements of the universal soul of Adam. For to the Messiah, in whom dwells a pure, immaculate soul, are unfolded the mysterious depths of the higher worlds, essences, and divine creation, even the Divine Being Himself. The Messiah of the seed of David would, to a certain extent, be the original man (Adam Kadmon) incarnate, part of the Godhead.

This Luryan mysticism dazzled the bewildered brain of the Smyrna youth, and produced such confusion and giddiness, that he thought he could easily usher in this spiritual redemption, which would be immediately followed by that of the body. In what manner this haughty wish to play the part of a Messiah germinates and breaks forth in enthusiastic minds, is an impenetrable riddle. Sabbataï Zevi was not the first to believe himself able to reverse the whole order of the world, by mystical hocus-pocus, and partly to succeed in the endeavor. Certain it is that the extravagant notions entertained by Jews and Christians with regard to the near approach of the time of grace worked upon Sabbataï's weak brain. That book of falsehoods, the Zohar, declared that in the year of the world 5408 (1648)

the era of redemption would dawn, and precisely in
that year Sabbataï revealed himself to his train of
youthful companions as the Messianic redeemer.
It happened in an apparently insignificant manner,
but the mode of revelation was of great import to
the initiated. Sabbataï Zevi uttered the full four-
lettered name of God in Hebrew (Jhwh, the Tetra-
grammaton) without hesitation, although this was
strictly prohibited in the Talmud and by the usage
of ages. The Kabbalists attached all sorts of mystical importance to this prohibition. During the
dispersion of Israel, the perfection of God Himself
was to a certain extent destroyed, on account of the
sinfulness of men and the degradation of the Jewish
people, since the Deity could not carry out His
moral plan. The higher and lower worlds were
divided from each other by a deep gulf; the four
letters of God's name were parted asunder. With
the Messianic period of redemption the moral order
of the world, as God had laid it down in the plan of
the universe, and the perfection and unity of God
would be restored. When Sabbataï Zevi permitted
himself to pronounce the name of God in full, he
thereby proclaimed that the time of grace had begun
with him.

However, despite his pious, mystical life, he had
too little authority at the age of two and twenty for
the rabbis to allow an infraction of the existing
order of things, which might lead to further inroads.
When Zevi's pretensions became known some years
later, the college of rabbis, at their head his teacher
Joseph Eskapha, laid him and his followers under a
ban. Many bickerings ensued in the community,
the particulars of which are not known. Finally he
and his disciples were banished from Smyrna (about
1651). The Messianic delusion appeared to have
been extinguished, but it smouldered on, and broke
out again, about fifteen years later, in a bright, consuming flame. This persecution, far from terrifying

Sabbataï Zevi, gave him a sense of his dignity.   The idea of a suffering Messiah had been transplanted from Christianity to Judaism; it was the accepted view that humiliation was the precursor of the Messiah's exaltation and glorification.   Sabbataï believed in himself, and his disciples, amongst them Moses Pinheiro, a man of mature age, highly esteemed for scientific acquirements, shared the belief with tenacity.   If the Messiah had been obliged to beg his way through the world, his illusion would not have long held its ground.   But Sabbataï was richly provided with means, he could maintain his independence and his presumed dignity, and win adherents to his cause.   At first, however, he kept himself in concealment, did not say much about his Messiahship, and thereby escaped ridicule.   Whither he betook himself after his banishment from his native city is not quite certain; probably to the Turkish capital, where dwelt the largest Jewish community, in which were so many clean and unclean elements, that everyone could find companions for plans and adventures.   Here he made the acquaintance of a preacher, Abraham Yachini, who confirmed him in his delusion.   Yachini stood in high repute on account of his talent as a preacher.   He was a needy and artful fellow, and made neat transcriptions for a Dutch Christian, who dabbled in Oriental literature. From selfish motives or delight in mystification, and to confirm Sabbataï Zevi in his delusion, Yachini palmed off upon him an apocryphal manuscript in archaic characters, which he alleged bore ancient testimony to Sabbataï's Messiahship.

"I, Abraham, was shut up for forty years in a cave, and wondered that the time of miracles did not make its appearance.   Then a voice replied to me, 'A son shall be born in the year of the world 5386 (1626), and be called Sabbataï.   He shall quell the great dragon: he is the true Messiah, and shall wage war without weapons.'"

This document, which the young fanatic himself appears to have taken for a genuine revelation,

became later on the source of many mystifications
and impostures.   However, it appeared inadvisable
to the dupe and the deceiver that he should appear
in Constantinople.   Salonica, which had always paid
homage to mysticism, seemed a more suitable field
for Kabbalistic extravagances.   Here, therefore,
Sabbataï resided for some time, gained adherents,
and came forward with greater boldness.   Here he
enacted one of his favorite scenes, by which he afterwards worked upon the imagination of the Kabbalists.   He prepared a solemn festival, invited his
friends, sent for the sacred book (Torah), and intimated to those present, that he was about to celebrate his mystical marriage with it.   In the language
of the Kabbala this meant that the Torah, the
daughter of heaven, was to be united indissolubly
with the Messiah, the son of heaven, or En-Sof.
This scene displeased the discreet rabbis of Salonica,
and they decreed his banishment.   Thence he betook himself to the Morea, probably to relatives and
friends of his father, and resided for some time at
Athens, where at that time there was a Jewish community.   When the Jews of this region heard of the
sentence pronounced upon him, they gave him no
encouragement.   This opposition, far from dis-
couraging him, only served to make him bolder ; he
probably regarded his sufferings as necessary for
the glorification of the Messiah.

At last, after long wandering, a prospect of realizing his dream presented itself at Cairo.   In the
Egyptian capital there was a Jewish mint-master
and tax-farmer, with the title of Saraph-Bashi, similar
to the Alabarchs at Alexandria in earlier ages.   At
that time (after 1656) the office was held by Raphael
Joseph Chelebi, of Aleppo, a man of great wealth
and open-handed benevolence, but of unspeakable
credulity, and ineradicable propensity to mysticism
and asceticism.   Fifty learned Talmudists and Kabbalists were supported by him, and dined at his

table.   Everyone who sought his compassion found
help and relief in his need.   While riding in the
royal chariot, and appearing in splendid robes, he
wore sackcloth underneath, fasted and bathed much,
and frequently at night scourged himself.   Samuel
Vital, a son of Chayim Calabrese, superintended his
constant penances according to the Kabbalistic precepts of Lurya (Tikkun Lurya).   These were intended, as has been stated, to hasten the coming of
the Messiah.   To be in Cairo and not to make
Raphael Joseph's acquaintance was an inconceivable
course for a Kabbalist.   Sabbataï Zevi thus came
into his circle, and won his confidence the sooner,
as, owing to his independent position, he did not
desire anything of him.   He appears to have partially revealed his Messianic plans to Raphael.   He
had grown older, maturer, and wiser, and knew how
to make men amenable to his wishes.   The Apocalyptic year, 1666, was drawing near, and it was
important to use the auspicious moment.

He betook himself to Jerusalem, perhaps under
the delusion that in the Holy Land a miracle would
take place to confirm his greatness.   The community at Jerusalem was at that time in every way
poor and wretched.   Besides being ground down
by the oppressions and extortions of Turkish officials, it suffered because the supplies from Europe
were exhausted on account of the constant massacres
of the Jews in Poland.   The consequence was that
the best men emigrated, leaving the government of
the community to thorough-going Kabbalists, devoted adherents of Lurya and Vital, or to a licentious set, who followed the impulses of bare-faced
selfishness.   There were at that time very few men
of repute and authority in Jerusalem.   A Marrano
physician named Jacob Zemach appears to have
stood at their head.   He had leapt, so to speak, in
one bound from a Portuguese church into the nest
of Kabbalists at Safet, and there, as later at Jeru-

salem, had become an unconscious tool for the mystifications practiced by Vital. Abraham Amigo, a Talmudist of the second or third rank, had similar aims. A man of some importance, to be sure, was Jacob Chages (1620-1674), who had migrated from Italy to Jerusalem, and who wrote Spanish well. Chages, however, had no official position, but lived the life of a recluse in an academy, which two brothers named Vega, of Leghorn, had founded for him. The thoughtless credulity of the people of Jerusalem of that time is instanced by the gross deception practiced upon them by Baruch Gad, one of their alms-collecting emissaries, which they, the learned and the unlearned, not only credited, but swore to as true. Baruch Gad had gone on a begging journey to Persia, where he pretended that he had experienced many adventures, and had been saved by a Jew of the tribe of Naphtali, who had given him a Kabbalistic letter from one of the "Sons of Moses" at the miraculous river Sabbation. It contained much about the riches, splendor, and daily miracles of the Sons of Moses, and said that they were momentarily awaiting the commencement of the Messianic epoch as a signal for coming forth. This story, certified by a circular, was brought by Baruch Gad to Jerusalem, where it found unquestioning credence. When the community of Jerusalem had fallen into great want in consequence of the Cossack massacre, ten so-called rabbis, Jacob Zemach at their head, sent to Reggio to their envoy Nathan Spira, of Jerusalem, a copy of this document from the Sons of Moses, which was kept in careful custody. It was to serve as a bait to draw more abundant alms.

The miracle which Sabbataï Zevi was expecting for himself in the Holy City was present in the credulity and mania for miracles on the part of the people of Jerusalem, who were inclined, like the lowest savages, to accept any absurd message as a divine revelation, if only it was brought before them in the right manner. At first the Smyrna enthusiast kept himself quiet, and gave no offense. He lived according to the precepts of the Kabbala, imposed the severest mortifications on himself, and often stayed by the graves of pious men in order to draw down their spirits. Thereby, aided by his pleasing, attractive, and reverential behavior and taciturn manner, he gradually gathered round him a circle of adherents who had blind faith in him. One of his devoted followers related with credulous simplicity, that Sabbataï Zevi shed floods of tears in prayer. He sang Psalms the whole night with his melodious voice, while pacing the room now with short, now with long strides. His whole conduct was out of the ordinary groove. He was also wont to sing coarse love songs in Spanish, with a mystical meaning, about the emperor's fair daughter Melisselda, with her coral lips and milk-white skin, as she rose out of the bath. Sabbataï used another means to win hearts. When he showed himself in the streets he distributed sweet-meats of all sorts to the children, who in consequence ran after him, and he thus gained the favor of their mothers.

An incident brought his eccentric ideas nearer their realization. The community at Jerusalem was sentenced by one of the pachas or some minor official to one of those oppressive exactions which frequently carried torture or death in their train. The impoverished members rested their hopes solely on Raphael Joseph Chelebi at Cairo, known to have the means and inclination to succor his afflicted brethren, especially the saints of Jerusalem. A messenger was to be sent to him, and Sabbataï Zevi was universally regarded as the most fitting, particularly as he was a favorite with the Saraph-Bashi. He undertook this task willingly, because he hoped to get the opportunity to play the part of saviour of the Holy City. His worshipers date from this journey to Egypt the beginning of his miraculous power, and assert that he accomplished many miracles at sea.   Sabbataï however traveled not by water, but by land, by way of Hebron and Gaza, probably joining a caravan through the desert.   He excited so much attention that all the Jews of Hebron, in order to observe him, refrained from sleep during the night of his stay.   Arrived at Cairo, he immediately received from Chelebi the sum required for the ransom of the community at Jerusalem, and, besides, an extraordinarily favorable opportunity presented itself to confirm his Messianic dreams.

During the massacre of the Jews in Poland by Chmielnicki, a Jewish orphan girl of about six was found by Christians, and put into a nunnery.   Her parents were dead, a brother had been driven to Amsterdam, the whole community broken up and put to flight, and no one troubled himself about the forsaken child, so that the nuns of the convent regarded the foundling as a soul brought to them and gave her a Christian conventual education.   The impressions received in the house of her parents were so lively, that Christianity found no entrance into her heart ; she remained faithful to Judaism. Nevertheless, her soul was nourished by fantastic dreams induced by her surroundings, and her thoughts took an eccentric direction.   She developed into a lovely girl, and longed to escape from the cloister.   One day she was found by Jews, who had again settled in the place, in the Jewish cemetery. Astonished at finding a beautiful girl of sixteen lightly clad in such a position, they questioned her, and received answer that she was of Jewish extraction, and had been brought up in a convent.   The night before, she said, she had been bodily seized by her father's ghost, and carried out of bed to the cemetery.   In support of her statement, she showed the women nail-marks on her body, which were said to come from her father's hands.   She appears to have learnt in the convent the art of producing scars on her body. The Jews thought it dangerous to keep a fugitive from the convent in their midst, and sent her to Amsterdam. There she found her brother. Eccentric by nature and excited by the change in her fortunes, she continually repeated the words, that she was destined to be the wife of the Messiah, who was soon to appear. After she had lived some years in Amsterdam under the name of Sarah, she came—it is not known for what purpose—by way of Frankfort-on-the-Main to Leghorn. There, as credible witnesses aver, she put her charms to immoral use, yet continued to maintain that she was dedicated to the Messiah, and could contract no other marriage. The strange history of this Polish girl circulated amongst the Jews, and penetrated even to Cairo. Sabbataï Zevi, who heard of it, gave out that a Polish-Jewish maiden had been promised to him in a dream as his spiritual wife. He sent a messenger to Leghorn, and had Sarah brought to Cairo.

By her fantastical, free, self-confident behavior and by her beauty, Sarah made a peculiar impression upon Sabbataï and his companions. He himself was firmly convinced of his Messiahship. To Sabbataï and his friends the immoral life of this Polish adventuress was not unknown. This also was said to be a Messianic dispensation; he had been directed, like the prophet Hosea, to marry an unchaste wife. No one was so happy as Raphael Joseph Chelebi, because at his house the Messiah met his bride, and was married. He placed his wealth at the disposal of Sabbataï Zevi, and became his most influential follower. The warm adhesion of so dignified, respected, and powerful a man brought many believers to Sabbataï. It was rightly said, that he had come to Egypt as a messenger, and returned as the Messiah. For, from this second residence at Cairo dates his public career. Sarah, also, the Messiah's fair bride, brought him many disciples. Through her a romantic, licentious element entered into the fantastic career of the Smyrna Messiah. Her beauty and free manner of life attracted youths and men who had no sympathy with the mystical movement. With a larger following than when he started, Sabbataï returned to Palestine, bringing two talismans of more effective power than Kabbalistic means—Sarah's influence and Chelebi's money. At Gaza he found a third confederate, who helped to smooth his path.

At Jerusalem there lived a man named Elisha Levi, who had migrated thither from Germany. The Jews of the Holy City dispatched him to all parts of the world with begging letters. Whilst he was roaming through northern Africa, Amsterdam, Hamburg, and Poland, his son Nathan Benjamin Levi (1644–1680) was left to himself, or the perverse education of that time. He developed, in the school of Jacob Chages, into a youth with superficial knowledge of the Talmud, acquired Kabbalistic scraps, and obtained facility in the high-sounding, but hollow, nonsensical Rabbinical style of the period, which concealed poverty of thought beneath verbiage. The pen was his faithful instrument, and replaced the gift of speech, in which he had little facility. This youth was suddenly raised from pressing poverty to opulence. A rich Portuguese, Samuel Lisbona, who had moved from Damascus to Gaza, asked Jacob Chages to recommend a husband for his beautiful, but one-eyed daughter, and he suggested his disciple Nathan Benjamin. Thus he became connected with a rich house, and in consequence of his change of fortune, lost all stability, if he had had any. When Sabbataï Zevi, with a large train of followers, came to Gaza on his way back from Cairo, posing as the Messiah, and accepted as such by the crowds gathering about him, Nathan Ghazati (*i.e.*, of Gaza) entered into close relationship with him. In what way their mutual acquaintance and attachment arose is not explained. Sabbataï's disciples declared that Nathan had dug up a part of the ancient writing, wherein Zevi's Messiahship was testified. It is probably nearer the truth, that Sabbataï, to convince Ghazati of his mission, palmed off on him the spurious document received from Abraham Yachini. At any rate Nathan became his most zealous adherent, whether from conviction or from a desire to play a prominent part, can no longer be discerned in this story, in which simple faith, self-deception, and willful imposture, border so close on one another.

After Nathan Ghazati and Sabbataï had become acquainted, the former a youth of twenty, the latter a man of forty, prophetic revelations followed close upon one another. Ghazati professed to be the risen Elijah, who was to pave the way for the Messiah. He gave out that he had received a call on a certain day (probably the eve of the Pentecost, 1665), that in a year and a few months the Messiah would show himself in his glory, would take the sultan captive without arms, only with music, and establish the dominion of Israel over all the nations of the earth. The Messianic age was to begin in the year 1666. This revelation was proclaimed everywhere in writing by the pretended prophet of Gaza, with the addition of wild fantasies and suggestive details. He wrote to Raphael Joseph acknowledging the receipt of the moneys sent by him, and begging him not to lose faith in Sabbataï; the latter would certainly in a year and some months make the sultan his subject and lead him about as a captive. The dominion would be entrusted to Nathan, until he should conquer the other nations without bloodshed, warring only against Germany, the enemy of the Jews. Then the Messiah would betake himself to the banks of the river Sabbation, and there espouse the daughter

of the great prophet, Moses, who at the age of thirteen would be exalted as queen, with Sarah as her
slave.   Finally, he would lead back the ten tribes to
the Holy Land, riding upon a lion with a seven-
headed dragon in its jaws.   The more exaggerated
and absurd Nathan's prophetic vaporings were, the
more credence did they find.   A veritable fit of intoxication took possession of nearly all the Jews of
Jerusalem and the neighboring communities.   With
a prophet, formerly a shy youth, proclaiming so
great a message, and a Messiah, more profoundly
versed in the Kabbala than Chayim Vital, who could
venture to doubt the approach of the time of grace?
Those who shook their heads at this rising imposture were laughed to scorn by the Sabbatians.

The rabbinical leaders of the Jerusalem community were unfavorably struck by this Messianic
movement, and sought to stifle it at its birth.   It
was sufficient to prejudice them against Sabbataï
that he stood in the foreground, and put them in the
shade.   He is said to have distributed the money
from Egypt according to his own discretion, and in
the division to have unduly favored his own followers.   Jacob Chages and his college threatened him
with the heaviest excommunication if he should per-
sist in his course.   Sabbataï Zevi appears to have
cared little for this, especially as a ban could have
no effect if the community was on his side.   Even
Moses Galante, the son-in-law of Jacob Chages, esteemed as an authority in the Holy Land, regarded
him with respect, although, as he afterwards declared, he did not believe in him unconditionally.
Sabbataï Zevi saw clearly that Jerusalem was not
the right place for his plans, as the rabbis would
place obstacles in his way.   Nathan Ghazati thereupon proclaimed in an ecstasy that Jerusalem had
lost its importance as the sacred city, and that Gaza
had taken its place.   At Smyrna, his native city—
an important gathering-place for Europeans and

Asiatics—Sabbataï thought he could obtain greater success. His rich brothers prepared a good reception for him by the distribution of money amongst the poor and needy, and Nathan's extravagant prophetic letters had kindled the imagination of the people. But before he left Jerusalem, Sabbataï took care to dispatch active missionaries of a fanatical and fraudulent character, to predict his Messianic appearance, excite men's minds, and fill them with his name. Sabbataï Raphael, a beggar and impostor from the Morea, enlarged in mountebank fashion on the Messiah's greatness; and a German Kabbalist, Matathias Bloch, did the same in blind simplicity.

Thus it came to pass that when Sabbataï Zevi left Jerusalem—of his own accord, as he pretended, banished, as others said—he was at once received in triumph in the large Asiatic community of Aleppo. Still greater was the homage paid him in his native city (autumn 1665). The ban pronounced against him was not remembered. He was accompanied by a man of Jerusalem, Samuel Primo, who became his private secretary, and one of his most zealous recruiting agents. Samuel Primo understood the art of investing trifles with an air of official seriousness and by a flowery style to give world-wide importance to the Messianic imposture. He alone remained sober in the midst of the ever-increasing fanaticism, and gave aim and direction to the enthusiasts. Primo appears to have heralded Sabbataï's fame from conviction; he had a secret plan to be accomplished through the Messiah. He appears to have made use of Sabbataï more than to have been employed by him. Sabbataï had tact enough not to announce himself at once at Smyrna as the Messiah; he commanded the believing multitude not to speak of it until the proper time. But this reserve, combined with other circumstances— the ranting letters of Nathan, the arrival of some

men of Jerusalem who brought him the homage of
the Holy City (though without being commissioned
to do so), the severe mortifications which the people
inflicted on themselves, to atone for their sins and
become worthy of the coming of the Messiah—all
this worked upon the minds of the multitude, and
they could scarcely wait for the day of his revelation.
He had the Kabbalists on his side through his mystical utterances. At length Sabbataï Zevi declared
himself publicly in the synagogue, with blowing of
horns, as the expected Messiah (New Year, September, or October, 1665), and the multitude shouted
to him, "Long live our King, our Messiah!"

The proverb that a prophet is least honored in
his own country was for once belied. The madness
of the Jews of Smyrna knew no bounds. Every
sign of honor and enthusiastic love was shown him.
It was not joy, but delirium to feel that the long-
expected Messiah had at last appeared, and in their
own community. The delirium seized great and
small. Women, girls, and children fell into raptures, and proclaimed Sabbataï Zevi in the language
of the Zohar as the true redeemer. The word of
the prophet, that God at the end of the world will
pour forth his spirit upon the young, appeared fulfilled. All prepared for a speedy exodus, the return to the Holy Land. Workmen neglected their
business, and thought only of the approaching kingdom of the Messiah. The confusion in men's brains
showed itself in the way in which the Sabbatians of
Smyrna strove to merit a share in the time of grace.
On the one hand, they subjected themselves to incredible penances—fasted several days in succession, refrained from sleep for nights, in order that,
by Kabbalistic prayers (Tikkunim) at midnight, they
might wipe away their sins, and bathed in extremely
cold weather, even with snow on the ground. Some
buried themselves up to the neck in the soil, and
remained in their damp graves until their limbs were

stiff with cold.   On the other hand, they abandoned themselves to the most extravagant delight, and celebrated festival after festival in honor of the Messiah, whenever Sabbataï Zevi showed himself— always with a large train of followers—or walked through the streets singing Psalms, "The right hand of the Lord is exalted, the right hand of the Lord bringeth victory," or preached in a synagogue, and proved his Messiahship by Kabbalistic interpretations of Scripture. He showed himself only in procession in public, waved a fan to cool himself, and whoever was touched with it was sure of the kingdom of heaven. The delirious joy of his followers knew no bounds. Every word of his was repeated a thousand times as the word of God, expounded, exaggerated, and intensified. All that he did was held as miraculous, published, and believed. The madness went so far that his adherents in Smyrna and elsewhere, as at Salonica, that Kabbalist hotbed of old, married their children of twelve, ten, and even younger, to one another—seven hundred couples in all—that, according to Kabbalistic ideas, they might cause the souls not yet born to enter into life, and thereby remove the last obstacle to the commencement of the time of grace.

The activity of Sabbataï Zevi in electrifying the minds of simple believers, now by public pomp and pageantry, now by silent retirement, was supplemented by Sarah, his wife, who by her loose conduct worked on the passions of the male population. The bonds of chastity, drawn much tighter among Eastern Jews than in Europe, were broken. The assembling of persons of both sexes in great multitudes, hitherto unheard of, was a slight innovation. In Messianic transports of delight men and women danced with one another as if mad, and in mystical fervor many excesses are said to have been committed. The voice of censure and caution was gradually silenced; all were drawn into the vortex,

and the unbelievers were rendered harmless. The
rabbi Aaron de la Papa (died 1674), an aged and
respectable man, who at first spoke against this
Messianic madness, and pronounced the ban against
its originator, together with other rabbis, was publicly reviled in a sermon by Sabbataï, removed from
office, and obliged to leave Smyrna.

Most unworthy was the behavior of the rabbi
Chayim Benvenisti (1603-1673), a very considerable
authority on the Talmud, and of astonishing learning, who, because he was a literary opponent of De
la Papa, not only suffered the latter's removal from
office, but allowed himself to be appointed in his
place by Sabbataï. Though at first harshly disposed towards the new Messiah, he became a
believer, and led the multitude by his authority.
The latter were instigated by Sabbataï to bloodthirsty fanaticism. Because a noble, rich, and respected man in Smyrna, Chayim Penya, who had
liberally supported Chayim Benvenisti, opposed
the widespread delusion with obstinate incredulity,
he was suddenly attacked in the synagogue, persecuted, and nearly torn to pieces by the raging
multitude. Sabbataï Zevi, the pretended incarnation of piety, commanded the synagogue to be
broken open and the vile heretic to be seized. But
when Penya's daughters, likewise attacked by the
madness, fell into raptures, and prophesied, the
father had no choice but to put a good face upon
the wretched business. He also assumed the air of
a zealous adherent. After Penya's subjugation Sabbataï Zevi became sole ruler in the community, and
could lead the Jewish population at will for good
or for evil. In this humor which lasted for some
months, the Jews of Smyrna feared their tyrants,
the Turkish cadis, very little; if they offered to
check the prevailing tendency, they were induced by
rich presents to remain inactive.

These events in the Jews' quarter at Smyrna

made a great sensation in ever-widening circles. The neighboring communities of Asia Minor, many members of which had betaken themselves to Smyrna, and witnessing the scenes enacted in that town, brought home exaggerated accounts of the Messiah's power of attraction and of working miracles, were swept into the same vortex. Sabbataï's private secretary, Samuel Primo, took care that reports of the fame and doings of the Messiah should reach Jews abroad. Nathan Ghazati sent circulars from Palestine, while the itinerant prophets, Sabbataï Raphael and Matathias Bloch, filled the ears of their auditors with the most marvelous accounts of the new redeemer. Christians also helped to spread the story. The residents, the clerks of English and Dutch mercantile houses, and the evangelical ministers, reported the extraordinary occurrences in Smyrna, and though they scoffed at the folly of the Jews, could not withhold half-credulous sympathy. Did they not see with their own eyes the ecstasies, and hear with their own ears the predictions, of the prophets and prophetesses of Sabbataï Zevi, the true redeemer? On the exchanges in Europe men spoke of him as a remarkable personage, and eagerly awaited news from Smyrna or Constantinople. At first the Jews were dazed by the reports that suddenly burst upon them. Was the long cherished hope, that one day the oppression and shame of Israel would be removed, and that he would return in glory to his home, at length to be realized? No wonder that nearly everywhere scenes similar to those in Smyrna were repeating themselves, that men's minds were filled with credulity, accepting mere rumors as accredited facts, or that wild excitement, ascetic living, and almsgiving to the needy, by way of preparation for the time of the Messiah, were followed here and there by prophetic ecstasies. Not only the senseless multitude, but nearly all the rabbis, and even men of culture and philosophical judgment, fell a prey to this credulity.

At that time not a single man of weight and importance recognized that the primary source of all these phenomena lay in the Kabbala and the Zohar. Jacob Sasportas, originally from Africa, had lived in Amsterdam and London and, at this time, was in Hamburg. He was born about 1620, and died 1698. A man of courage and keen penetration, whose word had weight through his Talmudical learning, Sasportas from the first combated this Messianic rage with passionate warmth. He was unwearied in sending letter after letter to the various communities and their guides in Europe, Asia, and Africa, to unmask the gross deceptions practiced, and to warn against the sad consequences. But even he was entangled in the snares of the Kabbala, and adopted its principles. On the ground of this spurious philosophy, thoroughgoing enthusiasts were more in the right than half-hearted adherents. Spinoza, who might have scattered this thick mist with his luminous ideas, was not only estranged from Judaism and his race, but even hostile to them, and regarded the prevailing perplexities with indifference or malice.

The accounts of Sabbataï Zevi and the Messianic excitement either came direct, or in a roundabout way by Alexandria, to Venice, Leghorn, and other Italian cities.

Venice was led by the bigoted Kabbalist Moses Zacut, Spinoza's very uncongenial fellow-student, who had formed the design of migrating from Amsterdam through Poland to Palestine, but stopped short in Venice. Far from opposing the delusion of the multitude, he encouraged it, as did the rabbinate of Venice. The news from Smyrna had most striking effect upon the great and the lesser Jerusalem of the North. The prophet of Gaza, who was not devoid of sober calculation, had directed his propagandist circulars to the most considerable and the richest communities—Amsterdam and Hamburg. These entered into close relationship with the new Messianic movement. The Jews of Amsterdam and Hamburg received confirmation of the extraordinary events at Smyrna from trustworthy Christians, many of whom were sincerely rejoiced thereat. Even Heinrich Oldenburg, a distinguished German savant in London, wrote to his friend Spinoza (December, 1665) :—

"All the world here is talking of a rumor of the return of the Israelites, dispersed for more than two thousand years, to their own country. Few believe it, but many wish it. . . . Should the news be confirmed, it may bring about a revolution in all things."

The number of believers in Amsterdam increased daily among the Portuguese no less than among the Germans, and numbers of educated people set the example ; the rabbis Isaac Aboab and Raphael Moses D'Aguilar, Spinoza's fellow-student Isaac Naar, and Abraham Pereira, one of the capitalists of Amsterdam and a writer on morals in Spanish, all became believers. Even the semi-Spinozist Dionysius Musaphia became a zealous adherent of the new Messiah. In Amsterdam devotion to the new faith expressed itself in contradictory ways— by noisy music and dancing in the houses of prayer, and by gloomy, monkish self-mortification. The printing presses could not supply enough copies of special prayer-books in Hebrew, Portuguese and Spanish, for the multitude of believers. In these books penances and formulas were given by which men hoped to become partakers in the kingdom of the Messiah. Many Sabbatian prayer-books (Tik-kunim) printed Sabbataï's likeness together with that of King David, also the emblems of his domin-ion, and select sentences from the Bible. In confi-dent expectation of speedy return to the Holy Land, the elders of one synagogue introduced the custom of pronouncing the priestly blessing every Sabbath.

At Hamburg, the Jews went to still greater lengths of folly, because they wished to make a demonstration against the bigoted Christians, who in many ways tormented them with vexatious restrictions, and when possible compelled them to listen to Christian sermons. Whoever entered the synagogue, and saw the Jewish worshipers hop, jump, and dance about with the roll of the Law in their arms, serious, respectable men withal, of Spanish stateliness, had to take them for madmen. In fact, a mental disease prevailed, which made men childish; even the most distinguished in the community succumbed to it.

Manoel Texeira, also called Isaac Señor Texeira, was born about 1630, and died about 1695. Some months before the death of his father, Diego Texeira, a Marrano nobleman who had emigrated from Portugal and settled at Hamburg, Manoel became resident minister, banker, and confidant of Christina, former queen of Sweden. She valued him on account of his honesty, his noble bearing, and his shrewdness. She exchanged letters with him on important affairs, conferred with him on the political interests of Europe, and credited him with deep, statesmanlike views. During her residence at Hamburg she took up her abode in Manoel Texeira's house, to the vexation of the local ecclesiastical authorities—who were hostile to the Jews—and remained quite unconcerned, although the Protestant preachers censured her severely from the pulpits. Men of the highest rank resorted to Texeira's house, and played with him for high stakes. This Jewish cavalier also belonged to Sabbataï's adherents, and joined in the absurd dances; as also the skillful and famous physician Bendito de Castro (Baruch Nehemiah), now advanced in years, for a time the physician of the queen during her residence in Hamburg. De Castro was at that time director of the Hamburg community, and by his order the

Messianic follies were practiced in the synagogue. Jacob Sasportas, who because of the outbreak of the plague in London at that time resided in Hamburg, used serious arguments and satire against this Messianic delusion ; but he could not make his voice heard, and only just escaped rough handling by the Sabbatians. The community recently established in London in the reign of Charles II, which had elected Jacob Sasportas as chief rabbi, was no less possessed with this craze. It derived additional encouragement from contact with Christian enthusiasts who hoped to bring about the millennium. Curious reports flew from mouth to mouth. It was said, that in the north of Scotland a ship had appeared, with silken sails and ropes, manned by sailors who spoke Hebrew. The flag bore the inscription, "The Twelve Tribes or Families of Israel." Believers living in London in English fashion offered wagers at the odds of ten to one that Sabbataï would be anointed king at Jerusalem within two years, and drew formal bills of exchange upon the issue. Wherever Jews dwelt, news of the Kabbalistic Messiah of Smyrna penetrated, and everywhere produced wild excitement. The little community of Avignon, which was not treated in the mildest manner by the papal officers, prepared to emigrate to the kingdom of Judah in the spring of the year 1666.

If Sabbataï Zevi had not hitherto firmly believed in himself and his dignity, this homage from nearly the whole Jewish race must have awakened conviction. Every day advices, messengers, and deputations came pouring in, greeting him in most flattering terms as king of the Jews, placing life and property at his disposal, and overwhelming him with gifts. Had he been a man of resolute determination and strength of will, he might have obtained results of importance with this genuine enthusiasm and willing devotion of his believers. Even

Spinoza entertained the possibility, with this favor
able opportunity and the mutability of human things,
that the Jews might re-establish their kingdom,
and again be the chosen of God. But Sabbataï
Zevi was satisfied with the savor of incense. He
cherished no great design, or rather, he lived in the
delusion that men's expectations would fulfill themselves of their own accord by a miracle. Samuel
Primo and some of his confidants appear, however,
to have followed a fixed plan, namely, to modify the
Rabbinical system, or even to abolish it. That was
in reality implied in the reign of the Messiah. The
fundamental conception of the Zohar, the Bible of the
Kabbalists, is that in the time of grace, in the world
of order (Olam ha-Tikkun), the laws of Judaism, the
regulations concerning lawful and forbidden things,
would completely lose their significance. Now this
time, the Sabbatians thought, had already begun ;
consequently, the minute ritualistic code of the
Shulchan Aruch ought no longer to be held binding.
Whether Sabbataï himself drew this conclusion, is
doubtful. But some of his trusted adherents gave
this theory prominence. A certain bitterness
towards the Talmud and the Talmudic method of
teaching prevailed in this circle. The Sabbatian
mystics felt themselves confined by the close meshes
of the Rabbinical network, and sought to disentangle
it loop by loop. They set up a new deity, substi-
tuting a man-god for the God of Israel. In their
wanton extravagance the Kabbalists had so entirely
changed the conception of the deity, that it had
dwindled away into nothing. On the other hand,
they had so exalted and magnified the Messiah, that
he was close to God. The Sabbatians, or one of
them (Samuel Primo ?), built on this foundation.
From the Divine bosom (the Ancient of Days),
they said, a new divine personage had sprung,
capable of restoring the order in the world intended
in the original plan of Divine Perfection. This new

person was the Holy King (Malka Kadisha), the Messiah, the Primal Man (Adam Kadmon), who would destroy evil, sin, and corruption, and cause the dried-up streams of grace to flow again. He, the holy king, the Messiah, is the true God, the redeemer and saviour of the world, the God of Israel; to him alone should prayers be addressed. The Holy King, or Messiah, combines two natures—one male, the other female; he can do more on account of his higher wisdom than the Creator of the world. Samuel Primo, who dispatched circulars and ordinances in the name of the Messianic king, often used the signature, " I, the Lord, your God, Sabbataï Zevi." Whether the Smyrna fanatic authorized such blasphemous presumptuousness cannot be decided, any more than whether in his heart he considered the Jewish law null and void. For, although some Sabbatians, who uttered these absurdities, pretended to have heard them from his own lips, other disciples asserted that he was an adherent of traditional Judaism.

The truth probably is that Sabbataï Zevi, absorbed in idle ruminating, accepted everything which the more energetic among his followers taught or suggested. They began the dissolution of Judaism by the transformation of the fast of the tenth of Tebeth (Asara be-Tebeth) into a day of rejoicing. Samuel Primo, in the name of his divinity, directed a circular to the whole of Israel in semi-official form:

" The first-begotten Son of God, Sabbataï Zevi, Messiah and Redeemer of the people of Israel, to all the sons of Israel, Peace ! Since ye have been deemed worthy to behold the great day and the fulfillment of God's word by the prophets, your lament and sorrow must be changed into joy, and your fasting into merriment, for ye shall weep no more. Rejoice with song and melody, and change the day formerly spent in sadness and sorrow, into a day of jubilee, because I have appeared."

So firmly rooted in men's minds was faith in Sabbataï Zevi, that the communities which the letter reached in time discontinued this fast, although

they believed that they could enter into the kingdom
of the Messiah only by strict abstinence. The staunch
orthodox party, however, was shocked at this innovation.   They could not conceive the Messiah as other
than a pious rabbi, who, if possible, would invent
fresh burdens.   A thousand times had they read in
the Zohar, and repeated to one another, that in the
time of the Messiah the days of mourning would be
changed into days of feasting, and the Law in general would be no longer binding; but when words
were changed into deeds, horror seized them.
Those rabbis who before had regarded the movement half incredulously, or had not interfered with the
penances and deeds of active benevolence to which
many of the Sabbatians had felt prompted, thereby
giving silent assent, now raised their voice against
the law-destroying Messiahship.   There began to
be formed in every large community a small party
of unbelievers (Kofrim), chiefly men learned in the
Talmud, who desired to guard the established religion against attacks and disruption.

Rabbinical Judaism and the Kabbala, hitherto in
close confederation, began to be at variance with
each other; this doubtful ally showing herself at
last in her true form as the enemy of Rabbinism.
But this sobering discovery, that the Kabbala was
a serpent nursed into life by the rabbis themselves,
was recognized only by a few. They still remained true
to her, imputing the growing hostility to the Shulchan Aruch to Sabbataï and his aiders and abettors.
It was too late, their voices were drowned in shouts
of joy.   Solomon Algazi, and some members of the
Smyrna rabbinate who shared his opinions, tried to
oppose the abolition of the fast, but were nearly
stoned to death by the multitude of believers, and
were obliged, like Aaron de la Papa, to leave the
city in haste.

But the Messiah was at last forced to tear himself out of his fool's paradise and the atmosphere

of incense in Smyrna, in order to accomplish his work in the Turkish capital—either because his followers compelled him to put his light, not under a bushel, but upon it, that the world at large might see it, or because the cadi could no longer endure the mad behavior of the Jews, and did not wish to bear the sole responsibility. It is said that the cadi gave Sabbataï Zevi three days to go to Constantinople and appear before the highest Turkish authorities. In his delusion, Zevi perhaps believed that a miracle would fulfill the prophecies of Nathan Ghazati and other prophets, that he would easily be able to take the crown from the sultan. He prepared for his journey. Before he left Smyrna, he divided the world among his six-and-twenty faithful ones, and called them kings and princes. His brothers, Elijah and Joseph Zevi, received the lion's share; the former was named king of kings, the latter king of the kings of Judah. To his other faithful followers he disclosed, in Kabbalistic language, which soul of the former kings of Judah or Israel dwelt in each of their bodies, that is, had passed into them by transmigration. Among the better known names were those of the companion of his youth, Isaac Silveira, and Abraham Yachini at Constantinople, who had imparted to him the art of mysticism. Raphael Joseph Chelebi could least of all be passed over; he had been the first firm supporter of the Messiah, and was called King Joash. A Marrano physician, who had escaped from Portugal, and was his devoted adherent, received the crown of Portugal. Even his former opponent Chayim Penya received a kingdom of his own. A beggar, Abraham Rubio of Smyrna, was likewise raised to a throne, under the name of Josiah, and was so firmly convinced of his approaching sovereignty that he refused large sums for his imaginary kingdom

Sabbataï Zevi appears purposely to have started on his Messianic journey to Constantinople exactly

at the beginning of the mystic year 1666. He was
accompanied by some of his followers, his secretary
Samuel Primo being in his train. He had announced the day of his arrival at Constantinople,
but circumstances proved false to him. The ship
in which he sailed had to contend with bad weather,
and the voyage was prolonged by weeks. Since
the sea did not devour him, the Sabbatians composed marvelous stories describing how the storm
and the waves had obeyed the Messiah. At
some place on the coast of the Dardanelles the pas-
sengers of the weather-beaten vessel were obliged
to land, and there Sabbataï was arrested by Turkish
officers, sent to take him prisoner. The grand
vizir, Ahmed Coprili, had heard of the excitement
of the Jews in Smyrna, and desired to suppress it.
The officers had strict orders to bring the pretended
redeemer in fetters to the capital, and therefore
hastened to meet the ship by which he came. According to orders, they put him in fetters, and
brought him to a small town in the neighborhood of
Constantinople, because the eve of the Sabbath was
near. Informed by a messenger of his arrival at
Cheknese Kutschuk, his followers hastened from
the capital to see him, but found him in a pitiable
plight and in chains. The money which they
brought with them procured him some alleviation,
and on the following Sunday (February, 1666), he
was brought by sea to Constantinople—but in how
different a manner to what he and his believers had
anticipated! However, his coming caused excitement. At the landing-place there was such a crowd
of Jews and Turks who desired to see the Messiah,
that the police were obliged to superintend the dis-
embarkation. An under-pasha commissioned to
receive him welcomed the man-god with a vigorous
box on the ear. Sabbataï Zevi is said, however, to
have wisely turned the other cheek to the blow.
Since he could not play the part of the triumphant,

he at least wished to play that of the suffering Messiah with good grace. When brought before the deputy-vizir (Kaimakam), Mustapha Pasha, he did not stand the first test brilliantly. Asked what his intentions were, and why he had roused the Jews to such a pitch of excitement, Sabbataï is said to have answered that he was nothing more than a Jewish Chacham, come from Jerusalem to the capital to collect alms ; he could not help it if the Jews testified so much devotion to him. Mustapha thereupon sent him to a prison in which insolvent Jewish debtors were confined.

Far from being disappointed at this treatment, his followers in Constantinople persisted in their delusion. For some days they kept quietly at home, because the street boys mocked them by shouting, " Is he coming ? is he coming ? " (Gheldi mi, Gheldi mi.) But they soon began again to assert that he was the true Messiah, and that the sufferings which he had encountered were necessary, a condition to his glorification. The prophets continued to proclaim the speedy redemption of Sabbataï and of all Israel. A Turkish dervish filled the streets of Constantinople with prophecies of the Messiah, whose enemies said that Sabbataï's followers had bribed him. Thousands crowded daily to Sabbataï's place of confinement merely to catch a glimpse of him. English merchants whose claims were not satisfied by their Jewish debtors applied to the Messiah. An order in his handwriting, admonishing defaulters to do justice to their creditors, as otherwise they would have no share in his joy and glory, had the best effect. Samuel Primo took care that most fabulous accounts should reach the Jews of Smyrna and those at a distance, of the reverence paid the Messiah by the Turkish authorities. At heart, he wrote, they were all convinced of his dignity. The expectations of the Jews were raised to a still higher pitch, and the most exaggerated hopes fostered to a greater degree.   It was looked upon as a palpable miracle that summary Turkish justice allowed him, the rebellious Jew, to live.   Did not this act of mercy prove that he was feared?   The Turkish government in fact seems to have stood in awe of the Jewish Messiah.   The Cretan war was impending, which demanded all the energy of the half-exhausted Turkish empire.   The prudent grand vizir, Ahmed Coprili, did not like to sentence him to death, thus making a fresh martyr, and causing a desperate riot among the Jews.   Even the Turks, charmed by Sabbataï's manner, and deceived by extraordinary miraculous manifestations, especially by the prophecies of women and children, joined the ranks of his worshipers.   It seemed to Coprili equally dangerous to leave Sabbataï, during his absence at the war, in Constantinople, where he might easily add fuel to the ever-increasing excitement in the capital.   He therefore commanded, after Sabbataï had been imprisoned in Constantinople for two months—from the beginning of February to April 17—that he be taken to the castle of the Dardanelles at Abydos, where state-prisoners were wont to be kept in custody.   It was a mild confinement; some of his friends, among them Samuel Primo, were allowed to accompany him thither. The Sabbatians called this fortress by a mystical name, the Tower of Strength (Migdal Oz).

If Sabbataï Zevi had doubted himself for a moment, his courage rose through his change of abode, the respectful clemency shown him by the divan, and the steady and increasing devotion of the Jews. He felt himself the Messiah again.   On his arrival at the castle of the Dardanelles on April 19, the day of preparation for the Passover, he slew a Paschal lamb for himself and his followers, and ate it with the fat, which is forbidden by the laws of the Talmud. He is said, while doing so, to have used a blessing which implied that the Mosaic, Talmudic, and Rab-

binical law was abrogated—"Blessed be God, who
hath restored again that which was forbidden." At
Abydos he held regular court with the large sums
of money which his brothers and his rich adherents
sent him with lavish hand. His wife Sarah, who
was allowed to remain with him, demeaned herself
as the Messianic queen, and bewitched the multitude
by her charms. From the Turkish capital a number
of ships conveyed his followers to the castle of the
Dardanelles. The fare on vessels rose in consequence daily. From other countries and continents,
too, crowds of Jews streamed to the place of his
captivity, in the hope to be deemed worthy of be-
holding him. The governor of the castle reaped
advantage thereby, for he charged the visitors entrance money, and raised it to fifteen or thirty marks
a head. Even the inhabitants of the place profited,
because they could earn high prices for board and
lodging. A veritable shower of gold poured into
Abydos. The impression which these facts, industriously circulated and exaggerated, made on the
Jews in Europe, Asia, and Africa, and the effect
which they produced, are indescribable. With few
exceptions all were convinced of Sabbataï's Messiahship, and of a speedy redemption, in two years
at the latest. They argued that he had had the
courage to go to the Turkish capital, although he
had openly proclaimed the dethronement of the
sultan, yet had not forfeited his life, but had been
left in a sort of mock imprisonment. What more
was needed to confirm the predictions of prophets
of ancient and modern times? The Jews accordingly prepared seriously to return to their original
home. In Hungary they began to unroof their
houses. In large commercial cities, where Jews
took the lead in wholesale business, such as Amsterdam, Leghorn, and Hamburg, stagnation of
trade ensued. In almost all synagogues his initials,
S and Z, were posted up with more or less adorn-

ment. Almost everywhere a prayer for him was
inserted in the following form: "Bless our Lord
and King, the holy and righteous Sabbataï Zevi, the
Messiah of the God of Jacob." In Europe the eyes
of all communities were directed to Amsterdam, the
representatives of which adhered to the movement
most enthusiastically. Every post-day which brought
fresh letters was a holiday for them. The Amsterdam Jews showed their joy openly, and were afraid
neither of the Christian population nor of the magistrates. Isaac Naar, of Amsterdam, and the rich
Abraham Pereira, prepared themselves for a journey
to the Messiah, and the former ironically announced
it to the unbelieving Jacob Sasportas. The Hamburg community always imitated that of Amsterdam, or went beyond it. The council introduced
the custom of praying for Sabbataï Zevi, not only
on Saturday, but also on Monday and Thursday.
The unbelievers were compelled to remain in the
synagogue and join in the prayer with a loud Amen.
And all this was done at the suggestion of the educated physician Bendito de Castro. The believers
went so far as to threaten their opponents if they
ventured to utter a word of censure against Sabbataï. At Venice, on the Sabbath, a quarrel broke
out between the Sabbatians and their opponents,
and one of the latter nearly lost his life. When
Sabbataï was asked how the Kofrim (unbelievers)
should be dealt with, he, or Samuel Primo, answered
that they might be put to death without ado, even
on the Sabbath; the executors of such punishment
were sure to enjoy eternal bliss. A learned Talmudist at Buda, Jacob Ashkenazi of Wilna, whose
son and grandson became zealous persecutors of
the Sabbatians, was guided by the decision, and declared a member of the community worthy of death,
because he would not say the blessing for Sabbataï
Zevi. In Moravia (at Nikolsburg) there were such
violent dissensions and tumults in consequence of

the craze about the Messiah, that the governor of the province was obliged to post up notices to calm men's minds. At Salee, in the north-western part of Africa, the ruling Emir Gailan (Gailand) ordered a persecution of the Jews, because they too openly displayed the hope of their coming redemption.

Many Christians shared the delusive faith in the new Messiah, and the weekly tidings from the East concerning Sabbataï Zevi and his doings made an overwhelming impression on them. At Hamburg, for example, pious Protestants betook themselves to the proselytizing preacher Esdras Edzard, and asked him what was to be done:

"We have certain accounts, not only from Jews, but also from our Christian correspondents at Smyrna, Aleppo, Constantinople, and other places in Turkey, that the new Messiah of the Jews does many miracles, and the Jews of the whole world flock to him. What will become of the Christian doctrine and the belief in our Messiah?"

The attention bestowed by educated classes of Christians upon the extraordinary events, which were published as news of the day, in turn enhanced the credulity of the Jews. In short, every circumstance tended to increase the deception. Only Jacob Sasportas raised his warning voice against the imposture. He sent letters in all directions, here to point out the absurdity of current rumors, there to collect exact information. He failed to obtain striking evidence of Sabbataï's, or Nathan's, roguery. Forged letters and documents were the order of the day; conscientiousness and uprightness had utterly disappeared. Thus the mist of false belief grew thicker and thicker, and one was no longer able to get at the truth.

For three months, from April to July, Sabbataï had been leading the life of a prince in the castle of the Dardanelles, intent only upon his own apotheosis. Either from caprice or at Samuel Primo's suggestion, he declared the fast of the 17th Tammuz to be abolished, because on this day he had realized his

Messianic character.   Was this a mere freak, or was it done with the intention of accustoming his adherents to the abolition of Rabbinical Judaism?   At all events, he appointed the 23d of Tammuz (July 25th), a Monday, to be kept as a strict Sabbath.   More than four thousand Jews, men and women, who happened to be at Abydos, celebrated this new Sabbath with great scrupulousness.   Sabbataï, or his secretary, sent circulars to the communities directing them to celebrate the next fast, the ninth of Ab, his birthday, as a festival by a special service, with Psalms specially chosen, with eating of choice meats, and the sound of the harp and singing.   He is said to have contemplated the annulling of all the Jewish festivals, even the Day of Atonement, and the introduction of others in their stead.   But before this could be done, he was guilty in his pride of an act of folly which caused the whole fabric to collapse.

Among the many thousand visitors from far and near, two Poles from Lemberg made a pilgrimage to him, to confirm their faith and feast on his countenance.   One was Isaiah, son of a highly-esteemed Rabbinical authority, the aged David Levi (Ture Zahab), and grandson of the no less celebrated Joel Serkes; the other, his half-brother, Leb Herz. From these two Poles Sabbataï heard that in the distant land from which they came, another prophet, Nehemiah Cohen, was announcing the approach of the Messiah's kingdom, but not through Sabbataï. He gave Isaiah Levi a laconic letter to take to his father, in which he promised the Jews of Poland revenge for the massacre by the Cossacks, and peremptorily ordered Nehemiah to come to him with all speed.   He laid so much stress on Nehemiah's coming, that he made his followers eager for his arrival.   The two Poles traveled back delighted to Lemberg, and everywhere told of the splendor amid which they had seen the Messiah.   Nehemiah was ordered to hasten to Sabbataï, and he was not deterred by the length of the journey. When he arrived at Abydos at the beginning of September, he was immediately admitted to an audience which lasted several days. The Polish prophet and the Smyrna Messiah did not laugh in one another's faces, like two augurs, but carried on a grave discussion. The subject of their mystical conversation remained unknown, as may be imagined. It was said to concern the forerunner of the Messiah—the Messiah of Ephraim—whether or not he had appeared and perished, as had been predicted. Nehemiah was not convinced by the long argument, and did not conceal the fact. On this account, the fanatical Sabbatians are said to have secretly made signs to one another to do away with this dangerous Pole. He fortunately escaped from the castle, betook himself forthwith to Adrianople, to the Kaimakam Mustapha, became a Mahometan, and betrayed the fantastic and treasonable designs which Sabbataï Zevi cherished, and which, he said, had remained unknown to the government, only because the overseer of the castle of Dardanelles had an interest in the concourse of Jews.

The Kaimakam conveyed the intelligence to the sultan, Mahomet IV, and the course to be pursued with regard to Sabbataï was maturely considered, the mufti Vanni being also admitted to aid the deliberations. To make short work with the rebellious schemer appeared impracticable to the council, particularly as Mahometans also followed him. If he should fall as a martyr, a new sect might arise, which would kindle fresh disturbances. Vanni, a proselytizing priest, proposed that an attempt be made to bring Sabbataï over to Islam. This advice was followed, and the sultan's physician (Hakim Bashi), a Jewish renegade, by name Guidon, was employed as the medium. A messenger suddenly appeared at Abydos, drove away the Jews, who were besieging the Messiah with homage, conveyed him to

Adrianople, and brought him first to the Hakim
Bashi, who, as a former coreligionist, would be able
to convert him the more easily.   The physician represented to him the dreadful punishment that would
inevitably befall him—he would be bound, and
scourged through the streets with burning torches,
if he did not appease the wrath of the sultan by
adopting Islamism.   It is not known whether this
call to apostatize from Judaism cost the conceited
Messiah great mental conflict.   He had not much
manly courage, and Judaism, in its existing form, was
perhaps dead for him.   So he adopted Guidon's
advice.   The following day (Elul 13, September 14,
1666) he was brought before the sultan.   He immediately cast off his Jewish head-dress, in sign of contempt ; a page offered him a white Turkish turban
and a green instead of the black mantle which he
wore, and so his conversion to the Mahometan
religion was accomplished.   When his dress was
changed, it is said that several pounds of biscuit
were found in his loose trousers.   The sultan was
highly pleased at this termination of the movement,
gave him the name of Mehmed Effendi, and appointed him his door-keeper—Capigi Bashi Otorak
—with a considerable monthly salary; he was to
remain near the sultan.   The Messiah's wife, Sarah,
the Polish rabbi's fair daughter of loose behavior,
likewise became a Mahometan, under the name of
Fauma Kadin, and received rich presents from the
sultana.   Some of Sabbataï's followers also went
over to Islam.   The mufti Vanni instructed them in
the Mahometan religion.   Sabbataï is said to have
married a Mahometan slave, in addition to his wife
Sarah, at the command of the mufti.   Nehemiah
Cohen, who had brought about this sudden change,
did not remain in Turkey, but returned to Poland,
took off the turban, and lived quietly without breathing a word of what had happened.   He disappeared
as suddenly as he had come forward.   The ex-Mes-

siah impudently wrote, some days after his conversion, to his brothers at Smyrna: "God has made me an Ishmaelite ; He commanded, and it was done. The ninth day of my regeneration."   Nearly at the same time the rabbis and presidents of schools at Amsterdam assembled, and sent a letter of homage to Sabbataï Zevi, to testify their belief in and submission to him.   The semi-Spinozist Dionysius (Benjamin) Musaphia, vexed at not being invited, wrote a separate letter to Sabbataï Zevi, signed by himself and two members of the school (Elul 24th). A week later, twenty-four distinguished men of Amsterdam sent another letter of homage to the apostate Messiah.   At their head was Abraham Gideon Abudiente.   Did these letters reach the Mahometan Mehmed Effendi?   At Hamburg, where likewise his conversion was not suspected, the blessing was five times pronounced over the renegade Sabbataï, on the Day of Atonement (October 9, 1666).

But when the rumor of his apostasy went the rounds of the communities, and could no longer be denied, confidence was succeeded by a bewildering sense of disenchantment and shame.   The highest representative of Judaism had abandoned and betrayed it!   Chayim Benvenisti, the rabbi of Smyrna, who had invested the false Messiah with authority from motives far from honorable, almost died of shame.   Mahometans and Christians pointed with scorn at the blind, credulous Jews.   The street boys in Turkey openly jeered at Jewish passers-by.   But this ridicule was not all.   So widespread a commotion could not die out and leave no trace.   The sultan thought of destroying all the Jews in his empire, because they had formed rebellious plans, and of ordering all children under seven to be brought up in Islamism.   The newly converted Mahometan, Mehmed Effendi, in order to revenge himself, is said to have betrayed his own plans, and the consent of the Jews thereto. Two councilors and the sultana-mother are reported to have dissuaded the sultan from his design by the observation that the Jews ought to be regarded as having been misled. Fifty chief rabbis, however, because they had neglected their duty in teaching the people, were to be executed—twelve from Constantinople, twelve from Smyrna, and the remaining twenty-six from the other communities in Turkey. It was regarded as a special miracle that this resolution remained a dead letter, and that the Jews did not even have to pay a fine. The division in the communities might have had even worse consequences, if the unbelievers had heaped scorn and mockery upon the late devotees. But the colleges of rabbis in the East interposed, and sought to appease and reconcile, and threatened to excommunicate any one who, by word or deed, offended a former Sabbatian.

Although men's minds were calmed for the moment, it was long before peace was restored. After the first surprise at Sabbataï's conversion was over, his zealous followers, especially at Smyrna, began to recover. They could not persuade themselves that they had really been running after a shadow. There must be, or have been, some truth in Sabbataï's Messianic claims, since all signs so entirely agreed. The Kabbalists easily got over objections. Sabbataï had not turned Mahometan; a phantom had played that part, while he himself had retired to heaven or to the Ten Tribes, and would soon appear again to accomplish the work of redemption. As at the time of the origin of Christianity mystical believers (Docetæ) interpreted the crucifixion of Jesus as a phantasm, so now thoroughgoing mystics explained Sabbataï's apostasy from Judaism. Others, such as Samuel Primo, Jacob Faliachi, Jacob Israel Duchan, who had designed, through him, to bring about the fall of Rabbinical Judaism, and would not abandon their plan lightly, still

clung to him.   The prophets, who had been mani-
festly proved false through his conversion, were
most interested in remaining true to him.   They did
not care quietly to renounce their functions and
withdraw into obscurity, or be laughed at.   The
prophets residing at Smyrna, Constantinople,
Rhodes, and Chios were silenced; but the itinerant
prophets, Nathan Ghazati and Sabbataï Raphael, did
not choose to abdicate.   The former had remained
in Palestine during Sabbataï's triumph in order to
be paid homage on his own account.   After the
deception was unmasked he regarded himself as no
longer safe ; he made preparations to go to Smyrna,
and continued to send out his mystical, bombastic
letters.   From Damascus he warned the Jews of
Aleppo by letter not to allow themselves to be discouraged by strange circumstances in their belief
in the Messiah; there was a deep mystery shortly to
be revealed ; but wherein the mystery consisted
could not yet be disclosed.   By these circulars the
credulous were confirmed afresh in their delusion.
In Smyrna many synagogues continued to insert the
blessing for Sabbataï in their prayers.   Hence the
rabbis were obliged to interfere vigorously, especially the rabbinate of the Turkish capital.   They laid
under a ban all who should even pronounce the
name of Sabbataï, or converse with his followers,
and threatened to hand them over to the secular
arm.   Nathan Ghazati, in particular, was excommunicated, and everyone warned against harboring
him or approaching him (Kislev 12, December 9,
1666).   These sentences of excommunication were
so far effectual that Nathan could not stay anywhere
for any length of time, and even in Smyrna he could
remain only a short time in secret at the house of a
believer.   But the rabbis were not able entirely to
exorcise the imposture.   One of the most zealous
Sabbatians, probably Samuel Primo, who was ready
in invention, threw out a more effective suggestion

than that of the mock conversion. All had been
ordained as it had come to pass. Precisely by his
going over to Islam had Sabbataï proved himself
the Messiah. It was a Kabbalistic mystery which
some writings had announced beforehand. As the
first redeemer Moses was obliged to reside for some
time at Pharaoh's court, not as an Israelite, but to
all appearance an Egyptian, even so must the last
redeemer live some time at a heathen court, apparently a heathen, "outwardly sinful, but inwardly
pure." It was Sabbataï's task to free the lost
emanations of the soul, which pervade even Mahometans, and by identifying them with himself, as it were,
bring them back to the fountain-head. By redeem-
ing souls in all circles, he was most effectually
furthering the kingdom of the Messiah. This suggestion was a lucky hit ; it kindled anew the flame
of the imposture. It became a watchword for all
Sabbatians enabling them, with decency and a show
of reason, to profess themselves believers, and hold
together.

Nathan Ghazati also caught up this idea, and was
encouraged to resume his part as prophet. He had
fared badly so far ; he had been obliged secretly to
leave Smyrna, where he had been in hiding several
months (end of April, 1667). His followers, consisting of more than thirty men, were dispersed.
But by this new imposture he recovered courage,
and approached Adrianople, where Mehmed Effendi
presided, attended by several of his adherents, who
as pretended Mahometans lived and made fantastic
plans with him. The representatives of the Jewish
community at Constantinople and Adrianople
rightly feared fresh disturbances from the presence
of the false prophet, and desired to get rid of him.
Nathan Ghazati, however, relied on his prophecy,
which might possibly, he said, be fulfilled at the end
of the year. He expected the Holy Spirit to descend upon the renegade Mehmed on the Feast of

Weeks (Pentecost), and then he also would be able
to show signs and wonders.   Until then, he defiantly
replied to the deputies, he could entertain no propositions.   When the Feast of Weeks was over,
the people of Adrianople again urged him to cease
from his juggleries.   After much labor they obtained
only a written promise to keep at a distance of
twelve days' journey from the city, not to corres-
pond with Sabbataï, not to assemble people round
him, and if by the end of the year the Redeemer did
not appear, to consider his prophecies false.   In
spite of his written promise, this lying prophet continued his agitation, and admonished the Sabbatians
in Adrianople to make known their continued adhesion by the suspension of the fast on the 17th of
Tammuz.   In this city there was a Sabbatian conventicle under the leadership of a former disciple,
who stood in close connection with Mehmed Effendi.
The rabbinate of Adrianople did not know how to
check the mischievous course of this daring sect,
and were obliged to have recourse to falsehood.
They announced that the renegade had suddenly
appeared before the Jewish communal council, had
repented of his imposture, and laid the blame on
Nathan and Abraham Yachini, who had made him
their dupe.   In this way the rabbinate succeeded in
deceiving the Sabbatians.   The effect did not last
long.   Nathan on the one hand, and Mehmed
Effendi's circle on the other, awakened new hope,
the number of believers again increased, and they
made a special point of not fasting on the 9th of Ab,
the birthday of their Messiah.   The rabbinates of
Constantinople and Smyrna sought to repress this
imposture by the old means—excommunication and
threats of punishment (end of July)—but with little
success.   The Sabbatians had a sort of hankering
after martyrdom in order to seal their faith.   The
false prophet renewed his propagandism.   He still
had some followers, including two Mahometans.

At Salonica, the home of a swarm of Kabbalists, he fared badly. The more easily did he find a hearing in the communities of the islands of Chios and Corfu. His hopes were however directed principally to Italy.

Here also confusion continued to reign. The first news of Sabbataï's defection had not been confirmed, as in consequence of the war in Crete the ships of the Christians had been captured by the Turks. Thus the Sabbatians were left free to maintain their faith and denounce the report as false, especially as encouraging letters arrived from Raphael Joseph Chelebi of Cairo and others. The most absurd stories of Sabbataï's power and dignity at the Porte were published in Italy, and found credence. Moses Pinheiro, Sabbataï's old companion, Raphael Sofino at Leghorn, and the Amsterdam fanatics, Isaac Naar and Abraham Pereira, who had gone to Italy to search for the Messiah, had a special interest in clinging to straws; they feared ridicule as dupes. The ignorant mountebank and strolling prophet, Sabbataï Raphael, from the Morea, then residing in Italy, was bent upon deception and fraud, and appears to have reaped a good harvest there. When at last there could be no doubt of Sabbataï's change of religion, Raphael turned his steps to Germany, where, on account of defective postal arrangements and the slight intercourse of Jews with the outer world, they had only a vague idea of the course of events, and took the most foolish stories for truth. Sabbataï Raphael was there regarded as a prophet; but, as he expected greater gain from the rich Amsterdam community, he betook himself thither (September, 1667). Here also the imposture continued. Ashamed that they, the shrewd and educated Portuguese, should have been so signally deceived, they at first placed no faith in the news of Sabbataï's treachery. Even the rabbis Isaac Aboab, Raphael Moses d'Aguilar, and the philosophical sceptic Musaphia, remained staunch. Justly Jacob Sasportas laughed them to scorn, especially Musaphia, on account of his present un shaken faith as contrasted with his former incredulity.

Meanwhile Nathan Ghazati, the prophet of Gaza was pursuing his mischievous course in Italy. Coming from Greece, he landed at Venice (end of March, 1668), but the rabbinate and the council, who had had warning of him, would not allow him to enter the Ghetto. A Sabbatian interceded for him with some Christians of rank, and under such protection he could not be expelled. To cure those who had shared in the delusion, the rabbinate wrung from him a written confession, that his prophecies of Sabbataï Zevi's Messiahship rested on a freak of his imagination, that he recognized them as such, and held them to be idle. This confession was printed with an introduction by the rabbinate of Venice, in order at last to open the eyes of the Sabbatians in Italy. But it was not of much avail. The delusion, resting as it did on the Kabbala, was too deeply rooted. From Venice Ghazati was sent to Leghorn, with the suggestion to render him innocuous there, where Jews enjoyed more freedom; but Nathan Ghazati secretly escaped to Rome, cut off his beard, disguised himself, and is said to have thrown notes written in Chaldee into the Tiber, to bring about the destruction of Rome. The Jews recognized him, and, since they feared danger for themselves on papal soil from his fraudulent absurdities, they procured his banishment. Then he went to Leghorn, and found followers there also. Promising himself more honor and profit in Turkey, or more opportunity to satisfy his restless mind, Nathan returned to Adrianople. He did not pay great regard to word and oath. Nathan Ghazati compiled much Kabbalistic nonsense, but acquired no fame. He is said to have died at Sophia, and to have been laid in a vault dug by himself (1680). Other men appeared at the head of the Sabbatians who far surpassed him, and pursued a definite end.

Sabbataï, or Mehmed Effendi, at this time began his revolutionary chimeras afresh. Immediately after his apostasy he was obliged, under the direction of the mufti Vanni, to acquire Mahometan ways, and guard carefully against any appearance of inclination to Judaism and the Jews. He therefore figured as a pious Mahometan. Gradually he was permitted greater freedom, and to give utterance to his Kabbalistic views about God and the universe. Vanni, to whom much was new, heard his expositions with curiosity, and the sultan also is said to have listened to his words attentively. Probably Sabbataï won over some Mahometans to his Kabbalistic dreams. Weary of quiet, and anxious to play an active part again, he once more entered into close relations with Jews, and gave out that he had been filled anew with the Holy Spirit at Passover (end of March, 1668), and had received revelations. Sabbataï, or one of his aiders and abettors, published a mystical work (" Five Evidences of the Faith," Sahaduta di Mehemnuta) addressed to the Jews and couched in extravagant language, in which the following fantastic views were set forth: Sabbataï had been and remained the true Redeemer; it would be easy to prove himself such, if he had not compassion on Israel, who would have to experience the same dreadful sufferings as the Messiah; and he only persisted in Mahometanism in order to bring thousands and tens of thousands of non-Jews over to Israel. To the sultan and the mufti, on the other hand, he said that his approximation to the Jews was intended to bring them over to Islam. He received permission to associate with Jews, and to preach before them at Adrianople, even in synagogues. Thus he played the part of Jew at one time, of Mussulman at another. If Turkish spies were present, his Jewish hearers knew how to deceive them.   They threw away their Jewish headdress, and put on the turban.   It is probable that many Jews were seriously converted to Islam, and a Jewish-Turkish sect thus began to form round Sabbataï Zevi.   The Jews who had hitherto felt such horror of apostatizing, that only the outcasts amongst them went over to Christianity or Islam, became less severe.   They said without indignation that so and so had adopted the turban.   Through such jugglery Sabbatians at Adrianople, Smyrna, Salonica, and other cities, even in Palestine, allowed themselves to be confirmed in their obstinate faith in the Messiah.   Even pious men, learned in the Talmud, continued to adhere to him.

As though this complication were to become more involved, and the Kabbalistic-Messianic disorder were to be pursued to its utmost limits, a Sabbatian champion unexpectedly appeared in a man of European culture, not wanting in gifts, Abraham Michael Cardoso.   He was an original character, a living personification of the transformation of the Portuguese Jews after their expulsion.   Born of Marrano parents in a small town of Portugal, Celarico, in the province of Beïra, Miguel Cardoso, like his elder brother Fernando, studied medicine.   While the latter devoted himself earnestly to science, Miguel dawdled away his days amidst the luxury of Madrid, sang love-songs with the guitar under the balconies of fair ladies, and paid very little heed to Kabbala or Judaism.   What influenced him to leave Spain is not known.   Perhaps his more serious and thoughtful brother, who, after making a name in Spain as a medical and scientific author, out of love to Judaism migrated to Venice, where he plunged deeply into Jewish literature, infected him with enthusiasm.   Both brothers assumed Jewish names after their return to the religion of their forefathers.   The elder, Isaac Cardoso, gave up his name Fer-

nando ; the younger took the name of Abraham in
addition to that of Miguel (Michael). Both composed verses in Spanish. While the elder brother
led a regular life, guided by moral principles and a
rational faith, the younger fell under the sway of extravagant fancy and an eccentric manner of living.
Isaac Cardoso (born 1615, died after 1680) conferred renown on Judaism, while Abraham Michael
Cardoso (born about 1630, died 1706) was a disgrace to it.

The latter lived as a physician at Leghorn, but
not flourishing he accepted the position of physician
in ordinary to the Bey of Tripoli. His warm-
blooded, dissolute nature was a hindrance to his
advancement. Contrary to the custom of African
Jews, he married two wives, and instead of employing himself with his difficult science, he revolved
fantastical schemes. Cardoso appears to have been
initiated into the Kabbala and the Sabbatian delusion by Moses Pinheiro, who was living at Leghorn.

He continually had dreams and visions, which increased in frequency after the public appearance of
Sabbataï at Smyrna and Constantinople. He communicated his delusion to his wives and domestics,
who likewise pretended to have seen all sorts of apparitions. The apostasy of the false Messiah from
Judaism did not cure Cardoso of his delusion ; he
remained a zealous partisan, and even justified the
treachery of the Messiah by saying that it was necessary for him to be counted among sinners, in order that he might atone for Israel's sin of idolatry,
and blot it out. He sent circulars in all directions,
in order to support the Messianic claim of Sabbataï,
and figure as a prophet. In vain his more sober
brother, Isaac Cardoso, warned and ridiculed him,
asking him ironically, whether he had received the
gift of prophecy from his former gallantries and
from playing the guitar for the fair maidens of Madrid. Abraham Cardoso's frivolity was in no way

lessened, he even assumed a didactic tone towards
his grave elder brother, who despised the Kabbala
as he did alchemy and astrology, and sent him numberless proofs, from the Zohar and other Kabbalistic
writings, that Sabbataï was the true Messiah, and
that he must necessarily be estranged from Judaism.
By his zeal he gained many adherents for the Sabbatian delusion in Africa; but he also made enemies,
and incurred dangers.	He continued to prophesy
the speedy commencement of the Messiah's reign,
although often proved false by reality.	He put off
the event from year to year, performed Kabbalistic
tricks, set up a new God for Israel, and at last declared himself the Messiah of the house of Ephraim,
until he was rigorously prosecuted by an opponent
of these vagaries.	Cardoso was driven back to his
former uncomfortable position, forced to lead an
adventurer's life, and win bread for himself and his
family, so to speak, by his delusions, going through
all sorts of jugglery, at Smyrna, at Constantinople,
in the Greek islands, and at Cairo, and promoting
the Sabbatian delusions with his abundant knowl-
edge, eloquent tongue, and ready pen.	Thanks to
his education in Christian schools, he was far superior to other Sabbatian apostles, and knew how to
give an air of rationality and wisdom to nonsense,
thus completely blinding the biased, and stultifying
even those averse to the Sabbatian movement.

Encouraged by the support of the Jews, continued
in spite of his change of religion, Sabbataï persisted
in keeping up his character as Messiah, and asso-
ciated more and more with Jews.	His weak brain
had been turned by the overwhelming rush of events,
and he completely lost balance.	At one time he re-
viled Judaism and the God of Israel with foul words
of abuse, and is said even to have informed against
Jews as blasphemers of Islam before Turkish mag-
istrates.	At other times he held divine service ac-
cording to the Jewish ritual with his Jewish follow-

ers, sang psalms, expounded the Zohar, ordered
selections from the Torah to be read on the Sabbath,
and frequently chose seven virgins for that purpose.
On account of his constant intercourse with Jews,
whom he was not able to bring over wholesale to
Mahometanism, as he may have boastfully asserted,
Mehmed Effendi is said to have fallen into disfavor,
forfeited his allowance and been banished from Adrianople to Constantinople. He finally married
another wife, the daughter of a man learned in the
Talmud, Joseph Philosoph of Salonica. The Turkish patrol having surprised him in a village (Kuru
Gisme) near Constantinople, while singing psalms
in a tent with some Jews, and the Bostanji Bashi
(officer) having reported it, the grand vizir commanded the Kaimakam to banish him to Dulcigno,
a small town in Albania, where no Jews dwelt.
There he died, abandoned and forsaken, it was
afterwards said, on the Day of Atonement, 1676.

Spinoza, who had likewise broken away from
Judaism, may well have looked with great contempt
on this Messianic craze of his contemporaries. If
he had cared to dig the grave of Judaism and bury
it, he would have been obliged to recognize Sabbataï Zevi, his private secretary, Samuel Primo, and
his prophets, as allies and abettors. The irration-
ality of the Kabbala brought Judaism much more
effectually into discredit than reason and philosophy.
It is a remarkable fact that neither the one nor the
other could wean the numerous cultured Jews of
Amsterdam from the religion of their forefathers,
so strongly was it rooted in their hearts. At this
time when two forces of Jewish origin were antago-
nizing Judaism in the East and the West, the Portuguese community, increased to the number of four
thousand families, undertook (1671) the building of a
splendid synagogue, and after some years finished
the huge work, which had been interrupted by war
troubles. The dedication of the synagogue (Ab 10,

August 2, 1675), was celebrated with great solemnity and pomp. Neither the first Temple of Solomon, nor the second of Zerubbabel, nor the third of Herod, was so much lauded with song and eloquent speech as the new one at Amsterdam, called Talmud Torah. Copper-plate engravings, furnished with inscriptions in verse, were published. Christians likewise took part in the dedication. They advanced money to the Jews in the times of need, and a poet, Romein de Hooghe, composed verses in honor of the synagogue and the Jewish people in Latin, Dutch, and French.

Spinoza lived to see this rejoicing of the community from which he had become a pervert. He happened to be at Amsterdam just at the time. He was engaged in seeing through the press a treatise (Ethics) which reversed the views hitherto prevailing, and the second, enlarged edition of his other work, chiefly directed against Judaism. He may have laughed at the joy of the Amsterdam Jews, as idle ; but the building of this synagogue in a city which a hundred years before had tolerated no Jews and had supported a Spanish Inquisition, was loud testimony of the times, and contradicted many of his assertions. He died not long afterwards, or rather, passed gently away as with a divine kiss (February 21, 1677), about five months after Sabbataï Zevi. Against his will he has contributed to the glory of the race which he so unjustly reviled. His powerful intellect, logical acumen, and strength of character are more and more recognized as properties which he owed to the race from which he was descended. Among educated Jews, Isaac Orobio de Castro alone attempted a serious refutation of Spinoza's philosophical views. Though his intention was good, he was too weak to break through the close meshes of Spinoza's system. It was left to history to refute it with facts.

CHAPTER V.

LIGHT AND SHADE.

Jews under Mahometan Rulers—Expulsion from Vienna—Jews admitted by Elector Frederick William into the Mark of Brandenburg—Charge of Child-murder in Metz—Milder Treatment of Jews throughout Europe—Christian Champions of the Jews: Jurieu, Oliger Pauli, and Moses Germanus—Predilection of Christians for the Study of Jewish Literature—Richard Simon —Interest taken by Charles XI in the Karaites—Peringer and Jacob Trigland—German Attacks on Judaism by Wülfer, Wagenseil, and Eisenmenger—Circumstances of the Publication of *Judaism Unmasked*—The *Alenu* Prayer—Surenhuysius, Basnage, Unger, Wolf, and Toland.

1669—1700 C. E.

THE princes and nations of Europe and Asia showed great consideration in not disturbing the Messianic farce of the Jews, who were quietly allowed to make themselves ridiculous. A pause had come in the constantly recurring persecution of the Jews, which did not, however, last very long. The regular succession of accusations, vexations, and banishments soon re-commenced. The contrast between the followers of Mahomet and those of Jesus is very striking. In Turkey the Jews were free from persecution, in spite of their great excitement, and absurd dreams of a national Messiah. In Africa, Sid Gailand and later Muley Arshid, sultan of Tafilet, Fez, and Morocco, oppressed the Jews, partly on account of their activity, partly from rapacity. But this ceased with the next sovereign, Muley Ismail. He was a patron of the Jews, and entrusted several with important posts. He had two Jewish advisers, Daniel Toledano of Miquenes, a friend of Jacob Sasportas, a Talmudist and experienced in state affairs, and Joseph Maimaran, likewise from Miquenes.

Within Christendom, on the contrary, Jews were esteemed and treated as men only in Holland ; in other states they were regarded as outcasts, who had no rights, and no claim to compassion. Spain again led the way in decreeing banishments. That unfortunate country, becoming more and more de-populated through despotism, superstition, and the Inquisition, was then ruled by a foolish, fanatical woman, the dowager-regent Maria Anna of Austria, who had made her father-confessor, the German Jesuit Neidhard, inquisitor-general and minister with unlimited powers. Naturally, no toleration of other religions could be suffered at this big-oted court. There were still Jews in some parts of the monarchy, in the north-western corner of Africa, in Oran, Maxarquivir, and other cities. Many had rendered considerable services to the Spanish crown, in times of peace and war, against the native Arabs, or Moors, who endured with inward rage the dominion of the cross. The families of Cansino and Sasportas, the former royal interpreters, or drago-mans, for the province of Oran, had distinguished themselves especially by their fidelity and devotion to Spain ; and their conduct had been recognized by Philip IV, the husband of Maria Anna, in a special letter. Nevertheless, the queen-dowager suddenly ordered the banishment of the Jews from the dis-trict, because she could no longer tolerate people of this race in her realm. At the urgent request of Jewish grandees the governor allowed the Jews eight days' grace during the Passover, and admit-ted that they were banished, not because of mis-conduct or treason, but simply on account of the re-gent's intolerance (end of April, 1669). They were obliged to sell their possessions in haste at ridicu-lous prices. The exiles settled in the district of Savoy, at Villafranca, near Nice.

Like mother, like daughter. At about this time the banishment of Jews from Vienna and the arch-

duchy of Austria was decreed at the instigation of
the daughter of the Spanish regent, the empress
Margaret, an ally of the Jesuits.   The emperor did
not easily allow himself to be prejudiced against
Jews, from whom he derived a certain revenue.   The
community of Vienna alone, grown to nearly two
thousand souls, paid a yearly tax of 10,000, and the
country community of 4,000, florins.   Including the
income from Jews in other places, the emperor received from them 50,000 florins annually.   But an empress need not trouble herself about finance; she can
follow the inclinations of her heart, and Margaret's
heart, filled with Jesuitism, hated Jews profoundly,
and her father-confessor strengthened the feeling.
Having met with an accident at a ball, she wished
to testify her gratitude to heaven which had wonderfully preserved her, and could find no means more
acceptable to God than the misery of Jews.   More
urgently than before she entreated her imperial con-
sort to banish from the capital and the country the
Jews, described by her father-confessor as outcasts
of hell, and she received his promise.   With trumpet-
sound it was made known in Vienna (February 14,
1670) that by the emperor's command the Jews were
to quit the city within a few months on pain of death.
They left no measure untried to avert the stroke.
Often before had similar resolutions been recalled
by Austrian emperors.   The Jews cited the privileges accorded them in writing, and the services
which they had rendered the imperial house.   They
offered large sums of money (there were very rich
court Jews at Vienna), used the influence of persons
connected with the court, and, after a solemn service
in honor of the recovery of the emperor from sick-
ness, presented him as he left the church with a large
gold cup, and the empress with a handsome silver
basin and jug.   The presents were accepted, but the
command was not recalled.

At Vienna and at the court there was no prospect

of a change of purpose; the Jesuits had the upper
hand through the empress and her confessor. The
community of Vienna in despair thought to avert
the evil by another, roundabout course. The Jews
of Germany had felt sincere sympathy for their
brethren, and had implored heaven by prayer and
fasting to save them. The Jews of Vienna could
count confidently upon their zeal. Therefore, in a
pitiful letter to the most influential and perhaps the
richest Jew of that time, Isaac (Manoel) Texeira, the
esteemed agent of Queen Christina, they begged
him to exert his influence with temporal and church
princes, through them to make Empress Margaret
change her mind. Texeira had previously taken
active steps in that direction, and he promised to
continue them. He had written to some Spanish
grandees with whom he stood in close connection to
use their influence with the empress's confessor.
The queen of Sweden, who, after her romantic conversion to Catholicism, enjoyed great esteem in the
Catholic world, led Texeira to hope that, by letters
addressed to the papal nuncio, to the empress, and
to her mother, the Spanish regent, she might prevent the banishment of the Austrian Jews. The
Jews of Rome also did their part to save their
threatened brethren. But all these efforts led to
nothing. Unhappily there had just been a papal
election at Rome after the death of Clement IX, so
that the head of the church, though Jews were tolerated in his states, could not be prevailed upon to
assume a decided attitude. Emperor Leopold remained firm, and disposed of the houses of the Jews
before they had left them. He was only humane
enough to order, under pain of severe punishment,
that no harm be done to the departing Jews.

So the Jews had to submit to the iron will of necessity, and grasp their pilgrims' staffs. When 1,400
souls had fallen into distress, or at least into an
anxious plight, and many had succumbed, the re-

mainder, more than three hundred, again petitioned the emperor, recounting the services of Jews to the imperial house, and showing all the accusations against them to be groundless, at all events not proven. They did not shrink from declaring that to be a Jew could not be called a crime, and protested that they ought to be treated as Roman citizens, who ought not to be summarily expelled. They begged at least for a respite until the next meeting of the Reichstag. Even this petition, in which they referred to the difficulty of finding a refuge, if the emperor, the ruler of half of Europe, rejected them, remained without effect. All had to depart; only one family, that of the court factor, Marcus Schlesinger Jaffa, was allowed to remain in Vienna, on account of services rendered. The Jesuits were full of joy, and proclaimed the praise of God in a gradual. The magistrates bought the Jews' quarter from the emperor for 100,000 florins, and called it Leopoldstadt in his honor. The site of the synagogue was used for a church, of which the emperor laid the corner-stone (August 18, 1670) in honor of his patron saint. A golden tablet was to perpetuate the shameful deeds of the Jews:

"After the Jews were banished, the emperor caused their synagogue, which had been as a charnel-house, to be made into a house of God."

The tablet, however, only proves the mental weakness of the emperor and his people. The Talmud school (Beth ha-Midrash) was likewise converted into a church, and named in honor of the empress and her patron saint.

But this dark picture had also its bright side. A struggling state, which hitherto had not tolerated the Jews, now became a new, though not very hospitable, home, where the Jewish race was rejuvenated. The Austrian exiles dispersed in various directions. Many sought protection in Moravia,

Bohemia, and Poland. Others went to Venice and as far as the Turkish frontiers, others turned to Fürth, in Bavaria. Fifty families were received by Elector Frederick William, in the Mark of Brandenburg. This great prince, who laid the solid foundation for the future greatness of the Prussian monarchy, was not more tolerant than other princes of Louis XIV's century; but he was more clear-sighted than Emperor Leopold, and recognized that a sound state of finances is essential to the prosperity of a state, and that Jews retained somewhat of their old renown as financiers. In the Mark of Brandenburg no Jew had been allowed to dwell for a hundred years, since their expulsion under Elector John George. Frederick William himself took the step so difficult for many; he wrote (April, 1670) to his ambassador, Andrew Neumann, at Vienna, that he was inclined to receive into the electoral Mark from forty to fifty prosperous Jewish families of the exiles from Vienna under certain conditions and limitations. The conditions, made known a year later, proved in many points very harsh, but were more favorable than in other Protestant countries, as, for instance, in the bigoted city of Hamburg. The Jews might settle where they pleased in Brandenburg and in the duchy of Crossen, and might trade everywhere without hindrance. The burgomasters were directed to place no impediment in the way of their settlement and not to molest them. Every family had to pay eight thalers a year as a protective tax, a gold florin for every marriage, and the same for every funeral; on the other hand, they were freed from the poll-tax throughout the country. They might buy and build houses, on condition that after the expiration of a term they sell them to Christians. They were not permitted to have synagogues, but could have prayer-rooms, and appoint a school-master and a butcher (Shochet). This charter of protection was valid for only twenty years, but a prospect was held out that it would be prolonged by the elector or his successor. Of these fifty Austrian families, some seven settled in Berlin, and formed the foundation of the community afterwards so large and influential. One step led to another. Frederick William also admitted rich Jews from Hamburg, Glogau, and other cities, and thus communities sprang up at Landsberg and Frankfort-on-the-Oder.

It is evident that Frederick William admitted the Jews purely from financial considerations. But he occasionally showed unselfish good-will towards some. When he agreed to the quixotic plan of Skytte, a Swedish royal councilor, to found, at Tangermünde in the Mark, a university for all sciences and an asylum for persecuted savants, he did not fail, according to his programme, to admit into this Athens of the Mark, Jewish men of learning, as well as Arabs and unbelievers of every kind, but on condition that they should keep their errors to themselves, and not spread them abroad.

At another spot in Christian Europe a few rays of light pierced the darkness. About the same time that the Jews were expelled from Vienna, a false accusation, which might have had far-reaching consequences, cropped up against the Jews of a city recently brought under French rule. In Metz, a considerable community had developed in the course of a century from four Jewish families, and had appointed its own rabbi since the beginning of the seventeenth century. The Jews of Metz behaved so well that King Louis XIV publicly declared his satisfaction with them, and renewed their privileges. But as Metz at that time still had a German population, narrow guilds continued to exist, and these insisted upon limiting the Jews in their occupations. Thwarted by the magistrates, some of them roused in the populace a burning hatred of the Jews. A peasant had lost a child, and the news was quickly spread that the Jews had killed it to practice sorcery with its flesh. The accusation was brought specifically against a peddler, Raphael Levi. Scraps of paper with Hebrew letters, written by him during his imprisonment, served as proofs of his guilt. A baptized Jew, Paul du Vallié (Vallier, formerly Isaac), son of a famous physician in that district, with the aid of another Jewish convert, translated the scraps to the disadvantage of the accused.

Du Vallié had literally been decoyed into Christianity, and changed into a bitter enemy of his former co-religionists. He had been a good son, adored by his parents. He had also been a pious Jew, and had declared to two tempters who had tried to influence him to apostatize from Judaism that he would sooner be burned. Nevertheless, the priests continued their efforts until they induced him to accept Christianity. The news of his baptism broke the heart of his mother, Antoinette. A touching letter to her son, in French, is still extant, in which she entreats him to return to Judaism. Du Vallié however refused, and proved himself besides to be a bad man and a traitor. He brought false evidence against the poor accused Jew. Accordingly, Raphael Levi was stretched on the rack, and, though he maintained his innocence in the tone of convincing truth, he was condemned by the Metz parliament, and put to death with torture, which he resolutely bore (January, 1670). The parliament intended to continue the persecution. The enemies of the Jews, moreover, caused a document on the subject to be printed and widely circulated, in order to produce the proper effect. But the Metz community found a supporter in a zealous fellow-believer, Jonah Salvador, a tobacco dealer, of Pignerol. He was learned in the Talmud, and a follower of Sabbataï Zevi. Richard Simon, an eager student, sought him out in order to study Hebrew under his guidance. Jonah Salvador managed to interest this Father of the Oratory in the Metz community, and

inspired him to draw up a vindication of the Jews
respecting child-murder.   The tobacco merchant of
Pignerol delivered this document to persons at court
whose word had weight, and this turned the scale.
The king's council ordered the records of the Metz
parliament to be sent in, and decided (end of 1671)
that judicial murder had been committed in the case
of Raphael Levi.   Louis XIV ordered that henceforth criminal charges against Jews be brought before the king's council.

Inhuman treatment of Jews, banishment, false accusations against them, and massacres did not actually cease, but their number and extent diminished.
This phenomenon was a consequence of the increasing civilization of the European capitals, but a growing predilection for the Jews and their brilliant literature had a share in their improved treatment.   Educated Christians, Catholics as well as Protestants,
and sober, unbiased men, whose judgment had
weight, began to be astonished at the continued
existence of this people.   How was it that a people,
persecuted for ten centuries and more, trampled
under foot, and treated like a pack of venomous or
noisome beasts—a people without a home, whom all
the world treated roughly—how was it that this
people still existed—not only existed, but formed a
compact body, separate from other peoples, even in
its subjection too proud to mingle with more powerful nations ?   Numerous writers appeared as apol-
ogists for the Jews, urging their milder treatment,
and appealing earnestly to Christians not to destroy
or disfigure this living marvel.   Many went very far
in their enthusiasm for the Jews.   The Huguenot
preacher, Pierre Jurieu, at Rotterdam, wrote a book
(1685) on "The Fulfillment of Prophecy," in which
he expounded the future greatness of the Jews as
certain—that God had kept this nation for Himself
in order to do great wonders for it : the true Anti-
christ was the persecution of Jews.   A Dane, Oliger

(Holger) Pauli, displayed over-zealous activity for the return of the Jewish people to their former country. As a youth, he had had visions of the coming greatness of Israel, in which he also was to play a part. Oliger Pauli was so fond of the Jewish race that, although descended from Christian ancestors of noble rank, he always gave out that he had sprung from Jewish stock. He had amassed millions as a merchant, and spent them lavishly on his hobby, the return of the Jews to Palestine. He sent mystical letters to King William III of England and the dauphin of France to induce them to undertake the assembling and restoration of the Jews. To the dauphin the Danish enthusiast plainly declared that by zeal for the Jews, France might atone for her bloody massacre of St. Bartholomew and the dragonnades. John Peter Speeth of Augsburg, born of Catholic parents at Vienna, went still farther in his enthusiasm for Jews and Judaism. After writing a pamphlet in honor of Catholicism, he went over to the Socinians and Mennonites, and at last became a Jew at Amsterdam, and took the name of Moses Germanus (died April 17, 1702). He confessed that precisely the false accusations against Jews had inspired him with disgust for Christianity.

" Even at the present time much of the same sort of thing happens in Poland and Germany, where circumstantial tales are told and songs sung in the streets, how the Jews have murdered a child, and sent the blood to one another in quills for the use of their women in childbirth. I have discovered this outrageous fraud in time, and abandoned Christianity, which can permit such things, in order to have no share in it, nor be found with those who trample under foot Israel, the first begotten Son of God, and shed his blood like water."

Moses Germanus was Paul reversed. The latter as a Christian, became a zealous despiser of Judaism ; the former, as a Jew, an equally fanatical opponent of Christianity. He regarded its origin as gross fraud. One cannot even now write all that Moses Germanus uttered about the teaching of Jesus. He was not the only Christian who at this

time "from love for Judaism" exposed himself to
the painful operation and still keener shame and
reproach of circumcision.   In one year three Christians, in free Amsterdam to be sure, went over to
Judaism, amongst them a student from Prague.

Even more than the anticipated greatness of Israel, Jewish literature attracted learned Christians,
and inspired them with a sort of sympathy for the
people out of whose mine such treasures came.
The Hebrew language was studied by Christians
even more than in the beginning of the seventeenth
century.   In the middle and towards the close of
that century Hebrew Rabbinical literature was most
eagerly searched, translated into Latin or modern
languages, quoted, utilized, and applied. "Jewish
learning" was, not as before a mere ornament, but
an indispensable element, of learning.   It was regarded as a disgrace for Catholic and Protestant
theologians to be ignorant of Rabbinical lore, and
the ignorant could defend themselves only by abusing these Hebraists as semi-rabbis.

The first Catholic critic, Father Richard Simon,
of the congregation of the Oratory at Paris, contributed very much to the high esteem in which the
Jews and their literature were held.   This man, who
laid the foundation of a scientific, philological, and
exegetical study of the Old and New Testament, investigated Jewish writings with great zeal, and utilized them for his purpose.   He was gifted with a
keen understanding, which unconsciously led him
beyond the limits of Catholic doctrine.   Spinoza's
criticism of the Bible induced him to make original
inquiries, and since, as a genuine Frenchman, he
was endowed with sound sense rather than metaphysical imagination, he was more successful, and
his method is thoroughly scientific.   Richard Simon
was disgusted with the biblical exegesis of the Protestants, who were wont to support their wisdom and
their stupidity with verses of Holy Scripture.   He

undertook, therefore, to prove that the biblical knowledge and biblical exegesis of the Protestant church, on which it prided itself before Catholics and Jews, was mere mist and error, because it mistook the sense of the original text, and had no conception of the historical background, the coloring of time and place, of the books of the Bible, and in this ignorance multiplied absurd dogmas.

"You Protestants appeal to the pure word of God to do battle against the Catholic tradition ; I intend to withdraw the ground from under you, and to leave you, so to speak, with your legs dangling in the air."

Richard Simon was the predecessor of Reimarus and David Strauss. The Catholics applauded him —even the mild Bishop Bossuet, who at first had opposed him from conceit—not dreaming that they were nourishing a serpent in their bosom. In his master-piece, "The Critical History of The Old Testament," he set himself to prove that the written word in no way suffices for faith. Richard Simon appreciated with a master's eye, as no one before him, the wide extent of a new science—biblical criticism. Although he criticised freely, he proceeded apologetically, vindicated the sacred character of the Bible, and repelled Spinoza's attacks upon its trustworthiness. Richard Simon's writings, which were composed not in Latin, but in the vernacular, were marked by a certain elegance of style, and attracted well-deserved attention. They form an agreeable contrast to the chaos of oppressive learning of the time, and have an insinuative air about them. Hence they were eagerly read by the educated classes, even by women. Simon accorded much space to Jewish literature, and subjoined a list of Jewish writers. By this means Rabbinical literature became known to the educated more than through the efforts of Reuchlin, Scaliger, the two Buxtorfs, and the learned men of Holland who wrote in Latin. To gain a comprehensive knowledge of this litera-

ture, Richard Simon was obliged, like Reuchlin
before him, to seek intercourse with Jews ; in particular he associated with Jonah Salvador, the Italian
Sabbatian. By this means he lost a part of his
prejudice against Jews, which still existed in France
in its intensity. He was drawn to Jews in another
direction. Laying stress on Catholic tradition as
opposed to the literal belief of the Protestants, he
felt in some degree related to the Talmudists
and Rabbanites. They also upheld their tradition
against the literal belief of the Karaites. Richard
Simon, therefore, exalted Rabbinical Judaism in the
introduction and supplements which he added to his
translation of Leon Modena's "Rites." Familiar
with the whole of Jewish literature as few of his
time or of a later period, Richard Simon refrained
from making the boastful assertion, grounded upon
ignorance, that Christianity is something peculiar,
fundamentally different to Judaism and far more
exalted. He recognized, and had the courage to
declare, the truth that Christianity in its substance
and form was molded after the pattern of Judaism,
and would have to become like it again.

"Since the Christian religion has its origin in Judaism, I doubt not
that the perusal of this little book (the 'Rites') will contribute to the
understanding of the New Testament, on account of its similarity to,
and close connection with the Old. They who composed it were
Jews, and it can be explained only by means of Judaism. A portion
of our ceremonies also are derived from the Jews . . . . The Christian religion has this besides in common with the Jewish, that each is
based on Holy Scripture, on the tradition of the fathers, on traditional
habits and customs. . . . . One cannot sufficiently admire the
modesty and devotion of the Jews, as they go to prayer in the morning. . . . . The Jews distinguish themselves, not only by prayers, but
also by deeds of mercy, and one thinks one sees, in their sympathy
for the poor, the image of the love of the first Christians for their
brethren. Men obeyed in those times what the Jews have retained to
this day, while we (Christians) have scarcely kept up the remembrance of it."

Richard Simon almost deplored that the Jews,
formerly so learned in France, who looked upon
Paris as their Athens, had been driven out of that

country. He defended them against the accusation of their hatred of Christians, and emphasized the fact that they pray for the welfare of the state and its princes. His predilection for tradition went so far, that he maintained that the college of cardinals at Rome, the supreme court of Christendom, was formed on the pattern of the Synhedrion at Jerusalem, and that the pope corresponded to the president, the Nassi. Whilst he compared the Catholics to the Rabbanites, he called the Protestants Karaites, and jestingly wrote to his Protestant friends, "My dear Karaites." It has been mentioned that Richard Simon interested himself zealously in the Jews of Metz, when they were accused of murdering a Christian child. When other opportunities offered, he defended the Jews against false accusations and suspicions. A baptized Jew, Christian Gerson, who had become a Protestant pastor, at the beginning of the seventeenth century, in order to vilify the Talmud, had made extracts in the shape of ridiculous legends, printed and published in many editions. Richard Simon wrote to a Swiss, about to translate these German extracts into French, that Gerson was not guiltless of having passed off plays upon words and purely allegorical expressions in the Talmud as serious narratives. Gerson imputed to the whole Jewish nation certain errors, accepted only by the credulous, unable to distinguish fiction from fact, and he, therefore, abused the Talmud. It must not be forgotten that it was a distinguished ecclesiastic, moreover, a sober, moderate man, who spoke thus favorably of Judaism. His books and letters, written in a lively French style, and much read by the educated world, gained many friends for Judaism, or at least lessened the number of its enemies. The official Catholic world, however, appears to have reprimanded this eulogist of Judaism, and Richard Simon, who loved peace, was obliged partially to recant his praises.

"I have said too much good of this wretched nation, and through intercourse with some of them I have since learned to know them."

This cannot have been spoken from his heart, for he was not wont to judge a whole class of men by a few individuals.

The attention paid to Jews and their literature by Christian scholars and princes here and there produced droll occurrences. In Sweden, the most bigoted Protestant country, no Jew and no Catholic were allowed to dwell. Nevertheless King Charles XI felt extraordinary interest in the Jews, still more in the Karaites, who pretended to follow the simple word of God without the accretion of traditions, and were said to bear great resemblance to the Protestants. Would it not be easy to bring over to Christianity these people who were not entangled in the web of the Talmud? Charles XI accordingly sent a professor of Upsala, learned in Hebrew literature, Gustavus Peringer of Lilienblad (about 1690), to Poland for the purpose of seeking out the Karaites, informing himself of their manner of life and their customs, and especially buying their writings without regard to cost. Provided with letters of recommendation to the king of Poland, Peringer went first to Lithuania, where dwelt several Karaite communities. But the Polish and Lithuanian Karaites were even more degraded than their brethren in Constantinople, the Crimea, and Egypt. There were very few among them who knew any details about their origin and the history of their sect; not one had accurate information. At about this time the Polish king, John Sobieski, had ordered, through a Karaite judge, Abraham ben Samuel of Trok, who was in favor with him, that the Karaites, for some unknown object, scatter from their headquarters of Trok, Luzk, and Halicz, and settle also in other small towns; they obeyed, and dispersed as far as the northern province of Samogitia. These Polish Karaites, cut off from their center, isolated, avoiding intercourse with rabbis, and mixing only with the Polish rustic population, became more and more boorish, and sank into profound lethargy.

Whether Peringer even partially fulfilled the wish of his king is not known; probably he altogether failed in his mission. Some years later (1696-1697), two learned Swedes, probably also commissioned by Charles XI, traveled in Lithuania to visit Karaite communities and buy up their writings. At the same time they invited Karaites to visit Sweden, and give information respecting their doctrines. Zeal for conversion had certainly more share in the matter than curiosity about the unknown. A young Karaite, Samuel ben Aaron, who had settled at Poswol in Samogitia, and understood some Latin, resolved to make a journey to Riga, and hold a conference with John Puffendorf, a royal official. Through want of literary sources and the ignorance of the Karaites concerning the origin and development of their sect, Samuel ben Aaron could give only a scanty account in a work, the title of which proves that fancifulness had penetrated also to Karaite circles.

From another side the Karaites were the object of eager inquiry. A professor at Leyden, Jacob Trigland, fairly well acquainted with Hebrew literature, who intended to write a book about the old Jewish sects, no longer in existence, had his attention directed to the still existing Karaites. Inspired by the wish to get information concerning the Polish Karaites and obtain possession of their writings, he sent a letter with various questions through well-known mercantile houses to Karaites, to which he solicited an answer. This letter accidentally fell into the hands of a Karaite, Mordecai ben Nissan, at Luzk, a poor official of the community, who did not know enough to give the desired information as to the beginning and cause of the schism between Rabbanites and Karaites. He regarded it as a

point of honor to avail himself of this opportunity
to bring the forgotten Karaites to the remembrance
of the educated world through the instrumentality
of a Christian writer, and to deal blows at their
opponents, the Rabbanite Jews. He spared no
sacrifice to procure the few books by which he might
be able to instruct himself and his correspondent
Trigland. These materials, however, were not worth
much, and Mordecai's dissertation for Trigland
proved unsatisfactory, but for want of a better work
it had the good fortune to serve during nearly a
century and a half as the only source for the history
of Karaism. Some years later, when Charles XII,
the hero of the north, conquered Poland in his victorious career, and like his father was anxious to have
more precise intelligence respecting Karaites, he
also made inquiries concerning them. Mordecai
ben Nissan used this occasion to compose a work in
Hebrew for Charles XII, in which he freely indulged
his hatred against Rabbanites, and strained every
nerve to make Talmudical literature ridiculous.

The zealous attention paid by Christian scholars
to Jewish literature could not fail to cause annoyance
and inconvenience to Jews. They felt sorely bur-
dened by German Protestant literati, who, acquiring
cumbersome learning, strove to rival the Dutch
writers and Richard Simon in France, without possessing their mild and gentle toleration towards
Jews, or their elegance of style. Almost at the same
time three German Hebraists, Wülfer, Wagenseil,
and Eisenmenger, used their knowledge of Hebrew
literature to bring accusations against the Jews. All
three associated much with Jews, learned from them,
and devoted much study to Jewish literature, mastering it to a certain degree.

John Wülfer of Nuremberg, who was educated for
the church, and had studied with a Jew of Fürth and
afterwards in Italy, thoroughly acquainting himself
with biblical and Talmudical literature, sought after

Hebrew manuscripts and old Jewish prayer-books to found an accusation against the Jews. Christians, instigated by baptized Jews, took offense at a beautiful prayer (Alenu), which arose in a time and country in which Christianity was little known. Some Jews were wont to add a sentence to this prayer: "For they (the heathen) pray unto vanity and emptiness." In the word "emptiness," enemies of the Jews pretended to see an allusion to Jesus and to find blasphemy against him. The sentence was not printed in the prayer-books, but in many copies a blank space was left for it. This vacant space, or the presence of the obnoxious word, equally enraged the Protestants, and Wülfer, therefore, searched libraries to find authority for it, and when he found the word in manuscripts, he did not fail to publish his discovery. He praised Prince George of Hesse because he made his Jews swear an oath never to utter a blasphemous word against Jesus, and threatened to punish them with death in case of transgression. Wülfer, on the other hand, was candid enough to confess that the Jews had been long and cruelly persecuted by Christians, that the accusation against them of using blood was a mischievous invention, and that the testimony of baptized Jews deserved little credence.

John Christopher Wagenseil, a lawyer and professor at Altorf, was a good-hearted man, and kindly disposed towards the Jews. He had traveled farther than Wülfer, had penetrated through Spain into Africa, and took the greatest pains to hunt up such Jewish writings as attacked Christianity from the ground of Holy Scripture or with the weapons of reason. His discoveries filled his quiver "with the fiery darts of Satan." Wagenseil looked up that insipid compilation of the magical miracles of Jesus (Toldoth Jesho), with which a Jew, who had been persecuted by Christians, tried to revenge himself on the founder of Christianity, and he spent much money in hunting up this Hebrew parody of the Gospel. Few Jews possessed copies of it, and the owners kept them under lock and key for their own security. Because one Jew had once written these absurdities about Jesus, and some Jews had copies of the book in their possession, while others had defended themselves against attacks by Christians, Wagenseil felt assured that the Jews of his time were vile blasphemers of Jesus. He therefore implored the princes and civil magistrates to forbid the Jews most strictly to continue such blasphemy. He directed a pamphlet, "The Christian Denunciation," to all high potentates, urging them to impose a formal oath upon Jews, not to utter any word of mockery against Jesus, Mary, the cross, the mass, and other Christian sacraments. Wagenseil had two pious wishes besides. One was that the Protestant princes should take active steps for the conversion of the Jews. He had, it is true, convinced himself that at Rome, where since the time of Pope Gregory XIII a Dominican monk was wont on certain Sabbaths to hold forth, in a sleepy manner, before a number of Jews, they either ignored him or mocked at him. But he thought that the Protestant princes, more zealous Christians than the Catholics, ought to devise a better plan. It also grieved this thorough scholar that the colleges of rabbis presumed to criticise writings concerning the Jewish religion, and that they ventured to express their approval or disapproval; this was an infringement of the rights and the dignity of Christians! Withal Wagenseil, as has been said, was kindly disposed to the Jews. He remarked with emphasis that he thought it wrong and unworthy to burn Jews, to rob them of all their property, or to drive them with their wives and children out of the country. It was excessively cruel that in Germany and other countries children of Jews should be baptized against the will of their parents, and compelled to accept Christian-

ity. The oppressions and insults to which they were
exposed at the hands of the Christian rabble were
by no means to be approved.   It was not right that
they were compelled to say " Christ is risen," that
they were assailed with blows, had dirt and stones
thrown at them, and were not allowed to go about
in safety. Wagenseil wrote a pamphlet to expose
the horrible falsehood of the charge, that the Jews
use the blood of Christians. For the sake of this
pamphlet, which spoke so warmly for the Jews, his
other absurdities should be pardoned. Wagenseil
expressed his indignation at the horrible lie:

"It might pass if the matter stopped with idle gossip ; but that on
account of this execrable falsehood Jews have been tormented, punished, and executed by thousands, should have moved even stones to
compassion, and made them cry out."

Is it credible that in the face of this judgment,
spoken with firm conviction by Wülfer and Wagenseil, who not only had associated with Jews for
years, but were accurately acquainted with Jewish
literature, and had penetrated into its innermost re-
cesses as none before them, their contemporaries
should seriously revive the horrible falsehood, and
justify it with ostentatious learning?   A Protestant,
John Andrew Eisenmenger, professor of Oriental
languages, repeated the accusation, a thousand times
branded as false, and furnished posterity with abundant material for charges against the Jews.   Eisenmenger belonged to the class of insects which sucks
poison even out of flowers. In confidential converse
with Jews, pretending that he desired to be converted to Judaism, and in the profound study of
their literature, which he learned from them, he
sought only the dark side of both.

He compiled a venomous book in two volumes,
the title of which in itself was an invitation to Christians to massacre the Jews, and was synonymous
with a repetition of earlier scenes of horror for the
Jews.

"Judaism Unmasked; or a Thorough and True Account of the Way in which the Stubborn Jews frightfully blaspheme and dishonor the Holy Trinity, revile the Holy Mother of Christ, mockingly criticise the New Testament, the Evangelists, the Apostles, and the Christian Religion, and despise and curse to the Uttermost Extreme the whole of Christianity. Much else besides, either not at all or very little known, and Gross Errors of the Jewish Religion and Theology, as well as Ridiculous and Amusing Stories, herein appear. All proved from their own Books. Written for the Honest Information of all Christians."

Eisenmenger intended to hurl Wagenseil's "fiery darts of Satan" with deadly aim at the Jews. If he had merely quoted detached sentences from the Talmudical and later Rabbinical literature and anti-Christian writings, translated them, and drawn conclusions from them hostile to the Jews, he would only have proved his mental weakness. But Eisenmenger represented most horrible falsehoods, as Wagenseil had called them, as indisputable facts. He adduced a whole chapter of proofs showing that it was not lawful for Jews to save a Christian from danger to life, that the Rabbinical laws command the slaughter of Christians, and that no confidence should be placed in Jewish physicians, nor ought their medicines to be taken. He repeated all the false stories of murders committed by Jews against Christians, of the poisoning of wells by Jews at the time of the Black Death, of the poisoning of the elector of Brandenburg, Joachim II, by his Jewish mint-master, of Raphael Levi's child-murder at Metz —in short, all ever invented by saintly simplicity, priestly fraud, or excited fanaticism, and imputed to Jews. That the martyrdom of little Simon of Trent was a fabrication had been clearly proved by the doge and senate of Venice on authentic documents. Not only the Jewish writers Isaac Viva and Isaac Cardoso, but also Christians, like Wülfer and Wagenseil, recognized these documents as genuine, and represented the charge against the Jews of Trent as a crying injustice. Eisenmenger was not influenced by that, declared the documents to be forged, and maintained the bloodthirstiness of Jews with fiery zeal and energy. One would be justified in ascribing his proceedings against Jews to brutality or avarice. Although very learned in Hebrew, he was otherwise uncultured. He was willing to be bribed by solid coin into silence with regard to the Jews. But for the honor of humanity one would rather impute his course to blindness ; he had lived a long time at Frankfort-on-the-Main, formerly the center of hatred to Jews in Germany, and he may there have imbibed his bitter animosity, and have wished, at first from conscientious motives, to blacken the character of the Jews.

Some Jews had got wind of the printing of Eisenmenger's work at Frankfort, and were not a little alarmed at the danger threatening them. The old prejudices of the masses and the ecclesiastics against Jews, stronger amongst Protestants than Catholics, still existed too strongly for a firebrand publication to appear in German without doing mischief wherever it came. The Jews of Frankfort therefore placed themselves in communication with the court-Jews at Vienna in order to meet the danger. Emperor Leopold I, who, at the instigation of the empress and her father-confessor, had expelled the Jews from Vienna, being in need of money in consequence of the Turkish wars, fifteen years later allowed some rich Jews to settle in the capital. Samuel Oppenheim, of Heidelberg, a banker, one of the noblest of Jews, whose heart and hand were open to all sufferers, had probably brought about this concession. As before, several Jewish families, alleged to be his servants, came with him to Vienna. Samuel Oppenheim zealously endeavored to prevent the circulation of Eisenmenger's book against the Jews. He had the same year experienced what a Christian rabble instigated by hatred of Jews could do. A riotous assault was made upon his house, which was broken into, and everything

there, including the money-chest, was plundered
(July 17, 1700).   Hence from personal motives
and on public grounds Samuel Oppenheim exerted
himself to prevent the 2,000 copies of Eisenmenger's work from seeing the light of day.   He
and other Jews could justly maintain that the publication of this book in German, unattractive though
its style was, would lead to the massacre of the Jews.
An edict was therefore issued by the emperor forbidding its dissemination.   Eisenmenger was doubly
disappointed; he could not wreak his hatred on the
Jews, and he had lost the whole of his property,
which he had spent on the printing, and was obliged
to incur debts.   All the copies, except a few which
he had abstracted, were in Frankfort under lock
and key.   He entered into negotiations with Jews,
and proposed to destroy his work for 90,000 marks.
As the Jews offered scarcely half that sum, the con-
fiscation remained in force, and Eisenmenger, deceived in all his hopes, died of vexation.

But the matter did not terminate there.   Frederick I, the newly-crowned king of Prussia, took a
lively interest in the book.   The attention of this
prince was keenly directed to the Jews from various
causes.   At the beginning of the eighteenth century
more than a thousand Jews dwelt in his domains.
The community of Berlin had grown in thirty years,
since their admission, from twelve to some seventy
families.   Frederick I, who was fond of show and
pomp, had no particular partiality for Jews, but he
valued them for the income derived from them.
The court jeweler, Jost Liebmann, was highly
esteemed at court, because he supplied pearls and
trinkets on credit, and thus held an exceptionally
favorable position.   It was said that Liebmann's
wife had taken the fancy of the prince; she later
obtained the liberty of entering the king's apartment
unannounced.   Through her the Jews received permission to have a cemetery in Königsberg; but

Jewish money was more highly prized by this king than Jewish favorites. Frederick, who while elector had thought of banishing the Jews, tolerated them for the safety tax which they had to pay—100 ducats yearly—but they were subjected to severe restrictions, amongst others they could not own houses and lands. Yet they were allowed to have synagogues, first a private one granted as a favor to the court jeweler Jost Liebmann and the family of David Riess, an immigrant from Austria, and then, owing to frequent disputes about rights and privileges, a public synagogue as well.

Two maliciously disposed baptized Jews, Christian Kahtz and Francis Wenzel, sought to prejudice the new king and the population against the Jews. "Blasphemy against Jesus"—so runs the lying charge. The prayer "Alenu" and others were cited as proofs that the Jews pronounced the name of Jesus with contumely, and that they spat in doing so. The guilds not being well disposed to the Jews utilized this excitement for fanatical persecution, and such bitter feeling arose in the cities and villages against the Jews, that (as they expressed themselves, perhaps knowingly exaggerating) their life was no longer safe. King Frederick proposed a course which does honor to his good heart. He issued a command (December, 1700) to all the presidents of departments to call together the rabbis and, in default of them, the Jewish school-masters and elders on a certain day, and ask them on oath whether, in uttering or silently using the blasphemous word "va-rik," they applied it to Jesus. The Jews everywhere solemnly declared on oath that they did not refer to Jesus in this prayer at the place where the lacuna was left in the prayer-books. John Henry Michaelis, the theologian, of Halle, who was asked respecting the character of the Jews, pronounced them innocent of the blasphemy of which they were accused. As the king continued to suspect the Jews of reviling Jesus in thought, he issued orders characteristic of the time (1703). He said that it was his heart's wish to bring the people of Israel, whom the Lord had once loved and chosen as His peculiar possession, into the Christian communion. He did not, however, presume to exercise control over their consciences, but would leave the conversion of the Jews to time and God's wise counsel. Nor would he bind them by oath to refrain from uttering in prayer the words in question. But he commanded them on pain of punishment to refrain from those words, to utter the prayer "Alenu" aloud, and not to spit while so doing. Spies were appointed to visit the synagogues from time to time, as eleven centuries before in the Byzantine empire, in order to observe whether this concluding prayer was pronounced aloud or in a whisper.

Eisenmenger before his death, and his heirs after him, knowing that the king of Prussia was inclined to listen to accusations against the Jews, had applied to him to entreat Emperor Leopold to release the book against the Jews, entitled "Judaism Unmasked," from ban and prohibition. Frederick I interested himself warmly in the matter, and sent a kind of petition to Emperor Leopold I (April 25, 1705) very characteristic of the tone of that time. The king represented that Eisenmenger had sunk all his money in this book, and had died of vexation at the imperial prohibition. It would seem a lowering of Christianity if the Jews were so powerful as to be able to suppress a book written in defense of Christianity and in refutation of Jewish errors. There was no reason to apprehend, as the Jews pretended, that it would incite the people to a violent onslaught against them, since similar writings had lately appeared which had done them no harm. Eisenmenger's book aimed chiefly at the promotion of Christianity, so that Christians might not, as had repeatedly happened some years ago, be induced to revolt from it and become adherents of Judaism. But Emperor Leopold would not remove the ban from Eisenmenger's book. King Frederick repeated his request three years later, at the desire of Eisenmenger's heirs, to Emperor Joseph I. With him also King Frederick found no favorable hearing, and the 2,000 copies of "Judaism Unmasked" remained at Frankfort under ban for forty years. But with Frederick's approval a second edition was brought out at Königsberg, where the imperial censorship had no power. For the moment it had no such effect as the one side had hoped and the other feared; but, later on, when the rights of Jews as men and citizens were considered, it proved an armory for malicious or indolent opponents.

King Frederick I was often urged by enemies of the Jews to make his royal authority a cloak for their villainy. The bright and the dark side of the general appreciation of Jewish literature appeared clearly. In Holland, likewise a Protestant country, a Christian scholar of this period cherished great enthusiasm for the Mishna, the backbone of Talmudical Judaism. William Surenhuysius, a young man of Amsterdam, in the course of many years translated the Mishna with two commentaries upon it into Latin (printed 1698-1703). He displayed more than the usual amount of Dutch industry and application. Love certainly was needed to undertake such a study, persevere in it, and finish the work in a clear and attractive style. No language and literature present so many difficulties as this dialect, now almost obsolete, the objects which it describes, and the form in which it is cast. Surenhuysius sat at the feet of Jewish teachers, of whom there were many at Amsterdam, and he was extremely grateful for their help. But their assistance did not enable him to dispense with industry and devotion. He was influenced by the conviction that the oral Law, the Mishna, in its main contents is as divine as the written word of the Bible.   He desired that Christian youths in training for theology and the clerical profession should not yield to the seductions of classical literature, but by engaging in the study of the Mishna should, as it were, receive ordination beforehand.

"He who desires to be a good and worthy disciple of Christ must first become a Jew, or he must first learn thoroughly the language and culture of the Jews, and become Moses's disciple before he joins the Apostles, in order that he may be able through Moses and the prophets to convince men that Jesus is the Messiah."

In this enthusiastic admiration for the corner-stone of the edifice of Judaism, which the builders up of culture were wont to despise, Surenhuysius included the people who owned these laws.   He cordially thanked the senate of Amsterdam because it specially protected the Jews.

"In the measure in which this people once surpassed all other peoples, you give it preference, worthy men !   The old renown and dignity, which this people and the citizens of Jerusalem once possessed, are yours.   For the Jews are sincerely devoted to you, not overcome by force of arms, but won over by humanity and wisdom ; they come to you, and are happy to obey your republican government."

Surenhuysius was outspoken in his displeasure against those who having learned what served their interest from the Scriptures of the Jews, reviled and threw mud at them, "like highwaymen, who, having robbed an honest man of all his clothes, beat him to death, and send him away with scorn."   He formed a plan to make the whole of Rabbinical literature accessible to the learned world through the Latin language.   While Surenhuysius of Amsterdam felt such enthusiasm for this, not the most brilliant, side of Judaism, and saw in it a means to promote Christianity (in which view he did not stand alone), a vile Polish Jew, named Aaron Margalita, an apostate to Christianity for the sake of gain, brought fresh accusations of blasphemy before King Frederick of Prussia against an utterly harmless part of Jewish literature—the old Agada.   An edition of

the Midrash Rabba (1705), published at Frankfort-
on-the-Oder, was accordingly put under a ban by
the king's command, until Christian theologians
should pronounce judgment upon it.

The best result of this taste for Jewish literature
on the part of learned Christians, and of the literary
works promoted thereby was an interesting historical work concerning Jews and Judaism, which may
be said to have terminated the old, and foreshadowed
a new epoch. Jacob Basnage (born 1653, died
1723), of noble character, a Protestant theologian, a
solid historian, a pleasant author, and a person held
in high esteem generally, rendered incalculable service to Judaism. He sifted the results of the laborious researches of scholars, popularized them, and
made them accessible to all educated circles. In
his assiduous historical inquiries, especially as to the
development of the Church, Basnage met Jews at
almost every step. He had a suspicion that the
Jewish people had not, as ordinary theologians
thought, become utterly bankrupt through the loss
of its political independence and the spread of Christianity, a doomed victim, the ghost of its former self.
The great sufferings of this people and its rich literature inspired him with awe. His sense of truth
with regard to historical events would not allow him
to dismiss facts or explain them away with empty
phrases. Basnage undertook to compile the history
of the Jews or the Jewish religion, so far as it was
known to him, from Jesus down to his own times.
He labored on this work for more than five years.
It was intended to continue the history of the Jewish
historian Flavius Josephus after the dispersion of
the Jewish people. Basnage strove, as far as was
possible for a staunch Protestant at that time, to
present and judge events in an impartial manner.

"Christians may not be surprised that we often acquit the Jews of
crimes of which they are not guilty, since justice so requires. No partiality is implied in accusing those of injustice and oppression who

have been guilty of them.   We have no intention to injure the Jews
any more than to flatter them. . . . In the decay and dregs of centuries men have adopted a spirit of cruelty and barbarism towards the
Jews. They were accused of being the cause of all the disasters which
happened, and charged with a multitude of crimes of which they
never even dreamed.   Numberless miracles were invented to convict
them, or rather the better to satisfy hatred under the shade of religion.
We have made a collection of laws, which councils and princes published against them, by means of which people can judge of the malice
of the former and the oppression of the latter.   Men did not, however,
confine themselves to the edicts, but everywhere military executions,
popular riots, and massacres took place.   Yet, by a miracle of Providence, which must excite the astonishment of all Christians, this hated
nation, persecuted in all places for a great number of centuries, still
exists everywhere. . . . Peoples and kings, heathens, Christians, and
Mahometans, opposed to one another in so many points, have agreed
in the purpose of destroying this nation, and have not succeeded.
The bush of Moses, surrounded by flames, has ever burned without
being consumed.   The Jews have been driven out of all the cities of
the world, and this has only served to spread them abroad in all cities.
They still live in spite of the contempt and hatred which follow them
everywhere, while the greatest monarchies have fallen, and are known
to us only by name."

Basnage, who by the revocation of the Edict of
Nantes through the Catholic intolerance of Louis
XIV was banished to Holland, could to some degree
appreciate the feelings of the Jews during their long
exile. He had acquired sufficient knowledge of
Jewish literature to consult the authorities in the
execution of his work. The historical works of
Abraham ibn Daud, Ibn Yachya, Ibn Verga, David
Gans, and others were not neglected; they served
Basnage as building material wherewith to rear the
great fabric of Jewish history of the sixteen centuries
since the origin of Christianity.

But Basnage was not sufficiently an artist to unroll before the eye in glowing colors, even if in images fleeting as the mist, the sublime or tragic scenes
of Jewish history. Nor had he the talent to mass
together or marshal in groups and detachments facts
widely scattered in consequence of the peculiar
course of this people's history. One can feel in
Basnage's presentation that he was oppressed and
overpowered by the superabundance of details. He
jumbled together times and occurrences in motley

confusion, divided the history into two unnatural halves, the East and the West, and described in conjunction events without connection. Of the deep inner springs of the life and deeds of the nation he had no comprehension.   His Protestant creed hindered him; he saw Jewish history only through the thick mist of Church history.   Despite his efforts to be impartial and honest, he could not rid himself of the belief that the "Jews are rejected because they have rejected Jesus."   In short, Basnage's " History of the Religion of the Jews" has a thousand faults. Hardly a single sentence can be regarded as perfectly just and in accordance with the truth.

Yet the appearance of this work was of great importance to the Jews.   It circulated in the educated world a mass of historical information, crude and distorted though it was, because it was written in the fashionable French language, and this seed shot up everywhere luxuriantly. A people, which, despite bloody persecutions, without a home, with no spot on the whole earth where it could lay its head or place its foot, yet possessed a history not wholly devoid of splendor—such a people was not like a gipsy horde, but must find ever-increasing consideration. Without his knowledge or intention, even whilst casting many an aspersion upon the Jewish race, Basnage paved the way to raising it from its abject condition.   Christian Theophilus Unger, a pastor in Silesia, and John Christopher Wolf, professor of Oriental languages in Hamburg, who were busily and earnestly engaged in the study of Jewish literature and history, became Basnage's disciples, and without his work could not have effected so much as they did in this field.   Both, especially Wolf, filled many gaps which Basnage had left, and evinced a certain degree of warmth for the cause.

The admiration, or at least sympathy, felt for the Jews at this time, induced John Toland (an Irishman, the courageous opponent of fossilized Christianity) to raise his voice on behalf of their equality with Christians in England and Ireland. This was the first word spoken in favor of their emancipation. But the people, in whose favor this remarkable revulsion of sentiment had taken place in the educated world, was without knowledge of it, and felt no change in popular sentiment.

CHAPTER VI.

GENERAL DEMORALIZATION OF JUDAISM.

Low Condition of the Jews at the End of the Seventeenth Century—
Representatives of Culture: David Nieto, Jehuda Brieli—The
Kabbala—Jewish Chroniclers—Lopez Laguna translates the
Psalms into Spanish—De Barrios—The Race after Wealth—
General Poverty of the Jews—Revival of Sabbatianism—Daniel
Israel Bonafoux, Cardoso, Mordecai of Eisenstadt, Jacob Querido,
and Berachya—Sabbatianism in Poland—Abraham Cuenqui—
Judah Chassid—Chayim Malach—Solomon Ayllon—Nehemiah
Chayon—David Oppenheim's Famous Library—Chacham Zevi
—The Controversy on Chayon's Heretical Works in Amsterdam.

1700—1725 C. E.

At the time when the eyes of the civilized world
were directed upon the Jewish race with a certain
degree of sympathy and admiration, and when, at
the dawn of enlightenment in the so-called philosophical century, ecclesiastical prejudices were beginning to disappear, the members of this race were
making a by no means favorable impression upon
those with whom they came into contact. Weighed
in the balance, they were found wanting even by
their well-wishers. The Jews were at no time in so
pitiful a plight as at the end of the seventeenth and
beginning of the eighteenth century. Several circumstances had contributed to render them utterly
demoralized and despised. The former teachers
of Europe, through the sad course of centuries, had
become childish, or worse, dotards. Every public
or historical act of the Jews bears this character of
imbecility, if not contemptibility. There was not a
single cheering event, hardly a person commanding
respect who could worthily represent Judaism, and
bring it into estimation. The strong-minded, manly
Orobio de Castro (died in 1687), the former victim

of the Inquisition, whose fidelity to conviction, whose
dignity, and the acumen with which he contested
Christianity commanded the respect of the leading
opponents of Judaism, was indeed still living. But
he left no successor of equal standing within the
highly cultured community of Amsterdam, certainly
not outside of it, where the conditions for an independent Jewish personality possessed of culture
were entirely wanting. The leaders of the community were for the most part led astray, wandering
as in a dream, and stumbling at every step. But
few rabbis occupied themselves with any branch of
knowledge beyond the Talmud, or entered on a new
path in this study. The exceptions can be counted.
Rabbi David Nieto, of London (born 1654, died
1728), was a man of culture. He was a physician,
understood mathematics, was sufficiently able to defend Judaism against calumnies, and, besides many
platitudes, wrote much that was reasonable. The
Italian rabbi, Jehuda Leon Brieli, of Mantua (born
about 1643, died 1722), was also an important personage—a man of sound views, of solid, even philosophical knowledge, whose style in the vernacular
was elegant, and who knew how to defend Judaism
against Christian aggressiveness. Brieli had the
courage to disregard two customs, which was accounted worse than criminal by his contemporaries :
he remained unmarried all his life, and though a
rabbi, did not wear a beard. But Brieli's influence
on his Jewish contemporaries was very slight. He
knew the weaknesses of Christianity, but had not
the same sharp vision for the faults of Judaism and
the Jews. Of the mischievous nature of the Zohar
and the Kabbala generally, however, Brieli was
thoroughly aware ; he wished that they had not seen
the light of day ; but his critical knowledge extended
no further.

For the rest, the rabbis of this period were not
models, the Poles and Germans being for the most

part pitiable figures, their heads filled with unprofit-
able knowledge, otherwise ignorant and helpless as
little children.   The Portuguese rabbis presented a
dignified, imposing appearance, but they were
shallow.   The Italians bore more resemblance to
the Germans, but had not their learning.   Thus,
with no guides acquainted with the road, sunk in ignorance, or filled with conceit, beset with phantoms,
the Jews in all parts of the world without exception
were passing from one absurdity to another, and
allowing themselves to be imposed upon by jugglers
and visionaries.   Any absurdity, however transparent, provided it was apparently vindicated with
religious earnestness, and interlarded with strained
verses of Scripture, or sayings from the Talmud
artificially explained, or garnished with scraps of
the Kabbala, was persistently believed and pro-
pagated.   "The minds of men, estranged from life
and true knowledge, exhausted their powers in
subtleties and the superstitious errors of the Kabbala.   Teachers spoke seldom or only in the words
of the Talmud to their scholars ; no attention was
paid to delivery, for there was no language and no
eloquence."   The culminating point of the Middle
Ages was reached in Jewish history at a time when
it had been passed by the most of Western Europe.
The spread of superstitious usages with a coating
of religion was in no wise checked.   To write
amulets (Kamea) for the exorcism of diseases was
required of the rabbis, and they devoted themselves
to this work ; many wished to be thought conjurors
of spirits.   A rabbi, Simon Baki at Casale in Italy,
complained to his master, the foolish Kabbalist
Moses Zacut at Venice, that he had used the prescribed formulas of conjuration for a woman at Turin
supposed to be possessed, without any successful
result.   Thereupon the latter gave him more efficacious means, viz., whilst using God's name in
prayer, he was to hold burning sulphur to the nose

of the possessed.   The more sensitive she was, and the more she struggled against the remedy, the more might he be convinced that she was possessed by an evil spirit.   An instructed Jew of the Kabbalist school of Damascus once boasted seriously before the free-thinking critic Richard Simon, that he could evoke a genius of a high order, and began to make preparations.   The incredulous Father followed his movements with a satirical smile, and the conjuror got out of the predicament with the remark that the soil of France was not suited for apparitions.

To elevate Judaism in the eyes of the nations and to represent it in a manner worthy of respect was at this time not in the power of the Jews.   They rather degraded and made it contemptible.   Thoughtful Christians stood astonished before this wonderful monument of history, this people with its learning and its alternately glorious and tragic destiny ; but its own sons were too dull to feel their own greatness, or sought it only in silly stories and absurd actions.   Whilst Christians industriously and with feelings of amazement investigated the history of the Jews during three thousand years, the Jews had no such feeling, not even the cultivated Portuguese Jews.   Manasseh ben Israel had outlined a history of the Jews, and probably suggested Basnage's work, but he did not accomplish his own design. Three historians, indeed, are named as belonging to this time—the itinerant rabbi David Conforte, secondly, Miguel (Daniel) de Barrios, a Marrano, born in Portugal, who returned to Judaism at Amsterdam, and lastly the Polish rabbi Jechiel Heilperin, of Minsk.   But all three resemble the monkish chroniclers of the barbarous ages, and their style is more repulsive than attractive.

If literature is the true photograph of the thoughts and aspirations of an age, then the century between Spinoza and Mendelssohn, judged by its literary productions, must have had very ugly features. A good deal, it is true, was written and published; every rabbi by a fresh contribution to the already stupendous pile of Rabbinical matter essayed to perpetuate his name, to secure his future bliss, and withal to earn a pittance. Subtle Rabbinical commentaries, insipid sermons, and books of devotion, acrimonious controversial writings were the emanations of the Jewish mind or lack of mind at this time. The flower of poetry found no soil in this quagmire. This age produced only two Jewish poets, genuine sons of the Jewish muse, who lived at a great distance from each other, one in the island of Jamaica, the other in Italy—Lopez Laguna and Luzzatto—as if the old Jewish trunk, crownless and leafless, wished to reveal the life at its heart and prove its capability to renew its youth even under the most unfavorable circumstances. Lopez Laguna, born a Marrano in France (about 1660, died after 1720), came when but a youth to Spain, where he made the acquaintance of the horrible Inquisition. In his night of suffering, the Psalms, full of tender feeling, brought light and hope to him as to so many of his companions in sorrow. Released from prison, and having escaped to Jamaica, Laguna, under the Jewish name of Daniel Israel, attuned his harp to the holy songs which had revived his soul. To make the Psalms accessible to others, especially to Marranos ignorant of Hebrew, he made a faithful translation of them into melodious, elegant Spanish verse. This psalter, "a mirror of life," Daniel Israel Lopez Laguna took to London, where his work procured him a triumphant reception from several minor poets and also from three Jewish poetesses, Sarah de Fonseca Pinto y Pimentel, Manuela Nuñez da Almeida, and Bienvenida Coen Belmonte, who addressed him in Latin, English, Portuguese, and Spanish verses.

Moses Chayim Luzzatto, a victim to the dreary

errors of this time, composed two Hebrew dramas full of beauty and youthful freshness. With the exception of these poetical flowers this long period shows a colorless waste. Daniel de Barrios, captain, historian, and beggar, cannot be reckoned a poet, although he composed an astonishing number of Spanish, as well as Hebrew rhymes, besides several Spanish dramas, and he sang before, and without shame begged of, nearly every Jewish and Christian magnate who possessed a full purse.

Not only the scientific and artistic spirit, but also the moral sense was lost, or at least blunted in this general demoralization. The fundamental virtues of the Jewish race continued to exist even at this time in undiminished strength—idyllic family love, brotherly sympathy towards one another, and chastity. Gross vices and crimes occurred even then but seldom in the tents of Jacob. Thoroughly corrupt outcasts were considerate enough to leave it, and to pollute the church or the mosque with their immorality. But the feeling of right and honor amongst Jews was on the whole weakened. There was a lowering in tone of that tender conscience, which with a sort of maiden shame avoids even what the precepts of religion and the paragraphs of the civil code leave unforbidden. To make money was so imperious a necessity that ways and means became indifferent, and were not exposed to censure. To take undue advantage, and to overreach, not merely a hostile population, but even their own co-religionists, was regarded for the most part not as a disgrace, but rather as a kind of heroic action. From this sprang worship of Mammon, not merely love, but also respect for gold, no matter how impure its source. The democratic equality hitherto maintained amongst Jews, who refused to recognize distinctions of class and caste, was lost in the furious dance round the golden calf. The rich man was held worthy of honor—one to whom those less kindly favored by fortune looked up as to something higher, and in whom they therefore overlooked many failings. The richest, not the most worthy, were made the managers of the community, and were granted a charter for arbitrary conduct and arrogance. A satire of the period scourges very severely the almighty power of money, to which all bowed down. "The dollar binds and looses, it raises the ignorant to the chief offices in the community."

Increasing poverty among Jews was partly the cause of this state of affairs. Only among the small number of Portuguese Jews at Amsterdan, Hamburg, Leghorn, Florence, and London, there were men of considerable wealth. Isaac (Antonio) Suasso, created Baron Alvernes de Gras by Charles II, of Spain, was able to advance to William III, for his semi-adventurous expedition to London to obtain the English crown, two million florins without interest, with the simple words, "If you are fortunate, you will repay them to me; if not, I am willing to lose them." The millionaires at Amsterdam were the Pintos, the Belmontes, David Bueno de Mesquito, Francisco Melo, who rendered many services to Holland by his wealth. One of the De Pintos bequeathed several millions for noble objects, making provision for Jewish communities, the state, Christian orphanages, clergy, clerks, and sextons. At Hamburg there were the Texeiras, who were related by marriage to Suasso, and Daniel Abensur, able to make large advances to the poor rulers of Poland. On the other hand, the Polish, German, and also the Italian and the Oriental Jews, were extremely impoverished. The changes which commerce had experienced brought about this alteration. The Jews could no longer practice usury, they had no capital, or rather Christian capitalists competed with them. Poorest of all were the Polish Jews,— they who used to lord it over all the Jews in Europe.

They could not recover from the wounds which the Cossack disturbances had inflicted on them, and the disruption of the Polish kingdom that followed caused them fresh troubles. The increasing poverty of the Polish Jews every year drove swarms of beggars to the west and south of Europe. They resorted to the large communities to procure shelter and food from their rich brethren. Polish students of the Talmud, superior to all other Jews in knowledge of the Talmud, went principally to the important rabbinates, Prague, Nikolsburg, Frankfort-on-the-Main, Amsterdam, and Hamburg, and even to Italian communities. Every Polish emigrant was, or proclaimed himself to be, a rabbi or preacher, and was so regarded. Many of them were a disgrace to the rabbinical office, for which they had no qualifications, either mental or moral. They fawned on the rich from need and habit. From them sprang the ever-increasing demoralization among Jews. To their care, or rather to their neglect, were entrusted the Jewish youth, who, as soon as they could talk, were introduced to the Talmud, after the sophistical, artificial method. Through this perversity the language of the German Jews, like that of the Poles, degenerated into a repulsive stammer, and their manner of thinking and love of disputation into crabbed dogmatism that defied all logic. Their feeling for simplicity and truth was lost, and even the Portuguese Jews, who kept themselves aloof from the odious jargon, did not remain uncontaminated by the perverse manner of thinking prevalent at the time.

Added to this was the fact that the mud-streams of Sabbatian fanaticism burst forth afresh. They besmirched all who came in contact with them, but, nevertheless, they were regarded as a pure stream from the fountain-head of the Deity. Their one good effect was that they stirred up, and set in motion the stagnant swamp ; or, to speak without met-

aphor, the sluggish routine in which the Jews lived
was broken, and the rabbis, dull with unfruitful learning, were roused to a certain degree of passion and
energy.   After Sabbataï's death one of his followers, Daniel Israel Bonafoux, an ignorant officiating
reader (Chazan) at Smyrna, kept up the faith in the
dead Messiah by all sorts of jugglery.   At one time
he pretended to have seen a moving fire-ball ; at
another, to have heard a voice say that Sabbataï
was still alive, and would reign forever.   The community at Smyrna bribed the Kadi to banish him
from the city, but Daniel Israel took up his residence
in the neighborhood of Smyrna, and encouraged the
sect to persevere in its belief.   He was aided and
abetted by Abraham Michael Cardoso of Tripoli,
who reappeared on this stage, where he found a conventicle of Sabbatian associates, who flocked round
him, because with his scientific education, his culture,
and fluency of speech, he was far superior to them.
Cardoso announced dreams and visions, declared
himself Sabbataï Zevi's successor, the Ephraimite
Messiah, practiced extraordinary impositions, and
visited graves to be inspired by departed spirits, and
obtain predictions to suit his theory.   This consisted
in the blasphemous assumption that there are two
Gods—one the First Cause, incomprehensible, without will and influence over the universe ; the other
the God of Israel, the actual Creator of the world,
and Lawgiver of the Jewish people, who alone should
be worshiped.   But the rabbis of Smyrna put a stop
to Cardoso's proceedings, threatened him with death,
and compelled him to leave Sabbataï Zevi's birth-
place.   He betook himself thence to Constantinople
with his Smyrna adherents, later pursued his mischievous behavior at Adrianople, Rhodosto, in Egypt,
the Archipelago, and Candia ; now as Messiah, now
as physician, composed numerous treatises on the
advent of the Messianic kingdom, expounded his
theosophical-dualistic theory, incurred debts, drew

women into his Kabbalistic conventicle, and is said
to have lived immorally even to old age. At last
Cardoso was stabbed by his nephew, who believed
that he had been cheated by him (1706). His imposture did not cease with his death; for his writings, a mixture of sense and nonsense, were eagerly
read, and inflamed men's minds. Abraham Michael
Cardoso remained at least faithful to Judaism, did
not reverence Sabbataï Zevi as divine, vehemently
contended against this blasphemy, and did not go
over to Mahometanism. His prophet, Daniel Israel
Bonafoux, on the other hand, assumed the turban,
probably on account of the persecution suffered at
the hands of the rabbinate of Smyrna.

Far more important was the Kabbalistic fanaticism
spread by an itinerant Sabbatian preacher, and
transplanted to Poland, where it found congenial
soil, and maintained its ground tenaciously. Mordecai of Eisenstadt (Mochiach), even after the death
of the renegade, remained his faithful follower. A
disciple of Nathan and partisan of Cardoso, he returned to his home from the East, was of prepossess-
ing appearance and awe-inspiring features, lived an
ascetic life, fasted eleven days in succession, preached
in Hungary, Moravia, Bohemia, and Italy with much
impressiveness on penitence and contrition—in fact,
played the part of a Jewish Vincent Ferrer. The
applause which his preaching excited awakened his
confidence, and he gave himself out as a prophet.
In word and writing the preacher of Eisenstadt
maintained that Sabbataï Zevi was the true Messiah,
obliged to become a Mussulman by high mystical
dispensation. The Hungarian, Moravian, and Bohemian Jews listened to these Sabbatian preachings
and prophecies with eager interest. The Sabbatian
frenzy had so blunted their power of thought that
they were not offended at the notion of a new Messiah who had apostatized from Judaism. Mordecai
went further in his folly, gave himself out as the true

Messiah of the house of David, and maintained that he was Sabbataï Zevi risen from the dead. The latter had not been able to accomplish the work of redemption, because he was rich. The Messiah must be poor; therefore he, Mordecai, being poor and persecuted, was the true redeemer. All this nonsense was accepted with credulous devotion. Some Italian Jews formally invited the Hungarian Messiah to come to them, and he obeyed the summons. At Modena and Reggio he was received with enthusiasm. He talked of his mission—that he must go to Rome in order to make Messianic preparations in the sinful city. He cunningly hinted that he might be obliged to assume a Christian disguise, as Sabbataï Zevi had been obliged to veil himself in Turkish clothing: that is, in case of need he would apparently submit to baptism. Some Jews appear to have betrayed his plans to the Roman Inquisition, and his Italian followers advised him to leave Italy. He went once more to Bohemia, but could not find a footing there, and emigrated to Poland. Here, whither only a dim rumor of Sabbataï and the Sabbatians had penetrated, he found, it appears, numerous followers; for a sect was formed there which pursued its baneful career until the beginning of the age of Mendelssohn, and even beyond that period.

At the same time the old imposture reappeared under new forms in Turkey. Sabbataï Zevi had left a widow, the daughter of Joseph Philosoph of Salonica, a learned Talmudist. She is said either from ambition or, as her enemies declared, from licentious motives, to have led the Sabbatians into fresh frenzy. Having returned to Salonica, she is said to have passed off her brother, Jacob (surnamed Querido, the favorite), as her son by Sabbataï Zevi. This boy, who received the name of Jacob Zevi, became an object of devout reverence to the Sabbatians. They believed that in him the united souls

of the two Messiahs of the houses of Joseph and
David were born again ; he was therefore to be regarded as the true redeemer, the genuine successor
of Sabbataï. This new fantastic idea found the more
adherents because Querido's own father, Joseph
Philosoph, a man deeply versed in the Talmud, and
another learned Talmudist, Solomon Florentin,
joined the believers, and supported the new claim-
ant. The widow of the Messiah and her brother
Querido are said straightway to have recommended
and practiced sexual indulgence as a means of promoting the work of redemption. The sinfulness of
the world, they maintained, could be overcome only
by a superabundance of sin, by the extremest degree
of licentiousness. Among these Salonica Sabbatians, then, shameless profligacy, even incest, were
openly practiced—so their enemies declared. One
thing only is certain, marriage was not regarded as
sacred among these people. According to the perverse teachings of the Luryan school of Kabbalists,
women who were not acceptable to their husbands,
being a hindrance to a harmonious mystical marriage,
could be divorced without further ceremony, and
made over to others, who felt themselves attracted
to them. This precept was only too eagerly obeyed
in the mystical circle. It was a peculiar sort of
"elective affinity." Several hundreds in Salonica
belonged to this Sabbatian sect, chiefly young
people. Amongst them was a young man named
Solomon Ayllon, afterwards rabbi in London and
Amsterdam, who shared in the prevailing loose life.
He married a wife, as the one appointed by heaven,
whom another man had forsaken without formal divorce, and she was carried off from him by a third.
The Sabbatians of Salonica stood in close connection with other members of the sect in Adrianople
and Smyrna.

The rabbis could not regard this disorder with
indifference, and denounced the offenders to the

Turkish authorities. The latter instituted investigations, and sentenced them to severe punishments.
But the Sabbatians had learned from their founder
a means of appeasing the anger of Turkish rulers.
They all, to the number of four hundred it is said,
assumed the white turban (about 1687), and displayed more earnestness than Sabbataï in their
newly-adopted faith. The pseudo-Messiah Jacob
Zevi Querido with many of his followers made a pilgrimage to Mecca, in order to pray at the tomb of
the prophet Mahomet. On the journey back he
died at Alexandria. The leadership of the Turco-
Jewish sect at Salonica was afterwards undertaken
by his son Berachya, or Barochya (about 1695-1740).
He also was regarded as the successor of Sabbataï
Zevi, as the embodiment of the original soul of the
Messiah, as the incarnate Deity. His followers
lived under the name Dolmäh (properly Donmäh),
that is, apostates from Judaism, a sect distinct alike
from Jews and Turks, who married only one another,
and attended the mosques now and then, but more
frequently assembled in secret for their own mystical
service, to worship their redeemer and man-God.
There are still in Salonica descendants of the sect
of Sabbataï–Querido–Berachya, who observe a
mixture of Kabbalistic and Turkish usages. Of Judaism they retained only circumcision on the eighth
day and the Song of Solomon, the love dialogues and
monologues of which left them free play for mystical
and licentious interpretations. Recently the sultan
granted the Donmäh, now said to number 4,000
members, the free exercise of their religion.

In spite, perhaps on account of these excesses on
the part of the Sabbatians of Salonica, opposed
alike to Judaism and morality, they continually
found fresh supporters, who clung to the delusion
with pertinacity, deceived themselves and others,
and gave impostors an opportunity to profit by this
fanatical humor. From the East and from Poland

secret Sabbatians crossed to and fro, from the latter as itinerant preachers, from the former as pretended messengers from the Holy Land, and continually incited to fresh errors. The emissary Abraham Cuenqui, from Hebron, who in Poland and Germany claimed charity for the poor of that city, at the request of a mystic gave a glowing description of the life of Sabbataï, whom he had seen and admired in his youth. This biography, a sort of Sabbatian gospel, is an excellent example of how in the field of religion history takes the shape of myth, and myth again transforms itself into history. In Poland, probably at the instigation of the crazy Mordecai of Eisenstadt, there arose a Sabbatian sect, which believed that it was hastening the advent of the kingdom of heaven by penitence. At its head stood two men, Judah Chassid (the pious) of Dubno, a narrow-minded simpleton, and Chayim Malach, a cunning Talmudist. Both agitated the people by exciting sermons, and found an applauding audience, who joined them in penances and Kabbalistic extravagances. The association was called Chassidim. In Poland ignorance was so great that the rabbis themselves did not recognize the power and mischievous tendency of these Sabbatian enthusiasts. From 1,300 to 1,500 of this sect, under Judah Chassid, emigrated from Poland at the beginning of the year 1700, intending to journey to the Holy Land, to await redemption there. Like the Christian flagellants of old, these so-called devotees distinguished themselves by fasting many days, and by mortifications of every kind. The leaders wore on the Sabbath white garments of satin or cloth, whereby they intended to signify the time of grace. Wherever they went in Germany, they preached, and exhorted to strict penance. Judah Chassid by his powerful voice, his gestures, and bitter tears, carried away his hearers. He wrought especially upon the weak minds of women, to whom, contrary to custom, he was wont to preach, with a Torah roll under his arm, in the women's gallery. While the greater number of the Chassidim were assembling in Moravia and Hungary, Judah Chassid traveled with about 150 persons through Germany from Altona to Frankfort-on-the-Main and Vienna, everywhere preaching, wailing, and warning. The sect, especially in the larger communities, was richly supported. On account of the concourse of men and women who flocked to these sectarians, the rabbis did not venture to oppose their proceedings. Samuel Oppenheim, the rich court Jew at Vienna, supported the Chassidim richly, and procured passports for them to the East.

The enthusiasm of this sect soon came to an end. On the first day after their arrival in Jerusalem their principal leader Judah Chassid died; his followers were helpless, and instead of speedy redemption found only horrible misery. Some of the Chassidim, therefore, disappointed and in despair, went over to Islam. The rest dispersed in all directions. Many were baptized as Christians, amongst them Judah Chassid's nephew, Wolf Levi of Lublin, who took the name of Francis Lothair Philippi; another nephew, Isaiah Chassid, afterwards caused fresh Sabbatian disturbances. Chayim Malach, however, who made the acquaintance of the aged Samuel Primo, Sabbataï Zevi's private secretary and counselor, remained for several years in Jerusalem, and presided over a small Sabbatian sect. He also taught the doctrine of two Gods or three Gods, and of the Divine incarnation, paid Sabbataï Zevi divine reverence, and is said to have carried about his image, carved in wood, in the synagogue, to be worshiped, and his followers are said to have danced round it. Chayim Malach aimed at the destruction of Rabbinical Judaism or Judaism in general. It is incomprehensible how the community of Jerusalem could have witnessed his proceedings for years

without opposing them. Probably the rabbis there
shared the Sabbatian idolatry, or profited by it.
However, Chayim Malach seems at length to have
been banished from Jerusalem. He then betook
himself to the Mahometan Sabbatians at Salonica,
the Donmäh, took part in their extravagances, then
went about preaching in several Turkish communities, and openly taught the Sabbatian imposture.
At Constantinople he was excommunicated, and on
his second residence in that community was banished
by Chacham Bashi (about 1709). He thereupon
returned through Germany to Poland, scattering the
seed of Sabbatian heresy, destined to undermine
Judaism. His death is said to have been due to
excessive drinking.

At the same time that Malach was sowing seed-
grains in Poland for the process of dissolution, the
torch of discord was hurled into the Jewish camp by
two disguised Sabbatians, Chayon and Ayllon.
The one through imposture, the other through stub-
bornness and dogmatism, promoted a movement
which presents very unpleasant features. Solomon
Ayllon (born about 1667, died 1728), of Spanish
descent, was born at Safet, and his mind was filled
with the errors of the Kabbala. In his youth he fell
in with the Sabbatians of Salonica, and in part
shared their extravagances. Later he went to
Leghorn, and after the death of the worthy and
accomplished rabbi, Jacob Abendana, was invited to
London to fill his place (1696-1707). Ayllon had
enemies in London who, having heard of his not
wholly irreproachable youth, implored one rabbi
after another to procure his dismissal from office.
From dread of the public scandal which would arise
were it known that a former adherent of the notorious Sabbataï had officiated as rabbi, all who were
consulted advised that the ugly story be forgotten.
Ayllon was not distinguished in any branch of
learning, not even in knowledge of the Talmud, nor

could he have had an over-scrupulous conscience.
While treating for the post of rabbi at Amsterdam,
the London community being unwilling to lose him,
he swore a solemn oath that he would not accept
the post offered to him, although he had already
given his consent to the Amsterdam council, and
actually accepted the office. He palliated his conduct in a sophistical and Jesuitical manner. His
youthful predilection for Sabbatian errors, which he
does not appear entirely to have abandoned even
as rabbi of Amsterdam, induced Ayllon to give his
aid to an arrant rogue, and thereby to help in
producing profound dissensions in the Jewish world.

This arch-impostor, who in hypocrisy, audacity,
and unscrupulousness had but few equals in the
eighteenth century, so rich in impostors, was
Nehemiah Chiya Chayon (born about 1650, died
after 1726). He took especial delight in mystification and extravagances, and from his youth led an
adventurous, easy life of dissimulation. The career
of this Kabbalistic adventurer is characteristic of the
demoralization of the age in various ways. Chayon
received his Talmudical instruction at Hebron,
where the Sabbatian intoxication had made many
victims. He possessed considerable logical acuteness, was ready at discovering contradictions and
incongruities; but his giddy brain and cold heart,
bent on the satisfaction of low cravings, induced him
to make corrupt use of his powers. Of the Talmud
and Rabbinical literature he understood enough to
be able to appear at home in them, but he had no
real attraction to these studies, nor any religious
feeling. He was observant from hypocrisy; when
not watched, he disregarded the demands of religion
and morality. He could assume a serious, awe-
inspiring manner, and held men enthralled by his
attractive appearance, his Kabbalistic scraps, and
his mysterious demeanor. He generally enacted
the part of a saint, at the same time singing love-

songs and associating with women. He was, as he
himself confessed, in close relation with the Sabbatians at Salonica, and had taken trouble to get
possession of their writings. He frequently conversed with their leader, Samuel Primo, about
Kabbalistic projects. It is said that in one of these
interviews he proposed a new doctrine of a Trinity.
He composed a work in which he maintained that
Judaism, to be sure Kabbalistic Judaism, inculcated
belief in a triune God. With this manuscript in his
otherwise empty coffer he went to Smyrna, in the
spring of the year 1708, intending to seek his fortune
either with the Sabbatians or with their opponents.
He did, in fact, succeed in hoodwinking some rich
men of Smyrna. His patrons pledged themselves
mutually and to Chayon to give him powerful
support. The arch-rogue was treated at Smyrna
as a holy prophet, and nearly the whole community
escorted him to the ship which was to convey him
back to Palestine. His schemes were for the
moment crowned with success. But before Chayon
could settle down, the rabbinate of Jerusalem
launched a sentence of excommunication against
him, condemned his work, which they had not even
read, to be burned (June 1708), and refused to give
a hearing to the author. This gross blunder re-
venged itself afterwards. For the moment, however, Chayon was defeated. As one formally interdicted by the chief college in Palestine, he could not
settle anywhere. The enthusiasm of his patrons in
Smyrna was extinguished as quickly as it had blazed
up, for the favor of men is changeable.

Thus Chayon after a few days of good fortune
was again reduced to mendicancy. In Italy, whither
he had gone after leaving Egypt, and where he
spent some years begging (1709-1711), his schemes
met with little sympathy. At Venice only he met
with some consideration from rabbis and the
laity. Here he printed a small pamphlet, an extract

from his larger work, wherein he openly set forth the Trinity as an article of the Jewish faith, not the Christian Trinity, but three persons (Parzufim) in the Godhead, the holy Primeval One, or Soul of all Souls, the Holy King, or incarnation of Deity, and a female Person (the Shechina). This nonsense, an insult to Judaism and its conception of God, was repeated by Chayon in doggerel, which he recommended as edifying prayers for the especially pious. Bold and venturesome, he interwove with the first verses the words of a low Italian song, " Fair Margaret." And this blasphemous pamphlet (" Secret of the Trinity," " Raza di Yechuda ") was accepted and recommended by the rabbinate of Venice, either because they had not seen it before it was printed, or because by reason of Kabbalistic stupidity they did not perceive its drift. Chayon did not stay long at Venice. He betook himself to Prague, where he found credulous faith, favorable to his work of deception. The leaders of the community, old and young rabbis and students of the Talmud, were all filled with it.

David Oppenheim, chief rabbi of Prague, more famous for his rich collection of books than on account of his deeds and literary work, was an inveterate Kabbalist. To be sure he had no leisure to concern himself about the itinerant preacher Chayon, or the affairs of the community and the interest of Judaism. He needed his time for money transactions with the funds which, together with a considerable library, his rich uncle at Vienna, Samuel Oppenheim, had left him. David Oppenheim, therefore, seldom met Chayon ; but his son Joseph, who was enchanted with his Kabbalistic juggling, took him into his house. He was well received also by the Kabbalistic rabbi, Naphtali Cohen, who was then living at Prague, and whose thaumaturgy had cost him dear. And if the house of Oppenheim, and Naphtali Cohen paid him homage, who would fail to exert himself for the pretended preacher or emissary from Palestine, as Chayon professed to be? No wonder that industrious youthful students of the Talmud, thirsting for knowledge, thronged to Chayon! Among these was Jonathan Eibeschütz, afterwards so notorious, who was living at that time in Prague. Chayon preached sermons at Prague, and entranced his hearers by his sophistical and witty manner, which made the most inconsistent things appear reconcilable. Now and then he allowed the erroneous doctrine of the Salonica Sabbatians to crop out, viz., that sin can be overcome only by a superabundance of sinfulness, by the satisfaction of all, even the most wicked, desires, and by the transgression of the Torah. He told his Prague adherents, or caused it to be circulated by his Venetian companion, that he conversed with the prophet Elijah, that he could compel the Godhead to reveal itself to him, and that he was able to call the dead to life and to create new worlds—all of which found credence. He wrote amulets, which were eagerly sought after, and at the same time in secret led a profligate life. The money derived from imposture he wasted in card-playing. At last he ventured to submit his heretical work, his Sabbatian confession of faith in the Trinity, to Naphtali Cohen for his opinion, and showed him forged testimonials from Italian rabbis. From admiration for Chayon's person Naphtali Cohen, without even having glanced at the manuscript, expressed not simply his approval, but gave him a glowing recommendation—a careless habit characteristic of the rabbis of that time, which on this occasion was destined to revenge itself bitterly.

Provided with forged and filched recommendations, Chayon deceived many other communities, those of Vienna, Nikolsburg, Prosnitz, Breslau, Glogau, and Berlin. He succeeded in passing himself off as a prophet before the credulous German Jews, and in being maintained by them. Secretly he entered into close relations with a Sabbatian enthusiast or impostor, Löbele Prosnitz, who cut out the four Hebrew letters of the name of God in gold tinsel, stuck it on his breast, and made it shine before the dazzled eyes of the credulous by means of burning alcohol and turpentine. Like savages, the Moravian Jews gazed at Löbele Prosnitz's alcohol miracle. At Berlin, where Chayon spent several months, he enjoyed the best opportunity to fish in troubled waters. The community of Berlin, increased to more than a hundred families, had fallen into disunion, apparently through two mutually hostile families at court. The widow of the court jeweler, Liebmann, was a favorite of King Frederick I, and was therefore disliked by the crown prince, afterwards Frederick William I. The latter had his own Jew in attendance, Marcus Magnus, the mortal enemy of the house of Liebmann, not merely from complaisance to the successor to the throne. The feud between the two Jewish houses in Berlin spread to the whole community, divided it into two parties, and affected even the synagogue. When the fire of faction burned most furiously, Chayon came to Berlin, and turned the quarrel to his own advantage. He joined the Liebmann party, which, though the weaker of the two, was rich, and therefore more willing to make sacrifices. The rabbi of Berlin, Aaron Benjamin Wolf, son-in-law of the court Jewess Liebmann, a simple fellow, treated Chayon with honorable distinction. Naphtali Cohen, who had come to Berlin, could have unmasked Chayon, but was afraid, as he said, to inflame the quarrel still further. Thus Chayon without molestation was able in Berlin to print his heretical book, with which he had begun his mischievous proceedings five years before at Smyrna. He gave his work the artful title, "The Belief of the Universe" ("Mehemenuta de Cola"). The main text, the production of a Sabbatian (some thought of Sabbataï Zevi himself), proclaims the "holy king," the Messiah, the incarnate Deity, as the God of Israel, and as the exclusive object of reverence and worship. Chayon added two sophistical commentaries, wherein he proved in various ways that the God of Judaism was the Trinity. In the prayer, "Hear, O Israel, God is one," every Jew must needs think of this Trinity, otherwise he cannot attain to salvation, even if he fulfills all religious and moral duties. This belief alone can make a man certain of bliss. So low had Judaism sunk, that such blasphemy was printed before the eyes and with the consent of a rabbi—Aaron Benjamin Wolf, at Berlin—probably at the expense of the Liebmann party! Chayon had the audacity to order forged testimonials of rabbis to be prefixed, as though they had read the book and recommended it. With this work he hastened by way of Hamburg to Amsterdam, to make his fortune in that Jewish Eldorado, and thus schism was introduced into the Jewish world.

The community of Amsterdam had been sufficiently warned of the machinations of the Sabbatians. The Jerusalem rabbi, Abraham Yizchaki, who had been appointed an emissary to collect alms, behaved like a papal legate, invested with supremacy over everything religious, and like a grand inquisitor commissioned to destroy the heresy which had been gaining ground. At Smyrna the heretical writings of the fanatic Abraham Michael Cardoso were in the hands of a few secret Sabbatians. At Yizchaki's suggestion these had to be given up by their owners under threat of excommunication and severe temporal punishment, and they were burned. The community of Smyrna thereby felt itself freed from a heavy burden, and was thankful to its liberator. Yizchaki had also come to Amsterdam, and had warned the rabbis and the communal council against Sabbatian emissaries, and drew attention to the hint of the Smyrna rabbinate, that a secret Sabbatian was on his way to print Cardoso's writings. In fact a Sabbatian emissary did come to Amsterdam for that purpose. Chayon at first conducted himself modestly, and affiliated with the Portuguese. He presented the council with a copy of his work on the Trinity printed at Berlin, in order to obtain leave to sell it. He appears to have passed himself off as an emissary from Palestine. Hereupon bickerings arose, which began with personal feeling and ended in wide-spread dissension.

The rabbi of the German community, Zevi Ashkenazi, called Chacham Zevi, was much excited at the news of Chayon's presence in Amsterdam. This man, whose father had belonged to the most zealous Sabbatians, while he himself and his son, Jacob Emden, were destined to fight against them with vehement zeal, was gifted with a clear head, and combined thoroughness with acuteness in the study of the Talmud. In his eighteenth year he had been consulted as an expert in the Talmud. Pampered, sought after, married while young to the daughter of a rich man at Buda and thereby rendered independent, he became proud, self-conscious, and vain of his knowledge of the Talmud. On account of his Talmudical learning he was invited to be chief rabbi of the German community at Amsterdam (1710); he preferred to be called Chacham. Here he looked down with great contempt upon his Portuguese colleagues, especially upon Solomon Ayllon, and would never regard him as his equal in rank. "Chacham Zevi wishes to rank higher even than the prophet Moses," was the judgment passed upon him by Ayllon.

As soon as the name of Chayon reached the ears of the German Chacham, he connected it with a former enemy of his at Bosna-Seraï in Bosnia, where Zevi had been rabbi for a short time, and he immediately intimated to the Portuguese authorities that it would be wise to show no sort of favor to the stranger, as he was a man of evil notoriety. Nehemiah Chayon explained that the mistake in his identity was caused by similarity of names, and behaved so very humbly towards Chacham Zevi, that the latter soon informed the council that he had nothing to urge against the stranger, whose identity he had mistaken.   Chayon appeared to have removed every obstacle from his path at Amsterdam, when Moses Chages, of Jerusalem, who was in Holland, sounded the alarm against him, perhaps because he feared him as a Palestinian rival.   The heretical work printed at Berlin was put before him for examination, as some members of the council did not trust their Chacham Ayllon.   Scarcely had he looked into it, when he raised the cry of heresy.   In fact, it did not need lengthy search in the book to find an explicit enunciation of the doctrine of the Trinity. The German Chacham, having had his attention drawn by Moses Chages to Chayon's suspicious doctrine, again notified, almost ordered, the Portuguese council, to banish instead of favoring the stranger.   The council, not disposed to accept such abrupt orders, requested Chacham Zevi either to point out the heretical passages in Chayon's book, or to join with some members nominated by the council as a committee to examine it.   Chacham Zevi, at the advice of Chages, rejected both proposals flatly, saying that as rabbi he was not obliged to bring forward proofs, but simply to pronounce final judgment.   Still less did he choose to take council with Ayllon, as this would have been tantamount to recognizing him as a Talmudist of equal rank with himself.   The haughty behavior of the Chacham, on the one hand, and Ayllon's sensitiveness, on the other, kindled a spark into a bright flame.

The Portuguese Chacham had reason to feel himself slighted and to complain.   His own congregation had passed him over in this matter, shown distrust towards him, and set his opponent over him

as a higher authority.　Besides, he appears to have
feared the cunning adventurer, who if persecuted
might reveal more than was desirable of Ayllon's
past history and relations to the Salonica heretics.
He felt it his interest to remain on Chayon's side
and protect him against the threatened banishment
from Amsterdam.　It was not difficult for him to
prejudice a member of the Portuguese council,
Aaron de Pinto, a resolute, unbending, hard man,
indifferent to spiritual problems, against the German
Chacham, and persuade him of his duty to guard
the independence of the old, respectable, and superi-
or Portuguese, against the presumptuousness of the
hitherto subordinate German, community.　Ayllon
converted the important question of orthodoxy and
heresy into one of precedence between the communities.　De Pinto treated the affair in this light,
and the other members of the council conformed to
his resolute will.　He straightway rejected the interference of the German Chacham in an affair of
concern only to the Portuguese community, broke
off all negotiations with him, and commissioned
Ayllon to appoint a committee of Portuguese to examine and report on Chayon's work.　Ayllon added
to the college of rabbis four men, of whom only one
understood the question.　This one hesitated to
join the committee, but was compelled to do so.
The others were totally ignorant of theology, and
accordingly dependent on Ayllon's judgment.
Ayllon and the council, that is, Pinto, made the
members of the committee swear to let no one see
the copies of Chayon's work handed to them for
examination, in fact, to keep everything secret until
the final judgment was pronounced.　The petty
question of tolerating or expelling a begging adventurer thus attained great importance.

Whilst the Portuguese committee was still apparently engaged in the business of examination, Chacham Zevi, in conjunction with Moses Chages,

hastened to pronounce sentence of excommunication against Chayon and his heretical book, because "he sought to draw Israel away from his God and to introduce strange gods (the Trinity)." No one was to have dealings with the author until he recanted his error. His writings in any case were to be committed to the flames. This sentence of condemnation was printed in Hebrew and Portuguese, and circulated as a pamphlet. A great portion of the objections raised by these two zealots against Chayon's writings was equally applicable to the Zohar and other Kabbalistic books. Short-sighted as they were, they saw only the evil consequences of the Kabbalistic errors, not their original cause.

Great was the excitement of the Jews of Amsterdam over this step. Chacham Zevi and Moses Chages were affronted and abused in the streets by Portuguese Jews, and it was asserted that Ayllon employed disreputable people for this purpose. When Chages appeared the rabble shouted, "Stone him, slay him." Attempts at reconciliation failed; partly through the dogmatism of Ayllon, who refused to admit himself wrong, partly through the firmness of De Pinto, who simply had in view the dignity of the Portuguese community. Pamphlets increased the bitter feeling.

The quarrel of the Amsterdam Jews made a great stir elsewhere, and was the cause of party strife. Ayllon and De Pinto forbade the members of their community, under threat of excommunication, to read pamphlets, or to express themselves either verbally or in writing upon the matter. They also hastened the delivery of the verdict, which, however, was drawn up by Ayllon alone. It declared, in direct opposition to the decision of Chacham Zevi and Chages, that Chayon's work taught nothing offensive or dangerous to Judaism; it contained only the doctrines found in other Kabbalistic writings. It was officially made known in the synagogues (August

14, 1713) that Chayon was acquitted of the charge of heresy brought against him, and that he had been innocently persecuted. The day after, the original cause of the strife was carried in triumph into the Portuguese chief synagogue, and to the vexation of his opponents, almost worshiped. The false prophet, who had openly declared, "Come, let us worship false gods," was loaded with homage by the Portuguese who had staked life and property for the unity of God. They cheered Chayon in the synagogue, and cried "Down with his adversaries." In secret Chayon probably laughed at the complications he had caused, and at the credulity of the multitude. De Pinto took care that Chacham Zevi should not be supported by his own German community, but should be left exposed, without protection, to the rough treatment of his opponents. He found himself entirely isolated, almost like a person under interdict.

But help came to Chacham Zevi from without. The rabbis whose pretended letters of recommendation Chayon had prefixed to his work declared them to be forged. The deepest impression was made by the letters of the highly respected, aged rabbi of Mantua, Leon Brieli, who, well acquainted with the past history of the impostor, unmasked him, and approved of the sentence of condemnation against his heretical book. Brieli wrote urgently to the Amsterdam council, and to Ayllon, in Hebrew and Italian, imploring them not to lend their authority to so bad a cause. But they remained stubborn, answered him politely, yet evasively. The quarrel rose higher every day in the Amsterdam community; every one took one side or the other, defending his view with bitterness, passion, and frequently with vigorous action. Peace vanished from this pattern community, and dissension was carried into family life. Matters had gone so far that the leaders could not yield. Ayllon and De Pinto went to

greater lengths in their obstinacy. They suggested
that the Portuguese council summon Chacham Zevi,
the rabbi of the German community (over whom it
had no authority whatever), before its tribunal, with
the intention of shaming him or of inducing him to
recant. When he paid no heed, it laid him and
Moses Chages under the ban, most strictly forbidding the members of the community to have dealings
with them, protect them, or intercede for them with
the civic authorities.

As though the council and the rabbinate had been
infected by Chayon's baseness, they committed one
meanness after another. In justification of their
course of action they distorted the actual state of
the case, and made use of notorious falsehoods.
They encouraged, or at least countenanced, Chayon
in calumniating his opponents with the vilest and
most revolting aspersions, not only Chacham Zevi
and Chages, but even the wise and venerable rabbi,
Leon Brieli, and supported Chayon in all his audac-
ities. The Portuguese council and the rabbinate,
or rather De Pinto and Ayllon, for their colleagues
were mere puppets, persecuted Chayon's opponents
as though they were lost to all feeling of right.
With Moses Chages they had an easy game. He
lived on the Portuguese community; and when they
withdrew the means of sustenance, he was compelled to leave Amsterdam with his helpless family
and migrate to Altona. They also pressed Chacham
Zevi hard, annoyed him, accused him before the civil
authorities, and prevented any one's assisting him.
He, too, left Amsterdam, either De Pinto procuring
his banishment at the hands of the magistrates, or
Chacham Zevi, in order to anticipate scandalous
expulsion, going into banishment of his own accord.
He repaired to London, in the first instance, then
by way of Breslau to Poland, and was everywhere
honorably received and treated.

His opponents, Chayon, Ayllon, and De Pinto, were

not able to enjoy the fruits of their victory. The apparently trivial dispute had assumed large dimensions. Almost all the German, Italian, Polish, and even some African communities with their rabbis espoused the cause of the persecuted Chacham Zevi, and hurled sentences of excommunication upon the unscrupulous heretic. These anathemas were published, and unsparingly revealed Chayon's villainy, bringing to light the sentence passed upon him years before at Jerusalem. The exposure of his character by witnesses who came from countries where his past history was well known, contributed to ruin the false prophet of the new Trinity.

But the Portuguese of Amsterdam, or at least their leaders, would not drop him, either because they believed his audacious lies or from a sense of shame and obstinacy. They saw clearly, however, that Chayon must take steps to calm the storm raised against him. They therefore favored his journey to the East, providing him with money and recommendations to influential Jews and Christians, who were to aid him in loosing the ban passed upon him in the Turkish capital. But the journey proved full of thorns for Chayon; no Jew admitted him into his house, or gave him entertainment. Like Cain, curse-laden, he was obliged to flee from place to place in Europe. At last he had to take ship in haste to Constantinople. He was followed by fresh accusations of heresy, not only from Chages and Naphtali Cohen, but also from the highly esteemed Kabbalist Joseph Ergas, and the London preacher David Nieto, who calmly exposed, in Hebrew and Spanish, the heresy, falsehood, and villainy of this hypocritical Sabbatian.

At Constantinople Chayon was avoided by the Jews, and treated as an outcast; but his Amsterdam letters of recommendation paved the way for him with a vizir, who ordered his Jewish agents to accord him support. In spite of his artifices, however, the

rabbinate of Constantinople refused to remove the
sentence against him, but referred him to the college
of Jerusalem, the first to proscribe him.   Several
years elapsed before three rabbis, probably intimidated by the vizir, declared themselves ready to
free Chayon from the ban, but they added the condition that he should never again teach, preach, or
publish Kabbalistic doctrines.   Chayon bound himself by a solemn oath, given to be broken at the
first opportunity.   With a letter, which testified to
his re-admission into the Jewish communion, he
hastened to Europe for fresh adventures and impostures.

Meanwhile the Sabbatian intoxication had spread
in Poland, especially in Podolia and the district of
Lemberg.   There are revolting evidences extant
of the immorality of the Podolian Sabbatians : how
they wallowed in a pool of shameless profligacy, all
the while pretending to redeem the world.   Their
violation and contempt of Tadmudical Judaism were
for a long time kept secret, but they strove to win
adherents, preaching, and explaining the Zohar to
support their immoral theories.   As their sect grew,
they raised the mask of piety a little, came out more
boldly, and were solemnly excommunicated by the
Lemberg rabbinate with extinguished tapers in the
synagogue.   But this sect could not be suppressed
by such means.   Its members were inspired with a
fanatical desire to scorn the Talmud, the breath of
life of the Polish Jews, and to set up in its place the
Kabbala and its Bible, the Zohar, and this plan they
endeavored to put into execution.

Their leaders secretly sent (1725) an emissary in
the person of Moses Meïr Kamenker into Moravia,
Bohemia, and Germany, to establish a connection
with the Sabbatians of these countries, and perhaps
also to beg for money for their undertaking.   Kamenker traveled through several communities without
being found out.   Who could divine the thoughts

of this begging Polish rabbi, who understood how
to dispute in the manner of the Talmud, and rolled
his eyes in a pious, hypocritical manner? Moses
Meïr entered into relations with Jonathan Eibeschütz
at Prague, who though young was regarded as a
most thorough and acute Talmudist, but who was
entangled in the snares of the Sabbatian Kabbala.
Moses Meïr pressed on unrecognized to Mannheim,
where a secret Sabbatian of Judah Chassid's following
passed himself off among his companions as the
Messiah returned to earth. From Mannheim these
two Polish Sabbatians threw out their nets, and
deluded the simple with sounding phrases from the
Zohar. Their main doctrine was that Jews devoted
to the Talmud had not the right faith, which was
rooted only in the Kabbala. At the same time a
work, apparently Kabbalistic, was disseminated
from Prague. Its equal can scarcely be found for
absurdity, perversity, and blasphemy; the coarsest
notions being brought into connection with the
Godhead in Talmudic and Zoharistic forms of expression. It also develops the doctrine of persons
in the Godhead—the Primeval One and the God
of Israel, and hints that from a higher standpoint
the Torah and the laws have no significance. It
was reported at the time that Jonathan Eibeschütz
was the author of this production, as revolting as it
is absurd.

Chance brought these underhand proceedings to
light. Moses Meïr was enticed to Frankfort by
promises, and in the house of Rabbi Jacob Kahana
his conduct was exposed. Many heretical writings
were found upon him as well as letters by Sabbatians, amongst them letters from and to Eibeschütz.
An examination of witnesses was held by three rabbis
(July, 1725). Several witnesses denounced Moses
Meïr, Isaiah Chassid, and Löbele Prosnitz as closely
allied fanatical Sabbatians, Eibeschütz also being
connected with them. These three, indeed, regarded

him as Sabbataï's successor, as the genuine Messiah. The witnesses averred that they had received Kabbalistic heretical writings about the Song of Solomon, and others, from Moses Meïr. They pretended also to have heard many blasphemies that could not be repeated. Because of the writings found upon Moses Meïr Kamenker and the testimony of witnesses, the rabbinate of Frankfort pronounced upon him, his companions, and all Sabbatians, the severest possible sentence, decreeing that no one should have dealings with them in any form whatever, and that every Jew should be bound to inform the rabbis of the secret Sabbatians, and reveal their misconduct without respect of persons. The rabbis of the German communities of Altona-Hamburg and Amsterdam joined in this sentence; they ordered it to be read in the synagogues for the information of all, and had it printed. The same was done at Frankfort-on-the-Oder at fair-time in the presence of many Jews from other towns, and several Polish rabbis did the same. They at last realized that only by united forces and continuous efforts could an end be put to the follies of the Sabbatians.

Just at this time Chayon returned to Europe, and increased the confusion. To protect himself from persecution, he secretly approached Christians, obtained access to the imperial palace at Vienna, partly severed his connection with the Jews, reviled them as blind men who reject the true faith, let it be understood that he, too, taught the doctrine of the Trinity, and that he could bring over the Jews. Provided with a letter of protection from the court, he proceeded on his journey, and again played a double game, living secretly as a Sabbatian, openly as an orthodox Jew released from the interdict. It is hardly credible, as contemporaries relate of Chayon, that at the age of nearly eighty, he took about with him as his wife a notorious prostitute, whom he had picked up in Hungary. He did not meet with so good a reception this time; distrust had been excited against secret Sabbatians, especially against him. At Prague he was not admitted into the city. At Berlin, Chayon wrote to a former acquaintance that, if the money he needed were not sent him, he was resolved to be baptized to the disgrace of the Jews. At Hanover, his papers were taken from him, which exposed him still more. Thus the rogue dragged himself to Amsterdam in the hope of again finding enthusiastic friends. But Ayllon would have nothing more to do with him; he is said to have repented having favored Chayon. The latter was included in the proscription of the Sabbatians and excommunicated (1726). Moses Chages, formerly persecuted by him, now occupied an honored position in Altona. He was considered the chief of the heresy judges, so to say, and he dealt Chayon the last blow. The latter could not hold his own in Europe or in the East, and therefore repaired to northern Africa, where he died. His son was converted to Christianity, and, whilst at Rome, through his false, or half-true accusations, he drew the attention of the Inquisition to ancient Jewish literature, which he declared to be inimical to Christianity.

CHAPTER VII.

THE AGE OF LUZZATTO, EIBESCHÜTZ, AND FRANK.

Poetical Works of Moses Chayim Luzzatto—Luzzatto ensnared in the Kabbala—His Contest with Rabbinical Authorities—Luzzatto's last Drama—Jonathan Eibeschütz—Character and Education of Eibeschütz—His Relations with the Jesuits in Prague—The Austrian War of Succession—Expulsion of the Jews from Prague—Eibeschütz becomes Rabbi of Altona—Jacob Emden—Eibeschütz charged with Heresy—The Controversy between Emden and Eibeschütz—The Amulets—Party Strife—Interference by Christians and the Civil Authorities—Revival of Sabbatianism—Jacob Frank Lejbowicz and the Frankists—The Doctrine of the Trinity—Excesses of the Frankists.

1727–1760 C. E.

THE disgrace and disappointment caused by visionaries and impostors during almost a whole century, the lamentable effects of the careers of Sabbataï Zevi and his band of prophets—Cardoso, Mordecai of Eisenstadt, Querido, Judah Chassid, Chayim Malach, Chayon, and others—failed to suppress Kabbalistic and Messianic extravagances. As yet these impostors only invited fresh imitators, who found a credulous circle ready to believe in them, and thus new disorders were begotten. The unhealthy humors which, during the lapse of ages, had been introduced into the organism of Judaism appeared as hideous eruptions on the surface, but this might be considered the sign of convalescence. Corruption had seized even the most delicate organs. A gifted youth, endowed with splendid talents, who in ordinary circumstances would have become an ornament to Judaism, was tainted by the general degradation, and under the spell of mysticism misapplied his excellent gifts, and contributed to error. It is impossible to resist a feeling of sorrow at finding this amiable man with his ideal character falling into

errors which bring him down to the level of such
impure spirits as Chayon and Löbele Prosnitz—a
many-colored sunbeam extinguished in a swamp. If
we denounce the Kabbala, which has begotten such
unspeakable misconceptions of Judaism, and are
justly wrathful against its authors and propagators,
we feel specially indignant when we find two noble
young men of high endowments and purity of life,
Solomon Molcho and Luzzatto, following its chimeras, and thereby precipitating themselves into the
abyss. Both literally sacrificed their lives for dreams,
the confused imagery of which was suggested by the
dazing medley of the Kabbala. Although Luzzatto
did not meet with a tragic end like the Portuguese
Marrano who shared his convictions, yet he, too,
was a martyr, none the less because his wounds had
been inflicted by himself under the influence of excitement.

Moses Chayim Luzzatto (born 1707, died 1747)
was the son of very wealthy parents, natives of
Padua. His father, who carried on an extensive silk
business, spared no expense in educating him. The
two ancient languages, Hebrew and Latin, which in
Italy were in a measure a literary necessity, the one
among Jews, the other among Christians, Luzzatto
acquired in early youth; but they had an influence
on his mind altogether different from that which
they obtained over his contemporaries. Both enriched his genius, and promoted its higher development. Latin opened for him the realm of the beautiful, Hebrew the gates of the sublime. Luzzatto had
a poet's delicately-strung soul, an Æolian harp,
which responded to every breath with harmonious,
tuneful vibrations. His poetic gift displayed at once
power and sweetness, wealth of fancy and richness
of imagery, combined with due sense of proportion.
A believer in the transmigration of souls might have
said that the soul of the Hebrew-Castilian singer,
Jehuda Halevi, had been born again in Luzzatto, but

had become more perfect, more matured, more tender, and endowed with a more delicate sense of harmony, encompassed as he was by the musical atmosphere of his Italian fatherland.   Even in early boyhood every event, joyful or sad, was to him a complete picture, a little work of art, wherein color and euphony were revealed together.   A youth of seventeen, he discerned with such remarkable clearness the hidden charm of language, the laws of harmony, deducible from the higher forms of eloquence as from poetry, and the grace of rhythm and cadence, that he composed a work on the subject, and illustrated it by beautiful examples from sacred poetry. He contemplated introducing a new meter into modern Hebrew poetry, in order to obtain greater variety in the succession of long and short syllables, and thus produce a musical cadence.   The Hebrew language is usually classified among the dead tongues.   To Luzzatto, however, it was full of life, vigor, youth, clearness, and euphony.   He used Hebrew as a pliant instrument, and drew from it sweet notes and caressing melodies ; he renewed its youth, invested it with a peculiar charm, in short, lived in it as though his ear had absorbed the rich tones of Isaiah's eloquence.   Incomparably more gifted than Joseph Penso de la Vega, Luzzatto, likewise in his seventeenth year, composed a drama on the biblical theme of Samson and the Philistines. This early work gives promise of the future master. The versification is faultless, the thoughts original, and the language free from bombast and redundancy.   His Hebrew prose, too, is an agreeable contrast to the insipid, ornate, and laboriously witty style of his Jewish contemporaries ; it has much of the simplicity, polish, and vivacity of the biblical narrative.   Before his twentieth year Luzzatto had composed one hundred and fifty hymns, which are only an imitation of the old psalter, but the language of which is marked by fervor and purity.   It was perhaps during the same period that he composed his second Hebrew drama, in four acts—" The High Tower, or The Innocence of the Virtuous"—beautiful in versification, melodious in language, but poor in thought. The young poet had not yet seen life in its fullness, nor keenly studied its contrasts and struggles. He was acquainted only with idyllic family life and academic peace. Even virtue and vice, love and selfishness, which he desired to represent in his drama, were known to him but by hearsay. His muse becomes eloquent only when she sings of God's sublimity. Isolated verses are faultless, but the work as a whole is that of a schoolboy. He was too dependent on Italian models—still walked on stilts.

This facility and versatility in clothing both platitudes and original thoughts in new as well as borrowed forms, and the over-abundance of half-matured ideas, which, if he could have perfected them, might have proved a blessing to Judaism and to himself, were transformed into a curse. One day (Sivan, 1727) he was seized with the desire to imitate the mystic language of the Zohar, and he succeeded as well as in the case of the psalms. His sentences and expressions were deceptively similar to those of his model, just as high-sounding, apparently full of meaning, in reality meaningless. This success turned his head, and led him astray. Instead of perceiving that if the Kabbalistic style of the Zohar is capable of imitation, that book must be the work of a clever human author, Luzzatto inferred that his own creative faculty did not proceed from natural endowments, but, as in the case of the Zohar, was the product of a higher inspiration. In other words, he shared the mistaken view of his age with respect to the origin and value of the Kabbala. Isaiah Bassan, of Padua—who instructed Luzzatto in his early years—had infused mystical poison into his healthy blood. However, any other teacher

would also have led him into the errors of the Kabbala, from which there was no escape.   The air cf
the Ghettos was impregnated with Kabbala.   From
his youth upwards Luzzatto heard daily that great
adepts in mysticism possessed special tutelar spirits
(Maggid), who every day gave them manifestations
from above.   Why should not he, too, be vouchsafed
this divine gift of grace?   Some of the mystical
writings of Lurya, at that time still a rarity, fell into
his hands.   He learnt them by heart, became entirely absorbed in them, and thus completed his de-
rangement.   Luzzatto was possessed by a peculiar
delusion.   His naturally clear and methodical intellect, his fine sense of the simplicity and beauty of
the poetry of the Bible, and his æsthetic conceptions
with regard to Italian and Latin literature urged
him to seek clearness and common sense even in
the chaos of the Kabbala, the divine origin of which
was accepted by him as a fact.   He in no way resembled the wild visionaries Moses Zacut and Mordecai of Eisenstadt ; he did not content himself with
empty formulas and flourishes, but sought for sound
sense.   This he found rather in his own mind than
in the Zohar or in the writings of Lurya.   Nevertheless, he lived under the delusion that a divine
spirit had vouchsafed him deep insight into the Kabbala, solved its riddles, and disentangled its meshes.
Self-deception was the cause of his errors, and religious fervor, instead of protecting, only plunged
him in more deeply.   His errors were fostered by
the conviction that existing Judaism with its excrescences would be unintelligible without the Kabbala,
the theories of which could alone explain the phenomena, the strife, and the contradictions in the
world, and the tragical history of the Jewish people.
Israel—God's people—the noblest portion of creation, stands enfeebled and abased on the lowest
rung of the ladder of nations ; its religion misjudged, its struggles fruitless.   To account for this

bewildering fact, Luzzatto constructed a system of cobwebs.

It flattered the vanity of this young man of twenty to gain this insight into the relations of the upper and the lower worlds, to explain them in the mystical language of the Zohar, and thus become an important member in the series of created beings. Having firmly convinced himself of the truth of the fundamental idea of the Kabbala, he accepted all its excrescences—transmigration of souls, anagrams, and necromancy. He wrote reams of Kabbalistic chimeras, and composed a second Zohar (Zohar Tinyana) with appropriate introductions (Tikkunim) and appendices. The more facility he acquired, the stronger became his delusion that he, too, was inspired by a great spirit, and was a second, perhaps more perfect Simon bar Yochaï. Little by little there crept over him in his solitude the fantastic conviction that he was the pre-ordained Messiah, called to redeem, by means of the second Zohar, the souls of Israel and the whole world.

Luzzatto could not long bear to hide his light under a bushel. He began operations by disclosing to Israel Marini and Israel Treves, two young men of the same way of thinking as himself, that his guardian spirit had bidden him grant them knowledge of his new Zohar. His disciples in the Kabbala were dazzled and delighted, and could not keep the secret. The result was that Venetian Kabbalists sought out the young and wealthy prodigy at his home in Padua, and thus confirmed him in his fanaticism. A vivacious, energetic, impetuous Pole, Yekutiel (Kussiel) of Wilna, who had come to Padua to study medicine, joined Luzzatto's circle. To hear of the latter, join him, abandon his former studies, and devote himself to mysticism was for the Pole a rapid, easy resolution. It was far harder for him to keep the secret. No sooner had he been initiated by Luzzatto than he blazoned forth this new miracle

to the world.   Kussiel circulated extravagant letters
on the subject, which came into the hands of Moses
Chages in Altona.   The latter, who had stoutly opposed and effectually silenced Chayon and the other
Sabbatian visionaries, was, so to speak, the recognized official zealot, whose utterances were decisive
on matters of faith ; and the rabbi of the so-called
"three communities" of Altona, Hamburg, and
Wandsbeck, Ezekiel Katzenellenbogen, who had
excommunicated Moses Meïr Kamenker and his
confederates, was subservient to him.   Chages
therefore requested the Venetian community to
suppress the newly-born brood of heretics before
the poison of their doctrine could spread further.

The Venetian community, however, was not disposed to denounce Luzzatto as a heretic, but treated
him with great forbearance, probably out of consideration for his youth, talents, and the wealth of his
family, and merely ordered him to justify himself.
The enthusiastic youth rebelled against this demand,
proudly gave Chages to understand that he did not
recognize his authority, repudiated the suspicion
of Sabbatian heresy, and insisted that he had been
vouchsafed revelations from Heaven.   He referred
him to his instructor Bassan, who would never refuse
to testify that his orthodoxy was above suspicion.
In this Luzzatto was perfectly right.   Bassan was
so infatuated with his pupil that he would have
palliated his most scandalous faults, and encouraged
rather than checked his extravagances.   In vain
Chages and Katzenellenbogen threatened him and
the Paduan community with the severest form of
excommunication, if he did not abandon his pretensions to second sight and mystical powers.   Luzzatto remained unmoved : God had chosen him, like
many before, to reveal to him His mysteries.   The
other Italian rabbis showed themselves as lukewarm
in the matter as those of Padua and Venice.   Moses
Chages called on three rabbis to form a tribunal,

but all three declined to interfere.   He exerted himself so zealously, however, that he persuaded several German rabbis (June, 1730) to excommunicate all who should compose works in the language of the Zohar in the name of angels or saints.   This threat proved effectual.   Isaiah Bassan was obliged to repair to Padua and obtain a promise from his favorite disciple to discontinue his mystical writings and his instruction of young Kabbalists, or emigrate to the Holy Land.   At last the Venetian rabbinate was stirred up to intervene, and sent three representatives to Padua—Jacob Belillos, Moses Menachem Merari, and Nehemiah Vital Cohen,—in whose presence Luzzatto was obliged to repeat his promise under oath.   He was compelled to deliver his Kabbalistic writings to his teacher Bassan, and they were placed under seal.   Thus the storm which had threatened him was averted.

Luzzatto appears to have been sobered by these events.   He occupied himself with his business, wrote more poetry, and resolved to marry.   He was a happy father, lived in concord with his parents and brothers and sisters, and was highly respected. The evil spirit, however, to whom he had sold himself would not release him, and led him back to his youthful follies.   A quarrel in the family and business misfortunes in connection with his father's house, in which he was a partner, appear to have been the cause of this renewal of his former studies.   Disquieted and troubled in the present he sought to learn the future by means of Kabbalistic arts.   He began once more to write down his mystical fancies, and ventured to show them to Bassan, from whom he obtained permission to publish them.   It was whispered that Luzzatto performed incantations by means of magic, and that his teacher had handed him for publication some of the sealed writings in his custody.   The Venetian council of rabbis, owing to certain reports, was especially excited and pre-

judiced against him. Luzzatto had written a sharp
reply to Leon Modena's forcible work against the
Kabbala ; and as the latter was a Venetian rabbi,
though of doubtful sincerity, the members of the
Venetian council, Samuel Aboab and his five colleagues, considered any attack upon him an insult to
their own honor. Their *esprit de corps* roused them
to greater activity than had zeal for their faith, when
seemingly in peril. True Venetians, they had in
their service a spy, Salman of Lemberg, who watched
and reported Luzzatto's movements to them. As
long as he was prosperous and surrounded by friends
the Venetian rabbis had treated him with remarkable indulgence, and bestowed on him a title of
honor ; but after his family fell into misfortune,
when he was on the verge of ruin, and deserted by
his friends and flatterers, their regard for him ceased,
and they could not find enough stones to throw at
him. They believed one of their number who
asserted that he had found implements of magic in
Luzzatto's house. Absurdly enough, too, they reproached Luzzatto with having learnt Latin ; to a
man who had studied this language of Satan no
angel, they said, could appear ! The members of
the Venetian council of rabbis believed, or pretended to believe that Luzzatto had boasted that
in the Messianic age his psalms would take the
place of David's psalter. They now showed themselves as active as they had previously been negli-
gent in the persecution of the unfortunate author.
They sent three inquisitors to Padua to examine
him, search his house for writings, and make him
declare on oath that he would publish nothing without first submitting it to the censorship of the Venetian council of rabbis. The poet, deeply mortified,
haughtily answered that this council had no authority whatever over him, a member of the community
of Padua. The Venetian rabbis then excommunicated him, and condemned his writings to the flames

(December, 1734), taking care to give notice of their proceedings to all the communities in Germany, particularly to the "big drum," Chages. The Paduan community also abandoned the unfortunate Luzzatto. To the honor of his teacher Isaiah Bassan be it said, that he adhered to him as staunchly in misfortune as in prosperity. The rabbi Katzenellenbogen, or rather his crier Chages, on this occasion made the sensible suggestion that the study of the Kabbala be altogether forbidden to young men, to prevent their falling into deplorable errors, as had hitherto been the case; but the proposition failed to meet with the approbation of other rabbis. Twenty years later the evils produced by the Kabbala became so patent, that the synod of Polish Jews enacted a decree to the above effect without encountering opposition.

The unfortunate, excommunicated dreamer was obliged to leave his parents, his wife and child, and go forth a wanderer; but what grieved him even more was separation from his fellow Kabbalists and his mystic conventicle. He cherished the hope of being able to print his Kabbalistic writings in Amsterdam. Alas for his want of experience! Who would help him after fortune had turned her back! At Frankfort-on-the-Main he was rudely awakened from his pleasant dream. As soon as the rabbi, Jacob Kahana, heard of his arrival, he insisted that he should promise on oath to abandon his Kabbalistic illusions, and to refrain from writing on or instructing any one in the doctrines of the Zohar (January 12, 1735). One liberty, however, Luzzatto reserved for himself: to pursue his favorite studies at the age of forty in the Holy Land. Many rabbis of Germany, Poland, Holland, and Denmark, who were informed of Luzzatto's concessions, agreed in advance to his excommunication in case he should break his word. The name of Chages was of course upon the list.

Deeply humiliated and disappointed, Luzzatto repaired to Amsterdam. Here a gleam of sunlight smiled on him again. The Portuguese community received him kindly, as though desirous of atoning for the injustice he had experienced at the hands of the Germans and Poles. They granted him a pension; and he found a hospitable home in the house of Moses de Chaves, a wealthy Portuguese, and became instructor to his son. To be independent, he applied himself, like Spinoza, to the polishing of lenses, and this led him to study physics and mathematics. He found himself so comfortably settled that he induced not only his wife, but also his parents to come to Amsterdam, and they were well received by the Portuguese community. This favorable turn in his fortunes encouraged him to resume his chimerical theories. He repeatedly exhorted his disciples in Padua to remain true to their Kabbalistic studies; whereupon the council of rabbis at Venice, which had received intelligence of his proceedings, pronounced sentence of excommunication in the synagogues and in the Ghetto against all who possessed Kabbalistic writings or psalms of Luzzatto, and failed to deliver them to the council.

In addition to his various occupations, with the Kabbala for his spiritual wants and the polishing of lenses for his temporal needs, Luzzatto published a masterpiece second to none in Hebrew poetry; a drama, perfect in form, language, and thought; a memorial of his gifts calculated to immortalize him and the language in which it is composed. Under the unpretentious form of an occasional poem in honor of the wedding of his disciple, Jacob de Chaves, with the high-born maiden Rachel de Vega Enriques, he published his drama, "Glory to the Virtuous" (La-Yesharim Tehilla). It differs materially from his earlier works. The poet had in the interval enjoyed various opportunities of gaining pleasant and painful experiences, and of enriching his mental powers. His muse, grown more mature, had become acquainted with the intricacies of life. Luzzatto had learnt to know the vulgar herd well enough to see that it resembles a reed swaying to and fro in the water, and is kept by the fetters of Deceit in a state of ignorance and infirmity against which Wisdom herself is powerless. He had been taught by experience how Folly yoked with Ignorance makes merry over those born of the Spirit, and mocks at their labors, when they measure the paths of the stars, observe the life of the vegetable world, behold God's works, and account them of more value than Mammon. Superficiality sees in all the events of life and of nature, however powerfully they may appeal to the heart, only the sport of Chance or the inflexible laws of heartless Necessity. Luzzatto had proved in his own case that Craft and Pride closely united can deprive Merit of its crown, and place it on their own heads. None the less he cherished the conviction that Merit, though misjudged and calumniated, at last wins the day, and that its acknowledgment (Fame) will fall to its share like a bride, if only it allows itself to be led by Reason and her handmaid Patience, averting its gaze from ignoble strife, and becoming absorbed in the wonders of Creation. "Could we, with undimmed eyes, for a moment see the world as it is, divested of pretense, we should see Pride and Folly, which speak so scornfully of Virtue and Knowledge, deeply humbled." Through an extraordinary occurrence, a kind of miracle, Truth is revealed, Deceit unmasked, Pride becomes a laughing-stock, and the fickle mob is led to recognize true Merit.

Luzzatto in his dramatic parable clothes and vivifies this train of ideas, and enunciates them in monologues and dialogues through the mouth of acting, or, more correctly, speaking characters. Luzzatto's masterpiece is indeed not a drama in the strict sense of the word. The characters represented are not of flesh and blood, but mere abstractions : Reason and Folly, Merit and Deceit, are placed on the stage. The dramatic action is slight. It is in truth a beautiful wreath of fragrant flowers of poesy, a series of delightful monologues and dialogues. In it Luzzatto embodies deep thoughts, difficult to quicken into life or to paint in poetical colors ; but he succeeded. The wonderful evolution of the vegetable world, the extraordinary phenomena of light, are treated in dramatic verse by Luzzatto with the same facility as the appropriate subjects for poetry, and this too in the Hebrew language, not readily lending itself to new forms of thought, and with the self-imposed fetters of a meter never sinned against. His style is dignified, and he employed a diction quite his own, replete with youthful charms, beauty, and harmony. Thereby he supplied a new impulse for the coming age. When the mists of error passed away, the general chaos of thought was reduced to some sort of order, and a happier period opened, young poets derived inspiration from the soft warm rays diffused by the genius of Luzzatto. A modern Hebrew poet who helped to accomplish the transition from the old to the new period, David Franco Mendes, owes his inspiration to Luzzatto.

What might not Luzzatto have accomplished if he could have liberated his mind from the extravagant follies of the Kabbala ! But it held him captive, and drew him not long after the completion of his drama (about 1744) to Palestine. Here he hoped to be able to follow unmolested the inspirations of his excited fancy, or play the *rôle* of a Messiah. From Safet, too, he continued his communications with his band of disciples ; but before he could commence operations he fell a victim to the plague, in the fortieth year of his age. His body was buried in Tiberias. The two greatest modern Hebrew poets,

Luzzatto and Jehuda Halevi, were to rest in Hebrew soil. Even the tongues of the slanderous Jews of Palestine, to whom Luzzatto, with his peculiarities, must have seemed an enigma, could only speak well of him after his death. Nevertheless he sowed bad seed. His Italian followers reintroduced the Kabbala into Italy. His Polish disciple, Yekutiel of Wilna, whose buffooneries had first got him into trouble, is said to have led an adventurer's life in Poland and Holland, playing scandalous tricks under the mask of mysticism. Another Pole, Elijah Olianow, who belonged to Luzzatto's following, and proclaimed him as Messiah and himself as his Elijah, did not enjoy the best of reputations. This man took part in the disgraceful disorders which broke out in Altona after Luzzatto's death, and which, again stirring up the Sabbatian mire, divided the Jews of Europe into two hostile camps.

The foul pool which for centuries, since the prohibition of free inquiry and the triumph of its enemy the Kabbala, had been in process of formation in Judaism was, with perverse stupidity, being continually stirred up, defiling the pure and the impure. The irrational excitement roused by the vain, false Messiah of Smyrna was not suppressed by the proscription of Chayon and the Polish Sabbatians, but showed a still more ill-favored aspect, forcing its way into circles hitherto closed against it. The rabbis, occupied with the practical and dialectical interpretation of the Talmud, had hitherto refused admission to the Kabbala on equal terms, and only here and there had surreptitiously introduced something from it. They had opposed the Sabbatian heresy, and pronounced an anathema against it. But one influential rabbi espoused its cause, invested it with importance, and so precipitated a conflict which undermined discipline and order, and blunted still more the sense of dignity and self-respect, of truth and rectitude. The occasion of the conflict was the petty jealousy of two rabbis. Its true origin lay deeper, in intellectual perversity and the secret dislike on the one hand to the excess of ritualistic observances, and on the other to the extravagances of the Kabbala. The authors of this far-reaching schism—two Polish rabbbis of Altona—each unconsciously had taken a step across the threshold of orthodoxy. Diametrically opposed to each other in faculties and temperament, they were suited by their characters to be pitted against each other. Both Jonathan Eibeschütz and Jacob Emden had taken part in the foregoing conflicts, and eventually gave these quarrels a more extended influence.

Jonathan Eibeschütz, or Eibeschützer (born at Cracow 1690, died 1764), was descended from a Polish family of Kabbalists. His father, Nathan Nata, was for a short time rabbi of the small Moravian town of Eibenschitz, from which his son derived his surname. Endowed with a remarkably acute intellect and a retentive memory, the youthful Jonathan, early left an orphan, received the irregular education, or rather bewildering instruction of the age, which supplied him with only two subjects on which to exercise his brains—the far-reaching sphere of the Talmud, with its labyrinthine mazes, and the ensnaring Kabbala, with its shallows full of hidden rocks. The one offered abundant food for his hungry reason, the other for his ill-regulated fancy. With his hair-splitting ingenuity he might have made an adroit, pettifogging attorney, qualified to make out a brilliant and successful justification for the worst case; or, had he had access to the higher mathematics of Newton and Leibnitz, he might have accomplished much in this field as a discoverer. Eibeschütz had some taste for branches of learning beyond the sphere of the Talmud, and also a certain vanity that made him desire to excel in them; but this he could not satisfy. The perverted spirit of the Polish and German Jews of the time closed to

every aspiring youth the gates of the sciences based
on truth and keen observation, and drove him into
the mazes of Rabbinical and Talmudic literature.
From lack of more wholesome food for his active
intellect, young Eibeschütz filled his brain with per-
nicious matter, and want of method forced him into
the crooked paths of sophistry. He imagined
indeed, or wished it to be supposed, that he had
acquired every variety of knowledge, but his writings
on subjects not connected with the Talmud, so far
as it is possible to judge of them, his sermons, his
Kabbalistic compositions, and a mass of occasional
papers, reveal nothing that can be described as
wisdom or solid learning. Eibeschütz was not even
familiar with the Jewish philosophers who wrote in
Hebrew; he was at home only in the Talmud. This
he could manipulate like soft clay, give it any form
he desired, and he could unravel the most intricately
entangled skeins. He surpassed all his contemporaries and predecessors not only in his knowledge
of the Talmud, but also in ready wit.

But Eibeschütz did not derive complete satisfaction from his scholarship; it only served to sharpen
his wits, afford him amusement, and dazzle others.
His restless nature and fiery temperament could
not content themselves with this, but aspired to a
higher goal. This goal, however, was unknown
even to himself, or was only dimly shadowed before
his mind. Hence his life and conduct appear enigmatical and full of contradictions. Had he lived in
the age of the struggle for reform, for the loosening
of the bands of authority, he would have been among
the assailants, and would have employed his Talmudical learning and aggressive wit as levers to
upheave the edifice of Rabbinical Judaism, and oppose the Talmud with the weapons it had supplied.
For he was easy-going, and disliked the gloomy
piety of the German and Polish Jews; and though
impressed by it, he lacked fervor to yield to its in-

fluence. He therefore found mysticism as interpreted by the followers of Sabbataï very comforting :
the Law was to be abolished by the commencement
of the Messianic era, or the spirit of the Kabbala
demanded no over-scrupulousness with regard to
trifles. Nehemiah Chayon appears to have made a
great impression on young Eibeschütz in Prague or
Hamburg. With the Sabbatian Löbele Prosnitz,
he was in constant, though secret intercourse. He
studied thoroughly the works of Abraham Michael
Cardoso, though they had been publicly condemned
and branded as heretical. Eibeschütz had adopted
the blasphemous tenets of these and other Sabbatians—namely, that there is no relation of any
kind between the Most High God, the First Cause,
and the Universe, but that a second person in the
Godhead, the God of Israel, the image and prototype of the former, created the world, gave the Law,
chose Israel, in short governs the Finite. He appears to have embraced also the conclusions deduced
from this heretical theory, that Sabbataï Zevi was
the true Messiah, that the second person of the
Godhead was incorporated in him, and that by his
appearance the Torah had ceased to have any
importance.

But Eibeschütz had not sufficient strength of
character or determination to act in conformity with
his convictions. It would have been contrary to his
nature to break openly with Rabbinical Judaism, and
by proclaiming himself an anti-Talmudist, as had
been done by several Sabbatians, to wage war
against the whole of Judaism. He was too practical and loved ease too well to expose himself to
the disagreeable consequences of such a rupture.
Should he, like Chayon, wander forth a fugitive
through Asia and Europe, and back again? Besides, he loved the Talmud and Rabbinical literature
as food for his wit, and could not do without them.
The contradictions in his career and the disorders

which he originated may be traced to want of harmony between his intellect and his temperament.
Rabbinical Judaism did not altogether suit him, but
the sources from which it was derived were indispensable to him, and had they not been in existence
he would have created them.   Fettered by this contradiction he deceived not only the world, but also
himself; he could not arrive at any clear understanding with himself, and was a hypocrite without
intending it.

At one-and-twenty Eibeschütz directed a school
in Prague, and a band of subtlety-loving Talmud
students gathered round him, hung on his lips, and
admired his stimulating method, and playful way of
dealing with difficulties. He captivated and inspired
his pupils by his genial, one might almost say
student-like, manners, by his sparkling wit, and
scintillating sallies, not always within the bounds of
propriety. His manner towards his pupils was
altogether different from that of rabbis of the ordinary type. He did not slink along gloomily, like a
penitent, and with bowed head, and he imposed no
such restraints on them, but allowed them great
freedom. Social life and lively, interesting conversation were necessities to him. For these reasons
the number of Eibeschütz's disciples yearly increased, and counted by thousands. At thirty he
was regarded not alone in Prague, but far and wide
as an authority.

It has been stated that the council of rabbis of
Frankfort-on-the-Main had clear proofs of Eibeschütz's connection with Löbele Prosnitz and the
Podolian Sabbatians. Only his extensive influence
and the great number of his disciples protected him
from being included in the sentence of excommunication pronounced against the others. He had the
hardihood to meet the suspicions against himself
by excommunicating the Sabbatians (1725). Moses
Chages, the man without "respect of persons," the

"watchman of Zion" of that age, predicted that for-bearance would prove hurtful. In fact, Eibeschütz was at that time deeply committed to the Sabbatian heresies, confessed the fact to Meïr Eisenstadt, the teacher of his youth, who knew his erring ways, and, apparently ashamed and repentant, promised amendment. Thanks to this clemency Eibeschütz maintained his reputation, increased by his erudition, his ever-growing body of disciples, and his activity. The suspicion of heresy was by degrees forgotten, and the community of Prague, in recognition of his merits, appointed him preacher (1728).

In another matter Eibeschütz left the beaten path, and placed himself in a somewhat ambiguous light. Either from vanity or calculation, he entered into intimate relations with the Jesuits in Prague. He carried on discussions with them, displaying a cer-tain sort of liberality, as though he did not share the prejudices of the Jews. He associated, for instance, with that spiritual tyrant, Hasselbauer, the Jesuit bishop of Prague, who frequently made domiciliary visits among Jews, to search for and confiscate Hebrew books that had escaped the vigilance of the censor. Through this intimacy Eibeschütz obtained from the bishop the privilege to print the Talmud, so often proscribed by the Church of Rome. Did he act thus from self-interest, with the view of compelling the Bohemian Jews to use only copies of the Talmud printed by him, and in this way create a remunerative business, the profits to be shared with the Jesuits? This was most positively asserted in many Jewish circles. Eibeschütz obtained permission to print from the episcopal board of censors, on condition that every expression, every word in the Talmud which, in howsoever small a degree, appeared to be antagonistic to Christianity be expunged. He was willing to perpetrate this pro-cess of mutilation (1728-1739). Such obsequious pli-ability to the Jesuits excited the displeasure of many

Jews. The community of Frankfort-on-the-Main
spent a considerable sum—Moses Chages and perhaps David Oppenheim being at the bottom of the
movement—in their efforts to obtain from the emperor a prohibition against the publication of the
Prague edition. Eibeschütz, on the other hand,
used his connection with Christian circles to avert
perils impending over the Bohemian Jews.

Eibeschütz's early heretical leanings were not
absolutely forgotten. When the post of rabbi at
Metz became vacant, he applied for it. When the
council were occupied with the election, the gray-
haired widow of the late rabbi appeared at the
meeting, and warned them not to insult the memory
of her dead husband and the pious rabbis who had
preceded him, by appointing a heretic, perhaps
worse (a Mumar), their successor. This solemn
admonition from the venerable matron who was related to the wife of Eibeschütz so impressed the
council that his election fell through. Jacob Joshua
Falk was appointed at Metz. He remained there
only a few years, and, on his removal to Frankfort-
on-the-Main, Eibeschütz was chosen in his place.
Before he entered on his duties, the Austrian War
of Succession broke out, a struggle between youthful,
aspiring Prussia, under Frederick the Great, and
decrepit Austria, under Maria Theresa. A French
army, in conjunction with Prussia and the anti-
emperor Charles VII, occupied Prague. The sys-
tematically brutalized population of Bohemia and
Moravia conceived the false notion that the Jews
were treacherously taking part with the enemy. It
was said that Frederick the Great, the Protestant
heretic, was an especial patron of the Jews. In
Moravia, whither the Prussians had not yet penetrated, occurred passionate outbursts of fury against
the Jews. An Austrian field-marshal in Moravia,
under the delusion of the Jews' treachery, issued a
decree that the communities, within six days, should

"pay down in cash 50,000 Rhenish gulden at Brünn, failing which, they would all be delivered over to pillage and the sword." Through the devoted exertions of Baron de Aguilar and the wealthy rabbi, Issachar Berush Eskeles—two members of the Vienna community—this decree was revoked by the empress, Maria Theresa (March 21). These men had another opportunity to avert a crushing disaster from their brethren.

Jonathan Eibeschütz, having been appointed rabbi of Metz, either from self-conceit or in order to secure for himself the post of rabbi in French Lorraine, imprudently fraternized with the French soldiery who occupied the town. He obtained from the French commandant a safe-conduct enabling him to travel unmolested to France, and thereby aroused in the Bohemian population the suspicion that he had a treasonable understanding with the enemy. After the departure of the French (end of 1742), the Austrian authorities held an inquiry into his conduct; and all his property, which had not been seized by the Croats, was sequestered. Eventually all the Moravian and Bohemian Jews were suspected of treason. The most Catholic empress, who was at once good-natured and hard-hearted, published a decree, December 18, 1744, for Bohemia, January 2, 1745, for Moravia, that all Jews in these royal provinces should, "for several important reasons," within a brief period be banished; and that Jews found in these crown lands after the expiration of this period should be "removed by force of arms." Terrible severity was shown in enforcing this decree. The Jews of Prague, more than 20,630 souls, were obliged in the depth of winter hurriedly to leave the town and suffer in the villages; and the royal cities were forbidden to harbor them even temporarily. The position of the Bohemian and Moravian Jews was pitiable. Whither should they turn? In the eighteenth century Jews were not in request or made welcome on account of their wealth as they had been before. As though Eibeschütz felt himself in a measure to blame for their misfortunes, he took trouble to obtain relief for them. He preached on their behalf in Metz, addressed letters to the communities in the south of France, Bayonne and Bordeaux, asking for aid, and wrote to the Roman community begging them to intercede with the pope on behalf of their unhappy brethren. It was all of but little avail. More efficacious appears to have been the intercession of De Aguilar, Berush Eskeles, and other Jews connected with the court of Vienna. The clergy, too, spoke on their behalf, and the ambassadors of Holland and England interceded warmly and urgently for them. The empress revoked her severe decree, and permitted the Jews in both the royal provinces to remain for an indefinite time (May 15, 1745). In the case of the Prague community alone, which was chiefly under suspicion, the strictness of the decree was not relaxed. Not till some years later, in consequence of a declaration by the states of the empire "that their departure would entail a loss of many millions" was the residence of all Jews prolonged to ten years, but under degrading conditions. They were to be diminished rather than be permitted to increase, their exact number being fixed. Only the eldest son was permitted to found a family. Some 20,000 " Familianten," as they were called, were allowed in Bohemia and 5,100 in Moravia, who were obliged to pay annually to the imperial treasury a sum of about 200,000 gulden. These restrictions were maintained almost up to the Revolution of 1848. Jonathan Eibeschütz rightly or wrongly was declared a traitor to his country, and forbidden ever to set foot on Austrian soil.

If, during the first years passed in Metz, he was so popular that the community would not allow him to accept the post of rabbi at Fürth, offered to him,

he must have made himself disagreeable later on, as
during his difficulties, he could not find supporters
there, nor any witnesses to his innocence. If he
committed only a small portion of the mean actions
with which he was reproached, his life must have
presented a striking contrast to the sermons which
he composed. Eibeschütz did not feel at home in
Metz; he missed the bustling, argumentative band
of young admirers, and the wide platform on which
to display his Talmudical erudition. In France
there were fewer students of the Talmud. It was
therefore pardonable that he strenuously exerted
himself to obtain the post of rabbi of the "three
communities" (Hamburg, Altona, and Wandsbeck).
Thanks to the efforts of his connections and
admirers, and his fame as the most distinguished
of Talmudists and miracle workers, the choice fell
on him. As the Jews of the three towns had their
own civil jurisdiction, based on Rabbinical law, they
required an acute rabbi, a lawyer, and they could
not, from this point of view, have made a better
selection.

But an evil spirit seems to have entered Altona
with his instalment, which threw into disorder not
only the three communities, but also the whole of
German and Polish Judaism. Eibeschütz, though
not free from blame, must not alone be made
answerable. The tendency of the age was culpable,
and Jacob Emden, an unattached rabbi, was more
especially the prime mover in the strife. He desired
to unmask hypocrisy, and in doing so laid bare the
nakedness of his Jewish contemporaries.

Jacob Emden Ashkenazi (abbreviated to Jabez;
born 1698, died 1776) resembled his father Chacham
Zevi, as a branch its parent stem; or rather he made
the father whom he admired extravagantly his model
in everything. The perverted spirit of the age prevented his following his natural bent and inspirations.
A true son of the Talmud, he seriously believed that

a Jew ought to occupy himself with other branches of knowledge only during "the hour of twilight," and considered it unlawful to read newspapers on the Sabbath. He, too, was well versed in the Talmud, and set a high value on the Kabbala and the Zohar, of the dangerous extravagances of which he at first knew nothing. Philosophy, although he possessed no knowledge of it, was an abomination to him. In his perverseness he maintained it to be impossible that the philosophical work, "The Guide," could have been composed by the orthodox rabbi, Maimuni. In character he was just, truth-loving, and staunch, herein forming a sharp contrast to Jonathan Eibeschütz. Whatever he considered as truth or false, he did not hesitate forthwith to defend or condemn with incisive acuteness; it was contrary to his nature to conceal, dissimulate, hide his opinions, or play the hypocrite. He differed from Eibeschütz in another respect. The latter was agreeable, pliant, careless, cheerful, and sociable; Emden, on the contrary, was unsociable, unbending, earnest, melancholy, and a lover of solitude. Well-to-do, and maintaining himself by his business, Emden was always disinclined to undertake the office of a rabbi. He was too well aware of his own craving for independence, his awkwardness, and impetuosity. Only once was he induced to accept the office of rabbi, in Emden (from which he derived his surname); but he relinquished it after a few years on account of his dislike to the work and from ill-health, and settled in Altona. He obtained from the king of Denmark the privilege of establishing a printing-press; built a house with a private synagogue, and, with his family and a few friends, formed a community within the community. He indeed visited the exchange, but he lived enwrapped in a dream-world of his own.

Emden was on the list of candidates for the appointment of rabbi to the "three communities."

His few friends worked for him, and urged him to exert himself to try and obtain the post. He, however, resisted all their solicitations, and declared decidedly, that he would not accept the election even if the choice fell on him, but he was none the less aggrieved that he obtained only a few votes, and entertained an unfriendly feeling towards Eibeschütz, because he was preferred. There was another peculiarity in Emden's character: his antipathy to heretics. His father Chacham Zevi had undauntedly pursued Nehemiah Chayon and the other Sabbatians, and had brought himself into painful positions by so doing. Emden desired nothing more ardently than to follow his father, and would not have shunned martyrdom in the cause. Since the return of Moses Chages to Palestine, he considered himself the watchman on behalf of orthodoxy among his fellow-believers. He was a Jewish grand inquisitor, and was in readiness to hurl the thunders of excommunication whenever heresy, particularly the Sabbatian, should show itself. The opportunity of exercising his unpaid office of inquisitor, of proving his zeal for orthodoxy, and even of suffering in its behalf, was granted him by Jonathan Eibeschütz.

At the time when Eibeschütz entered on his duties as rabbi a painful agitation was prevalent among the Jews of the "three communities." Within the year several young women had died in childbirth. Every wife in expectation of becoming a mother awaited the approaching hour with increasing anxiety. The coming of the new rabbi, who should drive away the destroying angel by whom young women had been selected as victims, was awaited with eager longing. At that time a rabbi was regarded as a protector against every species of evil (Megîn), a sort of magician, and the wives of Hamburg and Altona expected still greater things from Jonathan Eibeschütz, who had been heralded by his admirers as the most gifted of rabbis and a worker of miracles. How would he respond to these exaggerated expectations? Even if he had been honest, Eibeschütz would have been forced to resort to some mystification to assert his authority in his new office. Therefore, immediately after his arrival, he prepared talismans—writings for exorcising spirits (Cameos, Kameoth)—for the terrified women, and indulged in other forms of magic to impose upon the credulous. He had distributed similar amulets in Metz, Frankfort-on-the-Main, and other places. From Frankfort a rumor had reached Altona that the talismans of Eibeschütz were of an altogether different nature to what they usually were, and that they were heretical in character. Out of curiosity one of the amulets distributed by the chief rabbi Jonathan Eibeschütz, was opened in Altona, and was found to contain the following invocation:

"O God of Israel, Thou who dwellest in the adornment of Thy might [a Kabbalistic allusion], send through the merit of Thy servant Sabbataï Zevi healing for this woman, whereby Thy name and the name of Thy Messiah, Sabbataï Zevi, may be sanctified in the world."

It is hard to tell which is more surprising— Eibeschütz's stupid belief in and attachment to the impostor of Smyrna, who had apostatized from Judaism, or his imprudence in thus exposing himself. He had indeed altered the words a little, and put certain letters to represent others ; but he must have known that the key to his riddle was easy to find. These attempts at deception naturally did not remain a secret. The amulets came into the hands of Emden, who no longer entertained a doubt that Eibeschütz still adhered to the Sabbatian heresy. Though he rejoiced greatly at having found an opportunity to exercise his office of inquisitor, he in a measure recoiled from the consequences of doing so. Was it wise to begin a contest with a man who had an extensive reputation as the most learned

Talmudist of his day, as an orthodox rabbi, whose numerous disciples—over 20,000 it was said—were rabbis, officials of communities, and holders of influential posts, who clung to him with admiration, and were ready to form a phalanx round him and exert all their energies in his defense? On the other hand, the matter could not be suppressed, it having been discussed in the Jews' quarter and on exchange. The elders felt obliged to interrogate Eibeschütz on the matter, and he replied by a pitiful evasion. The council, whether believing Eibeschütz or not, was bound to lend him a helping hand in burying the matter. What a disgrace for the highly respected "three communities," which a quarter of a century earlier had condemned and branded the Sabbatians as heretics, that they themselves should have chosen a Sabbatian as their chief rabbi! Jacob Emden, from whose zeal the worst was to be dreaded, was partially beguiled by flatteries, partially intimidated by threats, to refrain from publishing the affair. But these threats against him necessarily led to publicity. Emden solemnly declared in his synagogue that he held the writer of the amulets to be a Sabbatian heretic who deserved to be excommunicated, that he did not charge the chief rabbi with their composition, but that the latter was in duty bound to clear himself from suspicion. This declaration caused a deep sensation in the "three communities," and aroused vehement animosity. The council, and the greater part of the community, regarded it as a gross piece of presumption and as an encroachment upon their jurisdiction. The friends of Eibeschütz, especially his disciples, fanned the flame. Religious hero-worship was so prevalent that some did not hesitate to declare that if their rabbi believed in Sabbataï Zevi, they would share his belief. Without putting Emden on trial the council arbitrarily decreed that no one, under pain of excommunication, should attend his synagogue, which was to be closed, and that he should not publish anything at his printing establishment. And now began a struggle which at first produced abundant evil, but which in the end had a purifying effect. Jonathan Eibeschütz published the affair far and wide among his numerous friends and disciples in Bohemia, Moravia, and Poland, and painted himself as an innocent man unjustly accused, and Jacob Emden as an audacious fellow who had the presumption to brand him as a heretic. He was hurried along from one untruth to another, from violence to violence; but he nevertheless had many partisans to support him. Jacob Emden on the contrary stood well-nigh alone, for the few who adhered to him had not the courage to come forward openly. He however informed his friends, Eibeschütz's enemies, on the same day of what had occurred. The foolish affair of the amulets thus acquired a notoriety which it was impossible to check. Every Jew capable of forming an opinion on the subject took one side or the other; the majority adhered to Eibeschütz. Many indeed could not conceive it possible that so distinguished a Talmudist could be a Sabbatian, and the accusation against him was accounted base slander on the part of the irascible and malignant Emden. Great ignorance prevailed with regard to the character and history of the Sabbatians (or Shäbs, as they were termed), for a quarter of a century had passed since they had been everywhere excommunicated. Public opinion was therefore at first in Eibeschütz's favor.

Eibeschütz thoroughly understood how to win over opponents to his side, and to soothe them with illusions. He convened a meeting in the synagogue, and took a solemn oath that he did not adhere to a single article of the Sabbatian creed; if he did, might fire and brimstone descend on him from heaven! He went on to anathematize this sect with all kinds of maledictions, and excommunicated

his adversaries who had slandered him, and originated these elements of strife.   This solemn
declaration made a deep impression.   Who could
doubt the innocence of a rabbi of such high standing
when he called God to witness respecting it?   The
council of the "three communities" considered itself
fully justified in ordering Emden, as a common
slanderer, to leave Altona.   As he refused, and referred to the charter granted him by the king, he
was cut off from all intercourse with others, pursued
by intrigues, and relentlessly persecuted.   This
treatment only aroused Emden to more strenuous
efforts.   Letters had meantime been sent from
Metz with other amulets (1751), which Eibeschütz
had distributed there, and the genuineness of which
he had himself admitted, clearly demonstrating that
he revered Sabbataï Zevi as the Messiah and saviour.
The Metz amulets were in the main of the same
character :—

"In the name of the God of Israel . . . . of the God of his
anointed Sabbataï Zevi, through whose wounds healing is come to us,
who with the breath of His mouth slays the Evil One, I adjure all
spirits and demons not to injure the bearer of this amulet."

A judicial examination of these amulets had been
made by the council of rabbis and elders ; and all
who had any in their possession were commanded
to deliver them up under pain of excommunication.
A royal procurator confirmed their authenticity ;
that is to say, they were proved by the evidence of
witnesses under oath to be the work of Eibeschütz ;
who did not find one person of note in Metz to
maintain his honor.   It was some small satisfaction
to Jacob Emden to know that he did not stand
alone in his conflict ; but concurrence in his views
did not profit him much.   The members of the
"three communities," with the exception of a small
minority, adhered to Eibeschütz, and made his cause
their own.   It was forbidden to speak a slanderous
word against the chief rabbi.   Elsewhere his enemies

made plans—he received notice from all quarters as
to what was designed against him—but there was
no definite scheme. His disciples, on the other
hand, were extraordinarily zealous in his behalf.
One of these, Chayim of Lublin, had the courage,
in glorification of Eibeschütz and in defamation of
his opponents, to excommunicate three of the latter
in his synagogue, Jacob Emden, Nehemiah Reischer,
and an elder in Metz, Moses Mayo, because they
had dared slander "that most perfect man, Jonathan,
in whom God glorified Himself." This decree of
excommunication was distributed throughout Poland
for observance and imitation. The remaining Polish
rabbis agreed with it, either being supporters of
Eibeschütz, or having been bribed, or being indifferent in the matter. By way of Königsberg and
Breslau, for example, large sums were sent to Poland
to commend the case of Eibeschütz to the rabbis of
that country. Matters did not stop at excommuni-
cations and anathemas ; in Altona (Iyar 25=May)
they culminated in a riot. A hand-to-hand fight
took place, and the police had to be called in. In
consequence, Jacob Emden, believing his life to be
endangered through the fury of Eibeschütz's partisans, fled to Amsterdam on the next day, and was
kindly received there. Emden's wife was ordered
by the council not to part with any of his property,
as an action for damages would be brought against
him.

Eibeschütz was acute enough to perceive that the
residence of Jacob Emden in Amsterdam might
prove dangerous, as he would have full scope, by
means of his trenchant pen, to expose the rabbi's
past history through the press. To counteract this,
Eibeschütz issued to his followers in Germany,
Poland, and Italy, an encyclical (Letter of Zeal, Sivan
3, 1751), in which, under the guise of an exhortation
to bear testimony to his orthodoxy, he besought
them to make his cause their own. He urged them

to prosecute his adversary with all their energy and by every possible means : it would be set to their account as a special merit by the Almighty. It greatly resembled the command of a popular general to thousands of his soldiers to attack, and pitilessly ill-treat defenseless men. To complete the delusion, he induced two men, devotedly attached to mysticism, but not to truth—Elijah Olianow and Samuel Essingen—to declare that his amulets contained nothing dangerous or heretical, but a great deal of deep orthodox mysticism intelligible only to the few.

Eibeschütz had not yet just grounds for rejoicing. The excess of insolence of the newly-fledged rabbi of Lublin in excommunicating gray-haired rabbis aroused the leading men in the communities. A cry of horror resounded from Lorraine to Podolia at this arrogance, justly suspected to be due to the instigation of Eibeschütz. Three rabbis at length combined, Joshua Falk, Leb Heschels, and Heilmann, and others joined them. Eibeschütz was challenged to exculpate himself before a meeting of rabbis regarding the amulets ascribed to him, which undeniably were heretical. As was to be anticipated, Eibeschütz declined to justify himself in any way, and the confederates took council as to what further steps to take against him. The scandal continued to increase. The newspapers reported the quarrel amongst the Jews regarding the rabbi of Altona. Christians naturally could not comprehend the nature of the dispute. It was said that a vehement controversy had arisen amongst the Jews as to whether the Messiah had or had not already appeared. The Jews were derided, because they preferred to believe in the impostor Sabbataï Zevi, rather than in Jesus. This reacted on the Jews, and the two parties imputed to each other the offense of this scandal, this "profanation of God's name." An energetic man, Baruch Yavan, of Poland, transferred the schism to that country. He was a disciple of Falk, agent to the notorious Saxon minister Brühl, and enjoyed considerable reputation in Poland.   Through his intrigues, a Polish magnate deprived Chayim Lublin of his office as rabbi, and ordered him and his father to be thrown into prison (Elul=September, 1751).   In Poland the controversy assumed an ugly character—bribery, information through spies, acts of violence, and treachery being among its leading features.   Seceders from each party betrayed the secrets of one to the other. Every fair and every synod were battlefields, where the partisans of Eibeschütz and Falk contended. The proceedings at the synods were more disorderly than those in the Polish Reichstag.   When the defenders of either side proved more numerous or more energetic, the weaker party was excommunicated.   The supporters of Eibeschütz were in the main more active.   Count Brühl made them as many empty promises of protection, as he bestowed on their opponents through Baruch Yavan.

In Germany, naturally, matters were conducted with more moderation.   The triumvirate of rabbis published a decision to the effect that the writer of the Sabbatian amulets should be cut off from communion with Israel.   Every devout Jew lay under obligation to persecute him to the utmost of his power.   No one might study the Talmud under his guidance.   All who supported his cause were to be excommunicated.   No mention was made of Eibeschütz's name.   Many German rabbis concurred in this moderate decision, as also the Venetian rabbis who had excommunicated Luzzatto. The resolution was delivered to Eibeschütz and the council of the "three communities" (February, 1752), and notice was given to Eibeschütz that within two months he must clear himself before a rabbinical court of arbitration of the suspicion that he was the author of heretical amulets, failing which his name would be publicly stigmatized.   This sentence of excommunication was to be printed by the Venetian council of rabbis, and published throughout the East and Africa. But Eibeschütz understood how to meet this blow craftily. The Italian rabbis were, for the most part, reluctant to burn their fingers in this violent quarrel, and declined to participate in any way. The council of rabbis at Leghorn, especially Malachi Cohen, the last of the Italian rabbinical authorities, inclined towards the side of Eibeschütz. The Portuguese in Amsterdam and London designedly kept themselves aloof from this domestic squabble among the Germans and Poles. One broker of Amsterdam, David Pinto, alone espoused Eibeschütz's cause, and threatened Emden with his anger if he continued his hostility. The council of rabbis in Constantinople, dazzled by Eibeschütz's illustrious name, or in some way deceived, declared decidedly for him, but would not pronounce a direct sentence of excommunication against his antagonists. What they neglected was done by a so-called envoy from Jerusalem, Abraham Israel, a presumptuous mendicant, who as a representative of the Holy Land and the Jewish nation, imprecated and anathematized all who should utter a slanderous word against Eibeschütz. Thus almost the whole of Israel was excommunicated; on the one side those who showed enmity towards the illustrious chief rabbi of the "three communities," and on the other those who supported that heretic. Thus the effects of excommunication were nullified, or rather it became ridiculous, and with it a phase of rabbinical Judaism disappeared.

A new turn was given this disagreeable controversy when it was transferred from its home to the law courts of the Christians. The fanaticism of Eibeschütz's followers was more to blame than the conduct of their opponents. One of the elders of Altona, who had so far remained true to the cause of the persecutors, in a letter to his brother

showed himself somewhat doubtful of its justice.
This letter was opened by the followers of Eibeschütz, and the writer was set down as a traitor,
expelled from the council, ill-treated, and threatened
with banishment from Altona. There remained no
alternative for him but to address himself to the
government of Holstein, to the king of Denmark,
Frederick V, and unsparingly expose all the illegali-
ties, meannesses, and violence of which Eibeschütz
and his party had been guilty. The injustice of the
council towards Jacob Emden and his wife was
discussed in connection with the affair. An authenticated copy of the suspected amulets was translated
into German. The trial was conducted with extreme
bitterness; both parties spared no expense. The
plaintiff and his faction in their anger did not confine
themselves to necessary statements, but treacherously stigmatized as a crime much that was of an
innocent nature. King Frederick, who loved justice,
and his minister Bernstorff, gave judgment against
the followers of Eibeschütz (June 3, 1752). The
council of Altona was severely censured for its illegal
and harsh treatment of Jacob Emden, and punished
with a fine of 100 thalers. Emden was not only permitted to return to Altona, but the use of his synagogue and his printing establishment was restored.
Eibeschütz was deprived of authority as rabbi of the
Hamburg community, and ordered to clear himself
with regard to the incriminating amulets, and to
answer fifteen questions propounded to him. Events
thus took an unfortunate turn for him. Even the
well-intentioned letter of a partisan sent from Poland
served to show how desperate his case was. Ezekiel
Landau (born 1720, died 1793) as a young man had
aroused hopes that he would become a second
Jonathan Eibeschütz in rabbinical learning and
sagacity. His opinion as rabbi of Jampol (Podolia)
carried great weight. Landau wrote with youthful
simplicity and straightforwardness to Eibeschütz

that the amulets which he had seen were without
doubt Sabbatian and heretical.   He, therefore, could
not believe that the honored and devout rabbi of
Altona had written them.   For that reason he was
as much in favor of condemning the amulets, as of
upholding Jonathan Eibeschütz and declaring war
against his adversaries.   He entreated Eibeschütz
to condemn the amulets as heretical, and when
occasion offered clear himself from the accusation
that he was the author of the slanderous writings,
full of unworthy expressions about God, and to
condemn them leaf by leaf.   This was a severe
blow from the hand of a friend.   As Eibeschütz
had acknowledged the amulets to be genuine, and
had only sophistically explained away their heresy,
he was now in evil case.   A follower of Emden's
in addition published the correspondence and decisions of Eibeschütz's enemies, which stigmatized his
conduct, together with an account of the amulets
and their true interpretation ("The Language of
Truth," printed August, 1752).   Emden himself
published the history of the false Messiah, Sabbataï
Zevi, and the visionaries and knaves who had succeeded him, down to Chayon and Luzzatto, vividly
describing the errors and disorderly excesses of
the Sabbatians for his own generation, which was
careless with regard to historical events, and had
but scanty, confused knowledge on the subject.
Thus it was made clear to many that the Sabbatian
heresy aimed at nothing less than the dethronement
of the God of Israel in favor of a phantom, and
the dissolution of Judaism by means of Kabbalistic chimeras.   But the worst that befell Eibeschütz
was that Emden himself returned unmolested to
Altona, and had the prospect of being indemnified
for his losses.

The danger in which Eibeschütz found himself of
being unmasked as a heretic in the courts of law,
and before the eyes of the world, determined him to

a step which a rabbi of the old stamp of honest piety, even under peril of death, would not have taken. He associated himself with an apostate baptized Jew, formerly his pupil, in order to obtain assistance from him in his difficulties. Moses Gerson Cohen, of Mitau, who, on his mother's side, was descended from Chayim Vital Calabrese, had studied the Talmud under Eibeschütz in Prague for seven years, then traveled in the East, and, after his return to Europe, had been baptized in Wolfenbüttel under the name Charles Anton. He was appointed by his patron, the duke of Brunswick, Reader in Hebrew in Helmstädt. It was afterwards proved that this convert had become a Christian solely from self-interest.

To him the chief rabbi of the "three communities" secretly repaired in order to induce him to compose a vindication, or rather a panegyric, of his conduct. It is evident on the face of it, even at the present day, that the work was written "to order," and it transpired that Eibeschütz had dictated it to Charles Anton. He is extolled as the most sagacious and upright Jew of his time, as a man versed in philosophy, history, and mathematics, and as a persecuted victim. Jacob Emden, on the other hand, is represented as an incompetent, envious fellow. Anton dedicated this work to the king of Denmark, and commended to him the case of the alleged innocent and persecuted man. This work, with another cunningly chosen expedient, had favorable results for Eibeschütz. He had screened himself not only behind a baptized Jew, but behind a princess. King Frederick V had married, as his second wife, a princess of Brunswick, Maria Juliana, and a Jewish agent—a partisan of Eibeschütz—did business at the court of Brunswick. The latter made the most of his direct and indirect influence with the young Danish princess, and said a good word to her on behalf of the chief rabbi under accu-

sation of heresy. With the comment that the majority of rabbis except some litigious, malevolent individuals sided with Eibeschütz—proof of the justice
of his cause—the court suppressed the amulet case.
A royal decree, forbidding the continuation of this
controversy, was read aloud in the Altona synagogue (February 7, 1753). At the suggestion of
the government the vote of the community with regard to Eibeschütz was again taken, and resulted in
his favor. He then took the oath of fealty to the
king, and his position was more assured than ever.
His sagacity had a second time gained the day, but
his success was only transitory. The number of his
enemies had materially increased even in Altona
through the far-reaching dissensions and the better
knowledge of his character gleaned little by little.
His adversaries did not allow themselves to be
silenced by the king's arbitrary decision without
making another effort; and the rabbinical triumvirate urged them to petition for a revision of the
heresy proceedings against Eibeschütz, and try to
convince the king that the assertion that the majority of the rabbis were his partisans was entirely
false, that, on the contrary, he was supported only
by his relatives and disciples. The three rabbis
and the rabbi of Hanover laid before the council a
demand to consider Eibeschütz as excommunicated,
and forbid him to exercise any rabbinical function
until he repented of his heresy, and promised
amendment. Hostile writings by Emden and
others fed the fire of dissension; they were written in vehement, pitiless language and were full
of petty gossip. To calm the public wrath, the Altona council with great difficulty induced Eibeschütz
to make a binding declaration that he was prepared
of his own free-will to justify himself before an impartial rabbinical court of arbitration, and submit to
its decision (beginning of 1753). This only inflamed
the strife. Eibeschütz proposed as his judges

two rabbis, of Lissa and Glogau, men but little
known, who were to add a third to their number.
But the opposite party insisted that the court be
composed of Joshua Falk and his colleagues. This
angered Eibeschütz, who lost the calmness of mind
he had hitherto maintained. At one time he desired to submit his cause to the rabbis of Constantinople, at another he proposed the Synod of the Four
Polish Countries, to meet in Jaroslav late in the
summer of 1753. He appears to have reckoned on
obtaining a favorable sentence from this assemblage
of many rabbis and influential persons. Relying on
this, he believed that he could easily free himself
from the compact forced upon him, of submitting to
arbitration. He is said to have managed this by
giving information at court that the royal preroga-
tive had been encroached upon by this proposed
appeal from the judgment of the sovereign to that
of the rabbis. Both parties were therefore fined by
the magistrates. This only increased his enemies,
and several of his warmest supporters, former members of the communal council, renounced him, and
proclaimed him, not only a heretic, but an intriguer.
These opponents complained once more to the king
with regard to the prevalent dissensions in the community, of which he was the cause. They could
not, they said, obtain impartial judgment from him
in their lawsuits, because he allowed himself to be
guided in his decisions by spite and passion. The
justice-loving king gave these complaints his attention. He desired to arrive at a definite conclusion
with regard to the case, whether Eibeschütz was an
arch-heretic, as his opponents maintained, or a persecuted innocent, as he described himself.

With this in view the king ordered certain Christian professors and theologians versed in Hebrew,
to give him their opinion with regard to the amulets.
Eibeschütz felt uneasy at the turn affairs had taken;
he feared that the matter might prove disastrous to

him. To place himself in a favorable light he resolved on a course which he had hitherto hesitated
to adopt—to dispose public opinion in his favor
through the press. As things then stood, there was
no other course open to him, and he therefore composed a defense—"The Tables of Testimony," completed Tammuz 18, end of June, 1755, the first production of his pen. As might have been expected
from a man of his ability, it is skillfully worked out ;
and he places his case in a favorable light. But
Eibeschütz was unable to convince either his impartial contemporaries or posterity of his innocence.
On the contrary, his vindication, and much of the
evidence adduced, clearly betray his guilt. Emden
and his disciple David Gans did not fail to publish
refutations, drawing attention to weak points, and
throwing doubt on the testimony in favor of
Eibeschütz.

A publication by a professor and pastor, David
Frederick Megerlin, early in 1756, made a fresh
diversion, apparently in Eibeschütz's favor, with
respect to this vexed question. This confused
babbler and proselytizer, induced by the order of
the Danish king to pronounce an opinion upon the
matter, imagined that he had discovered the key to
the enigmatical amulets of Eibeschütz, the disputed
characters which his opponents explained as referring to Sabbataï Zevi being nothing less than a mystic allusion to Jesus Christ ! The chief rabbi of Altona and Hamburg was at heart attached to the
Christian faith, Megerlin maintained, but dared not
come out openly through fear of the Jews. He
himself, it is true, and his disciple, Charles Anton,
had explained these amulets in quite another way,
not in a Christian sense ; but the latter had not
comprehended the deeper meaning, and Eibeschütz
had composed his vindication only for Polish Jews.
In his heart of hearts the chief rabbi was a true believer in Christianity. Megerlin, therefore, called

on the king of Denmark to protect Eibeschütz
against the persecutions of the Jews, especially
against the calumnies of Jacob Emden, who hated
and persecuted the Christians, as his father had
persecuted Chayon, also a secret Christian. In his
folly Megerlin exhorted Eibeschütz most earnestly
to throw off his mask, resign the post of rabbi of the
"three communities," and allow himself to be baptized. He also addressed a circular letter to the
Jews, urging them to arrange a general convention
of rabbis and openly glorify Christianity. Had
Eibeschütz possessed a spark of honor he would
have repudiated, even at the risk of losing the king's
favor, his supposed adherence to Christianity. But
he did not take the smallest step to answer the
charge of hypocrisy ; he was content to profit by it.
Megerlin's arguments, foolish as they were, convinced King Frederick. He revoked the suspension
from office with which Eibeschütz was threatened,
and decreed that the Jews of the Altona community
should show him obedience. The Hamburg senate,
also, again acknowledged him as rabbi of the German community. Eibeschütz exulted, and his admirers prepared a solemn triumph for him
(Chanukkah—middle of December, 1756). His disciples, clad as knights, marched through the streets
shouting, till they reached the rabbi's house, where
they arranged a dancing-party. The six years of
strife which had aroused every evil passion among
the Jews, from Lorraine to Podolia, and from the
Elbe to the Po, ended apparently in a dance. But
at the same time Eibeschütz in another direction
suffered defeat, which branded him in the eyes of
those who had hitherto spoken favorably of him and
supported him.

Facts flatly contradicted his assertion, put forward
through his mouthpiece, Charles Anton, that "there
were no longer any Sabbatians." They raised their
serpent heads and shot forth their tongues full of

poisonous rage at this very moment. The seed which Chayim Malach had scattered in Poland was by no means checked in growth by the anathemas of the rabbis. They had only forced the Sabbatians to disguise themselves better, and to counterfeit death; but they flourished secretly, and their following increased. Some towns in Podolia and Pakotia were full of Talmudists who, in Sabbatian fashion, scoffed at the Talmud, rejected the law of Judaism, and, under the mask of ascetic discipline, lived impure lives. The disorders to which the dispute regarding Eibeschütz had given rise in Poland encouraged the Polish Sabbatians to venture from their hiding-places and raise their masks a little. The time seemed favorable for an attempt to cast aside odious religious rites, and openly to come forward as anti-Talmudists. They needed a spirited leader to gather the scattered band, give it cohesion, and mark out a line of action. This leader now presented himself, and with his appearance began a new movement which threw the whole Jewish world of Poland into intense agitation and despair. This leader was the notorious Jacob Frank.

Jankiev Lejbovicz (that is, Jacob son of Leb) of Galicia, was one of the worst, most subtle, and most deceitful rascals of the eighteenth century. He could cheat the most sagacious, and veil his frauds so cleverly that after his death many still believed him an admirable man, who bore through life, and carried to the grave, most weighty secrets. He understood the art of deception even in his youth, and boasted how he had duped his own father. As a young man he traveled in Turkey in the service of a Jewish gentleman, and in Salonica entered into relations with the Sabbatians or Jewish Moslems there. If he did not learn from them how to work deceptive and mystifying miracles, he at all events learnt indifference towards all forms of religion. He became a Mahometan, as afterwards a Catholic, for so long as it served his purpose, and changed his religion as one changes one's clothes. From his long sojourn in Turkey he acquired the name of Frank, or Frenk. Ignorant of Talmudical literature, as he himself confessed, he was acquainted with the Zoharist Kabbala, explained it to suit his purpose, and took peculiar pleasure in the doctrine of metempsychosis, by virtue of which the successive Messiahs were not visionaries or impostors, but the embodiment of one and the same Messianic soul. King David, Elijah, Jesus, Mahomet, Sabbataï Zevi, and his imitators, down to Berachya, were one and the same personality, which had assumed different bodily forms. Why should not he himself be another incarnation of the Messiah? Although Jacob Frank, or Lejbovicz, loved money dearly, he accounted it only a lever by which to raise himself; he wished to play a brilliant part and surround himself with a mysterious halo. Circumstances were exceptionally favorable to him. He married in Nicopolis (Turkey) a very beautiful wife, through whom he attracted followers. He collected by degrees a small number of Turkish and Wallachian Jews, who shared his loose principles, and held him to be a superior being—the latest embodiment of the Messiah. He could not, however, carry on his mischievous schemes in Turkey, where he was persecuted.

Frank appears to have obtained intelligence of the schism in Poland caused by the Eibeschütz controversy, and thought that he might utilize the propitious moment to gather round him the Sabbatians of Podolia, and play a part among them, and by means of them. He came suddenly amongst them, visiting many towns of Podolia and the Lemberg district, where secret Sabbatians resided, with whom he may have been in communication previously. They fell, so to speak, into his arms. Frank needed followers, and they were seeking a leader. Now they found one who had come to them with a full purse, of the

contents of which he was not sparing. In a trice
he won the Sabbatians of Podolia. Frank disclosed
himself to them as the successor of Sabbataï, or,
what was the same thing, as the new-born soul of
the Sabbatian chief Berachya. What this manifes-
tation signified was known to the initiated. They
understood by it the blasphemous and at the same
time absurd theory of a kind of Trinity, consisting of
the Holy and Most Ancient One, the Holy King,
and a female person in the Godhead. Frank, like
his predecessors, attributed the chief importance to
the Holy King, at once the Messiah and God incarnate, and possessed of all power on earth and in
heaven. Frank ordered his followers to address
him as the Holy Lord. In virtue of his participation in the Godhead, the Messiah was able to do
all things, even miracles, and Frank did perform miracles, as his followers maintained. The adherents
whom he brought in his train, and whom he gathered
round him in Poland, believed so strongly in his
divine nature that they addressed to him mystic
prayers in the language of the Zohar, with the same
formulas that the Donmäh of Salonica were wont to
address to Jacob Querido and Berachya. In short,
Frank formed a sect from the Sabbatians of Podolia,
called by his name, "Frankists." Their founder
taught his disciples to acquire riches for themselves,
even by fraudulent and dishonest means. Deceit
was nothing more than skillful artifice. Their chief
task was to undermine rabbinical Judaism, and to
oppose and annihilate the Talmud. This task they
undertook with a passion which perhaps owed its
origin to the constraints imposed upon them through
fear of persecution. The Frankists opposed the
Zohar to the Talmud, and Simon bar Yochaï, its
alleged author, to the other authorities of the
Talmud, as though in earlier times the former had
combated the latter and accused them of being the
falsifiers of Judaïsm. The true teaching of Moses

was said to be contained only in the Zohar, which
had declared the whole of rabbinical Judaism to be
on a lower level—a fact which blundering Kabbalists
had so long overlooked.   The Frankists, more clear-
sighted, had discovered the half-concealed secret of
the Zohar.   They rightly called themselves anti-
Talmudists as well as Zoharites.   With a certain
childish frowardness they did exactly those things
which rabbinical Judaism strongly prohibited, and
neglected those which the latter prescribed, not
only in points of ritual, but also with regard to
marriage and the laws of chastity.   Among these
anti-Talmudic Frankists were found rabbis and so-
called preachers (Darshanim, Maggidim), Jehuda
Leb Krysa, rabbi of Nadvorna, and Rabbi Nachman
ben Samuel Levi of Busk.   Of especial reputation
among Polish Sabbatians was Elisha Schor of
Rohatyn, an aged man, descended from distinguished Polish rabbis.   He, his sons, his daughter
Chaya (who knew the Zohar by heart, and was considered a prophetess), his grandson, and sons-in-law
were from an early period thoroughgoing Sabbatians, to whom it was a positive pleasure to deride
rabbinical precepts.

During the first months after his return to
Poland, Frank held secret conferences with the
anti-Talmudists of Podolia, as a public demonstration was attended with danger.   One day,
he with about twenty of his followers was surprised in Laskorun in a conventicle.   The Frankists declared that they had been singing psalms
in the Zohar language, while their adversaries
asserted that they had been performing an indecent
dance around a half-naked woman, and kissing her.
Many gathered about the inn to force their way in;
others ran to the police to give information that a
Turk had stolen into Podolia to pervert the Jews
to the Mahometan religion and make them emigrate
to Turkey, and that those who had joined him were

leading an Adamite, that is to say dissolute, life. The
police immediately interposed, broke open the
barricaded doors, and expelled the Frankists.
Frank was dismissed next day as a foreigner, and
repaired to the neighboring Turkish territory ; and
the Podolian Frankists were kept in custody. The
incident made a sensation, and was perhaps intentionally exaggerated. Like wild-fiie the news concerning the Sabbatians spread. It can be imagined
what this defiance of Rabbinical Judaism meant in
those days, especially in Poland, where the most
insignificant religious rites were sedulously observed.
It was now discovered that, in the midst of the
excessive piety which characterized the Poles, a
number of persons, brought up in the knowledge of
the Talmud, scoffed at the whole system of Rabbinical Judaism. The rabbis and elders forthwith
began to employ the usual weapons of excommunication and persecution against the offenders, and
the secret heretics were hunted out. Won over
by large sums, the Polish authorities energetically
supported the persecutors. Those in distress showed
signs of repentance, and made public confession of
their misdeeds, which, be they accurate or exaggerated, present a sad picture of the deterioration of
the Polish Jews. Before the council of rabbis in
Satanov, in open court, several men and women
stated that they and their friends had not only treated
the rites of Judaism with contempt, but had abandoned themselves to fornication, adultery, incest,
and other iniquities, and had done so in accordance
with Kabbalistic-mystic teachings. The penitents
declared that Frank had taught his followers to
scoff at chastity.

In consequence of this evidence a solemn sentence
of excommunication, during the reading of which
tapers were extinguished, was pronounced in Brody
against the Frankists: no one might intermarry
with them, their sons and daughters were to be

treated as bastards, and none who were even suspected could be admitted to the post of rabbi, to any religious office, or to the profession of teacher. Every one was in duty bound to denounce and unmask the secret Sabbatians. This excommunication was repeated in several communities, and finally ratified by a great synod in Konstantinov on the Jewish New Year (September, 1756). The document was printed, distributed, and ordered to be read aloud every month in the synagogues for observance. This sentence of excommunication contained one point of great importance. No one under thirty years of age was to be permitted to study the Kabbala. Necessity at length opened the eyes of the rabbis to the recognition of the impure spring, which since the time of Lurya had poisoned the sap of the tree of Judaism. More than four centuries had passed since philosophical inquiry had been forbidden, and the young Kabbala encouraged. In their blindness, the rabbis had imagined that they were strengthening Judaism in placing folly on the throne of wisdom. This course produced that book of lies, the Zohar, which impudently set itself above the Holy Writings and the Talmud. Finally, the delusions of the Kabbala declared a life and death war against rabbinical Judaism. Such were the fruits of blindness. The members of the synod of Konstantinov turned in their perplexity to Jacob Emden, who, since his controversy with Eibeschütz, was accounted the representative of sound orthodoxy. He, too, enjoyed a triumph, though of an altogether different kind from the one his antagonist was at the same time celebrating in the midst of his noisy admirers. The Polish Jews at last began to be aware that secular knowledge and cultivated eloquence are after all not altogether objectionable, since they can render assistance to Judaism. They were desirous that a cultured Portuguese should come to Poland, endowed with knowledge and readiness of speech, who would represent them before the Polish magistracy and clergy, in order to suppress the dangerous Frankist sect.

Jacob Emden, deeply affected by the despairing appeal of his Polish brethren, came to a conclusion of great importance for succeeding ages. Sabbatians of all shades appealed to the Zohar as a sacred authority, as the Bible of a new revelation, excusing all their blasphemies and indecencies by quotations from it. What if the Zohar should prove not to be genuine, but only a supposititious work? And this was the conclusion to which Emden came. The repulsive incidents in Poland first suggested the inquiry to him, and it became clear to him that at least a portion of the Zohar was the production of an impostor.

To the question whether it would be lawful to persecute the Frankists, Jacob Emden answered emphatically in the affirmative. He held them, according to the accounts received from Poland, to be shameless transgressors of the most sacred laws of decency and chastity, turning vice into virtue by means of mystical jugglery. No persuasion, however, was required from him; when persecution became necessary in Poland the will to inflict it was never wanting. The Frankists were denounced to the magistracy and clergy as a new sect, and handed over to the Catholic Inquisition, and the bishop of Kamieniec, Nicolas Dembowski, in whose diocese they were apprehended, had no objection to erect a stake. Frank was cunning enough to avert from his followers the blow aimed at them and to direct it against their enemies. From Chocim, where after a brief imprisonment he had settled in safety, he counseled them to emphasize two points in their defense: that they believed in a Trinity, and that they rejected the Talmud as a compilation full of error and blasphemy. His counsel meeting with opposition, he secretly assembled some of his followers in a small town in Poland, and reiterated his advice, with the addition that twenty or thirty of them must quickly be baptized to give more emphasis to their assertions that they acknowledged the Trinity and rejected the Talmud. To Frank change of religion was a small matter. The Talmud Jews of the district heard of Frank's secret conference with his confederates, collected a band, attacked them, and after using them roughly placed them in confinement. This proceeding provoked the anti-Talmudists to revenge. They would not, indeed, be baptized, but they declared before the tribunal of Bishop Dembowski that they were *almost* Christians, that they believed in a Divine Trinity, that the rest of the Jews, who repudiated this doctrine, did not hold the true faith, and persecuted them on account of their superiority. To make their breach with Judaism unmistakable, or to revenge themselves in a very sanguinary way, they made false accusations, namely, that believers in the Talmud make use of the blood of Christians, and that the Talmud inculcates the murder of Christians as a sacred duty. There was no difficulty in trumping up evidence in favor of the accusation. It was only necessary that some Christian child should be missing. Something of the kind must have occurred in Jampol in Podolia (April, 1756), and immediately the most respected Jews of the town were placed in chains, and the other communities menaced. Bishop Dembowski and his chapter, rejoiced at their good luck, favored the Frankists in every way in return for their false evidence, freed them from prison, protected them from persecution, allowed them to settle in the diocese of Kamieniec, permitted them to live as they pleased, and were delighted to foster their hatred of the Talmud Jews. The bishop flattered himself that, through the Frankists, among whom were several rabbis, he would be able to con-

vert many Polish Jews to Catholicism. The new
sect passed into the state in which the persecuted
becomes the persecutor.

In order to drive their adversaries to desperation,
the Frankists (1757) petitioned Bishop Dembowski
to arrange a disputation between themselves and
the Talmudists, and bound themselves to prove both
the doctrine of the Trinity and the harmful nature
of the Talmud, from the Scriptures and the Zohar.
To this the bishop willingly consented.   One of the
Frankist rabbis—perhaps old Elisha Schor, of
Rohatyn—composed a confession of faith, which,
almost unequaled for audacity and untruthfulness,
is so artful in its explanation of Sabbatian-Kabbal-
istic doctrines as to have led the bishop to suppose
that they were in consonance with the Catholic faith,
and to drive their adversaries into a corner.   The
Frankist confession of faith contains nine articles.
The religion revealed by God to man contains so
many deep mysteries, that it must be thoroughly
searched out and examined ; without higher inspiration, however, it cannot be understood.   One of
these mysteries is that the Godhead consists of
three Persons, equal to one another, at once a
Trinity and a Unity.   Another mystery is that the
Godhead assumes human form to manifest itself
visibly to all men.   Through the mediation of these
deities incarnate, mankind is redeemed and saved—
not through the Messiah expected to assemble the
Jews and lead them back to Jerusalem.   The latter
is a false belief : Jerusalem and the Temple will
never be rebuilt.   The Talmud, indeed, interprets
revealed faith otherwise ; but its interpretation is
baneful, and has led its adherents into error and
unbelief.   The Talmud contains most revolting
statements ; such as that Jews are permitted, indeed,
obliged, to deceive and slay Christians.   The Zohar,
which is diametrically opposed to the Talmud, offers
the only true and correct interpretation of the Holy

Writings.   All these absurd statements, the Frankist confession of faith supported by passages from
the Bible and the Zohar; and to vilify the Talmud,
passages in it were intentionally misrepresented.
The creed was printed and published in the Hebrew
and the Polish language.   The representatives of
the Polish community—the Synod of the Four
Countries—were painfully sensible, in their desperate
situation, of the want of education prevalent among
them.   They could not produce a single man who
could expose the imposture of the Frankists and
the hollowness of their creed in well-turned or even
tolerable language.   The proud leaders of the
Synod behaved like children in their anxiety.   They
helplessly devised extravagant schemes, wished to
appeal to the pope, and to incite the Portuguese in
Amsterdam and Rome to protect them from the
machinations of their vindictive enemies.

Bishop Dembowski consented to the proposition
of the Frankists, and issued a command that the
Talmudists send deputies to a disputation at
Kamieniec, failing which he would punish them and
burn the Talmud as a book hostile to Christianity.
In vain the Polish Jews referred to their ancient
privileges, screened themselves behind great nobles,
and spent large sums of money.   They were obliged
to prepare for the disputation and render account
to the enemies they had so greatly despised.   Only
a few rabbis appeared.   What could the representatives of the Talmud, with their profound ignorance
and halting speech, effect against the audacious denunciations of the Frankists, particularly as they also
acknowledged the Zohar as a sacred book, and this,
as a matter of fact, formulates the doctrine of a kind
of Trinity !   What happened at the disputation of
Kamieniec has never transpired.   The Talmudists
were accounted as vanquished and refuted.   Bishop
Dembowski publicly declared (October 14, 1757),
that, as the anti-Talmudists had set down in writing

and proved the chief points of their confession of
faith, they were permitted everywhere to hold dis-
putations with the Talmudists. Copies of the Talmud were ordered to be confiscated, brought to
Kamieniec, and there publicly burned by the hangman. Dembowski was permitted arbitrarily to favor
the one party and condemn the other. The king
of Poland and his minister, Count Brühl, troubled
themselves but little about internal affairs, still less
about the Jews. Hence Dembowski, who at about
that time was made archbishop of Lemberg, was
allowed with the aid of the clergy, the police, and
the Frankists, to search for copies of the Talmud
and other rabbinical writings in the towns of his
bishopric, collect them at Kamieniec, and drag them
through the streets in mockery. Only the Bible
and the Zohar were to be spared, as in the time of
the Talmud persecution under Popes Julius IV and
Pius V. Nearly a thousand copies of the Talmud
were thrown into a great pit at Kamieniec and burnt
by the hangman. The Talmudists could do nothing,
but groan, weep, and proclaim a rigorous fast-day
on account of "the burning of the Torah." It was
the Kabbala that had kindled the torches for the
funeral pile of the Talmud. The clergy, in conjunction with the anti-Talmudists, daily made domiciliary visits into Jewish houses to confiscate copies
of the Talmud.

To free themselves and all other Jews from the
oft repeated, and as often refuted, accusation of
child-murder, which the abject Frankists had confirmed, the Jewish Talmudists sent Eliakim Selig
(Selek) to Benedictus XIV, to procure an official
exposure of the falsehood of the charge brought
against Jews. Eliakim's determination and persis-
tence succeeded in obtaining this authoritative ac-
quittal in Rome at the end of 1757.

Suddenly Bishop Dembowski died (November 17,
1757) a violent death, and this led to a new devel-

opment in the controversy.   Persecution of the
Talmudists immediately ceased, and from that time
the Frankists were persecuted, imprisoned, and declared outlaws.   Their beards were shaved off as a
mark of disgrace and to make them easily recog-
nizable.   The majority, no longer able to maintain
themselves in Kamieniec, fled to the neighboring
province of Bessarabia.   But they were even more
disturbed under Turkish jurisdiction.   Their persecutors informed the Jewish community of the arrival
of the anti-Talmudists in their district and of their
injuriousness to Judaism, and the former had only
to notify the Pasha and the Cadi that these supposed Polish Jews were not under the protection of
the Chacham Bashi (chief rabbi) of Constantinople
in order to invite the Turks to fall upon the new-
comers and mercilessly rob and ill-treat them.
In despair the Frankists wandered restlessly about
the borderlands of Podolia and Bessarabia.   At
length they addressed the king of Poland, and implored him to confirm the privilege tolerating their
worship granted them by Bishop Dembowski.   Augustus III, the weakling and martyr of the seven
years' war, thereupon issued a decree (June 11,
1758) permitting the Frankists to return unmolested
to their homes, and reside in Poland wherever they
pleased.   The decree was not enforced with sufficient energy, and the Frankists continued to be
persecuted by their opponents aided by the nobles.
In their trouble some of their body were sent to beg
Frank, who had so long forsaken them, to assist
them with his advice.   While affecting to demur, he
willingly obeyed their call and repaired again to
Podolia (January, 1759).

With his appearance the old game of intrigue
began once more.   Frank was from that time the
life and soul of his followers, and without his commands they undertook nothing.   He saw clearly
that the hypocrisy of simply declaring that the anti-

Talmudists believed in the Trinity must not be repeated, but that they must make more of a concession to Christianity. By his advice six Frankists, the majority foreigners, repaired to Wratislav Lubienski, Archbishop of Lemberg, with the declaration (February 20, 1759), "in the name of their whole body," that they were all willing, under certain conditions, to be baptized. In their petition they used phrases savoring of Catholicism, and breathed vengeance against their former co-religionists. Lubienski had this petition of the Zoharites printed, in order, on the one hand, to proclaim the victory of the Church, on the other, to keep the members of this sect to their word; but he did nothing for them. Although in their Catholic and Kabbalistic language they declared that they were languishing for baptism "like the hart for the water-brooks," they did not in the least contemplate an immediate formal secession to Christianity. Frank, their leader, whom they blindly followed, did not consider the time ripe for this extreme measure. He reserved it to extort favorable terms, which were embodied in an address presented to the king and Archbishop Lubienski (May 16, 1759) by two deputies. They insisted especially on a disputation with their opponents, adducing as a reason, that they wished to show the world that they were led to embrace Christianity, not from necessity and poverty, but through conviction. They wished, moreover, to give an opportunity to their secret confederates to publicly avow themselves believers in Christianity, which they would infallibly do if their righteous cause should triumph in public argument. Finally they hoped in this way to open the blinded eyes of their antagonists. To this cunningly devised petition breathing malice against their enemies, the king made no reply, while Lubienski answered evasively that he could only promise them eternal salvation if they allowed themselves to be baptized;

the rest would follow as a matter of course.   He
displayed no zeal whatever for the conversion of
these ragged fellows whom he believed to be dis-
semblers.   The papal nuncio in Warsaw, Nicholas
Serra, did not regard with favor the idea of the conversion of the anti-Talmudists.

The position of affairs changed, however, when
Lubienski withdrew to Gnesen, his arch-episcopal
seat, and the administrator of the archbishopric of
Lemberg, the canon De Mikulski, showed more zeal
for conversion.   He immediately promised the
Frankists to arrange a religious conference between
them and the Talmudists, if they would exhibit a
sincere desire for baptism.   On this the deputies,
Leb Krysa and Solomon of Rohatyn, in the name
of the whole body, made a Catholic confession of
faith (May 25), which savored of Kabbalism: "the
cross is the symbol of the Holy Trinity and the seal
of the Messiah."   It closed with these words: "The
Talmud teaches the use of the blood of Christians,
and whosoever believes in it is bound to use this
blood."   Thereupon Mikulski, without consulting
the papal nuncio Serra, made arrangements for a
second disputation in Lemberg (June, 1759).   The
rabbis of this diocese were summoned to appear,
under pain of a heavy fine, and the nobility and
clergy were requested in case of necessity to compel them.   The nuncio Serra, to whom the Talmudists complained, was in the highest degree dissatisfied with the idea of the disputation, but did
not care to prevent it because he wished to learn
with certainty whether the Jews used the blood of
Christians.   This appeared to him the most important point of all.   Just at this time Pope Clement
XIII had given a favorable answer on this question
to the Jewish deputy Selek.   Clement XIII proclaimed that the Holy See had examined the
grounds on which rested the belief in the use of
human blood for the feast of the Passover and the

murder of Christians by Jews, and that the Jews must not be condemned as criminals in respect of this charge, but that in the case of such occurrences legal forms of proof must be used. Notwithstanding this, the papal envoy at this very time, deceived by the meanness of the Frankists, partially credited the false accusation, and notified the Curia of it.

The religious conference which was to lead to the conversion of so many Jews, at first regarded with indifference, began to awaken interest. The Polish nobility of both sexes purchased admission cards at a high price, the proceeds to go to the poor people who were to be baptized. On the appointed day the Talmudists and Zoharites were brought into the cathedral of Lemberg; all the clergy, nobility, and burghers crowded thither to witness the spectacle of Jews, apparently belonging to the same religion, hurling at each other accusations of the most abominable crimes. In reality it was the Talmud and the Kabbala, formerly a closely united pair of sisters, who had fallen out with each other. The disputation failed miserably. Of the Frankists, who had boastfully given out that several hundreds of their party would attend, only about ten appeared, the rest being too poor to undertake the long journey and attire themselves decently. Of the Talmudists forty were present owing to their dread of the threatened fine. How Judaism had retrograded in the century of "enlightenment" when compared with the thirteenth century! At that time, on a similar occasion, the spokesman of the Jews, Moses Nachmani, proudly confronted his opponents at the court of Barcelona, and almost made them quake by his knowledge and firmness. In Lemberg the representatives of Talmudic Judaism stood awkward and disconcerted, unable to utter a word. They did not even understand the language of the country —their opponents, to be sure, were in like case— and interpreters had to be employed. But the

Catholic clergy in Poland and the learned classes also betrayed their astounding ignorance. Not a single Pole understood Hebrew or the language of the rabbis sufficiently to be an impartial witness of the dispute, whilst in Germany and Holland Christians acquainted with Hebrew could be counted by hundreds. The Talmudists had a difficult part to play in this religious conference. The chief thesis of the Frankists was that the Zohar teaches the doctrine of the Trinity, and that one Person of the Godhead became incarnate. Could they dare to deny this dogma absolutely without wounding the feelings of the Christians, their masters? And that leanings toward this doctrine were to be found in the Zohar they could not deny. Of course, they might have refuted completely the false charge of using the blood of Christian children and of the bloodthirsty nature of the Talmud, or might have cited the testimony of Christians and even the decisions of popes. They were, however, ignorant of the history of their own suffering, and their ignorance avenged itself on them. It is easy to believe that the Talmudic spokesmen, after the three days' conference, returned home ashamed and confused. Even the imputation of shedding Christian blood continued to cling to their religion.

The Zoharites who had obtained their desire were now strongly urged by the clergy to perform their promise, and allow themselves to be baptized. But they continued to resist as if it cost them a great struggle, and only yielded at the express command of their chief, Frank, and in his presence. The latter appeared with great pomp, in magnificent Turkish robes, with a team of six horses, and surrounded by guards in Turkish dress. He wished to impress the Poles. His was the strong will which led the Frankists, and which they implicitly obeyed. Some thousand Zoharites were baptized on this occasion. Frank would not be baptized in Lemberg, but appeared suddenly, with dazzling magnificence, in Warsaw (October, 1759), aroused the curiosity of the Polish capital, and requested the favor that the king would stand godfather to him. The news-papers of the Polish capital were full of accounts of the daily baptisms of so many Jews, and of the names of the great nobles and ladies who were their godparents. But the Church could not rejoice in her victory. Frank was watched with suspicion by the clergy. They did not trust him, and suspected him to be a swindler who, under the mask of Chris-tianity, as formerly under that of Islam, desired to play a part as the leader of a sect. The more Frank reiterated the demand that a special tract of country be assigned to him, the more he aroused the suspicion that he was pursuing selfish aims and that baptism had been but a means to an end. The Talmud Jews neglected nothing to furnish proofs of his impostures. At length he was un-masked and betrayed by some of his Polish followers, who were incensed at being neglected for the foreign Frankists, and showed that with him belief in Chris-tianity was but a farce, and that he had commanded his followers to address him as Messiah and God Incarnate and Holy Lord. He was arrested and examined by the president of the Polish Inquisition as an impostor and a blasphemer. The depositions of the witnesses clearly revealed his frauds, and he was conveyed to the fortress of Czenstochow and confined in a convent (March, 1760). Only the fact that the king was his godfather saved Frank from being burnt at the stake as a heretic and apostate. His chief followers were likewise arrested and thrown into prison. The rank and file were in part condemned to work on the fortifications of Czen-stochow, and partly outlawed. Many Frankists were obliged to beg for alms at the church doors, and were treated with contempt by the Polish pop-ulation. They continued true, however, to their

Messiah or Holy Lord. All adverse events they accounted for in the Kabbalistic manner: they had been divinely predestined. The cloister of Czenstochow they named mystically, "The gate of Rome." Outwardly they adhered to the Catholic religion, and joined in all the sacraments, but they associated only with each other, and like their Turkish comrades, the Donmäh, intermarried only with each other. The families descended from them in Poland, Wolowski, Dembowski, Dzalski, are still at the present day known as Frenks or Shäbs. Frank was set at liberty by the Russians, after thirteen years' imprisonment in the fortress, played the part of impostor for over twenty years elsewhere, in Vienna, Brünn, and at last in Offenbach; set up his beautiful daughter Eva as the incarnate Godhead, and deceived the world until the end of his life, and even after his death; but with this part of his career Jewish history has nothing to do.

For all these calamitous events, Jonathan Eibeschütz was in some measure to blame. The Frankists regarded him, the great Gaon, as one of themselves, and he did nothing to clear himself from the stigma of this suspicion. He was implored to aid the Polish Jews, to make his influence felt in refuting the charge of the use of Christian blood. He remained silent as if he feared to provoke the Frankists against himself. Some of his followers who had warmly upheld him began to distrust him, among them Ezekiel Landau, at that time chief rabbi of Prague. Jacob Emden had won the day, he could flourish over him the scourge of his scorn; and he pursued him even beyond the grave as the most abandoned being who had ever disgraced Judaism. The rabbinate had placed itself in the pillory, and undermined its own authority. But it thereby loosened the soil from which a better seed could spring forth.

Whilst Eibeschütz and his opponents were squabbling over amulets and Sabbatian heresy, and Jacob Frank Lejbowicz was carrying on his Zoharistic frauds, Mendelssohn and Lessing were cementing a league of friendship, Portugal was extinguishing its funeral fires for the Marranos, and in England the question of the emancipation of the Jews was being seriously discussed in Parliament.

CHAPTER VIII.

THE MENDELSSOHN EPOCH.

Renaissance of the Jewish Race—Moses Mendelssohn—His Youth—
Improves Hebrew Style—Lessing and Mendelssohn—Mendels-
sohn's Writings—The Bonnet-Lavater Controversy—Kölbele—
The Burial Question—Reimarus—Anonymous Publication of his
Work—Lessing's "Nathan the Wise"—Mendelssohn in
"Nathan"—Mendelssohn's Pentateuch—Opposition to it—The
"Berlin Religion"—Montesquieu—Voltaire—Portuguese Mar-
ranos in Bordeaux—Isaac Pinto—His Defense of Portuguese
Jews—Dohm and Mendelssohn—Joseph II of Austria—Michaelis
—Mendelssohn's "Jerusalem"—Wessely: his Circular Letter—
Mendelssohn's Death.

1750—1786 C. E.

CAN "a nation be born at once"—or can a people
be regenerated? If the laboriously constructed
organism of a nation has lost vitality, if the bonds
connecting the individual parts are weakened, and
internal dissolution has set in, even the despotic
will which keeps the members in a mechanical union
being wanting; in short, if death comes upon a
commonalty in its corporate state, and it has been
entombed, can it be resuscitated and undergo a revival? This doom has overtaken many nationalities
of ancient and modern times. But if in such a
people a new birth should take place, *i.e.*, a resurrection from death and apparent decomposition, and
if this should occur in a race long past its youthful
vigor, whose history has spread over thousands of
years,—then such a miracle deserves the most at-
tentive consideration from every man who does not
stolidly overlook what is marvelous.

The Jewish race has displayed miraculous phenomena, not only in ancient days, the age of miracles, but also in this matter-of-fact epoch. A community which was an object of mockery not merely

to the malicious and ignorant, but almost more to
benevolent and cultured men; despicable in its own
eyes ; admirable only by reason of its domestic virtues and ancient memories, both, however, disfigured
beyond recognition by trivial observances; scourging
itself with bitter irony ; of which a representative
member could justly remark, "My nation has become so estranged from culture, that the possibility
of improvement is doubtful"—this community
nevertheless raised itself from the dust ! It revived
with marvelous rapidity from its abjection, as if a
prophet had called unto it, " Shake thyself from the
dust ; arise . . . . loose thyself from the bands
of thy neck, O captive daughter of Zion !" And
who caused this revival? One man, Moses Mendelssohn, who may be considered the incarnation
of his race—stunted in form, awkward, timid, stut-
tering, ugly, and repulsive in appearance. But
within this race-deformity breathed a thoughtful
spirit, which only when misled pursued chimeras,
and lost its self-esteem only when proscribed. No
sooner did it understand that it was the exponent
of the truth, than it dismissed its visionary fancies,
its spirit transfigured the body, and raised the bent
form erect, the hateful characteristics disappeared,
and the scornful nickname of " Jew" was changed
almost into a title of honor.

This rejuvenescence or renaissance of the Jewish
race, which may be unhesitatingly ascribed to Mendelssohn, is noteworthy, inasmuch as the originator
of this great work neither intended nor suspected
it ; in fact, as already remarked, he almost doubted
the capacity for rejuvenescence in his brethren. He
produced this altogether unpremeditated glorious
result not by means of his profession or his public
position. He was not a preacher in the wilderness,
who urged the lost sons of Israel to a change of
mind ; all his life he shrank from direct exercise of
influence. Even when sought after, he avoided

leadership of every kind with the oft-repeated confession, that he was in no way fitted for the office. Mendelssohn played an influential part without either knowing or desiring it: involuntarily, he aroused the slumbering genius of the Jewish race, which only required an impulse to free itself from its constrained position and develop. The story of his life is interesting, because it typifies the history of the Jews in recent times, when they raised themselves from lowliness and contempt to greatness and self-consciousness.

Moses Mendelssohn (born at Dessau, August, 1728, died in Berlin, January 4, 1786) was as insignificant and wretched an object as almost all poor Jewish children. At this time even infants seemed to possess a servile appearance. For quick-witted boys there was no period of youth; they were early made to shiver and shake by the icy breath of rough life. They were thus prematurely awakened to think, and hardened for their struggle with unlovely reality. One day Mendelssohn, a weakly, deformed lad in his fourteenth year, knocked at the door in one of the gates of Berlin. A Jewish watchman, a sort of police officer, the terror of immigrant Jews, who was ordered to refuse admission to those without means of subsistence, harshly addressed the pale, crippled boy seeking admission. Fortunately, he managed bashfully to stammer out that he desired to enroll himself among the Talmudical pupils of the new rabbi of Berlin. This was a kind of recommendation, and enabled him to dispense with a full purse. Mendelssohn was admitted, and directed his steps towards the house of the rabbi, David Fränkel, his countryman and teacher, who had shortly before been called from Dessau to the rabbinate of Berlin.

He took an interest in the shy youth, allowed him to attend his rabbinical lectures, provided for his maintenance, and employed him in copying his

Commentary to the Jerusalem Talmud, because Mendelssohn had inherited a beautiful handwriting as his only legacy from his father, a writer of scrolls of the Law. Even if Mendelssohn learnt from Fränkel nothing besides the Talmud, yet the latter exerted a favorable influence upon the mind of his disciple, because his method, exercising itself upon virgin soil, the Jerusalem Talmud, was not so distorted, hair-splitting, and perverse as that of most expounders of the Talmud, who made the crooked straight, and the straight crooked. Mendelssohn's innate honesty and yearning for truth were not suppressed or hindered by his first teacher, and this was of value.

Like the majority of Talmud disciples (Bachurim) Mendelssohn led the life of poverty which the Talmud in a measure makes a stipulation for study :—

"Eat bread with salt, drink water by measure, sleep upon the hard earth, live a life of privations, and busy thyself with the Law."

His ideal at this time was to perfect himself in the knowledge of the Talmud. Was it chance that implanted in Berlin the seed destined to produce such luxuriant fruit? Or would the result have been the same, if he had remained with Fränkel in Dessau, or if the latter had been called to Halberstadt, or Fürth, or Metz, or Frankfort? It is highly improbable. Retired though Mendelssohn's life was, yet a fresh breeze was wafted from the Prussian capital into the narrow chambers of his Rabbinical studies. With the accession of Frederick the Great, who besides war cultivated the Muses (though in a French garb), literary dilettanteism, French customs, and contempt for religion began to grow into fashion among Berlin Jews. Although their condition under Frederick was restricted, yet, because several became wealthy, the new spirit did not pass over them without leaving an impression, however inadequate and superficial. An impulse towards culture, the spirit of innovation, and imitation of Christian habits began to manifest themselves.

A Pole first introduced Mendelssohn to the philosophical work of Maimuni, which for him and through him became a "Guide of the Perplexed." The spirit of the great Jewish thinker, whose ashes had lain in Palestine for more than five hundred years, came upon young Mendelssohn, inspired him with fresh thoughts, and made him, as it were, his Elisha. What signified to Mendelssohn the long interval of many centuries? He listened to the words of Maimuni as if sitting at his feet, and imbibed his wise instruction in deep draughts. He read this book again and again, until he became bent by constant perusal of its pages. From the Pole, Israel Zamosc, he also learned mathematics and logic, and from Aaron Solomon Gumpertz a liking for good literature. Mendelssohn learned to spell and to philosophize at the same time, and received only desultory assistance in both. He principally taught and educated himself. He cultivated firmness of character, tamed his passions, and accustomed himself, even before he knew what wisdom was, to live according to her rules. In this respect also Maimuni was his instructor. By nature Mendelssohn was violent and hot-tempered; but he taught himself such complete self-mastery that, a second Hillel, he became distinguished for meekness and gentleness.

As if Mendelssohn divined it to be his mission to purify the morals and elevate the minds of his brethren, he, still a youth, contributed to a Hebrew newspaper, started by associates in sympathy with him for the purpose of ennobling the Jews. The firstlings of his intellect are like succulent grass in the early spring. He abandoned the ossified, distorted, over-embellished Hebrew style of his contemporaries, which had debased the Hebrew language into the mere mumbling of a decrepit tongue. Fresh and clear as a mountain-stream the Hebrew outpourings of Mendelssohn welled forth. Philosophical-religious views pervaded these early works, not only where he desired to depict trust in God and the inefficacy of evil, but also the rejuvenescence of nature in her spring vesture, and the delight of the pure mind of man at this beautiful change. The school of suffering through which he had passed for so many years, instead of dragging him down, had awakened, elevated, and ennobled his spirit. His struggles for a livelihood ceased when he obtained the situation as tutor in a rich family (that of Isaac Bernard), which, though not over-lucrative, sufficed for his frugal habits. His journeyman days were, however, not yet at an end. The old and the new, tradition and original views agitated his mind; clearness and self-consciousness were to flow into it from another source.

To the great minds which Germany produced in the eighteenth century belongs Gotthold Ephraim Lessing. He was the first free-thinking man in Germany, probably more so than the royal hero Frederick, who had indeed liberated himself from bigotry, but still had idols to whom he sacrificed. With his gigantic mind, Lessing burst through all bounds and regulations which depraved taste, dry-as-dust science, haughty orthodoxy, and pedantry of every kind had desired to set up and perpetuate. The freedom that Lessing brought to the Germans was more solid and permanent than that which Voltaire aroused in depraved French society with his biting sarcasm ; for, his purpose was to ennoble, and his wit was only a means to this end. Lessing wished to exalt the theatre to a pulpit, and art to a religion. Voltaire degraded philosophy into light gossip for the drawing-room.

It was an important moment for the history of

the Jews, when these two young men, Mendelssohn and Lessing, became acquainted. It is related that a passionate lover of chess, named Isaac Hess, brought them together at the chess-board (1754). The royal game united two monarchs in the kingdom of thought. Lessing, the son of a pastor, was of a democratic nature: he sought the society of outcasts, and those despised by public opinion. As shortly before he had mixed with actors in Leipsic, and as afterwards he associated with soldiers in Breslau, so now he was not ashamed to converse in Berlin with despised Jews. He had before this dedicated the first-fruits of his art, which to him appeared the highest art, to the pariah nation. By his drama, "The Jews," he desired to show that a Jew can be unselfish and noble, and he thereby aroused the displeasure of cultivated Christian circles. The ideal of a noble Jew which Lessing had in mind while composing this drama, he saw realized in Mendelssohn, and it must have pleased him to find that he was not mistaken in his portraiture, and that reality did not disprove his dream.

As soon as Lessing and Mendelssohn became acquainted, they learned to respect and love each other. The latter admired in his Christian friend his ability and unconstraint, his courage and perfect culture, his overflowing spirit, and the vigor which enabled him to bear a new world upon his broad shoulders; and Lessing admired in Mendelssohn nobility of thought, a yearning for truth, and firmness of character based upon a moral nature. They were both so imbued with lofty nobility of mind that the one prized in the other whatever perfection he could not attain to equally with his friend. Lessing suspected in his Jewish friend "a second Spinoza, who would do honor to his nation." Mendelssohn was completely enchanted by Lessing's friendship. A friendly look from him, he confessed, had such power over his mind that it banished all

grief.   They exerted perceptible influence upon
each other.   Lessing, at that time a mere "Schön-
geist," as it was termed, aroused in Mendelssohn
an interest for noble forms, æsthetic culture, poetry,
and art; the latter in return stimulated Lessing to
philosophical thought.   Thus they reciprocally gave
and received, the true relationship in a worthy
friendship.   The bond of amity became so strong,
and united the two friends so sincerely, that it lasted
beyond the grave.

The stimulus that Mendelssohn received from his
friend was extraordinarily fruitful both for him and
for the Jews.   It may be said without exaggeration
that Lessing's influence was greater in ennobling
the Jewish race than in elevating the German people, due to the fact that the Jews were more eager
for study and more susceptible to culture.   All that
Mendelssohn gained by intercourse with his friend
benefited Judaism.   Through his friend, who by
reason of a genial, sympathetic nature exerted
great attraction upon talented men, Mendelssohn
was introduced into his circle, learned the forms of
society, and threw off the awkwardness which was
the stamp of the Ghetto.   He now devoted himself
zealously to the acquisition of an attractive German
style—a difficult task, as the German language was
strange to him, and the German vocabulary in use
among Jews was antiquated and misleading.   Nor
had he any pattern to follow; for, before Lessing
enriched German style with his genius, it was un-
wieldy, rugged, and ungraceful.   But Mendelssohn
overcame all difficulties.   He withdrew, as he expressed it, "a portion of his love from the worthy
matron (philosophy), to bestow it upon a wanton
maiden (the so-called *belles-lettres*.)"   Before a
year's intimacy with Lessing elapsed, he was able
to compose in excellent form his "Philosophical
Conversations" (the beginning of 1755), in which
he, the Jew, blamed the Germans, because, misap-

prehending the depth of their own genius, they bore the yoke of French taste: "Will, then, the Germans never recognize their own worth? Will they always exchange their gold for the tinsel of their neighbors?" This rebuke was applicable even to the philosophical monarch Frederick II, who could not sufficiently scorn native talent, nor sufficiently admire that of foreign lands. The Jew was more German than most of the Germans of his time.

His patriotic feelings for Judaism did not suffer diminution thereby; they were united in his heart with love for German ideals. Although he could never overcome his dislike to Spinoza's revolutionary system, yet in his first work he strove to save the latter's birthright in the new metaphysics. The "Philosophical Conversations" Mendelssohn handed to his friend, with the jesting remark that he could produce something like Shaftesbury, the Englishman. Without his knowledge Lessing had them printed, and thus contributed the first leaves to his friend's crown of laurel. Through Lessing's zeal to advance him in every way, Mendelssohn became known in the learned circle in Berlin. When a "Coffee-house of the Learned," for an association of about one hundred men of science, was established in the Prussian capital, hitherto deficient in literary interests, the founders did not pass over the young Jewish philosopher, but invited him to join them. Every month some member delivered a discourse upon a scientific subject. Mendelssohn, however, was prevented from reading in public by modesty and an imperfection of speech; he presented his contribution in writing. His essay was called an "Inquiry into Probability," which must replace certainty in the limited sphere of human knowledge. While it was being read aloud, he was recognized as the author, and was applauded by the critical audience. Thus Mendelssohn was made a citizen in the republic of literature, took an active part in the literary productions of the day, and contributed to the "Library of the Fine Arts," which had been founded by his friend Nicolai. His taste became more refined every day, his style grew nobler, and his thoughts more lucid. His method of presentation was the more attractive because he seasoned it with incisive wit.

That which the Jews had lost through the abasement of thousand years of slavery, Mendelssohn now recovered for them in a short space of time. Almost all, with the exception of a few Portuguese and Italian Jews, had lost pure speech, the first medium of intellectual intercourse, and a childish jargon had been substituted, which, a true companion of their misfortunes, appeared unwilling to forsake them. Mendelssohn felt disgust at the utter neglect of language. He saw that the Jewish corrupt speech contributed not a little to the "immorality of the average man," and he hoped for good results from the attention beginning to be paid to pure language. It was one of the consequences of the debasement of language, that the German and Polish Jews had lost all sense of form, taste for artistic beauty, and æsthetic feeling. Oppression from without and their onerous duties, which had reduced them to veritable slaves, had banished from their midst these, together with many other, ennobling influences. Mendelssohn recovered these lost treasures for his brethren. He acquired so remarkable a sense for the beautiful, that he was afterwards recognized by the Germans as a judge in questions of taste. The perverse course of study pursued by the Jews since the fourteenth century had blunted their minds to simplicity. They had grown so accustomed to all that was artificial, distorted, super-cunningly wrought, and to subtleties, that the simple, unadorned truth became worthless, if not childish and ridiculous, in their eyes. Their train of thought was mostly perverted, uncultivated, and defiant of logical discipline. He who in a short time was to restore their youthful strength, so schooled himself that twisted methods and thoughts became repugnant to him. With his refined appreciation for the simple, the beautiful, and the true, he acquired a profound understanding of biblical literature, whose essence is simplicity and truth. Through the close layers of musty rubbish, with which commentaries and super-commentaries had encumbered it, he penetrated to the innermost core, and was able to cleanse the beautiful picture from dust, and to understand and render comprehensible the ancient Revelation as if it were a new one. Though not gifted with the ability of expressing his thoughts poetically or rythmically, he had a delicate perception of the poetic beauties of every literature, especially of those in the holy language. And what formed the crowning-point of these attainments was, that his moral views were characterized by extreme delicacy; he was painfully conscientious and truthful, as if there flowed through his veins the blood of a long series of noble ancestors, who had chosen for their life's task all that is honorable and worthy. Almost childlike modesty adorned him, modesty quite remote however from self-despising subservience. He combined in himself so many innate and hardly acquired qualities, that he formed a striking contrast to the caricatures which German and Polish Jews of the time presented. There was but one feeling wanting in Mendelssohn—and this deficiency was detrimental to the near future of Judaism. He lacked an appreciation for history, for things petty on close view, but great in perspective, for the comic and tragic course of the human race during the progress of time. "What do I know of history!" he observed, in half-apologetic, half-scornful tones; "whatever is called history, political history, history of philosophers, I cannot understand." He shared this deficiency with his prototype Maimuni, and infected his surroundings with it.

Some of his brilliant qualities shone out from Mendelssohn's eyes and features, and won him more hearts than if he had striven to gain them. Curiosity about "this Jew" began to be aroused even at the court of Frederick the Great. He was considered the embodiment of wisdom. The dauntless Lessing infused such courage into him, that he ventured to criticise in a periodical the poetical works of the Prussian sovereign, and gently hint at their faults (1760). Frederick the Great, who regarded verse-making as poetry, and dogmatism as philosophy, worshiped the Muse in the court language of the day, thoroughly despised the German tongue, at this time pregnant with real poetry, and mocked at intellectual treasures sacred to solid thinkers. Mendelssohn, the Jew, felt hurt at the king's hatred of German, as well as by his superficial judgments. However, as one dare not tell the truth to monarchs, he cleverly, through the trumpet of praise, emitted a soft note of blame, clear enough to the acute reader.

Skillfully as Mendelssohn had concealed his censure of the king, yet a malicious courtier, the preacher Justi, discovered it, and also the name of the fault-finder, and denounced him, "a Jew, who had thrown aside all reverence for the most sacred person of His Majesty in insolent criticism of his poetry." Suddenly, Mendelssohn received a harsh command to appear on a Saturday at Sans-Souci; an act in accordance with the coarseness of the age. Full of dread, Mendelssohn made his way to Potsdam to the royal castle, was examined, and asked whether he was the author of the disrespectful criticism. He admitted his offense, and excused himself with the observation, that "he who makes verses, plays at nine-pins, and he who plays at ninepins, be he monarch or peasant, must be satisfied with the judgment of the boy who has charge of the bowls as to the merit of his playing." Frederick was no doubt ashamed to punish the Jewish reviewer for his subtle criticism in the presence of the French cynics of his court, and thus Mendelssohn escaped untouched.

Fortune was extraordinarily favorable to this man, unwittingly the chief herald of the future. It gave him warm friends, who found true delight in exalting him, though a Jew, in public opinion. It secured for him a not brilliant, yet fairly independent situation as book-keeper in the house where he had hitherto held the toilsome position of resident tutor. It bestowed on him a trusty, tender, and simple life companion, who surrounded him with tokens of devoted love. Fortune soon procured a great triumph for him. The Berlin Academy had offered a prize for an essay upon the subject, "Are philosophical (metaphysical) truths susceptible of mathematical demonstration?" Modestly Mendelssohn set to work to solve this problem. He did not belong to the guild of the learned, had not learnt his alphabet until grown up, at an age when conventionally educated youths have their heads crammed with Latin. When he became aware that his friend, the young, highly-promising scholar Thomas Abt, was also a competitor, he almost lost courage, and desired to withdraw. Still his work gained the prize (June, 1763), not alone over Abt, but even over Kant, whose essay received only honorable mention. Mendelssohn obtained the prize of fifty ducats and the medal. The Jew, the tradesman, had defeated his rivals of the learned guild. Kant's disquisition went deeper into the question, but that of Mendelssohn had the advantage of clearness and comprehensibility. "He had torn the thorns from the roses of philosophy." Compelled to acquire each item of his knowledge by great labor, and having only with difficulty become conversant with the barbarous dialect of the schools, he did not content himself with dry formulæ, but exerted himself to render intelligible, both for himself and others, metaphysical conceptions and truths. This circumstance gained him the victory over his much profounder opponent. His essay, which together with that of Kant was translated into French and Latin at the expense of the Academy, earned for him assured renown in the learned world, which was enhanced by the fact that the prize-winner was a Jew.

In the same year (October, 1763), he received a distinction from King Frederick, characteristic of the low condition of the Jews in Prussia. This honor was the privilege of being a protected Jew (Schutz-Jude), *i. e.*, the assurance that he would not some fine day be expelled from Berlin. Hitherto, he had been tolerated in Berlin only as a retainer of his employer. The philosophical King Frederick sympathized with the antipathy of his illustrious enemy Maria Theresa to the Jews, and issued anti-Jewish laws worthy of the Middle Ages rather than of the eighteenth century, so boastful of its humanity. He wished to see the Jews of his dominions diminished in number, rather than increased. Frederick's "general privilege" for the Jews was an insult to the age. Marquis d'Argent, one of Frederick's French courtiers, who in his naïveté could not conceive that a wise and learned man like Mendelssohn might any day become liable to be driven out of Berlin by the brutal police, urged Mendelssohn to sue for the privilege of protection, and the king to grant it. However, a long time elapsed before the dry official document granting it reached him. At last Mendelssohn became a Prussian "Schutz-Jude."

The philosophical "Schutz-Jude" of Berlin now won great success with a work, which met with almost rapturous admiration from his contemporaries

in all classes of society.   Two decades later this
production was already obsolete, and at the present
day has only literary value.   Nevertheless, when it
appeared, it justly attained great importance.
Mendelssohn had hit upon the exact moment to
bring it forward, and he became one of the celebrities of the eighteenth century.   For almost sixteen centuries Christianity had educated the nations
of Europe, governed them, and almost surfeited
them with belief in the supernatural.   It had employed all available means to effect its ends, and
finally, when the thinkers awakened from their
slumber induced by its lullabies, to inquire into the
certainty secured by this announcement of salvation which promised so much, serious people said
with regret—whilst sceptics chuckled with brutal
delight—that it offered delusive fancies in the place
of truth.

In serious compositions, or in satires, the French
thinkers of the eighteenth century—the whole body
of Materialists—had revealed the hollowness of the
doctrine, in which the so-called civilized peoples
had found comfort and tranquillity for many centuries.   The world was deprived of a God, the
heavens were enshrouded in mist; all that had
hitherto seemed firm and incapable of being dis-
placed was turned topsy-turvy.   The doctrine of
Jesus had lost its power of attraction, and become
degraded in the eyes of the earnest and thoughtful
to the level of childish fables.   Infidelity had become a fashion.   With the undeifying of Jesus
appeared to go hand-in-hand the dethronement of
God, and doubt of the important dogma of the immortality of the soul, which Christian theology had
borrowed from Greek philosophy and, as always,
adorning itself with strange feathers, had claimed
as its original creation.   Thereupon depended not
merely the confidence of mankind in a future existence, but also the practical morals of the present.

If the soul is mortal and transient, they thought in the eighteenth century, then the acts of man are of no consequence! Whether he be good or evil, virtuous or criminal, on the other side of the grave there was no retribution. Thus, after the long dream of many centuries, the civilized portion of mankind again fell into the despondency prevalent in the Roman society of the empire; they were without God, without support, without moral freedom, without stimulus to a virtuous life. Man had been degraded to a complicated machine.

Mendelssohn was also biased by the prejudice that the dignity of man stands and falls with the question of the immortality of the soul. He therefore undertook to restore this belief to the cultured world, to discover again the lost truth, to establish it so firmly and ward off materialistic attacks upon it so decisively, that the dying man should calmly look forward to a blissful future and to felicity in the after-life. He composed a dialogue called "Phædon, or the Immortality of the Soul." It was to be a popular book, a new doctrine of salvation for the unbelieving or sceptical world. Therefore he gave to his dialogue an easily comprehensible, attractive style, after the pattern of Plato's dialogue of the same name, from which he copied also the external form. But Plato supplied him with the mere form. Mendelssohn caused his Socrates to give utterance to the philosophy of the eighteenth century through the mouth of his pupil, Phædon.

His starting-point, in proving the doctrine of the immortality of the soul, is the fact of the existence of God, of which he has the highest possible certainty. The soul is the work of God, just as the body is; the body does not actually perish after dissolution, but is transformed into other elements; much less, then, can the soul, a simple essence, be decomposed, and perish. Further, God has acquainted the soul with the idea of immortality, has

implanted it in the soul.   Can He, the Benevolent
and True One, practice deception ?

"If our soul were mortal, then reason would be a dream, which
Jupiter has sent us that we may forget our misery ; and we would be
created like the beasts, only to seek food and die."

Every thought inborn in man must for that reason
be true and real.

In demonstrating the doctrine of immortality,
Mendelssohn had another noble purpose in view.
He thought to counteract the malady of talented
youths of the day, the Jerusalem-Werthers, who,
without a goal for their endeavors, excluded from
political and elevating public activity, lost in whimsical sentimentality and self-created pain, sank to
thoughts of suicide, which they carried out, unless
courage, too, was sicklied over.   Mendelssohn,
therefore, in his " Phædon" sought to inculcate the
conviction, that man, with his immortal soul, is a possession of God, and has no manner of right to decide
arbitrarily about himself and his life, or about the
separation of his soul from his body—feeble argu-
mentation, but sufficient for that weakly, effeminate
generation.

With his " Phædon," Mendelssohn attained more
than he had intended and expected, viz., " conviction
of the heart, warmth of feeling," in favor of the doctrine of immortality.   " Phædon " was the most popular book of its time, and was perused with heart
and soul.   In two years it ran through three editions,
and was immediately translated into all the European languages, also into Hebrew.   Theologians,
philosophers, artists, poets, such as Herder, Gleim,
and Goethe, then but a youth, statesmen, and princes
—men and women—were edified by it, reanimated
their depressed religious courage, and, with an enthusiasm which would to-day appear absurd, thanked
the Jewish sage who had restored to them that
comfort which Christianity no longer afforded.   The

deliverance by Mendelssohn, the Jew, was as joyfully welcomed by the world grown pagan, as in
an earlier epoch that effected by the Jews, Jesus and
Paul of Tarsus, was welcomed by the heathens.
His contemporaries were delighted both with the
contents and the form, with the glowing, fresh, vigorous style, a happy, artistic imitation of Plato's
dialogues.   From all sides letters of congratulation
poured in upon the modest author.   Everyone of
the literary guild who passed through Berlin eagerly
sought out the Jewish Plato, as one of the greatest
celebrities of the Prussian capital, to have a word
with him.   The Duke of Brunswick seriously thought
of securing the services of Mendelssohn for his
state.   The Prince of Lippe-Schaumburg treated
him as a bosom friend.   The Berlin Academy of
Sciences proposed him as a member.   But King
Frederick struck the name of Mendelssohn off the
list, because, as it was said, he desired at the same
time to have the Empress Catherine admitted into
the learned body, and she would be insulted in having a Jew as a companion.   Two Benedictine friars
—one from the convent of Peter, near Erfurt, the
other from the convent of La Trappe—addressed
Mendelssohn, the Jew, as the adviser of their conscience, for instruction in moral and philosophical
conduct.   The book " Phædon," out of date in twenty
years, as remarked above, raised its author to the
height of fame.   He was fortunate, because he introduced it to the world exactly at the right moment.

An incident vexatious in itself served to exalt
Mendelssohn to an extraordinary degree in the eyes
of his contemporaries, and to invest him with the
halo of martyrdom.   John Caspar Lavater, an
evangelical minister of Zürich, an enthusiast who
afterwards joined the Jesuits, thought that he had
found in Mendelssohn's intellectual countenance a
confirmation of his deceptive art, the reading of the
character and talents of a man from his features.

Lavater asserted that in every line of Mendelssohn's face the unprejudiced could at once recognize the soul of Socrates. He was completely enchanted with Mendelssohn's head, raved about it, desiring to possess a well-executed model, in order to bring honor upon his art. Mendelssohn having caused his Phædon to speak in so Greek a fashion that no one could have recognized the author as a Jew, Lavater arrived at the fantastic conclusion that Mendelssohn had become entirely estranged from his religion. Lavater had learned that certain Berlin Jews were indifferent to Judaism, and forthwith reckoned Mendelssohn amongst their number. There was the additional fact that, in a conversation reluctantly entered upon with Lavater, Mendelssohn had pronounced calm, sober judgment upon Christianity, and had spoken with a certain respect of Jesus, though with the reservation, "if Jesus of Nazareth had desired to be considered only a virtuous man." This expression appeared to Lavater the dawning of grace and belief. What if this great man, this incarnation of wisdom, who had become indifferent towards Judaism, could be won over to Christianity! This was the train of thought which arose in Lavater's mind after reading "Phædon." Ingenuous or cunning, he spread his net for Mendelssohn, and thus showed how ignorant he was of his true character. About this time, a Geneva professor, Caspar Bonnet, had written in French a weak apology, entitled "Investigation into the Evidences of Christianity against Unbelievers." This work Lavater translated into German, and sent to Mendelssohn, with an awkward dedication, which looked like a snare (September 4, 1769). Lavater solemnly adjured him to refute publicly Bonnet's proofs of Christianity, or, if he found them correct, to do "what sagacity, love of truth, and honesty would naturally dictate, what a Socrates would have done, if he had read this treatise, and found it unanswerable." If Lavater had been really acquainted with the secrets of the heart, as he prided himself, he would have understood that, even if Mendelssohn had severed all connection with Judaism, Christianity was still more repugnant to him, and that sagacity, that is to say, regard to profit and the advantages of a pleasant existence, was altogether lacking in his character. Lavater did not desire to expose him before the public, but he wished to create a sensation, without thinking what pain he was causing the shy scholar of Berlin.

Mendelssohn later had reason to thank Lavater for having through thoughtlessness or pious cunning drawn him out of his diffidence and seclusion. Mendelssohn had indeed expressed his relations to Judaism and his co-religionists so vaguely that on-lookers might have been misled. In public life he was a philosopher and an elegant writer, who represented the principles of humanity and good taste, and apparently did not trouble about his race. In the darkness of the Ghetto he was a strictly ortho-dox Jew, who, apparently unconcerned about the laws of beauty, joined in the observance of every pious custom. Self-contained and steadfast though he was in reality, he seemed to be a twofold per-sonality, revealing the one or the other as he was in Christian or in Jewish society. He could not stand up in defense of Judaism without, on the one hand, affronting Christianity by his philosophical convictions, and, on the other, showing, if ever so lightly, his dissatisfaction with the chaotic traditions of the synagogue, and so offending the sensibility of his co-religionists and quarreling with them. Neither of these courses, owing to his peace-loving character, entered his mind. He would have been able to pass his life in an attitude of silence, if Lav-ater's rude importunity had not dragged him out of this false position, altogether unworthy of a man with a mission. Painful as it was to reveal his innermost thoughts upon Judaism and Christianity, he could not hold his peace at this challenge, without being considered a coward even by his friends. These reflections weighed heavily upon him, and caused him to take up the glove.

He skillfully carried on the contest thus forced upon him, and was ultimately victorious. At the end of 1769, in a public letter addressed to Christendom and Lavater, its representative, Mendelssohn in the mildest form wrote most cutting truths, whose utterance in former times would inevitably have led to bloodshed or the stake. Mendelssohn had examined his religion since the days of his youth, and found it true. Philosophy and *belles-lettres* had with him never been an end, but the means to prepare him for testing Judaism. He could not possibly expect advantage from adherence to it; and as for pleasure—

"O my worthy friend, the position assigned to my co-religionists in civil life is so far removed from all free exercise of spiritual powers, that one's satisfaction is not increased by learning the true rights of man. He who knows the state in which we now are, and has a humane heart, will understand more than I can express."

If the examination of Judaism had not produced results favorable to it, what would have chained him to a religion so intensely and universally despised, what could have prevented him from leaving it? Fear of his co-religionists, forsooth? Their secular power was too insignificant to do any harm.

"I do not deny that I have noticed in my religion certain human additions and abuses, such as every religion accepts in course of time, which unfortunately dim its splendor. But of the essentials of my faith I am so firmly and indisputably assured, that I call God to witness that I will adhere to my fundamental creed as long as my soul does not assume another nature."

He was as opposed to Christianity as ever, for the reason which he had communicated to Lavater verbally, and which the latter should not have concealed, namely, that its founder had declared himself to be God.

"Yet, for my part, Judaism might have been utterly crushed in every polemical text-book, and triumphantly arraigned in every school composition, without my ever entering into a controversy about it. Without the slightest contradiction from me, any scholar or any sciolist in subjects Rabbinic might have constructed for himself and his readers the most ridiculous view of Judaism out of worthless books which no rational Jew reads, or knows of. The contemptible opinion held of Jews I would desire to shame by virtue, not by controversy. My religion, my philosophy, and my status in civil life are the weightiest arguments for avoiding all religious discussion, and for treating in public writings of truths equally important to all religions."

Judaism was binding only upon the congregation of Jacob. It desired proselytes so little, that the rabbis had ordained that any person who offered to unite himself to this religion was to be dissuaded from his design.

"The religion of my fathers does not care to be spread abroad; we are not to send missions to the two Indies or to Greenland, to preach our belief to remote nations. I have the good fortune to possess as friends many excellent men not of my creed. We love each other dearly, and never have I said in my heart, 'What a pity for that beautiful soul!' It is possible for me to recognize national prejudices and erroneous religious opinions among my fellow-citizens, and nevertheless feel constrained to remain silent, if these errors do not directly affect natural religion or natural law (morality), but are only accidentally connected with the advancement of good. It is true that the morality of our actions does not deserve the name, if based upon error. . . . . But as long as truth is not recognized, as long as it does not become national, so as to work as powerful an effect upon the great mass of the people as ingrained prejudice, the latter must be almost sacred to every friend of virtue. These are the reasons that religion and philosophy give me to shun religious disputes."

Besides, being a Jew, he had to be content with toleration, because in other countries even this was denied his race. "Is it not forbidden, according to the laws of your native city," he ask Lavater, "for your circumcised friend even to visit you in Zürich?" The French work of Bonnet he did not find so convincing, he said, as to cause his convictions to waver; he had read better defenses of Christianity written by Englishmen and Germans; also it was not original, but borrowed from German writings. The arguments were so feeble and so little tending to prove Christianity that any religion could be equally well or badly defended by them. If Lavater thought that a Socrates could have been convinced of the truth of Christianity by this treatise, he only showed what power prejudice exerts over reason.

If the evangelical consistory, before whom Mendelssohn offered to lay his letter for censorship before printing it, did not regret granting him permission to print whatever he pleased, " because they knew his wisdom and modesty to be such that he would write nothing that might give public offense," still he undoubtedly did give offense to many pious persons.

Mendelssohn's epistle to Lavater naturally made a great sensation. Since the appearance of Phædon, he belonged to the select band of authors whose works every cultivated person felt obliged to read. Besides it happened that the subject of the controversy was attractive at the time. The freethinkers—by no means few at this time—were glad that at last some one, a Jew at that, had ventured to utter a candid word about Christianity. Owing to his obtrusiveness and presumptuous advocacy of Christianity, Lavater had many enemies. These read Mendelssohn's clever reply to the zealous conversionist with mischievous delight. The hereditary prince of Brunswick, who, as said above, was charmed with Mendelssohn, expressed (January 2, 1770) his admiration, that he had spoken " with such great tact and so high a degree of humanitarianism " upon these nice questions. Bonnet himself, less objectionable than his servile flatterer, admitted the justice of Mendelssohn's cause, and complained of Lavater's injudicious zeal. A letter of his dated January 12, 1770, was almost a triumph for Mendelssohn. He said that his dissertation, with which Lavater had desired to convert the Jew, had not been addressed to the honorable " House of Jacob," for which his heart entertained the sincerest and warmest wishes; much less had it been his intention to give the Jewish philosopher a favorable opinion of Christianity. He was full of admiration for the wisdom, the moderation, and the abilities of the famous son of Abraham. He indeed desired him to investigate Christianity, as it could only gain by being subjected to a close inquiry by the wise son of Mendel. But he did not wish to fall into Lavater's mistakes, and make it burdensome for him. However, in spite of his virtuous indignation, Bonnet perpetrated a bit of knavery against Mendelssohn. Lavater himself was obliged in a letter to publicly beg Mendelssohn's pardon for having placed him in so awkward a position, entreating him at the same time to attest that he had not intentionally been guilty of any indiscretion or perfidy. Thus Mendelssohn had an opportunity of acting magnanimously towards his opponent. On the subject proper under dispute, however, he remained firm; he did not surrender an iota of his Judaism, not even its Talmudical and Rabbinical peculiarities, and with every step his courage grew.

Mendelssohn did not wish to let pass this propitious opportunity of glorifying Judaism, which was so intensely contemned, and make it clear that it was in no way opposed to reason. Despite the warnings of timid Jews, to allow the controversy to lapse, so as not to stir up persecutions, he pointed out with growing boldness the chasm which Christianity had dug between itself and reason, whereas Judaism in its essence was in accord with reason. "The nearer I approach this so highly-esteemed religion," he wrote in his examination of Bonnet's "Palingénésie," "the more abhorrent is it to my reason." It afforded him especial delight when strictly orthodox Christians thought that they were abusing Judaism by declaring it to be equivalent to natural religion (Deism).

"Blessed be God, who has given unto us the doctrine of truth. We have no dogmas contrary to, or beyond reason. We add nothing, except commandments and statutes, to natural religion ; but the fundamental doctrines of our religion rest upon the basis of understanding." "This is our glory and our pride, and all the writings of our sages are full of it."

Frankly Mendelssohn spoke to the hereditary prince of Brunswick of the untenability of Christian, and the reasonableness of Jewish, dogmas. He thought that he had not yet done enough for Judaism.

"Would to God, another similar opportunity were granted me ; I would do the same. . . . . When I consider what we ought to do for the recognition of the sanctity of our religion."

Those who had not wholly parted company with reason declared Mendelssohn to be in the right, and his defense to be just. They beheld with astonishment that Judaism, so greatly despised, was yet vastly superior to celebrated, official, orthodox Christianity. Through its noble son, Judaism celebrated a triumph. The unhappy ardor of Lavater, and the refined yet daring answer of Mendelssohn for a long time formed the topic of conversation in cultured circles in Germany, and even beyond its borders. The journals commented upon it, and noted every incident. Anecdotes passed backwards and forwards between Zürich and Berlin. It was said that Lavater had asserted that if he were able to continue for eleven days in a state of complete holiness and prayer, he would most positively succeed in converting Mendelssohn to Christianity. When Mendelssohn heard this saying—whether authentic or not it is characteristic of Lavater—he smilingly said, "If I am permitted to sit here in my armchair and smoke a pipe philosophically, I have no objections !" There was more talk of the contest between Mendelssohn and Lavater than of war and peace. Every fair brought pamphlets written in German and French, unimportant productions, which did not deserve to live long. Only a few were

on Mendelssohn's side, the majority took the part
of Christianity and its representatives against the
"insolence of the Jew," who did not consider it an
honor to be offered admission into the Christian
community.

The worst of these was by a petty, choleric
author, named John Balthasar Kölbele, of Frankfort-on-the-Main, who, from hatred of the Jews, or
from distemper of body and soul, hurled such coarse
insults against Mendelssohn, the rabbis, the Jews,
and Judaism, that his very violence paralyzed his
onslaught. Kölbele had on a previous occasion
attacked Mendelssohn, and jeered at him by means
of a lay figure in one of his forgotten romances. He
desired to write, or said that he had written, an
"Anti-Phædon" against Mendelssohn's "Phædon."
His whole gall was vented in a letter to "Mr. Mendelssohn upon the affair of Lavater and Kölbele"
(March, 1770). Against the assertions of Mendelssohn as to the purity of Judaism, he brought forward
the calumnies and perversions of his brother in feeling, Eisenmenger. Mendelssohn's pure, unselfish
character was known in almost all cultivated and
high circles of Europe. Nevertheless, Kölbele cast
the suspicion upon him of adhering to Judaism from
self-interest, "because a Jewish bookkeeper is in a
better position than a Christian professor, and the
former besides derives some profit from attendance
in the antechambers of princes." To Mendelssohn's
asseveration that he would cling to Judaism all his
lifetime, the malignant fool or libeler rejoined,
"How little value Christians attach to the oath of a
Jew!" Mendelssohn disposed of him in a few words
in the postscript of a letter addressed to Lavater.
Nothing more was required; Kölbele had condemned himself. Mendelssohn profited by these
vilifying attacks, inasmuch as respectable authors,
who in their hearts were not a little irritated by his
independent and bold action, left him in peace,

rather than be associated with Kölbele. Mendelssohn emerged victorious from this conflict, trifling only at first sight, which had lasted for nearly two years ; he rose in public opinion, because he had manfully vindicated his own religion.

It had brought upon him also the reproaches of pious Jews. That which his discernment had feared took place. From love of truth he had publicly declared, that he had found in Judaism certain human additions and abuses, which only served to dim its splendor. This expression offended those who reverenced every custom, however un-Jewish, as a revelation from Sinai, because it was sanctified by time and the code. The entire Jewish world, including the Berlin community, with the exception of the few who belonged to Mendelssohn's circle, would not admit that rust had accumulated upon the noble metal of Judaism. He was therefore questioned on this point, probably by Rabbi Hirschel Lewin, and asked for an exact explanation of the phrase. He was very well able to give a reply, which probably satisfied the rabbi, who was no zealot. But his orthodoxy was still suspected by the strictly pious people whom he termed "the Kölbeles of our co-religionists." He was obliged to exculpate himself from the imputation of having pronounced the decisions of Talmudical sages "as worthless trash." Young Poles, adventurous spirits, thirsting for knowledge, "with good minds, but confused thoughts," both pure and impure elements, forced themselves upon Mendelssohn, and brought him into bad repute. The majority had broken not alone with the Talmud, but also with religion and morality ; they led a dissolute life, and considered it the mark of philosophy and enlightenment. Out of love to mankind and independent thought, Mendelssohn entered into relations with them, held discussions with them, advanced and aided them, which also cast a false light upon his relations to Judaism.

The frivolity and excesses of these young men were imputed to him, and they were regarded as his protégés and disciples.

He soon gave occasion for an increase of this suspicion.   The Duke of Mecklenburg-Schwerin, to avoid the dangers of premature interment, had in a mild, fatherly way (April, 1772) forbidden the Jews of his land to bury the dead at once, according to Jewish usage.   Jewish piety towards the deceased, which forbids keeping the dead above the earth long enough for decomposition to set in—a feeling petrified in the ritual code—was affronted by this edict, as though the duke had commanded disregard of a religious practice.   The representatives of the congregations of Schwerin supplicated Jacob Emden, of Altona, the aged champion of orthodoxy, to demonstrate from Talmudic and Rabbinic laws, that prolonged exposure of a corpse was an important infringement of Jewish law.   Emden, who knew his inability to compose a memorial in German, referred the people of Schwerin to Mendelssohn, whose word had great influence with princes. They followed his advice.   How astounded were they to learn, from a letter of Mendelssohn's (May, 1772), that he agreed with the ducal order, that the dead should not be buried before the third day; because, according to the experience of competent physicians, cases of apparent death were possible; and that it was right, in fact, compulsory, to rescue human life in spite of the most stringent ordinances of the religious code!   Mendelssohn proved besides that in Talmudical times precautions were taken for the prevention of hasty burial in doubtful cases.   His opinion was, with the exception of one blunder, faultlessly elaborated in the Rabbinical manner.   Nevertheless, true to his peaceful, complaisant nature, he sent the formula of a petition to the duke to mitigate the decree.   Emden, however, in his orthodox zeal, stamped this disputed question

almost as an article of faith. A custom so universal among Jews, among Italians and Portuguese as
well as Germans and Poles, could not be lightly set
aside. Not much value was to be attached to the
sayings of doctors. Mendelssohn's Talmudical
proofs were not conclusive. In a letter Emden
gave him clearly to understand that he was reprov-
ing him for his own benefit, to remove the suspicion
of lukewarm belief, which he had aroused by his
evil surroundings. Thus arose petty discord between Mendelssohn and the rigidly orthodox party,
which afterwards increased.

Meanwhile, his friend Lessing, just before his
death, had unintentionally stirred up a storm in
Germany which caused the Church to tremble, and,
under the spell of discontent and an artistic impulse, he had glorified Mendelssohn, together with
all Jews, in a perfect poetic creation. The first
cause of this tempest, which shook Christianity to
its core, was Mendelssohn's dispute with Lavater.
Lessing was so indignant at the certainty of victory
assumed by the representative of Church Christianity that he had strenuously encouraged his Jewish
friend to engage in valorous conflict.

"You alone dare and are able to write and speak thus upon this
matter, and are therefore infinitely more fortunate than all other honest people, who cannot achieve the subversion of this detestable
structure of unreason otherwise than under the pretense of building a
new substructure."

He did not suspect that even then he was holding
a thunderbolt in his hands, which he would soon be in
a position to hurl against the false gods who thought
that they had conquered heaven. During his restless life, which corresponded to his constantly agitated spirit, Lessing came to Hamburg, where he
made the acquaintance of the respected and free-
thinking family of Reimarus. Hermann Samuel
Reimarus, a profound inquirer, indignant at the
fossilized and insolent Lutheran Christianity of the

Hamburg pastors, had written a "Defense of the
Rational Worshipers of God," in which he rejected
every revealed religion, endeavoring to secure to
reason the rights denied it, and depreciating particularly the founder of Christianity.   Reimarus,
however, had not courage to utter boldly what he
recognized as true, and lay bare publicly, in accordance with his convictions, the weaknesses of the
dominant religion.   He left this treatise, which contained dangerous and inflammatory material, to his
family and to a secret order of free-thinkers, as a
legacy.   Eliza Reimarus, a noble daughter worthy
of her father, handed fragments of this incendiary
manuscript to Lessing, who read them with interest,
and thought of publishing them.   However, he had
not sufficient confidence in himself to give a decision upon points of theological discussion, and, therefore, sent these fragments to his Jewish friend, who
was capable of judging them.   Mendelssohn did
not, indeed, find this work very convincing, because
the author, embittered by the credulity of the
Church, had fallen into the opposite error of advocating the most spiritless form of infidelity, and, according to the shortsighted view of that age, of
finding only petty intrigues in great historical movements.   Despite Mendelssohn's judgment, his friend
continued to think that this book would be of service in humiliating the Church.   He seriously
thought of hurling the inflammatory writings of
Reimarus, under a false name, at the Church.   But
the Berlin censorship would not allow them to be
printed.   Then Lessing formed another plan.   His
position as superintendent of the ducal library of
Brunswick in Wolfenbüttel permitted him to publish the manuscript treasures of this rich collection.
In the interest of truth he perpetrated a falsehood,
asserting that he had discovered in this library these
"Fragments of an Unknown," the work of an author
of the last generation.   Under this mask, and pro-

tected by his immunity from censorship in publishing contributions "to history and literature from the treasures of the library at Wolfenbüttel," he began to issue them. He proceeded step by step with the publication of these fragments. The first installments were couched in an entreating tone, asking for support of the religion of reason against the religion of the catechism and the pulpit. He then ventured a step further—to prove the impossibility of the miracles upon which the Church was based, and especially to make apparent the unhistorical character and incredibility of the resurrection of Jesus, one of the main pillars of Christianity, with which it stands and falls. Finally, Lessing produced the most important of the fragments at the beginning of 1778, "Upon the Aim of Jesus and His Disciples." Herein it was explained that Jesus had only desired to announce himself as the Jewish Messiah and King of the Jews. To this end he had made secret preparations with his disciples, formed conspiracies to kindle a revolution in Jerusalem, and attacked the authorities in order to cause the downfall of the High Council (the Synhedrion). But when this plan of subversion failed, and Jesus had to suffer death, his disciples invented another system, and declared that the kingdom of Jesus was not of this world. They proclaimed him the spiritual redeemer of mankind, and gave prominence to the hope of his speedy reappearance; thus the Apostles had concealed and disfigured the original system of Jesus.

This treatment of the early history of Christianity, fairly calculated to overthrow the whole edifice of the Church, descended like a lightning-flash. It was sober, convincing, scientifically elaborated, yet comprehensible by everyone. Amazement and stupefaction were the effect, especially on the publication of the last fragment. Statesmen and citizens were as much affected as theologians.

Public opinion upon the matter was divided. Earnest youths about to begin a theologic career hesitated; they did not care to yield their life's activity to what was perhaps only a dream, and chose another vocation. Some affirmed that the proofs against Christianity were irrefutable. The anonymity of the writer heightened the excitement. Conjectures were made as to who the author might be; Mendelssohn's name was publicly mentioned. Only a few knew that this blow had been struck by Reimarus, revered by theologians, too. The anger of the zealots was discharged upon the publisher, Lessing. He was attacked by all parties, and had no companion in arms. His Jewish friend would willingly have hastened to his assistance, but how could he mix himself up in these domestic squabbles of the Christians? Among the numerous slanders circulated by the orthodox about Lessing it was said that the wealthy Jewish community of Amsterdam had paid him one thousand ducats for the publication of the Wolfenbüttel fragments. Accustomed to single-handed combat against want of taste and reason, Lessing was man enough to protect himself. It was a goodly sight to behold this giant in the fray, dealing crushing strokes with light banter and graceful skill. He defeated his enemies one after the other, especially one who was the type of blindly credulous, arrogant, and malicious orthodoxy, the minister Göze in Hamburg. As his pigmy opponents could not overcome this Hercules by literary skill, they summoned to their aid the secular arm. Lessing's productions were forbidden and confiscated, he was compelled to deliver up the manuscripts of the "Fragments," his freedom from censorship was withdrawn, and he was expected not to write any more upon this subject (1778). He struggled against these violent proceedings, but he was vulnerable in one point. The greatest man whom Germany had hitherto produced was without means, and his position as librarian being imperiled, he was obliged to seek for other means of support. During one of his sleepless nights (August 10, 1778), a plan struck him which would simultaneously relieve him from pecuniary embarrassments and inflict a worse blow than ten " Fragments" upon the Lutheran theologians. They thundered against him from their church pulpits ; he would try to answer them from his theatre pulpit. The latest, most mature, and most perfect offspring of his Muse, "Nathan the Wise," should be his avenger. Lessing had carried this idea in his mind for several years ; but he could not have executed it at a more favorable time.

To the annoyance of the pious Christians who, with all their bigotry, uncharitableness, and desire for persecution, laid claim to every virtue on account of their belief in Jesus, and denounced the Jews, one and all, as outcasts, Lessing represented a Jew as the immaculate ideal of virtue, wisdom, and conscientiousness. This ideal he had found embodied in Moses Mendelssohn. He illumined him and the greatness of his character by the bright light of theatrical effects, and impressed the stamp of eternity upon him by his immortal verses. The chief hero of Lessing's drama is a sage and a merchant, like Mendelssohn, "as good as he is clever, and as clever as he is wise." His nation honors him as a prince, and though it calls him the wise Nathan, he was above all things good :

> " The law commandeth mercy, not compliance.
> And thus for mercy's sake he's uncomplying :
> . . . . How free from prejudice his lofty soul—
> His heart to every virtue how unlocked—
> With every lovely feeling how familiar . . . .
> . . . . O what a Jew is he ! yet wishes
> Only to pass as a Jew."

A son of Judaism, Nathan had elevated himself to the highest level of humane feeling and charitableness, for such his Law prescribed. In a fanatical

massacre by Crusaders, ferocious Christians had
slaughtered all the Jews in Jerusalem, with their
wives and children, and his beloved wife and seven
hopeful sons had been burnt. At first he raged,
and murmured against fate, but anon he spake with
the patience of Job :

> "This also was God's decree : So be it !"

In his terrible grief a mounted soldier brought
him a young, tender Christian child, an orphan girl,
and Nathan took it, bore it to his couch, kissed it,
flung himself upon his knees, and thanked God that
the lost seven had been replaced by at least one.
This Christian maiden he loved with all the warmth
of a fatherly heart, and educated her in a strictly
conscientious manner. Not one religion in preference to another, still less his own, did he instil
into the young soul of Recha, or Blanche, but only
the doctrines of pure fear of God, ideal virtue, and
morality. Such was the representative of Judaism.

How did the representative of Christianity
behave ? The Patriarch of Jerusalem, who, with
his church, was tolerated in the Mahometan city by
the magnanimous Sultan Saladin, by virtue of a
solemnly ratified treaty, meditates treacherous plans
against the sultan, concocts intrigues against him :

> "But what is villainy in human eyes
> May, in the sight of God, the patriarch thinks,
> Not be villainy."

For Nathan, he desires to kindle a pyre, because
he has fostered, loved, and raised to a lovely,
spiritual maiden, a forsaken Christian child. Without the compassion of the Jew, the child would have
perished :

> "That's nothing !   The Jew must still be burnt."

Daya, another representative of Church Christianity, who knows Recha's Christian origin, has
misgivings when she sees the Christian child bask-

ing in the warm love of a Jew. She is won over from these scruples by costly presents, but she still contemplates depriving Nathan of the most precious object to which his soul clings, even though danger should thereby befall him.

The Templar, Leon of Filnek, represents yet another phase of Christianity. A soldier and at the same time a cleric, who, spared by Saladin although he had broken his word, rescues Recha, the supposed Jewish maiden; he behaves with Christian insolence towards Nathan, speaking roughly and harshly to him, whilst the latter is pouring forth heartfelt gratitude for the rescue of his adopted daughter. Then, gradually, through the wonderful power of love, the Templar lays aside the coarse, hateful garb of Christian prejudice. In his veins there flows Mahometan blood. Only the holy simplicity of the friar Bonafides combines human kindness with monastic ecclesiasticism; but he knows only one duty—obedience—and at the command of the fanatically cruel Patriarch would commit the most horrible crimes.

These lessons Lessing preached from his theatre pulpit to the obdurate minds of the followers of Christ. The wise Jew, Nathan—Mendelssohn—has arrived at the highest level of human sympathy; while the best Christian, the Templar, every cultivated Christian—the Nicolais, the Abts, the Herders—have yet to free themselves from their thick-skinned prejudices, to attain to that height. It is a delusion to claim the possession of the one true religion and the only means of salvation. Who possesses the real ring? How can the real one be detected from the false? Only by meekness, heartfelt tolerance, true benevolence, and most fervent devotion to God; in short, by all those qualities which the official Christianity of the time did not display, and which were perfectly realized in Mendelssohn.

In every way Lessing scourged fossilized, persecuting Christianity, and glorified Judaism through
its chief representative.   As if this splendid drama,
the beautiful first-fruits of German poetry, was to
belong to the Jews, although given to the world by
a Christian poet, a son of Israel aided its production.
Lessing, besieged by theological foes, and fighting
against dire necessity, would not have been able to
complete it, if, during its composition, he had not
been enabled to live without anxiety.   He required
a loan, and found no helper among the Christians.
Moses Wessely, in Hamburg, the brother of the
neo-Hebraic poet, Naphtali Wessely, who afterwards
made a name for himself in Jewish history, advanced
the desired sum, although he was not a wealthy Jew,
and only wished to have the honor of possessing
something in Lessing's handwriting.

Lessing had not been wrong in thinking that this
drama would vex pious Christians much more than
ten controversial pamphlets against Göze.   As soon
as it appeared (spring, 1779), intense wrath was felt
against the poet, as if he had degraded Christianity.
The "Fragments" and his polemics against Göze
had not made him so many enemies as "Nathan."
Even his friends greeted him coldly, shunned him,
excluded him from the social reunions he loved, and
left him to the persecution of his adversaries.
Through this silent excommunication he felt himself
aggrieved, lost more and more of his bright humor
and elasticity of spirit, and became wearied, down-
cast, and almost stupefied.   The treatment of pious
Christians terribly embittered the last year of his
life.   He died in vigorous manhood like an aged
man, a martyr to his love of truth.   But his soul-
conquering voice made itself heard on behalf of tolerance, and gradually softened the discordant notes
of hatred and prejudice.   In spite of the ban placed
upon "Nathan," as well as upon its author, both in
Protestant and Catholic countries, this drama be-

came one of the most popular in German poetry, and as often as the verses inspired by conviction resound from the stage, they seize upon the hearts of the audience, loosening the links of the chain of Jew-hatred in the minds of Germans, who find it most difficult to throw off its shackles. "Nathan" made an impression on the mind of the German people, which, despite unfavorable circumstances, has not been obliterated. Twenty years before, when Lessing produced his first drama of "The Jews," an arrogant theologian censured it, because it was altogether too improbable that among a people like the Jews, so noble a character could ever be formed. At the appearance of "Nathan" no reader thought that a noble Jew was possible. Even the most stubborn dared not assert so monstrous an absurdity. The Jewish ideal sage was a reality, and lived in Berlin, an ornament not alone to the Jews, but to the German nation. Without Mendelssohn, the drama of "Nathan" would not have been written, just as without Lessing's friendship Mendelssohn would not have become what he did to German literature and the Jewish world. The cordiality of the intimacy between these two friends showed itself after Lessing's death. His brothers and friends, who only after his demise realized his greatness, turned, in the anguish of their loss, to Mendelssohn, as if it were natural that he should be the chief mourner. And in very sooth he was; none of his associates preserved Lessing's memory with so sorrowful a remembrance and religious a reverence. He was beyond all things solicitous to protect his former friend against misapprehension and slander.

As Mendelssohn, without knowing or desiring it, stimulated Lessing to create an ideal, and through him helped to dispel the bias against Jews, so at the same time, without aiming at it, he inaugurated the spiritual regeneration of his race. The Bible,

especially the Pentateuch—the all in all of the
Jews—although very many knew it by heart, had
become as strange to them, as any unintelligible
book.   Rabbinical and Kabbalistic expositors had
so distorted the simple biblical sense of the words,
that everything was found in it except the actual
contents.

Polish school-masters—there were no others—
with rod and angry gestures, instructed Jewish boys
in tender youth to discover the most absurd perversities in the Holy Book, translating it into their
hateful jargon, and so confusing the text with their
own translation, that it seemed as if Moses had
spoken in the barbarous dialect of Polish Jews.

The neglect of all secular knowledge, which increased with every century, had reached such a
pitch that every nonsensical oddity, even blasphemy,
was subtly read into the verses of Scripture.   What
had been intended as a comfort to the soul was
changed into a poison.   Mendelssohn acutely felt
this ignorance and wresting of Bible words, for he
had arrived at the enlightened view that Holy Writ
does not contain "that which Jews and Christians
believe they can find therein," and that a good, simple translation would be an important step towards
the promotion of culture among Jews.   But in his
modesty and diffidence it did not occur to him to
employ these means to educate his brethren.   He
compiled a translation of the Pentateuch for his
children, to give them a thorough education and to
introduce the word of God to them in an undisfig-
ured form, without troubling (as he observed)
"whether they would continue to be compelled, in
Saxe-Gotha, on every journey, to pay for their Jewish heads at a game of dice, or to tell the story of
the three rings to every petty ruler."   It was only
at the urgent request of a man whose word carried
weight with Mendelssohn, that he decided to publish his translation of the Pentateuch into German

(in Jewish-German characters) for Jewish readers.
It cost him an effort, however, to attach his name
to it.

He knew his Jewish public too well not to understand that the translation, however excellently it
might be done, would meet with little approval, unless it were accompanied by a Hebrew exposition.
Of what value to the depraved taste of Jewish
readers was a book without a commentary? From
time immemorial, since commentaries and super-
commentaries had come into existence, these had
been much more admired than the most beautiful
text. Mendelssohn, therefore, obtained the assistance of an educated Pole, named Solomon Dubno,
who, a praiseworthy exception to his countrymen,
was thoroughly acquainted with Hebrew grammar,
to undertake the composition of a running commentary. The work was begun by securing the
necessary subscribers, without whom no book could
at that time be issued. It became apparent that
Mendelssohn had already many supporters and admirers among his brethren, within and beyond Germany. His undertaking, which was to remove from
the Jews the reproach of ignorance of their own literature, and of speaking a corrupt language, was
hailed with joy. Most of the subscribers came from
Berlin and Mendelssohn's native town, Dessau,
which was indeed proud of him. From Poland also
orders for the Germanized "Torah" arrived, mostly
from Wilna, where Elijah Wilna, to a certain extent
a liberal thinker, and the visionary perversities of
the New-Chassidim had drawn attention to the
Holy Scriptures. As a sign of the times, it may
also be noticed that the translation was purchased
by Christians, professors, pastors, court preachers,
consistorial councilors, court councilors, and the
nobility. Mendelssohn's Christian friends were,
indeed, extraordinarily active in promoting his work.
Eliza Reimarus, Lessing's noble friend, even collected subscriptions.

Glad as were Mendelssohn's admirers to receive
the news of a Pentateuch translation from his hand,
so disturbed were the rigid adherents to antiquity
and obsolete habit.   They felt vividly, without being
able to think it out clearly, that the old times, with
their ingenuous credulity—which regarded everything with unquestioned faith as an emanation from
a Divine source—would now sink into the grave.

No sooner was a specimen of the translation
published, than the rabbis of the old school were
prejudiced against it, and planned how to keep the
enemy from the house of Jacob.   To these opponents of Mendelssohn's enterprise belonged men
who brought honor upon Judaism, not alone by
their Rabbinical scholarship and keen intellects, but
also by their nobility of character.   There were especially three men, Poles by birth, who had as little
appreciation of the innovations of the times as of
beauty of form and purity of speech.   One of them,
Ezekiel Landau (chief rabbi of Prague, from the
year 1752; died in 1793), enjoyed great respect
both within and outside his community.   He was a
clever man, and learned in time to swim with the
tide.   The second, Raphael Cohen, the grandfather
of Riesser (born 1722, died 1803), who had emigrated from Poland, and had been called from Posen
to the rabbinate of the three communities of Hamburg, Altona, and Wandsbeck, was a firm, decided
character, without guile or duplicity, who as judge
meted out justice without respect to persons, considering justice the support of God's throne.   The
third and youngest was Hirsch Janow, a son-in-law
of Raphael Cohen, who, on account of his profound
acumen in Talmudical discussions, was called the
"keen scholar" (born 1750, died 1785).   His acute
mind was equally versed in the intricate problems
of mathematics as in those of the Talmud.   He was
thoroughly unselfish, the trifling income that he received from the impoverished community of Posen

he gave away to the unfortunate; he distributed alms with open-handed benevolence, and without asking questions whether the recipients were orthodox or heretics, whilst he himself starved. He contracted debts to save the needy from misery. Solomon Maimon, a deep thinker, who had opportunities of knowing men from their worst side, called this rabbi of Posen and Fürth "a godly man," an epithet not to be considered an exaggeration from such lips. To these three rabbis a fourth kindred spirit may be added, Phineas Levi Hurwitz (born 1740; died 1802), rabbi of Frankfort-on-the-Main, also a Pole, educated in the Chassidean school. These men, and others who thought like them, and who regarded the perusal of a German book as a grievous sin, from their point of view were right in opposing Mendelssohn's innovation. They perceived that the Jewish youth would learn the German language from the Mendelssohn translation more than an understanding of the "Torah"; that the former would strongly tend to become the chief object of study; the attention to Holy Writ would degenerate into an unimportant secondary matter, whilst the study of the Talmud would be completely suppressed. Though Mendelssohn himself enjoyed good repute from a religious point of view, his adherents and supporters were not invariably free from reproach. Unworthy men, who had broken with Judaism, and conceitedly termed themselves Mendelssohnians, were energetic in advancing the sale of the translation, and thus brought it into suspicion with the rigidly orthodox party.

Raphael Cohen, of Hamburg, a man of hasty temper, was the most zealous agitator against the German version of the Bible. But as Mendelssohn had relatives on his wife's side in this town, and also many admirers, no action could be taken against him there or in Prague, where there were freethinkers among the Jews. Fürth, therefore, was looked upon as the fittest place whence the interdict (about June, 1779) against "the German Pentateuch of Moses of Dessau" should be launched. All true to Judaism were forbidden, under penalty of excommunication, to use this translation.

Meanwhile the conflict between the old and the new Judaism was conducted with calmness, and no violent symptoms showed themselves. If Jacob Emden had been alive, the contest would have raged more fiercely, and evoked more disturbance. Mendelssohn was too unselfish, too gentle and philosophically tranquil to grow excited on hearing of the ban against his undertaking, or to solicit the aid of his Christian friends of high rank in silencing his opponents. He was prepared for opposition. "As soon as I yielded to Dubno to have my translation printed, I placed my soul in my hands, raised my eyes to the mountains, and gave my back to the smiters." He regarded the play of human passions and excessive ardor for religion as natural phenomena, which demanded quiet observation. He did not wish to disturb this peaceful observation by external influence, by threats and prohibitions, or by the interference of the temporal power. "Perhaps a little excitement serves the best interests of the enterprise nearest to my heart." He suggested that if his version had been received without opposition, its superfluity would have been proved. "The more the so-called wise men of the day object to it, the more necessary it is. At first, I only intended it for ordinary people, but now I find that it is much more needful for rabbis." On the part of his opponents, however, no decided efforts were made to suppress his translation, which appeared to them so dangerous, or to denounce its author. Only in certain Polish towns, such as Posen and Lissa, it was forbidden, and it is said to have been publicly committed to the flames. Violent action

world was opened to them. The Hebrew commentary served as a guide to a proper understanding of the translation. As if touched by a magic wand, the Talmud students, fossils of the musty schoolhouses, were transfigured, and upon the wings of the intellect they soared above the gloomy present, and took their flight heavenwards. An insatiable desire for knowledge took possession of them ; no territory, however dark, remained inaccessible to them. The acumen, quick comprehension, and profound penetrativeness, which these youths had acquired in their close study of the Talmud, rendered it easy for them to take their position in the newly-discovered world. Thousands of Talmud students from the great schools of Hamburg, Prague, Nikolsburg, Frankfort-on-the-Main, Fürth, and even from Poland, became little Mendelssohns ; many of them eloquent, profound thinkers. With them Judaism renewed its youth. All who, towards the end of the eighteenth and the beginning of the nineteenth century, were in various ways public workers, had up to a certain period in their lives been one-sided Talmudists, and needed the inspiration of Mendelssohn's example to become exponents and promoters of culture among Jews. In a very short time a numerous band of Jewish authors arose, who wrote in a clear Hebrew or German style upon matters of which shortly before they had had no knowledge. The Mendelssohn translation speedily resulted in a veritable renaissance of the Jews. They found their level in European civilization more quickly than the Germans, and—what should not be overlooked—Talmudic schooling had sharpened their intelligence. Mendelssohn's translation of the Pentateuch, together with his paraphrase of the Psalms, has produced more good than that of Luther, because instead of fossilizing, it animated the mind. The inner freedom of the Jews, as has been said, dates from this translation.

The beginning of the outward liberation of the Jews from the cruel bondage of thousands of years was also connected with Mendelssohn's name, and like his activity for their internal freedom was unconscious, without violence or calculation. It seems a miracle, though no marvelous occurrence accompanied it. It secured to the Jews two advocates, than whom none more zealous, none warmer could be desired : these were Lessing and Dohm.

Since the middle of the eighteenth century the attention of the cultured world had been directed towards the Jews without any action on their part. Montesquieu, the first to penetrate to the profound depths of human laws and reveal their spirit, was also the first to raise his weighty voice against the barbarous treatment of the Jews. In his widely-read, suggestive work, "Spirit of the Laws," he had demonstrated, with convincing arguments, the harm that the ill-treatment of the Jews had caused to states, and branded the cruelty of the Inquisition with an ineradicable stigma. The piercing cry of agony of a tortured Marrano at sight of a stake prepared for a "Judaizing" maiden of eighteen years of age in Lisbon had aroused Montesquieu, and the echo of his voice resounded throughout Europe.

"You Christians complain that the Emperor of China roasts all Christians in his dominions over a slow fire. You behave much worse towards Jews, because they do not believe as you do. If any of our descendants should ever venture to say that the nations of Europe were cultured, your example will be adduced to prove that they were barbarians. The picture that they will draw of you will certainly stain your age, and spread abroad hatred of all your contemporaries."

Montesquieu had rediscovered the true idea of justice, which mankind had lost. But how difficult was it to cause this idea to be fully recognized with reference to Jews !

Two events had brought the Jews, their concerns, their present, and their past before public notice : their demand for a legal standing in England, and

Voltaire's attacks upon them.   In England, where
a century before they had, as it were, crept in, they
formed a separate community, especially in the capital, without being tolerated or recognized by law.
They were regarded as foreigners—as Spaniards,
Portuguese, Dutchmen, or Germans, and had to pay
the alien duty.   However, the authorities, especially
the judges, showed regard for the Jewish belief ; for
instance, they did not summon Jewish witnesses
on the Sabbath.   After the Jews settled in the
American colonies of England had been naturalized,
a bill was presented in Parliament by merchants
and manufacturers, Jews and their friends, to be
sure, begging that they be treated as natives of
England, without being compelled to obtain civil
rights by taking the sacrament, as the law prescribed.   Pelham, the minister, supported the petition, and pointed out the advantages that would accrue to the country by the large capital of the Portuguese Jews and their warm attachment to England.
By their opponents, however, partly self-interest,
partly religious prejudices were brought to bear
against them.   It was urged that, placed on an equal
footing with English citizens, the Jews would acquire
the whole wealth of the kingdom, would obtain possession of all the landed property, and disinherit
Christians : the latter would be their slaves, and the
Jews would choose their own rulers and kings.
Orthodox literalists argued that according to Christian prophecies they were to remain without a home
until gathered to the land of their fathers.   Sur-
prisingly enough, a bill was passed by the Upper
House permitting Jews who had resided in England
or Ireland for three consecutive years to be naturalized ; but they were not to occupy any secular or
clerical office, nor to receive the Parliamentary franchise.   The lords and the bishops, then, were not
opposed to the Jews.   The majority of the Lower
House also agreed to the bill, and George II ratified

it (March, 1753). Was the decision of the Three
Estates really the expression of the majority of the
nation? This at once became doubtful: imprecations were immediately thundered from pulpits,
guilds, and the taverns against the ministry which
had urged the Naturalization Act for Jews. In our
days it seems hardly credible that the London merchants should have feared the ruin of their trade by
the influx of Jewish capitalists. Deacon Josiah
Tucker, who took the part of the Jews, and defended
the Naturalization Act, was attacked by the opposition in Parliament, in the newspapers, and in
pamphlets, and his effigy, together with his defense
of the Jews, was burnt at Bristol. To the vexation
of the liberal-minded, the ministry were weak
enough to yield to the clamor of the populace arising
from mercantile jealousy and fanatical intolerance,
and to annul their own work (1754) "because it had
provoked displeasure, and the minds of many loyal
subjects had been disquieted thereby." For, even
the most violent enemies of the act could not impute
evil to the Jews of England; they created a good
impression upon Englishmen by their riches, accumulated without usury, and by their noble bearing.
Public opinion warmly sided with them and their
claims for civil equality, and if, for the moment,
these were disregarded, yet no unfavorable result
ensued.

The second occurrence, although originating in a
single person, roused even more attention than the
action of the English Parliament towards the Jews.
This person was Arouet de Voltaire, king in the
domain of literature in the eighteenth century, who
with his demoniacal laughter blew down like a house
of cards the stronghold of the Middle Ages. He,
who believed neither in Providence nor in the moral
progress of mankind, was a mighty instrument of
history in the advancement of progress. Voltaire—
in his writings an entrancing wizard, a sage, in his

life a fool, the slave of base passions—picked a
quarrel with the Jews, and sneered at them and their
past. His hostility arose from personal ill-humor
and irritability. He maintained that during his stay
in London he lost eighty per cent of a loan of
25,000 francs, through the bankruptcy of a Jewish
capitalist named Medina. He cannot, however,
always be believed.

"Medina told me that he was not to blame for his bankruptcy:
that he was unfortunate, that he had never been a son of Belial.
He moved me, I embraced him, we praised God together, and I lost
my money. I have never hated the Jewish nation ; I hate nobody."

Yet, a low-minded Harpagon, who clung to his
money, Voltaire, on account of this large or small
loss, hated not only this Jew, but all Jews on earth.
A second incident excited him still more against
them. When Voltaire was in Berlin and Potsdam
as court poet, literary mentor, and attendant of
King Frederick, who both admired and detested
this diabolical genius, he gave a filthy commission
to a Jewish jeweler, named Hirsch, or Hirschel
(1750), which he afterwards, at the instigation of a
rival in the trade, named Ephraim Veitel, wished to
withdraw. Friction arose between Voltaire and
Hirschel, until some arrangement was made, which
the former afterwards desired to evade. In a word,
Voltaire practiced a series of mean tricks upon his
Jewish tradesman : cheated him about some diamonds, abused him, lied, forged documents, and
acted as if he were the injured party. At length a
complicated lawsuit sprang from these proceedings.
King Frederick, who had obtained information of
all this from the legal documents, and from a pamphlet, written ostensibly by Hirsch, in reality by
Voltaire's enemies, was highly enraged with the
poet and philosopher scamp. He resolved to banish him from Prussia, and wrote against him a comedy in French verse, called "Tantalus in the Lawsuit." Voltaire's quarrel with the Prussian Jew

created a sensation, and provided ample material for the mischievous delight of his opponents.

Next to avarice, revenge was a prominent feature in his character. It was too trifling for Voltaire to avenge himself upon the individual Jew who had contributed to his humiliation ; he determined to make the whole Jewish nation feel his hatred. Whenever he had an opportunity of speaking of Judaism or Jews, he bespattered the Jews of the past and the present with his obscene satire. This accorded with his method of warfare. Christianity, which he thoroughly hated and despised, could not be attacked openly without rendering the aggressor liable to severe punishment. Judaism, the parent of Christianity, therefore served as the target, against which he hurled his elegant, lightly brandished, but venomous darts. In one of his essays particularly he poured forth his gall against Jews and Judaism.

This partial and superficial estimate of the Jews, this summary judgment of a whole people, and a history of a thousand years, irritated many truth-loving men ; but no one dared provoke a quarrel with so dreaded an antagonist as Voltaire. It required a bold spirit, but it was hazarded by a cultured Jew, named Isaac Pinto, more from skillfully-calculated motives than from indignation at Voltaire's baseless defamation. Pinto (born in Bordeaux, 1715 ; died in Amsterdam, 1787) belonged to a Portuguese Marrano family, was rich, cultivated, noble, and disinterested in his own affairs ; but suffered from pardonable egoism, namely, on behalf of the community. After leaving Bordeaux he settled in Amsterdam, where he not only served the Portuguese community, but also advanced large sums of money to the government of Holland, and therefore held an honorable position. He always took warm interest in the congregation in which he had been born, and assisted it by word and

deed.   But his heart was most devoted to the Portuguese Jews, his brethren by race and speech ; on
the other hand, he was indifferent and cold towards
the Jews of the German and Polish tongues; he
looked down upon them with disdainful pride, as
Christians of rank upon lowly Jews.   Nobility of
mind and pride of race were intimately combined in
Pinto.   In certain unpleasant matters in which the
Portuguese community of Bordeaux had become
entangled, he displayed, on the one hand, ardent
zeal, on the other, hardness of heart.   In this prosperous commercial town, since the middle of the
sixteenth century, there had flourished a congregation of fugitive Marranos, who had fled from the
prisons and the autos-da-fé of the Spanish and Portuguese Inquisition.   These refugees had brought
considerable capital and an enterprising spirit, and
thus secured right of residence and certain privileges, but only under the name of new-Christians or
Portuguese merchants.   For a time they were
forced to undergo the hypocrisy of having their
marriages solemnized in the churches.   Their numbers gradually increased ; in two centuries (1550—
1750) the congregation of Bordeaux had grown to
200 families, or 500 souls.   The majority of the
Portuguese Jews, or new-Christians, of Bordeaux,
kept large banking-houses, engaged in the manu-
facture of arms, equipped ships, or undertook trans-
marine business with French colonies.   To their
importance as merchants and ship-owners they
united staunch uprightness, blameless honesty in
business, liberality towards Jews and non-Jews, and
the dignity which they had brought from the Pyrenean peninsula, their unnatural mother-country.
Thus they gained respect and distinction among
the Christian inhabitants of Bordeaux, and the
French court as well as the high officials connived
at their presence, and gradually came to recognize
them as Jews.   The important mercantile town also

attracted German Jews from Alsace, and French
Jews from Avignon, under papal government, who
obtained the right to settle by paying large sums
of money.   The Portuguese Jews were jealous ;
they feared that they would be placed on a level
with these co-religionists, who were little educated,
and engaged in petty trading or monetary transactions, and that they would lose their honorable
reputation.   Induced by these selfish motives they
exerted themselves to have the immigrant German
and Avignon Jews expelled from the town, by appealing to the old edict that Jews might not dwell
in France.   But the exiles contrived to gain the
protection of influential persons at court, and thus
obtained the privilege of sojourn.   Through the
connivance of the authorities, 152 foreign Jews had
already flocked to Bordeaux, several of whom had
powerful friends.   This was a thorn in the side of
the Portuguese, and to hinder the influx of strangers, they passed (1760) an illiberal communal law
against their foreign co-religionists.   They branded
every foreign Jew not of Portuguese origin as a
vagrant and a beggar, and as a burden to the
wealthy.   They calumniated the strangers, asserting that they followed dishonorable, fraudulent occupations, and thereby predisposed the citizens and
authorities against them.   According to their proposal, Portuguese Jews, or their council, should be
vested with the right to expel the foreign Jews, or
"vagrants," from the town within three days.   This
cruel and heartless statute had to be confirmed by
King Louis XV.   It was not difficult to obtain from
this monarch, who was ruled by his wives and his
courtiers, the most inhuman petitions.   A friend
and kinsman of Isaac Pinto undertook to get the
sanction of the court for this statute.

This was Jacob Rodrigues Pereira (born in Spain,
1715 ; died in Paris, 1780), grandfather of the famous and enterprising Emile and Isaac Pereira, a

man of talent and noble character, and an artist of a
peculiar kind, who had obtained wide renown.   He
had invented a sign language for the deaf and
dumb, and taught these unfortunate people a means
of expressing their thoughts.   As a Marrano, he
had taught the deaf and dumb in Spain.   Love for
the religion of his ancestors, or hatred of the bloodthirsty Catholic Church impelled him to leave the
land of the Inquisition (about 1734), and, together
with his mother and sister, to emigrate to Bordeaux.   Here, even before Abbé de l'Epée, he so
thoroughly verified his theory for the instruction of
those born dumb, in a specially appointed school,
that the king conferred a reward, and the first men
of science—D'Alembert, Buffon, Diderot, and Rousseau—lavished praises upon him.   Pereira afterwards became royal interpreter and member of the
Royal Society in London.   The Portuguese community of Bordeaux appointed him their representative in Paris, to ventilate their complaints and
accomplish their ends.   Moved with sympathy for
the unfortunate, he was yet so filled with communal
egoism, that he did not hesitate to inflict injury
upon his German and Avignon co-religionists.
The commission to secure from Louis XV the ratification of the proposed statute, he carried out but
too conscientiously.   But in the disorderly government of this king and his court there was a vast
difference between the passing and the administering of a law.   The higher officials were able to cir-
cumvent any law or defer its execution.   The expulsion of the Jews of German and Avignon origin
from Bordeaux lay in the hands of the governor,
the Duc de Richelieu.   Isaac Pinto, who was on intimate terms with him, was able to win his support.
Richelieu issued an urgent command (November,
1761) that within two weeks all foreign Jews should
be banished from Bordeaux.   Exception was made
only in favor of two old men and women whom the

hardships of the expulsion would have killed, and
of a man who had been of service to the town
(Jacob de Perpignan). All the rest were plunged
into unavoidable distress, as it was forbidden to
Jews to settle anywhere in France, and the districts
and towns where Jews already dwelt admitted no
new-comers. What a difference between the German Jew Moses Mendelssohn and the Portuguese
Jews Isaac Pinto and Rodrigues Pereira, who in
their time were ranked side by side ! The former
did not cease his efforts, until by his influence he
brought help to his unhappy brethren, or at least
offered them comfort. For the Jews in Switzerland,
who were tolerated only in two small towns, and
even there were so enslaved that they must have
died out, Mendelssohn procured some alleviation
through his opponent Lavater. Several hundred
Jews were about to be expelled from Dresden, because they could not pay the poll-tax laid upon
them. Through Mendelssohn's intercession with
one of his numerous admirers, Cabinet Councilor
Von Ferber, the unfortunate people obtained permission to remain in Dresden. To a Jewish Talmudical scholar unjustly suspected of theft and
imprisoned in Leipsic, Mendelssohn cleverly contrived to send a letter of consolation, whereby
he gained his freedom. Isaac Pinto and Jacob
Pereira, on the other hand, were zealous in
bringing about the expulsion of their brethren by
race and religion, which Mendelssohn considered
the hardest punishment of the Jews, "equal to annihilation from the face of God's earth, where
armed prejudice repulses them at every frontier."

The cruel proceedings of the Portuguese Jews
against their brethren in Bordeaux made a great
stir. If Jews might not tarry in France, why should
those of Portuguese tongue be tolerated ? The
latter, therefore, saw themselves compelled to put
themselves in a favorable light, and requested Isaac

Pinto, who had already appeared in public, and possessed literary culture, to write a sort of vindication for them, and make clear the wide difference between Jews of Portuguese descent and those of other lands. Pinto consented, or rather followed his own inclination, and prepared the "Reflections" upon Voltaire's defamation of Judaism (1762). He told this reckless calumniator that the crime of libeling single individuals was increased when the false accusations affected a whole nation, and reached its highest degree when directed against a people insulted by all men, and when the responsibility for the misdeeds of a few is laid upon the whole body, whose members, moreover, widely scattered, have assumed the character of the inhabitants of the country in which they live. An English Jew as little resembles his co-religionist of Constantinople, as the latter does a Chinese mandarin; the Jew of Bordeaux and he of Metz are two utterly different beings. Nevertheless, Voltaire had indiscriminately condemned them, and his sketch of them was as absurd as untrue. Voltaire, who felt called upon to extirpate prejudices, had in fact lent his pen to the greatest of them. He does not indeed wish them to be burnt. but a number of Jews would rather be burnt than so calumniated. "The Jews are not more ignorant, more barbarous, or superstitious than other nations, least of all do they merit the accusation of avarice." Voltaire owed a duty to the Jews, to truth, to his century, and to posterity, which would justly appeal to his authority when abusing and trying to crush an exceedingly unhappy people.

However, as already said, it was not so much Pinto's aim to vindicate the whole of the Jewish world against Voltaire's malicious charges as to place his kinsmen, the Portuguese or Sephardic Jews, in a more favorable light. To this end, he pretended that a wide gulf existed between them and those of other extraction, especially the German and Polish Jews. He averred, with great exaggeration, that if a Sephardic Jew in England or Holland wedded a German Jewess, he would be excluded from the community by his relatives, and would not even find a resting-place in their cemetery. This arose from the fact that the Portuguese Jews traced their lineage from the noblest families of the tribe of Judah, and that their noble descent had always in Spain and Portugal been an impulse to great virtues and a protection against vice and crime. Among them no traces of the wickedness or evil deeds of which Voltaire accused them were to be found. On the contrary, they had brought wealth to the states which received them, especially to Holland. The German and Polish Jews, on the other hand, Pinto abandoned to the attacks of their detractors, except that he excused their not over honorable trades and despicable actions by the overwhelming sufferings, the slavery, and humiliation which they had endured, and were still enduring. He succeeded in obtaining what he had desired. In reply, Voltaire paid him and the Portuguese Jews compliments, and admitted that he had done wrong in including them in his charges, but nevertheless continued to abuse Jewish antiquity.

Pinto's defense attracted great attention. The press, both French and English, pronounced a favorable judgment, and espoused the cause of the Jews against Voltaire. But they blamed Pinto for having been too partial to the Portuguese, and too strongly opposed to the German and Polish Jews, and, like Voltaire, passing sentence upon all indiscriminately, because of the behavior of a few individuals. A Catholic priest under a Jewish disguise took up the cause of Hebrew antiquity. He addressed "Jewish Letters" to Voltaire, pretending that they came from Portuguese and German Jews ; these were well meant but badly composed. They were widely read, and helped to turn the current of public opinion in favor of the Jews against Voltaire's savage attacks. They did not fail to remind him that owing to loss of money sustained through one Jew he pursued the whole race with his anger. This friendly pamphlet on behalf of the Jews being written in French, then the fashionable language, it was extensively read and discussed, and found a favorable reception.

Sympathy for the Jews and the movement to elevate them from their servile position were most materially stimulated by a persecution which humane thinkers of the time considered surprising and unexpected, but which has often been repeated in the midst of Christian nations. This persecution kindled passions on both sides, and awakened men to activity. In no part of Europe, perhaps, were the oppression and abasement of Jews greater than in the originally German, but at that time French province of Alsace, to which Metz may be reckoned. All causes of inveterate Jew-hatred—clerical intolerance, racial antipathy, arbitrariness of the nobility, mercantile jealousy, and brute ignorance—were combined against the Jews of Alsace, to render their existence in the century of enlightenment a continual hell. Yet the oppression was so paltry in its nature that it could never stimulate the Jews to offer heroic resistance. The German populace of this province, like Germans in general, clung tenaciously to their hatred of the Jews. Both the nobles and citizens of Alsace turned a deaf ear to the voice of humanity, which spoke so eloquently in French literature, and would not abate one jot of their legal rights over the Jews, who were treated as serfs. In Alsace there lived from three to four thousand Jewish families (from fifteen to twenty thousand souls). It was in the power of the nobility to admit new, or expel old families. In Metz the merchants had had a law passed limiting Jews to four hundred and eighty families. This condition of affairs had the same consequences as in Austria and Prussia: younger sons were condemned to celibacy, or exile from their paternal home, and daughters to remain unmarried. In fact, it was worse than in Austria and elsewhere, because German pedantry carefully looked to the execution of these rigorous Pharaonic laws, and stealthily watched the French officials, lest any attempt be made to show indulgence towards the unfortunate people. Naturally the Jews of Alsace and Metz were enclosed in Ghettos, and could only occasionally pass through the other parts of the towns. For these privileges they were compelled to pay exorbitant taxes.

Louis XIV had presented a portion of his income derived from the Jews of Metz as a gift to the Duc de Brancas and the Countess de Fontaine. They had to pay these persons 20,000 livres annually; besides poll-taxes, trade-taxes, house-taxes, contributions to churches and hospitals, war-taxes, and exactions of every sort under other names.

In Alsace they were obliged to pay protection-money to the king, tribute to the bishop of Strasburg, and the duke of Hagenau, besides residence-taxes to the nobles in whose feudal territory they dwelt, and war-taxes. The privilege of residence did not descend to the eldest son, but had to be purchased from the nobleman, as if the son were a foreign applicant for protection. The Jews had to win the good opinion, not alone of their lord, but also of his officials, by rich gifts at New Year, and on other occasions. Whence could they procure all these moneys, and still support their synagogues and schools?

Almost every handicraft and trade were forbidden them in Alsace: legally they could engage only in cattle-dealing, and in trading in gold and silver. In Metz the Jews were allowed to kill only such animals as they required for private consumption, and the appointed slaughterers had to keep a list of the animals slain. If they wished to make a journey outside their narrow province, they had to pay a poll-tax, and were subjected to the vexations of passports. In Strasburg, the capital of the province, no Jew could stay over night. What remained but to obtain the money indispensable for their wretched existence in an illegal way—through usury? Those who possessed money made advances to the small tradesmen, farmers, and vinedressers, at the risk of losing the amounts lent, and demanded high interest, or employed other artifices. This only caused them to be more hated, and the growing impoverishment of the people was attributed to them, and was the source of their unspeakable sufferings. They were in the sad position of being compelled to make themselves and others unhappy.

This miserable condition of the Alsatian Jews a villainous man sought to turn to his own advantage, and he almost brought on a sanguinary persecution. A lawyer, not without brains and literary culture, named Hell, belonging to a poor family, and ardently wishing for a high position, being acquainted with the devices of the Jewish usurers, actually learned the Hebrew language, to be able to levy blackmail on them without fear of discovery. He sent threatening letters in Hebrew, saying that they would inevitably be accused of usury and deception, if they did not supply him with a stated sum of money. This worthless lawyer afterwards became district judge to several Alsatian noblemen, and thus the Jews were given wholly into his power. Those who did not satisfy his continually increasing demands, were accused, ill-treated, and condemned. Meantime his unjust conduct was partially exposed: he was suspected, and this excited him against the Jews of Alsace. He devised a plan to arouse fanaticism against them. He pointed out to debtors a way to escape the oppressive debts which they owed Jewish money-lenders, by producing false receipts as for payments already rendered.　Some of his creatures traveled through Alsace, and wrote out such acquittances.　Conscientious debtors had their scruples silenced by the clergy, who assured them that robbing the Jews was a righteous act. The timid were pacified by a rogue especially despatched for that purpose, who distributed orders and crosses, presumably in the name of the king, to those who accepted and presented the false receipts, and were ready to accuse the Jews of oppression and duplicity.　Thus a menacing feeling, bordering on actual violence, developed against the Jews of Alsace.　The debtors united with common ruffians and clergymen to implore the weak-minded king Louis XVI, to put an end to all disturbances by expelling the Jews from the province.　To crown his work, the villainous district magistrate strove to exasperate the populace against them.　He composed a venomous work against them (1779), "Observations of an Alsatian upon the Present Quarrels of the Jews of Alsace," in which he collected all the slanderous accusations against Jews from ancient times, in order to present a repulsive picture of them, and expose them to hatred and extermination.　He admitted that receipts had been forged, but this was in consequence of the decrees of Providence, to whom alone vengeance was becoming.　They hoped by these means to avenge the crucifixion of Jesus, the murder of God.　This district judge aimed at the annihilation, or, at least, the expulsion of the Jews.　But the spirit of toleration had acquired sufficient strength to prevent the success of such cunning designs.　His base tricks were revealed, and, at the command of the king, Hell was imprisoned, and afterwards banished from Alsace.　A decree of the sovereign ordered (May, 1780) that lawsuits against usurers should no longer be decided by the district courts of the nobility, but by the chief councilor, or state councilor (Conseil Souverain) of Alsace.

One result of these occurrences was that the Alsatian Jews finally roused themselves, and ventured to state that their position was intolerable, and to entreat relief from the throne of the gentle king Louis XVI. Their representatives (Cerf Berr?) drew up a memorial to the state council upon the inhuman laws under which they groaned, and made proposals for the amelioration of their lot. They felt, however, that this memorial should be written so as to influence public opinion, at this time almost as powerful as the king himself. But in their midst there was no man of spirit and ability who could compose a fitting description of their condition.

To whom could they turn except to Mendelssohn, looked upon by European Jews as their advocate and powerful supporter in distress? To him, therefore, the Alsatian Jews—or, more correctly, their distinguished representative Cerf Berr, who knew Mendelssohn—sent the material with the request, to give the necessary polish and an impressive form to their petition. Mendelssohn had neither the leisure, nor perhaps the skill to carry out their request. Fortunately, he had found a new friend and admirer, who, by knowledge and position, was better able to formulate such a memorial. Christian William Dohm (b. 1751, d. 1820), owing to his thorough knowledge of history, had shortly before been appointed by Frederick the Great—with the title of military councilor—to superintend the archives. Like all ambitious youths and men who frequented Berlin, Dohm had sought out the Jewish philosopher, at this time at the summit of his fame; and like all who entered his circle Dohm felt himself attracted by his intellectuality, gentleness, and great wisdom. During his stay in Berlin

he was a regular visitor at the house of Mendelssohn, who, on Saturday, his day of leisure, always
assembled his friends around him.   Every cultivated
Christian who came in contact with Mendelssohn
was pleasantly attracted by him, overcame his bias
against Jews, and experienced mingled admiration
and sympathy for a race that had endured so much
suffering, and produced such a personality.   Dohm
had already thrown aside his innate or acquired antipathy against Jews.   His interest in mankind
rested not upon the shifting ground of Christian
love, but upon the firm soil of human culture, characteristic of the eighteenth century, and included
also this unhappy people.   He had already planned
to make the "history of the Jewish nation since the
destruction of their own state" the subject of his
studies.

Dohm evinced his readiness to draw up the memorial for the Alsatian Jews in a pleasing form, in
conjunction with Mendelssohn.   Whilst engaged on
this task, the thought struck him to publish a plea,
not alone for protection for the few, but on behalf
of all the German Jews, who suffered under similar
oppression.   Thus originated his never-to-be-for-
gotten work, "Upon the Civil Amelioration of the
Condition of the Jews" (finished August, 1781), the
first step towards removing the heavy yoke from
the neck of the Jews.   With this pamphlet, like
Lessing with his " Nathan," Dohm partly atoned for
the guilt of the German nation in enslaving and degrading the Jews.   Dohm's apology has no clerical
tinge about it, but was addressed to sober, enlightened statesmen, and laid particular stress upon the
political advantages.   The noble philanthropist
who first pleaded for the emancipation of the negroes had fewer difficulties to overcome than Dohm
in his efforts for the freedom of the Jews.   The
very circumstances that ought to have spoken in
their favor, their intelligence and activity, their

mission to teach Christian nations pure doctrines on God and morality, their ancient nobility—all tended to their detriment. Their intellectual and energetic habits were described as cunning and love of gain; their insistence upon the origin of their dogmas as presumption and infidelity, and their ancient nobility as pride. It is difficult to over-estimate the heroism required to speak a word on their behalf, in face of the numerous prejudices and sentiments against the Jews prevailing among all classes of Christian society.

In his apology Dohm, as already noted, omitted all reference to the religious point of view, and dwelt solely upon the political and economical aspect. He started by asserting that it was a universal conviction that the welfare of states depended upon increase of population. To this end many governments spent large sums of money to attract new citizens from foreign countries. An exception was made only in the case of Jews. "Almost in all parts of Europe the tendency of the laws and the whole constitution of the state is to prevent, as far as possible, the increase of these unfortunate Asiatic refugees. Residence is either denied them, or granted, at a fixed sum, for a short time. A large proportion of Jews thus find the gates of every town closed against them; they are inhumanly driven away from every border, and nothing is left to them except to starve, or to save themselves from starvation by crime. Every guild would think itself dishonored by admitting a Jew as a member; therefore, in almost every country, the Hebrews are debarred from handicrafts and mechanical arts. Only men of rare genius, amidst such oppressive circumstances, retain courage and serenity to devote themselves to the fine arts and the sciences. Even the rare men who attain to a high degree of excellence, as well as those who are an honor to mankind through their irreproachable righteousness, meet with respect only

from a few ; with the majority the most distinguished
merits of soul and heart can never atone for the
error of ' being a Jew.' What reasons can have induced the governments of European states to be so
unanimous in this attitude towards the Jewish
nation?" asked Dohm. Is it possible that industrious and good citizens are less useful to the state,
because they originally came from Asia, and are distinguished by a beard, by circumcision, and their
form of worship? If the Jewish religion contained
harmful principles, then the exclusion of its adherents
and the contempt felt for them would be justified ;
but that is not the case. " The mob, which considers
itself at liberty to deceive a Jew, falsely asserts that,
by his law, he is permitted to cheat the adherents
of another creed, and persecuting priests have spread
stories of the prejudices felt by the Jews, and thus
revealed their own. The chief book of the Jews,
the Law of Moses, is regarded with reverence also
by Christians."

Dohm reviewed the history of the Jews in Europe
—how, in the first centuries, they had enjoyed full
civil rights in the Roman Empire, and must have
been considered worthy of such privileges—how
they were degraded and deprived of their rights,
first by the Byzantines, then by the German barbarians, especially by the Visigoths in Spain. From
the Roman Empire the Jews had brought more culture than the dominant nations possessed ; they
were not brutalized by savage feuds, nor was their
progress retarded by monkish philosophy and superstition. In Spain amongst Jews and Arabs there
had existed a more remarkable culture than in
Christian Europe. Dohm then reviewed the false
accusations and persecutions against Jews in the
Middle Ages, painting the Christians as cruel barbarians and the Jews as illustrious martyrs. After
touching upon the condition of the Jews in the
various states, he concluded his delineation with the
words :

"These principles of exclusion, equally opposed to humanity and politics, which bear the impress of the dark centuries, are unworthy of the enlightenment of our times, and deserve no longer to be followed. It is possible that some errors have become so deeply rooted that they will disappear only in the third or fourth generation. But this is no argument against beginning to reform now; because, without such beginning, a better generation can never appear."

Dohm suggested a plan whereby the amelioration of the condition of the Jews might be facilitated, and his proposals formed a programme for the future. In the first place, they were to receive equal rights with all other subjects. In particular, liberty of occupation and in procuring a livelihood should be conceded them, so that, by wise precautions, they would be drawn away from petty trading and usury, and be attracted to handicrafts, agriculture, arts, and sciences, all without compulsion. The moral elevation of the Jews was to be promoted by the foundation of good schools of their own, or by the admission of their youth into Christian schools, and by the elevation of adults in the Jewish Houses of Prayer. But it should also be impressed upon Christians, through sermons and other effectual means, that they were to regard and treat the Jews as brothers and fellow-men. As a matter of course, Dohm desired to see freedom in their private religious affairs granted them: free exercise of religion, the establishment of synagogues, the appointment of teachers, maintenance of their poor, if considered wise, under the supervision of the government. Even the power of excluding refractory members from the community should be given them. Dohm, moreover, pleaded for the continuance, under certain restrictions, of independent jurisdiction in cases between Jews, the power to be vested in a tribunal of rabbis. He wished to debar them from only one privilege, from filling public offices, or entering the arena of politics. The ability to undertake these duties, he thought, was completely lacking in that generation, and would not manifest itself very con-

spicuously in the next. Besides there was a superabundance rather than a lack of competent state
officers. For this reason, it would, for the present,
be better both for the state and the Jews, if they
worked in warehouses and behind the plough rather
than in state offices. The immediate future disproved his doubts.

Dohm foresaw that his programme for the emancipation of the Jews would meet with violent and
stubborn opposition from the clergy and the theological school. He therefore submitted it to the
"wisdom of the governments," who at this time
were more inclined to progress and enlightenment
than the people. Dohm was filled with the seriousness and importance of his task; he was positive
that his proposals would lay the basis not only for
the welfare of the Jews, but also for that of the
states. It is not to be overlooked that Mendelssohn stood behind him. Even if he did not dictate
the words, yet he breathed into them his spirit of
gentleness and love of mankind, and illumined
the points which were strange and dark to Dohm,
the Christian and political writer. Mendelssohn is,
therefore, to be looked upon, if not as the father,
certainly as the godfather, of Dohm's work.

It was inevitable for such a treatise to create
great excitement in Germany. Must not this demand to treat Jews as equals have appeared to
respectable Christians as a monstrous thing; as if
the nobility had been asked to place themselves at
the same table with their slaves? Soon after its
appearance, Dohm's work advocating Jewish emancipation became extraordinarily popular; it was
read, discussed, criticised, and refuted by many,
and approved by only a few. The first rumor was
that Dohm had sold his pen to the Jews for a very
high price, although he had specially entreated protection for the poor homeless peddlers. Fortune
began to smile upon the Jews after having turned

its back upon them for so many centuries. Scarcely had the pamphlet appeared, when Emperor Joseph, the first Austrian ruler to allow himself in some degree to be guided by moral and humane principles, having snapt asunder the yoke of the Catholic Church, and having accorded a Toleration Edict to the Protestants, issued a series of laws relating to the Jews, which displayed sincere if rather fierce philanthropy.

By this new departure (October 19, 1781), the Jews were permitted to learn handicrafts, arts, and sciences, and with certain restrictions to devote themselves to agriculture. The doors of the universities and academies, hitherto closed to them, were thrown open. The education of the Jewish youth was a matter of great interest to this emperor, who promoted "philosophical morality." He accordingly decreed the establishment of Jewish primary and high schools (normal schools), and forced adults to learn the language of the country, by decreeing that in future only documents written in that language would possess legal force. He considerately removed the risk of all possible attempts at religious compulsion. In the schools everything that might be offensive to any creed was to be omitted from the curriculum. An ordinance enjoined (November 2) that the Jews were to be everywhere considered "fellow-men," and all excesses against them were to be avoided. The Leibzoll (body-tax), more humiliating to Christians than to Jews, was also abolished by Joseph II of glorious memory, in addition to the special lawtaxes, the passport-duty, the night-duty, and all similar oppressive imposts which had stamped the Jews as outcasts, for they were now to have equal rights with the Christian inhabitants (December 19). Joseph II did not intend to concede complete citizenship to the Jews; they were still forbidden to reside in those cities whence Christian intolerance had hitherto banished them. Even in Vienna Jews were allowed to dwell only in a few exceptional cases, on payment of protection-money (toleration-tax), which protection did not extend to their grown-up sons. They were not suffered to have a single public synagogue in Vienna. But Joseph II annulled a number of vexatious, restrictive regulations, such as the compulsory wearing of beards, the prohibition against going out in the forenoon on Sundays and holidays, or frequenting public pleasure resorts. The emperor even permitted Jewish wholesale merchants, notables, and their sons, to wear swords (January 2, 1782), and especially insisted that Christians should behave in a friendly manner towards Jews.

A notable beginning was thus made. The ignominy of a thousand years, which the uncharitableness of the Church, the avarice of princes, and the brutality of nations, had cast upon the race of Judah, was now partly removed, at least in one country. Dohm's proposals in consequence met with earnest consideration; they were not regarded as ideal dreams, but as political principles worthy of attention. Scholars, clergymen, statesmen, and princes began to interest themselves seriously in the Jewish question. Every thoughtful person in Germany and elsewhere took one side or the other. Various opinions and ideas were aired; the most curious propositions were made. A preacher, named Schwager, wrote:

"I have always been averse to hating an unfortunate nation, because it worships God in another way. I have always lamented that we have driven the Jews to deceive us by an oppressive political yoke. For, what else can they do, in order to live? in what other way can they defray their heavy taxes?"

Diez, Dohm's excellent friend, one of the noblest men of that epoch, afterwards Prussian ambassador to the Turkish court, thought that Dohm had asked far too little for the Jews.

"You aver most truly," he remarked, "that the present moral depravity of the Jews is a consequence of their bondage.   But to color
the picture, and weaken the reproaches leveled at the Jews, a representation of the moral depravity of the Christians would have been
useful ; certainly it is not less than that of the Jews, and rather the
cause of the latter."

John von Müller, the talented historian of the
Swiss, with his wide attainments in general history,
also admired the glorious antiquity of the Jews,
praised Dohm's efforts on behalf of the Jews, and
supplied him from the treasures of his knowledge
with new proofs of the unjust and pitiless persecution of the mediæval Jews, and their demoralization
by intolerable tyranny.   He wished the writings of
Maimuni, "the Luther of the Jews," to be translated
into one of the European languages.

Naturally, hostile pamphlets were not wanting.
Especially noteworthy was an abusive tract, published in Prague, entitled "Upon the Inutility of the
Jews in the Kingdoms of Bohemia and Moravia," in
which the author indulged in common insults
against the Jews, and revived all the charges of
poisoning wells, sedition, and other pretexts for
their expulsion.   This scurrilous work was so violent, that Emperor Joseph forbade its circulation
(March 2, 1782).   A bitter opponent of the Jews at
this time was Frederick Traugott Hartmann.   And
why?   Because he had been cheated out of a few
pennies by Jewish hawkers.   On account of their
venomous tone, however, these writings harmed the
Jews less than those of the German pedants.

To these belonged a famous scholar of authority,
John David Michaelis, the aged professor at Göttingen.   His range of vision had been widened by
travels and observation, and he had cut himself
adrift from the narrowness of Lutheran theology.
Michaelis was the founder of the rationalist school
of theologians, who resolved the miracles and the
sublimity of the Holy Scriptures into simple natural
facts.   Through his "Mosaic Law," and cultivation

of Hebrew grammar and exegesis, he gained high
repute. But Michaelis had exactly that proportion
of unbelief and belief which made him hate the Jews
as the bearers of revealed religion and a miraculous
history, and despise them as antagonists of Christianity. A Jewish officer in the French army, when
it was stationed in Göttingen, had given but a
grudging salute in return for the slavish obeisances
of the professors, which they held as due to every
Frenchman. This was ground enough for Michaelis
to abominate the Jews one and all, and to affirm
that they were of despicable character. Michaelis
had several years before remarked, on the appearance of Lessing's drama "The Jew," "that a noble
Jew was a poetic impossibility." Experience had
disproved this assertion through Mendelssohn and
other persons ; but a German professor cannot be
mistaken. Michaelis adhered to his opinion that the
Jews were an incorrigible race. Now he condemned
the Jews from a theological point of view, now from
political considerations. It is hard to say whether
it is to be called insensibility, intellectual dullness,
or malice, when Michaelis blurts out with :

"It seems to me, that here in Germany they (the Jews) already have
everything that they could possibly desire, and I do not know what he
(Dohm) wishes to add thereto. Medicine, philosophy, physics, mathematics, they are not excluded from,—and he himself does not wish
them to have offices."

He even defended the taking of protection-money
from the Jews.

It cannot be said that the anti-Jewish treatise of
Michaelis injured them at the time, for in no case
would the German princes and people have emancipated them, had not the imperious progress of
history compelled it. But in after years Michaelis
was employed as an authority against the Jews. The
agitation excited by Dohm, and the views *pro* and
con had only resulted in forming public opinion
upon Judaism, and this affected not Germany, but

France. Miraculous concatenation of historical events! The venomous Alsatian district judge wished to have the Jews of Alsace annihilated, and through his malice he actually facilitated the liberation of the Jews in France.

Mendelssohn prudently kept himself in the background in this movement: he did not desire to have attention drawn to him as a prejudiced defender of his brethren in religion and race. He blessed the outbreak of interest in his unhappy kinsmen.

"Blessed be Almighty Providence that has allowed me, at the end of my days, to see the happy time, when the rights of humanity begin to be realized in their true extent."

However, two things induced him to break silence. He found that the arrows hurled by Dohm had been insufficient to pierce the thick-skinned monster of Jew-hatred.

"Reason and humanity have raised their voices in vain, for grey-headed prejudice is deaf."

Dohm himself did not appear to him to be free from the general prejudice, because he admitted that the Jews of the present day were depraved, useless, even harmful; therefore he suggested means to improve them. But Mendelssohn, who knew his coreligionists better, did not find them so greatly infected with moral leprosy—or differing so widely from Christians of the same class and trade—as arrogant Christians in their self-glorification were wont to assert. In a very clever way Mendelssohn made not alone the Göttingen scholars Michaelis and Hartmann, but also Dohm, understand that they had misconceived the Jewish question.

"It i wonderful to note how prejudice assumes the forms of every century in order to act despotically towards us, and place difficulties in the way of our obtaining civil rights. In superstitious ages we were said to insult sacred objects out of mere wantonness; to pierce crucinxes and cause them to bleed; secretly to circumcise children and stab them in order to feast our eyes upon the sight; to draw Christian blood for our Passover; to poison wells.

"Now times have changed, calumny no longer makes the desired impression. Now we, in turn, are upbraided with superstition and ignorance, lack of moral sentiments, taste, and refined manners, incapacity for the arts, sciences, and useful pursuits, especially for the service of war and the state, invincible inclination to cheating, usury, and lawlessness; all these have taken the place of coarse indictments against us, to exclude us from the number of useful citizens, and reject us from the motherly bosom of the state. They tie our hands, and reproach us that we do not use them. . . . . . Reason and the spirit of research of our century have not yet wiped away all traces of barbarism in history. Many a legend of the past has obtained credit, because it has not occurred to any one to cast doubts upon it. Some are supported by such important authorities that few have the boldness to look upon them as legends and libels. Even at the present moment there is many a city of Germany where no circumcised person, even though he pays duty for his creed, is allowed to issue forth in open daylight unwatched, lest he kidnap a Christian child or poison the wells; while during the night he is not trusted under the strictest surveillance, owing to his well-known intercourse with evil spirits."

The second point in Dohm's memoir which did not please Mendelssohn was, that it demanded the recognition of the state for the Jewish religion, inasmuch as the government was to grant it the right of excluding unruly members by a sort of excommunication. This did not harmonize with his conception of a pure religion. In order to counteract the errors of Dohm's well-meant apology, and the obstinate misapprehension of the Jews as much as possible, Mendelssohn caused one of his young friends, the physician Marcus Herz, to translate from the English original the "Vindiciæ Judæorum" of Manasseh ben Israel against the numerous slanderous charges brought against them. He himself wrote a preface full of luminous, glowing thoughts (March, 1782), called "The Salvation of the Jews," as an appendix to Dohm's work. Manasseh's Apology was buried in a book little read; Mendelssohn made its excellent truths known among the cultured classes, and by a correct elucidation gave them proper emphasis. In this preface he insisted, that while the church arrogates the right of inflicting punishment upon its followers, religion, the true faith, based upon reason and love of humanity, "requires neither an arm nor a finger for its purpose; it concerns only the spirit and the heart. Moreover it does not drive sinners and renegades from its doors." Without knowing the whole extent of the harm caused by it in the course of Jewish history, Mendelssohn detested the interdicting power. He therefore adjured the rabbis and elders to give up their right of excommunicating.

"Alas! my brethren, you have felt the oppressive yoke of intolerance only too severely; all the nations of the earth seem hitherto to have been deluded by the idea that religion can be maintained only by an iron hand. You, perhaps, have suffered yourselves to be misled into thinking the same. Oh, my brethren, follow the example of love, as you have till now followed that of hatred!"

Mendelssohn now held so high a position in public opinion, that every new publication bearing his name was eagerly read. The fundamental thought of the preface to Manasseh ben Israel's "Vindication," that religion has no rights over its followers and must not resort to compulsory measures, struck its readers with astonishment. This had never occurred to any Christian believer. Enlightened Christian clergymen, such as Teller, Spalding, Zollikofer, and others, gradually fell in with the new idea, and tendered its originator public applause. Bigoted clerics and obdurate minds, on the other hand, beheld therein the destruction of religion. "All this is new and difficult; first principles are denied," said they. In Jewish circles also many objections were made to Mendelssohn's view. It seemed as if he had suddenly discarded Judaism, which certainly owns an elaborate system of penalties for religious crimes and transgressions. From the Christian camp a pamphlet called "Inquiry into Light and Truth" was launched against him, which asserted that he had finally dropped his mask; that he had embraced the religion of love, and turned his back upon his native faith, which execrates and punishes.

A second time Mendelssohn was compelled to emerge from his retirement, and give his views upon religion. This he did in a work entitled " Jerusalem," or "Upon Ecclesiastical Power and Judaism" (spring, 1783), whose purity of contents and form is a memorial of his lofty genius. The gentleness that breathes through this book, the warmth of conviction, the frankness of utterance, its child-like ingenuousness, yet profoundly thoughtful train of ideas, the graceful style which renders even dry discussion enjoyable—all these qualities earned contemporary approval for this work, and will always assure it a place in literature. At the time it excited great surprise. It had been believed, that, owing to his ideas upon religion and Judaism, Mendelssohn, if he had not entirely broken away from Judaism, had yet declared many things therein to be worthless. He now showed that he was an ardent Jew, and would not yield a tittle of existing Judaism, either rabbinical or biblical ; that he, in fact, claimed the highest privileges for it. All this was in accord with his peculiar method of thought.

Judaism recognizes the freedom of religious convictions. Original, pure Judaism, therefore, contains no binding articles of belief, no symbolical books, by which the faithful were compelled to swear and affirm their incumbent duty. Judaism prescribes not faith, but knowledge, and it urges that its doctrines be taken to heart. In this despised religion everyone may think, opine, and err as he pleases, without incurring the guilt of heresy. Its right of inflicting punishment begins only when evil thoughts become acts. Why? Because Judaism is not revealed religion, but revealed legislation. Its first precept is not, "thou shalt believe or not believe," but, "thou shalt do or abstain from doing."

"In the divinely-ordained constitution, state and religion are one. Not unbelief, false teaching, and error, but wicked offenses against the principles of the state and the national constitution are chastised.

With the destruction of the Temple, *i. e.*, with the downfall of the state, all corporal and capital punishment, as well as money fines, ceased. The national bonds were dissolved ; religious trespasses were no longer crimes against the state, and religion, as such, knows no punishments."

For those who seriously or jestingly had reported that Mendelssohn had separated from Judaism, he laid stress upon two points not wholly germane to his subject, viz., that the so-called ceremonial law of Judaism is likewise, indeed particularly, of divine origin, and that its obligatory character must continue "until it pleases the Supreme to abrogate it as plainly and publicly as it was revealed."

The effect of this detailed apology was greater than Mendelssohn could have expected. Instead of defending himself he had come forward as an accuser, and in a manner at once gentle and forcible he had laid bare the hateful ulcers of the church and state constitution. Two authoritative representatives of the age pronounced flattering opinions upon him and the subject which he was discussing. Kant, who had already testified to his greatness of thought, wrote that he had read "Jerusalem" with admiration for its keenness of argument, its refinement, and cleverness of composition.

"I consider this book the herald of a great reform, which will affect not alone your nation, but also others. You have succeeded in combining your religion with such a degree of freedom of conscience as was never imagined possible, and of which no other faith can boast. You have, at the same time, so thoroughly and clearly demonstrated the necessity of unlimited liberty of conscience in every religion, that ultimately our Church will also be led to reflect how to remove from its midst everything that disturbs and oppresses conscience, which will finally unite all men in their view of the essential points of religion."

Michaelis, the rationalistic anti-Semite, stood baffled, embarrassed, and ashamed before the bold ideas of the "Jerusalem." Judaism, which he had scornfully disdained, now fearlessly and victoriously raised its head. The Jew Mendelssohn, whom he would not have trusted with a penny, appeared the incarnation of conscientiousness and wisdom. Michaelis was sorely perplexed in passing judgment upon this remarkable work. He was obliged to admit many things. Thus, without selfish motives, impelled only by circumstances, Mendelssohn glorified Judaism, and shook off disgrace from his people. In the meantime Dohm was aiding him. He continued to expound Judaism in the most favorable light, and refute all objections, the honest as well as the malicious ones; he had come to regard the quarrel as his own. But Dohm effected most by enlisting through his writings in favor of Jews the sympathies of Mirabeau, a man with shoulders strong enough to bear a new system of the world, and he continued the work of Dohm.

At the same time, and in the same way, that is, indirectly, Mendelssohn again urged the internal rejuvenescence of the Jews, which was to accompany their emancipation. From modesty or discretion, he would not come to the front; he had stimulated Dohm to do battle for their emancipation, and for their regeneration he brought forward another friend, who appeared born for the task. Owing to Mendelssohn, Wessely became a historical personage, who worked with all his energy for the improvement of the Jews, completing the deficiency of Mendelssohn's retiring character. Hartwig (Hartog, Naphtali-Herz) Wessely (born in Hamburg, 1725; died in the same town, 1805) was of a peculiar disposition, combining elements not often associated. His grandfather had established a manufactory for arms in Holstein, and had been a commercial councilor and royal resident. His father also conducted an important business, and had frequent intercourse with so-called great people. In this way Hartwig Wessely came with his father to Copenhagen, where a Portuguese congregation, and also a few German Jews had settled. His early education was the same as that of most

boys of that time; he learnt to read Hebrew
mechanically, and to mis-translate the Bible, to be
launched, a boy of nine, into the labyrinth of the
Talmud. But a traveling grammarian, Solomon
Hanau, promoted the development of the germs
within him, and inspired him with love for the
Hebrew language. His labor was not in vain.
The seed sown by Hanau was to bear thousand-fold
fruit. Wessely's chief interest was the study of the
Holy Writings in the original tongue; it was the
aim of his life to understand them from all points of
view. Owing to his father's frequent contact with
non-Jewish circles, in the course of business,
Wessely obtained an insight into actual life, and
absorbed other branches of knowledge, the modern
languages, geography, history, descriptions of travels. These only served as auxiliary sciences to be
employed in his special study of the Scriptures, and
by their means to penetrate deeper into their
thought and spirit. Like Mendelssohn, Wessely
was self-taught. Very early he developed taste, a
sense for beauty, feeling for purity of speech and
form, and repugnance to the mixed dialects and the
jargon commonly used among German Jews.

Wessely again resembled Mendelssohn in character, distinguished as he was by strict conscientiousness and elevated feelings of honor. In him,
too, thoughts, sentiments, words, and deeds, showed
no discrepancy. He was of deep, pure piety, an
unswerving adherent to Judaism. His nature, however, did not display the gentle pliancy of Mendelssohn's. He was stiff and pedantic, more inclined to
juggle with words and split hairs than to think
deeply, and he had no correct idea of the action of
world-moving forces. All his life Wessely remained
a visionary, and saw the events of the real world
through colored glasses. In one way Wessely was
apparently superior to Mendelssohn; he was a
poet. In reality, however, he only possessed un-

common facility and skill in making beautiful, well-sounding verses of blameless refinement, of graceful symmetrical smoothness, and accurate construction.

Wessely was greatly charmed by the laws of Emperor Joseph in favor of the Jews, especially by the command to erect schools ; he beheld therein the dawn of a golden age for the Jews, whilst Mendelssohn, with his keen perception, from the first did not expect great results. He remarks, "It is perhaps only a passing idea, without any substance, or, as some fear, it has a financial purpose." Wessely, however, composed a glowing hymn of praise to the noble rule and the magnanimity of Emperor Joseph. As soon as he was informed that the rigidly orthodox party in Vienna regretted the order to establish schools as an interference with their liberty of conscience, he addressed a Hebrew letter (March, 1782), called "Words of Peace and Truth," to the Austrian congregations, exhorting them to welcome it as a benefit, to rejoice in it, and at once execute it. He explained that it was a religious duty of the Jews, recommended even by the Talmud, to acquire general culture, that the latter must even precede a knowledge of religion, and that only by such means could they remove the disgrace which, owing to their ignorance, had weighed upon them for so long a time. Wessely emphasized the necessity of banishing the barbarous jargon from the midst of the Jews, and of cultivating a pure, euphonious language. He sketched a plan of instruction in his letter, showing how the Jewish youth should be led, step by step, from elementary subjects to the study of the Talmud. This letter, written with fervor, impressive eloquence, and in a beautiful Hebrew style, could not have failed to produce great effect, had not Wessely, in his fantastic manner, recommended that all Jewish youths, without distinction of talents and future profession should be taught, not only history and geography but also natural sciences, astronomy, and religious philosophy, because only by this preliminary knowledge could a thorough understanding of Holy Writ and of Judaism be acquired !

This epistle bore him both sweet and bitter fruit. The community of Trieste, chiefly comprising Italian and Portuguese Jews, who, unlike the Germans, did not consider culture as heresy, had applied to the governor, Count Zinzendorf, declaring their readiness to establish a normal school, and begging him to advise them how they might procure text books on religion and ethics. Zinzendorf directed them to Mendelssohn, whose celebrated name had penetrated to that distant place. Accordingly, Joseph Chayim Galaïgo, in the name of the congregation of Trieste, addressed a petition to the Jewish sage of Berlin for his writings. On this occasion, Mendelssohn called the attention of the people of Trieste to his friend Wessely and to his circular letter, recommending the founding of Jewish schools, and the community forthwith entered into negotiations with him. Thus his fervent words met with early encouragement.

From the strictly pious people, however, a storm now broke out against him. They were particularly indignant at his hearty approval of Emperor Joseph's reforms. The unamiable manner in which princes were wont to concede freedom, the force brought to bear upon the Jews, a natural aversion to forsake the past, the legitimate fear that through school education and partial emancipation young men would be seduced from Judaism, and that the instruction given at the normal schools would supersede the study of the Talmud—all these things had induced the rabbis and the representatives of tradition to oppose the reforming Jewish ordinances of Emperor Joseph. Besides, men of doubtful piety, such as Herz Homberg, eagerly pressed forward to obtain appointments at the newly-founded training schools, and to tempt the youthful students to innovations. There were, to be sure, intelligent men, especially in Prague, who greeted the new laws as salutary measures, and hoped that by these means the Jews would rise out of their wretched, demoralized condition. But this minority was denounced by the orthodox as innovators and triflers. Religious simplicity, which at every puff of wind feared the downfall of the edifice of faith, and the desire of gain, which fattened upon ignorance, and the perverse method of instruction in a corrupt dialect, worked hand in hand to predispose the communities against school reforms. Wessely destroyed the whole opposition with one blow. He who had hitherto been respected as an orthodox believer, now supported the new order of things. Further, in his incautious way, he had quoted the Talmudical sentence, "A Talmudist who does not possess knowledge (general culture), is uglier than a carcass." This expression greatly angered the orthodox. The Austrian rabbis dared not attack him openly, because he had only followed the emperor in his ideas. They appear therefore to have incited certain Polish rabbis to condemn his circular letter and excommunicate him.

Although the zealots were without support from Berlin, they continued in their heretic-hunting, causing the pulpits to re-echo with imprecations against Wessely; and in Lissa his letter was publicly burnt. He had the bitter experience of standing alone in this conflict. None of his adherents publicly sided with him, although he was contending for a just cause by noble methods and in a most becoming manner. Mendelssohn did not like such disputes, and at this time was suffering too much, bodily and mentally, to take part. Thus Wessely had to conduct his own defense. He published a second letter (April 24), supposed to be addressed to the Trieste congregation, in which he again dwelt upon the importance of regular instruction, and of the abolition of old practices, and disproved the charges against him. Gentle and forbearing as he was, he avoided retorting severely upon his opponents; but he permitted words of censure against orthodoxy and the one-sided, perverse Talmudic tendency to slip from him. It was, indeed, the irony of history, that the most orthodox among the followers of Mendelssohn, without wishing it, opened fire on Rabbinism, as the Kabbalist Jacob Emden had given the first violent blow to the Kabbala. By and by, several Italian rabbis of Trieste, Ferrara, and Venice, spoke in favor of Wessely, and recommended culture, although they were unable to bridge over the chasm between it and Rabbinism. Wessely was victorious; and the opposing rabbis laid down their arms. Schools for regular instruction arose here and there, even in Prague. But the strict Talmudists were right. Their suspicions foreboded the future more truly than Mendelssohn's and Wessely's confidence. The old rigid form of Judaism could no more assert itself. Both these men, who had felt so much at ease in the old structure, and wished only to see it cleansed here and there from cobwebs and fungus growths, contributed to sap its foundations.

Wessely, ever deserted by fortune, lived to see this decay with weeping eyes. Mendelssohn, more fortunate, was spared this pain. Death called him away in time, before he perceived that his circle, even his own daughters, treated with contemptuous scorn and rejected what his heart held to be most sacred, and what he so earnestly strove to glorify. Had he lived ten years longer, even his wisdom would perhaps not have availed him to tide over this anguish. He who without a trace of romance had led an ideal life, died ideally transfigured, at the right moment. The friendship and the philosophy which had elevated his life and brought him fame broke his heart. When Mendelssohn was about to raise a memorial to his unforgotten friend, to

show him in his true greatness to future generations, he learned from Jacobi that shortly before his death Lessing had manifested a decided
liking for the philosophy of Spinoza. "Lessing a
Spinozist!" This pierced Mendelssohn's heart as
with a spear. Nothing was so distasteful to him as
the pantheistic system of Spinoza, which denied a
personal God, Providence, and Immortality, ideas
with which Mendelssohn's soul was bound up.
That Lessing should have entertained such convictions, and that he, his bosom friend, should
know nothing whatsoever about them! Jealousy
that Lessing had communicated to others the secret
so carefully concealed from himself, and deep disappointment that his friend had not shared his own
convictions took possession of Mendelssohn. He
suspected, that his philosophy, if it was true that
Lessing had not been pleased with it, would become
obsolete, and be thrust aside. His whole being
rose in resistance against such doubts. These
thoughts robbed the last years of his life of rest,
made him passionate, excited, feverish. While
composing his work in refutation of Jacobi's, "To
the Friends of Lessing," excitement so overpowered
him that it brought on his death (January 4, 1786).
This ideal death for friendship and wisdom worthily
concluded his life, and showed him to posterity as
he appeared to his numerous friends and admirers,
an upright, honest man, in whom was neither falsehood nor guile. Almost the entire population of
the Prussian capital, and many earnest men in Germany and beyond its borders mourned the man
who, forty years before, with heavy heart had
knocked at one of the gates of Berlin, in fear that
the Christian or the Jewish beadle would drive him
away. The attempt of his Christian friends, Nicolai, Biester, and Engel, the tutor of the Crown
Prince Frederick William III, in conjunction with
Jewish admirers, to erect a statue to Mendelssohn

in the Opera Square next to those of Leibnitz, Lambert, and Sulzer, although it did not meet with approval, characterizes the progress of the time. The deformed son of the so-called " Ten Commandments writer" of Dessau had become an ornament to the city of Berlin.

CHAPTER IX.

THE NEW CHASSIDISM.

The Alliance of Reason with Mysticism—Israel Baalshem, his Career and Reputation—Movement against Rabbinism—The "Zaddik" —Beer Mizricz, his Arrogance and Deceptions—The Devotional Methods of the Chassidim—Their Liturgy—Dissolution of the Synods "of the Four Countries"—Cossack Massacres in Poland —Elijah Wilna, his Character and Method of Research—The Mizricz and Karlin Chassidim—Circumstances prove Favorable to the Spread of the New Sect—Vigorous Proceedings against them in Wilna—Death of Beer Mizricz—Progress of Chassidism despite the Persecution of its Opponents.

1750—1786 C. E.

As soon as an historical work has performed its service, and is to undergo a change, new phenomena arise from various sides, and assume a hostile attitude, either to alter or destroy it. It might have been foreseen that the rejuvenescence of the Jewish race, for which Mendelssohn had leveled the way, would produce a transformation and decomposition of religious habits among Jews. The innovators desired this, and hoped, and strove for it ; the old orthodox party suspected and dreaded it. The process of dissolution was brought about also in another way, upon another scene, under entirely different conditions, and by other means, and this could not have been foreseen. There arose in Poland a new Essenism, with forms similar to those of the ancient cult, with ablutions and baths, white garments, miraculous cures, and prophetic visions. Like the old movement, it originated in ultra-piety, but soon turned against its own parent, and perhaps hides within itself germs of a peculiar kind, which, being in course of development, cannot be defined. It seems remarkable that, at the time when Mendelssohn declared rational thought to be the essence of Judaism, and founded, as it were, a widely-extended order of enlightened men, another banner was unfurled, the adherents of which announced the grossest superstition to be the fundamental principle of Judaism, and formed an order of wonder-seeking confederates.   Both these new bodies took up a hostile position to traditional Judaism, and created a rupture.   History in its generative power is as manifold and puzzling as nature.   It produces in close proximity healing herbs and poisonous plants, lovely flowers and hideous parasites.   Reason and unreason seemed to have entered into a covenant to shatter the gigantic structure of Talmudic Judaism.   The attempt once before made by history, to subvert Judaism by the contemporaneous existence of Spinoza and Sabbataï Zevi, was now repeated by the simultaneous attacks of representatives of reason and unreason.   Enlightenment and Kabbalistic mysticism joined hands to commence the work of destruction.   Mendelssohn and Israel Baalshem, what contrasts !   Yet both unconsciously undermined the basis of Talmudic Judaism.   The origin of the new Chassidim, who had already become numerous, and who sprang up very rapidly, is not so clear as the movement started by Mendelssohn.   The new sect, a daughter of darkness, was born in gloom, and even to-day proceeds stealthily on its mysterious way.   Only a few circumstances which contributed to its rise and propagation are known.

The founders of the new Chassidism were Israel of Miedziboz (born about 1698 ; died 1759) and Beer of Mizricz (born about 1700 ; died 1772).   The former received, alike from his admirers and his antagonists, the surname of " The Wonderworker by means of Invocations in the Name of God," Baalshem, or Baal-Shemtob, in the customary abbreviated form, Besht.   As ugly as the name, Besht, was the form of the founder and the order that he called into existence. The Graces did not sit by his cradle, but the spirit of belief in wonderworking, and his brain was so filled with fantastic images that he could not distinguish them from real, tangible beings. The experiences of Israel's youth are unknown. So much, however, is certain; he was left an orphan, poor and neglected, early in life, and passed a great portion of his youth in the forests and caves of the Carpathian mountains. The spurs of the Carpathian hills were his teachers. Here he learnt what he would not have acquired in the dark, narrow, dirty hovels called schools in Poland— namely, to understand the tongue which nature speaks. The spirits of the mountains and the fountains whispered secrets to him. Here he also learned, probably from the peasant women who gathered herbs on the mountain-tops and on the edges of rivers, the use of plants as remedies. As they did not trust to the healing power of nature, but added conjurations and invocations to good and evil spirits, Israel also accustomed himself to this method of cure. He became a miracle-doctor. Necessity, too, was his teacher; it taught him to pray. How often, in his forsaken and orphaned condition, may he have suffered from want even of dry bread, how often may he have been surrounded by real or imaginary dangers! In his distress he prayed in the usual forms of the synagogue; but he spoke his words with fervor and intense devotion, or cried them aloud in the solitude of the mountains. His audible prayer awakened the echoes of the mountains, which appeared as an answer to his supplications. He seems to have been often in a state of rapture, and to have induced this condition by frantic movements of the whole body while praying. This agitation drove the blood to his head, made his eyes glitter, and wrought both body and soul into such a condition of over-excitement that he felt a deadly weakness come over him. Was this magnetic tension of the soul caused by the motions and the shouting, singing, and praying?

Israel Baalshem asserted that, in consequence of these bodily agitations and this intense devotion, he often caught a glimpse of infinity. His soul soared upward to the world of light, heard and saw Divine secrets and revelations, entered into conversation with sublime spirits, and by their intervention could secure the grace of God and prosperity, and especially avert impending calamities. Israel Miedziboz also boasted that he could see into the future, as secrets were unveiled to him. Was this a deliberate boast, self-deception, or merely an over-estimation of morbid feelings? There are persons, times, and places, in which the line of demarcation between trickery and self-delusion cannot be distinguished. In Poland, in Baalshem's time, with the terrible mental strain created by the Kabbala in connection with the Sabbatian fraud, the feverish expectation of imminent Messianic redemption, everything was possible and everything credible. In that land the fancy of both Jews and Christians moved among extraordinary and supernatural phenomena as in its natural element. Israel steadfastly and firmly believed in the visions seen when he was under mental and physical excitement; he believed in the power of his prayers. In his delusion he blasphemously declared that prayer is a kind of marriage union (Zivug) of man with the Godhead (Shechina), upon which he must enter whilst in a state of excitement. Equipped with alleged higher knowledge of secret remedies and the spirit world, to which he thought he had attained through Divine grace, Israel entered the society of men to prove his higher gifts. It must be acknowledged to his credit that he never misused these talents. He did not make a trade of them, nor seek to earn his livelihood with them. At first he followed

the humble occupation of a wagoner, afterwards he
dealt in horses, and when his means permitted it he
kept a tavern.

Occasionally, when specially requested, he employed his miraculous remedies, and thereby gained
so great a reputation that he was consulted even by
Polish nobles. He became conspicuous by his
noisy, delirious praying, which must have so transfigured him that men did not recognize the wagoner
or horse-dealer whom they knew. He was admired
for his revelation of secrets. In Poland not only
the unlearned and the Jews considered such gifts
and miracles possible ; the Jesuits and the Kabbalists had stultified the Christians and the Jews of
their country, and plunged them into a state of prim-
itive barbarism.

It would have been a remarkable thing if such a
wonder-doctor, who appeared to have intercourse
with the spirit world, had not found adherents, but
he can hardly have designed the formation of a new
sect. He was joined by persons of a similar disposition to his own, who felt a religious impulse, which
could not be satisfied, they thought, by a rigorous,
penitential life, or by mechanical repetition of prescribed prayers. They joined Israel, in Miedziboz,
to pray with devotion, *i. e.*, in a sing-song tune, clap-
ping their hands, bowing, jumping, gesticulating, and
uttering cries. At almost the same time there
arose, in Wales, a Christian sect called "the Jump-
ers," who resorted to similar movements during
prayer, and induced trances and mesmeric dreams.
At the same time there was established, in North
America, the sect of the Shakers, by an Irish girl,
Johanna Lee, who likewise in the delirium of prayer
pursued mystic Messianic phantoms. Israel need
not have been a trickster to obtain followers. Mysticism and madness are contagious. He particularly
attracted men who desired to lead a free and merry
life, at the same time hoping to reach a lofty aim,

and to live assured of the nearness of God in serenity and calmness, and to advance the Messianic future. They did not need to pore over Talmudical folios in order to attain to higher piety.

It became the fashion in neo-Chassidean circles to scoff at the Talmudists. Because the latter mocked at the unlearned chief of the new order, who had a following without belonging to the guild of Talmudists, without having been initiated into the Talmud and its appendages, the Chassidim depreciated the study of the Talmud, avowing that it was not able to promote a truly godly life. Covert war existed between the neo-Chassidim and the Rabbanites; the latter could not, however, harm their opponents so long as Israel's adherents did not depart from existing Judaism. After the death of the founder, when barbarism and degeneracy increased, the feud grew into a complete rupture under Beer of Mizricz.

Dob Beer (or Berish) was no visionary like Israel, but possessed the faculty of clear insight into the condition of men's minds. He was thus able to render the mind and will of others subservient to him. Although he joined the new movement only a short time before Israel's death, yet, whether at his suggestion or not, Israel's son and sons-in-law were passed over, and Beer was made Israel's successor in the leadership of the neo-Chassidean community. Beer, who transferred the center to Mizricz—a village in Volhynia—was superior to his master in many points. He was well read in Talmudical and Kabbalistic writings, was a fluent preacher (Maggid), who, to further his purpose, could make the most far-fetched biblical verses, as also Agadic and Zoharic expressions, harmonize, and thus surprise his audience. He removed from the Chassidim the stigma of ignorance, especially disgraceful in Poland, and secured an accession of supporters. He had a commanding appearance, did not mingle with the people, but lived the whole week secluded in a small room—only accessible to his confidants—and thus acquired the renown of mysterious intercourse with the heavenly world. Only on the Sabbath did he show himself to all who longed to be favored with his sight. On this day he appeared splendidly attired in satin, his outer garment, his shoes, and even his snuff-box being white, the color signifying grace in the Kabbalistic language. On this day, in accordance with the custom introduced by Israel Besht, he offered up prayers together with his friends, with the strangers who had made a pilgrimage to him, with the new members, and those curious to see the Kabbalistic saint and wonderworker. To produce the joyous state of mind necessary to devout prayer, Beer indulged in vulgar jokes, whereby the merriment of the bystanders was aroused; for instance, he would joke with one of the circle, and throw him down. In the midst of this child's play he would suddenly cry out, " Now serve the Lord with gladness."

Under Beer's guidance, the constitution of Chassidism remained apparently in the same form as under his predecessor: fervent, convulsive praying, inspiration (Hithlahabuth), miraculous cures, and revelations of the future. But as these actions did not, as with Israel, flow from a peculiar or abnormal state of mind, they could only be imitated—artifice or illusion had to supply what nature withheld. It was an accepted fact that the Chassidean leader, or Zaddik, the perfectly pious man, had to be enthusiastic in prayer, had to have ecstatic dreams and visions. How can a clever plotter appear inspired? Alcohol, so much liked in Poland, now had to take the place of the inspiring demon. Beer had not the knowledge of remedial herbs, which his teacher had obtained in the Carpathian mountains. He, therefore, devoted himself to medicine, and if his remedies did not avail, then the sick person died of his sinfulness. To predict the future was a more difficult task, yet it had to be accomplished; his reputation as a thaumaturgist depended upon it. Beer was equal to the emergency. Among his intimates were expert spies, worthy of serving in the secret police. They discovered many secrets, and told them to their leader; thus he was enabled to assume an appearance of omniscience. Or his emissaries committed robberies; if the victims came to the "Saint" in his hermitage to find them out, he was able to indicate the exact spot where the missing articles were lying. If strangers, attracted by his fame, came to see him, they were not admitted, as mentioned, until the following Saturday, to take part in the Chassidean witches' Sabbath. Meantime his spies, by artful questions and other means, gleaned a knowledge of the affairs and secret desires of these strangers, and communicated them to the Zaddik. In the first interview Beer, in a seemingly casual manner, was able, in a skillfully arranged discourse, to bring in allusions to these strangers, whereby they would be convinced that he had looked into their hearts, and knew their past. By these and similar contrivances, he succeeded in asserting himself as omniscient, and increasing the number of his followers. Every new convert testified to his Divine inspiration, and induced others to join.

In order to strengthen respect for him, Beer propounded a theory, which in its logical application is calculated to promote most harmful consequences. Supported by the Kabbalistic formula, that "the righteous or the pious man is the foundation of the world," he magnified the importance of the Zaddik, or the Chassidean chief, to such an extent that it became blasphemy. "A Zaddik is not alone the most perfect and sinless human being, he is not alone Moses, but the representative of God and His image." All and everything that the Zaddik does and thinks has a decided influence upon the upper and lower worlds. The Deity reveals Himself especially in the acts of the Zaddik; even his most trifling deeds are to be considered important. The way he wears his clothes, ties his shoes, smokes his pipe, whether he delivers profound addresses, or indulges in silly jokes—everything bears a close relation to the Deity, and is of as much moment as the fulfillment of a religious duty. Even when drawing inspiration from the bottle, he is swaying the upper and nether worlds. All these absurd fancies owed their origin to the superstitious doctrines of the Kabbala, which, in spite of the unspeakable confusion they had wrought through Sabbataï Zevi and Frank, in spite of the opposition which their chief exponent, the Zohar, had encountered at about this time at the hands of Jacob Emden, still clouded the brains of the Polish Jews. According to this theory, the Zaddik, *i. e.*, Berish Mizricz, was the embodiment of power and splendor upon earth. In his "Stübel," or "Hermitage," *i. e.*, in his dirty little retired chamber, he considered himself as great as the papal vicar of God upon earth in his magnificent palace. The Zaddik was also to bear himself proudly towards men; all this was "for the glory of God." It was a sort of Catholicism within Judaism.

Beer's idea, however, was not meant to remain idle and unfruitful, but to bring him honor and revenue. While the Zaddik cared for the conduct of the world, for the obtaining of heavenly grace, and especially for Israel's preservation and glorification, his adherents had to cultivate three kinds of virtues. It was their duty to draw nigh to him, to enjoy the sight of him, and from time to time to make pilgrimages to him. Further, they were to confess their sins to him. By these means alone could they hope for pardon of their iniquities. Finally, they had to bring him presents, rich gifts, which he knew how to employ to the best advan

tage. It was also incumbent upon them to attend
to his personal wants. It seems like a return to the
days of the priests of Baal, so vulgar and disgusting
do these perversities appear. The saddest part of
all is that this teaching, worthy of a fetish worshiping people, met with approbation in Poland, the
country distinguished by cumbersome knowledge of
Jewish literature. It was just this excess, this over-
activity of the spiritual digestive apparatus, that
produced such lamentable phenomena. The intellect of the Polish Jews had been so over-excited,
that the coarsest things were more pleasing to them
than what was refined.

Beer despatched abroad as his apostles bombastic preachers who seasoned his injurious teachings
with distorted citations from the Scriptures. Sim-
ple-minded men, rogues, and idlers, of whom there
were so many in Poland, attached themselves to the
new Chassidim; the first from inclination to enthusiasm and belief in miracles ; the cunning, in order
to procure money in an easy way, and lead a pleasant existence; and the idlers, because in the court
of the Zaddik they found occupation, and gratified
their curiosity. If such idlers were asked what they
were thinking of, as they strolled about pipe in
mouth, they would reply with seriousness, " We are
meditating upon God." The simple people, however, who hoped to win bliss through the Chassidean discipline, engaged continually in prayer, until through exhaustion they dropped unconscious.

Neo-Chassidism was favored by two circumstances, the fraternization of the members and the
dryness and fossilized character of Talmudic study
as carried on in Poland for more than a century.
At the outset the Chassidim formed a kind of
brotherhood, not indeed with a common purse, as
among their prototypes, the Essenes and the Judæo-
Christians, but having regard to the wants of needy
members. Owing to the closeness of their union,

their spying system, and their energy, it was easy
for them to provide for those who lacked employment or food.   On New Year and the Day of
Atonement people, even those who dwelt at long
distances, undertook pilgrimages to the Zaddik, as
formerly to the Temple, and left their wives and
children to pass the so-called holy days in the company of their chief, to be edified by his presence and
actions.   Here the Chassidean disciples learned to
know one another, discussed local affairs, and rendered mutual help.   Well-to-do merchants found
opportunity at these assemblies, in conversation
with fellow-believers, upon whose fidelity and brotherly attachment they could rely, to discover fresh
sources of income.   Fathers of marriageable daughters sought and easily found husbands for them,
which at that time in Poland was considered a highly
important matter.   The common meals on the
afternoons of Saturdays and the holidays strengthened the bonds of loyalty and affection among
them.   How could meals for so many guests be
provided?   The wealthy Chassidim regarded it as
a duty to support the Zaddik liberally.   A special
source of income was the superstitious belief prevalent among the Chassidim that the Zaddik for
certain sums (Pidion, Redemption) could ward off
threatening perils and cure deadly diseases.   Pressure was brought to bear upon wealthy but weak-
minded persons, and they were terrified into believing that they could escape impending calamities
only by rich gifts.   Whoever desired to enter upon
a hazardous transaction consulted the Zaddik as an
oracle, and had to pay for his counsel.   The cunning
Chassidim knew everything, were ready with counsel
in any emergency, and by their craftiness were
able to afford real assistance.   The Zaddik, however miserly he might be, had to assist the poor
and distressed with his revenues.   Thus every member received help here.   Full of enthu-

siasm they returned home from their journey; the feeling that they belonged to a brotherhood elevated them, and they ardently looked forward to the return of the holy time. The poor and forsaken, the fanatical and the unprincipled, could not do better than join this union, this easy-going yet religious order.

Earnest men, also, desirous of satisfying their spiritual wants, felt themselves attracted to the Chassidim. Rabbinical Judaism, as known in Poland, offered no sort of religious comfort. Its representatives placed the highest value upon the dialectic, artificial exposition of the Talmud and its commentaries. Actual necessity had besides caused that portion of the Talmud which treated of civil law to be closely studied, as the rabbis exercised civil jurisdiction over their flocks. Fine-spun decisions of new, complicated legal points occupied the doctors of the Talmud day and night. Moreover, this hair-splitting was considered sublimest piety, and superseded everything else. If any one solved an intricate Talmudic question, or discovered something new, called Torah, he felt self-satisfied, and assured of his felicity hereafter. All other objects, the impulse to devotion, prayer, and emotion, or interest in the moral condition of the community, were secondary matters, to which scarcely any attention was paid. The mental exercise of making logical deductions from the Talmud, or more correctly from the laws of Mine and Thine, choked all other intellectual pursuits in Poland. Religious ceremonies had degenerated, both amongst Talmudists and the unlearned, into meaningless usages, and prayer into mere lip-service. To men of feeling this aridity of Talmudic study, together with the love of debate, and the dogmatism and pride of the rabbis arising from it, were repellent, and they flung themselves into the arms of the new order, which allowed so much play for

the fancy and the emotions. Especially preachers,
semi-Talmudists who were looked upon and treated
by erudite rabbi-Talmudists as inferior and contemptible, who eked out a wretched living, or
almost starved, leagued themselves with the neo-
Chassidim, because among them their talents of
preaching were appreciated, and they could obtain
an honorable position, and be secured against need.
By the accession of such elements the circle of neo-
Chassidim became daily augmented. Almost in
every town lived followers of the new school, who
occasionally had intercourse with their brother-
members and their chief.

With advancing strength the antipathy of the
neo-Chassidim to the rabbis and Talmudists increased. Without being aware of it they formed a
new sect, which scorned intercourse with the Talmud Jews. With Beer at their head, they felt
themselves strong enough to introduce an innovation, which would naturally bring down the anger of
the rabbis upon them. Since prayer and the rites
of Divine service were the chief consideration for
them, they did not trouble themselves about the
prescriptions of the ritual law as to how many
prayers should be said, nor at what time the different services should commence and terminate, but
were entirely guided by the feeling of the moment.
Through their daily ablutions, baths, and other preparations for public worship they were seldom ready
for prayer at the prescribed time, but began later,
prolonged it by the movements of their bodies and
their intoning, and suddenly came to an end after
omitting several portions. They were especially
averse to the harsh interpolations in the Sabbath
and festival prayers (the Piyutim). These inser-
tions interrupt the most important and suggestive
portions of the service. To abolish these at a
blow, Beer Mizricz introduced the prayer-book of
the arch-Kabbalist, Isaac Lurya, which for the

greater part conforms to the Portuguese ritual, and does not contain poetical (poetanic) additions. In the eyes of the ultra-orthodox this innovation was an enormous, or rather a double crime, permitting, as it did, the omission of interpolations hallowed by custom, and the exchange of the German ritual for the Sephardic.

This innovation would probably have been severely visited upon the neo-Chassidim, but that at this time, when the political power of Poland lay crushed, the firm political connection of the Polish Jews had also been dissolved. Poland was distracted by civil war. "In this country," as the Primate of Gnesen complained at the opening of the Reichstag, March, 1764, "freedom is oppressed, the laws are not obeyed, justice cannot be obtained, trade is utterly ruined, districts and villages are devastated, the treasury is empty, and the coin of the realm has no value." It had been enfeebled by the Jesuits, and was already regarded by Russia as a sure prey. Its king—Stanislaus Augustus Poniatowski—was a weakling, the plaything of internal factions and external foes (September, 1764). In the first year of his reign, Poniatowski among other laws issued a regulation which destroyed the communal union of the Polish Jews. The synod of the Four Countries, composed of delegates, rabbis and laymen (Parnassim), with authority to pronounce interdicts and levy fines, was not permitted to assemble, pass resolutions, or execute them.

The dissolution of the synod was very fortunate for the neo-Chassidim. They could not be excommunicated by the representatives of the Polish Jewish world, but each individual congregation had to proceed against them and forbid their meetings. Even this step was not taken at once, as the terrible death-struggle in which Poland engaged before its first partition was severely felt by the wealthy Jews, who trembled for their lives. The Confeder-

ation War broke out, which made many districts a
desert; Poland was punished by eternal Justice in
the same way as it had sinned.   In the name of the
pope and the Jesuits it had always persecuted dissenters, and excluded them from public offices,
and, in the name of the dissenters, Catherine
plunged the land into fratricidal war.   The Russians, for the second time, let loose against Poland
the Zaporogian Cossacks—the savage Haidamaks—
who inflicted death, by every known method, upon
the Polish nobles, the clergy, and the Jews.   The
Haidamaks hung up together a nobleman, a Jew, a
monk, and a dog, with the mocking inscription,
"All are equal."   Most inhuman cruelties were inflicted upon captives and the defenseless.   In addition came the Turks, who, in the guise of saviours
of Poland, murdered and plundered on every side.
The Ukraine, Podolia, in general the southern provinces of Poland, were turned into deserts.

These misfortunes were more advantageous than
injurious to the neo-Chassidim.   They spread in
the north, and whilst hitherto they had been able to
carry on their cult only in small, comparatively
young communities, from this time they gained
ground in the large and old congregations.   Their
numbers had already grown to such an extent that
they formed two branches—the Mizriczians and the
Karlinians—the former called after their original
home, the latter after the village of Karlin, near
Pinsk.   The Karlinians spread as far as Wilna and
Brody.   At first they proceeded cautiously.   As
soon as at least ten persons had assembled, they
looked for a room (Stübel) in which to conduct their
services; there they practiced the rites of their
creed, and sought to gain new adherents; but all
this was skillfully done, so that nothing came to
light before they had secured a firm foothold.   In
Lithuania their system was not yet known, and thus
at first they aroused no suspicion.

The first violent attack upon them was made by a man whose influence was blessed during his lifetime, and even after death, and who, in a more favorable environment, might, like Mendelssohn, have effected much for the moral advancement of his coreligionists. Elijah Wilna (born 1720; died 1797), whose name, with the title of "Gaon," is still mentioned by the Lithuanian Jews with reverence and love, was a rare exception among the mass of the Polish Jews. He was of the purest character, and possessed high talents, which he did not put to perverted uses. It suffices to say of his character that in spite of his comprehensive and profound Talmudical erudition, he refused a post as rabbi, in contrast to most scholars in Poland, who were office-seekers, and obtained rabbinates by artifice. In spite of the marvelous fertility of his pen in many domains of Jewish literature, he allowed nothing to be published during his lifetime, again in contradistinction to contemporary students, who, in order to make a name and to see their ideas in print, scarcely waited till the ink of their compositions was dry. In his disinterestedness, Elijah Wilna realized the ideal of the Talmud, that a teacher of Judaism "should use the Law neither as a crown to adorn himself therewith, nor as a spade to dig therewith." In spite of the superiority of his knowledge and the full and general recognition accorded him, he modestly and conscientiously avoided asserting himself. The gratification that results from research, from the seeking of knowledge, completely satisfied him. His intellectual method corresponded in its unaffected simplicity with his character and life. As a matter of course, the Talmud and all the branches connected with or dependent on it filled his mind. But he disliked the corrupt method of his countrymen, who indulged in hairsplitting, casuistry, and subtleties. His sole aim was to penetrate to the simple sense of the text;

he even made an attempt at the critical examination and emendation of texts, and by his undistorted explanations he blew down the houses of cards which the subtle Talmudists had erected upon quicksand.

It required extraordinary mental force to swim against the high tide of custom and rise above the aberrations into which all the sons of the Talmud in Poland had fallen. In point of fact Elijah Wilna stood isolated in his time. It seemed as though from his youth he had been afraid of following the errors of his compatriots, for he attached himself to no special school, but, strange to say, was his own teacher in the Talmud. Talmudical studies did not exclusively occupy his mind. Elijah Wilna devoted great attention to the Bible—a rarity in his circle— and, what was still more unusual, he acquainted himself with the grammar of the Hebrew language. Unlike his compatriots, he by no means despised a knowledge of extra-Talmudic subjects, but studied mathematics, and wrote a book upon geometry, algebra, and mathematical astronomy. He exhorted his disciples and friends to interest themselves in profane sciences, and openly expressed his conviction that Judaism would be the gainer from such studies. Only his scrupulous piety, his immaculate conduct, his unselfishness, and his renunciation of every office and position of honor, saved him from the charge of heresy on account of his pursuing extra-Talmudical branches of knowledge.

Elijah Wilna, above all, implanted a good spirit in the Lithuanian Jews. He taught his sons and disciples to seek simplicity and avoid the casuistry of the Polish method. In Elijah Wilna the beautiful Talmudical saying was exemplified, " He who flees from honors is sought out by them." At an early age he was recognized, even outside of Poland, as an authority and a man of truth. Yet even Elijah was subject to the delusion that the hateful

Kabbala was a true daughter of Judaism, and contained true elements.   He deeply lamented the moral ruin wrought by the Kabbala among Podolian and Galician Jews, through the rascally Frank, who had driven them into the arms of the Church, and made them enemies to the Synagogue ; yet he could not free himself from it.   Even when the danger of these false doctrines was brought home to him by the rise of the Chassidim, and he was compelled openly to oppose them, he could not relinquish his blind fondness for the Kabbala.

The neo-Chassidim, or Karlinians, had crept into Wilna, and had established a secret "Stübel" for their noisy conventicles.   A trusty friend of their leader, and an emissary sent by him, had stealthily introduced their cult into the town, and won over several members of the Wilna community.   Their meetings, their proceedings, and their derision of the Talmudists, were betrayed.   The whole congregation were greatly excited at this.   They were indignant that the Karlinians impudently asserted of the respected Elijah Wilna, that, like his occupation and his belief, his life was a lie.   The elders and rabbis forthwith took counsel.   The Chassidic conventicles were straightway attacked, investigations set on foot, and trials instituted.   Writings were found among the Chassidim, which contained the principle that all sadness was to be avoided, even in the repentance for sins.   But greatest uneasiness was aroused by the alterations in the liturgy and the disrespectful utterances against the rabbis.   Elijah Wilna, who, although he filled no official position, was always invited to the council meetings, and had an important voice in its decisions, took a very serious view of the matter.   He beheld in the Chassidic aberration a continuation of Frank's excesses and corrupting influence.   The otherwise gentle and meek man became a veritable fanatic.   The rabbis and the chiefs of the commu-

nity, together with Elijah Wilna, addressed a letter
to all the large communities, directing them to keep
a sharp eye upon the Chassidim, and to excommunicate them until they abandoned their erroneous
views. Several congregations immediately obeyed
this injunction. In Brody, during the fair, in the
presence of many strangers, the ban was published
against all those who prayed noisily, deviated from
the German synagogue ritual, wore white robes on
Sabbath and the festivals, and were guilty of other
strange customs and innovations. Elijah Wilna's
circle launched a vigorous denunciatory pamphlet
against the offenders. This was the first blow that
the Chassidim experienced. In addition, their
leader, Beer Mizricz, died in the same year (1772)—
the rabbis imagined in consequence of the excommunication—and thus they felt themselves utterly
deserted. Owing to the weakness of the king, and
the greed of the neighboring nations, the kingdom
of Poland was dismembered. Through this disorganization the union of the Chassidim was broken,
and the separated members became dependent
upon the legislature, or the arbitrary treatment, of
various governments.

However, this storm did not crush them; they
remained firm, and did not display the slightest
sign of submitting to their opponents (Mithnagdim).
On the contrary, the struggle made them more
active and energetic. They were not deeply
moved by the ban under which they had been
placed; this weapon, blunted since the contest for
and against Jonathan Eibeschütz, could no longer
inflict wounds. The Chassidim, grown to the number of fifty or sixty thousand, formed themselves
into small groups, each with a leader, called Rebbe.
Their itinerant preachers encouraged the individual
communities to persevere in their tenets, and to
accept persecution as a salutary trial. The connection of the groups with one another was maintained

in this way ; a chief from the family of Beer Mizricz was placed at the head as the supreme Zaddik,
to whom the various Rebbe were subordinate, and
for whose use they were to set aside a portion of
their income.   The possible apostasy of members
through the onslaughts from Wilna was met by the
order that the Chassidim might read no work that
had not received the approval of the Chassidic
authorities.   Obedience towards their leaders had
taken so deep a root in the minds of the Chassidim that they never transgressed this prohibition.
Their chiefs distributed among them the sermons
or collections of sayings supposed to have been
written by Israel Baalshem, or Beer Mizricz, which
emphasized the high importance of the Zaddik, of
the Chassidic life, and of scorn for the Talmudists—
vile writings, which were nevertheless read with admiration by the members, who were kept in a constant state of intoxication.   What had hitherto been
optional and individual was raised by these writings
to the rank of statutes and stringent laws.

After Beer's death, two men chiefly contributed
to the exaltation of Chassidism, one through his
unbounded enthusiasm, the other by his scholarship.
These men, neither of whom is open to suspicion,
were Israel of Kozieniza (north of Radom) and
Salman of Liadi, both Beer's disciples.

So strong did the Chassidim again become, that
a second interdict had to be fulminated against
them.   This time also the persecution originated in
Wilna, and was instigated by Elijah Wilna.   The
Chassidim were declared to be heretics, with whom
no pious Jew might intermarry (summer of 1781).
Two messengers were sent from Wilna to the Lithuanian congregations to induce them to support the
ban.   In consequence of this, the collections of
Chassidic sermons and other writings, although they
contained sentences from Holy Writ, were publicly
burnt in Brody and Cracow.   In Selvia, near

Slonim, during the fair, in the presence of large numbers of Jews, the ban was publicly promulgated against the Chassidim and their writings (August 21, 1781); but these obsolete methods were of little use. In the Austrian Polish provinces (Galicia) other means were employed by the disciples of the Mendelssohn school against the stultifying system of the Chassidim. The decree of Joseph II, that schools for instruction in German and elementary subjects be established in all Jewish communities, encountered vigorous resistance from all Jews, but especially from Chassidim. In the belief that culture would improve the demoralized and barbarous state of the people, a small body of men, Mendelssohn's admirers, strove zealously to oppose them. Among the most ardent workers for the enlightenment of the Galician Jews was Alexander Kaller. Kaller and his associates probably obtained a decree from the court at Vienna, commanding that no Chassidic or Kabbalistic writings be admitted into Galicia (1785). After the second partition of Poland, denunciations were also leveled against the Chassidim in Russian Poland as dangerous to the state. Salman of Liadi was dragged in chains to St. Petersburg. Elijah Wilna is said to have been the instigator of this charge, too; indeed, he persecuted the sect as long as he lived. After his death the Chassidim took vengeance upon him by dancing upon his grave, and celebrating the day of his decease as a holiday, with shouting and drunkenness. All efforts made to suppress the Chassidim were in vain, because in a measure they represented a just principle, that of opposing the excesses of Talmudism. Before the end of the eighteenth century they had increased to 100,000 souls. At the present day they rule in congregations where they were formerly persecuted, and they are spreading on all sides.

CHAPTER X.

THE MEASFIM AND THE JUDÆO-CHRISTIAN SALON.

The Progressionists—The Gatherer (Meassef)—David Mendes—
Moses Ensheim—Wessely's Mosaid—Marcus Herz—Solomon
Maimon—Culture of the Berlin Jews—Influence of French Liter-
ature—First Step for Raising the Jews—The Progressive and
Orthodox Parties—The Society of Friends—Friedländer and
Conversion—Depravity of Berlin Jewesses—Henrietta Herz—
Humboldt—Dorothea Mendelssohn—Schlegel—Rachel—Schlei-
ermacher—Chateaubriand.

1786—1791 C. E.

The state of the German Jews, among whom the
battle against unreason began, was more satisfactory than that of the Polish Jews. In Germany
youthful activity and energy asserted themselves,
an impulse to action that promised to repair in a
short space of time the neglect of centuries. Great
enthusiasm suddenly sprang up, which produced
wonderful, or at least surprising, results, and overcame the benumbing effects of apathy. Young men
tore the scepter from the grasp of the aged, and
desired to preach new wisdom, or rather to rejuvenate the old organism of Judaism with new sap.
The synagogue might well have exclaimed, "Who
hath begotten me these, seeing I have lost my
children, and am desolate, a captive, and removing
to and fro? and who hath brought up these?" A
new spirit had come upon these youths, which, in
one night, put an end to their isolation, and transformed them into organs for historical reconstruction. As if by agreement they suddenly closed the
ponderous folios of the Talmud, turned away from
it, and devoted themselves to the Bible, the eternal
fount of youth. Mendelssohn's Pentateuch translation poured out a new spirit over them, furnished

them with a new language, and infused new poetry into them. Whence this body of spirited young men? What had hitherto been their course of education? Why were they so powerfully influenced? Suddenly they made their appearance, prophesied a new future, without knowing exactly what they prophesied, and, scarce fledged, soared aloft. From Poland to Alsace, from Italy to Amsterdam, London, and Copenhagen, new voices were heard, singing in harmonious union. Their significance lay wholly in their harmony; singly, the voices appear thin, piping, and untrained; only when united do they give forth a pleasant and impressive tone. Those who had but recently learnt to appreciate the beauties of Hebrew, came forward as teachers, to re-establish in its purity a language, so greatly disfigured, so generally used, and so continually abused. Inspired by ideals which the sage of Berlin had conjured up, they desired to pave the way to a thorough understanding of Holy Writ, to acquire a taste for poetry, and awaken zeal for science. Carried away by ardor, they ignored the difficulties in the way of a people, internally and externally enslaved, which seeks to raise itself to the heights of poetry and philosophy, and therefore they succeeded in accomplishing the revival. On the whole they achieved more than Mendelssohn, their admired prototype, because the latter was too cautious to take a step that might have an untoward result. But these youths pressed boldly forward, for they had no reputation to lose, and represented no interests that could be compromised.

This result was produced by a material and an ideal circumstance. Frederick's eagerness for money, his desire to enrich the land, almost compelled the Jews, especially those of Berlin, to accumulate capital. Owing to their manufactories, speculations, and enormous enterprises on the one hand, and their moderate manner of living on the other, the first Jewish millionaires arose in Berlin, and by their side many houses in affluent circumstances. But what could be done with these riches? To the nobility and the court, Jews were not admitted; the Philistine burghers closed their doors against these Jewish upstarts, whom they regarded with envy. There thus remained for wealthy Jews only literary intercourse, for which they have always had a preference. All or the majority had in their youth made the acquaintance of the Talmud, and were intimate with the world of books. This circumstance gave their efforts an ideal character: they did not worship Mammon alone; reading in their leisure hours was a necessity to them. As soon as German literature had been naturalized in their midst through Mendelssohn, they included it in their circle of studies, either with the serious object of cultivating themselves or to be in accord with fashion. In this matter they excelled the Christian citizens, who as a rule did not care for books. Jewish merchants, manufacturers, and bankers interested themselves in literary productions, as if they belonged to a guild of learned men, using for them the time that Christian citizens and workmen passed in drinking.

The first movement was made in Königsberg, a kind of colony to Berlin. In this town certain men had acquired wealth by their industry and circumspection, and shared in the culture dawning in Germany under the influence of French literature. Three brothers named Friedländer (Bärmann, Meyer, and Wolf) were the leaders. To this family belonged David Friedländer (born 1750, died 1834), a servile imitator of Mendelssohn, who by means of his connection by marriage with the banking-house of Daniel Itzig, obtained influence in Berlin (since 1771), and brought about close intercourse between Berlin and Königsberg. He also took part in the promotion of the revival among Jews. It was an event in the history of the Königsberg jews, when Mendelssohn stayed there for several days while on a business journey. He was visited by distinguished persons, professors and authors, and was treated with extraordinary attention. Immanuel Kant, the profound thinker, publicly embraced him. This trifling occurrence gave to the cultured Jews of Königsberg a sort of consciousness that the Jew can by self-respect command the regard of the ruling classes. Moreover, the Königsberg University, at the instigation of certain liberal-minded teachers, especially Kant, admitted Jewish youths thirsting for knowledge as students and academical citizens. Among these young men, trained partly on Talmudical, partly on academical lines, there were two who awakened a new spirit, or rather, continued the quiet activity of Mendelssohn with greater effect. These were Isaac Abraham Euchel and Mendel Bresselau, both tutors employed by the wealthy, culture-loving Friedländers. Isaac Euchel, through Mendelssohn and Wessely, had acquired a dignified, correct Hebrew style contrasting most favorably with the corrupt language hitherto employed. His younger companion, Mendel Bresselau, who afterwards took part in the great contest against the old school, was of more importance. He was truly an artist in the Hebrew tongue, and without elaboration or ambiguity he applied biblical phraseology to modern conditions and circumstances. He took as his model the poet Moses Chayim Luzzatto, and like him composed a moral drama, entitled "Youth." Supported by two young members of the wealthy Friedländer family, Euchel and Bresselau, during the lifetime of Mendelssohn, and at the time of Wessely's conflict with the ultra-orthodox (spring, 1783), issued a summons to the whole Jewish world to establish a society for the promotion of the Hebrew language (Chebrath Dorshe Leshon Eber), and to found a journal to be

called "The Gatherer" (Meassef). They had
reckoned upon the support of Wessely, already
recognized as an authority upon style, and had
asked contributions from him, who, as they expressed themselves, "had taken down the harps
from the willows of Babylon, and had drawn forth
new songs from them." The aged poet gladly
joined the young men, but, as if he had had a fore-
boding of the ultimate result, he warned them
against turning their darts against Judaism, and
in general against employing satire. Their summons found widespread response. They had
chosen the right means to advance culture, and they
satisfied a real want. The Hebrew language in its
purity and chastity could alone accomplish the
union between Judaism and the culture of the day.

"The Gatherer" found most encouragement in
Berlin, the capital of Jewish culture. Here numerous literary contributions and material support
were forthcoming. In this city lived a number of
youths moved by the same aspirations as Euchel
and Bresselau, who fostered enthusiasm for the
Hebrew language, and renewed its youth. Not too
proud to enter into rivalry with beginners, Mendelssohn also contributed a few Hebrew poems
anonymously. It is characteristic of the newly-
aroused spirit, that the fine introductory Hebrew
verses in the periodical are represented as being
written by a young child who modestly begs ad-
mittance, as if henceforth, not the grey-headed
Eliphaz, but the youthful Elihu was to be spokesman, and lay down the law. Fresh names appeared in the newly-established organ, and their
owners, under the collective name of Measfim, contributors to "The Gatherer" (Meassef, first published in the autumn of 1783), mark a definite
tendency, a *Sturm und Drang* period of neo-
Hebraic literature. Another pair of friends of
Euchel and Bresselau afterwards undertook the

editorship; these were Joel Löwe and Aaron Halle, or Wolfssohn—the one an earnest inquirer, the other a bold iconoclast, who first verified Wessely's fears, and, in a dialogue between Moses Maimonides and Moses Mendelssohn, subjected unprogressive Judaism to scathing criticism.

Two Poles residing in Berlin, Isaac Satanow and Ben-Zeeb, most accomplished masters of Hebrew style, also belonged to the Measfim, but their studies in German culture had an injurious effect upon their moral character. Besides, the small number of contributors to the "Gatherer" was swelled by Wolf Heidenheim, a strange man, who equally abhorred the crudeness and folly of the old system, and the frivolity and sophistry of the new, and banished his ill-humor by pedantically exact grammatical and Masoretic studies on the lines of the old masters. By his carefully arranged editions of old writings, if he did not destroy, he at least curbed, the old habits of slovenliness and carelessness.

The cultivators of Hebrew stretched out friendly hands to each other across widely-sundered districts, and formed a kind of brotherhood which spread to Holland, France, and Italy. David Friedrichsfeld was also an enthusiast for the Hebrew language and biblical literature. He possessed such delicate appreciation of the beauties of the language, that an ill-chosen Hebrew word caused him pain. He constantly insisted upon pure forms and expressions, and was a cultivated and severe judge. In his youth, Friedrichsfeld had chosen the better fate, by turning his back upon Prussia, so cruel to the Jews, and emigrating to the free city of Amsterdam. He heartily welcomed, with youthful ardor, the plan for the study of Hebrew, and lived to enjoy the good fortune of celebrating in Hebrew verse the complete emancipation of the Jews in Holland. At his proposition, the Jewish poets in Holland joined

the ranks of the Measfim.   The most renowned was
David Franco Mendes in Amsterdam (born 1713;
died 1792).   He was descended from a Marrano
family, was a disciple of the poet Luzzatto when the
latter lived in Amsterdam, and took him as a pattern.   A series of occasional poems, in the form of
the Judæo-Spanish poetry of the seventeenth century, had gained him a name which was increased
by his Hebrew historical drama, "The Punishment
of Athalia" (Gemul Athalia).   It distressed Franco
Mendes to see how the Jews turned away from
Hebrew to the fashionable French literature, because the latter produced beautiful, artistic works,
whilst the Hebrew language seemed smitten with
sterility.   This disgrace Mendes desired to blot
out, and, following in the wake of Racine and
Metastasio, he undertook to dramatize the interesting history of the royal boy Joash who, to be protected from murderous hands, was brought up
secretly in the Temple, and of the downfall of the
bloodthirsty queen Athalia.

In France the Hebrew literature of the Measfim
was represented by Moses Ensheim (Einsheim), or
Moses Metz, who for several years was private
tutor to Mendelssohn's children.   He was a mathematician of great repute, whose work has been
praised by qualified authorities of the first rank.
Thus he wrote a work upon Integral and Differen-
tial Calculus, which won the applause of Lagrange
and Laplace.   But he never published any of his
writings.   He only gave voice to triumphal songs
in Hebrew upon the victory of freedom over slavery
in France, and some of these were sung in the
synagogues.   Ensheim influenced an advocate
(Grégoire) of the liberation of his co-religionists in
France, and provided him with material wherewith
to defend them.   Ensheim formed a contrast to an
older teacher in Mendelssohn's house, Herz Homberg, a great favorite with Mendelssohn.   The

latter was deceived in him, and trusted in him too far
when he invited his co-operation in the Pentateuch
translation.   Homberg was of a prosaic nature,
actuated wholly by selfish motives, and was somewhat of a place-hunter.   Through Homberg, during
his stay in Görz, and Elijah Morpurgo, who corresponded with Mendelssohn and Wessely, the educa-
tional influence of the Measfim penetrated to Italy ;
and the younger generation, which afterwards
united with the French Jews, drew inspiration from
that source.

In this manner, the Hebrew language and neo-
Hebraic poetry became a bond of union for the
Jews of Western Europe, to some extent embracing
also the Jews of Poland, and led the way to an
astonishingly swift and enduring revival.   The Hebrew tongue was known to almost all Jews, with'the
exception of a few ignorant villagers, and afforded
an excellent medium for propagating European culture.   Thousands of youths who studied the Talmud
in various colleges, gradually, for the greater part
secretly, took an active share in the movement, and
drank deep draughts from the stream of innovation.
Thus, with the expected deliverance from political
oppression, which had already been realized in various places, there arose a peculiar excitement and
confusion.   The old and the new mingled, forming
a kind of a spiritual hotch-potch.   The question was
raised whether or not, beside the Talmud, it was
allowed to engage in biblical studies and profane
literature, to cultivate philosophy, and in general to
study the sciences (Chochmoth).   The great rabbis,
Ezekiel Landau, Raphael Cohen, and others, condemned such studies, whilst Mendelssohn and
Wessely, blamelessly pious men, not only permitted,
but even recommended them for the elevation of
Judaism.   Of the old and respected authorities,
some permitted them and even occupied themselves
therewith, whilst others prohibited and held aloof

from them, as from some seductive sin. These important questions presented themselves to thinking Jewish young men, and gave rise to much disquietude. For the greater number the charm of novelty, the attractive language of the representatives of the new tendency, or the inclination to cast off burdensome ritual fetters decided the question. The number of those interested in the periodical, "The Gatherer," increased from year to year. The death of Mendelssohn also exerted a decided influence. His pupils—as such, all the Measfim regarded themselves—deified him, glorified him in bright colors, idealized him and his eventful history in prose and verse, pointed him out as an ideal worthy of imitation, and turned his renown to advantage in their cause. They went a step further, or widened the extent of their activity, aiming not merely at ennobling the Hebrew language, but at refinement in general. They called themselves "The Society for the Good and the Noble" (from 1787), without being able to define their purpose. The all-powerful stream of innovation could not be stemmed by the adherents of the old school. Unskillfully they attempted to vindicate the old system, exaggerating the dangers, and thereby losing all influence.

Thus in almost every large community, there arose a party of the "Enlightened" or "the Left," which had not yet broken with the old school, but whose action bordered upon secession. By the ultra-orthodox they were denounced as heretics, on account of their preference for pure language and form, both in Hebrew and European literature. This abusive name hurt them but little, and rather afforded them a certain amount of satisfaction. The outcome of the work of the Measfim was that they stirred men's minds, extending their range of observation, and leading them to ennobling thoughts and acts ; but these writers did not leave any permanent results. Not a single production of the circle has enduring value. Their best performance was Wessely's swan-song, which possesses literary, if not artistic worth. Roused perhaps by the astonishment of Herder, the admirer of ancient Hebrew poetry, that no poet had celebrated the miracles of the departure from Egypt—whose center was the sublime prophet Moses—Wessely determined to compose a neo-Hebraic epic. Animated by the spirit of the prophets, there poured from his pen smooth, well-rounded, euphonious verses, which unroll before the eye the grand events that occurred from the cruel bondage in Egypt till the miraculous passage of the Red Sea and the wanderings in the wilderness. "Songs of Glory" Wessely called his Hebrew heroic poem, his Mosaid. In fact his verses and strophes are beautifully arranged and perfect in form. It is the best work that the school of the Measfim produced. Wessely's epic was so much admired that two Christian poets, Hufnagel and Spalding, rendered the first two cantos into German. The Mosaid is, however, by no means a masterpiece; it lacks the breath of true poetry, fancy and loftiness of conception. It is merely a history of the origin of the Israelites transcribed into verse, or, more correctly, a versified commentary on the Pentateuch. This criticism holds of the school as a whole; its disciples were good neo-Hebraic stylists, but as poets their ability was not even mediocre.

The appearance of the "Gatherer" aroused attention in Christian circles. The old assailant of the Jews, Michaelis, could not remain silent. Others greeted it as the dawn promising a fair day; it was in fact daybreak for the Jewish race. What is the distinction of a cultured people? Next to gentle manners, it consists in taste for harmonious forms and in the power to produce artistic creations. This taste and power, lost through external oppression and internal disorganization, were re-awakened

among the Jews by the organ of the Measfim. To
elevate the Jewish race to the rank of the cultured
nations, nothing new was required ; it was merely
necessary that a comprehension of the beauties
and sublimities of their own literature be inculcated.

In this period, the Jews owned profound philosophical thinkers, if not of the first, certainly of
the second rank, who in acuteness of intellect
almost surpassed Mendelssohn. Three are especially to be mentioned, who, though trained in the
Mendelssohnian system, soon recognized its weaknesses, and directed their minds to new paths:
these were Marcus Herz, Solomon Maimon, and
Ben-David. The events of their lives picture on a
small scale how the Jewish race as a whole worked
its way from degradation and ignorance to freedom
and enlightenment. Marcus (Mordecai) Herz (born
in Berlin, 1747, where he died 1803) was the son
of poor parents, and his father, like Mendelssohn's,
supported himself and his family by copying
Hebrew manuscripts. He received his Talmudical
education in the school founded by Ephraim Veitel.
Owing to poverty he was unable in spite of his
talents to continue his studies, but at fifteen years
of age was compelled to go to Königsberg as an
apprentice. The desire for knowledge soon withdrew him from business and led him to the University, as the Albertina at that time admitted Jewish
youths to the medical department. Philosophy,
however, exerted greater attraction upon him.
Herz was regarded as being gifted with the " keen
mind peculiar to the Jewish nation." Kant, then
at work upon his monumental system, saw Herz in
his audience as often as the medical professors saw
him in theirs. He distinguished him, drew him
into the circle of his intimates, and treated him as
his favorite disciple. When entering upon his
professorship, according to an absurd and antiquated
custom Kant had to argue in public upon a philo-

sophical subject, and found no one better fitted than
Herz to act as his assistant. Several University
representatives objected that a Jewish student,
however talented and superior to his Christian
companions, should be allowed equal privileges
with them. Kant, however, insisted upon his
demand. Pressed by pecuniary difficulties, and
because a Jew could not receive the degree at the
Königsberg University, Herz returned to his native
town and joined Mendelssohn's circle. He was,
however, an advocate of the Kantian philosophy.
He became at the same time a skilled physician,
and practiced his art with conscientiousness and
zeal. By his marriage with Henrietta de Lemos,
he secured a large practice and numerous acquaintances as assistant-physician to his Portuguese
father-in-law ; and through his incisive wit and
versatile knowledge he became a noted personage
in the Prussian capital. When he delivered philosophical lectures upon the Kantian philosophy, still
new and but little understood, many distinguished
men were among his auditors. Had not progress
been great, if notabilities sat at the feet of a Jew to
hear his instruction upon the highest truths, whilst
men like Michaelis roundly denied all possibility of
culture in the Jews ? Herz afterwards delivered
discourses upon physics, and illustrated the mar-
vellous laws of nature by experimental demonstration. These lectures were still more crowded ;
even the Crown Prince (afterwards King Frederick
William III) and other princes did not disdain to
enter the house of a Jew and be taught by him.
His philosophical lucidity, acquired from Kant and
Mendelssohn, contributed towards rendering his
lectures upon medicine, as well as upon other subjects, enjoyable and appreciated. Herz was not,
however, an independent thinker, able to illumine
the dark ways of human knowledge by brilliant
ideas ; but he succeeded in explaining the profound

thoughts of others and in making them intelligible
to the average mind.   Through his personality and
his social position, Herz deeply influenced not alone
the culture of Berlin Jews, but also of Christian
circles.

Of the remarkable capacity of Jews for culture,
Solomon Maimon was a still more striking example.
This Pole, whose real name was Solomon of
Lithuania, or of Nieszwiez (born about 1753, died
1800), rose from the thickest cloud of Polish ignorance to pure philosophical knowledge, attaining
this height by his unaided efforts, but owing to his
scepticism, he fell a prey to shocking errors.   The
story of his life is full of travel and restlessness,
and is a good example of the versatility of Jews.

As in the case of Mendelssohn, Maimuni's philosophical religious work, "The Guide of the Perplexed" (More Nebuchim), was the cause of
Solomon's intellectual awakening.   He read the
book until it became part of him, consequently
assumed the name of Maimon, swore by the name
of the Jewish sage whenever evil desire prompted
him to sin, and conquered by its aid.   But whereas
Mendelssohn reached the right way through Maimuni, Solomon Maimon was led into error, doubt,
and unbelief, and to the end of his life lived an
aimless existence.   In despair he snatched at the
Kabbala, wishing to become a Jewish Faust, to
conjure up spirits who would obtain deep wisdom
for him ; he also made a pilgrimage to the leader
of the Chassidim, Beer of Mizricz.   But the deception practiced disgusted him, and he quickly turned
away from him.   But what was he, with his spirit of
scepticism, to do in a narrow world of rigid
orthodoxy ?   Continually play the hypocrite ?   Rumor
had carried a report to Poland, that in certain towns
of Germany a freer religious system prevailed, and
that more scope for philosophical inquiry was given.
At this period a Pole felt no scruples in forsaking

wife, children, and home, and wandering abroad. It cost Maimon the less effort, seeing that his wife had been thrust upon him when he was a child, and it was to his vexation that children were born to him. To appease his conscience he deceived himself by the pretext that he would study medicine in Germany, and be enabled to maintain himself and his family.

Thus Maimon left Lithuania (spring, 1777), at the age of twenty-five, "with a heavy, dirty beard, in torn, filthy clothes, his language a jargon composed of fragments of Hebrew, Judæo-German, and Polish, together with grammatical errors," as he himself says, and in this guise he introduced himself to some educated Jews in Königsberg, saying that he desired to devote himself to science. In this ragged Pole was a brain full of profound thoughts, which, as he grew older, developed into maturity. His journey from Königsberg to Berlin by way of Stettin was a succession of pitiful troubles. In Berlin the authorities refused to grant him residence. Those Poles who had severed themselves from the Talmud, and devoted themselves to science, lived in the odor of the worst heresy, and often gave occasion to suspicion. Maimon was sincere enough to admit the justice of this opinion. A moral life, activity of any kind, participation in the work of mankind, utilization of talent in the conquest of nature, man's liberation from the shackles of self-interest, the awakening of his moral impulse to act for the welfare of his brethren, the realization of the heavenly kingdom of justice and beneficent love— of all these ideals Maimon had no appreciation. These were indifferent matters, with which a thinker need not trouble himself. In this unsound state of mind he shunned all active work; to meditate idly and draw up formulas were his chief occupations. He attained no fixed goal in life, but staggered from folly to folly, from misery to misery.

To the general public he was first known through his "Autobiography," wherein he revealed the weak points of the Polish Jews, to him the only representatives of Judaism, as well as his own, with unsparing, cynical severity, as some years previously Rousseau had done in his "Confessions." He thereby performed an evil service for his co-religionists. His opinions concerning his brethren, originating in ill-humor, were accepted to their detriment as universal characteristics; and what he depicted as hateful in the Polish Jews was attributed to all Jews.

This kind of confession was considered extraordinary, and aroused great attention, in stiff, pedantic Germany. The "Autobiography" found its way into numerous circles, and gained many readers. The two great German poets, Schiller and Goethe, were absurdly fond of the cynical philosopher; and Goethe expressed the wish to have him live near him. His fame made Maimon neither better nor happier, and he did honor to the Jewish race only with his mental powers; in his actions he altogether dishonored it.

The third Jewish thinker of this time, Lazarus Ben-David (born in Berlin 1762; died there 1832), had neither the tragic nor the comic history of Maimon. He was a prosaic, pedantic personality, who in any German university could have filled the chair of logic and mathematics, and year after year given the same instruction unabridged and unincreased. For the philosophy of Kant, however, Ben-David possessed ardor and enthusiastic devotion, because he recognized it as the truth, and faithfully conformed to its moral principles. This philosophy was well suited to Jews, because it demanded high power of thought and moral action. For this reason Kant, like Aristotle in former days, had many Jewish admirers and disciples. Ben-David was also learned in the Talmud, and a good mathematician. It was perhaps a mistake on his

part to go to Vienna to lecture upon the Kantian
philosophy. At first the University permitted his
discourses in its halls,—a Jew lecturing on a philosophy which denied the right of Catholicism to
exist! He soon however had to discontinue them;
but Count Harrach offered him his palace as a
lecture-room. Meeting with obstacles here, too, he
left the imperial city, continued his discourses in
Berlin, and for some time acted as editor of a
journal. Ben-David produced but little impression
upon the course of Jewish history.

The German Jews, however, under Mendelssohn's
inspiration, not only elevated themselves with great
rapidity to the height of culture, but unmistakably
promoted the spread of culture in Christian circles.
Intellectual Jews and Jewesses created in Berlin
that cultured public tone which has become the distinction of this capital, and has influenced the whole
of Germany. Jews and Jewesses were the first to
found a salon for intellectual intercourse, in which
the elements of elevated thought, taste, poetry, and
criticism mingled together in a graceful, light way,
and were discussed, and made accessible to men of
different vocations. The Christian populace of
Berlin at the time of Frederick the Great and his
successor greatly resembled that of a petty town.
The nobility and high dignitaries were too aristocratic and uneducated to trouble themselves about
intellectual and social affairs and the outside world.
For them the court and the petty events of every-
day life were the world. The learned formed an
exclusive guild, and there was no high or wealthy
class of burghers. The middle classes followed the
narrow path of their old-fashioned German fathers;
met, if at all, over the beer-jug, and were continually engaged in repeating stories of "old Fritz's
victories." Particularly, the women lived modestly
within their four walls, or occupied themselves
wholly with the concerns of their family circles.

With the Jews of Berlin it was entirely different.
All, or most of them, had been more or less engaged with the Talmud in their youth ; their mental
powers were acute, and susceptible to fresh influences.   These new elements of culture Mendelssohn gave them through his Bible translation, and
his philosophical and æsthetic writings.   In Jewish
circles, knowledge procured more distinction than
riches ; the ignorant man, however wealthy, was
held up as a butt for contempt.   Every Jew, whatever his means, prided himself on possessing a
collection of old and new books, and, when possible,
sought to know their contents, so that he might not
be wanting in conversation.   Every well-informed
Jew lived in two worlds, that of business, and that
of books.   In consequence of the impulse given by
Mendelssohn, the younger generation occupied itself with *belles-lettres*, language, and philosophy.
The subjects of study had changed, but the yearning
for knowledge remained, or became still stronger.
Amongst the Jews of Berlin, shortly after the death
of Mendelssohn, were more than a hundred young
men burning with zeal for knowledge and culture,
from whose midst the contributors to the periodical
" Ha-Meassef " were supplied.

To this honest inclination for study, there was
added a fashionable folly.   Through Frederick the
Great, French literature became acclimatized in
Prussia, and Jews were especially attracted by the
sparkling intellectuality of French wit.   Voltaire
had more admirers in the tents of Jacob than in
German houses.   Jewish youths ravenously flung
themselves upon French literature, and acquired its
forms ; French frivolity naturally made its entry at
the same time.   The clever daughters of Israel also
ardently devoted themselves to this fashionable
folly ; they learned French, at first, to be sure, for
the purpose of conversing in the fashionable language with the youthful cavaliers who borrowed

money from their fathers. It was one more ornament with which to deck themselves. Through the influence of Mendelssohn and Lessing, such trifling gave way to earnest endeavors for the acquisition of solid knowledge, in order that they might occupy an equally exalted footing with the men. Mendelssohn's daughters, who were continually in the society of cultivated men, led the way, and stirred up emulation. In no town of Germany were there so many cultured Jewish women as in Berlin, for they learned easily, were industrious, and altogether superior to their Christian sisters in knowledge of literature.

Mendelssohn's house became the center for scientific and literary intercourse, and was the more frequented as his friends might expect to meet distinguished strangers there who were attracted by his wide-spread renown, and from whom something new might be learned. His daughters were admitted to this witty and charming society, to which they also introduced their young companions. After Mendelssohn's death David Friedländer and Marcus Herz took his place. Friedländer was, however, too stiff and plain to exercise attraction. Thus Herz's house became headquarters for Mendelssohn's friends, who became the nucleus of a large circle. Herz was a popular physician, and had numerous acquaintances among distinguished Jewish and Christian families. His lectures attracted people of every rank to his house, and those eager for knowledge were admitted into the intimacy of the family circle. Herz was gifted with caustic wit, with which he seasoned the conversation. But more powerful than his science and his genius was the influence of his wife. Hers was a magic circle, into which every native or foreign personage of importance in Berlin was magnetically drawn. Intercourse with the beautiful and gifted Jewess Henrietta Herz was, next to the court circle, the most sought after in Berlin.   Had she not been misled by seductive influences, she might have been a source of rich blessings to Judaism.

This beautiful woman, then, made her house the gathering-place of the select society of Berlin, and illustrious strangers pressed for the honor of an introduction to her.   Here the Christian friends of Mendelssohn, already accustomed to intercourse with Jews, mingled freely with cultured Jews, but also new men, who filled high positions, and diplomatists were to be met there.   Mirabeau, in whose mind the storm-charged clouds of the Revolution were already forming, and to whom the Jews owed so much, during his secret diplomatic embassy (1786) to Berlin was more in the society of Henrietta Herz than in that of her husband.   Gradually ladies of high degree and education also entered into relations with Madame Herz and her friends, attracted by the charm of refined, social communion. But her salon exercised most powerful attraction upon cultured Christian youths, by reason of its beautiful Jewish damsels and ladies, the satellites of the fair hostess.   These Jewish beauties, however, did not merely form the ornament of the salon, but took an active part in the intellectual entertainment, and distinguished themselves by their originality. Gentz called them "the clever women of Jewry." Among them were two who shone by superior intellectual qualities, and combined modern culture with Jewish keenness of mind and wit : Mendelssohn's eldest daughter Dorothea, and Rachel Levin, afterwards the wife of Varnhagen von Ense.   Both possessed eminent talents, in addition to which Rachel Levin had an inflexible love for truth, united with gentleness and amiability.

Almost at the same time a brilliant salon, where authors, artists, nobles, and diplomatists, native and foreign, came together, was opened in Vienna, by a Berlin Jewess, Fanny Itzig, daughter of the

banker Daniel Itzig. She was witty, amiable and
noble, and was married to Nathan Adam von Arn-
stein, who had been made a baron. Like her friends
in Berlin she brought about the social intermingling of Jews with Christians in Vienna. These Jewish coteries most triumphantly refuted the foolish
remark of the insolent scholar of Göttingen, "that
gypsies would sooner undergo the transformation
into a people than Jews." The prejudice of a
thousand years was blown away with one breath
more effectually than by a hundred learned or eloquent disquisitions.

The social equalization of the Jews in cultivated
circles of Prussia caused them to hope, if not for
complete civil rights, at least fo a lightening of the
oppressive taxes and the humiliations imposed upon
them. Between the social position of cultured Jews
and their legal standing there was a deep chasm.
In the burgher classes, the Jews of Berlin were the
first millionaires—no indifferent matter considering
the important place held by money at that time—
yet, according to the law, they were treated like
peddlers. Humane treatment could not be expected from the philosophical king. Dohm's apology for the Jews did not exist for him. Hope was
aroused among the Berlin Jews on the accession of
Frederick William II, who was of a weak but kindly
nature. Urged on by David Friedländer, who, the
successor of Mendelssohn, was at the same time
considered the representative of Jewish interests,
the chiefs and elders of the Berlin community presented a petition for the abolition of the Jewish
poll-tax, the repeal of barbarous laws against the
Jews, and the concession of freedom of movement.
They received a favorable reply, directing them to
"choose honest men from their midst," with whom
the government might negotiate. Their proposal
to select delegates from amongst the Jews in the
provinces was assented to, and a commission was

established to investigate the complaints of the Prussian Jews and make suggestions for improvement. As general deputies of the Jews there were selected Friedländer and his rich father-in-law, Daniel Itzig, who, with great independence and courage, laid bare the barbarous and venal legislation of Frederick the Great in reference to the Jews.

The deputies drew up a list of the imposts extorted from the Jews, bearing ridiculous titles ; for instance, the exportation of porcelain, which bound them to purchase articles of the worst quality for an exorbitant price (called in mockery " Jews' porcelain ") from the royal manufactory and to sell them abroad ; and taxes for the support of manufactories for caps, stockings, pocket-handkerchiefs, and veils. They pointed out burdensome restrictions, how in courts of justice they were not treated as the equals of Christian suitors, and they especially complained of the responsibility laid upon all for each, and boldly demanded complete equalization, not mere permission to engage in agriculture and trades, but also to fill public offices and university chairs (May, 1787). The expectations of the Jews of Berlin and Prussia were however baffled. Only the law to deal in bad porcelain was annulled for a sum of four thousand thalers. The degrading body-tax was also repealed for native Jews journeying from province to province, and for strangers when frequenting the fair at Frankfort-on-the-Oder (December, 1787 ; July, 1788.) This release from slavery had been effected by Joseph II and by Louis XVI of France several years previously. The high officials therefore advised the abolition of the Jewish poll-tax from shame. But the gain was not great, for, as Prussian Jews had to prove themselves such at every public gate, the stigma was not removed. The ultimate result of the petition of the Jewish deputies was lamentable. What was given with one hand,

was taken away with the other. It redounds to the
honor of the deputies that they frankly rejected the
paltry, narrow-minded concessions, remarking, " The
intended favors are below our expectation, and
hardly accord with the joyful hopes entertained at
the accession of the king." They declared that
they were not empowered to accept the reforms
offered, " which contain few advantages and many
restrictions," especially as regarded the enlistment
of common soldiers. Only certain individual Jews
received exceptional equalization of rights. Orders
were given that in official acts they should not be
treated as Jews. Otherwise everything continued
as of old, only slight relief being given to the Jews
in Silesia.

Thus a nucleus for the elevation of the Jewish
race was formed in the Berlin community, and their
efforts were encouraged, if not by the state, at least
by public opinion. In two ways their action influenced a wider circle—through the Free School
(Chinuch Nearim), and the printing establishment
connected with it. The Free School, conducted by
David Friedländer and his brother-in-law, Itzig
Daniel Itzig, was not managed according to
Wessely's ideal plan. The curriculum was composed mainly of the subjects of a general education,
and gradually everything Jewish (Hebrew, the
Bible, the Talmud) was crowded out. In ten years
(1781-1791) over five hundred well-taught pupils
were graduated from the school—apostles of the
Berlin spirit, who spread its influence in all directions. It became a model school for German and
other communities. With similar ends in view the
printing-press sent into the Ghettos a large number
of instructive works in Hebrew and German. The
spirit engendered thereby was at first one of scepticism, of superficial enlightenment. Its aim was to
eradicate from Jewish life and manners everything
that offended cultured taste or made the Jews

objects of derision, but it included in its attack whatever did not at once recommend itself to the sober-minded, and so tended to obliterate everything that recalled the great events of the past, and that caused the Jews to appear as a separate race in the eyes of Christians. The dearest ambition of the advocates of this movement was to resemble Christians in every respect. "Enlightenment, Culture" were their passwords, the idols of their worship, to which they sacrificed everything. Mendelssohn had left no disciple of any importance able to recognize the great truths of Judaism, and bring them into accord with culture. Men like Euchel, Löwe, Friedländer, Herz, and almost all the Measfim, possessed mediocre minds and limited views; they were unable to scatter abroad fruit-bearing germs of thought. Despite their enthusiasm for Mendelssohn, they did not appreciate the essence of his nature, and thought that he was still in their midst, when they had long forsaken him. Even his own children, not excepting his accomplished daughters, misunderstood him; and this misconception resulted in great confusion.

With every step forward taken by the Berlin school of enlightenment, it became more opposed to the main body of Judaism, vexing its susceptibilities, and thereby frustrating its own efficacy. Misunderstandings, bitter feelings, friction, and strife were the direct consequences.

The ultra-orthodox party, however, numbered still fewer men of importance than the advanced school. The most eminent leader among them, or the one regarded as such, Ezekiel Landau, in Prague, had not the slightest sympathy with the new tendency, but thoughtlessly clung to every usage however unjustifiable, and thereby injured the cause he represented. He had only condemnation and denunciation as heretics for those who withdrew from the well-trodden path.

Owing to the friction between the progressive

and the orthodox parties, both of whom exceeded
all proper bounds, an exciting quarrel sprang up in
the Berlin community. Young men—private tutors,
merchants' apprentices, the sons of the rich, and
fashionable youths—boasted a frivolous philosophy,
and proudly despised their hoary religion, considering everything that interfered with their pleasures
as superstition, prejudice, and Rabbinical folly.
The adherents of the old views therefore grew the
more tenacious, and held to everything that bore a
religious stamp. As the orthodox communal leaders
still had the upper hand in the benevolent institutions, they refused support to the partisans of
enlightenment, especially to strangers, would not
admit their sick into the Jewish hospital, and denied
the dead honorable burial. In short all the phenomena that usually accompany religious party
conflicts appeared. Those without families, among
whom were two prominent Measfim, Euchel and
Wolfssohn, determined to unite together so as not
to stand isolated against the orthodox party. They
desired to form a union for the protection of its
members. Mendelssohn's eldest son, Joseph, was
very zealous in promoting such a union, and on the
strength of his name it met with abundant encouragement. Thus the "Society of Friends" was
formed (1792), a community of *illuminati* within
the community, comprising solely unmarried men,
whose chief aim was to regard each other as
brothers, and to support each other in distress and
illness ; but their collateral intention was to spread
culture and promote enlightenment. The "Friends"
took a saying of Mendelssohn as their motto, "To
seek for truth, to love the beautiful, to desire the
good, to do the best." A bundle of staves was
their symbol. In the first year of its existence, the
union numbered more than a hundred members in
the capital. Young men in Königsberg, Breslau,
and Vienna, joined the ranks. A bond of cordial

brotherhood held the members together, and to the present day, a fraternal feeling of delicate benevolence has survived in the Society. But it was a morbid symptom. The Society floated in the air without a firm basis; it had roots neither in its own midst, nor in Judaism, nor did it attach itself to any great political ideal. It aimed at bodily welfare and quietude, as if civilized men could live by bread only: the catchwords and phrases of culture and enlightenment did not avail much. The struggle against the old régime was but weak; all that they succeeded in doing was to keep their deceased friends longer above ground. In short, the "Society of Friends" lacked the leaven of inspiration, the only quality which ultimately bears fruit.

If the members of this Society took up no firm attitude, those who never knew an ideal, nor even a dreamy striving, the commonplace men who were mere slaves, and sought their whole happiness in mixing with Christians, acted yet more culpably. The old system had no charms for them, and the new one no tangible form to attract them. The example of the court and high circles of society exercised an evil influence also upon the Jews of the large towns of Prussia. "Under Frederick William II," as Mirabeau remarks from his own observation, "Prussia had fallen into a condition of rottenness, before having attained the stage of maturity." Jewish youths of wealthy houses followed the general inclination to sensual pleasures. Not secretly, but openly in the light of day, they overleapt all bounds, and with contempt of Judaism united contempt for chastity and morality. They aped other apes. Earnest men, such as David Friedländer, Lazarus Ben-David, and Saul Asher, deplored the decay of morality among the Jews, without noticing that their own shallow desire for enlightenment had contributed to it.

"Vices have spread in our midst, which our fathers knew not, and which at any price have been bought too dearly. Irreligion, voluptuousness, and effeminacy, weeds that spring from the misuse of enlightenment and culture, have alas! taken root amongst us, and especially in the principal towns we are exposed to the danger that the stream of luxury along with our boorishness is sweeping away our severe and simple morals."

Having broken loose from the bond of a national religion existing for thousands of years, superficial reasoners and profligates passed over to Christianity in a body. "They were like moths, fluttering around the flame, till they were consumed." Of what use was it to be galled by the fetters of the "general privilege," of what use to continue to bear the disgrace of being "protected" Jews, if by the repetition of an empty formula they could become equal to the Christians! So they washed away the mark of the yoke and its shame with the waters of baptism. The congregations of Berlin, Breslau, and Königsberg beheld daily the apostasy of their members, of the richest and outwardly the most cultured people. It appeared as if the words of the prophet would be verified, "I will leave in the midst of thee an afflicted and poor people." It must be considered a miracle that the entire Jewish party of enlightenment in Germany did not abjure Judaism. Three invisible powers kept them from following *en masse* the example of treachery and apostasy: deep aversion to the dogma of Divine Incarnation, indestructible attachment to their families and to their great past of thousands of years, and love for the Hebrew language and literature. Without suspecting it, they felt themselves united as a nation, a link in the long chain of the history of the Jewish race, and they could not persuade themselves to separate from it. The revival of Hebrew through the Measfim had had beneficial influence in this direction. Whoever could comprehend the beauties and elevated thoughts of biblical literature, and could imitate the language, remained a Jew in spite of secret doubts, degradation, and disgrace. Thus Mendelssohn provided the new generation both with a poison and its antidote.

David Friedländer alone proved an exception to this rule. Neither Jewish antiquity, nor Hebrew poetry, nor family ties, had power to keep him loyal to his banner, even with half-hearted devotion. The tearing asunder of all family connections, the casting aside of the duties of the religious brotherhood, did indeed oppress him. Nevertheless, he proceeded to sever himself from the Jewish community and to desert to the hostile camp. He had striven to obtain for himself and his whole family an exceptional naturalization with all its rights and duties, but had not succeeded. This pained him, and instead of hiding his annoyance in the pride of ancestry and martyrdom, instead of working on behalf of his co-religionists so as to surpass the haughty Christians, he coveted the honor of joining them. Friedländer, however, did not desire to effect this desertion alone or absolutely. He therefore, together with other fathers of families similarly disposed, in a cowardly manner directed a letter, without mentioning either himself or others by name, to the chief consistorial councilor Teller, who was on friendly terms with Jews. This letter expressed their desire for conversion and baptism, under the condition that they might be excused from believing in Jesus, and from participating in the rites of the church, or that at least they might be allowed to explain Christian dogmas in their own manner—a suggestion equally silly and dishonorable. Friedländer could not deny that, among the Jews, "virtue was general, benevolence inherent, parental and filial love, and the sanctity of marriage deeply rooted, self-sacrifice for the sake of others frequent; and that, on the other hand, gross crimes—murder, robbery, and outrage—were rare." But this bright side of their servile state seemed to him only a secondary matter. Therefore, in this foolish letter, he libeled his people and its past, called the Talmud (that mental tonic) mysticism, spoke in illogical confusion now of the harmful character, now of the utility of the ritual laws of Judaism, and sketched the development of Jewish history in a way not to be excelled for perversity.

Teller disposed of the Jewish fathers who craved a Christianity without Jesus politely, but decisively, as they deserved. They might remain what they were, for Christianity had no desire for such infidel believers. Friedländer had met with an ignominious experience; he remained a Jew, but his children pressed forward to be baptized without conditions or qualifications. His letter however aroused more attention than it deserved.

If the German Jews, especially those of Berlin, through their intercourse with Christian society, and their interest in literature, gained in external conduct, in forms of politeness, and social manners— advantages not to be underrated—they lost something for which there was no compensation. The chastity of Jewish women and maidens during their isolation had been of inviolable sanctity; the happiness of family life rested upon this precious basis. Jewish women were seldom married for love—the Ghetto was not the place for the dallyings of love— but after marriage duty induced love. This sanctuary, the pride of Israel, which filled earnest Christians with admiration, and led them highly to esteem the Jews, became dishonored by their association with Christians of the corrupt higher ranks.

If the enemies of the Jews had designed to break the power of Israel, they could have discovered no more effectual means than infecting Jewish women with moral depravity, a plan more efficacious than that employed by the Midianites, who weakened the men by immorality. The salon of the beautiful Henrietta Herz became a sort of Midianite tent.

Here a number of young Jewish women assembled, whose husbands were kept away by their business. The most prominent male member of this circle was Frederick von Gentz, the embodiment of selfishness, licentiousness, vice, and depravity, whose chief occupation was the betrayal of women. Henrietta Herz was the first to be confused and led astray by homage to her beauty. It was the time when German romanticism, the product of Goethe's muse, began to act upon the minds of men, urging them to translate lyrical emotions into reality, and transfigure life poetically. This romantic tendency resulted in fostering sentimentality and in infamous marriages which were contracted and dissolved at pleasure. A so-called Band of Virtue (Tugend-Bund) was formed, of which Henrietta Herz, two daughters of Mendelssohn, and other Jewesses, together with Christian profligates, were members. The Jewish women felt themselves exalted and honored by their close intimacy with Christians of rank ; they did not see the fanged serpent beneath the flowers. With William von Humboldt, an ardent youth, afterwards a Prussian minister, Henrietta secretly maintained an amatory correspondence behind her husband's back.

When William von Humboldt married, and forgot Henrietta, who had been misled by her vanity, she entered into an ambiguous relation with Schleiermacher, the modern apostle of the new Christianity. Their conspicuous intimacy was mocked at by acquaintances, even more than by strangers. Both parties denied somewhat too anxiously the criminality of their intimate intercourse. Whether true or not, it was disgrace enough that evil tongues should even suspect the honor of a Jewish matron of good family.

Schleiermacher's companion was Frederick Schlegel, who stormed heaven with childish strength,—a chameleon in sentiments and views, enthusiastic now for the republic, now for monarchical despotism, who conjured up the specters and evil spirits of the Middle Ages. Introduced into the salon of Herz, he became the bosom friend of Schleiermacher, and at once resolved to seduce Dorothea Mendelssohn. Her father had died with the knowledge that she was joined in happy wedlock to the banker Simon Veit Witzenhausen. Her husband surrounded her with marks of attention and love. Two children were the issue of this marriage. Nevertheless, she allowed herself to be led into faithlessness by the treacherous voice of the romantic Schlegel. It was the fashion in this society to complain about being misunderstood and the discord of souls. The immoral teachings of Goethe's elective affinities had already taken root in Jewish families. The thought of parting from her husband and children did not restrain Dorothea from going astray, and Henrietta Herz acted as go-between. Dorothea therefore left her husband, and lived with Schlegel, at first in unlawful union. All the world was astounded at this immorality, which dragged Mendelssohn's honorable name in the mud. Doctor Herz forbade his wife to hold intercourse with this depraved woman. But she herself was at heart an adulteress, and informed her husband that she would not forsake her friend. Schleiermacher, the preacher, also took but little offense at this dissolute conduct. Dorothea followed her romantic betrayer from one folly to another, was baptized as a Protestant, and finally, together with him, became converted to Catholicism. It was a lamentable sight when Mendelssohn's daughter kissed the toe of the pope. The younger sister, Henrietta Mendelssohn, was not handsome enough to enthrall the libertines of the salon. It suffices to indicate her bent of mind to say that she also went over to Catholicism. The consequence of this internal corruption was to render the participators out of sorts with life.

Rachel Levin, another high-spirited woman, was too clever to take part in the frivolity of the Band of Virtue. She desired to pursue her own way. But her wisdom and clear mind did not secure her against the contamination of immorality. In one respect she was superior to her sinful Jewish sisters ; she was truthful, and wore no mask. When Rachel first made the acquaintance of the heroic but dissolute Prince Louis Ferdinand, she undertook to teach him "garret-truths"; but she rather learned from him the follies of the palace. Herself unmarried, she consented to become the intermediary between him and the abandoned Pauline Wiesel. Rachel Levin, or, as she was also called, Rachel Robert, in whose veins flowed Talmudic blood, which endowed her with a bright and active mind, and enabled her to penetrate to the very foundation of things, and pursue the soul and its varying instincts in their subtlest manifestations, ignored her own origin. She desired to distinguish the breath of God in the mutations of history, yet had no appreciation of the greatness of her race. She despised it, considering it the greatest shame and her worst misfortune to have been born a Jewess. Only in the hour of death did a faint suspicion of the great importance of Judaism and the Jews cross her mind.

"With exalted delight I meditate upon my origin and the web of history, through which the oldest reminiscences of the human race are united with present affairs, despite distance of time and space. I, a fugitive from Egypt, am here, and find assistance. What all my life I considered my greatest disgrace, I now would not give up for any price."

But even in that hour her mind did not see clearly, her thoughts were disordered, and she exhausted herself in fantastic dreams.

These talented but sinful Jewish women did Judaism a service by becoming Christians. Mendelssohn's daughters and Rachel were converted publicly, while Henrietta Herz, who had more regard for appearances, received baptism in a small town to avoid hurting her Jewish friends, and took this step only after her mother's death.

Schleiermacher again inoculated the cultivated classes in Germany with a peculiar, scarcely definable, antipathy to Judaism. He was in no way a Jew-baiter, in the usual sense of the term, and indignantly protested against being called so; but his mind was agitated with a vague, disagreeable feeling towards the Jews, from which he could not escape. When Friedländer's foolish letter on the admission of certain families into Christianity divested of the dogma of the Trinity, was published, Schleiermacher expressed himself adverse to their admission. The state might concede to the Jews the rights of citizenship, but should tolerate them only as a special sect, inasmuch as they would not surrender their hope in the Messiah. It was quite in accordance with his romantic neo-Christianity, that from ignorance and confusion he depicted Judaism as a mummy "around which its sons sit moaning and weeping." He would not even acknowledge Judaism as the forerunner of Christianity. " I detest this sort of historical relationship in religion." Hitherto, Christendom had been conscious of a certain connection with Judaism, and the Old Testament, the Bible, had been the common ground upon which the insolent daughter and the enslaved mother met, and for the moment forgot their hatred. To this connection, or its recognition, the Jews owed their salvation in the sad days of excess of Christian faith, or they would have been altogether annihilated in Europe. The papacy protected them, " because the Saviour had come from their midst." This bond Schleiermacher destroyed at a breath. To have anything in common with the Jews enraged him. But were not Jesus, the Apostles, and the early Fathers of the Church, Jews? Schleiermacher would willingly have denied this fact, if he could possibly have done it ; but as this was impracticable, he enshrouded it in mystery.

"What ? we are to believe that Jesus was only a Jewish Rabbi, with philanthropic sentiments, and some Socratic morality; with certain miracles, or at least what some consider as such, and with the talent of composing neat riddles and parables—some follies will even then have to be forgiven him, according to the first three Evangelists ; and such a man could have established a new religion and a Church—a man who cannot be compared with Moses and Mahomet ?"

This fact Schleiermacher could not tolerate ; for in such case, not only Moses the prophet, but also Moses Mendelssohn, the sage of Berlin, would have been greater. Therefore Schleiermacher removed his Jesus far away from Judaism ; he had only had the accident of birth in common with the Jews, but he was superhuman, and still a man, "whose consciousness of God may properly be called existence of God within him," as it is expressed in this mystic, extravagant, romantic teaching, which thus took its own chief under its protection. Schleiermacher's sermons were filled with this kind of word-juggling, to which the Berlin Jews, especially the women, listened as devoutly as their ancestors to the lying tricks of the false prophets. The school of Schleiermacher, which became the leading influence in Germany, made this intense contempt of Judaism its password and the basis of its orthodoxy.

At the same time, another romanticist, Chateaubriand, invented new, flimsy supports for Christianity, which was in ruins and almost forgotten in France. Even though he traced the origin of the arts, music, painting, architecture, eloquence, and poetry, to Christianity, he, at least, did not deny a share in these merits to Judaism, though only with the intention of claiming for Christianity the noblest features in Hebrew literature and history. "There are only two bright names and memories in history, those of the Israelites and the Pelasgians (Greeks)." When Chateaubriand desired to prove his assertion that the poetry of nature is the invention of Christianity, he cited as examples the beautiful descriptions in Job, in the Prophets, and the Psalms, to whose poetry the works of Pindar and Horace were much inferior. Chateaubriand gathered the flowers of Hebrew poetry to weave a beautiful garland for his crucified god. But he did not, like Schleiermacher, crush Judaism into the dust by denying the paternity of the child grown to be so powerful.

A new Judæophobia sprang from the neo-Christian school, which, as its originators obtained political influence, grew much stronger than that of old orthodox Christianity. It is remarkable that the two-fold reaction, that of the Church, brought about by Schleiermacher, and that of the political world, which is connected with Gentz, had its rise in the Judæo-Christian salon in Berlin. But in the same year when the effeminate Schleiermacher, in his romantic delineation of himself, calumniated Judaism by describing it as a mummy, there arose a man, a hero, a giant in comparison with these wretched dwarfs, who issued a summons for the Jews to gather round his standard. He wished to conquer the Holy Land of their fathers for them, and, a second Cyrus, to rebuild their Temple. The freedom which the Berlin Jews desired to attain by the surrender of their peculiarities, and by humiliation before the Church, they now obtained through France, without paying this price and without disgraceful bargaining.

CHAPTER XI.

THE FRENCH REVOLUTION AND THE EMANCIPATION OF THE JEWS.

Foreshadowing of the French Revolution—Cerf Berr—Mirabeau on the Jewish Question in France—Berr Isaac Berr—The Jewish Question and the National Assembly—Equalization of Portuguese Jews—Efforts to equalize Paris Jews—Jewish Question deferred—Equalization of French Jews—Reign of Terror—Equalization of Jews of Holland—Adath Jeshurun Congregation—Spread of Emancipation—Bonaparte in Palestine—Fichte's Jew-hatred—The Poll-Tax—Grund's "Petition of Jews of Germany"—Jacobson—Breidenbach—Lefrank—Alexander I of Russia: his Attempts to improve the Condition of the Jews of Russia.

1791—1805 C. E.

HE who believes that Providence manifests itself in history, that sins, crimes, and follies on the whole serve to elevate mankind, finds in the French Revolution complete confirmation of this faith. Could this eventful reaction, which the whole of the civilized world gradually experienced, have happened without the long chain of revolting crimes and abominations which the nobility, the monarchy, and the Church committed? The unnatural servitude inflicted by the temporal and spiritual powers produced liberty, but nourished it with poison, so that liberty bit into its own flesh, and wounded itself. The Revolution was a judgment which in one day atoned for the sins of a thousand years, and which hurled into the dust all who, at the expense of justice and religion, had created new grades of society. A new day of the Lord had come "to humiliate all the proud and high, and to raise up the lowly." For the Jews, too, the most abject and despised people in European society, the day of redemption and liberty was to dawn after their long slavery

among the nations of Europe. It is noteworthy
that England and France, the two European countries which first expelled the Jews, were the first to
reinstate them in the rights of humanity. What
Mendelssohn had thought possible at some distant
time, and what had been the devout wish of Dohm
and Diez, those defenders of the Jews, was realized
in France with almost magical rapidity.

However, the freedom of the French Jews did
not fall into their laps like ripe fruit, in the matur-
ing of which they had taken no trouble. They
made vigorous exertions to remove the oppressive
yoke from their shoulders; but in France the result
of their activity was more favorable and speedy
than in Germany. The most zealous energy in
behalf of the liberation of the French Jews was displayed by a man, whose forgotten memory deserves
to be transmitted to posterity. Herz Medelsheim
or Cerf Berr (born about 1730, died 1793) was the
first to exert himself by word and deed to remove
the prejudices against his co-religionists, under
which he himself suffered severely. He was
acquainted with the Talmud, in good circumstances,
warm-hearted enough to avoid the selfishness bred
by prosperity, and sufficiently liberal to understand
and spread the new spirit emanating from Mendelssohn. He was intimately acquainted with the
Berlin sage, and undertook to disseminate the Pentateuch translation in Alsace. Owing to his position, Cerf Berr was enabled to work for the emancipation of his brethren. He furnished the French
army with the necessaries of war, and therefore had
to be in Strasburg, where no Jew was allowed to
live. At first he was allowed in Strasburg only one
winter, but having performed great services to the
state, during the war and a famine under Louis
XV, the permission to stay was repeatedly prolonged by the minister, and he utilized this favor to
take up his permanent residence there. Cerf Berr

drew other Jews to Strasburg. Secretly he purchased houses for himself and his family, and owing
to his services to the state, he obtained from Louis
XVI all the rights and liberties of royal subjects,
especially the exceptional privilege of possessing
landed property and goods. He also established
factories in Strasburg, and tried to have the work
done by Jews, so as to withdraw them from petty
trading and deprive their accusers of all excuse for
their prejudices.

Although Cerf Berr was a useful member of
society, and brought profit to the town, the Germans
in Strasburg viewed the settlement of Jews within
their walls askance, and made every conceivable
effort to expel Berr and his friends. This Philistine
narrow-mindedness on the one hand, and Dohm's
advocacy of the Jews on the other, as well as the
partial relief afforded by Emperor Joseph, impelled
Berr seriously to consider the emancipation of the
Jews, or at least their admission to most of the
French towns, and to endeavor to carry the measure
at court. To win public opinion, he energetically
spread Dohm's Apology in France. The proposals
of Cerf Berr were favorably received at court.
From other quarters, also, the French government
was petitioned to lighten the oppressive measures,
which weighed especially on the Jews of Alsace and
Lorraine. The good-natured Louis XVI was inclined
to remove any abuse as soon as it was placed
before him in its true light. The noble Malesherbes,
enthusiastic for the well-being of mankind, probably
at the instigation of the king, summoned a commission of Jews, which was to make suggestions for
the amelioration of the condition of their brethren in
France. As a matter of course, Cerf Berr was
invited. As representative of the Jews of Lorraine,
his ally, Berr Isaac Berr of Nancy, was summoned,
who afterwards developed the greatest zeal for the
emancipation of his co-religionists. Portuguese

Jews from Bordeaux and Bayonne, the two towns where they resided, were also included in the commission. Furtado, who subsequently played a part in the history of the Revolution, Gradis, Isaac Rodrigues of Bordeaux, and Lopes-Dubec, were members of this commission instituted by Malesherbes. These eminent men, all of them animated with zealous sympathy for their languishing brethren, undoubtedly insisted upon the repeal of exceptional laws, but their proposals are not known. Probably in consequence of their efforts, Louis XVI abrogated the poll-tax, which had been particularly degrading to the Jews in the German-speaking provinces of France.

More effectually than Cerf Berr and the Jewish commission, two men worked for the liberation of the Jews who in a measure had been inspired by Mendelssohn and his friends, and were the incarnation of the Revolution. They were Mirabeau and the Abbé Grégoire, no less zealous for liberty than the former. Count Mirabeau (born 1749; died 1791), who was always on the side of the oppressed against the oppressors, was first induced, by his intimacy with Mendelssohn's circle, to raise his voice of thunder on behalf of the Jews.

Filled with admiration for the grand personality of Mendelssohn, and inspired by the thought of accomplishing the deliverance of an enslaved race, Mirabeau wrote his important work "Upon Mendelssohn and the Political Reform of the Jews" (1787). Of the former he drew a brilliant picture. The Jewish sage could not have wished for a warmer, more inspired, more clear-sighted interpreter. The liking he entertained for Mendelssohn Mirabeau transferred to the Jews in general.

"May it not be said that his example, especially the outcome of his exertions for the elevation of his brethren, silences those who, with ignoble bitterness, insist that the Jews are so contemptible that they cannot be transformed into a respectable people?"

This observation was the introduction to Mirabeau's vindication of the Jews, in which he gave a
correct exposition of what Dohm had adduced and
what he himself had experienced. He surveyed the
long, tragic history of the Jews, discovering traits
very different from those found by Voltaire. Mirabeau saw the glorious martyrdom of the Jews and
the disgrace of their oppressors. Their virtues he
extolled freely, and attributed their failings to the
ill-treatment they had received.

"If you wish the Jews to become better men and useful citizens,
then banish every humiliating distinction, open to them every avenue
of gaining a livelihood; instead of forbidding them agriculture,
handicrafts, and the mechanical arts, encourage them to devote
themselves to these occupations."

With telling wit, Mirabeau refuted the arguments
of the German anti-Semites, Michaelis and the Göttingen guild of scholars, against the naturalization
of the Jews. It was only necessary to place the
different objections side by side to demonstrate
their absurdity. On the one hand, it was maintained that, in their rivalry with Christians, the Jews
would gain the upper hand, and from another point
of view it was demonstrated that they would always
remain inferior. "Let their opponents first agree
among themselves," he remarked, "at present they
refute each other." Mirabeau foresaw, with prophetic clearness, that in a free and happy condition
the Jews would soon forget their Messianic king,
and that therefore the justification of their permanent exclusion, derived from their belief in the Messiah, was futile.

"There is only one thing to be lamented, that so highly gifted a
nation should so long have been kept in a state wherein it was impossible for its powers to develop, and every far-sighted man must
rejoice in the acquisition of useful fellow-citizens from among the
Jews."

On all occasions Mirabeau seized the opportunity
of speaking warmly on behalf of the Jews. He was

devoted to them and their biblical literature, and
scattered the clouds of prejudice with which Voltaire had enveloped them.   When Mirabeau undertook the defense of any matter, the victory was
already half won.   His suggestions for reform
came at the right moment.

Among the thousand matters that occupied public opinion on the eve of the Revolution was also
the Jewish question.   The Jews, especially in Alsace, complained of their unendurable misery, and
the Christian populace, of their intolerable impoverishment through the Jews.   In Metz an anti-
Jewish pamphlet had appeared, entitled "The
Citizen's Cry against the Jews," which inflamed the
worst passions of the people against them.   The
pamphlet was indeed prohibited ; but what slanderous assertion, however incredible, has ever been
without result?   Appearances, in point of fact, were
against the Jews.   A young Jewish author, the first
Alsatian Jew who wrote in French, published a
stinging reply (1787), which justified the expectation
that the Jews would no longer, as in Voltaire's time,
permit such insults to pass unnoticed, but would
emerge from their attitude of silent suffering.
Isaiah Berr Bing (born 1759 ; died 1805), well-edu-
cated and eloquent, better acquainted with the
history of his people than his Jewish contemporaries,
including even the Berlin leaders, rebutted every
charge with convincing emphasis.

Through these writings for and against the Jews,
the Jewish question became prominent in France.
The Royal Society of Science and Arts in Metz
offered a prize for the best essay in answer to the
question, "Are there means to make the Jews
happier and more useful in France?"   Three replies, all in favor of the Jews, were sent in—by
two Christian inquirers, and one Jewish, the Abbé
Grégoire, Thiery, the member of Parliament for
Nancy, and Salkind Hurwitz the Pole, of Kovno

(on the Niemen), who had emigrated to Paris. That of Grégoire, however, had the greatest effect. Grégoire was a simple nature, and in the midst of universal corruption had preserved a pure, child-like mind.

When these apologetic pamphlets appeared, the storm-charged clouds of the Revolution, which were to bring about destruction and reorganization in the world, had already gathered. The fetters of a double slavery, beneath which European nations groaned, that of the State and the Church, were at length, in one country at least, to be broken. As if touched by a magic wand, France turned into a glowing furnace, where all the instruments of serf-dom were consumed, and out of the ashes arose the French nation, rejuvenated, destined for great things, the first apostle of the religion of freedom, which it loved with passionate devotion. Was it not natural to expect the hour to strike for the redemption of the most abased people, the Jews? Two of their most ardent defenders sat in that part of the National Assembly which, truly representa-tive of the nation, restored inalienable rights to those so long disinherited by Church and State. These representatives were Mirabeau, one of the fathers of the Revolution, and the Abbé Grégoire, who owed his election to his essay in defense of the Jews.

At the outbreak of the Revolution, there lived in France scarcely 50,000 Jews—almost half of whom (20,000) dwelt in Alsace—under the most oppres-sive yoke. In Metz, the largest, "the pattern com-munity," only 420 Jewish families were tolerated, and in the whole of Lorraine only 180, and these were not allowed to increase. In Paris, in spite of stringent prohibitions, a congregation of about 500 persons had gathered (since 1740); about as many lived in Bordeaux, the majority of them of new-Christian or Portuguese descent. There were also some communities in the papal districts of Avignon and Carpentras. In Carpentras there dwelt about 700 families (over 2,000 souls) with their own rabbinate. Those in the best condition were the Jews of Bordeaux and the daughter community of Bayonne. Among the Jews of the various provinces there was as little connection as among those in other European countries. Misfortune had separated them. Thus it happened that no concerted action was taken to obtain naturalization from the National Assembly at once, although Grégoire, the Catholic priest, true love for mankind in his heart, exhorted them to seize this favorable opportunity. They indeed boasted men of energy, filled with love for their race, and ready for self-sacrifice, men of tact, such as Cerf Berr, Furtado, Isaac Berr, and David Gradis, but at first no measures were taken. An appeal for united action may possibly have been made, but the pride of the Portuguese probably made it ineffectual. Therefore, in the first stormy months of the Revolution, nothing was undertaken for the emancipation of the Jews. The deputies in the States General or the National Assembly were sufficiently occupied without thinking of the Jews. Besides, they adhered rather closely to the programme enumerating the wishes of their electors, on which the emancipation of the Jews was not mentioned. The deputies of Alsace and Lorraine, in fact, had received instructions to attack the Jews. The assaults made upon the Jews in the German provinces, as a result of the disorders of the Revolution, first moved the victims to bring their complaints before the National Assembly. It was, perhaps, an advantage that the ripe fruit of liberty did not fall into their laps, but that they had to exert themselves energetically to obtain it; for thus liberty became the more precious to them.

The storming of the Bastille had finally torn the scepter from the deluded king, and handed it over to the people.   The Revolution had tasted blood, and began to inflict punishment upon the tyrants. In many parts of the land, as if by agreement, castles were burnt down, monasteries destroyed, and the nobility maltreated or slain.   The people, brought up in ignorance by the Church, and now released from the chains of slavery, knew not how to distinguish friend from foe, and rushed recklessly upon what lay nearest their stupid gaze.   In Alsace the lower classes of the people at the same time made a fierce attack upon the Jews (beginning of August, 1789)—perhaps incited by secret Jew-haters —destroying their houses, plundering their property, and forcing them to flee half-naked.   They, who hitherto had been humiliated and enslaved by the nobles and the clergy, were now fellow-sufferers with their tyrants.   The Alsatian Jews mostly escaped to Basle, and although no Jew was allowed to live there, the fugitives were sheltered and sympathetically treated.   Complaints were made to the National Assembly of the excesses after the first draught of liberty; from that Assembly all expected help, no longer from the monarchy, which had already become a mere shadow.   Every deputy received detailed reports of disquieting, sometimes sanguinary, events.   The ill-treated Jews of Alsace had turned to Grégoire, and he sketched (August 3) a gloomy picture of the outrages upon the Jews, and added that he, a servant of a religion which regards all men as brothers, requested the interference of the powerful arm of the Assembly on behalf of this despised and unhappy people.   He also published a pamphlet, called "Proposals in Favor of the Jews," to influence public opinion.   Then followed the memorable night of the Fourth of August, which covered the French nation with eternal fame, when the nobles sacrificed their privileges on the altar of freedom, and acknowledged the equality of all citizens—the birth-hour of a new order of things.   In consequence of this agitation, and dreading that they might fall victims to anarchy, the Jews of the various provinces resolved to present petitions for admission into the fraternity of the French people ; but again they acted singly, and to some extent preferred contradictory requests. The Jews of Bordeaux had already joined the National Guard, and one was even appointed captain. They had only one desire, that their equalization be sealed by law, and this wish their four deputies, David Gradis, Furtado, Lopes-Dubec, and Rodrigues, publicly expressed. About a hundred Parisian Jews were also enrolled in the National Guard, and rivaled the other citizens in patriotism and revolutionary spirit. They sent eleven deputies to the National Assembly, who prayed for the removal of the ignominy which covered them as Jews, and for equalization by law, saying that the example of the French people would induce all the nations of the earth to acknowledge the Jews as brothers. The community of Metz desired besides that their oppressive taxes be removed, and the debts which they had contracted in consequence of the taxes be made void. The communities of Lorraine sent a delegate to the National Assembly, Berr Isaac Berr (born 1744; died 1828), who, a man of many virtues and merits, and an admirer of Mendelssohn and Wessely, had great influence. He drew up a petition containing the special request that the authority and autonomy of the rabbis in internal affairs be established and recognized by law. The deputies for Luneville and an adjacent community protested against this. It was a long time, however, before the Jewish question became the distinct order of the day. The National Assembly seemed to shrink from discussing the point, for fear of stirring up public opinion still more passionately in the German provinces with their obstinate prejudices and hatred of Jews.

Religious intolerance manifested itself even in

the Assembly. On the 23d of August an exciting sitting was held. The subject of debate was whether the inviolable rights of man, to be placed at the head of the constitution, were to include religious freedom of conscience and freedom of worship. A deputy, De Castellane, had formulated this point plainly: "No man shall be molested on account of his religious opinions, nor disturbed in the practice of his belief." Against this motion a storm arose on the part of the Catholic Clergy and other representatives of Catholicism. They continually spoke of a dominant religion or confession, which, as hitherto, should be supported by the State, whilst other creeds might be tolerated. In vain Mirabeau raised a bold protest against such presumptuousness.

"The unrestricted freedom of belief is so sacred in my eyes, that even the word tolerance sounds despotic to me, because the very existence of an authority empowered to tolerate, injures freedom, in that it tolerates, because it might do the reverse."

But his powerful voice was drowned by the opposing clamor. The clever speech of another deputy, Rabaud Saint Etienne, however, gained the victory for freedom of conscience. He spoke also on behalf of the Jews.

"I demand liberty for the nation of the Jews, always contemned, homeless, wandering over the face of the whole globe, and doomed to humiliation. Banish forever the aristocracy of thought, the feudal system of opinion, which desires to rule others and impose compulsion upon them."

Amidst strong opposition the law was passed, which has since become the basis of the European constitution:

"No one shall be molested on account of his religious opinions, in so far as their outward expression does not disturb public order as established by law."

Therewith one point in the petition of the French Jews was disposed of. But when the Jewish question afterwards came on for treatment (September 3),

it was postponed, and handed over to a committee.
Three weeks later the Assembly was again obliged
to deal with the Jewish question. Persecutions
which the Jews underwent in certain places forced
it upon them. Those in Nancy were threatened
with pillage, because they were reproached with
having bought up provisions and raised the prices.
The Jewish question became so pressing, that the
order of the day (on September 28) was interrupted
by it. It was again Grégoire who defended the
persecuted. He was supported by Count Clermont-Tonnerre, a sincere friend of liberty. With
glowing eloquence he pointed out that Christian
society was guilty of the degradation of the Jews,
and that it must offer them some atonement. The
Assembly thereupon resolved that the president
address a circular letter to the various towns,
stating that the declaration of the rights of man,
which the Assembly had accepted, comprehended
all men upon earth, therefore also the Jews, who
were no longer to be harassed. The king, with
his enfeebled authority, was asked to protect the
Jews from further persecutions. This action, however, produced no results for the sufferers. The
Jews of Alsace remained exposed to attack, as
before. The Jewish representatives of the three
bishoprics of Alsace and Lorraine lost patience,
seeing that their equalization was being constantly
deferred. They therefore strove to obtain a hearing
for themselves. Introduced by the deputies of
Lorraine to the National Assembly (October 14),
Berr, the indefatigable advocate of his co-religionists, delivered a speech, in which he portrayed the
sufferings of a thousand years, and implored humane
treatment for them. He worthily fulfilled his task.
He was obliged to be brief; the Assembly, which
had to establish a new edifice upon the ruins of the
old kingdom, could not spare time for long speeches.
President Preteau replied that the Assembly would

feel itself happy to be able to afford rest and happiness to the Jews of France. The meeting applauded his words, permitted the Jewish deputies to be present as guests at the proceedings, and promised to take the equalization of the Jews into consideration at the next sitting. From this time the French Jews confidently hoped that their emancipation would be realized.

Meanwhile, the Revolution had again made a gigantic stride forward: the people had brought the proud French sovereign like a prisoner from Versailles to Paris. The deputies also moved to Paris, and the capital became more and more infected with revolutionary fever. The youthful Parisian Jews, as well as the immigrants, took great interest in all occurrences. Even the middle classes aided the cause of the fatherland by supplying funds. At length the Jewish question was to be settled. A deputy was appointed to report upon it, and a special sitting called. But it was brought into connection with another question, namely, the franchise of executioners, actors, and Protestants, to whom the Catholic population in some towns did not wish to grant permission to vote.

The report was sent in by Clermont-Tonnerre, and spoke most logically in favor of all four classes. All sincere friends of liberty, Robespierre, Duport, Barnave, and, of course, Mirabeau, expressed themselves in favor of the Jews and their fellow-sufferers. The followers of the old school opposed them with determination, chief among them Abbé Maury, Bishop LaFare of Nancy, and the bishop of Clermont. Only one ultra-revolutionist, Reubell, from Alsace, spoke against the Jews, maintaining that it was dangerous forthwith to grant complete rights of citizenship to those resident in Alsace, against whom there was deeply-rooted hatred. Abbé Maury produced utterly false, or partially true statements, as arguments for unfriendly behavior towards the Jews.

He even quoted Voltaire's anti-Jewish writings in order to prejudice the Assembly. The Assembly hesitated; it feared to attack the gross prejudice entertained by the populace of the eastern provinces against the Jews. At the representation of one of the deputies, the equalization of the Jews was separated from that of the Protestants, and the resolution ran in this equivocal manner: that the Assembly reserved to itself the right of deciding about the Jews, without determining upon anything new concerning them. This reservation was repeated at the discussion of the laws for the election of municipal officers (January 8, 1790), from which Jews were excluded.

This evasive decision grossly offended the Portuguese Jews of Bordeaux. Hitherto they had tacitly enjoyed all the rights of citizens, and in their turn fulfilled all their duties with self-sacrificing readiness. Now they were to be kept in uncertainty about their civil status, in company with the German Jews, against whom they bore an antipathy not less than that of hostile Christians. They therefore hastily despatched a deputation to Paris to cause this injurious resolution to be rescinded. As the population were on better terms with the Portuguese, their request was easily obtained. The deputy for Bordeaux, De Sèze, spoke warmly on their behalf. Talleyrand, then bishop of Autun, was appointed to report upon the matter, and concisely suggested (February 28), that those Jews who had hitherto enjoyed civil rights as naturalized Frenchmen should continue to enjoy that privilege. The enemies of the Jews, of course, opposed this motion, fearing that it would apply also to German Jews.

Nevertheless, the majority decided that those Jews in France who were called Portuguese, Spaniards, or Avignonese (of Bordeaux and Bayonne) should enjoy full privileges as active citizens, and the king at once approved of this law. It was the first legal recognition of the Jews as citizens, and, though only a partial recognition, it at least would serve as a precedent.

The deputies of the Jews from German districts did not so easily attain success ; they had to struggle hard for equality. At the same time they lighted upon a means whereby to bring pressure to bear upon the National Assembly, and induce them to concede them full citizenship. There were five men who worked most perseveringly to remove all obstacles. They won over to their side the fiery, eloquent advocate Godard, to plead their cause with pen and tongue. They knew that power was no longer in the hands of the National Assembly, but had been seized by the parties of the capital, who, with their revolutionary ardor, held complete sway over Paris, the deliberating Assembly, the king, almost the whole country. The Jewish representatives from Paris, Alsace, and Lorraine therefore turned to them for help. They had Godard draw up a petition to the National Assembly, stating that the emancipation of the Jews was not only demanded by the principles of the Constituent Assembly and by justice, but that it was cruelty to withhold it. For, so long as their equality was not legally established, the people would believe that they were indeed the outcasts their enemies had described them to be. But even more efficacious than this petition was a scene which the Parisian Jews arranged with their advocate, before the General Assembly of the Paris Commune ; it decided the question. Fifty Jewish members of the National Guards, adorned with cockades, among them Salkind Hurwitz, the Pole, appeared as deputies before the Assembly of the Commune, and petitioned that the city of Paris itself should energetically set about obtaining equality for the Jews. Godard delivered a fiery speech in their support. The president of the General Assembly, Abbé Mulot, replied to this vigorous address with the fervid eloquence peculiar to the orators of the Revolution : " The chasm between their religious conceptions and the truth which we as Christians profess, cannot hinder us as men from approaching each other, and even if we reproach each other with our errors and complain of each other, at least we can love each other." In the name of the meeting he promised to support the petition of the Paris Jews for equalization. Next day (January 29, 1790), the Jews of Paris obtained a certificate, couched in most flattering terms, and testifying to their excellent reputation, from the inhabitants of the district of the Carmelites, where most Jews dwelt at this time.

The six deputies appointed for the district of the Carmelites then went to the City Hall, to support the resolution in favor of the Jews. One of them, Cahier de Gerville, afterwards a minister, delivered an impressive address. "Do not be surprised," said he, "that this district hastens to be the first to make public recognition of the patriotism, the courage, and the nobility of the Jews who dwell in it. No citizen has proved himself more zealous for the gaining of liberty than the Jew, . . . none has displayed more sense of order and justice, none shown more benevolence towards the poor, and readiness in voluntarily contributing towards the expenses of the district. Let us attack all prejudices, and attack them with determination. Let not one of the monstrosities of despotism and ignorance survive the new birth of liberty and the consecration of the rights of man . . . Take into consideration the just and pressing demands in favor of our new brethren, and join your wishes to their petition, so that thus united they may come before the National Assembly. Do not doubt but that you will obtain, without trouble, for the Jews of Paris that which was not denied the Jews of Portugal, Spain, and Avignon. What reason is there for showing a preference for this class? Do not all Jews hold the same doctrines? Are not our political conditions alike for the one as for the other? If the ancestors of those Jews on whose behalf we plead experienced more bitter suffering and persecution than the Portuguese Jews, then this long, cruel oppression which they have sustained should give them a new claim to national justice. For the rest, look to the origin of these strange and unjust distinctions, and see whether any one to-day dares set up a distinction of rights between two classes of the same people, two branches of the same stem, basing his action upon apocryphal tradition, or rather upon chimeras and fables."

To this speech the President Abbé Mulot replied, bringing into prominence the fact that the report from the district of the Carmelites was to be considered of great weight in favor of the Jews.

The next speech, that of Abbé Bertolio, at length induced the meeting to add its favorable testimony to the Jews of Paris, and to express the wish to the National Assembly that these Jews, most of them of German birth, be put on an equal footing with the Portuguese. Mayor Bailly and his committee on the same day passed the resolution, that as soon as the other districts announced their approval, the whole weight of the influence of the municipality of Paris be exerted on behalf of the equalization of the Jews. In the course of the following month all the city districts, with the exception of that of the Halles, sent in their approval of the decision of the Carmelite district. Accordingly, a deputation of the Commune, together with its president, Abbé Mulot, officially commissioned by the capital (February 25), presented itself at the meeting of the National Assembly, to request, or rather by moral suasion to compel, that body to extend to Jews resident in Paris the decree declaring the Portuguese Jews full citizens.

After some delay, certain deputies demanded (April 15) that the Jewish question be placed on the order of the day. Abbé Maury again opposed the motion, and promised to present a memorial which the Jews should be called upon to answer. In order, however, to protect the Jews of Alsace from the attacks of mobs, the Assembly again decreed that they were under protection of the laws, and that the magistrates and the National Guard were to take precautions for their security. In this way they appeased their consciences. The king forthwith sanctioned (April 18) the law of protection for the Alsatian Jews, after which the question was not broached for three months.

Fortunately the Jewish question did not stand isolated, but was connected with other questions. The Jews of Alsace, especially those of Metz, had to pay high protection-taxes. When the subject of finances came on for discussion, the Assembly had to determine whether this tax should continue or cease. They came to a liberal decision, although the deputies were sorely troubled about the deficit thus created. The secretary of the committee of the crown land, Vismes, first showed how unjust it was that the community of Metz, which Louis XIV, once when in good humor, had given to the Duke of Brancas and the Countess De Fontaine, should pay annually to the house of Brancas 20,000 francs. He therefore proposed that the Jew taxes should be remitted without any indemnification, and that every tribute, under whatever name—protection-money, residence-tax, or tolerance-money—should cease. This proposal was passed into law (July 20) almost without opposition. Louis XVI, who by this act saw another remnant of the Middle Ages vanish, at first showed himself tardy in confirming the law (August 7). Ten years previously the Jews of Alsace had in vain presented a memorial to the state council detailing the misery of their condition;

it received no notice.   Owing to the sudden revolution of affairs, they now achieved in less than an hour more than they had ever dared hope for.

But the National Assembly would not proceed to deal with the chief demand of the Jews of the Lower Rhine—as these districts were then called—to grant them civil rights.   Several had expressed themselves favorably, when the Duc de Broglie intervened with a violent speech.   He asserted that the proposed resolution would engender new causes of excitement in Lorraine and Alsace, already in a state of ferment owing to the action of the clergy who refused to take the oath.   Strasburg was likewise greatly excited on account of the Jews, who desired to settle there, where hitherto no Jew had been permitted.   De Broglie further remarked that the general body of Jews in Alsace was utterly indifferent to citizenship ; that the petition presented in their name was an intrigue carried on by four or five Jews ; especially one, who had amassed a great fortune at the expense of the state (Cerf Berr), was scattering large sums of money most liberally in Paris, to gain adherents for the scheme of equalization.   His motion to adjourn this question till the Constitution was finished was carried.

But the Constitution was definitely fixed and ratified by the king (September, 1791), and the German-speaking Jews of France did not obtain the equality so often promised.   Only the paragraph in the "Rights of Man," which said that no one might be molested on account of his religious opinions, benefited them.   At last, a few days before the dissolution of the National Assembly, the Jews were remembered by one of the friends of liberty, Duport, a member of the Jacobin Club, formerly a parliamentary councilor.   In a speech of a few words he procured the equality they so much desired.   He drew the natural conclusion from the above-quoted rights of religious freedom, and said, "I believe that freedom of thought does not permit any distinction in political rights on account of a man's creed. The recognition of this equality is always being postponed. Meanwhile the Turks, Moslems, and men of all sects, are permitted to enjoy political rights in France. I demand that the motion for adjournment be withdrawn, and a decree passed that the Jews in France enjoy the privileges of citizenship (citoyens actifs)." This proposition was accepted amid loud applause. In vain did Reubell strive to oppose the motion, he was interrupted. Another member suggested that every one who spoke against this motion be called to order, because he would be opposing the Constitution itself. Thus the National Assembly adopted (September 27, 1791) Duport's proposal, and next day formulated the law that all exceptional regulations against Jews be abrogated, and that the German Jews be admitted to the oath of citizenship. Two days later the National Assembly was dissolved, to make way for a still more violent revolutionary assembly. A few days later Louis XVI confirmed this full equalization of the French Jews (November 13, 1791). They were not required to swerve one iota from their religion as the price of emancipation; all demanded of them being that they forego certain ancient privileges.

Berr Isaac Berr was justified in rejoicing at this success, in which he had had a large share. He at once despatched a letter of congratulation to his co-religionists, to rouse enthusiasm for their newly-attained freedom, and at the same time incline them to appropriate improvements.

"At length the day has arrived on which the veil is torn asunder which covered us with humiliation! We have at last again obtained the rights of which we have been deprived for eighteen centuries. How deeply at this moment should we recognize the wonderful grace of the God of our forefathers! On the 27th September we were the only inhabitants of this great realm who seemed doomed to eternal humiliation and slavery, and on the very next day, a memorable day which we shall always commemorate, didst Thou inspire these immortal legislators of France to utter one word which caused 60,000 unhappy beings, who had hitherto lamented their hard lot, to be suddenly plunged into the intoxicating joys of the purest delight."

"God chose the noble French nation to reinstate us in our due privileges, and bring us to a new birth, just as in former days He selected Antiochus and Pompey to degrade and oppress us . . . . . This nation asks no thanks, except that we show ourselves worthy citizens."

Berr added certain important, timely remarks, in which he gently pointed out to his French co-religionists faults growing out of their former wretched plight, and admonished them to remove these faults.

He also supplied the French Jews with means to enable them to become thorough Frenchmen and at the same time remain members of the House of Jacob. The Bible was to be rendered into French on the basis of Mendelssohn's German translation, and put into the hands of the young, so that the corrupt German language which they used might be completely banished from their midst. Berr thus attacked a foolish prejudice which regarded the German or Jewish-German dialect as akin in sanctity to the Hebrew, therefore a more worthy organ for Divine Service than the language of Voltaire.

Berr was thoroughly imbued with the conviction that Judaism was in every way compatible with liberty, civilization, and patriotism for the country which had restored to his co-religionists their rights as men. Berr was a better disciple of Mendelssohn than David Friedländer and the Berlin Jews.

With great assiduity and self-sacrifice, most of the French Jews interested themselves in the welfare of the state which had given them a fatherland, liberty, and equality. They destroyed at one blow all the calumniations of their opponents, who had asserted that as Jews they would not be able to fulfill the duties of citizens. They came to the front whenever the state stood in need of help. A large number of Jews in this feverish time calling forth courageous action, threw aside with wonderful rapidity the shy, grovelling manner which had debarred them from intercourse with the world, and had subjected them to general ridicule. When the French legions, inspired by freedom, had put to rout the mercenary troops of Germany, Moses Ensheim, the Hebrew poet of the Mendelssohn school, composed a fiery triumphal hymn, similar to the song of Deborah, which was solemnly chanted in the synagogue. The Jews, however, took no part whatever in the bloody atrocities of the Revolution.

In the frenzy of the Reign of Terror, which like a scourge of God fell upon the innocent and the guilty, some Jews also suffered. The familiarity of the Jews with persecutions, their acuteness, and the dexterity with which they effaced themselves, their obedience to the precept, " Bend thy head a moment, till the storm is passed," protected them against wide-spread massacre. In general, they were not stirred by the ambition to thrust themselves forward, or a desire to take part in affairs ; nor did they give offense to the rulers of the hour. Thus the storm of the Revolution rushed over them without serious results.

The attack upon a belief in God, when the two blaspheming deputies, Chaumette and Hebert, succeeded in inducing the convention (November, 1793—May, 1794) to set up the religion of Reason, had likewise no effect upon the Jews. The intense hostility and anger felt to religion and the Divinity were directed only against Catholicism, or Christianity, by whose servants mankind had ever been degraded, who themselves had sacrificed myriads of victims, and during the Revolution had fomented a civil war. The Reign of Terror, the Massacre of September, and the Guillotine, had been conjured up by them almost as a sad, stern necessity, because, together with the feudal aristocracy, they were bitter enemies of freedom. The decree of the Convention ran thus : " The Catholic faith is annulled, and replaced by the worship of Reason." This represented not alone the mood of the most advanced, the Jacobins; it was the inclination of the French people to oppose the Church and its followers fiercely, because of a feeling that they are naturally hostile to liberty. Twenty days after the resolution of the Convention had been passed, more than 2,300 churches were transformed into Temples of Reason. The law included no provisions against Jews and Protestants. Only the magistrates or fanatically inclined members of clubs in the provinces, principally, it appears, in the old German districts, extended the order for the suppression of religion to the Jews also. In Nancy an official demanded of the Jews of the town, in the name of the city council, that they attend on an appointed day at the National Temple, and together with the clergy of other creeds renounce "their superstition," and further surrender all the silver and golden vessels of the synagogue. Brutal and riotous men forced their way into the synagogues, tore the Holy Writings from the Arks and burnt them, or searched the houses for books written in Hebrew in order to destroy them. Prayers in the synagogues of certain congregations were forbidden just as in the churches. By reason of the spy system which the revolutionary clubs supported, to enable them to oppose the imminent counter-revolution, even private meetings for religious purposes were attended with great danger. When the order of the Convention was issued, decreeing that every tenth day be observed as a day of rest, and making Sunday a working day, the Mayors of certain cities, as of Strasburg and Troyes, extended this decree also to the Sabbath. They commanded that Jewish merchants display their wares for sale on the Sabbath. In agricultural districts Jews were compelled, on the Sabbath and on Jewish Holidays, to mow and gather in the crops, and rabbis as well as bishops were molested. David Sinzheim, who lived in Strasburg, and afterwards became president of the great French Synhedrion, was forced to flee from town to town to escape imprisonment or death. In Metz the Jews dared not openly bake their Passover cakes, until a clever Jewish matron had the courage to explain to the officers of the Revolution that this bread had always been a symbol of freedom with the Jews. In Paris Jewish schoolmasters were compelled to conduct their pupils to the Temple of Reason into which the church of Notre Dame had been transformed on the Décadi. However, this persecution passed away without any serious effects. With the victory of the Thermidorians (9 Thermidor—July 27, 1794) over Robespierre, the Reign of Terror began to die out. The populace was anxious to resort to milder means. The equalization of the French Jews, once definitely settled, remained untouched through all changes of government. The new Constitution of the year Three of the Republic, or the Constitution of the Directory (autumn of 1795), recognized the adherents of Judaism, without further difficulty, as on an equal footing with all around them ; moreover, it wiped away the last trace of inequality, inasmuch as the Catholic Church was no more than the synagogue acknowledged to be the state church. The law laid down the fundamental proposition, that no one can be compelled to contribute to the expenses of a church establishment, as the Republic subsidized none. Only the community of Metz had to suffer under some baneful effects of the Middle Ages.

Together with the victorious French troops of the Republic, the deliverance of the Jews, of the most oppressed race of the ancient world, advanced from one place to another. It took firm root in Holland, which had been changed into a Batavian Republic (beginning of 1795). Here several energetic

Jews, among them Asser (Moses and Carolus), De Lemon, and Bromet, had joined a club, called Felix Libertate, which had taken the motto of the French Republic—Liberty, Equality, and Fraternity.

These state maxims were on the whole adopted by the assembled States General (March 4, 1795). Although the 50,000 Jews of Holland, who formed the thirty-ninth part of the whole population of the country, and were divided into the Portuguese and German communities, might justly have regarded this land as their Paradise, they had hitherto been laboring under many disadvantages as compared with Christians. They were suffered to exist only as corporate bodies, little commonwealths, as it were, in the midst of larger ones. That they were excluded from public offices did not trouble them. But they were also debarred from several trade-guilds, and this was a matter of great importance to them. They had to contribute to the ruling church establishment and to its schools without deriving any benefit therefrom. Also, there was no lack of vexatious grievances. In Amsterdam, for instance, when a Jewish couple went to register their wedding, they were compelled to wait till Christians had been attended to, and, besides, to pay double fees. On this account the demand for equalization became pressing, more on the part of the German than on that of the Portuguese Jews, the latter, wealthy and of noble birth, being generally treated with distinction by the patricians, whilst the Germans were despised as wretched Poles. In the first excitement of the agitation several disabilities of the Jews of Holland or Batavia were removed, and voices were raised in favor of their admission to full civil rights. But later on, as in France, writings hostile to the Jews roused public opinion against them. Amongst these Van Swieden's work, entitled "Advice to the Representatives of the People," especially produced a great impression.

He asserted that owing to their origin, their character, their history, and their belief in the Messiah, the Jews remained strangers, and could not be absorbed by the state. This statement was in a measure accepted by the official representatives of Judaism as correct. For strangely enough the rabbis and administrators of Jewish affairs, especially the powerful Parnassim in Amsterdam, alike in the Portuguese and German communities, were averse to equalization. They feared that Judaism would suffer from the great freedom of the Jews and from their new duties, such as military service.

In a circular letter they declared that the Jews renounced citizenship, seeing that it was opposed to the commands of Holy Writ. Within a short time this declaration was covered with more than one thousand signatures. Although Jews were invited, but few took part in the election of the first Batavian National Assembly (Nationale Vergadering). Thus it happened that Amsterdam, which contained more than 20,000 Jews, did not return a single Jewish deputy. The Jewish friends of liberty in Holland were in a sorry plight, having to combat enemies within and without. They were driven to exert all their energy to overcome this double difficulty. David Friedrichsfeld, a member of the school of the Measfim, who had settled in Amsterdam, composed an excellent work (about 1795) against the assailants of the Jews, called "Investigation of Van Swieden's Work in Reference to the Civil Rights of the Jews." Beside him, six distinguished and intelligent Jews— most of them of German descent—developed the greatest zeal to accomplish the emancipation of the Jews of Holland. They were: Herz Bromet, who had long lived in Surinam, where he was recognized as a free citizen, and whence he had brought a knowledge of politics and a fortune; Moses Asser, who had been appointed knight of the Belgian Order of the Lion; another Asser, Carolus, and

Isaac de Jonghe, all distinguished members of the German community.   Only two of the Portuguese community participated in the endeavor to obtain equalization of rights : the highly respected physician Herz de Lemon, and Jacob Sasportas.   They presented a petition to the Batavian National Assembly (March 29, 1796), which held its sittings at the Hague, demanding the emancipation of the Batavian Jews as a right ; inasmuch as they were citizens of the Batavian Republic, possessing the franchise, and had already exercised civil rights, they prayed the Assembly to declare that they might enjoy this privilege in its entirety.   The National Assembly considered the petition, and appointed a commission to advise and decide upon it.   When the Jewish question came on for discussion (August, 1796), excitement ran high, and the tension between the parties was great.

Although the emancipation of the Jews in the Batavian Republic had been recognized in principle, and practically acknowledged by the permission to vote at the election, there were still many opponents to contend against, almost more than in France. The conservative Dutch deputies in their hearts believed firmly in the Bible, and they considered as the word of God the writings of the New Testament, in which it was said that the Jews were outcasts, and should remain so.   The relatively large number of Jews, their wealth, respectability, and intelligence, gave cause for grave fears that they would make their way into the highest offices of the state, and expel the Christians.   Sixty or a hundred thousand Jews, in the great territory of France, were lost like a grain of sand in an immense plain, but fifty thousand among two millions, especially twenty thousand Jews in Amsterdam among two hundred thousand Christians, might make themselves felt, and effect their purpose.   One of the deputies, Lublink de Jonghe, dwelt upon this state of affairs with great emphasis. If the friends of the Jews pointed to America, where, as in France, they had recently attained to full civil rights, then he brought into prominence the unequal proportion of numbers; in Holland their great number would soon invest the populace with Jewish characteristics. The noble Portuguese might be admitted to full rights ; but as to the German Jews, the majority of whom were outcasts, Lublink de Jonghe quoted Pinto's work against Voltaire, in which he, a Jew himself, had plainly shown the vast difference between the Portuguese and the German Jews. Thus the artificial caste feeling, within the fold of Judaism, brought about its own revenge. The fear was still greater that the number of the Jews in Holland might be considerably increased by immigrants from Germany and Poland, whose goal, for a long time past, had been Amsterdam. Opponents to the scheme of equalization could further adduce the argument that the majority of Jews did not desire emancipation, and that the six petitioners had acted without authority. Noel, the French ambassador, in somewhat imperious fashion, took the first step in favor of the equalization of the Jews. After a long debate, the complete equality of the Batavian Jews was finally decreed (September 2, 1796), with the addition, for those who wished to make use of it. Thereupon all earlier provincial and municipal laws which referred to their disabilities were abolished.

The Jews in Holland did not receive the announcement of this decision with joy, as those in France, when the rights of equality had been granted them. They had not felt the deprivation of liberty enough to go into ecstasies about their new freedom. They had no ambition to obtain state offices, and saw in citizenship only a burden and a danger to religion. They therefore were embittered against those who had procured their equalization, and so had broken asunder the bonds which held the two congregations together as corporate bodies.   Thus there arose causes for dispute and internal dissension in Amsterdam.

The liberal-minded, most of whom belonged to the German community, demanded that the regulations which endowed the rabbis, and to a greater extent the Parnassim, or wardens, with powerful authority over the members, should be altered in accordance with the spirit of the age.   The leaders of the community not only refused this demand, but even threatened the petitioners with fines. Upon this the advanced left the existing synagogue, established their own congregation, and declared that they constituted the real community (Adath Jeshurun, formed at the end of 1796).   The conservative members of the old community thereupon passed a kind of interdict upon the separatists, forbade their own congregants to have any intercourse, or to intermarry with them.   The political divergence of opinion at the same time became a religious one ; for the supporters of the new congregation, Adath Jeshurun, initiated a sort of reform. They struck out of their ritual the formula of imprecation (v'la-Malshinim), which had originally been directed against the apostate Jewish Christians, but by misinterpretation was afterwards applied to all Christians.   They abolished the practice of hastily burying the dead, and erected a new, clean communal bath,—innocent reforms, which, however, were regarded by the strictly orthodox as grave offenses against Judaism.   The new congregation succeeded in having the fanatical leaders of the German community, who were more inconsiderate than the Portuguese in their opposition to those who had withdrawn from their midst, removed from their posts, probably through the action of the French ambassador Noel.   Among the new council officers, members of the new congregation were elected.   Gradually many of the old party became reconciled to the new order of things and to the aspirations of the liberal-minded section. The orthodox were also greatly flattered when two Jews, Bromet and De Lemon, were elected as deputies for Amsterdam. Several attended at the Hague at the opening of the second National Assembly (September 1, 1797), to participate in the honor of the Jewish deputies. They were still more pleased with the idea of equalization when the Jewish deputy, Isaac da Costa Atias, was successively elected a member of the city council, of the National Assembly, and finally to the position of President of the same (1798). The head of the Batavian Republic, the Grand Pensioner Schimmelpenink, was in earnest about the emancipation of the Jews, and without hesitation appointed able Jews to public offices. The first appointment to public posts in Europe was made in Holland.

It was natural that a sense of self-importance and honorable pride should be awakened in the breasts of the liberal members of the new congregation, among whom state offices were distributed. Indignation seized them when they saw that the Jews under the German princes were still treated as outcasts or wild beasts. They therefore laid a proposal before the National Assembly, entreating that the Batavian ambassador to the French Republic be instructed to move at the Peace Congress held at Rastadt, that the Dutch Jews in Germany should no longer be compelled to pay poll-tax, and to threaten that, unless this was granted, all Germans journeying through Holland would be subjected to the same dishonorable treatment. The National Assembly agreed to this proposition.

Righteous judgment soon overtook the German princes and people, who, stubborn as Pharaoh and the Egyptians, refused to loosen the chain of slavery from the Jews. They themselves were soon forced to become the *servi cameræ* of the French

Republic, and to pay a poll-tax. Wherever in Germany and Italy the courageous French obtained firm footing, the Jews were made free. The walls of the Ghetto were burst open, and bent figures stood erect.

The name of the invincible French, who had achieved wonderful victories in Italy, quickly spread abroad, even beyond Europe, and aroused terror and surprise in the most remote countries. A new Alexander, the Corsican Bonaparte, a god of war when scarcely thirty years old, set out with a comparatively small army to subdue Egypt, and hoped to penetrate to India. In less than six months (July—November, 1798) Egypt lay crushed at his feet. But a Turkish army was on its way to meet him, against which Bonaparte advanced into Palestine. Thus, through a marvelous series of historical events, the Holy Land became the scene of a bloody war between the representatives of the old and the new spirit in Europe.

El Arish and Gaza in the south-west of Palestine fell into the hands of the French army, which scarcely numbered 12,000 men (17th and 25th February, 1799). The Jewish community of Gaza had fled. In Jerusalem the news of French victories and cruelty created a panic. It was rumored that Napoleon was about to enter the Holy City. At the command of the sub-pasha, or Motusallim, the inhabitants began to throw up ramparts, the Jews taking part in the work. One of their rabbis, Mordecai Joseph Meyuchas, encouraged and even assisted them in their operations. The Turks had circulated the report that the French treated Jews particularly in a cruel manner. Bonaparte had issued a summons to the Asiatic and African Jews to march under his banners, promising to give them the Holy Land, and restore ancient Jerusalem to its pristine splendor. But the Jews in Jerusalem appear either not to have trusted in these flattering

words, or to have been utterly ignorant of the proclamation.   Probably it was only a trick on the
part of Bonaparte, intended to win over to his side
the Jewish minister of the pasha of Acco, Chayim
Maalem Farchi (assassinated in 1820), the soul of
the defense of the important sea-fortress of Acco.
Had Bonaparte succeeded in conquering Syria and
carrying the war into the heart of Turkey, he would
perhaps have assigned a share in his government to
members of the Jewish nation upon whom the
French could rely.   But the appearance of Bonaparte in Palestine was like that of a terrible meteor,
which disappears after causing much devastation.
His dream to become Emperor of the East, and restore Jerusalem to the Jews, quickly faded away.

The glowing enthusiasm for France, where his
enthralled co-religionists had been freed, had created a Jewish poet in Elia Halevi, while a Jewish
youth was aroused to become a spirited orator,
whose eloquence was always tinged with poetry.
Michael Berr (born 1780, died 1843), a worthy son
of Isaac Berr, who had so zealously striven for the
emancipation of the Jews of France, in his youth
aroused great hopes, by reason of his handsome,
noble form, and his manifold talents.   In him for
the first time Jewish and French spirit met in harmonious combination.   He was the first Jewish
attorney in France.   Animated by the ambition of
courageous youth and in the glow of his fiery spirit,
this young man conceived a bold idea, at the beginning of the new century, when peace was concluded.
A Congress of the princes of Europe was expected
to take place.   To them and their people Michael
Berr addressed a "Summons" in the name of "all
the inhabitants of Europe professing the Jewish
religion," praying them to free his co-religionists
from oppression, and to guarantee to them the
justice so long withheld.   This youth voiced the
hopes of rejuvenated Israel.   Berr's summons was

especially directed to the Germans, both to princes
and nations, who still treated the Jews living in
their midst as branded *servi cameræ.*

Berr, who was inspired with love for his co-religionists, preached to deaf ears, his burning words
and convincing arguments finding no response in
the hearts of the Eastern European people. In
Austria, Prussia, and the numerous smaller German
states, the Jews remained in their former abasement.
In Berlin itself, the seat of enlightenment, Jewish
physicians, however honorable their reputation,
were not included in the list of their Christian fellow-
practitioners, but were enumerated by themselves,
relegated, as it were, to a medical Ghetto. Two
men of the first rank, the greatest poet and the
greatest thinker of the time, Göthe and Fichte,
shared in the prejudices of the Germans against the
Jews, and made no secret of it. Göthe, the representative of the aristocratic world, and Fichte, the
defender of democratic opinion in Germany, both
desired to see the Jews removed like plague
patients beyond the pale of Christian society.
Both were on bad terms with the Church, both
looked upon Christianity with its belief in miracles
as a folly, and both were considered atheists. Nevertheless they abhorred the Jews in the name of
Jesus. Göthe's intolerance against the Jews cannot be taken as the expression of his personal prejudice; he only showed how the current of opinion
flowed in cultured German circles.

Fichte, the one-sided complement of Kant, was
still more savage and embittered against the Jews.
Like most German metaphysicians, his philosophy
was of a visionary nature before the outbreak of the
French Revolution.

Apparently Fichte bestowed great honor upon
the Jews when he put them on a level with the
nobility and the clergy. But he did not wish in any
way to honor them, but rather to accuse them before

the bar of public opinion. Fichte, the philosophical thinker, cherished the same ill-will against the Jews and Judaism as Göthe, the aristocratic poet, and Schleiermacher, the Gnostic preacher.

Should civil rights be granted to Jews? Fichte opposed it in a most decided fashion; not even in the Christian state, in his view a petty state, contrary to right and reason, should they be emancipated. "The only way I see by which civil rights can be conceded to them (the Jews) is to cut off all their heads in one night, and to set new ones on their shoulders, which should contain not a single Jewish idea. The only means of protecting ourselves against them is to conquer their promised land and send them thither." History judged otherwise: new heads have not been set on the Jews, but on the Germans themselves. His view was that Jews should not be persecuted, that, in fact, the rights of men should be granted them, "because they are men," but that they should be banished altogether. Even the clerical opponents of emancipation in France, Abbé Maury and Bishop La Fare, had not spoken of the Jews in so perverse and hateful a manner. Fichte may be regarded as the father and apostle of national German hatred of the Jews, of a kind unknown before, or rather never before so clearly manifested. Even Herder, although filled with admiration for Israel's antiquity and the people in its biblical splendor,—the first to examine sacred literature from a poetical point of view—felt an aversion to the Jews, which became apparent in his relations with Mendelssohn, whom it cost him an effort to treat in a friendly manner. Herder, it is true, prophesied a better time, when Christian and Jew would work together in concord on the structure of human civilization. But like Balaam of old, he pronounced his blessings upon Israel in a half-hearted way. This growing hostility to the Jews among the Germans was not noticed by educated Jews who dwelt in their midst, at least they did not combat it vigorously.   Only one pamphlet from the pen of a Jewish author appeared at this time.   Saul Asher wrote his "Eisenmenger the Second, an open letter to Fichte," but hardly any notice was taken of it.

If the Jews met with no favor in the eyes of those who formed public opinion in Germany, who had raised it from antiquated customs to a brilliant height of culture, both in the democratic and in the aristocratic camps, but experienced at their hands only repulse and scorn, how much worse was their relation to the great mass of the populace, still engulfed in the depths of darkest ignorance and crudeness ! Two noble-minded Christians addressed to the Congress of Rastadt the soundest arguments that the German Jews should be raised from their ignominious condition.   One of them, an unknown philanthropist, hurled the shaft of ridicule at the stupidity and bombastic haughtiness of the German Jew-haters, and the other, Christian Grund, demonstrated with pitiless logic the injustice with which the Jews were treated.   Both desired to support the demand of the Dutch Jews to the diplomatic representatives, that the princes of Germany be compelled to respect the Jews, and that influence be brought to bear upon public opinion to that effect.   Grund acted as a clever advocate for the Jews ; he complimented the Germans in order to win favor with them. "The German Jews," said he, "venture to approach the German nation, capable of great deeds, the creator of its own destinies, not merely an imitator of the actions of other peoples, uniting their voice with that of their brethren, to petition the representatives of the nation at Rastadt most respectfully for the abolition of those distinctions under which they live, and for the acquisition of greater rights." The answer of the German princes and rulers was not very encouraging.

The most disgraceful degradation and humiliation of the Jews consisted in the poll-tax, an impost unknown outside of Germany. Of what advantage was it that Emperor Joseph of Austria and Frederick William II had remitted it? It still existed in all its hideousness in Central and Western Germany, in the districts of the Main and the Rhine, where diminutive states bordered close on other diminutive states of the extent of a square mile, and where turnpike after turnpike at short intervals presented itself. If a Jew took a day's journey, he passed through different territories, and at the borders of each had to pay a poll-tax. A Jewish beggar, accompanied by his young son, once exhibited his poll-tax bills, which amounted to a florin and a half for six days, paid in various places. The way in which the tax was levied was more degrading than the duty of paying it. Very often the tax amounted to a few kreuzers, which only the poor, who were not exempt from it, felt as a burden. But the brutal procedure of the officers, and the ignominious treatment at each frontier-line offended also the rich. As long as the French armies were encamped in German territory, the Jews escaped paying the poll-tax. But no sooner was the peace of Lüneville concluded, and the French troops withdrawn, than the petty German princes re-imposed the tax, not in order to raise the small income derivable from this source, but to humiliate the Jews. They inflicted the insult also upon French Jews who crossed the Rhine for business purposes, defending their action by a literal construction of one of the articles of the peace of Campo Formio, which stated: " All business and intercourse shall for the present continue under the same conditions as before the war." The French Jews, proud of their citizenship, would not submit, severed their business connections with Germany, and complained of the injustice to the French government, by whom the question was not lightly passed over. The government commissioner Jollivet despatched a circular letter (1801) to the agents of the French Republic resident at German courts, instructing them not to permit French citizens of the Israelite faith to be degraded to animals. They were to make earnest representations to the governments concerned, and menace them with retaliation. Several small princes, like those of Solms, gave heed, and forthwith removed the poll-tax; from fear of the French the French Jews were freed from it, but it still weighed heavily upon German travelers. Every step towards the removal of oppressive restrictions in Germany was the result of great exertions.

In consequence of the peace of Lüneville, the Holy Roman Empire was now for the first time dismembered. The representatives of the Empire, assembled in Ratisbon, were driven to seek means of bringing their disunited members into some sort of order, or to decide upon the indemnity for the damage suffered. To this conference of the ambassadors of eight princes, occupied with traffic in territory, and regarded by the short-sighted as representing the German nation, the German Jews presented a petition asking for passive citizenship (November 15, 1802). This entreaty was drawn up "in the name of the Jews of Germany," by state attorney Christopher Grund. Which congregation, or what individuals zealous for emancipation had commissioned him to do this is not exactly known. It appears that the petition originated in Frankfort. It prayed that the representatives of the Empire remove from the German Jews the burdensome distinctions under which they labored; that the narrow confines in which they were forced to reside be thrown open, so that for the sake of health and free enjoyment of life, they might select their own dwelling-place in the cities. Further, that the bonds by which their population, their trade, and their industry were restricted to a fatal degree be loosened, and that, in short, the Jewish community be considered worthy, by the grant of civil rights, to constitute one united people with the German nation. The Jews, or their attorney Grund, cited the fact that they were "classed with dishonorable persons, outlaws, and serfs." The miserable condition of the Frankfort community, which, after the orders promulgated for the regulation of the town in 1616, had been deprived of natural freedom, and crowded together into the narrowest limits, served as a conclusive proof. The example of France and the Batavian Republic in emancipating the Jews was adduced; but the Jews could hardly have deceived themselves with the fond hope that the representatives of the Empire would concede so much to them. They hoped at least to have one restriction removed, viz., that of the poll-tax, and this point was insisted upon with great vigor. "The most degrading of all these disabilities," they said, "is the poll-tax, which removes the name of Jew from the category of rational beings, to place it among wild beasts, and forces him to pay his way when he sets foot upon one soil or another." Contrary to expectation, this petition to the representatives of the Empire was handed in and supported by the most distinguished member among them, the ambassador from the Electorate of Bohemia or Austria. He proposed the motion "that the Jews of Germany be allowed civil rights" (at the end of 1802). Meantime the Indemnification Congress had other affairs to engross its attention, and its members were unable to occupy themselves with the Jewish question. The petition was buried under a pile of state papers.

Nothing was to be expected from the German people, as those who watched the course of affairs readily perceived. The Jews therefore directed their zeal towards inducing the various governments to remit the poll-tax. Two men made their names famous in the struggle to remove this odious impost, viz., Israel Jacobson and Wolff Breidenbach. The former, court agent and finance counselor to the Prince of Brunswick, succeeded in procuring the abolition of the poll-tax in the territories of Brunswick-Lüneburg (April 23, 1803). During a number of years Wolff Breidenbach strove in the same cause, and effected more far-reaching results. Breidenbach was born in a village of that name near Cassel, 1751, and died at Offenbach 1829. He was a man of high culture, noble ideals, and so modest that his name has almost been forgotten in spite of all the sacrifices he made on behalf of the German Jews. He did not, like Jacobson, make provisions to have his name spread far and wide.

Deeply moved by the annoyances, and the contemptuous treatment inflicted on Jewish travelers in places where the tax was imposed, which came daily under the notice of Breidenbach in his business journeys, he determined at least to have the poll-tax remitted, and applied himself with all his energy to this task. Quietly he strove to have the chain loosened, where it weighed most heavily. He perceived that large sums of money would be required to provide presents for the police magistrates and the city clergy under the pretense of giving alms to the poor, and also " to erect beautiful monuments in honor of magnanimous princes" who would allow themselves to be influenced to leave the Jews untaxed and unoppressed. He was not able to meet this enormous expense out of his own means. He therefore issued a summons to German and foreign Jews (September, 1803), asking them to subscribe to a fund, from which the cost of abolishing the poll-tax might be defrayed. It was well known at the time who circulated this appeal, but out of modesty, Breidenbach did not append his name. By these means, and through negotiations with the minor German princes at the Diet in Ratisbon, carried on with the friendly help of the imperial chancellor, Dalberg, and finally by the recommendations of the princes themselves, who learned to esteem him, Breidenbach succeeded in obtaining the right of free passage for the Jews throughout the Rhineland and Bavaria. Even the narrow-minded, Jew-hating, most noble council of Frankfort was moved by Breidenbach's petition to abolish the poll-tax exacted at the gates and bridges.

The petition of the Jews to the representatives of the Empire for civil privileges, however restricted, the feeling displayed by several princes in favor of removing their bonds, and other signs, made the Jew-haters of Germany suspect that the old condition of imperial serfdom would soon vanish. They were terror-struck; they could not conceive the idea that the down-trodden Jews should be raised from their abasement in Germany. This painful idea induced a host of authors, most of them jurists, as if by mutual agreement, to employ all their efforts in various parts of Germany in opposing the deliverance of the Jews from slavery. Among these men were Paalzow, Grattenauer, Buchholz, and many anonymous writers, who persisted in their hostility for several years (1803-1805). They displayed hatred to the Jews, so malignant that it savored of the days of the Black Death, of Capistrano, Pfefferkorn, and the Dominicans. They produced an artificial fog, to prevent the spread of rays of enlightenment. In former days it had been the servants of the church who had branded the Jews with dishonor. Now the priests of justice assumed this part, and by perversion of justice sought to keep the Jews in servitude, for which course Fichte had prepared the way. As soon as the petition of the Jews reached the representatives of the Empire in Ratisbon, a jurist of South Germany opposed it, urging that a thousand reasons existed why Jews were unworthy of becoming citizens of the Empire and the pro-

vinces. The greater number and the most obstinate
of the representatives of this Jew-baiting movement
had their seat in Berlin, the city of enlightenment
and of the Christianity taught by Schleiermacher.
The character, teachings, and history of the Jews,
even their prophets and patriarchs, in fact, everything Jewish, was attacked by these cowardly writers,
most of whom wrote anonymously, and was made
the subject of foulest abuse and vituperation.

The leaders of Berlin Judaism were at a loss how
to oppose these systematic onslaughts. David
Friedländer remained silent. Ben-David resolved
to write an answer, but wisely abstained. The
parts were now changed. In the days of Mendelssohn, and for some time afterwards, the German
Jews had acted as guardians to the French Jews
whenever the latter had any grievances to redress.
Now freedom had made the French Jews so powerful and confident that they repulsed every attack
upon themselves and their belief with courage and
skill. The Berlin Jews, who had always been ready
enough to boast of their courage, at the first hostile
attack found themselves helpless as babes. In their
perplexity they solicited the aid of the police, who
issued an order that no pamphlet either for or
against the Jews should be published. This step
was regarded by their antagonists as a sign of
cowardice or a confession of powerlessness. A new
abusive tract, entitled "Can the Jews remain in their
present condition without harm to the state?" gave
additional weight to the accusations against them.

"What were a number of the most wealthy Jews or their fathers
twenty or thirty years ago? Hawkers, who crawled about the streets
in ragged clothes, annoying the passers-by with their importunity to
buy some yards of Potsdam hair riband; or rustics, who, under the
pretext of trading, stole into Christian dwellings, and often did damage
to their owners."

This writer proposed to render the Jews harmless
by means more revolting than those employed in
the Middle Ages.

"Not only must the Jews again be enclosed in a Ghetto, and be placed under continual police supervision ; not only should they be compelled to wear a patch of noticeable color upon their coat sleeves, but in order to prevent their increase, the second male child of each Jew should be castrated."

Protestant theology and German philosophy proposed regulations against the Jews unrivaled by the canonical decrees of Popes Innocent III and Paul IV.

In Breslau appeared similar libels which inflamed the hatred of the populace against the Jews. Even the well-meaning writings composed in their defense by Christians, such as Kosmann and Ramson—"A Word to the Impartial"—admitted the low character of the Jews, and seemed to imply that in every way it would be better for Christians if there were no Jews among them; but seeing that the evil existed, it must be endured. The honor of the Germans was partly redeemed by a man who belonged to the olden time, Freiherr von Diebitsch, once a major in the Russian service, to whom love of mankind was no empty phrase. He warmly defended the Jews against the venomous attacks of Grattenauer and his malicious allies (1803 and 1804), and thereby laid himself open to the charge of having been bribed. In view of the general prejudice against the Jewish race, he was prepared to see himself "caricatured, and represented as riding upon a sow or an ass." His kindly but pedantic pamphlets in defense of the Jews were not sufficient to close the mouths of their opponents.

Equally inadequate and fruitless were the attempts at vindication made by Jewish writers outside of Berlin, who found it necessary to lift their voice in opposition to the general outcry against their people.

Two Jews, one from Königsberg, the other from Hamburg, hit upon an excellent plan. Both recognized that the Jew hatred of the Germans could not be refuted by solid and weighty arguments, but might be silenced by ridicule. They were the forerunners of Börne and Heine, one being an unknown physician, the other writing anonymously (Lefrank). The former, in a satirical pamphlet written under the name of Dominicus Haman Epiphanes, expressed the opinion that unless all Jews were speedily massacred, and all Jewesses sold as slaves, the world, Christianity, and all states, must necessarily perish. Mankind would benefit enormously by the sale of the Jews: all immorality would thereby at once diminish, and the immortal Grattenauer, who had originated the glorious idea and had disseminated his noble abhorrence of the Jews, would everywhere be acknowledged a benefactor of mankind, and be deservedly commemorated by temples and monuments.

The other satirist, Lefrank, called his work "Bellerophon," (or the defeated Grattenauer). He wished to kill the chimerical monster "Jew hatred" in Grattenauer by mounting Pegasus. He addressed the Jew-baiter with the scornful "thou."

"Thou who hast grafted with so much success jurisprudence upon theology, thou who didst lick salt in Halle—not indeed Attic salt—thou who hast studied ignorance and stupidity under the great Semler, if thou art so proud of thy Christianity, that with contempt thou dost look down upon Jews, then pray let me ask thee why thy prisons are crammed with criminals condemned upon charges of high treason, murder, poisoning, robbery, and adultery? First remove from thy midst the scaffold, the gallows, the rack, the scourge, and all the ghastly instruments of torture and death, not one of which was invented by Jews. Divest thyself of the demon, and then wilt thou pity a people condemned to engage in traffic against its will, and accused because it does traffic. Deceit is said to be a widespread vice among Jews. Thy Christian tailor robs thee, thy bootmaker gives thee bad leather, thy grocer false measure and weight, thy baker despite prosperous harvests undersized loaves. Thy wine is adulterated, thy man-servant and thy maid-servant combine to cheat thee. Thou thyself—in the innocence of thy heart—offerest for sale wretched lies and spiteful malice written upon blotting-paper, for six farthings, which are not worth six pins, and thou darest assert that fraud is peculiar to Jews. See whether among all the bankruptcies now occurring in London and Paris there is a single Jewish failure." "Thou dost foolishly repeat the silly prattle of the great Fichte, when thou dost remark that the Jews constitute a state within the state. Thou canst not forgive the Jews the crime of speaking correct German, of dressing more respectably, and often judging more justly than thou. They no longer wear beards, which thou canst pull; they no longer speak gibberish, which thou mightest mimic. . . . . The Jew for over twenty years has striven to approach the Christian, but how has he been received? How many alterations has he made in his canonical laws to be able to join you; but from pure humanity ye turn your backs upon him. . . . . Yet thy pamphlet appears to me to be a good omen. The average man believes that winter can be parted from summer only by terrible thunder and hail-storms. Thus is it with thee. Persecution, fanaticism, and superstition are at their last gasp, and by mighty raging make their final effort through thee, before their spirit becomes entirely quenched."

The self-confidence manifested by Lefrank was the surest sign of the ultimate victory of the Jews.

Under existing conditions, in view of the fact that the Jews were apt to underrate and despise their own power, the hope of emancipation was deceptive. In Protestant as well as in Catholic countries, in Prussia as well as in Austria, the people were even more blindly opposed to them than their princes. That an Austrian voice might not be wanting in the chorus of Jew-baiters, a German-Austrian official, named Joseph Rohrer (1804), wrote against the "Jew people." He drew a dreadful picture, especially of the Jews of Galicia, without hinting that the Galician peasants were in a still lower state, and that the nobility was more degenerate than either class. Paalzow, Grattenauer, Buchholz, Rohrer, and their allies succeeded in their design. The idea of the emancipation of the Jews in Germany could not yet be entertained. With all his zeal, Breidenbach could not effect the abolition of the capitation-tax in all places. It still remained in force, a sad reminder and disgrace, in certain German provinces. Cannon had to be brought into the field to destroy these putrefying, deeply implanted prejudices.

A ray of light from the sun of freedom shining on the Jews of France penetrated even to Russia. The heart of Emperor Alexander I was filled with mercy towards the numberless Jews dwelling in his kingdom. He appointed a commission to consider a proposal for improving their condition. But a

Russian commission takes time over its work, and after two years' careful consideration of the interests of Christians, and of the most effectual way of benefiting the Israelites, an ukase was at length published in 1804.   By this law, farmers, manufacturers, artisans, those who had acquired a university education, or who had visited the upper or lower schools, were exempt from the exceptional laws against Jews.   To wean them from using the jargon, special privileges were granted to those who would learn one of three languages—Russian, Polish, or German.   The culture of the Jews within his kingdom was desired by Alexander, who hoped that another Mendelssohn would spring from their midst.   Attendance at schools was not enforced; it therefore depended on the Jewish community to support boys' schools (Chedarim) as best they could. Nor could it be otherwise amongst the millions of serfs in Russia, not one of whom was permitted to visit a school.

A limitation was, however, introduced at that time which nullified all privileges in favor of the Jews.   Those who dwelt in the country were ordered to depart within a short space of time and crowd together in the cities.   Cruel subtlety dictated this order.   The Polish landowners, who from indolence had given over the care of their breweries and the sale of produce to industrious and trustworthy Jewish managers and farmers, were ruined by the removal of the Jews from the villages, and thus rendered incapable of revolt.   This law could not be carried out for the time being, but remained in existence as a dead letter, until later days.   The worst result was that the Jews were treated as strangers, although they had been more than half a century in the Polish provinces.   Naturally they did not advance in culture, being hindered and persecuted by Rabbinism, and even more so by Neo-Chassidism.

CHAPTER XII.

SINCE the days of the Romans, the world had not witnessed such sudden changes and catastrophes as in the beginning of this century, when a new Empire was founded with the intention of establishing a universal monarchy. All the powers bent even lower before Napoleon, Emperor of the French, than before the First Consul Bonaparte. The pope, who in his heart cursed him and the whole new order, did not hesitate to anoint him successor to Charlemagne. The German princes were the first to recognize cringingly this innovation, the elevation of an upstart over themselves. As if Napoleon by contact with the Germans during his wars against Austria and Prussia had become infected with their Jew-hatred, his feelings with reference to them from that time underwent a change. Although he had before shown admiration for the venerable antiquity and gigantic struggles of the Jewish race, he now displayed a positive dislike to them. His unfavorable attitude towards the Jews was used by the Germans in Alsace to induce him to deprive the French Jews of their privileges and reduce them to their former state of abasement.

The storms of the Revolution had put an end to the old accusations against the Jews of Alsace.

Jewish creditors, usurers, Christian debtors were alike impoverished by the Reign of Terror; the olden times were swept away. When quiet was restored, many Jews, who through their energy had acquired some property again, went back to their former trades. What else could they do? To commence to learn handicrafts and agriculture could not be expected of men advanced in years. Even young men found it difficult, as bigoted Christian employers in the German-speaking provinces did not care to take Jewish apprentices. A numerous class of the populace of Alsace offered well-to-do Jews a source of income. The peasants and day-laborers, before the Revolution serfs, had been liberated through it, but possessed no means wherewith to purchase land and commence work. Their cattle and even their implements of agriculture were lost during the stormy years; and many of them had fled to escape military service. These peasants, on the return of peace, had addressed themselves to Jews for advances of money, to obtain small parcels of the national land for cultivation.

The Jewish men of substance had responded, and probably demanded high rates of interest. The peasants, however, were not the losers, for, although originally destitute of means, they had greatly improved their condition. In a few years their possessions in landed property amounted to 60 million francs, the sixth part of which they owed to Jews. It was, indeed, hard for the peasants of Alsace to obtain ready money to discharge debts to their Jewish creditors, especially as the wars of Bonaparte called them away from the plough to bear arms, and many lawsuits ensued against the debtors. The Strasburg Trade Court of Justice alone, during the years 1802-4, had to decide upon summonses for debt between Jewish creditors and Christian debtors amounting to 800,000 francs. The defaulting peasants were sentenced to hand over their fields and vineyards to the Jewish creditors, some of whom may have acted harshly in these matters.

These circumstances were made use of by the Jew-haters. They generalized the misdeeds of the Jews, exaggerated the sufferings of the Christian debtors forced to pay, and stamped the Jews as usurers and bloodsuckers, so as to deprive the French Jews living in their provinces of their recently-acquired equalization, or if possible to prepare some worse fate for them. As at all times, the citizens of the German town of Strasburg took the most prominent part in this movement against the Jews. They had made a vain attempt to keep the Jews out of their city and to persecute them during the Reign of Terror. With fierce rage they beheld the number of Jewish immigrants increase. There were no Jewish usurers in their midst; on the contrary, there were wealthy, highly respected, and educated Jews, such as the families of Cerf-Berr, Ratisbonne, and Picard, most of whom lived from their estates. Nevertheless the people of Strasburg raised the loudest clamors against the Jews, as if the latter were the cause of their impoverishment. The prefect of Strasburg, a German, aided and abetted the merchants. When Napoleon stayed in Strasburg (January, 1806), after the campaign of a hundred days against Austria, he was besieged by the prefect and a deputation of the people of Alsace with complaints showing how harmful to the state were the Jews; how like a crowd of ravens they ruined the Christian populace, so that whole villages passed into the possession of Jewish usurers, how half the estates of Alsace were mortgaged to Jewish creditors, and other malicious charges. Napoleon thereupon called to mind that during his campaign some Jews near Ulm had bought stolen articles from the soldiers, which had greatly displeased him. The Jew-haters suggested that these may have been Strasburg Jews, who followed in the track of the

army in order to enrich themselves by means of the
booty ; and that all Jews were usurers, hawkers, and
ragmen.   To incite the emperor still more to acts
of hostility, the following grave statement was
added—that, in the whole of Alsace, indeed, in all
the (German) Departments of the Upper and Lower
Rhine, the people were so embittered against the
Jews that a general massacre, scenes such as were
witnessed in the Middle Ages, might ensue.   In
taprooms the question of slaughtering the Jews
was often discussed.   His mind filled with such evil
impressions, Napoleon left Strasburg, promising
redress of these grievances.   That this impression
might not fade away, the enemies of the Jews
besieged the minister of justice with loud complaints
about the baseness and hurtfulness of the Jews.
Judges, prefects, all German-speaking officials vied
with each other in attempts to deprive the Jews of
their civil rights.   The minister of justice, carried
away by the complaints, was actually on the point of
putting an exceptional law into force against the
Jews of France, forbidding them for a time to do any
business in mortgages.

Mingled with this Jew-hatred, which arose from
the petty jealousy of guild members, and from fear
of excessive competition, were the bigoted and
gloomy views of the reactionary party, who commenced to spin their network of schemes in order
to suppress mental freedom, the mother, so to speak,
of political liberty.   One of the chief representatives
of this party, hostile to liberty, and skilled in intrigues,
was Louis Gabriel Ambroise Bonald, a man
of kindred spirit to Gentz, Adam Müller, and others
of like caliber, who, together with the romanticist
Chateaubriand, and Fontanes, a past-master of
flattery, brought about the most terrible religious
and political reaction.   Bonald, who, after short-
lived enthusiasm for liberty, unfurled the flag of the
Bourbon Legitimists, and glorified it with mystical-

Catholic inanities, beheld in the liberation of the
Jews a diminution of the power of the Church, and
employed means to undermine their equalization in
France. He wished to lower them to the level of
such despicable beings as the Church required for
its purposes. In a paper which he issued conjointly
with Chateaubriand for the purpose of maintaining
the Ultramontane power, he attacked the Jews with
sophistical eloquence. He envied the Germans
because, more reasonable and prudent than the
French, they had remitted only the capitation-tax, and
and had otherwise kept the Jews in subjection. He
blamed the National Assembly for having conceded
all rights without considering that when the French
Jews were released from the yoke, they might easily
act in concert with their co-religionists in other
countries to secure all influence and all wealth to
themselves and enslave the Christians. Bonald
again gave utterance to that venomous slander
which a venal, unscrupulous Alsatian had circulated
in a pamphlet before the Revolution. His recurring
statements were that the Jews were ever in conflict
with morality, that they formed a state within a
state, and that most of them were vampires and
petty traders, among whom the high-minded disappeared. Bonald concluded his list of charges with
an opinion which stigmatized the French nation
as much as the Jews. "If the latter are ever
permitted to enjoy independence and frame laws,
then a Jewish Synhedrion would not establish more
nonsensical or unworthy laws than the Constituent
Assembly of philosophers has established."

It was a fortunate circumstance for the future of
the Jews that the enemies of freedom as well as
orthodox Christians included Jew-hatred in their
programme, because this impelled friends of liberty
to defend the cause of the Jews in part as their own.
But for the moment, Bonald's Jew-hating attempts
greatly harmed them. They were approved by

those who strove to retard the advancing spirit of the age, and in a roundabout way were dinned into the ear of Napoleon. The French Jews had no idea of the extent of this agitation, they imagined that it concerned only the Jewish usurers in Alsace, and that it did not affect the honor, position, and existence of all, and therefore they did not sufficiently oppose it.

Matters now assumed a serious complexion. Napoleon laid the Jewish question for discussion before his council, which entrusted it to a young member, a Count Molé, known in later French history as the prototype of ambiguity. To the surprise of all the elder and more influential members of the council, Molé, whose great-grandmother was a Jewess, presented a report decidedly hostile to the Jews, suggesting that all French Jews be placed under exceptional laws, which meant that their legally acknowledged and practically realized equality was to be taken from them. His report was received with deserved derision by the oldest members of the council, who were so imbued with the principle of absolute equality sanctified by the Revolution, that they could not conceive that a creditor suing for payment from his debtor could have a right to inquire into his religious belief. They suspected that Molé was in league with the reactionary politicians Fontanes and Bonald, who were anxious to offer up the Jews as the first sacrifice to their retrograde policy. Molé, however, appears to have sought to curry favor with the emperor, who, as he knew, was not kindly disposed towards the Jews. Although all the councilors were in favor of their unabridged civil rights, the Jewish question was to be brought up at the regular session of the state council under the presidency of Napoleon (April 30, 1806), who attached great importance to the matter.

It was a fateful moment when these questions,

settled long ago, again came up for discussion. The weal and woe not alone of the French and Italian Jews, but of those in all Europe, depended upon the issue of this consultation. For if the equalization of the Jews of the former countries was in any way threatened, those of other countries would be doomed to remain in a state of degradation and oppression for a long time to come. The sitting was stormy. It happened unfortunately that a recently elected state councilor named Beugnot, who in the absence of the emperor had spoken with great spirit and address in favor of the Jews, wished to display his eloquence before the emperor. He therefore made use of the following unlucky phrase: "To deprive the Jews of their full civil rights were like a battle lost on the field of justice." Napoleon was annoyed. Both the tone and matter of Beugnot's speech sorely displeased him. It vexed him that his prejudices against the Jews should be regarded as unfounded. Beugnot aroused his passion, he spoke against theorists and propounders of principles, and allowed his anger to outrun his discretion. He spoke of the Jews as Fichte had done, saying that they constituted a state within a state, being the feudal nobles of the time; that they could not be placed in the same category with Catholics and Protestants, because, besides not being citizens of the country, they were a dangerous element. The keys of France, Alsace and Strasburg, should not be allowed to fall into the hands of a nation of spies. It would be prudent to suffer only 50,000 Jews in the districts of the Upper and Lower Rhine, to scatter the remainder throughout France, and prohibit them from engaging in trade, because they corrupted it by usury. He made other accusations which he had learnt from the Jew-haters. In spite of this speech, two councilors of importance, Regnault and Ségur, ventured to speak on behalf of the Jews, or of justice.

They pointed out that the Jews in Bordeaux, Marseilles, and the Italian cities belonging to France, like those in Holland, were held in the highest esteem, and that the offenses charged against the Jews of Alsace should not be imputed to Judaism, but rather to their unhappy condition. They succeeded in mollifying Napoleon's wrath for the moment, and a second session decided the matter.

Meantime some influential persons succeeded in impressing Napoleon with a better opinion of the Jews. They called to his attention how quickly they had become proficient in the arts and sciences, in agriculture and handicrafts. Persons were pointed out to him who had been decorated with the Order of the Legion of Honor, or who had received pensions for courage in war, and that, therefore, it was slander to call all Jews usurers and hawkers. At the second sitting of the state council (May 7, 1806) Napoleon spoke in a milder tone of the Jews. He rejected the proposal made to him to expel Jewish peddlers, and endow the tribunals of justice with unlimited authority over usurers. He desired to do nothing that might be disapproved by posterity, or darken his fame. Nevertheless, he could not free himself from the prejudice that the Jewish people, from the most ancient times, even from the days of Moses, had been usurers and extortioners. He was, however, determined not to permit any persecution or neglect of the Jews. He then conceived the happy thought—or it may have been suggested to him—to bring together a number of Jews from various provinces, who were to tell him whether Judaism demanded of its adherents hatred and oppression of Christians. The Jews themselves, through the medium of their representatives, were to decide their fate.

The decree which announced this resolution (May 30, 1806) was couched in harsh terms. Napoleon himself, it appears, gave it the last touches whilst in an angry mood. The first part of the decree ran as follows: "The claims of Jewish creditors in certain provinces may not be collected within the space of a year." The second part ordered the assembly of Jewish notables. The reason for their meeting was such as to satisfy the Bonalds. Certain Jews in the northern districts having by usury brought misery upon many peasants, the emperor had deprived them of civil equality. But he had also considered it necessary to awaken in all who professed the Jewish religion in France a feeling of civic morality, which, owing to their debasement, had become almost extinct amongst them. For this purpose Jewish notables were to express their wishes and suggest means whereby skilled work and useful occupations would become general among Jews. Thus, for a time at least, a portion of the Jews of France were deprived of their rights of equality. But balm might be expected from the Assembly of Notables for the wounds inflicted by Napoleon. The prefects were required to select prominent persons from among the rabbis and the laity, who, on a fixed day, should present themselves "in the good city of Paris." Not only the congregations of the old French provinces, but also those in the new ones, in the district on the left bank of the Rhine, were to be represented by deputies. The Italian Jews, who applied for permission to take part in this meeting, were likewise admitted.

Although the notables were somewhat arbitrarily chosen by the magistrates, on the whole their selections were fortunate. Among the hundred and more notables of French, German, and Italian speech, the majority were fully aware of the magnitude and importance of their task. They had to defend Judaism before the eyes of all Europe—a difficult but grateful task. Among them were men who had already gained fame, such as Berr Isaac Berr, his promising son, Michael Berr (who had issued the summons to princes and nations, to release the Jews from bondage), and Abraham Furtado, the partisan of the Girondists, who had suffered for his political opinions, and was a man of noble mind and great foresight. His descent is interesting. His parents were Marranos in Portugal, but in spite of the family's outward adherence to the Church during two hundred years, his mother had not forgotten her origin and her attachment to Judaism. When the terrible earthquake made Lisbon a heap of ruins, Furtado's parents were overwhelmed by their falling house—his father killed, but his mother, who was with child, entombed in a living grave. She vowed that if God would save her from this danger, she would, in spite of all difficulties, openly embrace Judaism. A fresh shock opened her tomb. She succeeded in escaping from this place of horror, made her way to London, and there publicly returned to Judaism. Here her son Abraham was born, whom she brought up as a Jew. Abraham Furtado was well acquainted with Jewish literature; he collected materials for a Jewish history, and paid particular attention to the Book of Job; but his Jewish knowledge was mere dilettanteism, without thoroughness. His favorite study was natural science. During the Revolution, Furtado belonged to the commission appointed to make proposals for ameliorating the condition of the French Jews. During the Reign of Terror, and as a supporter of the Girondists, his life was endangered and his property confiscated. By assiduous industry he had enabled himself to purchase an estate in Bordeaux. Next to the elder and younger Berrs, Furtado was the brightest ornament of the assembly; he was an eloquent speaker, and possessed great tact in public affairs.

A happy choice was that of Rabbi Joseph David Sinzheim, of Strasburg (born 1745, died 1812). He was a man of almost patriarchal character, of the deepest moral earnestness, and of a most lovable, gentle nature. Well furnished with means, and the brother-in-law of the wealthy Cerf Berr, Sinzheim devoted himself to the study of the Talmud, not from any mercenary purpose, but from inclination. His acquaintance with Talmudical and Rabbinical literature was astounding, but he was lacking in depth. His education prevented his being interested in other branches of science, but at least he had no antipathy to them. During the Reign of Terror, which caused the Jews in Jew-hating Strasburg to suffer severely, he was compelled to flee for safety, and could not return until peace was restored. The number of the Jews in Strasburg increased under the Directory and Napoleon. They formed themselves into a congregation, appointing Sinzheim as their first rabbi. Thence he was summoned to Paris to attend the Assembly of Notables. He was considered the most eminent French Talmudist, and became the leader of the orthodox party. Besides Sinzheim, only one rabbi was prominent, the Portuguese Rabbi Abraham Andrade, from Saint-Esprit; the majority of the members were laymen.

With trembling hearts about a hundred Jewish Notables from the French and German departments assembled. They had no plan, as they did not know precisely what were the emperor's intentions. A summons from the minister, addressed to each member singly (July 23, 1806), enlightened them but little. They learnt that in three days' time, on a Sabbath, they were to hold a meeting in a hall of the Hôtel de Ville set apart for them. There the assembly was to organize, and they were to answer the questions which imperial commissioners would lay before them. The purpose was to make useful citizens of the Jews, bring their religious belief into agreement with their duties as Frenchmen, refute the charges made against them, and remedy the

evils which they had occasioned. The selection of
Molé as imperial commissioner, together with Por-
talis and Pasquier, who were to treat officially with
the Assembly, was not calculated to quiet their fears.
Molé had been the first to serve as a medium
for the spread of the anti-Jewish slanders of Bonald
and others. On the day before the opening of the
Assembly (July 25), there appeared in the official journal, the "Moniteur," an account of the history of the
Jews from the return from Babylon till that time.
The French nation was thus to be acquainted with
the importance of the questions now to be submitted
to the Jews themselves. In rapid sequence the
following circumstances were depicted :— The
independence and the dependence of the Jewish
people, their victories and defeats ; their persecution during the Middle Ages and the protection they
found ; their scattered condition and their massacres ;
the accusations directed against them; their abasement and oppression in different countries inflicted
by monarch after monarch, and by fluctuating opinions and policies. Jewish history thus received, so
to speak, an official seal. That there were many
errors and false statements in this account was not
to be wondered at. At the command of the emperor,
the Jewish religion, or Judaism, was officially
expounded, with even greater display of ignorance.
Two points were particularly emphasized, viz., that
the religious and moral separation of the Jews from
the rest of the world, and the pursuit of usury to the
injury of members of other creeds, if not prescribed,
was at any rate tolerated by the Jewish law. "How
otherwise is the fact to be explained," it was
remarked at the conclusion of the official document,
"that those Jews who at the present time extort
high rates of interest, are most religious and follow
the laws of the Talmud most faithfully ? " The
inference was to the last degree false. "Do we
not see that the Portuguese Jews, who do not sully

themselves with usury, are less strict in their adherence to the Talmud?   Had the distinguished Jews in
Germany, such as their famous Mendelssohn, great
reverence for the rabbis?   Finally, are those men
among us who devote themselves to the sciences
orthodox Jews?"   Thus Talmudical Judaism was
once again represented as a stumbling-block in the
way of the progress of the Jews, not, indeed, in that
spirit of hatred which prevailed in Germany; but it
was laid open to attack, and that, too, before a public, so to say a European, tribunal.

On the same day that the Jews formed the topic
of conversation in Paris, the deputies assembled to
decide upon a question of conscience.   The first official meeting was to be held on Saturday, and the first
business was the election of a president and of
secretaries by means of written votes.   It was
the first time that representatives of the French,
German, and Italian Jews came together, and the
contrasts and variations developed during the last
half century by the changes in the times, became
apparent,—all shades were represented, from the politician Furtado, to the rabbis who had spent all their
lives in schools.   They were expected to harmonize.
At first they could not understand each other, but
had to employ German and Italian interpreters.
Was the public activity of the Jewish deputies to commence with the desecration of the Sabbath?   Or
should they strictly adhere to the religious prohibition, and thus give a handle to enemies of the Jews,
who asserted that Judaism was incompatible with
the exercise of civil functions?   These serious
questions occupied the minds of the members.
The rabbis and the party of Berr Isaac Berr were of
opinion that the first sitting should be postponed to
another day, or at least that no election should take
place.   The less critical party, the politicians, urged
that they prove to the emperor that Judaism can
subordinate itself to the law of the land; and the
debate grew very violent.

Thus the first Jewish Parliament in Paris assembled on a Sabbath, in a room of the Hôtel de Ville, decorated with appropriate emblems. The deputies attended in full force, none were absent ; some of them intentionally came in carriages. Some of the stricter members again tried to have the first meeting postponed, but in vain. The dread of Napoleon's authority terrified those who as a rule paid scrupulous regard to religious ordinances. Under the chairmanship of Rabbi Solomon Lipmann, the oldest member, the election now proceeded. The orthodox had provided themselves with ballot tickets, but most of the others wrote them out unabashed before the very eyes of the rabbis, whilst a few had theirs written for them. Only two men were qualified for the presidency, Berr Isaac Berr and Furtado. The former was supported by the orthodox party, the latter by the politicians. Furtado obtained the majority of votes. With parliamentary tact he presided over the meeting. The deputies became fully conscious of the grave responsibility resting upon them, and proved themselves equal to their task. All were animated by a strong desire for unanimity.

Even the German rabbis, who hitherto had been buried in the seclusion of the academies amidst the Talmud volumes, quickly adapted themselves to the new circumstances and to parliamentary forms. Certain deputies contributed to impress all present with a feeling of concord. The speech of the deputy Lipmann Cerf Berr had a remarkable effect, especially the following words :—

"Let us forget our origin ! Let us no longer speak of Jews of Alsace, of Portugal, or of Germany. Though scattered over the face of the globe, we are still one people worshiping the same God, and as our law commands us, we are to obey the laws of the country where we live."

When the officer of the guard of honor furnished for the meeting approached the newly-elected presi-

dent to receive his orders, and when at the departure
of the deputies, the guard greeted them with military honors and beat of drums, they felt themselves
exalted, and their fear was turned to hope.

This joyful expectation revived their courage, and
enabled them to oppose the attacks of Jew-hating
writers.   Meantime the whole body of deputies from
the kingdom of Italy arrived, and created a favorable
impression by their bearing.   Amongst them the
spirit of the age manifested itself in difference of
religious views and opinions, although not so sharply
marked as among the French and German Jews.

The most distinguished among the Jewish-Italian
deputies was Abraham Vita di Cologna (born 1755,
died in Trieste, 1832).   He was well versed both
in Rabbinical and scientific learning, of prepos-
sessing appearance, and an elegant speaker.   While
rabbi of Mantua, he was elected a member of the
Parliament of the Italian kingdom.   His Talmudical
and secular knowledge, however, was neither comprehensive nor deep.   Cologna was in favor of the new
tendency, which removed Judaism from its isolated
position to imbue it with European ideas ; but both
the means and end were not clearly defined in his
mind, and he took no steps to carry out his wishes.
An elder member of the Italian notables, Joshua
Benzion Segre (born about 1720, died 1809), at once
owner of an estate, rabbi, and municipal councilor of
Vercelli, was also in favor of scientific studies, and
belonged to the advanced party.   The follies of the
Kábbala still found many supporters among educated
Italian Jews, although its first opponents had come
from Italy.   Benzion Segre was averse to the study,
while the Italian deputy Graziadio (Chanannel) Nepi,
rabbi and physician in Cinto (born 1760, died 1836),
was a firm believer in it.   He was exceedingly well
read in Jewish literature, and compiled an alpha-
betical register of the names of Jewish authors of
ancient and modern times.

At the second sitting (July 29), the three imperial commissioners solemnly propounded twelve questions, which the Assembly were to answer conscientiously. The chief points were, whether the French Jews regarded France as their country, and Frenchmen as their brothers; whether they considered the laws of the state as binding upon them, and, by way of deduction from these two points, the incisive third question, "Can Jews legally intermarry with Christians," and, lastly, whether usury in the case of non-Jews is permitted or forbidden. The remaining points referred to polygamy, divorce, and the authority of the rabbis, and were of a subordinate nature. Most of the members could not listen to these queries without feeling pain that their love of country and their attachment to France should be called into question, notwithstanding that Jews had attested their patriotism by shedding their blood upon battlefields. From many sides rose a cry at these questions, "Aye, unto death." The address delivered by Molé on submitting these twelve questions was cold and to some extent offensive. Its contents were nearly as follows :—The charges against various Jews had been proved. The emperor was, however, not satisfied to check the evil himself, but desired the assistance of the deputies. They were to state the whole truth in replying to the questions laid before them. The emperor permitted full liberty of discussion, but wished them to bear in mind that they were Frenchmen, and would be relinquishing that honor unless they showed themselves worthy of it. The assembly now knew what was expected. They were brought face to face with the alternative of renouncing their equality or damaging Judaism.

Furtado, in his reply to the speech of the commissioner, very cleverly turned the mistrust of the emperor into a semblance of trust. He said that the Jews welcomed the opportunity of answering these questions, to lay bare all errors and put an end to the prejudices entertained against them. The speech which Berr Isaac Berr delivered at this meeting was more sincere, more manly, and altogether more fervent. Furtado represented the Jews, but not Judaism; he caused it to be understood that the Assembly should consider it a duty and an honor to obey every hint of the emperor. Berr gave dignified expression to the claims of Judaism. The duty of replying to the questions was assigned to a commission, which included, besides the president, the secretary, and the auditors, the four most eminent rabbis, Sinzheim, Andrade, De Cologna, and Segre, and two learned laymen.

This commission handed over the chief part of their work to Rabbi David Sinzheim, the most scholarly and esteemed member of the assembly, who in a very short time completed his task to the satisfaction of his colleagues, of the imperial commissioners, and eventually of the emperor (July 30 till August 3). His report was submitted to the commissioners, who reported it to the emperor before it was brought up for public discussion. Napoleon was so pleased with the behavior of the Assembly that he announced his intention to grant an audience to all the members. In fact, their parliamentary tact, as displayed in the proceedings, filled him with such high regard towards them that he partially overcame his prejudices against the Jews. He had always pictured them as ragmen and usurers, with cringing, bent forms, or as sly, cunning flatterers lying in ambush for their prey ; and to his astonishment he beheld among the members men of fine character, intelligence, and imposing appearance. He thus acquired a better opinion of the Jews. It must be admitted that the incense offered him by the Assembly, as to a deity, did not leave him unmoved. On the other hand, the serious task placed before the Jewish deputies made them greater, exalted them above the common level, ideal-

ized them. Their harmonious work aroused
their enthusiasm, the orations intoxicated them, and
even the sober German members became infected.

At the third sitting (August 4), at the debate upon
the replies to the various questions, the deputies
were filled with self-confidence and the certainty of
victory. No difficulty was offered by the first two
questions—whether polygamy was allowed among
Jews, and whether the validity of a divorce granted
by the French law was acknowledged by their religious and moral code. These were decided according
to the desire of the emperor without any injury to
Judaism. But the third question aroused painful
excitement, and revealed the opposition which had
divided the Jews since the time of Mendelssohn—
"May a Jewess marry a Christian, or a Christian
woman a Jew?" This question had given rise to
heated debates in the commission, how much more
in public assembly. Even the orthodox party felt
that to reply unconditionally in the negative would
be extremely perilous. The commission, however,
had already supplied a clever answer, and if it is
owing to Sinzheim's efforts, it redounds to his intellect and tact. At the outset it was skillfully explained
that, according to the Bible, only marriages
with Canaanite nations were forbidden. Even by
the Talmud intermarriages were allowed, because
the nations of Europe were not considered idolaters.
The rabbis, to be sure, were opposed to such unions,
seeing that the usual ceremonies could not be performed. They would refuse to bless such an union,
as the Catholic priests refused their assistance on
such occasions. This refusal, however, was of little
consequence, as civil marriages were recognized by
the state. At all events, the rabbis considered a
Jew or Jewess who had contracted a union of this
kind as a full co-religionist.

The remaining questions were settled without
any excitement in two sittings (August 7th and

12th). The questions whether the Jews regarded Frenchmen as their brothers, and France as their country, were answered by the Assembly with a loud, enthusiastic affirmative. They were able to refer to the doctrines of Judaism, which in its three phases—Biblical, Talmudical, and Rabbinical—had always ·emphasized humanity and the brotherhood of man. Only one point in the report of the commission gave rise to a certain amount of friction, viz., that which seemed to ascribe a kind of superiority to the Portuguese Jews, as if through their conduct they were held in higher esteem by Christians than the German Jews. This clause was therefore struck out.

In answering the two questions relative to usury, the Assembly was able to demolish a deeply-rooted prejudice and place Judaism in a favorable light.

The commissioner Molé, the first to yield to Jew-hatred and propose to exclude Jews from state offices, had now to declare publicly (September 18) that the emperor was satisfied with the intentions and zeal of the assembly. His speech on this occasion struck quite a different note to former ones. "Who, indeed," he exclaimed, "would not be astonished at the sight of this assembly of enlightened men, selected from among the descendants of the most ancient of nations? If an individual of past centuries could come to life, and if this scene met his gaze, would he not think himself transplanted within the walls of the Holy City? or might he not imagine that a thorough revolution in the affairs of man had taken place?" "His Majesty," continued Molé, "guarantees to you the free practice of your religion and the full enjoyment of your political rights ; but in exchange for these valuable privileges, he demands a religious surety that you will completely realize the principles expressed in your answers."

What could the surety be? Napoleon then

announced a surprising message, which filled the assembly with joyful astonishment and electrified them. "The emperor proposes to call together the great Synhedrion!" This part of their national government, which had perished together with the Temple, and which alone had been endowed with authority in Israel, was now to be revived for the purpose of transforming the answers of the Assembly into decisions, which should command the highest respect, equally with those of the Talmud, with Jews of all countries and throughout all centuries. Further, the Assembly was to make known the meeting of the great Synhedrion to all the synagogues in Europe, so that they send to Paris deputies capable of advising the government with intelligence, and worthy of belonging to this assembly. That the revived Synhedrion might possess the honorable and imposing character of its model, it was to be constituted on the pattern of the former one; it was to consist of seventy-one members, and have a president (Nasi), a vice-president (Ab-Beth-Din), and a second vice-president (Chacham). This announcement made the deputies feel as if the ancient glory of Israel had suddenly risen from the tomb and once more assumed a solid shape. Three months previously they had been summoned to rescue their civil rights which were endangered, and now a new vista opened before them; they seemed to behold their glorious past revived in the present, and assisted in the accomplishment of the dream; and they were filled with amazement.

Naturally, on receipt of this announcement, the Assembly passed enthusiastic motions and votes of thanks. They expressed their approval of everything which the commissioners had proposed or intimated. The Synhedrion was to be composed of two-thirds rabbis and one-third laymen, and was to include all the rabbis in the Assembly of Notables, together with others to be afterwards elected. The true importance of the Assembly now came to an end; its duties now were merely perfunctory. The proclamation issued to the whole Jewish world (Tishri 24—October 6) was its only momentous action thereafter. It aimed at rousing the Jews to take an interest in the Synhedrion and to send deputies. This proclamation was written in four languages, Hebrew, French, German, and Italian, and expressed the feelings which animated members of the Assembly, and the hopes entertained for the great Synhedrion:

"A great event is about to take place, one which through a long series of centuries our fathers, and even we in our own times, did not expect to see, and which has now appeared before the eyes of the astonished world. The 20th of October has been fixed as the date for the opening of a Great Synhedrion in the capital of one of the most powerful Christian nations, and under the protection of the immortal Prince who rules over it. Paris will show the world a remarkable scene, and this ever memorable event will open to the dispersed remnants of the descendants of Abraham a period of deliverance and prosperity."

The Jewish Parliament, and the re-establishment of a Synhedrion created much interest in Europe. The world was accustomed to Napoleon's feats of war and brilliant victories; the power of his arms had ceased to astonish men. But that this admired and terrible hero should descend to the most ancient people, to raise and restore them to some of their lost splendor, caused, perhaps, more general surprise among Christians than among Jews. It was looked upon as a miraculous event, as marking a new era in the history of the world, in which a different state of things would prevail. Some Christian writers in Bamberg, at their head a Catholic priest (Gley), expected such abundant and important results from the Jewish assembly in Paris that they established a special newspaper, a kind of journal for the Jews. Only the Berlin *illuminati*— David Friedländer's circle—experienced an uncomfortable sensation at the news, because they feared that, through the Synhedrion in France, ancient Judaism might be revived in a new garb. They therefore declared the Synhedrion a juggler's performance, provided by Napoleon for his Parisians. Patriotism was also involved in this sense of uneasiness, for the Prussian Jews participated in the deep grief into which the people of Prussia and the royal family had been plunged by the defeats at Jena and Auerstädt (October 14, 1806).

Four days after the dissolution of the Assembly of Notables (Adar 9—February 9, 1807), the Great Synhedrion, very different in character, assembled. It consisted, as mentioned above, for the greater part of rabbis, most of whom had been members of the Assembly of Notables. Twenty-five laymen from the same Assembly were added, and the ratification of the answers to the twelve questions according to the wishes of Napoleon was secured. To all appearances the great Synhedrion was to assemble and transact business according to its own pleasure. The commissioners were not to have any communications with it. The minister of the interior had chosen only the first three officials: Sinzheim as President (Nasi), the grey-headed Segre as first Vice-President (Ab-Beth-Din), and Abraham di Cologna as second Vice-President (Chacham).

After attending the synagogue, the Assembly made its way to the Hôtel de Ville, and there the seventy members, in a hall specially decorated for them, took their seats according to seniority, by ancient custom in a semi-circle around the president. The sittings were public, and many spectators were present at them. The members of the Synhedrion were suitably attired in black garments, with silk capes and three-cornered hats. The meeting was opened by a prayer specially composed by Sinzheim. The speeches of Sinzheim and Furtado, with which the first meeting commenced, were entirely appropriate to the situation.

The second sitting (February 12) was occupied
with the reading of the motions which the Synhedrion was to sanction, together with the presentation
of addresses from different congregations in France,
Italy, and the Rhineland, and especially in Dresden
and Neuwied, expressing their agreement with the
assembly, and the reception of messengers to the
Synhedrion from Amsterdam.

The Synhedrion felt itself at a loss for subjects to
discuss. The new matters which they had proposed
to settle were left untouched. The Franco-Prus-
sian war had caused the emperor to be forgetful of
the Synhedrion and the Jews in general. There
only remained for the members of the Synhedrion to convert the replies of the previous
assembly into definite, inviolable laws. The question as to the power of the new Synhedrion to
impose binding laws, or whether it could be placed
on the same basis as the ancient one, was not de-
bated. The rabbis overcame this scruple by arguing
that each generation was permitted by the Talmud
to institute suitable ordinances and make new
decisions, and therefore, without further discussion,
they declared themselves as constituted. Without
demur, the Synhedrion adopted Furtado's disinte-
grating view, that Judaism consisted of two wholly
distinct elements—the purely religious and the polit-
ical-legislative laws. The first mentioned are unal-
terable; the latter, on the other hand, which have lost
their significance since the downfall of the Jewish
state, can be set aside. The inferences from this
difference, however, could not be drawn by any
individual, but only by an authorized assembly, a
great Synhedrion, which owing to unfavorable circumstances had never been able to assemble. The
Synhedrion was, therefore, no innovation. The
following highly important paragraph with reference
to marriage was also passed without opposition:
That not only must the civil marriage precede the
religious ceremony, but that intermarriages between

Jews and Christians were to be considered binding, and although they were not attended by any religious forms, yet no religious interdict could be passed upon them. In this evasive manner the Synhedrion satisfied its own conscience and the suspicions of the imperial officers.

As the Synhedrion had no actual business to transact, the time of the sittings was filled up with speeches delivered by Furtado, Hildesheimer, the deputy from Frankfort, Asser, the deputy from Amsterdam, and finally by Sinzheim, who made the closing speech. The new decisions of the Synhedrion, drawn up in French and Hebrew, enacted the following : That it is prohibited for any Jew to marry more than one wife ; that divorce by the Jewish law was effective only when preceded by that of the civil authorities ; and that a marriage likewise must be considered a civil contract first ; that every Israelite was religiously bound to consider his non-Jewish neighbors, who also recognize and worship God as the Creator, as brothers ; that he should love his country, defend it, and undertake military service, if called upon to do so ; that Judaism did not forbid any kind of handicraft and occupation, and that, therefore, it was commendable for Israelites to engage in agriculture, handicrafts, and the arts, and to forsake trading ; and finally, that it was forbidden to Israelites to exact usury either from Jew or Christian.

These new laws of the Synhedrion were of very limited scope. The Synhedrion had in view only the present, and did not look into the distant future. The Jews in general were not satisfied with its action and results. An English Jew, in a letter addressed to the members, boldly reproached them for having disowned, not alone Judaism, but all revealed religion.

" Has any one of our brethren in Constantinople, Aleppo, Bagdad, Corfu, or one of our (English) communities been sent as a deputy to you, or have they recorded their approval of your decisions ?"

The French Government, however, had obtained the surety stipulated before the rights of citizenship would be legally recognized anew. At the proposition of the commissioners the Synhedrion dissolved, and their resolutions were submitted to Napoleon, whose attention had been fixed on the Prusso-Russian war, until owing to the decisive battle of Prussian Friedland the delusive peace of Tilsit was concluded. During Napoleon's absence, plans were secretly laid with the purpose of restricting the rights of the French Jews. The Jewish deputies, however, discovered this, and the indefatigable Furtado, together with Maurice Levy of Nancy, hastened from the Seine to the Niemen to acquaint the emperor with the agitation against the Jews ; and he remained prepossessed in favor of Judaism.

After the dissolution of the Synhedrion the Assembly of Notables again convened to present their formal report to the authorities (March 25—April 6, 1807).

After an interval of a year, Napoleon announced to the Jews his intentions with reference to legislation on their behalf. He expressed (March 17, 1808) his approval of the wretched consistorial organization which degraded the officials of the synagogue to the level of policemen, and regulated the civil position of the Jews, or rather made encroachments on their hitherto favorable condition, although he repeatedly assured them that their equalization would suffer no restrictions. He had deceived all the world, and everywhere trodden freedom under foot ; how could he be expected to keep his word with the Jews and to leave their freedom unmolested? The law suggests that the Jew-hating Molé framed it. It contained no word about the equalization of the Jews. No French Jew henceforth was to engage in any species of trade without having obtained the permission of the prefect, and his consent was to be granted only on the testimony of the civil magistrates and the consistory as to the good character of the applicant. Contracts of Jews who could not show a patent were null and void. The taking of pledges as security for a loan was also surrounded by limitations which savored of the Middle Ages. Further, no foreign Jew was to settle in the German departments, nor any from those departments in another district. Finally, the Jewish people were not allowed to procure substitutes for military service ; each Jew who was chosen as a soldier had to enter the ranks. These restrictive laws were to remain in force for ten years, " in the hope that by the end of that period, and by the enforcement of various regulations, no difference whatever would exist between the Jews and the other citizens."

Thus the Jews of France, the anchor of hope of their brethren in other countries, were once again humiliated and placed under exceptional legislation. The law enacted, indeed, that the Jews of Bordeaux and certain other departments who had given no cause for complaint should not be included under these new restrictions. Shortly afterwards, owing to their loud complaints, exceptions were made in favor of the Jews of Paris, Livorno, the department of the Lower Pyrenees, and of fifteen other districts in France and Italy, so that only the scapegoats, the German-speaking Jews in France, were deprived of their civil rights. But the odious stain which had been again fastened to the Jews adhered to the emancipated as well. Their opponents, who zealously strove to check the elevation of the Jews, could now point to France, and urge that the race was indeed incapable of amendment, seeing that even where its members had been emancipated long since, they had to be deprived of their rights of equality.

Napoleon's arm, powerful though it was, could not stem the flood once set in motion, by the liberation of oppressed nationalities and classes. By his own genius and impetuosity he increased the tumult of forces. After the subjection of Prussia, Napoleon called into existence, chiefly at the expense of this state, two new political creations, the duchy of Warsaw (avoiding the dangerous and magical title of kingdom of Poland), under the rule of the Electoral Prince of Saxony, and the kingdom of Westphalia under his brother Jerome (Hieronymus).

In the latter kingdom, formed from the territories of many lords, the Jews obtained freedom and equalization. Napoleon framed the constitution of the new kingdom with the assistance of the statesmen Beugnot, Johannes von Müller, and partially also of Dohm, who, being friends of the Jews, had made their emancipation a feature. Jerome, juster and more honest than his brother, issued an edict (January 12, 1808) declaring all Jews of his state without exception to be full citizens, abolishing Jewtaxes of every description, allowing foreign Jews to reside in the country under the same protection as that afforded to Christian immigrants, and threatening with punishment the malicious who should derisively call a Jewish citizen of his state "protection Jew" (Schutz-Jude). Michael Berr, the brave and pious defender of Judaism, was summoned from France to accept office in the kingdom of Westphalia. Jews and Christians alike were filled with hope at this just treatment of German Jews, and the Jew-hating German University of Göttingen elected Berr a member.

An important part was played at the new court in Cassel by Israel Jacobson (born at Halberstadt, 1769; died at Berlin, 1828), who had been court agent, or councilor of finance, at the court of Brunswick. Although he cuts a figure in modern Jewish history, and was pleased to consider himself a German Furtado, yet he bore only external resemblance to this earnest Jewish patriot. The similarity lay in the fact that Jacobson possessed extraordinary flow of language and great vigor in carrying out his projects, which talents, it must be admitted, he employed for ameliorating the condition of his co-religionists.   His wealth provided him with the means of realizing, or attempting, all the schemes which his active brain invented.   Noble-minded, good-natured, ready for any sacrifice, and energetic, he kept one aim before him, the removal of the hateful, repulsive exterior of the Jews and Judaism, and the endeavor to render them externally attractive and brilliant.

To commemorate the day of the emancipation of the Jews, Jacobson caused a gold medal to be struck with the emblem of the union of hitherto antagonistic beliefs, and the Latin inscription : "To God and the fatherly king, united in the kingdom of Westphalia."   At the instigation of Jacobson, the Jews of the kingdom of Westphalia were to be organized somewhat like their brethren in France. Twenty-two notables were summoned to Cassel, among whom the originator of the movement was naturally included.   Jerome received them kindly, and spoke the memorable words on the occasion : that he was pleased to find that the constitution of his kingdom, which had been forced upon him, confirmed the equality of all creeds, and in this respect entirely corresponded with his own ideas.   In the commission appointed to draw up the plan for a Jewish consistory in the kingdom of Westphalia, Jacobson was naturally elected to the presidency. Michael Berr was also a member.   The constitution of the consistory, on the model of the French, was published at about the same time as the latter (March 3, 1808).   In France a rabbi occupied the chief position, whilst in the German assembly Jacobson was to be president.   He desired to be considered a rabbi, and even represented himself as one.   The chief meeting-place of the Westphalian consistory was Cassel.   Its authority was acknowledged on many subjects, and Jacobson was all-powerful, being ordered to consult the magistrates only upon important occasions. The consistory was also to be employed as a means of rousing patriotic feelings in the hearts of old and young on behalf of the House of Bonaparte. It especially busied itself with the debts of the various congregations, which were to be divided among the several communities, and thus paid off easily.

Strange to say, one of the members of the consistory was a Christian, state councilor Merkel, who, acting as secretary, kept a watch upon the highest Jewish judicial authorities like a detective. In the French central consistory thoughtful, trusty men, who had given proofs of their abilities, were elected, such as David Sinzheim, the president, Abraham di Cologna, and Menahem Deutz, whose son afterwards obtained sad celebrity, men who knew how to bridge over the gap between the old times and the new; while Jacobson delighted in foolhardy leaps, and dragged his colleagues along with him. In transforming the condition of the congregations and the synagogues under his jurisdiction, he consulted with David Friedländer, standing almost within the pale of Christianity, and his colleagues among the Measfim. The desire of Jacobson was for reforms, or rather for the introduction of such practices into the Jewish Divine service as were observed in the Christian Church, especially such as appealed to the senses.

The first German prince who voluntarily conceded to the Jews at least a restricted amount of freedom was Duke Charles of Baden, one of the dependents of the family of Napoleon. Baden being on the borders of France became accustomed to the recognition of the Jews of the latter country as citizens; and public opinion was more favorable to them there than in other parts of Germany. To be sure, the German Prince of Baden was not so free from prejudice as the member of the Napoleon family who occupied a German throne. He declared the Jews citizens of the state, but did not give them the freedom of the cities, so that they could not dwell in such towns as had hitherto been closed to Jews; and even where they had always been tolerated, they were only to be regarded as "protected citizens." The duke, however, reserved the right to confer the freedom of the cities upon those who should give up petty trading. Their religious peculiarities were to be respected, "only in so far as they agreed with the Mosaic Law, but not with the Talmudical interpretations of the same."

Even the city of Frankfort for a moment succumbed to the equality intoxication, although petty, pedantic hatred of Jews was incorporated in every patrician. This hatred had greatly increased in intensity since the spread of revolutionary principles. The subjection of the Jews was to compensate for loss of independence. Not a single badge or ceremony which perpetuated Jewish degradation was removed from the Jews, who numbered about five hundred families. The laws of "Stättigkeit," defining their dependent status, which had existed for two hundred years, were still annually read in the synagogue. Every newly admitted Jew was compelled to take the oath of allegiance to the Senate. Restrictions continued to be imposed on Jewish marriages. Jew-taxes had to be paid, as if the Holy Roman Empire still held sway, instead of the all-powerful will of the Corsican, crushing emperors and kings. The Jews were obliged to dwell in the narrow, dirty, unhealthy Jewish quarter, and every Christian, however degraded, had the right of calling to the most refined Jew, "Mach Mores, Jud'!" of treating him as a despicable object, and even banishing him from the better parts of the city and from the parks.

The French general Jourdan had indeed freed the

Frankfort Jews from the Ghetto for a few years, when he bombarded the city and destroyed that portion of it. Under the eyes of the French victors, the patricians, sorely against their will, permitted Jews to rent houses in other districts; under no condition could they purchase or erect houses. When the Holy Roman Empire melted away like a snow-flake before the breath of Napoleon, when Frankfort fell under the sovereignty of the Arch-Chancellor or Prince Primate of the Rhenish Confederation, and the powerful aldermen themselves became subject, the serfdom of the Jews came to an end, though the change was not expressed in legal enactments. Karl von Dalberg, a liberal-minded man, and most favorably disposed towards the Jews, would gladly have removed their yoke, indeed he wrote to Grégoire, the advocate of emancipation, upon this subject. However, he was too well aware of the stubborn hatred of the Frankfort patricians towards the Jews, to venture upon their complete emancipation. He had only promised in a general way at the so-called coronation that the members of the Jewish nation should be protected against injury and insulting treatment. The urgent necessity of regulating the status of the Jews by law, was apparent to this Prince Primate, who discharged his duty only by half measures, such as were characteristic of the Germans. By the publication of a new order for the government and protection of the Jews, he conceded, in the spirit of the new era, that "previous laws, being opposed to the modern constitution of the Jewish nation," should be abrogated. At the same time he figured as the adherent of the anti-Jewish party by stating "that complete equality could not be granted so long as the Jews did not show themselves worthy of it, by forsaking their peculiarities and adopting the customs of the country." By these new ordinances they were treated as strangers on sufferance, who might enjoy the benefits of the law of nations and of humanity, but not the rights of citizens. The only relief measure was that the various protection-taxes were consolidated into an annual impost of 22,000 florins. Even the Ghetto was again held out to them as their residence; they were cautioned not to renew their leases in town with Christian landlords, because the day would soon dawn when they would have to return to their prison. Naturally, the Jews of Frankfort used their utmost endeavors to have these exceptional laws annulled, the more as their co-religionists in the neighboring kingdom of Westphalia were enjoying equality. When the Rhenish Confederation was dissolved and the Duchy of Frankfort created with a constitution of its own, recognizing the equality of all inhabitants, of whatever belief, Amschel, Gumprecht, and Rothschild (the first court-agent who made princes subject to himself), as representatives of the Jews, did not rest until they had induced the Archduke Dalberg and his council to establish their equalization by a special law in spite of all opposition. The new archduke being in want of funds, besides desiring the freedom and equality of the Jews, consented to grant these privileges for the sum of 440,000 florins (being twenty times the amount of the annual tax of 22,000 florins), 150,000 to be paid at once, then 50,000, and the remainder in annual payments of 10,000 florins. The law (published December 28, 1811) decreed, "that all Jews living in Frankfort under protection, together with their children and descendants, should enjoy civil rights and privileges equally with other citizens." The Jews took the oath of citizenship, entered upon their privileges and duties, and Louis Baruch (Börne), a Jew, was employed in the ducal police. The Jew-street, or what remained of it, lost its mournful privileges, and was swept out of existence or joined to adjacent quarters. The proud patricians gnashed their teeth at such unheard-of innovations. They had suffered a double loss by the abolition of serfdom and of the old laws regarding the Jewish inhabitants ; but for the time they had to acquiesce.

The northern Hanse Towns, where German guild-narrowness joined to ossified Lutheranism scarcely allowed the Jews to breathe, were compelled by order of the French garrison to grant them equality. Hamburg agreed to place all its inhabitants, including Jews, upon an equal level (1811), and also admitted them to seats in the civic council. The following testimony was afterwards adduced in their favor —

"With all the privileges of equality received, or guaranteed, their much-feared presumption did not obtrude itself, nor had any disadvantages accrued to the Christian citizens ; on the contrary, the Jews displayed a quiet, modest, and friendly demeanor in spite of additional prerogatives, and showed eagerness to work for the public weal. Several gained distinction by their great benevolence and patriotism."

The small town of Lübeck showed more opposition to the settlement and emancipation of a few Jews under French protection. Hitherto only about ten families were tolerated in the town as "protection Jews," who were forbidden to engage in trade, join the guilds, or obtain possession of houses. These privileges were regarded as exclusively Christian ; no Jews dared claim them. Only three Jews were allowed to come daily into Lübeck from the neighboring town of Moisling (under the dominion of Denmark or Holstein), and these were compelled to pay a sort of poll-tax at the gate. Any deputy of the merchants' guild could lay hands upon them, and take them before the police, if they sold goods, and everything found in the possession of such suspects was confiscated. With the advent of the French (1811-1814), about forty-two Jews from Moisling and fourteen foreigners with their families moved to Lübeck, thus bringing the number of families in Lübeck up to sixty-six. These sixty-six Jews aroused the fierce rage of the Lübeck patricians even more than Napoleon's sovereignty. The embargo laid by Napoleon upon the Continent to annoy England had attracted several Jewish families to North Germany, hitherto unfriendly to Jews.

In the Hanse Town of Bremen, which until then had known only traveling Jews, who paid toll on entering the town, Jews took up residence under French protection, not indeed in great numbers, but too many for the bigotry of the patricians. Here, too, they were allowed equal rights with other citizens. Even the Duke of Mecklenburg, Frederick Franz, granted the equalization of the Jews (February 22, 1812), and allowed marriages between Jews and Christians, a greater concession than those made by any other code. Prussia also could no longer resist the tide in favor of the Jews. In Prussia they had displayed much greater love for their native land, and brought more sacrifices during the times of trouble than many of the corrupt nobility, who had ingratiated themselves with their victorious enemies. But a long time elapsed before King Frederick William III could overcome his aristocratic and religious repugnance to them. He only abolished the insulting cognomen of "protection Jews," declaring them not only admissible to the citizenship of towns, but under compulsion to perform its duties. They were forced to take the oath as citizens of towns and to share in the burdens of the cities in which they lived. But they were not to be recognized as state citizens, their position being the reverse of that of the Jews in Baden. The prospect of equalization as state citizens was continually held out to them, but the promise remained unfulfilled for several years. When Hardenberg again assumed control of the disturbed affairs of the state, and insisted upon the repeal of decayed laws and the removal of rotten conditions, he favored the removal of the civil disabilities of the Jews, so that by their help new strength should be infused into the mutilated, bleeding, impoverished territory,—help which it could ill spare in its wretched state of deep depression. David

Friedländer and his friends, Berlin capitalists, used their utmost efforts to bring about the state equalization so long promised.   The king again and again delayed the ratification of the law submitted to him by the chancellor.   At length—moved, it is said, by the interest taken by the Berlin Jews in commemorating the death of the much-suffering, lamented Queen Louise,—Frederick William gave his assent (March 11, 1812) to the equalization of all Jews at that time settled in Prussia.   They were to be admitted to posts in schools and colleges ; but the king withheld the privilege of admission to state offices.   With the privileges, they were to assume the duties, especially as soldiers.   Their religious affairs were to be regulated afterwards : " When the plan for their religious organization is drawn up, such Jews as enjoy public confidence both on account of their knowledge and probity will be consulted."

Three German princes alone withstood the spirit of the age : those of Bavaria, Austria, and Saxony. The first, Maximilian Joseph, appointed king of Bavaria by Napoleon, promulgated an edict (June 10, 1813), which appeared to concede equality to Jews, at least to those who possessed the right of settlement.   But it was equality with many limitations.   In cities to which no Jew had hitherto been admitted, their settlement was to depend upon the royal pleasure, and even in those places where they had dwelt for a long time their numbers were not to be increased, but rather diminished.   In Austria, Leopold II and Francis I, the successors of Emperor Joseph, who had somewhat loosened the chains of the Jews, left the favorable intentions of their predecessor unexecuted, and imposed new humiliations. In addition to the unendurable burden of taxes in Bohemia, Moravia, Silesia, and Galicia,—taxes upon candles, upon wine, and meat—a collection-tax was imposed in Vienna, which was a toll upon every Jew who entered the capital.   Spies closely watched the Jew who stayed in Vienna for a short time unprovided with a passport, and treated him like a criminal. Marriages among Jews were still restricted, and could be contracted only by the eldest son of the family, or by one able to pay heavy bribes. Although Austria was so often overrun by the soldiers of liberty, yet, impenetrable as the wall of China, it resisted every innovation. In the newly-created kingdom of Saxony all the restrictions imposed in the time of the Electoral princes and the Lutheran Church were maintained in their fullest rigor. Saxony was rightly called the Protestant Spain of the Jews. Indeed they were not suffered to dwell in the country at all; only a few privileged Jews were admitted to the two towns of Dresden and Leipsic, but under the express condition that they could be expelled at any time. They were not allowed to have a synagogue, but only to meet for prayer in small rooms, on condition that they made no noise. In Leipsic and Dresden every privileged Jew was compelled to pay annually seventy thalers for himself, besides other sums for his wife, children, and servants. The Jews were rigidly constrained in their choice of trades and occupations, and were placed under strict supervision while traveling. When all other German districts had abolished the poll-tax, Saxony still retained it. The example of the two neighboring countries—Westphalia and Prussia—had no influence upon this district, which at that time was rendered doubly selfish by trade jealousy and religious prejudice. The reactionary movement found plenty of fuel in Germany.

CHAPTER XIII.

THE REACTION AND TEUTOMANIA.

The Jews in the Wars for Freedom—The Congress of Vienna—Hardenberg and Metternich—Rühs' Christian Germanism—Jew-hatred in Germany and Rome—German Act of Federation—Ewald's Defense of Judaism—Jew-hatred in Prussia—Lewis Way—Congress at Aix—Hep-hep Persecution—Hartwig Hundt—Julius von Voss—Jewish Avengers.

1813—1818 C. E.

LIKE the Persian monarch Xerxes, Napoleon, nitherto invincible, and grown haughty and brutal through his successes, summoned the nations and princes to a universal war, and they followed him as submissively as slaves follow their master. Proudly he led forth Europe, subdued by him, against Asiatic Russia. Within the memory of man such an immense expedition had not been known. But, if ever, the words of the text were fulfilled in this gigantic contest: "An horse is a vain thing for safety, neither shall he deliver any by his great strength"; if ever, Divine justice manifested itself in him who had trampled upon right and liberty. Napoleon was defeated, not by the power of his enemy, but by a Higher Hand which struck him with blindness—a blindness which permitted the glow of the flames at Moscow and the ice of a Russian winter to work his ruin. When God and fortune had forsaken him, the princes who had promised him service and allegiance fell away from him, and turned the points of their swords against him, and the people, which, relying upon his own warlike talents, he had so greatly despised, rose up against him. But the nations likewise were stricken with blindness; whilst breaking asunder one sort of bonds, they forged new ones for themselves. The two years (May, 1812—April, 1814) form an instructive chapter in history, from the moment when Napoleon led an army of more than half a million men against Russia, until the day when, abandoned by all, he was compelled to flee, in order to escape the threats and insults of the embittered French people. It was a sanguinary, horrifying drama.

No one could have suspected that the greater would drag down the less in its ruin, that by the downfall of Napoleon, the Jews whom he had liberated, though reluctantly, would be hurled into their former slavery. Jewish youths belonging to wealthy families had emulated their Christian friends in courage, and rushed to battle to help in slaying the giant. Large numbers of Jews, especially in Prussia, animated by burning love of country, had joined the volunteers, had rejoiced to be accepted in the ranks, and wipe away with their blood on the battlefield the stain of cowardice, so often imputed to them by the opponents to their emancipation. Jewish young men paid for the freedom accorded them on paper with their lives. Jewish physicians and surgeons sacrificed themselves in the camps and hospitals in their devoted attendance on the wounded and the plague-stricken. Jewish women and girls spared no efforts to bring help and comfort to the wounded. Again, as in the days of national independence, sons of the same race and religion were opposed to each other—German Jews engaged in deadly combat with French, Italian, and Dutch Jews, and recognized each other only in the last hour, in time to embrace as brothers. Those unfit to bear arms had shown their attachment to Germany and their worthiness of emancipation by sacrifices in other ways. Nevertheless, the seemingly forgotten Jew-hatred was rekindled in the hearts of the Germans, extended ever further, and robbed the Jews of the reward which the hard-won victories had promised to bring even to them.

With the fall of the hero began the rule of petty, intriguing, reckless speculators, who bartered both men and lands.   They misled the princes who earnestly desired to restore long banished freedom, and ensnared them with lying artifices.   In France these intriguers, the Talleyrands, reinstated the throne of the Bourbons.   In Germany Metternich and Gentz turned the struggles for freedom into mockery.   Only the more far-sighted knew that Europe, owing to the closer connection between the rulers, would be reduced to a more degrading state of slavery, because sloth and pettiness were the order of the day.

The Jews felt the first effects of the reaction now commencing in Germany.   It arose in Frankfort, the seat of unmitigated, mediæval anti-Semitism. As soon as the artillery of the retreating enemy had ceased within the precincts of this city, loud voices were heard encouraging each other to demand that boundaries be set at once to the unheard-of presumption of the Jews.   In Lübeck and Bremen, the citizens did not content themselves with depriving the Jews of their recently-acquired rights, but energetically strove to banish them altogether.   The proposal was seriously made to drive all adherents of the Mosaic religion from the town.   In Hanover, Hildesheim, Brunswick, and Hesse, they were at one blow divested of their rights of equality.   These events naturally gave great anxiety to the Jews throughout Germany.   If the privileges granted them by law, as in Frankfort, could be abolished, what security had they for the continuance of their equality?   What a contrast this reaction presented to that in France ! Here, although the nobility, who hated freedom and were thirsting for revenge, and the Catholic clergy were in power at the court of Louis XVIII, and looked upon the terrible events since 1789 as if they had not happened, yet the rights of the Jews were not abridged.

The Jews, concerned about their freedom, honor, nay, their very existence, especially in the so-called free towns, looked hopefully forward to the Congress of Vienna, which was to readjust dismembered Europe.   The monarchical and diplomatic members of the Congress, however, did not hasten to act the part of Providence assigned to them.   They opened the meetings in November instead of in August, and from the bosom of this Congress, intended to establish eternal peace, a desolating war arose. The community of Frankfort had sent two deputies to Vienna, one of them Jacob Baruch, the father of Börne, chosen because he had patrons at the Viennese court.   Baruch fulfilled his task in a disinterested manner worthy of his great son.   Together with his less known colleague, he presented a memorial (October, 1814) to the Congress, wherein the arguments in favor of the claim of the Frankfort Jews were clearly set forth.   They made the formal claim, that their equalization had been duly purchased for a large sum, and the patriotic claim, that they had taken part in the liberation of Germany.   Their chief aim was to remove the suzerainty of the Senate over them.

The Jews of the three Hanse Towns sent a Christian lawyer as deputy, to guard their interests in Vienna, who of his own accord had drawn up an appeal for the equalization of the Jews.   In combination with the deputies, certain influential personages worked quietly and unobtrusively.   The banking-house of Rothschild by its circumspection and fortunate enterprises had made itself a power in the money world ; and not even prying suspicion could find a trace of dishonesty in the accumulation of its riches, which might be used as a pretext by anti-Jewish opponents.   The founder of the house,

Mayer Amschel Rothschild, was held in the highest esteem in Frankfort, and in consequence of the equalization had a seat in the Electoral College. Happily he died before the beginning of the reaction (September, 1812), but his five sons increased the wealth left by their father. Although they appear to have adhered to the principle, not to throw the power of their riches into the scale on behalf of their co-religionists and their faith, yet they could not be indifferent to the attempt made in Frankfort, their home, to reduce the Jews again to a state of serfdom. One of the brothers probably addressed words of remonstrance to the most influential German members of the Congress against diminishing the rights of his co-religionists.

The statesmen who controlled German affairs in the Congress showed themselves favorable to the Jews. Hardenberg and Metternich in a letter on the subject expressed their disapproval of the oppressions to which the Jews in the Hanse Towns were subjected (January, 1815), and advised the Senate—advice which amounted to a command—to treat them in a humane, just spirit. Hardenberg pointed out to the Hanse Towns the example of Prussia and the edict of March 11, 1812, and remarked, with some sarcasm, that they would succeed in depriving the Jewish houses of the prosperity to which they had attained, and that constant oppression would compel them to withdraw their capital. In the sketch of the constitution for Germany drawn up by the Prussian plenipotentiary, William von Humboldt, which was submitted to Metternich, and accepted as a basis for discussion, the Jews were promised equality, even though they were mentioned separately. "The three Christian religious sects enjoy equal rights in all German states, and the adherents of the Jewish faith, so long as they undertake all the duties of citizenship, are to enjoy corresponding rights." But the goodwill of the two chancellors, even though their sentiments had been shared by the monarchs whom they represented, did not suffice at that time. A new enemy rose up against the Jews, tougher and more dangerous than envy and bourgeois pride. This terrible enemy who now turned his arms against the Jews was the German visionary. The yoke so long imposed on the Germans by the French, the compulsion under which they had been to obliterate their most characteristic peculiarities, had rendered hateful to them, not alone everything French, but all that was foreign, that did not bear the stamp of pure German origin. Allowances should certainly be made for a nation which, arriving at a consciousness of its strength and solidarity, breaks its fetters, if it conceives an exaggerated notion of its importance. But it was unpardonable and childish that grown men should dream in broad daylight, representing their dreams as truth and trying to foist them upon others. Extravagant Teutomania was a dream of this kind, and resulted in the ruin of the Germans. For the first time the German nation had acted as a unit; hitherto it had been the tool of princes in Italian expeditions, Turkish wars, or civil strife. The Germans sought analogous cases in their own history by which to regulate their conduct, and found them only in the Middle Ages, in the time of the Empire and the omnipotence of the papacy, or in early Teutonic times when uncouth barbarism and childish simplicity prevailed. The romantic school, the Schlegels, Arnims, and Brentanos, had shown them this grewsome specter of the Middle Ages in so wonderful a light, that the Germans in their delusion considered it an ideal, the realization of which was a holy task. To the Middle Ages belonged Christianity, credulity, unthinking clericalism, which became the dearest possessions of the Germans, because they were diametrically opposed to the unbelief of the French and the revolutionary epoch. From that time the hollow phrase, Christian-German (or Teutsch), arose, and speedily became a catchword.

But only the devoted followers of Catholicism, with the papacy as supreme authority, could be pious in the sense of the Middle Ages. Honest roman-ticists, such as Görres, Frederick Schlegel, Adam Müller, etc., logically went over to the Roman Church, and helped to re-establish the empire of the Jesuits and the Inquisition. As for the German Protestants, "God had poured out upon them the spirit of confusion and they tottered like drunken men." Instead of directing their attention to Vienna, where the Congress, amidst dancing and revelry, was running its quarry, the German people, to earth, the romanticists built castles in the air, and at once announced that certain people would be denied admission.

Christian Teutomania was the armed specter which for many decades robbed the German Jews of rest, honor, and joy in life. Because this race, strongly marked by descent and tradition, was dis-tinguished from the Germans by external marks, by features, carriage, and vivacity, although akin in language, feeling, and temperament, they were re-pelled as foreigners, as a force breeding disturbance and discomfort, and had the spirit of the times per-mitted they would have been expelled from German territory. But to find a reason for this blind hate, the enemies of the Jews had recourse to old con-temptible publications, and extracted rubbish from sources where others had found the rich intellectual treasures of the Jews, and drew such a portrait of them as to arouse terror both in themselves and others.

The first to clothe vague prejudice in words and heap abuse upon the Jews was not a knavish writer, but an academical professor named Friedrich Rühs, whom the newly-founded Berlin University had ap-pointed to the chair of history. He wished to investigate the decline of Germany, and hit upon the Jews, as though they had been the authors of Germany's disgrace during its occupation by foreign powers. Rühs discussed the "Claims of the Jews to German Citizenship," developed the unwholesome theory of a Christian state, and thence derived his justification, if not actually to expel the Jews from Germany, yet to humble them and thwart their growth. He drew up a complete programme for their treatment, which was afterwards conscientiously carried out.

Above all things he wanted the Jews to live merely on sufferance, and on no account to claim equal rights of citizenship. They were once more to pay protection-money, a Jew-tax, and limits were to be set to their increase. The cities which had hitherto not tolerated them were to be supported in this course, and naturally Jews were not to be admitted to any office, nor even permitted to defend their country. Rühs, moreover, insisted that the Jews should again wear a badge, not a repulsive yellow patch, but a "national cockade"; at any rate some mark of distinction, "that the German who could not recognize his Hebrew enemy by face, gait, or speech, might do so by the doubtful badge of honor." Above all things, Rühs exhorted the German states and the German people to promote the conversion of the Jews to Christianity ; that was most important. It was generally asserted, even in Christian quarters, that only bad and abandoned men exchanged Judaism for Christianity ; but that was prejudice.

Rühs' pamphlet excited great interest. Worthy and learned men declared their agreement with him. The learned German world at the time of Lessing, Abt, Kant, and Herder, the apostolic messenger of universal humanity, now talked the language of the Church Fathers, and stirred up hate and persecution. Schleiermacher and Fichte brought the representatives of German intellect so low that they actually competed with the ultra-Catholics in

hatred of the Jews. Pius VII, who in consequence
of the Restoration once more reigned in the Papal
States, and reintroduced the Inquisition, in order to
drive out godlessness by means of the auto-da-fé,
ordained that the Jews should forfeit the freedom
enjoyed under French rule. The Jews of Rome had
to forsake their beautiful houses in all parts of the
city and return to the dirty, unhealthy Ghetto ; the
Middle Ages had returned to the Papal States. The
Jews, as in the seventeenth century, had to attend
sermons for their own conversion on pain of punishment. Meantime history had enacted one of those
surprising interludes, which was to prove the insta-
bility of the reactionary Restoration. Napoleon had
contrived to land on French ground despite English
sea-guardianship. The props of the Bourbon throne
—the nobility, the clergy, and intriguers, who had
ostentatiously displayed their power,—collapsed
before a single shot had been fired, and Napoleon
entered Paris in triumph. The empire of the hundred
days was established. The whole of Europe armed
itself against one man, and the fortune of war decided
in favor of the allies on the Dutch battlefields at
Waterloo. In the Prussian army, which next to the
English had been most instrumental in turning the
tide of victory, there were many Jewish soldiers,
among them several militia officers.

What reward did the German Jews receive for
their sincere devotion to their country ? When the
Congress, alarmed by Napoleon's sudden reappearance, ceased to daily and began to hold regular
sittings, the Act of Federation for the German
states, which despite their union were to be auto-
nomous, was brought up for consideration, and a
paragraph in it devoted to the Jews. Citizenship
was to be assured them, and in countries where
obstacles to this reform existed, they were to be
removed as far as possible. But this paragraph
was accepted only by Prussia and Austria ; all the

other members of the league, especially those from the free towns, voted against it. To arrive at an agreement, a colorless compromise was proposed: "The Congress of the allies will consider how the civil improvement of those professing the Jewish faith in Germany is to be effected in the most harmonious manner, and how in particular the enjoyment of civil rights and participation in civil duties may be secured to them. The rights already conceded them in the several federated states will be continued."

The first portion was harmless, and could be accepted by all, since it remained open to every state to prevent its favorable interpretation. The latter portion, however, was apt to put the Free Towns into a delicate position. There the Jews through French influence were actually in possession of civil equality. Accordingly, the deputy for Frankfort (the syndic Danz) emphatically protested, and was supported by the Saxon deputies. To shame German narrow-mindedness, the Danish government, as if it had anticipated that the hatred of Jews in Germany would spread, ordered Bernstorff, its representative for Holstein, to declare that the adherents of the Jewish faith, if they fulfilled the duties of citizenship, might there expect a constitutional provision ensuring them against persecution, oppression, arbitrariness or uncertainty of legislation in respect of the rights conceded to them. The deputy for Bremen, Senator Schmidt, was cleverer; he did not protest, but defeated the suspicious resolution by a master-stroke. Remarking that the privileges of the Jews conferred by the French in North Germany (the 32d military division) could not be binding on the Germans, he stated that they need only change the word *in* into *by*, and everything would be right. Nobody at first took notice of this apparently insignificant change. Metternich and Hardenberg, who hitherto either from inclination or in pursuance of promises had appeared to favor the Jews, passed over this point in an incomprehensible manner. Thus the paragraph referring to the Jewish question in its final form read: "The rights already conceded the professors of the Jewish faith *by* the several federated states will be continued." Of the federated states, however, only Prussia and Mecklenburg, and perhaps also Baden, had conceded citizenship to the Jews. The enactment of the French authorities was thus made null and void, and Germany was saved. What did it matter to the delighted nation that this verbal change would cost so many tears?

The humiliation of the Jews soon showed itself in practical life. Lübeck, protected by the unfair interpretation of a paragraph, ordered more than forty Jewish families to leave the town (September, 1815). Bremen did the same with its Jews. Frankfort could not eject its Jewish inhabitants, but their lives were embittered; they were shut out from civil assemblies, Jewish functionaries were deposed, they were excluded from many trades and industries, marriage permits asked by Jewish couples were refused with the heartlessness of the Middle Ages, they were forbidden to live in certain parts of the town, and were treated as though they were still *servi cameræ*. But as the Senate knew that Prussia and Austria regarded it as a point of honor to preserve intact the civil rights of the Jews of Frankfort, and that the Federal Diet, at the instance of both great powers, might easily determine the controversy in favor of the Jews, it applied to three German juridical faculties, those of Berlin, Marburg, and Giessen, to have the question decided as one of law.

This struggle between the Frankfort Senate and the Jews, protracted during nine years (1815-24), and occasioning many vexations, will ever remain a stain on the time, a monument of German narrow-mindedness.   The Jews, relying on the assurance of the two German powers, believed that their civil rights were guarded as by a triple wall.

But just this manifest truth, the Teutomaniacs and sophists, suddenly developed into bigots, sought to obscure and cry down.   From all parts of Germany there resounded simultaneously outcries against the Jews, urging the nation, or the German federation, to enslave the Jews or destroy them.   Journals and pamphlets raged against them, as if Germany or Christendom could be saved only by the destruction of the Jews.

The most violent attack was that of a physician and professor of natural science at Heidelberg, J. F. Fries, "Danger to the Welfare and Character of the Germans through the Jews" (summer, 1816), in which he asserted that the Jews ought to be expelled the country, that the tribe must be exterminated root and branch, as among all secret and political societies they were most dangerous to the state.   "Ask man after man, and see, whether every peasant and every burgher do not hate and curse the Jews as national pests and bread robbers." The Jews, he said, had contrived to get more than half the entire capital of Frankfort into their hands. "Let them go on for forty years, and the sons of the first Christian houses will seek service among the Jews in the meanest capacities."   It is remarkable that in the face of such passionate incitement, wild outbreaks against the Jews did not occur at that time, especially as Fries' pamphlet was read in all taverns and public-houses.

Was no Christian voice raised against this injustice?   For the honor of the Germans it must be mentioned that some men had the courage to contend against crass prejudice and blind hatred.   A highly respected and learned councilor in Ratisbon, August Krämer, wrote a defense, "The Jews and their Just Claims on the Christian States; a Contribution to the Mitigation of the Cruel Prejudices against the Jewish Nation." Councilor Schmidt, in Hildburghausen, on the one hand, pictured the abominable scenes which Christian fanaticism had in the past enacted against Jews, and, on the other hand, showed the superiority of culture possessed by the latter over the Christians in Spain. But their most thorough-going advocate was Johann Ludwig Ewald, a reformed clergyman of Carlsruhe, of high position, and seventy years old. Rühs' and Fries' malignant statements about the Jews incensed him so deeply, that he denied himself a season's recreation in Baden, and employed the time in giving the lie to their impudent assertions in a pamphlet (1816). Ewald vindicated the downtrodden sons of Israel in the name of Christianity, whose representative he was. Every groundless complaint against them he dissolved into nothing. From England and France, too, admonitions reached the Germans not to expose their own pettiness by their insane hatred of the Jews. An English paper thought that the town of Lübeck, as well as all the free towns, ought to be deprived of their independence (of which they had made so infamous a use) by the German federation, on account of the ignorant intolerance displayed against the Jews. A French writer, M. Bail, vindicated the unhappy people in glowing language, and covered their German enemies with shame.

"The Jewish nation to a higher degree than any other possesses the ancient, sanctified character which excites astonishment. I never meet a rabbi adorned with a white beard without thinking of the venerable patriarchs. Nothing is more elevating about the Israelites than their solemn life, which makes them the most devoted and honorable people on earth. In their midst is to be found the illustration of all domestic virtues, of loving care for the needy, and profound reverence for parents. Happy, a thousand times happy, are the nations among whom the basis of morality has been preserved."

But if truth and justice had spoken with angels' tongues, the Germans of those days would have remained deaf to their voices. They were so deeply imbued with hatred of the Jews that they were irrational.

An organ of the Austrian government directed a sort of threat against the encroachments of the people of Lübeck upon the rights of the Jews.

"How can the future Federal Diet discuss the improvement of the condition of the Jews, if individual states anticipate it by the most cruel and arbitrary resolutions? This conduct exhibits want of respect as much towards the ensuing Federal Diet as towards the foremost courts of Germany, whose principles in regard to this matter have been often and loudly enough expressed."

What was done by Austria itself, which displayed such righteous indignation against Lübeck on behalf of the Jews? Francis I and his ruler Metternich completely forgot the benevolent intentions of Joseph II, and kept in mind only the hateful laws of Maria Theresa against the Jews. They did not indeed expel the Jews, as in Lübeck and Bremen, but they were relegated to Ghettos within Austria, beyond which they were not allowed to pass. Tyrol, the secluded mountain province, was closed to them as to Protestants. In Bohemia the mountain cities and villages were forbidden them, and in Moravia, in the great cities of Brünn and Olmütz, they were allowed to stay only over-night or for a short time. Everywhere there were Jew-streets; the restrictions imposed on the Jews of Austria had become proverbial, whilst in Galicia they met with greater oppression than in the Middle Ages. Even the benevolent regulations of Joseph II, in regard to compulsory school attendance and practical religious instruction, were carried out not so much to spread culture among the Jews as to torment and injure them. Emperor Francis ennobled a few Jews, but the others were humiliated; they were obliged to render military service, but the bravest were rarely admitted even to the lowest rungs of the military ladder.

Austria, to be sure, had made the Jews no promises, and had awakened no hope of freedom.   But Prussia, where they had already enjoyed full citizenship, conjured up a hobgoblin worthy of the Middle Ages, and wounded their honor the more deeply.   Frederick William III, who had confirmed the equality of the Prussian Jews by law, annulled it, or rather left it unexecuted, a dead letter.   Unconsciously he succumbed to the theory of the Christian state set up by the Teutomaniacs and sophists, who insisted that no place of honor be conceded the Jews.   The promised equalization of the Jews in the newly-acquired or reconquered provinces was continually delayed.   In the latter they remained subject to the restrictions of a former time, and Prussia's legislation regarding the Jews was a curious petrifaction.   There were twenty-one fundamental laws for their treatment, and they were divided into French, old Prussian, Saxon, and Polish Jews, naturally to their disadvantage.

The specific aim of Prussia was to make Jews despicable in society.   Whereas formerly the government had been at pains to avoid in official correspondence the words Jew, Jewish, as having an offensive connotation, they were now insisted upon.

The Judæophobist spirit in Prussia showed itself in a case which challenges comparison with France. The unjust Napoleonic law which had suspended the equality of the Jews of the German departments for ten years in respect of free migration and commerce was to fall into abeyance after the end of the respite (March 17, 1818), unless it was prolonged. The government of Louis XVIII, although besieged by clerical and political reactionaries, did not for a moment make an attempt to preserve the limitation. In the Chamber, which occupied itself with this point (February and March, 1818), only one hostile voice (Lathier) was raised against the Jews in Alsace.   This opponent of the Jews alleged that the whole country would soon be in the hands of the Jews, if a check was not put to their greed. Not even the Right, which was clerically disposed, uttered a word against the Jews in general and for the restriction of their liberties. The phantom of a Christian state was quite unknown to the French. The Chamber rejected Lathier's proposal, and thus the Jews of Alsace were restored to their former equality. A similar law had been passed against the Jews of the district on the left bank of the Rhine, which was added to Prussia, or the Rhine province and Westphalia. The Prussian government, on taking this former French territory, had permitted the continuance of restrictive legislation, and a cabinet order of March 3d, 1818, renewed it for an indefinite period.

About this time a distinguished Englishman, with the Old and New Testaments in his hand, advocated the equality and freedom of the Jews throughout Europe with extraordinary zeal. Lewis Way, a disciple of the Fifth Monarchy enthusiasts of the English War of Independence, accepted the prophecies of the Old Testament and the Apocalypse, and was convinced that the Jewish nation would be resurrected, and be restored in glory to the land of their fathers. Only when they had recovered their independence would they be converted to the doctrines of Jesus. It was therefore a matter of conscience with him to promote the welfare of the Jews. He made a journey to Poland to ascertain the number and condition of the Jews in that country. Way now elaborated a remarkable memorial in which he dwelt on the high significance of the Jews in the past, and also in the future. With this memorial he betook himself to Aix, where the king of Prussia and the emperors of Russia and Austria with their ministers and diplomatists were met in Congress (end of September, 1818). He sought to make a favorable impression on Emperor Alexander, whose mystical tempera-

ment was known to him. As soon as the Czar
showed himself in favor of the equalization of the
Jews, it could not be doubted that Frederick William
III and Emperor Francis would also be well disposed
towards it.

Way started with the supposition that the Jews
were a royal nation, and had not ceased to be so
even in exile, in the misfortunes of their tragical
career. This people possessed the key to the history
of the whole globe. The same divine grace which
had guided them in former times rested on them in
banishment and exile. The promises which the
prophets had foretold for the Israelite race would
not fail to be accomplished; they would once more
be gathered together in the land of their fathers.
All the nations of the earth which have received
salvation through them, were bound by gratitude to
show the Jews the greatest honors and boundless
beneficence, so as to wipe out the guilt incurred against
this divinely-gifted race by the cruel persecutions inflicted on them. The present moment was highly
favorable to their complete liberation. In some countries fanatical, narrow-minded clamorers had raised
their voices against the emancipatian of the Jews, but
they no more represented public opinion than the furious outcries of a few American planters against the
suppression of slavery. If Way was an enthusiast,
when he tried to prove the necessity of emancipation
in a mystical manner from prophetic and apocalyptic
verses, he was still true enough to the practical
instincts of the English race to be able to prove to
their majesties what profit the emancipated Jews
would bring the state. He conceded that much
about the Jews must be altered, but their national
peculiarity was holy property, which must not be
touched. It was the invisible tie which bound the
past of the Jews with their future, the past of mankind with its future: the fulfillment of prophecy
depended on Israel.

This mystical, yet sensible memorial was handed by Way to the Emperor of Russia, on whom it must have made an impression, for he delivered it to his plenipotentiaries, Nesselrode and Capo D'Istrias, charging them to bring it and the emancipation of the Jews under the notice of the Congress. Out of respect for Alexander, who at that time pulled the strings of European politics, the plenipotentiaries were obliged to give attention to the matter, if only in appearance. The protocol said (November 21, 1818) that, though they could not in every respect accept the point of view of the writer of the memorial, they must render justice to the tendency and laudable aim of his conclusions. The plenipotentiaries of Austria and Prussia (Metternich, Hardenberg, and Bernstorff) declared themselves ready to give any information with regard to the question in both monarchies, which might aid in solving a problem important to the statesman and the philanthropist ; but this was no more than a courtly phrase. Another voice addressed enthusiastic words in favor of the German and Polish Jews to the Congress at Aix-la-Chapelle. Michael Berr, like his father, untiringly active in the elevation of his co-religionists, poured forth the stream of his oratory in their cause.

"In Charlemagne's favorite city the monarchs will finally decide concerning the political existence of my co-religionists in Germany. The honor of Germany, the honor of the age and that of monarchs, loudly demand the reinstatement of the Jews in their civil and political rights. With justice are they exercised about laws, which still exist here and there to the disadvantage of the Jews."

The Italian Jews also combined to send a petition to the Congress of Aix-la-Chapelle concerning the abolition of their grievances and the cessation of persecution. They lost nothing by failure to carry out their design. The time had passed when princes and statesmen, sages and citizens, interested themselves in "the improvement of the condition of the Israelites," as the phrase ran.

The ill-feeling against the Jews in Germany continued to grow without ground or provocation. Jewish preachers celebrated the battle of Leipsic (October 18, 1818) in the synagogue with great enthusiasm, but to the Teutomaniacs this was no proof of their patriotic love. The hatred against Jews assumed so violent a character that a writer, one not badly disposed, saw reason to foretell the outbreak of popular attacks on life and property.

Germany was at that time intensely excited by the murder of Kotzebue, in Mannheim, by a half-mad Christian student, Karl Sand (March, 1819), and by the harsh regulations of the government against demagogic and Germanizing movements, which it had formerly fostered. The Germanizers panted for a sacrifice, and, as they could not attack the statesmen, such as the Metternichs, Gentzes, and Kamptzes, the helpless Jews were marked as victims. A series of brutal outbreaks occurred during several months. With the cry of " Hep, hep !" against the Jews, the Middle Ages revived again like a jeering ghost, and persecution was galvanized into life by the student and commercial classes.

The city of Würzburg commenced the attack. A new professor was inducted into office (August 2) amidst the rejoicings of the students, who were joined by a large number of people. Suddenly an old professor, Brendel, was noticed, who had shortly before written in favor of the Jews, for which it was alleged that he had received a box of ducats. On seeing him, there resounded from the mouths of the students the insane cry, "Hep, hep!" together with the outcry " Jude, verreck," *i. e.*, " Jew, die like a beast." The former expression, then used for the first time, meant in student's slang, " Jerusalem is destroyed" (Hierosolyma est perdita). Brendel was pursued, and had to flee for safety. Perfect fury took possession of the people of Würzburg, who

broke into the shops of the Jews, throwing the
goods into the streets, and when they defended
themselves with stones, the bitterness increased to
frenzy.   A regular battle ensued, many wounds
were received, and several persons killed.   About
forty citizens took part in the affray.   The military
had to be called out, or the Jews would have been
massacred.   The next day the burghers appealed
to the civic authorities to order the dismissal of the
Jews from Würzburg, and to this they had to submit.   Overcome with grief, about four hundred
Jews of all ages left the town, and encamped for
several days in the villages or under tents, looking
forward to a terrible future.   The persecution of the
Jews in Würzburg was repeated in Bamberg, and
in almost every town of Franconia.   Wherever a
Jew showed himself, he was assailed with the insulting cry of "Hep, hep!" and ill-treated.

This persecution of the Jews in Franconia was a
hint to the Frankforters how to humble their hated
fellow-citizens, who had dared bring an action
against the Senate, and were protected by the
Federal Diet.   Thus a riot was re-enacted here
(9th and 10th August), which began with the cry,
"Hep, hep!" and with the breaking of windows in
Jewish houses ; then the mob advanced to brutality,
and drove away all Jews from the promenades with
insults and outrage.   Artisans, workmen, shop
assistants, secretly encouraged by their employers,
as in the time of Vincent Fettmilch, two centuries
before, made violent attacks on Jewish houses.
The house of the Rothschilds in particular was
selected for attack, their wealth and political importance being a thorn in the side of Christian patricians.   In Paris at this time, all the ambassadors
and diplomatic representatives appeared at a ball
given by James Rothschild, and in Germany the
Rothschilds were still treated as peddlers.   Several
wealthy Jews left Frankfort after this outrage.   The

storm, which became frenzy in Frankfort, the seat
of the Diet, was not an indifferent matter to the
ambassadors. The moneys of the Diet were placed
in Rothschild's coffers for security. The president,
Count von Buol Schauenstein, summoned a conference of members, and it was resolved to call out
the federal troops, as the city militia could not be
trusted. The persecution of the Jews in Frankfort
aroused great attention throughout Europe, but the
excitement against them continued, in spite of the
arrival of the troops. Several Jews consequently
sold their houses, and even the Rothschilds put no
trust in the lull, and had serious thoughts of leaving
Frankfort; they would have had to emigrate to
France or England, as they were not safe anywhere
in Germany.

This massacre of the Jews spread like wildfire in
Germany, as if the people had everywhere waited
for a sign to break out. In Darmstadt and Bay-
reuth the riots were repeated (August 12). The
few Jews in Meiningen were expelled. In Carlsruhe, one morning, a placard was found posted on
the synagogue and the houses of prominent Jews—
"Death and destruction to the Jews!"

In Düsseldorf black marks and threatening pla-
cards were found on the doors of several Jewish
houses. In the territory of Baden, where Sand had
sealed the Teutomaniac folly with a murder, and
the excitement still lasted, the bitterness against
the Jews was so great that not one could appear in
the streets without being maltreated. In Heidelberg a tumult arose (beginning of September) in
consequence of a vulgar scene, which curiously illus-
trates German chivalry. A citizen had outraged a
Jewish maiden, and had been arrested by the police.
Nearly the whole populace immediately rushed to
rescue the hero and destroy the Jewish houses.
Cries of "Hep, hep!" resounded in the streets;
axes, crowbars, tools of all sorts were collected as

if to carry a place by storm.   The city guard, which ought to have dispersed the assaulting party, refused their services.   The city governor, Pfizer, instead of standing by the persecuted, assisted their assailants.   Blood would have been spilled, had not the Heidelberg students, humanized, perhaps, by contact with France, defended the unprotected people at their own risk, under the leadership of two professors, Daub and Thibaut.   When at length the armed force appeared, and patrols swept through the whole province of Baden, and every small town and village was made responsible for the attacks of certain of their number upon the Jews, the outbreaks against the Jews gradually subsided, but the hatred against them was only intensified.

"From Germany the spark of Jew-hatred flew even into the capital of the Danish state," which a few years before had extended citizenship to the Jews, and had refused to revoke it.   In Copenhagen the mob rose up (September), and commenced by throwing stones at the Jews, and ended with acts of violence.   The government proclaimed martial law.   The citizens, in the few cities where Jews lived, stood by them, and the preachers preached tolerance and love to them from the pulpit.   In Germany the ministers of religion did not utter a single protest during these outrageous scenes. That no feature of the persecution of the Jews of the Middle Ages might be wanting, a synagogue was stormed in a small Bavarian place, and the scrolls of the Law rudely torn to pieces.   Even where actual violence could not be resorted to, the insulting cry of " Hep, hep!" was hurled at the Jews in small and large towns, to the amusement of the spectators.   The police or military force which appeared against the rioters and disturbers secretly took part against the Jews, and the governments which protected them did so more from fear, because they suspected a demagogical movement behind the outbreaks against the Jews. Reference was afterwards made to these outrages, as illustrating the feeling, or rather ill-feeling towards the Jews, to withhold equal rights from them.

The zenith of Teutomaniac Jew hatred was reached by the inflammatory pamphlet which appeared at this time of excitemen , "The Mirror of the Jews" (November, 1819). Hartwig Hundt, a man of adventurous life, boldly advocated the slaughter of the Jews. He made most laudable propositions, which, he flattered himself, would satisfy the "Hep, hep" people.

"Although I for my part hold the killing of Jews neither a sin nor a crime, but only a police offence, I would nevertheless never counsel that they be condemned and punished unheard, as seems to be the fashion now."

What then ? His proposals were :—

"Let the children of Israel be sold to the English, who could employ them in their Indian plantations instead of the blacks. That they may not increase, the men should be emasculated, and their wives and daughters be lodged in houses of shame. The best plan would be to purge the land entirely of this vermin, either by exterminating them, or as Pharaoh and the people of Meiningen, Würzburg, and Frankfort did, by driving them from the country."

The "Hep, hep" storm and Hundt's murderous lessons were the poisonous fruit of the seeds which Fichte and Schleiermacher had sown, and which had shot up quickly and abundantly.

Hundt's inflammatory book, in which every word is an abomination, was as ravenously swallowed by the German reading public, as his bad novels. Only at the request of Jews it was forbidden and confiscated by the censorship, which had become omnipotent through the Carlsbad regulations. In Portugal, at about the same time, a motion was brought forward in the Cortes to re-admit the banished Jews and atone for the crime perpetrated against them, whilst in Germany authors and statesmen justified this crime, and wished it to be repeated in the nineteenth century. Hundt did not stand

alone in his advocacy of the extirpation of the Jews.
Who cares to enumerate all the virulent, hostile
writings against the Jews of the years of the "Hep,
hep" storm? Conversation on questions of the
day, however remote from the subject of the Jews,
always ended in abuse of them. If an author glorified Sand and his murder of Kotzebue, and praised
his Christian religious spirit, he did not fail to add
that "Christian hate would call down a day of judgment upon the Jews, the accomplices of financiers
who worked the ruin of the state, even though no
writer had ever printed a syllable to the disadvantage of the Jews."

Thus every man's hand was against them; no
defender of any weight or influence appeared for
them, whose word, if it could not silence, might at
least curb the opposition. The aged Jean Paul
(Friedrich Richter) did not raise his voice for them,
although he had a predilection for the Jews; nor
Varnhagen von Ense, although Rachel was his wife,
and was included in the general obloquy. Only one
writer overcame his prejudice, and defied public
opinion in order to take up cudgels on behalf of the
universally despised and downtrodden Jews. This
was the comedy writer Julius von Voss, whose voice
certainly had no great weight, and whose disordered
affairs roused the suspicion that Jewish liberality
encouraged his venturesomeness. Voss himself in
his comedies and novels had exposed the Jews to
ridicule, but from regret and remorse, he confessed,
he desired to protect the Jews against the "Hep,
hep" insults. His words were little regarded, and
even were derided. Still less impression was created
by the anonymous writings of various freemasons in
favor of the Jews, but their goodwill should be recognized. The converted Jews conducted themselves at this juncture in a shameful manner. Not
one of them, except Börne, came forward, in behalf
of their former brethren, with that just indignation

which violence against the defenseless ought to
inspire.   Rachel von Varnhagen, it is true, wrote
to her brother, Ludwig Robert, who had been a
witness of the "Hep, hep" storm, in the following
manner:—

> "I am intensely moved, as I have never yet been, on account of the
> Jews. They are to be preserved, but only for torture, for contumely,
> for insult, for brutal outrage. The hypocritical newborn love for the
> Christian religion (God forgive me for my sin!), for the Middle Ages
> with their art, poetry, and hideousness, incites the people to the only
> abomination to which, mindful of all past experiences, it can still be
> incited.   It is not the action of the people, who are taught to cry
> "Hep, hep." The professors Fries and Rühs, and others, such as
> Arnim, Brentano, ' our connections,' and yet greater persons are
> filled with prejudices."

She thought that the Christian priests ought to step
forward to check the outrages of the people. " Aye,
the priests."   But neither Rachel, nor her brother
Robert, nor her husband Varnhagen, who elaborated their periods for every childish folly, and had a
voice in public opinion, raised it against violence,
and against the rule of oppression.

The Jews had, it is true, their own literary exponents to protect them.   In Germany alone there
were nearly forty Jewish writers who could address
the German public.   They possessed two Jewish
organs, and the daily journals occasionally opened
their pages to them.   They advanced boldly to the
battle-field to ward off the universal accusations
against their race.   Even the aged David Friedländer raised his voice, wrung his hands over the
enemies of the Jews and their persecutions in Germany in the nineteenth century, and could not conceive—he who considered official Christianity and
the State as ideal—how these gods could wallow in
so much filth.   He addressed himself to the Countess Von der Recke, and reminded her of the time
when eminent Christians conversed pleasantly with
Jews, and both received instruction from each other.
This sounded like a forgotten fairy tale from
ancient days.   But the Jewish combatants only

threw light missiles, and could scarcely prick the
thick hide of prejudice. For this purpose sharp and
heavy harpoons were necessary. At this point the
Guide of all history, who had not abandoned the
Jews, awakened for them two avenging angels, who
with fiery scourges lashed the perverseness of the
Germans. These avenging spirits, who brought
the Germans more blessings even than their guardian angels, were Ludwig Börne and Heinrich
Heine.

CHAPTER XIV.

BÖRNE AND HEINE.

Börne and Heine—Börne's Youth—His Attitude to Judaism—His Love of Liberty—His Defense of the Jews—Heine : his Position with Regard to Judaism—The Rabbi of Bacharach—Heine's Thoughts upon Judaism—Influence of Börne and Heine.

1819—1830 C. E.

WHY should not Börne and Heine have a page in Jewish history? Not only did Jewish blood flow in their veins, but they were imbued with true Jewish spirit.

The lightning darts which they flashed across Germany, now in the colors of the rainbow, again in glaring sheets, were charged with the electricity of Jewish Talmudism. Both Börne and Heine renounced Judaism, but only like combatants who, appropriating the enemy's uniform and colors, can all the more easily strike and annihilate him. Both expressed, with a clearness which left nothing to be desired, how much they cared for the religion of the cross, which they professed. There is, therefore, not the slightest reason why Christianity should count Börne and Heine as members of its flock on account of the idle ceremony through which they passed in church. One of them, in spite of his changing moods, at heart remained truer to Judaism than the Friedländers who constituted themselves its representatives. These two gifted individuals, the pride of Germany, are still greater ornaments to Judaism. To these two Jews, the Germans owe their pure taste, their feeling for truth, and their impulse for liberty—to these two Jews persecuted through life by the abominable " Hep, hep." The mists of the Middle Ages, with which the Germans artificially surrounded themselves in order to obscure the truth, were dispersed by the flashes of wit of Börne and Heine, and light in its purity was restored.   They grafted wit and life on German literature, and banished that clumsiness and awkwardness which had aroused the ridicule of the neighboring nations.

In their childish spite against the Jews, the Teutomaniacs, the Rühses and Hundts, asserted that Judaism could not produce a man of forcible character, or gifted with a true sense of art.   History at once gave them the lie, and put them to shame.   Judaism furnished forth a vigorous apostle of liberty, with language recalling that of the prophets and the Roman Catos, who confounded all the ideas of the Germans concerning law ; and it supplied a poet, with artistic sense characterized by a mixture of pathos and cutting irony, who abolished all their hard and fast rules of art.   The rich, varied blossoms of the Börne-Heine mind sprang from Jewish soil, and were only watered by European culture.   Hence the close connection between them in spite of their dissimilarity and mutual antipathy.   Not only was their wit Jewish, but also their love of truth, their aversion to vain display, their hatred of veiling and palliating wrongs, their contempt for official pomp, for obscuring clouds of incense, for ringing of bells, ambrosial organ tones covering slavery, perversion of justice, and oppression.   The democratic, freedom-loving spirit, noticeable in Börne more than in Heine, and the analytical, Spinoza-like mode of reasoning, more characteristic of Heine than of Börne, are Jewish to the core.   Had they been born Christians, and brought up in the atmosphere of red-tapeism, neither of them would have developed as rescuing powers, which with laughing mien helped to banish deeply-rooted perversions and absurdities.   The slaves became deliverers, and saved their enemies from the double yoke of political and social inferiority.   The Teutomaniacs almost deserve thanks for having tormented the Jews with their reactionary measures. They roused, if not Heine, certainly Börne, who was inclined to idle speculation, and furnished him with the dart that wounded the enemy.

Ludwig Börne, or Löb Baruch (born in Frankfort-on-the-Main, 1786; died in Paris, 1837), saw the light in the same year when it was extinguished for Mendelssohn, as though history wished to compensate the bereaved Jews for the loss of the sage of Berlin. Börne resembled Mendelssohn in some respects: in his timid, bashful, somewhat awkward bearing, in his self-control, his strength of character, and his strict adherence to an adopted system of morality. Both became the objects of admiration by accident, in spite of themselves. Both drew up for themselves æsthetic rules of conduct without having been trained to do so.

Börne despised the Jews of his time, and spoke of them as if he were their arch-enemy. Jewish antiquity, misrepresented to him in his youth, and still more dimmed by his Berlin and Halle friends, he looked upon as a caricature. The ancient Jews from the day of Abraham until the time of "wealthy Solomon" appeared to him "as if they had wished to parody history." He did not suspect how much his inward self, the truthfulness of his nature, owed to Judaism. The filth of Lucinde, consecrated by Schleiermacher, so disgusted Börne at the age of sixteen, that even a stealthy perusal of the book possessed no charm. The sobriety with which Judaism had endowed him showed Börne the right way of balancing his ideal nature, and avoiding too harsh a discord with the real world. At an early age he became acquainted with a goddess to whom he was devoted in extravagant love, and to whom he remained faithful until his dying breath. "The true nature of virtue may be expressed in a few words. What is virtue? Virtue is bliss. And bliss? It is liberty. We cannot further inquire, what is liberty, for liberty is in accord with reason, in accord with God, and in accord with the unconditional— it explains itself." So thought Börne, and so he wrote in his diary at the age of eighteen; and this idea governed his inner being as long as he lived, and was the motive power of all his actions. Virtue is liberty, and liberty is virtue; they necessitate and produce bliss. Yet Börne limited his love of liberty; he guarded himself from overstepping that narrow boundary at which the pursuit of an ideal turns to madness.

May not his Jewish blood, or at any rate, the sad pages of Jewish history, explain his worship of liberty, which influenced his body and mind? How hard and degrading the absence of liberty was could be felt only by a Jew, in comparison with whom an Indian or a Russian bondsman was a free man. Frankfort, the birth-place of Börne, with its disgraceful laws concerning the residence of Jews, effectually taught him love of liberty. When, only a boy, he was prohibited from walking on the footpath, and had to keep to the dusty road for vehicles, when every ragged Christian beggar, or drunkard, was allowed to call to him, " Mach Mores, Jud !" the thought may have struck him that the absence of liberty was damnation and the presence of liberty salvation. "I, a slave from my birth, love liberty more than you ; yea, because I was trained in servitude, I understand liberty better than you !" he often said. His much admired style, his perfect, captivating manner, his profound epigrams, recall the gnomic wisdom of Bible and Talmud. In short, Börne owes his favorable points to Judaism. But he neither was grateful for his gifts, nor did he acknowledge their origin, which he estimated no more than did his Berlin friends. On one occasion, indeed, he said :

"I should not deserve to enjoy the light of the sun, were I, on account of mockery upon which I have always looked with contempt, ungrateful for God's great favor, in having made me at once a German and a Jew : for I know how to value the undeserved fortune of being at the same time a German and a Jew, to be able to strive after all the virtues of the Germans without participating in their faults."

He added, addressing the Germans :—

"I pray you, do not despise my Jews. If only you were as they are, you were better. You have deprived the Jews of air, they have thus been preserved from rottenness ; you have strewn the salt of hatred into their hearts, their hearts have thus been kept fresh. You have imprisoned them for the whole long winter in a cellar, and stopped up the cellar door with dung ; but you, exposed to the frost, were half frozen to death. When spring arrives, we shall see who will blossom first, Jew or Christian."

Börne did not, however, himself believe in the endurance of the Jews, and he gave utterance to those words only because he was vexed, or in order to vex the Germans. He said at the same time, ironically : "You know how my heart beats for the Jews."

Since the time when his mind began to mature, he beheld in the Jews only money-makers, as on the Exchange at Frankfort, or deriders of religion ashamed of their race, as in the salon of Henriette Herz; moreover, his education had made Judaism seem so despicable that he did not judge it worthy of consideration. Thus Börne never understood what was most sacred to the Jews, and he was unable to fathom the depths of his own mind, and discriminate between what he owed to the general state of culture and what to Judaism.

His healthy spirit, however, and love for the oppressed guarded him from the unprincipled conduct of Rachel, of those who frequented the salons at Berlin, and of many others who turned their backs contemptuously upon the Jews. Even as a youth Börne hated the idea that the word "Jew" might be insultingly cast at him.

"And when they come and tell you that you are a Jew," he wrote in his diary, "how they bandy about the Jewish jargon, so that one must almost die of laughter.

"Oh! when I think of that, my mind is tossed as by a storm, my soul would fain burst from its dwelling-place, and seek the body of a lion, that it might meet the villain with jaw and claw."

His anticipations proved correct, he was not spared the insult, and his lion's claw was shown. While a student, he procured from the police of Frankfort a passport, in which the spiteful police-clerk had inserted the words : " Jew of Frankfort."

" My blood stood still, but I could neither say nor do anything, for my father was present. I then swore in my heart : only wait, the time will come when I shall write a passport for you, a passport for all of you."

For a moment it seemed as if Börne would forget his oath. The Jews of Frankfort had bought equality for half a million of money, and Börne, who had studied law and shown himself a young man of promise, was one of the first to receive a position in the Frankfort police department. But if Börne was inclined to forget that he was a Jew, and remembered only that he was a German, the people of Frankfort did not forget it, and imprudently and brutally reminded him of his secret oath. He was the first victim of the reaction ; he was expelled from office, as soon as the Jews of Frankfort were driven back into the Ghetto. The insolent manner in which they were cheated out of trebly pledged freedom revolted Börne's feeling for liberty, and he sharpened his first arrows in defense of the members of his own race. They were directed against the narrow-minded citizens of Frankfort, who in the nineteenth century had restored the laws of 1616 concerning the residence of the Jews, "that romance of malice," as Börne called them. The feelings which agitated him during the years of ever-increasing reaction against the Jews he put into the mouth of a Jewish officer in a novel :

"You stole from me the pleasures of childhood, you arrant knaves ! You threw salt into the sweet cup of my youth, you placed malicious slander and hateful derision in my road in manhood ; arrest me you could not, but fatigued, vexed, without joyfulness, I reached my goal. . . . . That I cannot even revenge myself, that I should not have the power to forgive, nor the weakness to chastise! They are out of my reach in their fox-hole! . . . . You ask me why I shun my fatherland. I have none; I have never left my home. My home is in dungeons; where there is persecution I breathe the atmosphere of my childhood. The moon is as near to me as is Germany."

Instead of revenging himself for the wounds inflicted upon him and the members of his race by German Jew-hatred, Börne undertook the difficult task of extinguishing this hatred. In the "Waage," his organ, he erected ideal standards, by which he measured the narrow, petty circumstances of the Germans, and their short-sightedness.

Before Louis Baruch undertook his campaign against German faults and prejudices, or rather before he undertook the education of the Germans, he renounced Judaism, was baptized in Offenbach, and assumed the name Karl Ludwig Börne (June 5, 1818). How little he cared for the Christian faith we may judge from his remark that he "repented the money spent on baptism." He did not wish the effect of his missiles to be lessened by the prejudice which might arise from the fact of their being discharged by a Jew. It is, however, difficult to excuse a man of Börne's character for deserting, without any such struggle as Heine's with himself, the colors of the weak and oppressed, who should have been ennobled in his eyes by the very pain of degradation; deserting for a cause, moreover, in which he did not believe. Germany soon discovered that she had gained an author of Lessing's caliber. Börne's wit was felt the more keenly, because at every turn one could perceive the correctness of the picture and observe the genuineness and integrity of the painter. A glance revealed that he wrote with "the blood of his heart and the sap of his nerves," hence his words made the impression of weighty deeds.

He could not behold in silence the folly and cruelty of the "Hep, hep" year, and he wrote "for the Jews." "I should have said for right and liberty; but if these terms were understood, nothing need be said." He pointed his finger at fools, and threw light on the faces of villains. "A sort of fatal necessity," he said, "was connected in past times with Jew-massacres. They seem to have arisen from an indistinct, inexplicable feeling inspired by Judaism, which, like a scoffing and threatening spirit, like the ghost of a murdered mother, accompanied Christianity from its cradle." Börne analyzed German Jew-hatred into its constituents, and showed the absurdity of each. On another occasion (1820) he told them the stern truth :

"I pardon the German nation for its Jew-hatred, for it is a nation of children, and for this reason, just like an infant, needs a go-cart to enable it some day to stand firm, so that by means of the barriers to liberty it may learn to do without barriers. The German nation would collapse a hundred times a day if it were without prejudices. But individual adults I cannot pardon for their Jew-hatred."

Dr. Ludwig Holst, a newly-fledged Jew-hater, who had developed his cult into a philosophical system, and who, as Börne says, sounded "a metaphysical Hep-hep," was attacked by him with scoffs and sneers.

"Hatred of Jews is one of the Pontine bogs which poison the beautiful land of our liberty. We see the hopeful friends of the fatherland with pale faces wandering about hopelessly. German minds dwell on Alpine heights, but German hearts pant in damp marshes. Holst wishes to kill the Jews, and if they resist, he turns round to his circle of onlookers and says : 'Now you see that I am right in taxing the Jews with unparalleled insolence ; they will not suffer their heads to be struck off ever so little, and they sulk.' . . . . You hate the Jews, not because they have earned hatred, but because they earn money. . . . . What you call human rights, which, it must be conceded you grant Jews, are only animal rights. The right of seeking food, of devouring it, of sleeping, and of multiplying, are enjoyed also by the beasts of the field—until they are slain, and to the Jews you grant no more. . . . . Men of Frankfort, Hamburg, Lübeck, and Bremen, answer me. You complain that Jews are all usurers, yet you prevent the mental development of those who abandon usury ! I will not be turned away ; I demand a reply. Men of Frankfort, tell me : Why should the practice of medicine be restricted to four Jews, and that of the law be allowed to none ? . . . In the same way in which you in your free city now storm against the Jews, did you not twenty years ago storm against Catholics? . . . . Do you doubt the arrival of the day which will command you to look upon Jews as your equals? But you wish to be *forced!* The German is deaf. You will not obey voluntarily; fate will have to take hold of you and drag you hither and thither. Shame upon you!" Börne remarks in conclusion: "I love neither Jew as Jew, nor Christian as Christian; I love them because they are human beings, and born to be free. Liberty shall be the soul of my pen, until it becomes blunted, or my hand is lamed."

But Börne wished the Jews to forget as a bad dream their history of a thousand years, and to become Germans. He did not possess the far-sightedness of Heine.

Heinrich Heine (born in Düsseldorf, 1799, died in Paris, 1854) in his innermost self was infinitely more of a Jew than Börne; indeed, he possessed to a great extent all the favorable and unfavorable characteristics of Jews. Who can paint this "wicked favorite of the Graces and Muses" (as he was called), this scoffing romancer and lyrical philosopher, with his chameleon-like nature? Börne's mind resembled transparent spring-water, which trickles over pebbles, and foams only when attacked by winds. Heine's mind, on the other hand, resembled a whirlpool, upon whose surface the sunbeams play in prismatic colors, but which drags approaching vessels into its roaring depths, and dashes them to pieces unless they are of the strongest build. For Heine was as deep a thinker as he was an artistic poet, as unrelenting a critic as he was an amiable scoffer, as full of original thoughts as he was of verses. Heine had not to search for Truth; Truth flew to Heine. She, like the Muse, revealed herself to him, jesting and playing with him as her favorite. Behind his banter there often was more earnest conviction than in the litany of a morose moralist. Heine longed for ideals which his mind could revere, and because he did not find them he scoffed at the false gods who allowed themselves to be worshiped. He has certainly given profound solutions to problems of history. He never sacrificed substance to form, when the former was of greater value than the latter. It is true that he often changed his opinions, but he did not play with his convictions. His religious views changed also; but he did not change his mind. He never wrote or acted against such convictions as he entertained at the time. If for a time he was slave to the false philosophical theory which makes a god of man, he afterwards acknowledged his error, and derided it thoroughly. Heine was certainly no pattern of virtue, neither was he so great a sinner as his sharp pen and tongue might lead one to suppose. He never lost his profound, noble nature, nor his sense of the sublime; neither did he roll in the mud of sensuality, as he would have his readers believe. He painted himself blacker than he was. He had his share of that acute sensitiveness which is the lot of poets, actors, and preachers, and this morbid state was in Heine's case connected with severe nervous suffering. In his sensitive condition he wrote things of which his sober judgment disapproved, but which he was ashamed to recall.

Heine had an advantage over Börne by reason of his sincere affection for his mother. Betty von Geldern came of a respected, it is said, an ennobled Jewish family. This educated mother, to whom he owed his bent of mind, was a religious woman, and brought up her children in the knowledge of the Jewish faith. The religious discord which had early alienated Börne from Judaism was unknown to Heine, and in his youth he strictly avoided the transgression of Jewish customs. He did not indeed learn so much Hebrew as Börne, but because he imbibed with love the little that he did learn, that little never left him, nor did he forget it later in life, whilst Börne wiped Hebrew entirely from his memory. Heine's love of Judaism, which, in spite of his mockery, was never quite dead, and especially his deep understanding of it, sprang from the fond memories of his youth, which remained with him like sweet, pleasing dreams. His soul was also filled with the charm of true Jewish family life, which gave him the proper standard by which to measure what men call virtue and happiness.

He had a warm though vague attachment to Judaism or the Jewish race, to its pathetic history and sacred books, and he was forcibly impressed by the antiquity of Judaism and its continuity of existence, defying time and myriads of obstacles. Now and again Heine felt proud of belonging to this ancient aristocracy. He felt what he wrote late in life:

"Now I perceive that the Greeks were only handsome youths, but the Jews have always been men, powerful, stubborn men, not only in days of yore, but even at present, in spite of eighteen centuries of persecution and misery. I have since learned to know them better, and to value them more highly, and if pride of descent were not always a foolish contradiction, I might feel proud of the fact that my progenitors were members of the noble house of Israel, that I am a descendant of those martyrs who have given a God and morality to the world, and who have fought and suffered on all the battle-fields of thought."

This consciousness slumbered gently in him from his youth onwards. But he did not clearly define to himself his attitude towards Judaism. The Jews, in whom solidity, high virtue, and morality were still to be found, repelled him by their unæsthetic exterior and religious ceremonies, which he did not understand. He felt his sense of beauty wounded by the repulsive exterior of Judaism and its representatives. His eye could not penetrate through ugly veils. The circle of more refined Jews, which in early manhood he joined in Berlin—the older men, Friedländer, Ben-David, Jacobson, and their young imitators—did not cherish Judaism so deeply as to infuse into him the spirit of sacrifice for the faith. And in the semi-Jewish circle which also he frequented during his stay in Berlin, as in that of Rachel von Varnhagen, at this time already baptized, he beheld only thorough contempt for Jews and

Judaism, and an enthusiastic, romantic predilection for Christianity.

But Heine, unlike Börne, had too independent a judgment to be lured into idolatrous worship of the intellectual idols of the day. Sophistry could not undermine his devotion to Judaism. On the contrary, Heine joined the society of a number of young men whose object was to promote culture among Jews, and as one of its members, he subscribed to their tacit vow, not to suffer themselves to be baptized for the sake of a government appointment. The impulse by which he and the other members were actuated was no doubt vague; but at any rate it manifests the desire to do his share towards the improvement of his brethren. He undertook to aid in strengthening the society and in widening its scope. Heine's opinion even of the much-despised Polish Jews was not utterly unfavorable, and they found a champion in him.

Heine would have espoused the cause of Judaism with heart and soul, if Judaism itself, *i. e.*, its sons, had developed powers of mind and character, if the freshness of youth and attractive charms had been coupled with the dignity of its old age, its purport, and calling, and if it could have inspired respect in the educated world. In his impatience he wished to see Judaism, like the legendary Messiah chained at Rome, suddenly divest itself of its ragged cloak, its leprous skin, throw off its aspect of servitude, and be transformed into a richly adorned, blooming, commanding youth. The process of rejuvenescence seemed to him too slow, the means employed too petty, the bearing of those who wished to further it, especially their coquetry with the dominant Church, seemed to him to be weak, apish, and undignified.

Israel lacks energy. Chiropodists (David Friedländer and Co.) have sought to heal the body of Judaism of its fatal excrescences, and on account of their unskillfulness and their cobweb bandage of reason, Israel must bleed to death. Would that the delusion that impotency, privation of strength, one-sided negation are glorious, might soon cease. . . . We no longer have the courage to wear a beard, to fast, to hate, and by reason of hatred to suffer. This is the motive of our reformation. Those who have received their enlightenment and education from comedians wish to give Judaism new decorations and new scenes, and the prompter is to wear white bands instead of a beard. They wish to pour the ocean into a neat little hand-basin . . . Others desire evangelical Christianity under Jewish names." . . . "Even I do not possess the strength of mind (he frankly confessed) to wear a beard, and to allow myself to be called, 'dirty Jew.'"

We see clearly his attachment to Judaism in the case of his pardonable hatred of the oppressor and despiser of his race, of the enemy who had received salvation from Judaism, which he imprisoned and spat upon. In the renewed pain of old wounds, inflicted upon the Jews by heathen and Christian Rome, he compressed a world of boiling anger into the word Edom. Thus he jeered in a poem to Edom :—

> " For a thousand years or longer
> We bear with each other in a brotherly way ;
> Thou dost endure that I should breathe,
> I endure that thou shouldst rave.

> " Only sometimes, on dark days,
> Was thy mood a curious one,
> And thy pietistic claws
> Didst thou color with my blood.

> " Now our friendship waxeth stronger,
> And daily increaseth in strength ;
> For I myself began to rave,
> And I become almost like to thee."

Still greater was Heine's hatred towards deserters, traitors, Jews who for the sake of personal gain turned their back upon their suffering brethren, and went over to the enemy. Heine could not believe that a Jew ever was baptized from earnest conviction ; baptism was in his opinion self-delusion, if not a lie. The Gospel, preached in vain to the poor of Judæa, was now, as he averred, prospering among the rich. Heine gave vent to this hatred in his dramatic poem "Almansor" (completed in 1823).

But he found it unsuitable to introduce the characters
as Jews, to tell in glowing verses of their affliction
and the contempt in which they were held. He therefore put these verses into the mouths of the Mussulmans of Granada, who through devilish malice were
experiencing the same cruel fate as the Jews, and
who felt a yawning chasm in their hearts at having
been forced to embrace Christianity. It is unmistakable that these verses breathe forth Jewish
suffering. The Jewish poet, however, incurred
bitter enmity by this drama.

It is proof of Heine's warm attachment to his race
that when he was deeply vexed by private and
public disappointments, he proceeded to glorify it.
The enthralling psalm, once sung by a Hebrew bard
at Babel's waters, was constantly in his mind :

> " May my tongue cleave parched
> To the roof of my mouth, and my right hand
> Wither, if ever
> I forget thee, O Jerusalem."

For affronts put upon him in connection with the
performance of " Almansor," it was his intention to
take thorough revenge on his German-Christian
enemies, and to hold up a mirror to them in a
Jewish novel. In the " Rabbi of Bacharach " he
described vividly, as only he could, the sad and the
glorious scenes of Jewish history, and to this end he
carefully studied the Jewish chronicles, as he wished
to keep strictly to history. His imagination only
illuminated facts, but did not invent them, there
being material enough at his disposal. Heine did
not shrink from ransacking the rubbish contained in
old books, such as Schudt's " Jewish Curiosities,"
"that memorial of Frankfort Jew-hatred"; and he
succeeded in extracting something even from chaff
and straw. "The spirit of Jewish history reveals
itself more and more to me, and the pursuit of it
will no doubt prove useful to me in the future." In
the course of Jewish history, outlined by acts of

heroism and by sacrifices, he beheld a connection between the plans of Providence: "In the same year in which the Jews were expelled from Spain, the new land of religious liberty was discovered." The golden period of mediæval Jewish history—the history of the Spanish Jews—had greatest charm for him.   In the foreground of this stage he wished to introduce proud Jews, who would not bow their necks beneath the yoke of German restrictions and canonical arrogance, and who professed their religion with pride; but this epoch was not well known at that time, and Heine longed in vain for sources whence to draw pregnant information.   Instead of facts, those to whom he applied gave him only threshed straw.   But Heine allowed no difficulty to prevent his collecting interesting historical material for his novel; this production was to be the child, not of his hate, but of his love.   He fairly basked in it: "Since it proceeds from love, it will be an immortal book, an ever-burning lamp in the palace of God—no fitful theatrical light."

Heine's romance was indeed grandly conceived. The scene of action was laid in Germany, but the history of the Jews of Spain, their expulsion, and enforced baptism, were to be the main incidents.

However, at the time when Heine was earnestly engaged in the study of Judaism, and became enthusiastic for its history, and hated Christianity most fiercely, he quietly passed over to the Christian fold (June 28, 1825), and assumed the baptismal name of Christian Johann Heinrich.   He had fought for a long time against this temptation.   He expressed his opinion upon the question plainly:—

"Not one of my family is opposed to it except myself. This act may be of importance to me, as through it I may the better devote myself to the cause of my unhappy coreligionists. But I should consider it a blot upon my dignity and honor, if I were to be baptized in order to obtain a post in Prussia—in dear Prussia! . . . . Vexation may drive me to become a Catholic, and hang myself."

In spite of this declaration he became a convert, in order to obtain a position in Prussia, and also to escape from humiliating dependence upon his uncle. In his diary he wrote the following verses upon the subject :—

> "And unto the cross now bendest thou low,
>   To the cross that erstwhile thou didst despise ;
> Which but a few short weeks ago
>   Seemed so vile in thy scornful eyes."

Shortly afterwards (July 20, 1825) he passed his law examination. But he pursued phantoms, and had made a vain sacrifice of his honor. He was unable to procure employment, and could not dispense with his uncle's support. Shamefaced as a girl guilty of some fault, Heine communicated the fact of his conversion in allegorical language to his bosom friend Moser :

"A young Spanish Jew, at heart a Jew, who, owing to the demands of pleasure, had abjured his faith, corresponded with the youthful Judah Abrabanel, and sent him a poem translated from the Moorish. Perhaps he was loth to tell his friend in plain terms of his not very creditable performance ; still he sends the poem.—Do not meditate about it."

Through his apostasy, Heine became only the more embittered against Christianity, as though it were directly responsible for his faithlessness, his loss of dignity, and his disloyalty to his better self. "I assure you," he wrote to his intimate friend, "if the law had permitted the stealing of silver spoons, I should not have been baptized." When at about the same time, Edward Gans, the leader of young Israel, founder of the Society of Culture, and one of its active promoters, also embraced Christianity, Heine could not forgive him, for he had not been compelled by poverty to take the step. Heine was

yet more indignant when informed that Gans had
induced weak-minded Jews to forsake their belief.

"If he does it out of conviction, he is a fool ; if out of hypocrisy, he
is a rascal."

It also vexed him that his opponents would not
forget his Jewish origin, but, as in the case of Börne,
reminded him of it at every opportunity.   To
appease his conscientious scruples in a measure, he
continued to work at the romance, " The Rabbi of
Bacharach."   Through its medium he desired to
make known his secret attachment to the Jews, and
he wished to publish it in spite of the advice of his
friend Moser, who was not blind to the glaring contradiction between thought and act, and the enmity
it would necessarily draw down upon him.

Heine was not, however, so constituted as to
allow remorse to trouble him for any length of time.
Once having turned his back upon Judaism, he
sought to lull his conscience.   His pleasure-seeking
after his conversion was only a means to this end.
Heine ingeniously labored to discover faults in the
Jews and Judaism, and thus to justify himself.   In
this impulse originated his hostile sallies against
Judaism—that it is, for instance, " not a religion,
but a misfortune."   Afterwards, he sought to make
the dividing line between Judaism and Christianity
very faint ; he characterized both faiths as self-torturing, monkish, and Nazarite ; he vilified them
equally, disregarded both, and acknowledged a
Hellenistic religion of the " revival of the flesh."
Nevertheless, it may be said that, in bright moments,
his old love of Judaism revived, and he again showed
his thoughtful conception of it.   It annoyed Heine
that Shakespeare should be reckoned among the
Jew-baiters because he had created " Shylock," and
he employed his brilliant eloquence to remove this
blemish from the Jews and Shakespeare.

"Did Shakespeare aim at depicting a Jewess in Jessica? Certainly not. He portrayed only a daughter of Eve, one of those pretty birds who, as soon as they are fledged, flutter forth from the home-nest to their lovers. . . . . In Jessica there is especially noticeable a certain timid shame which she cannot overcome in donning male garments. In this trait one may, perhaps, recognize the modesty characteristic of her race, which endows its daughters with so marvelous a charm. The chastity of the Jews is probably the consequence of the aversion which they felt to Oriental sensuality and the immoral worship which flourished among their neighbors, the Egyptians, Assyrians, and Babylonians, and has continued, changing only its outward form, to the present day. The Jews are a chaste, abstemious, so to speak, an abstract people, and in purity of morals, approach the German nations. . . . The Greeks and Romans were devoted to the soil. . . . the later Northern immigrants to the person of their chieftains. . . . whilst the Jews from ancient times were attached to the law, to abstract thought, like our modern cosmopolitan Republicans. . . . . liberty and equality were their religion."

Advanced in years, when a severe nervous affliction had still more cleared the mirror of his thoughts, Heine became conscious of the superiority of morality based upon piety over beauty, and returned with his whole heart to the love of his youth, his reverence for Judaism. His "Confessions" (1853-54) are inspired hymns to Jewish history and the Jewish people, and it is apparent that they are sincere. He was always enthusiastic on behalf of the Bible.

"The Jews may console themselves for the loss of Jerusalem and the Ark of the Covenant; this loss is but trifling when compared with the Bible, the indestructible treasure which they have saved. . . . . I owe the re-awakening of my religious feelings to that Holy Book (the Bible), and it has become for me equally the source of salvation and the object of most ardent admiration. . . . . I think I may flatter myself that I comprehend the character of Moses as revealed in the first portion of the sacred book (of the Old Testament). I consider his a most imposing figure. What a giant form! How small Sinai appears when Moses stands upon it! This mountain is only the pedestal for the feet of the man, whose head reaches up to the heavens, where he speaks with God. . . . . Formerly, I felt no especial affection for Moses, probably because the Hellenic spirit was paramount in me, and I could not pardon the legislator of the Jews his hatred against the plastic arts. I did not see that, notwithstanding his hostility to art, Moses was a great artist, and possessed the true artistic spirit! But this spirit was directed by him, as by his Egyptian compatriots, to colossal and indestructible undertakings. . . . He built human pyramids, carved human obelisks; he took a poor shepherd family and created a nation from it, a great, eternal, holy people, a people of God, destined to outlive the centuries, and to serve as a pattern to all other nations, even as a prototype to the whole of mankind: he created Israel . . . . . As of the artist, so also I have not always spoken with sufficient respect of his work, the Jews. . . . . . The history of the Middle Ages, and even of other times, seldom inscribed in its annals the names of these knights of the holy spirit, because they usually fought with closed visor. The deeds of the Jews, as well as their peculiar character, are little known to the world. One thinks one knows them, because their beards are visible, but nothing else has come in view; and now, as in the Middle Ages, they are a profound mystery, which may perhaps be revealed on the day of which the prophet speaks. . . . .

"Yes, to the Jews, to whom the world owes its God, it also owes His Word, the Bible; they saved it from the wreck of the Roman Empire, and in the frantic scramble of migrating tribes they preserved the precious book, until Protestantism sought it with them, translated the discovered work into the vernacular, and disseminated it through the whole world. . . . . . . In the North of Europe and America, the influence of Palestine has grown to be so great, that one can fancy oneself transplanted into the midst of Jews. . . . . . I will not speak of most of the new communities of the United States where the life of the Old Testament is pedantically imitated. . . . . but the caricature will not disappear, and the real, imperishable, and true portion, namely, the morality of ancient Judaism, will also flourish in those countries as luxuriantly as in former days on the banks of the Jordan and upon the heights of Lebanon. No palms are needed for man to be good; and to be good is better than to be beautiful. . . . . Judæa has always appeared to me as a piece of the West lost in the East. In fact, with its spiritual belief, its severe, pure, almost ascetic morals, its abstract inner life, this land and its people have ever formed a remarkable contrast to the surrounding countries and their inhabitants, who paid homage to the most licentious and infamous nature cults, and dissipated their existence in bacchanalian orgies. Israel piously sat beneath its fig-tree, and sang the praise of the invisible God, and practised virtue and justice; whilst in the temples of Babylon, Nineveh, Sidon, and Tyre, sanguinary and immoral rites were celebrated, the description of which even now strikes us with horror. When one thinks of its surroundings, this early greatness of Israel cannot be sufficiently admired. Of Israel's love of liberty, whilst slavery was justified not alone in its immediate vicinity but by all the nations of antiquity, even by philosophers—of this I would rather not speak, in order to avoid compromising the Bible with our present rulers. . . . . Instead of wrestling with the impossible, instead of foolishly decreeing the abolition of property, Moses strove to render it moral; he endeavored to bring the possession of property into harmony with morality, with the law of reason, and this he effected by the institution of the Jubilee, when all alienated hereditary property, which amongst an agricultural people was land, reverted to the original owners, no matter how they had lost possession thereof. This ordinance offers a most decided contrast to the law of prescription among the Romans. . . . . Moses did not wish to abolish the holding of property; his plan was that every one should possess some land, that no one should become a slave, with slavish propensities, through poverty, for freedom was the ultimate aim of the great emancipator, and this desire breathes through all his laws dealing with pauperism.   He detested slavery immoderately, almost fiercely. . . . If a slave, however, freed by law, refused to leave the house of his master, Moses commanded that the incorrigible rascal be nailed by his ear to the door-post of his master's house. . . . . . O Moses, our teacher, Moshe Rabbenu, exalted enemy of serfdom, I pray thee furnish me with hammer and nails, that I may nail our willing slaves, in their liveries of black and red and gold, by their long ears to the Brandenburg Gate."

The spirit of the Jewish law and of Jewish history had indeed come upon this erratic son of Israel, and revealed to him what few of his predecessors had thoroughly grasped, and none had so luminously delineated. Heine appreciated equally the profound wisdom displayed in the laws and the intellectual contests in the centuries of Jewish history, as also the precious ore of poetry, which streamed forth from the greatest Jewish poet of the Middle Ages. Scarcely had Michael Sachs, the preacher with the Psalmist soul and prophetic speech, unveiled the hidden beauties of the "Religious Poetry of the Jews in Spain," and more especially the almost forgotten glory of the poet Jehudah Halevi Alhassan, before Heine, deeply moved, set up a memorial to this singer and brother in race and art. With his magic wand he invoked the shade of Jehudah Halevi from the grave, and depicted him in his complete ideality and the full glow of his inspiration.

Until his last breath the struggle continued within Heine's breast between the two great principles in the construction of the world's history, the pure morality of Judaism and the symmetrical beauty of Hellenism, both of which he reverenced, but was unable to reconcile :—

> " The contrasts are boldly paired,
> Love of pleasure in the Greek, and the thought of God in the Judæan,
> *   *   *   *   *
> Oh ! this conflict will never end,
> The true must always contend with the beautiful. "

He suspected that the harmonious intermingling of the two elements was the task of European civilization ; but he was unable to effect it in himself.

From this conflict his aberrations arose, and also his impulse to dominate them by ridicule, and thus prevent their mastering him.

The Jewish world is greatly indebted to its two apostate sons, Börne and Heine. They did not indeed destroy all German anti-Jewish feeling, but they at least subdued it. Referring to the absurd cry of "Hep, hep," Heine once said, "This can never occur again, for the press is a weapon, and there are two Jews who possess German style, the one being myself, the other Börne." His prediction was nearly fulfilled, for since the appearance of these two, such fierce outbreaks against Jews have not recurred. Germany has not produced more talented, more artistic, more refined writers than these two Jews.

Young Germany, which originated the present state of culture, and created the Year of Liberation, 1848, is the offspring of these two Jewish fathers. Invective, calumny, and the secret police were perfectly correct in designating the leaders of young Germany as Jews, because without the influence of the Jewish spirit they would not have become the champions of freedom. Jew-haters thought that they were inflicting disgrace on the fair-haired combatants in calling them Jews, whilst actually they only bestowed honor upon them. But the list of Börne's and Heine's services to Germany is not yet exhausted. They induced the French to respect the staunchness of the German spirit. Börne and Heine were the first to draw France and Germany together, to unite German depth of thought with French elegance. They first dispelled the clouds which separated these two nations, causing the French people to ascend and the Germans to descend the mountain, meet each other half-way, and, regardless of mutual antagonism and of their oppressors, stretch forth their hands in brotherly union. This Messianic time, when it arrives, will have been prepared by two Jews, who were fulfilling their national mission.

CHAPTER XV.

REFORM AND YOUNG ISRAEL.

Segregation of the Jews—Its Results—Secession and Obstinate Conservatism— Israel Jacobson — His Reforms — The Hamburg Reform Temple Union—Gotthold Salomon—Decay of Rabbinical Authority—Eleazar Libermann—Aaron Chorin—Lazarus Riesser—Party Strife—Isaac Bernays—His Writings—Bernays in Hamburg—Mannheimer—His Congregation in Vienna—Berlin Society for Culture—Edward Gans—His Baptism—Collapse of the Society for Culture.

1818—1830 C. E.

THE advance of the Jews in Germany had been completed in an amazingly short time, as appears when we contrast Mendelssohn's reticence in touching upon religious and political conditions in Christendom with the boldness of Börne and Heine, who displayed them in their naked form. And mark the progress made in France ! Here the Jews had become men, dauntlessly encountering every opponent, and ready to avenge with the sword insulting remarks on their origin. Judaism, however, was less rapid in casting off servile forms than its followers. For nearly two thousand years it had struggled for existence against every new people and every new tendency which appeared on the stage of history. With Greeks and Romans, Parthians and Neo-Persians, Goths and Slavonic tribes, with Arabs and mediæval knights in armor, with monks of every order and fanatic Lutherans, it had maintained ever-recurring contests, and had of necessity become covered with disfiguring scars and foul dust. To defend itself against the assaults of so many hostile powers and during so long a period, Judaism had been compelled to surround itself with an impenetrable coat of mail, to isolate itself completely, or withdraw into a shrine of its own, every access to which was carefully barricaded. So accustomed had the Jews become to their heavy armor, that it seemed to have grown into their very being ; nor could it be discarded so long as new battles were imminent.   Left to its own resources, and excluded from the external world, especially since the expulsion of its members from Spain and Portugal, and their simultaneous banishment from many German districts, Judaism had created a dreamland for itself.   It had admitted magical formulas into its world of thought and fancy to distract the minds of its adherents from pangs of torture, so that they might endure them with greater ease, or forget them entirely. Suddenly its sons were awakened from their dreams by the dazzling sunlight, and beheld the real world, to which they were utter strangers.   At first they closed their eyes the tighter, in order to retain the pleasant dream-pictures.   In this new age, and in the new conditions, they could not at once find their proper level, and they feared that the altered state of affairs was a mere stratagem, a novel method of warfare in disguise, which their ancient enemies expected to use against Judaism.

During its long journey through the world, and its acquaintance with many nations, Judaism, in spite of its exclusiveness, had admitted various perverse ideas, which became as thoroughly a part of itself, as if derived from the original stock.   Memory had been weakened through persecution and martyrdom ; the power of thought had also suffered somewhat through daily increasing afflictions.   At first it was too distracted to apply tests, to distinguish foreign and unfit elements from native and essential parts and remove them.   Among the Jews in Germany, England, and France, the adoption of the uncultivated Polish manner had conferred a barbarous aspect upon Judaism, and among the

Portuguese and Italian Jews, owing to Isaac Lurya and Chayim Vital, it had assumed a Kabbalistic form. This disfigurement of Judaism existing among the Portuguese along with external decorum, and its neglected condition in Polish and German communities, affected every element of religious life—divine service, sermons, marriages, interments, in short, every ceremonial, especially those of a public nature. The official representatives and expounders of Judaism, the rabbis and leaders of divine service, were repulsive, either semi-barbarians or visionaries. The foreign additions and excrescences, the fungous growth attached to the original trunk, were regarded by these leaders of Judaism as integral elements. The times had not yet matured men, who, by a delicate perception of the inner kernel of Judaism (as contained in the Bible and the Talmud), by wide vision, and clear insight, could recognize the abuses that had accumulated in the course of time, and separate them from the essential parts. To remove these objectionable excrescences gradually, and with a gentle hand, without giving offense, required profound understanding. A necessary reform, not prompted by external considerations, had been suggested several centuries earlier by far-sighted men; but the modern generation had no knowledge thereof. Neither was there any adequate representative body in the Jewish world. There was, to be sure, an organization, possessing, or in a position easily to obtain, a sort of official character and authority, namely, the French Synhedrion and Consistory. But the chiefs, David Sinzheim and Abraham di Cologna, had not the needful discernment to accomplish the ennoblement and rejuvenescence of Judaism. Sinzheim was only an orthodox Talmudist, and Di Cologna an interesting preacher. The right men were wanting to undertake and promote this much-needed reform, not of the religion itself—for neither the leaders nor the rank and file had lost any degree of morality through the deterioration of Judaism—but of its exterior, to beautify it and remove excrescences. No men being forthcoming, time effected the changes, and so quarrels and contentions were produced. It was destined to be no easy work for Judaism to cast its slough.

The changes in Judaism, like those in the Jews, began in Germany. To the German Jews (because Mendelssohn had come from their midst) a task was allotted similar to that achieved in earlier times by the Alexandrian and Spanish, and in part by the Provençal Jews, that of reconciling Judaism with culture. But when these efforts commenced, the situation was already one of great confusion, and the method by which they were conducted only intensified the difficulties. During the struggles of the German Jews to secure emancipation, when every step towards freedom was accomplished only after the most strenuous exertions, when each advance was met with scorn and neglect, when they were continually being hurled back into their humiliated condition and reminded of their despised state, two equally unpleasant phenomena manifested themselves. Those who, improved by culture and education, swam with the stream, estranged themselves from Judaism, disowned all connection with its official acts, and despised it as the obstacle to their civil or social advancement. To them Judaism appeared as a mummy, a petrifaction, or a specter, which restlessly and aimlessly flitted through the centuries, a picture of grief beyond help. Only a few of this educated class, like Heine in his bright moments, when not led astray by wantonness, were clear-sighted enough to recognize life in this mummy, capable some day of bursting its cerements and engaging in combat with its enemies. On the other hand, the majority of the Jews, who still bore in their hearts deep love for the wrinkled

mother of all religions, clung to those unessential
forms to which from youth they had been accustomed, because they perceived the treachery of the
opposite party, and did not wish to be classed
amongst the betrayers of Judaism.   "They loved
stones, and treasured dust."   Theirs was no longer
the innocent piety of bygone days which had no
opposition to contend with, but an active, passionate feeling.   The representatives of the old school
became anxious and suspicious about the growing
weakness of religious feeling, the loosening of all
bonds of union, the manifest symptoms of apostasy,
and the contempt for their origin.   Judaism seemed
a gigantic structure composed of tiny cubes, supporting each other and the whole.   They feared the
downfall of the whole edifice, if a single support
became loose.   They had no confidence in the per-
manence of the structure, for whose maintenance
they were ready to sacrifice their lives.   They
would give up not even the use of their miserable
jargon, defiant of every grammatical law, in the
ritual, nor their indecorous habits, nor any particular
of their disorderly system.   Every sign of yielding,
any departure from the old order, appeared to them
an act of treachery to Judaism.

It seemed impossible to find a means of uniting
these opposites.   Nevertheless, an attempt was
made, but in a rough, unskillful manner, the result
being that the advance of Judaism was retarded for
a considerable time.   The first to undertake some
sort of reform was Israel Jacobson.   He was especially fitted for the leadership of a new party by his
attachment to his faith, his admiration for beauty
and external qualities, his activity, wealth, and high
position.   Immediately after the Westphalian Consistory had been appointed, and he had been placed
at its head, he came forward with innovations of a
two-fold nature.   From the public service in the
synagogue connected with the newly-erected school

in Cassel, he removed all objectionable and noisy features, especially the sing-song reading so much in use. He naturally insisted upon the delivery of sermons in German. He also introduced new forms and methods borrowed from the Church, such as German as well as Hebrew prayers, insipid German songs by the side of the psalms pregnant with thought, and the ceremony of confessing the faith (Confirmation) for half-grown boys and girls—an idea without meaning in Judaism.

Jacobson exercised such power over his associates in the Westphalian Consistory, that they unresistingly accepted these innovations. He then proceeded to introduce his reforms into all the communities of Westphalia, with the threat that he would have such synagogues as refused to adopt his regulations closed. This compulsion, however, aroused the feelings of the orthodox party; the introduction of the German language into divine service being particularly objectionable to the majority. A rabbi of mild temperament, Samuel Eger of Brunswick (died 1842), had the courage to protest against the arbitrary conduct of the president of the consistory. He prophetically expressed the conviction, that by employing German prayers and hymns the Hebrew language would fall into disuse, and finally die out, and the bond uniting the Jews dispersed throughout the world would thereby be relaxed. Jacobson appears to have paid no heed to these warnings and signs of opposition. The dissatisfied Jews must have lodged complaints about him and his new schemes with King Jerome, for the king reprimanded him for his autocratic interference in matters of conscience and his ardor for reform.

Jacobson's glory ended with the speedy downfall of the Westphalian kingdom. Having moved to Berlin, he furnished a room in his house as a synagogue (1815), although he had formerly been opposed to private synagogues, and introduced his reformed service with German prayers, songs, and a choir.   At first there was no room for an organ. Afterwards Jacob Beer, the banker, the father of Meyer Beer, provided a large chamber (1817), where an organ could be put up.   After the victory of the Germans over Napoleon, it became the fashion to be religious, and it infected Jews who had previously not experienced the slightest necessity for devotional exercises, and had been quite indifferent to religious ceremonial.   Such sentimentalists, who had no regard for Judaism, attended the services of Jacobson, in order to "edify themselves," and "be devout," as the new phrases ran.   The "Society of Friends" furnished members.   This was the origin of a Reform party, a tiny community within the community, which however, as could be easily foreseen, had a future, owing to the energy displayed at the commencement and the repulsive form of the ordinary divine service.   The great attraction in the new form of service was the German sermon, which Jacobson usually delivered. His addresses exercised great power, because the so-called "homiletic discourses" of the rabbis and the Polish or Moravian itinerant preachers, were dull and unattractive.

But the private synagogue in Berlin, owing to complaints made by some of the orthodox party, was closed by the Prussian government.   The king of Prussia, Frederick William III, was averse to all innovations, even in Jewish circles, and hated them as being revolutionary plots.   A young preacher from the school of Jacobson thereupon betook himself to Hamburg, having been invited to conduct a free school established by certain rich Jews.   Here he set on foot the plan of erecting a reform temple on the model of Jacobson's.

This young minister, Kley, had brought from Jacobson's synagogue a complete scheme, which included German hymns and prayers, sermons, and the organ. He composed a so-called "religious song-book," in imitation of the Protestant liturgy, an empty and feeble work, suited only to a race of children, ignorant of the psalms, the pattern sources of religious devotion. But there were men in Hamburg who, although they approved of modern ideas, were yet unwilling to break entirely with Judaism and its past, and who decidedly objected to the omission of Hebrew in their prayers. The chiefs of this movement were M. J. Bresselau, himself a good Hebrew stylist, and Sæckel Fränkel (died in Hamburg, 1833), likewise a Hebrew scholar, who had retranslated several of the Apocryphal books into the sacred language. These two men compiled a selection from the Hebrew prayers in use, in order to amalgamate them with the newly-adopted German songs and prayers, a discordant medley in contents and form, which somewhat called to mind a friendly compromise among contending parties. About fifty families joined, and thus arose the Reform Temple Union in Hamburg. This mongrel birth was ushered into the world without love and enthusiasm. Its promoters were so prosaic that the anniversary of the battle of Leipsic was chosen for the day of the consecration of the Temple (October 18, 1818). The preacher Kley, in order to have ample material for a discourse, had to use as a starting point the German wars of freedom, which had caused the Jews in Germany to retrograde rather than to advance. Young maidens sang hymns with the young men, in order to create the sensation which the cause itself could not awaken, and this gave great offense. Kley could not have kept the Temple community together for long, had not the Templars, as they were called, found an efficient preacher in Gotthold Salomon, of Dessau (died 1862), who was well acquainted with biblical and Jewish literature, and knew how to conceal the bare-ness of the new movement. On the one hand, he invested the Temple with Protestant attributes, and on the other, by reason of his conceit and ostentation, he gave it an aggressive character. With Salomon the influence of the preacher among the German Jews commenced; the pulpit took the place of the school, and from it there often resounded the hollow phrases which conceal thought, or the lack of thought. The Temple Union had officially given up the belief in the Messiah, without exactly defining what position Judaism was to assume with reference to Christianity. Some of the zealous reformers meditated a complete rupture, and the refusal to contribute to the communal funds.

The originators and leaders were filled with the delusive idea, which at first appeared justifiable, that the Temple, through its modern and attractive form of service, would bring back to the fold those alienated from Judaism. They hoped that the less stringent religious forms would overcome the dislike felt by worldly men against everything Jewish. In a few instances those who had fallen away from Judaism were restrained from overstepping the threshold into the Church, but it was not a remedy with permanent effect. Nevertheless, the achievements of the Hamburg Temple, commonplace though its origin was, are not to be underrated. At one stroke, without much hesitation, it banished the rubbish of centuries from the synagogue, swept away with youthful impetuosity the holy cobwebs which no one had ventured to touch, and awakened a taste for a well-regulated service, for decorous behavior at divine worship, and for order and simplicity. The injury inflicted on Judaism by the aping of foreign customs, and the dilution of its own strength, cannot be altogether attributed to it.

Naturally the establishment of the Hamburg Temple produced a split in the Jewish world. Hitherto there had existed only the "old-fashioned" and the "new-fashioned" people, as they termed each other, but no distinct sects possessing a banner, a password, and a confession of faith. Not even the old-fashioned orthodox section constituted a definite party. For, although the adherents of the past, who would not swerve a hair's breadth from former practices, were so numerous, that even in Hamburg they might have suppressed the innovators if they had chosen, they did not act as a body. Only the faint remonstrance of single individuals was heard lamenting the ruin of Judaism through its betrayers, and these oft-repeated wailings were pitiful. The old party had no chiefs, no leaders; respect for the rabbis had vanished in a single generation. The wretched dispute for and against Jonathan Eibeschütz, and the satires of Hebrew writers of the period of the Measfim, had completely undermined their authority. In the larger German congregations the empty rabbinical chairs were permitted to remain untenanted. They no longer wished to have rabbis from Poland, because these could not speak the language of the land, and in Germany there were no great rabbis of recognized authority. Berlin set the example, which was followed by the community of Prague, after the death of the wise Ezekiel Landau, by Hamburg after the retirement of the zealot Raphael Cohen, and by Frankfort-on-the-Main after the death of the ultra-orthodox (Chassidic) Pinchas Hurwitz. The assistants (Dayanim) of the rabbis administered the rabbinical office—hybrid creatures, too dependent to have an opinion of their own, and too weak to oppose the demands of reckless leaders of communities.

As a result of the disregard in which the rabbis were held, the Talmudical schools fell into decay. Gifted Jewish youths, whose education formerly had begun with the Talmud, preferred to attend the gymnasiums and universities, and learned to despise the Talmud and Judaism. The most famous Talmudical academies in Prague, Frankfort, Altona and Hamburg, Fürth, Metz, and Halberstadt, which had boasted at least several hundred pupils (Bachurim), were gradually closed. This desolation spread to Poland, as the Talmud students no longer had hope of finding employment in Germany and France. They still made their way to Germany, but with the intention of studying science (Chochmoth), or if they remained at home, they devoted themselves to the ensnaring mysticism of Neo-Chassidism. There were but four rabbis of the younger generation who, on account of their profound knowledge of the Talmud and their pure, patriarchal character, enjoyed widespread authority : Mordecai Benet, in Nikolsburg, Jacob Lissa, Akiba Eger, and his son-in-law, Moses Sofer, of Frankfort-on-the-Main. These four rabbis, by their ingenious methods, kept alive the zeal for Talmudical study. Akiba Eger, owing to his astoundingly ingenious mind and high virtues —among which modesty was preëminent—enjoyed almost divine reverence from the thousands of disciples who came from his academies in Friedland and Posen. He was a quiet man, who never took the initiative, and was averse to aggressive opposition. Moses Sofer, on the other hand, was a fanatical zealot and an active heretic-hunter. He possessed courage and determination which disregarded consequences. He might have been a useful leader, but, like his companions, he was at too great a distance from the scene of action, to take part in the contest, or even to set up a standard. These rabbis had not the slightest conception of the new tendency which the times and the Jews had developed, and were therefore ignorant of the importance of the cause which they represented. They did not know the enemy whom they attacked, or despised him too much to be dangerous opponents. When a serious question or a critical situation arose, they were at a loss what to do, brought out their old rusty weapons, and damaged their cause by revealing its weakness. This awkwardness created an impression of feebleness and decrepitude. Thus the old orthodox party (as their opponents, borrowing the name from Church phraseology, termed them), or conservatives, were without a head, without a banner or a plan, utterly without unanimity or discipline, without consciousness of their own strength. They especially lacked eloquence, the indispensable means by which public opinion is influenced and ruled, and its follies and hollow emptiness are made apparent. Their utter want of education avenged itself bitterly upon the rigidly pious party.

On the other hand, the opposing section, the ardent innovators, the party of Jacobson, possessed what was wanting in the others: a daring leader, unity, and especially a wealth of passwords and phrases, such as, "spirit of the times, enlightenment," by which the thoughtless are captivated. Their victory and ultimate success could be foreseen. They had confidence and the courage of youth, were bold, and not over-particular as to the means employed. Jacobson, their chief, knew how to pursue and achieve an end, and how to utilize the means at his disposal. He saw that the Hamburg Temple would encounter difficulties, and would be condemned as heretical by the old rabbis. Jacobson was in correspondence with the founders, and knew that the Senate, instigated by the orthodox party, would, like the king of Prussia, forbid innovations. He also saw that many of the Hamburg Templars were too lukewarm to struggle against great difficulties. For this reason he strove to obtain in advance the ratification of the Temple ritual. Among the rabbis of Germany he could find no voice of approval for the new order of service. He, therefore, connected himself —a fact which throws no favorable light upon the cause—with a base adventurer, who, it appears, was bribed to help him. Eleazar Libermann from

Austria, a gambler, became his apostle of reform. To characterize the man, it suffices to note that he afterwards was baptized. At the bidding of the reformers, Libermann traveled in Austria. From him they learned that in Hungary and Italy there were rabbis or would-be rabbis, willing to pronounce a favorable opinion upon the new ritual. Jacobson addressed his inquiries to them, and his wishes were fulfilled. The first who allowed himself to be used by Libermann was Aaron Chorin (from Chorin), rabbi in Arad, Hungary, a tedious talker of superficial culture and mediocre Talmudical scholarship, who was capable of repeating absurdities in three languages—in Hebrew, German, and the Jewish-German jargon. He was devoted to the new movement without clearly understanding its bearings. Two Italian rabbis of low attainments also spoke in favor of the innovations. The opinions of all these men—not one of whom was of wholly sound mind—showed that the introduction of the organ was not against Rabbinical law. Chorin alone produced authorities in favor of the other reforms, and for German prayers. Libermann collated these opinions, strengthened them by his own pretended learning, adding the falsehood that not only all the rabbis of Leghorn, but even those of Jerusalem, had declared it permissible to use the organ in Jewish divine service. These opinions, which were printed and scattered broadcast, were intended to exonerate the Hamburg Reform Temple from blame at its very birth, and to remove the blot of illegitimacy which, as might have been foreseen, the rabbis of the old school would affix to it.

Whilst the reformers energetically tried to forestall every obstacle, the conservatives remained idle, and allowed the dangers which threatened their convictions to gather unnoticed. As already observed, Hamburg had at this time no rabbi at its head, but a college of three assistants (Dayanim) of little repute. Although these official representatives of Judaism had almost the entire Hamburg community to support them, they opposed the innovations with little vigor. Shortly after the opening of the Temple, the college ordered a feebly-written proclamation to be put up in the synagogues (October 26, 1818), that the new prayer-book should not be used by Israelites of pious sentiments, because contrary to usage essential passages had been omitted or altered. But this declaration lost its effect, when the lay heads of the community—whose assistance the Dayanim had not been able to win— took it down, and rebuked the authors, because "they had been guilty of intolerable presumption." The lay heads, at the recommendation of the college, afterwards invited the leaders of the Temple (November 8th) to a meeting, and requested them to discontinue the use of the prayer-book, as it did not agree with the ritual accepted by all Jewish communities. The Templars, however, laughed this demand to scorn.

The Temple Union unexpectedly received moral support from a person having great influence in Hamburg. Lazarus Riesser, the father of the indefatigable champion for the emancipation of the Jews in Germany, had always been reckoned one of the old orthodox party. As the son-in-law of Rabbi Raphael Cohen and his right hand, he was absorbed in the Talmud. He had published a Hebrew life of Raphael Cohen, in which he eulogized not only the author, but also his rabbinical views, and declared himself his faithful follower. How astonished, therefore, were the Hamburg Jews of both parties when a letter from Riesser suddenly appeared, entitled "To my Co-religionists in Hamburg" (the beginning of 1819), applauding the Temple innovations, and sharply rebuking the rabbinical college which had opposed them! He frankly called the opponents "sanctimonious hypocrites" who "nourish

contentions in Israel, and bar the way of the sons
desirous of returning to the favor of their father."
It appears that he wished to wreak a petty revenge
upon the members of the rabbinical college of
Hamburg, by whom he perhaps thought himself kept
in the background.

The orthodox party in Hamburg, who imagined
that no rabbi in the whole of Europe would approve
of the reforms, were bitterly disappointed; owing
to the activity of Jacobson and Libermann, the
Jewish public discovered that several rabbis in various districts upheld them.   The old rabbis were so
listless and indolent in the matter, that they had to
be addressed twice, before they pronounced judgment against the Temple.   In the first excitement
the Hamburg rabbis had unwisely condemned the
innocent and commendable customs which were
introduced into the Temple, such as the Portuguese
pronunciation of Hebrew, the omission of intoning
in reading from the Bible.   To rectify these mistakes, they afterwards limited their complaints to
three points—the abridgment of the prayers, especially with reference to the omission of Messianic
passages, prayers in German, and the use of the
organ.   To this programme the agreement of numerous distinguished rabbis and rabbinates was at
length secured; four in Germany (Fürth, Mayence,
Breslau, and Hanau), five in Italy (Trieste, Modena,
Padua, Mantua, and Leghorn), three in Prussian
Poland (Posen, Lissa, and Rawitz), and two in
Moravia (Nikolsburg and Trietsch).   Moses Sofer
in Presburg, the German rabbi in Amsterdam, and
the French chief rabbis of the consistory of Wint-
zenheim, also signed the document.   They all
declared the reforms in the Temple to be distinctly
heterodox.   Libermann's falsehoods now became
apparent, as the Leghorn rabbinate had not given
its assent to the use of the organ.   Samun, a would-
be rabbi of Leghorn, and Chorin of Arad, probably

under moral compulsion, revoked their former testimonials. The most zealous in their denunciations
of the Temple were Sofer of Presburg and Benet of
Nikolsburg, who declared the slightest deviation
from ancient usages as heresy. But the impression
which the authors of this document had hoped for
did not follow. It had been delayed too long, more
than seven months having elapsed before sentence
of heresy was promulgated; and meantime the
Temple Union had established itself. Eighteen
antagonistic rabbinates (in all forty rabbis) did not
seem many; and the most eminent of all, the Central Consistory of France, had remained silent.
The signers of the protest asserted that more opinions had been received; but this belated statement
was of no avail. The arguments adduced by the
rabbis against the Temple service were for the most
part void, some were thoroughly childish. The
letter of the law spoke against them. The diver-
sity of opinions among rabbinical authorities of various ages and countries, always made it possible to
find reasons for and against any question.

This weakness was mercilessly exposed by M. J.
Bresselau, one of the originators of the Hamburg
reform. In a Hebrew letter (1819) written in
beautiful Hebrew style and with such skillful man-
ipulation of biblical verses, that it seemed as though
the prophets and psalmists themselves were scourging the delusions of the obtuse rabbis, Bresselau
treated them now as ignorant boys, now as false
prophets, and especially as disturbers of the peace.
Every sentence in this seemingly earnest but
bitingly satirical epistle was a dagger-thrust against
the old perversions and their defenders. The
reformers also obtained reinforcement from Poland.
The old-fashioned party, on the other hand, were
unable to present a single Hebrew writer to defend
their cause. Even the Hebrew style used in the
document of the opposing rabbis was rugged and

coarse.   The Dayanim of Hamburg, indeed, caused
the testimonial to be in part translated into German—a concession that betrayed the weakness of
their cause—but the German version was not calculated to create a good impression.   For this they
had to employ Shalom Cohen, a turn-coat, who had
formerly belonged to the ranks of the reformers.
In short, the conservatives were unfortunate, because
they were unskillful and imprudent.

It also happened that the Temple quarrel took
place in the year when the " Hep, hep !" cry was
being raised, and Hamburg also participated in it.
The wealthy and worldly Jews were thereby restricted to the society of their own people, and actively
supported the banner that had been unfurled.   The
Jewish merchants of Hamburg, members of the
Temple Union, who were accustomed to attend the
fair at Leipsic during the chief festivals in the spring
and autumn, joined some Berlin merchants of similar opinions, and established a branch synagogue
(September 20, 1820).   Meyerbeer composed the
songs for the opening ceremony.   They appointed
a so-called fair-preacher (Messprediger), Jacob
Auerbach, and from this gathering-place of Jews
from various countries, the innovations spread to a
wider circle.   The Hamburg reforms thus were
adopted in some parts; and in other communities,
such as those of Carlsruhe, Königsberg, and
Breslau, where the entire programme was not carried out, at least the rite of confirmation, imitated
from the Church, was introduced.

The first attempt to set up an opposing party, so
as to dam the overflowing stream of reform, and
make it subside into a quiet bed, commenced on
account of the Temple innovations.   This opposing
party was established by a man who had himself
partially forsaken rabbinical Judaism, but who strove
to strengthen and vindicate it, under the correct
impression that development must take place upon

its own soil, with due regard to historical conditions, and along its peculiar lines, and especially without aping foreign Church forms. Isaac Bernays (born at Mayence, 1792; died at Hamburg, 1849) was the man who intelligently opposed the prevailing flaccidity of semi-enlightened reform and thought. In South Germany, in contradistinction to North Germany with its love for formal statements of doctrines, which never rose beyond the commonplaces of rationalism, a mystic philosophical school had been established, which promoted visionary notions. In all things, the smallest and the greatest, in nature and history, in the grouping of things, in numbers, colors, and names, this philosophy beheld a system, germs of ideas, the shattered ruins of a gigantic mirror reflecting fundamental thoughts in huge size. Isaac Bernays belonged to this school. To his vision Judaism in its literature and historical progress revealed itself half unveiled. Bernays' mind, with its overflowing wealth of ideas, found in all phenomena the harmonious systemization and development of a fundamental thought, which to manifest all its latent possibilities permeated passing events and historical achievements, and which had developed from the beginning of creation to the most recent fact. Bernays, much profounder than Mendelssohn, was the first to recognize the important rôle of Judaism in the history of the world, and at a glance to measure the range of its literature. His fault was, perhaps, that he was too rich in ideas, that therefore he sought out and discovered too much, and was not equal to the task of clothing his ideas in fitting form and language. From his superior altitude he looked with contemptuous pity upon the poverty of thought of Jewish reformers, who desired to contract and confine the giant spirit of Judaism (of which they had no conception) within the narrow bounds of a catechism for big and little children. In his eyes the followers of Friedländer were the embodiment of insipidity and narrowness. They impressed Bernays with the idea of a rabble who dwell in a Pyramid. and fit it up for petty household purposes.

"They, the disciples of Mendelssohn, ashamed of their antiquity, prefer, as foundlings of the present day, wildly to overleap the unfashionable limits of the Law, instead of listening in the school of their race, to hear what God has brought about at the present day."

The train of thought by which Bernays reconstructed Judaism in his mind from its original sources and history, is little known to us. He preferred oral to written instruction, and was averse to put his thoughts on paper. The "Biblical Orient," which is ascribed to him, is, so to speak, only the foundation of the vestibule of a reverence-inspiring temple. This work, odd as it was in form, is distinguished for its depth and originality; it starts with the idea, that to Judaism is allotted the task of bringing back to God men created in His image, and that the Jewish people was to serve as a type to mankind, showing how the lost likeness to God may be regained. The "Biblical Orient" endeavored to establish a more thorough comprehension of the Bible than had been effected by the Mendelssohnian school. They had regarded it merely from its poetical side, and had failed to see that it portrays the collision between two views of life. Bernays believed that his criticism dethroned the Mendelssohn school, together with its founder; for Mendelssohn himself, by his superficial treatment of Hebrew literature, had been the first to contribute to the enervation of Judaism.

According to the opinion of Bernays, the Hebrew cult differed from that of the heathen, and was intended to be a contrast. Idolatry expressed itself in plastic, Judaism in ritual, symbolism. Therefore the very aspect of Judaism which the reformers desired to abolish as unfitting and unworthy, should be preserved. Everything which in the course of

Jewish history had been assimilated and developed, according to Bernays, ought to have a place assigned to it, being a necessary part of the whole,—even Talmudism and the Kabbala.

This book contains many immature and unpolished ideas, much that borders on the ridiculous. But if the author only succeeded in awakening the idea that Judaism has an historical mission as an apostle to the nations, it should suffice to procure for him a place of honor in the records of Jewish history. Not that he could claim this as a new discovery, for the text-book of Judaism plainly points to it. It is the essence of the messages proclaimed by the prophets. It has been verified by history, that European and Asiatic nations have been delivered from their darkness by the light that came from Judaism. But the accumulated sufferings of the Jews, and the servile form assumed by Judaism, had caused this fact to be so entirely forgotten, that its own sons had no idea thereof. The merit of the man who again called it to mind is therefore of no mean degree.

The extraordinary talents and original ideas of Bernays directed the attention of Jewish society to him. Afterwards, it is true, he denied the authorship of the "Biblical Orient"; but if he did not actually compose it, he might have done so, for it is flesh of his flesh, or spirit of his spirit.

The Hamburg community, which sorely needed a power to withstand the Temple Union, in consequence of his renown chose Bernays for their spiritual guide. It was a good move on their part, and bore important results. The rabbis of the old school were ill prepared for the contest between two justifiable principles, the preservation of Judaism in its peculiar manifestations, and the assimilation of European culture by the Jews. Their weapons had grown rusty, and injured the owners more than their opponents. Fresh forces were

therefore required in their cause—men cognizant
of the wants of the age, who could utilize them
for the honor and purification of Judaism.   The
appointment of Bernays to the Hamburg rabbinate
(November, 1821) created a stir: he was the first
rabbi with a well-ordered secular education.   It was
a sign of the times that he dispensed with the title
of rabbi and preferred to be called Chacham, as was
customary among the Portuguese Jews : he did not
wish the despised title of rabbi to be a hindrance to
his activity.   True to his aversion for slavish imitation, he eschewed all clerical mummery in costume
and gestures, to which the reform preachers attached
great importance in the pulpit.   Bernays did not
claim to be the guardian of souls, only the teacher
of his congregation.   He also delivered sermons,
but the contents, form, and other details differed
entirely from those introduced by the Jacobson
school.   Owing to his peculiar mode of thought,
his addresses were not understood by the multitude ; but thoughtful hearers at least conceded to
him the merit of originality, which contrasted favorably with the insipidity of the Temple preachers.
When Heine, who at this time was still interested
practically in Judaism, was staying in Hamburg, he
was induced to hear Bernays' sermons, and to com-
pare them with those of other preachers.   Heine
understood the method and form of his thoughts,
and the opinion of the lyrical satirist ran as follows :

  " I have heard Bernays preach . . . , none of the Jews understand
him, he desires nothing for himself, and will never play any other
part ; but he is a man of mind, and has more life in him than Kley,
Salomon, and Auerbach I and II."

By unobtrusive work, Bernays succeeded in gaining the respect, not only of the community, but also
of the rigidly pious party elsewhere.   Their suspicious natures found nothing to blame in the religious conduct of the Chacham.   The changes that
he introduced, in reality reforms, met with approval

and imitation in orthodox congregations. By his penetration and his great erudition he exercised deep influence over the rising generation, to whom he opened up the rich treasures of Jewish literature, then but little known. He thereby imbued his disciples with joyous attachment to Judaism. As already stated, he did not care for writing. If his courage had kept pace with his knowledge and wealth of ideas, his activity would have had greater influence on modern Jewish history.

In another quarter, an equally beneficent and elevating, though differently constituted, personality, was at work. Isaac Noah Mannheimer (born at Copenhagen, 1793; died at Vienna, 1864), originally a disciple of the school of Jacobson, softened its crudities, and so caused the offensive alterations in the divine service to be received favorably; he struck the right note when making improvements. He may justly be considered the incarnation of Jewish refinement—every inch a man. In him the essential elements of peculiarly Jewish culture were harmoniously combined with the attractive forms of European civilization; indeed, in every respect his was a perfectly moulded nature. Gifted with genial humor and wit, enthusiasm and discretion, leading an ideal life, and possessing a sure practical instinct, endowed with poetic talents and sober thought, with childlike tenderness and cutting satire, great eloquence and earnest vigor, deep love of Judaism and delight in modern ideas—he combined these varied characteristics in the happiest manner. These brilliant qualities, together with his nobility of soul and disinterestedness, devotion to his convictions, and conscientiousness in all official duties, his delicacy of feeling, tact, aversion to vulgarity and forbearance with the vulgar—swiftly captivated all hearts, attracted the noble-minded, and even filled the unworthy with respect, and thus lightened his labors. Born and bred under the mild Danish

government, which at an early date had granted
equal rights to Jews, nor, like other states, withdrew or abridged them when circumstances changed,
Mannheimer from childhood learned to hold his
head high, and to represent his co-religionists and
utter his convictions without fear even in a country
where a servile conception of the position of bur-
gesses, peasants, and especially of the Jews, long
prevailed.   Mannheimer did not possess original
ideas or deep knowledge of Jewish literature; but
he was powerfully swayed by his own convictions,
which he cherished and disseminated, not hiding
them away as buried treasures.   This man of words
and action was placed by destiny in a situation,
where his peculiar nature and special gifts could
find scope, and ennoble wide circles.   Everyone
cognizant of the state of affairs then prevailing in
Austria, and the extent to which the Austrian Jews
have since progressed, must confess that Mannheimer was providentially fitted for his position in
the Austrian capital, on the boundary-line of semi-
barbarous countries, to raise the Jews of those
lands from the moral degeneracy into which they
had been plunged as much by Joseph II's benevolent despotism as by his mother's hostility, and to
repair the harm caused by the Herz Hombergs, the
Peter Beers, and the whole troop of so-called
"Normal teachers" and official religious instructors.

A chief who, in face of constant strife and danger,
founds a colony with a band of half savage men,
elevates it, and trains it to be a pattern to others,
can claim no greater praise than Mannheimer
deserved in founding the congregation of Vienna.
The camp of Metternich and Francis I tolerated no
Jews within its domains ; only by way of exception
a few rich families with their dependents were
tolerated under various extraordinary titles.   These
favored families had immigrated from various
countries, were in no way connected, had no rights

as a community, could not possess a synagogue, nor appoint a rabbi ; in short, by law almost everything was forbidden to them as a religious body. Nevertheless, certain adventurous persons amongst them desired to introduce a German order of service, founded on the model of the Hamburg Temple, and their efforts were alternately encouraged and frustrated by the government. When these enlightened men in Vienna undertook to build a Temple, they secured the aid of Mannheimer as preacher (June, 1825), but were compelled to evade the restrictive laws by inventing some insignificant title for him, so that he might be allowed to reside in Vienna.

Although Mannheimer was intimate with David Friedländer, Jacobson, and the young iconoclasts with whom destruction of the old Judaism was a principle, and had occasionally preached in the Reform synagogues of Berlin, Hamburg, and Leipsic, yet he was not so strongly attached to the new system that he did not recognize its fundamental errors. His first and his last word in his new sphere of action was that no rupture should be caused between Jews, no sectarianism should be encouraged, and that the old orthodox party should not be offended and repelled by daring movements, but should gradually be won over to the new forms. Actuated by these ideas, he carried a moderate change in the synagogue service, in opposition to the wishes of the man who had promoted him to his office. Mannheimer in the new synagogue removed only offensive excrescences, making the service dignified, and animating it by his impressive words, but he retained the Hebrew language, that strong bond of union, and, to the regret of his former brother reformers, dispensed with the organ and German hymns. Even more successfully than Isaac Bernays did Isaac Mannheimer pave the way to the reconciliation of old and new ideas.

In his pulpit eloquence, acknowledged by competent judges, Jews and Christians, to be of high quality, his power of harmoniously combining two apparently hostile elements was displayed. Mannheimer had discovered a noble treasure in Jewish literature and profited richly by it. In the Talmud and Agada— a mine of thoughtful sayings, parables, riddles, interesting observations and witty play upon words—he made himself thoroughly at home, discovered the golden grain, or, to speak more accurately, knew how to extract a pleasing meaning from the most insignificant saying, and employed the remarks of the old Agadists as interpreters of new views and thoughts. By utilizing the Agadic elements, his method of preaching acquired a peculiar character, and exercised strong attraction over the pious Jews and the rising generation. Portuguese Jews (Franks), who had migrated from Turkey to Vienna, also listened with pleasure to this lively and spirited preacher. The East and West were united in Mannheimer and in the new Viennese Temple, consecrated April, 1826. As if the congregation of this Temple were intended from the outset to complete the work of propitiation between old and new forms, they succeeded in securing the services of Sulzer, a skilled musician, who with his wealth of musical resources endowed the Hebrew prayers with almost magical expressiveness, and transformed the old objectionable intoning into soul-stirring melodies. These melodies rendered an organ superfluous. The soft, swelling chorals and solos of the Viennese Temple, as also Mannheimer's sermons, proved that the old possessions were not utterly useless, as violent reformers had represented them to be, but only required modifying to be impressive. Pulpit and choir, working in accord, produced great effect upon the minds of the growing congregation of Vienna, whose affection for inherited Judaism, and reverence for Jewish antiquity were

combined with a desire to satisfy the demands of
progress. Mannheimer's personality served to
strengthen the feeling so awakened. In the pulpit,
as in household and social affairs, he appeared, not
as a guardian of souls, as a clergyman, or priest—he
abominated a sanctimonious, unctuous manner—but
as a tender father, as a friend, adviser, and help.
As he did not shrink from censuring the objectionable side of old and new customs, he educated,
by word and example, a pattern community in which
each individual strove to maintain peace and suppress dissension.

It was in Vienna that the subservient humility
of the Jew was first turned into self-respect, and
this in spite of the political oppression which lasted
until the year of the Revolution. The aversion
felt by the barbarous Polish Jews to civilization
gradually disappeared, giving way to a desire
for self-improvement. The Viennese community
thereby obtained historical importance. The tones
that resounded from the pulpit and the choir, stirring
the members of the congregation, awoke a mighty
echo in the near and remote communities of Austria.
Pesth, Prague, and smaller communities in Hungary
and Bohemia followed the impulse given by Vienna,
influenced by the conciliatory manner with which the
" purified divine service" was there conducted, and
the movement commenced in Vienna extended to
Galicia.

The election of Chacham Bernays as head of the
Hamburg congregation, and Mannheimer's activity
in establishing the order of service in the Vienna
synagogue, gradually aroused the emulation of other
German communities. Educated rabbis were
preferred, and they restored dignity to the synagogue. The German Jews in turn made their
influence felt in France and Italy. The Franco-
Jewish consistories having neglected the favorable
opportunity to be leaders, offered by French suprem-

acy, had to content themselves with being followers. In Italy those of the communities that belonged to Austria also felt the impulse originating in Germany, although sermons in the vernacular or in Spanish had been delivered there since olden times, and the divine service, at least outwardly, showed no signs of neglect.

How great the harm that can be done through unsoundness of mind or nebulous theories even by distinguished men, or how, at least, they can nullify their own efforts, was proved by a striking example in Berlin, in most remarkable contrast to that in Vienna. At the time when the learned mob of Germany were flinging stones at the Jews with the cry of "Hep, hep!" three Jewish young men met together to plan a sort of conspiracy against the incorrigible Christian state, all three filled with earnest ideals. They pondered carefully the means to be employed in destroying the deeply-rooted hatred against Jews in Germany. The first of the three was Zunz who lived to grow grey in research; the second, Edward Gans, the champion and apostle of Hegel's philosophy and the assailant of the old ways of jurisprudence; and lastly, an accountant who lived in a literary world, Moses Moser, Heine's most trusted friend, whom he called, "The *édition de luxe* of a real man, the epilogue of Nathan the Wise." They combined (November 27, 1819) for the purpose of founding a "Society for the Culture and Science of the Jews." Gans, who was of a mercurial nature, and might have been the leader of a revolution, was the chief of this movement. These three young men secured the aid of two others similarly disposed, who were enthusiastic for science, freedom, and idealism. The two fossilized Mendelssohnians, Ben-David and David Friedländer, also became members of the society, and Jacobson was ready with advice and assistance. In all it numbered about fifty members in Berlin; in Hamburg it owned about twenty of the supporters of the Temple Union, and a few others scattered in one place and another. As already mentioned, Heine afterwards attached himself to it, and worked for its success.

The first condition made by the founders was that the members were to adhere faithfully to Judaism, to withstand bravely the allurements of the Church, and thus give to the young generation a brilliant example of constancy and independence. Had it remained true to this programme, the society would have been a beneficent factor in the advancement of Judaism, seeing that most of its members were talented, and occupied the heights of culture. But it started from false premises, aimed at results too far removed, and employed the wrong means to attain the end. Practical minds were wanting in the society. The false premise was, that if the Jews acquired solid culture, devoted themselves to arts and science, and carried on agriculture and handicrafts instead of trade, German anti-Semitism would vanish, the sons of Teut would fraternally embrace the sons of Jacob, and the state would not deny them equal privileges. Therefore the society desired—their multitudinous wishes seem almost ludicrous—to establish schools, seminaries, and academies for the Jews, to promote trades, arts, agriculture, and scientific studies, and even educate them in the forms of polite society. From the idea of founding academies, however, only a sort of private school resulted, where the cultured members of the society taught or caused to be instructed poor youths who had come to Berlin principally from Poland, students of the Talmud who escaped from its folios to learn " wisdom." The founders soon perceived that they had built castles in the air, and that the Society for Culture, on account of its pretentious character, met with no support. They therefore took up a less exalted position, limiting themselves to mere agitation, and to the promotion of the science of Judaism,—certainly a praiseworthy enterprise and a pressing necessity. They determined to deliver discourses in turn, and to establish a journal for the "Science of Judaism." But the leaders themselves did not exactly know what was meant by this term, nor how to commence their work.

Hegel, the profound thinker and great sophist, the court and church philosopher, introduced these young Jews, ardent in the pursuit of truth, into the labyrinths of his method, and confused their minds. Young Israel, the founders of the Society for Culture, at first listened to the utterances of this philosophical acrobat as to oracles. In a parrot-like manner they repeated after him, that Judaism is the religion of the spirit, which has given up the ghost, and that Christianity has united in itself the whole of ancient history, and radiates its ideas in a rejuvenated, ennobled form. They also accustomed themselves, like their master, to walk upon stilts. The simplest thoughts were presented in distorted forms, as though they did not wish to be understood. How, indeed, could feeling for Judaism have awakened in them? Edward Gans, it is true, was continually speaking of the "unrelieved pain of Judaism," but was all the time thinking of himself, who could not obtain a position in Prussia. What was the aim of the science of Judaism which this Society for Culture desired to promote? Gans expressed it in the hollow phrases of the Hegelian jargon, and it is apparent that the leader did not know what cause his followers were to defend.

"The Jews cannot perish, nor can Judaism be utterly destroyed. But in the great movement of the whole, it is to seem to have perished, still it is to continue to live, as the stream lives on in the ocean."

The Society desired to assist in demolishing the wall of separation dividing Jews from Christians, and the Jewish world from the European. It wished to abolish every dissimilarity existing between the Jewish and the universal system.

The journal of the Society for Culture testified to the uncertainty and obscurity of its aim. Its articles consisted chiefly of indigestible Hegelian phraseology, or of learned matter of use to an exceedingly limited circle as material for further work. Heine, who called a spade by its name, bluntly declared to the editor of the journal, "That the greater part of it is useless owing to its obscure form."

"Did I not know by chance what Marcus [one of the contributors] and Gans are aiming at, I should not understand anything of what they write. . . . . Insist upon culture of style with your contributors. Without this, the other culture cannot thrive."

Yet with this farrago of nonsense the Society hoped to elevate not only the Jews, but even Judaism, and were indignant that the former paid no regard to their efforts. Gans, in an article giving an account of their plans, complained that the founders were not understood. The reproach which he cast upon the Jews in general was especially true of the Society for Culture—

"Enthusiasm for religion, together with the solidity of ancient institutions, has vanished, but no new enthusiasm has come to light, and no new state of affairs has established itself. We have not gone beyond that negative enlightenment, which consists in despising and contemning things as they are, without troubling to infuse a new spirit."

This marvel could least of all be brought about by the Society for Culture, because it was deaf to the voice of God, which speaks in Jewish history, in Jewish law from its very commencement, and in the Jewish people. The Society inveighed against the whole world, and relieved its feelings in elegiac effusions. Gans, the chief mover, poured out his wrath over the rich men in Israel, who showed no sympathy with his world-awakening dreams.

Great was the disappointment of the founders of

the Society for Culture. Its supporters diminished rather than increased in number. The journal with its curiously confused language found no readers, supplies ran short, and the members themselves forsook the standard, and in spite of the tacit oath embraced Christianity. Edward Gans himself secretly cherished the idea of obtaining a professorship by means of baptism. The dissensions among the German Jews, the contemptuous tone in which the sons of Judaism spoke of their religion, and the numerous examples of baptism in their midst—up to the year 1823 there were no less than 1,236 conversions in Berlin, comprising half of the members of the community, and in other parts of Prussia there were 1,382—and the pietism of the Prussian court, brought about the formation in Berlin of a Society, "For the Promotion of Christianity among the Jews," which hoped to see the whole body of the Jews enter the Church. The election of talented Jews to academic posts was strenuously opposed. In vain did Hardenberg, the minister, intercede for Gans, to obtain for him the chair of historical jurisprudence, which was his specialty. Gans considered the possibility of becoming baptized whilst delivering long addresses before the Society for Culture. The Society dissolved, and at length died out quietly, uncared for, and unregretted. Gans, the chief mover, who possessed sufficient wealth to enable him to remain true to his vow, increased the number of sceptics and infidels professing Christianity. This so exasperated Heine, although he himself was a convert to Christianity, that two decades later, even after the grave had closed over him, he could not forgive Gans.

"The apostasy of Gans was the more revolting, because he played the part of agitator, and accepted the positive duties of a president. It is a traditional duty for the captain to be the last to leave the sinking ship ; Gans, however, was the first to save himself."

Moser, the second of the triumvirate of the Society for Culture, remained more steadfast to his

views, although he doubted the possibility of saving
Judaism, and proclaimed the wholesale baptism of
the Jews. The third member of the triumvirate was
the most steadfast, and alone remained thoroughly
true to his word. He was also filled with doubts,
but he did not despair of improvement. He pointed
out how the cure or the completion of the new
revival must commence. "What alone survives
and is imperishable in the midst of this 'Mabul'
(deluge) is the science of Judaism; it continues to
live, even though for centuries no finger has been
raised on its behalf. I confess that next to my submission to the justice of God, my hope and support
consist in the cultivation of this science. These
storms and experiences shall not so influence me as
to bring me into collision with myself. I have done
what I thought my duty. Because I saw that I was
preaching in a wilderness I ceased to preach, but
not in order to be faithless to the purport of my own
words. There remains naught for the members of
the Society to do, save to remain true, each man to
the work of his own limited sphere, and leave the
rest to God."

If the Society for Culture, which started on its
career with high aspirations, and ended so lament-
ably, succeeded in producing only this one result,
stirring up love for the science of Judaism, then its
dreams and attempts have not been entirely vain.
In history not even the slightest seed is wasted;
but no plant could blossom in soil covered with the
dust cast on it by Friedländer and Jacobson in
Berlin. As if smitten with a curse, the spot where
Mendelssohn began the work so full of promise,
nothing could be made to thrive or be of service in
the revival of Judaism. The rabbinical academy,
which the rabbinical assistant in Berlin, in conjunction
with excellent men, desired to call into existence,
never saw the light. From another quite unexpected
quarter, however, there arose the prospect, if not
of salvation, yet of its beginning.

CHAPTER XVI.

AWAKENING OF INDEPENDENCE AND THE SCIENCE OF JUDAISM.

Dawn of Self-respect—Research into Jewish History—Hannah Adams —Solomon Löwisohn—Jost—His History—The Revolution of July (1830) — Gabriel Riesser — His Lectures—Steinheim—His Works—His " Revelation "—Nachman Krochmal—Rapoport— Erter—His Poems—Rapoport's Writings—Zunz—Luzzatto—His Exegesis—Geiger—The " Nineteen Letters " of Ben Usiel—New School of Reform—Joel Jacoby.

1830—1840 C. E.

If for a moment fancy is allowed full play, one can imagine, not only that the houses, utensils, and pictures excavated from the ruins of Herculaneum and Pompeii were renewed, but also that the entombed men were suddenly aroused from their sleep of centuries, and enabled to collect their thoughts. If these resurrected Romans could recall their condition when the catastrophe befell them, could conjure up before their mind's eye the splendor of their greatness, remember the mighty institutions which they and their ancestors called into existence, realize the heroic power which the Roman people developed, and if they felt the same power still stirring within them, a not altogether unjustifiable self-esteem would seize them. This supposition is no fantastic idea: a nation actually did arise from the darkness of the tomb, the only example chronicled in the annals of man. This resuscitated people, the Jewish race, endeavored at its resurrection to collect its thoughts and memories, and recall a vision of its glorious past; feeling itself to be at once old and young, rich in memories and lacking in experience, chained to hoary antiquity by a perfect sequence of events, yet seeming as if of yesterday. The Jews first examined the monuments of their intellect, which had influenced the history of nations, and had brought forth a wealth of peculiar products. They served as signposts in the labyrinth of Jewish history. That is the science of Judaism—a vivid realization of its great history, and its peculiar doctrines. This effort of memory is not merely an amusing game, a pleasant pastime, the satisfaction of a desire for knowledge akin to curiosity, but an irresistible impulse of self-examination. It aroused the dormant strength in the breast of the inquirer, and inspired him with self-confidence to act in the future as in the past. Self-consciousness—the consciousness of being the people of God—was awakened in this old, resuscitated nation, and it at once entered into competition with the young nations, to assert its peculiar powers.

But history has not yet gone so far : it only shows that self-respect was awakened ; that the Jews no longer blush for their origin and confession ; no longer hesitate when questioned about them ; no longer, from false shame and their own evil plight, take a false step, pretending belief in a faith certainly more distasteful to them than to those born therein. As if this feeling of self-esteem were to be particularly favored by the generative force of history, there arose from the midst of the Jewish nation artists of great ability—artists in tone and color, and poets of the first rank, who by their steadfastness secured public recognition for their race. This self-respect of the Jews was the outcome of political maturity, the latter in turn being due to the wonderful inventions and the increase of general intelligence during the last decades, but it has chiefly been awakened, strengthened, and fostered by the science of Judaism and the achievements of talented Jews in connection therewith.

Although the history of this period is still in pro-

gression—at many points touches the fleeting present—and its results cannot be summed up like
those of bygone days, yet the fact cannot be denied
that the aim of Jewish life has been the attainment
of those two precious acquirements—self-reliance
and self-knowledge.   These qualities are intimately
connected, the one completing and promoting the
other.   Knowledge of their own experiences and
of history enabled the Jews to make a careful,
unprejudiced study of the origin and growth of their
nationality, and of the peculiarity of their teaching,
and to hide and ignore nothing.   Insight into their
own doctrines increased their self-reliance, and
induced them to remove the burdens assumed by
the generations that had lived under oppression.
The struggles in which the Jews had just been
engaged to secure civil, political, and social equality
and to bring about the reformation and refinement
of Judaism, stand in closest connection with these
two qualities—on the one hand, with the better
appreciation of their own nature, on the other, with
their growing self-reliance—influencing them, or
being influenced by them.

Step by step the mountain heaps of obstructive
rubbish had to be cleared away, an open space cut
out, new building materials procured or collected,
before it was possible, to think, not of putting the
crowning stone to the edifice, but of erecting the
frame of the structure.   Unconsciously the entire
generation, many members of which are still active,
set to work upon this gigantic task, which had not
been dreamed of fifty years before, still less considered in any way practicable.   Deep but almost
unconscious attachment to Judaism on the part of
enthusiastic spirits enabled them to attain a goal
which must be regarded as a marvel by posterity,
even though it has itself advanced beyond it.   Jewish science by laborious research and investigations
has developed three important points : the course

of Jewish history in its long chain of events and its significance, the precious basis of Jewish teaching in all its bearings, and, finally, the enduring faculty of the Jewish race, which defied so many persecutions, rendered certain qualities hereditary, accomplished such wondrous miracles of history, and was the means of bringing salvation to the world. These three aspects, the comprehension of history, of the tenets of Judaism, and of peculiar nationality, were developed one after the other. Each of these branches of knowledge had to be pursued from its commencement, and followed through a long course, and if not brought to a conclusion, it at least reached a state in which it could be clearly grasped and understood.

All nations desirous of asserting their independence and vitality seek to prove their age: they interest themselves in remembrances of the past, and bring to light their ancestral portraits and their armorial bearings, to demonstrate that they have passed through the vicissitudes of fortune and misfortune, the alternations of strength and weakness, victory and defeat, that they have given evidence of intellectual capacity, and therefore may lay claim to continued existence and development. The Jewish people had no need to make search for their famous exploits or the monuments of their intellectual powers; even in their apparently servile condition these were not wanting. Each century proclaimed this fact to the next, and it was only needful to give ear to, or not wholly to disregard this voice amid a crowd of selfish interests. The history of the Jews naturally bore most eloquent testimony to the people's greatness; but it was not easy to present it in its brilliancy. The history of the Jewish nation had been distorted by the thousand unjust prejudices of the ages. Under the cruel persecutions of their tormentors, the Jews could not retain the accumulated reminiscences of their great

past ; they knew them only in distorted fragments.
Christian scholars, attracted by the grandeur of the
theme, had indeed formed these disjointed fragments into a picture ; but it could not be a true one,
seeing that many component parts were wanting.
The bright colors had faded, and there was a pre-
ponderance of shadow, perhaps intentionally placed
there.   Even to well-disposed defenders of the
Jews, like Dohm and Grégoire, who had zealously
studied the annals of Jewish history, they did not
give a clear idea of its course.   More than a century had elapsed since the worthy French Protestant clergyman, Basnage, after diligently studying
Jewish history, had given to the world his somewhat
fragmentary researches, when the wife of an American clergyman, Hannah Adams, of Boston, struck
by the marvelous fate of the Jewish nation, delineated their history from the time of the return from
Babylon to recent days.   For many reasons she
was not qualified to give an intelligible outline of
Jewish history, but could only string together a
number of rough sketches without connection or
sequence.   This crude work, nevertheless, was
good enough for the purposes of the London Society for the Promotion of Christianity among the
Jews, which besides made several alterations in the
book in order to serve its ends.   Fidelity to history
and truth were entirely disregarded in the changes.

It was high time for Jews to take away the historian's pen from the hands of Christians who only
trifled with it.   However feeble might be their first
attempts, and inadequate though their conception
of the peculiarity of Jewish history was, yet it was
meritorious to remove the Christian seal, impressed
upon it by unconscious forgers, in order to claim it
as the property of the Church.   The first Jew who
bore in his heart the great characteristics of the
history of his race, and in part published it, deserves
a place of honor.   He was a talented youth whose

early death was due to insanity, so often the mark
of a true poet. Solomon Löwisohn (born in Moor,
Hungary, 1789, died 1822) had succeeded under
most unfavorable circumstances in acquiring secular
culture, and thereby had qualified himself to appreciate the value of his nation's treasures. Löwisohn
had a much truer comprehension of the beauty and
sweetness of Hebrew poetry, of its sublimity and
simplicity, than Herder, because he was better
acquainted with it. He regarded the history of his
people from the standpoint of poetry, as from that
of faith. In his "Lectures upon the Modern History of the Jews," from their dispersion till the
present day, he succeeded in unrolling a charming
picture. He also distinguished certain important
points, and correctly showed the lines to be followed,
to avoid losing oneself in this apparent chaos.

Jewish history assumed a better form in the hands
of Isaac Marcus Jost (born at Bernburg, 1793 ; died
at Frankfort-on-the-Main, 1860). He had greater
courage than a more gifted contemporary, and
although not possessed of sufficient resources he
undertook the gigantic task, and he deserves credit
for having pointed out a way through the vast labyrinth. When the bigoted Teutomaniacs desired to
banish the Jews from Teutonic soil, and the Jew-
haters searched the pages of history for an excuse
to slander them, Jost determined to show them in
a better light. He desired to prove that they had
always been peaceful citizens and faithful subjects.
They had certainly opposed the Roman Emperors,
and had maintained a vigorous war against them,
but this was the act of a few boisterous brawlers,
whose folly should not be visited upon the entire
people. On the whole, the Jews had proved themselves honest men, who had not slaughtered
Christian children, nor in any way deserved the
reproaches leveled against them. Only the Pharisees
and their descendants, the rabbis, detestable men,

filled with superstition, darkness, and arrogance, had
made hell hot for the people, the property of the
rabbis. This is the basis of Jost's delineation of
Jewish history. He wished to confute at the same
time the admirers and the antagonists of Jewish
history. No one at the present day can deny the
one-sidedness of his representation. Nevertheless
Jost performed a real service to his people by his
historical labors. He offered something new to his
age, and as accurately as possible laid down the indispensable foundations of history—time and space.
He cannot be reproached for utilizing the sources
of history without having investigated them; his
generation was not endowed with the faculty of carefully testing historical evidences. Jost's "History"
proved a good guide and instructor to statesmen
engaged in the amelioration of the condition of the
Jews.

But the main objection to Jost's narrative cannot
be disregarded, seeing that even in his old age, and
in spite of instructive criticism, he stubbornly
pursued his method. He gave to Jewish history,
undeniably heroic, a dry, Philistine character, despoil-
ing it of the brightness with which it was endowed
even in the eyes of unprejudiced Christian observers. He tore to shreds the heroic drama of
thousands of years. Between the old Israelites, the
ancestors and contemporaries of the Prophets and
Psalmists, and the Jews, the disciples of the rabbis,
Jost hollowed out a deep chasm, making a sharp
distinction between them, as if the latter were not
the descendants of the former, but of entirely different stock. And why? Because Jost, the pupil
of Friedländer and Jacobson, denied all miracles,
not only those involving changes in the laws of
nature, but also such as are brought about through
inspiration and steady endurance, the miracles of
history, arising out of the peculiar combination of
circumstances, blow following on blow, reaction on

action. He saw in history only an accumulation of contingencies subject to no law. Therefore the Jews were not to be considered the sons of the Israelites, nor the rabbis the successors of the Prophets, nor the Talmud the outcome of the Bible, otherwise the intervention of miracles had to be conceded.

In Europe, which had fallen into a state of almost glaring stupidity, there now occurred a historical marvel which caused a sensation from one end of the continent to the other. From the serene sky in the West there came a lightning flash; a thunderclap and terrifying crash followed, as if the end of the world had come—the Revolution of July (1830) was indeed a miracle. No one had expected it, or was prepared for it. Even the men who brought it about, and fought in it, were impelled by some dark feeling, were not aware of the force of their actions, were only the blind agents of the Ruler of history.

This revolution affected the Jews and consequently Judaism, like every important change in history. The equalization of the Jews in France, although sealed by the constitution, had suffered somewhat under the two Bourbons, Louis XVIII and Charles X, as the nobility and the Catholic clergy were possessed of great influence, and the officials understood their hint not to be too friendly to the Jews. The reactionary Catholic clergy began to renew their intolerance towards the Jews, and the police displayed hostility to the Jewish ritual. Had the Bourbons been able to gratify their own wishes by discrediting the constitution as well as liberty and equality, the French Jews would have been the first victims, and like their German co-religionists would once more have been placed under exceptional laws. The July Revolution was thus of momentous importance to them. The first assembly of deputies under King Louis Philippe, who desired to execute the Charter, at once considered the abolition of all existing inequalities, however slight, between Jews and Christians.   One of the deputies, Viennet, proposed (August 7, 1830) to remove from the constitution the recognition of a state religion. His proposition was supported on all sides. A few months later (November 13) the minister of public education, Mérilhou, brought forward a motion to place Judaism upon an equal footing with the other two creeds, to pay salaries from the public treasury to the Synagogue and the rabbis, as well as to the Church and its ministers. He praised the French Jews, saying that since the removal of their disabilities by the Revolution they had shown themselves worthy of the privileges granted them.   He exhorted the deputies to agree to the law of equality for the three creeds. His motion was adopted by a large majority.

In the chamber of peers it was more difficult to pass the law decreeing the equality of Judaism and Christianity. The advocates of the motion were eloquent in their recognition of Jewish virtues. The names of those Jews who had left behind them a glorious reputation in history were mentioned, such as Philo, the representative of Jewish philosophy in ancient times ; Maimonides, of that of " the Middle Ages and modern days "; Mendelssohn, "the sage, whom philosophic Germany was in the habit of comparing with Plato."

When the division was taken in the chamber of peers (January 1, 1831), the law for the complete equalization of the Jews was carried by 89 votes to 57. Thus the last barriers between the adherents of Judaism and their Christian neighbors were removed in France. King Louis Philippe, on the 8th of February, ratified the law, which enacted that the French rabbis, like the Catholic and Protestant clergymen, should receive part of their salary from the public exchequer. The High School (Collège

Rabbinique) for the training of rabbis, which a short time before had been founded in Metz, was also recognized as a state institution, and partly supported from the public budget. At the same time, the Senate at Frankfort-on-the-Main brought forward a motion to grant civil rights to the Jews, particularly abrogating the limitations to marriage. But of the 90 members of the legislative body, two-thirds voted against it.

The shock caused by the events of July, which was felt also in Germany, awakened a feeling of self-dependence; it dispelled all timidity and false shame in speaking about Jews and Judaism, which had hitherto been avoided, as if a loud word would have precipitated the avalanche of Judæophobia with destructive force. Even Jews belonging to so-called good society, who, for the sake of some material advantage, had been anxious to have people forget that they were members of an oppressed race, and had preferred to conceal or ignore the injustice done them, began to appreciate their own worth and ceased to be ashamed of being recognized as Jews. This change of sentiment manifested in different ways, like every change, was brought about by influential personalities.

Gabriel Riesser (born 1806, died 1860), a man of noble mind and great energy, took a prominent part in awakening this self-respect. However bitter the complaints of the German Jews of the disgrace brought upon them by immigrant Polish Jews, they were amply compensated by Riesser. His spirit of firm determination he derived more from his maternal grandfather, Rabbi Raphael Cohen, who had emigrated from Poland, than from his weak, good-natured German father. Gabriel Riesser in every respect belonged to modern times. Unlike most of the promoters of the new spirit, he was not rooted in the old order of things. His thoughts, feelings, and dreams were German, and

only slight traces of his Jewish origin are perceptible.   To Judaism in its national form, as the leaven
of history, Riesser was indifferent ; only the recol-
lections of his youth and his parental home bound
him to the faith.   Beyond that, he looked upon
it as an attenuated system of diluted doctrines,
which he tacitly professed without desiring to
defend them.   He suspected, however, that Judaism
might continue to flourish in a rejuvenated healthy
form, though he did not define clearly wherein this
revival should consist.   To promote it was altogether
outside his sphere.   Had he not been hampered in
his chosen vocation, he would have been a quiet
German citizen, a conscientious judge or lawyer,
without troubling himself to improve the world or
rectify a corrupt state of affairs.   German Jew-
hatred roused him to defend the derided cause of his
fellow-sufferers.   His first work as a jurist attracted
attention, and he tried to become an attorney in his
native town, but was rejected.   He next sought to
deliver lectures upon jurisprudence in Heidelberg,
but the professor's chair was refused him likewise.
His gentle, peaceable nature revolted against such
foolish exclusions.   Thus Riesser, who felt no
particular call to work for the general good, was
driven to become an agitator, not alone for the
freedom of his co-religionists, but also for that of
the whole German nation.   He made it his duty
in life to secure equal privileges for the Jews,
and to defend them whenever attacked.   "The
unspeakable sufferings throughout two centuries
of many millions of persons who patiently waited
for deliverance" weighed heavily upon him.   His
ideal was Lessing.   In his first pamphlet (1831) he
spoke with conscious pride, not alone against German rulers, but against the people, who refused permission to the Jews to ascend even the lowest rung
on the ladder of distinction.   Nor did he spare his
co-religionists who, on account of superior educa-

tion and social position, contemptuously looked down upon the mass of Jews, and were ashamed of the name of Jew. " If unjust hatred," he exclaimed, "clings to our name, should we not, instead of denying it, rather use all our strength to secure honor for it?" He contributed freely towards the removal of the contempt cast upon this name. Riesser aimed chiefly at defending the honor and dignity of the Jews. No selfish attainment of advantages withheld stimulated his action; but a desire to take part in the unceasing contest between freedom and oppression, justice and injustice, truth and falsehood. Filled with indignation he openly represented to the German rulers that the reason for depriving the Jews of their rights as men was the hope that they might thereby be induced to accept baptism. He also reproached the faint-hearted Jews who, having a comfortable position, separated themselves from the main body of their brethren, or by a false confession purchased equality, or handed over their children to the Church to smooth their path through life. Riesser desired to see societies established which should energetically work for the emancipation of the Jews. Sympathizers were to be united in a kind of covenant that, from a sense of honor, they might remain true to their fellow-sufferers, until the contest was decided. Ten years previously the Berlin Society for Culture had not dared to publish such a programme. But between Edward Gans and Gabriel Riesser came the July Revolution. Riesser also invited Christians to join, inasmuch as it behoved well-disposed men of every belief to participate in the release of an enslaved people.

Riesser's words produced their due effect; they came at an opportune moment, when men's minds had become susceptible. His mild though determined utterances made a deeper impression than Börne's with their incisive keenness. The tone of positive certainty with which Riesser foretold the ultimate victory of liberty infused hope into every heart. Various favorable events which now took place appeared to put a seal on his prophecy. For the first time the question of the emancipation of the Jews began to be discussed in the English Parliament, and the chief leaders in the House of Commons were in favor of the removal of the disabilities. A resolution was passed in the Electorate of Hesse, the first German province to legalize the emancipation of the Jews. This gave Riesser courage to pursue his ideal further. He was indefatigable in his efforts for the cause to which he had devoted his life, but he kept in view the honor and credit to be obtained, more than any desire for material gain. Not even the most unimportant ceremony might be sacrificed to obtain rights of citizenship, if they could be procured only at such a cost; a rule which he most emphatically laid down on two occasions.

The Jews of Baden, as a token of their gratitude, presented him with a beautifully designed picture by the Jewish painter Oppenheim, which artistically depicted the transition period in Jewish life, the separation of the old and the new. It was called "The Return of the Jewish Warrior," who is represented as surprising his parents and family in the repose of the Sabbath. In his letter acknowledging this gift, Riesser remarked, "The father is foolish who wishes to wrap his son in the garments of antiquity . . . . but wanting in dignity is the son ashamed of his father, the generation ashamed of the past." This deeply-rooted feeling was communicated to the younger generation with the more intensity, because it proceeded, not from an official representative of Judaism, but from a lawyer whose being was pervaded by the German spirit. Riesser made the emancipation question popular by his contest with the Judæophobists Paulus, Edward

Meyer, Pfizer, Streckfuss, and other driveling enemies of freedom in the German Assemblies of the
estates, who utilized the contempt attached to the
Jews to bring the whole struggle for liberty into
disrepute. Riesser further managed to have the
Jewish question placed on the programme of the
liberalists. Young Germany, and all who took part
against oppression, were thenceforth compelled to
inscribe religious liberty and the equality of all
classes upon their banner, however great might be
their antipathy against the Jews. But Riesser performed a far greater service, by rousing a feeling
of dignity in the Jews, and destroying that false
shame which so-called cultured people felt at the
name of Jew. The sincerity of his convictions and
the genuineness of his sentiments, as evinced in
every stroke of his pen, opened all hearts to him.

At this time men of commanding intellect were
not to be found in great numbers among the Jews ;
but the younger generation was rich in men of character who, as it were, compensated for the losses
occasioned by the Berlin Society for Culture. One
of these sterling characters was the bosom friend
of Riesser, a physician, Solomon Ludwig Steinheim
(born, Altona, 1790; died, Zurich, 1866). His was
a highly gifted nature, which dwelt upon the sunny
height of thought; and from this eminence the foolish pursuits of the multitude appeared like mist for-
mations, blown hither and thither by the wind.

In Steinheim was revealed, in all its splendor and
all its powers of redemption, the Jewish thought—
without which Judaism were merely a thousand
years' dream—that the Jewish people has a gigantic
mission, with which its teachings and fortunes are
in consonance. This idea may have been unconsciously aroused in Steinheim by Isaac Bernays.
Together with his wealth of thought, Steinheim was
skillful in clothing his ideas in an interesting form,
and adorning them with his rich gifts of eloquence.

He might be compared to Jehuda Halevi, the Castilian poet-philosopher, had he been gifted with higher poetical talents. His first production, "The Songs of Obadiah ben Amos in Exile," displayed germs of the fruitful seed of thought which he disseminated. A Jewish sage, Obadiah, in Egypt, describes to his son Eliakim, supposed to be living at the time of the Ptolemies, the different stages of greatness and abjection through which the Jewish people were to pass.

> "It is the design of Providence that a weak people, appointed to proclaim salvation, shall be persecuted, hunted down, and sacrificed among millions of enemies throughout thousands of years, and nevertheless continue alive and active. Our ancestors received for themselves and their descendants the consecrated office of the priesthood. The family of Jacob, since its beginning, has been alternately dispersed and gathered together, and thus trained for its vocation."

The Jewish people have entered upon their pilgrimage over the surface of the globe, to scatter the luminous seeds of pure worship of God and the ideal of exalted morality. From this moral pinnacle Steinheim beheld the past and the future of Judaism in the clearest light. All riddles were solved, all questions answered; the doctrines and history of Israel afforded satisfactory and comforting replies. The priestly mission of Israel was to be fulfilled through great sufferings; this saviour of the world was compelled to wear a crown of thorns, and to be humbled to the condition of a slave. Steinheim saw the past and the future of Israel as in a magic mirror, bright, clear, and rich in color. Only the present was puzzling to him. The estrangement of the sons of his people from their origin, their despair of themselves, their contempt for their teachings and descent, the daily recurring apostasies and desertion from the flag, appeared to him as omens of approaching downfall, as though the high priests of mankind were secularizing themselves, profaning their sanctity, exchanging their birthright for a mess of pottage. Such self-estrangement and self-debasement Steinheim desired to counteract. He therefore composed his "Songs of Obadiah in Exile," in which he worked out his system.

> "Such times are dangerous, when oppression is lessened, but not altogether removed, or when freedom is near, but not completely attained. At these periods, to desert the customs of bygone ages is deemed meritorious and advantageous, while a desire for transitory benefits gives rise to indifference to the eternal. This is the time for real lamentation, when every folly is taken seriously, and every serious thing is considered folly; when mockery is in every mouth, and insolence and license in every heart, and when, by reason of satirical laughter, there is no time for serious matters."

Steinheim's muse severely rebuked the unthinking who seceded from the Jewish religion.

He wished, however, not only to reprove, but also to instruct and convince. He did not address himself to the prosperous, the contented, and the rich, but to "youth with its pains and its ardent longings, its ready sensibility to light and justice." To these he dedicated his book so fertile in thought, "Revelation according to the System of the Synagogue" (February, 1835). Gifted with a philosophical mind, Steinheim submitted the whole system of the law to a searching examination, regarding it as the highest consideration, as the "miracle of miracles," by which alone the restless inquiring human mind can arrive at contentment. Boldly he attempted to give an answer to the question: What is this highly-praised and deeply-scorned Judaism? All Jewish thinkers had been happy in proving that its fundamental principles agreed with the axioms of mental philosophy, or, at least, were not in contradiction to them. If man were left solely to the guidance of reason or of natural philosophy, he would find no clue for his moral actions in the labyrinth of contradictions and uncertainties. It is, therefore, concluded Steinheim, a poor compliment to a religion to say that it is in accord with reason; for the latter is Chronos consuming his own offspring; building

up with one hand and destroying with the other.
The only religion in accordance with reason is
heathenism, or natural religion, in its various modi-
fications—the heathenism which was the origin of
so much mischief to morality, in which "robbers,
thieves, adulterers, and sodomites found their finest
examples in the highest beings."   If Christianity
renounces its joint origin with Judaism, the fashion
since Schleiermacher and Hegel, it thereby sinks to
the lowest depths of heathenism.   Love and hatred,
Ahriman and Ormuz, Christ and Satan, with all variations of the opposing principles, the eternal substance about which the two powers are ever contending, and inexorable necessity—these are the
fundamental ideas of natural religion : man himself
succumbs under the suffering inflicted by necessity :

> "Through eternal, immovable, mighty laws
>   Must we all complete the circle of our existence."

> "Like the gods, so are their priests and sages : like king, like
> herd."

In opposition to this sensual or perhaps refined
heathenism comes Judaism with its totally different
mode of thought.   It sets up a personal God who
is not identical with Nature, and is not divided into
two principles : it recognizes a "Creatio ex nihilo,"
without an eternal substance.   It lays stress upon
free will, consequently upon man's responsibility for
his moral actions.   These truths and others have
not been evolved by human reason, nor could they
be so evolved ; they had been revealed upon Sinai.
Although they were alien to reason, yet they are so
clear and convincing that it soon accepts them,
displacing the contradictory phases of thought
regarding the perplexing natural phenomena, whose
laws reason cannot explain.   Sinai, with its light-
ning-flashes, shed both light and warmth over the
world, clearness of thought and moral purity.   The
synagogue forms a sharply defined antithesis both

to mythological religion and the church. " Out of Zion shall go forth the law, and the word of the Lord out of Jerusalem": with inspired enthusiasm Steinheim subscribed to these prophetic, half-fulfilled words. When he had discovered, or thought he had discovered, the soul of Judaism, Steinheim became filled with ardent zeal, a striking phenomenon in a time of sober speculation. This love for Judaism so illumined his mind and facilitated his understanding of the past, that he even learned to value the activity and energy of the greatly despised rabbis.

In his "Revelation" Steinheim revealed many truths, or rather, he brought to light ancient truths which had been ignored or forgotten. No one either in his own or in the preceding age understood the fundamental principles of Judaism so thoroughly as he did, although several of his hypotheses and inferences cannot be completely established. He, however, made but a slight impression upon his contemporaries, although he set forth the grandeur of Judaism with almost prophetic inspiration, and in an attractive manner. Whence came his isolation? It arose from the fact that the life and actions of Steinheim did not accord with his thoughts and sentiments. In agreement with his words, he ought to have become intimately associated with the Synagogue which from ignorance "became daily more deserted," to have participated in its woes and ignominy, to have joined in the celebration of its days of festivity and sadness, and to have clothed himself with the pride of those who were externally slaves, but in their hearts freemen. But Steinheim did nothing of the kind: he kept himself aloof from the Jewish community and Jewish life. What he correctly recognized as the reason of the resistance to the doctrines of Judaism, "the simplicity and servile condition of its adherents," repelled even him.

"The name of the people, which has become its guardian, has degenerated into a by-word, and now it is demanded that a doctrine shall be accepted whose supporters are given up to hatred, contempt, and persecution."

To renounce Judaism altogether, like Heine, Edward Gans, and many others, appeared to Steinheim dishonorable and wanton ; and he therefore remained externally faithful.   But, although he had recognized the truth that the mission of Israel consisted in being not only priests, but also sacrifices, he did not permit this knowledge to influence his course of life.   This was not due to weakness of character in Steinheim, but to insufficient knowledge of Judaism in its many-sidedness.   In spite of his predilection for its intellectual treasury, he was more at home in every other subject than in Jewish literature.

A deeper knowledge of Judaism was unexpectedly aroused in a country which cultured Jews like Riesser and Steinheim were accustomed to despise. As it was formerly asked, What good can come out of Galilee? so now it was said, What good can come out of Poland?   Yet, from this very place there came fruitful seeds which developed into healthy blossoms.   Two men especially, Nachman Krochmal and Solomon Jehuda Rapoport, profitably employed the knowledge gained in Germany. Both seemed destined to fill a gap, to which the scholars of Jewish science in Germany and France were unequal.   They dug solid ore from the mines inaccessible in these countries, and showed how to procure and work it.   They stirred up a spirit of rivalry, which within the short space of three decades, was instrumental in removing the ruins covering the great past of Judaism, and in bringing to light the Divine image hidden beneath.   They were the founders of a new school, which may be called the Galician.

Nachman Cohen Krochmal (born at Brody, 1785;

died at Tarnopol, 1840), the son of a well-to-do
merchant interested in science, who was accustomed
to make journeys to Germany, caught up the pale,
dying light of the Mendelssohn school. Mendelssohn was the ideal upon which Krochmal
modeled himself. Married at the age of fourteen,
and transplanted to the little village of Zolkiew,
where the method of instruction so destructive to
science was still in vogue, Krochmal secretly became
absorbed in the study of Hebrew literature. He also
tried to obtain the writings of the German philosophers, especially of Kant, in order to expand and
clear his mind with earnest thoughts. The more
the strict Talmudists and heretic-hunting Chassidim
of Poland endeavored to discover those who occupied themselves with works other than the Talmud
or Kabbala, or who read a non-Hebraic book, in
order to denounce them—the more did Krochmal
and his fellows enjoy their stolen pleasure. Along
with a mass of knowledge from the Talmud, Krochmal stored up many thoughts of a character hostile
to Talmudism. But open war was never declared.
Krochmal, probably on account of his health,
enfeebled by continued mental activity, was too
timid to venture out of the beaten track : he avoided
disputes, and followed all the superstitiously pious
Polish customs, exaggerating them indeed, in order
not to jeopardize his peace of mind. He was too
earnest and too prudent to overstep the bounds of
habit ; nevertheless, he could not altogether escape
suspicion. He had carried on a harmless correspondence with a Karaite Chacham in the neighboring
village of Kukizow. Certain pious persons knew
this, and represented that he was hatching a conspiracy against the Talmud with the Karaites.
They obtained one of his letters from the unsus-
pecting Karaite, endeavored to extract heresies from
the innocent compliments paid his correspondent
in verse, and spread it throughout the large com-

munity of Lemberg in order to excite the mob against him. This intrigue greatly affected Krochmal, and becoming yet more timid and cautious, he locked up his thoughts within his own breast, and for a long time could not be induced to publish anything.

But he revealed the treasures of his mind to his trusty friends and disciples, not within treacherous walls, but in the open field. His hearers, schooled in the Talmud, and accustomed to unravel dark and difficult problems, quickly understood his hints without diffuse explanations. By his laconic method Krochmal could turn everything topsy-turvy, and unfold a series of investigations, every link of which, if made public, would have stamped him in the eyes of his countrymen as a wicked heretic. What made his method of instruction and his investigations especially fruitful, was the clearness and finish of his thoughts, which were arranged in admirable sequence. Thus his teaching was a wholesome antidote to the chaotic contradiction and confusion from which the best Polish minds greatly suffered. His acquaintance with German philosophy had schooled his mind, and taught him logical discipline. Krochmal did not develop original philosophic thoughts, which he nevertheless seems to have thought his strong point. He was the first to take a philosophical view of history, especially Jewish history, and make a clear survey of its intricacies. He also pointed out how the mine of the Talmud could be utilized, and rendered valuable in historical research. Krochmal himself devoted his attention to this neglected and little valued literature, and applied his results to the elucidation of Jewish history. He succeeded in throwing so much light on the period from the Babylonian Captivity until the conclusion of the Mishnah, which Jost and Christian scholars had completely failed to understand, that it was an easy task for succeeding inquirers to

follow in his path.   He was the first to teach scholars to examine Talmudical sources of history
through a microscope, or to reproduce half-obliter-
ated features.   This was, indeed, a great gain, and
an immense advance compared with Jost's clumsy
view of history.   Krochmal's results do not always
bear investigation, because having no access to
non-Hebraic writings, he was obliged to content
himself with secondary or tertiary sources.   But his
acuteness and sincere devotion to this study, did
not allow him to stray from the right track often.
He inspired his disciples to engage in research, and
gave them the key to these hieroglyphic sources.
Although he had not yet published many of his
discoveries, his fame extended beyond the boundaries of his own country.   The community of Berlin,
which since the time of Friedländer had felt deep
aversion to Poles and rabbis, entertained the idea
of calling him as their rabbi.   He was considered
one of the leaders of the young science of Judaism,
and had many admirers in Germany.

The most receptive and gifted among his disciples, Solomon Jehuda Rapoport (born Lemberg,
1790? died Prague, 1867), contested with him for
preëminence, and even overshadowed him, partly
by reason of his more fertile productions.   Rapoport was descended from a respected Jewish family,
a race of learned rabbis, one of whose branches had
been transplanted from Italy to Poland.   Traces
of his hereditary nobility were apparent in his bearing and appearance.   Of a gentle nature, which
won for him all hearts, having a fund of genial
humor, and of a sociable disposition, Rapoport was
a well-beloved and attractive person in every circle.
These qualities softened the severity of his astonishing learning.   Nothing of especial importance
occurred during his youth.   At an early age he was
admitted to the study of the Talmud, and soon was
at home in its labyrinths, owing to his extraordinary

memory and penetrating acuteness.   He also married young.

During his youth, Rapoport became partly false to Talmudical study, inasmuch as he favored its rivals—science and poetry.   He has graphically described the painful path trodden by him and his peers in order to arrive at the tree of knowledge. It was difficult to obtain any scientific book, most difficult to secure one written in a European language.   The index of books prohibited by public opinion was much more comprehensive than that of the popes.   If one thirsting for knowledge secretly procured such a book, and it was scented out by the prying eyes of his relatives or friends, he was implored to throw it aside, or his friends, on their own responsibility, confiscated the heretical work, so as to preserve the student from fanatical persecution by the Chassidim.   Even clear-minded men were doubtful whether, according to the Talmud, the study of profane sciences was not forbidden.

Rapoport was not alone in his longing for knowledge.   Here and there, in Galicia, the germs of a fresh spirit awoke, which struggled hard to remove the yoke of an unthinking, fanatical public opinion. Intercourse with Vienna, the Napoleonic wars, in general, communication with the world, caused many old forms to fall into abeyance.   The spread of the Chassidistic cult and its presumptuous, outrageous, and increasingly frantic actions, stimulated thoughtful, reasonable men to meet it with firm opposition, for it filled them with passionate hatred, and drove them to invent expedients whereby to crush it.   The most appropriate method seemed to be to remove the boorish ignorance in religious and secular matters and the childlike credulity, by means of education.   Although the Austrian government had declared it a duty of the Galician congregations to establish schools, the lower officials had not shown much zeal in causing this order to be carried into effect. This neglect was to some extent advantageous, as the self-deliverance of the Jews was the more effectual by reason of the struggle undergone. Since the wars with Napoleon, there had arisen small circles in the three largest Galician communities of Brody, Lemberg, and Tarnopol, banded together for self-culture, the promotion of education, and a war of annihilation against Chassidism. The beginning of this movement was made in Tarnopol by Joseph Perl (born at Tarnopol, 1773; died, 1839). With great sacrifice of time and money, and with unswerving perseverance, he founded a pattern High School for the middle classes. He made incisive attacks upon the Chassidim in a work, intentionally written in a corrupt, barbarous jargon, which was in no way inferior to "The Letters of Obscure Men" in the monkish Latin of Rubianus and Hutten, perhaps slightly more artistic. This bitter enemy of the Chassidim entered into communication with the Jewish representatives of education in Germany, and was elected an honorary member of the Berlin Society for Culture. In Brody, where Jews engaged in extensive foreign trade, the rich merchants, who traveled in Germany and Austria, introduced the desire to imitate the German Jews. In Lemberg, where Rapoport lived, a kind of literary circle was founded, at whose head was a wealthy, highly-cultured man, Jehuda Löb Mises (died 1831). He provided ambitious young men in Lemberg with money, counsel, and, what was of especial value to them, with an excellent library of Hebrew and European books.

From this circle arose an admired scholar, who deserves a golden page in the records of Jewish literature. This was Isaac Erter, born in a village near Przemysl, 1792, and died at Brody, 1851. He who by means of his magic poetry succeeds in showing the powers of renaissance dormant in a so-called dead language, unconsciously also demon-

strates the vitality of the race in whose midst such
artistic creations can arise, and can by many be understood, and admired.   Erter's object was to scourge
the perversity of Polish Judaism, the chaos of superstition and learning, and the coarseness of the
Chassidim; but by the noble form in which he
clothed his scorn and his righteous indignation he
attested the immortality of the Hebrew language
and people.   Born in a wretched Galician village,
he created beautiful Hebrew pictures, such as would
have delighted Isaiah and the most refined Psalmists.   Erter's father, though a poor man, little more
than a peasant, had nevertheless not neglected the
sacred duty of a Jew to have his talented son
instructed in Jewish writings.   The Talmud, to be
sure, was the only work with which young Erter
was thoroughly acquainted.   Of the beauties of
biblical poetry, like all Jews of Poland at that time,
he had no idea in his youth.   When he was thirteen
years old his father imposed the bonds of marriage
upon him, and shortly afterwards, having become a
widower, the boy married a second wife.   His second father-in-law, who had promised to support him,
did not keep his word, and thus Erter tasted the
bread of misery in his youth.   To dispel his bitter
cares he joined the merry Chassidim, taking part in
all their follies; but his innate love of the beautiful
made him feel disgust at the sight of their moral
and physical degradation, nor could he believe in
their miracles.   A fortunate accident acquainted
him with a cultured man, who introduced him to two
ideals, Maimuni and Mendelssohn, and so he learned
to understand, love, and imitate the highest models,
viz., the prophet Moses and Hebrew literature.
A new spirit was breathed into Erter by this old,
still ever new revelation, working a change in his
views and his relation to Judaism.   To increase his
culture Erter betook himself to Lemberg, where he
hoped to find better means for satisfying his thirst

for science.   Here he found struggling sympathizers of his own age, who, like himself, had married
early, had been tortured by material cares, but had
nevertheless directed all their energies to the cultivation of the mind.   Here he met Rapoport, to
whom as the more learned he looked up with reverence.   There was a peculiar charm in the intercourse of these young knowledge-seekers, each at
once master and pupil.   Whatever was beautiful
and true in European literature they elaborated, for
their own use and that of others, in the Hebrew
language, which they employed as if it were a living
language.   The difficulties which members of this
circle could not overcome were submitted to the
wise master, Krochmal, and to him they made pilgrimages to Zolkiew as to a wizard.   This intellec-
tually idyllic life, which they remembered even in
their old age as a golden dream, lasted for three
years.   But their occupation with profane literature
and their actions and aims gave great offense.

One day a ban of excommunication (in the name
of Rabbi Jacob Orenstein) was found affixed to the
gates of the synagogue.   It was directed against
four men, who were said to teach the young their
heretical views, viz., Rapoport, Erter, Natkes, and
Pastor.   The formal excommunication, customary
in olden days, had been forbidden in Galicia since
the time of Emperor Joseph : therefore the zealots
chose this method.   At the time when they had
brought Krochmal under the accusation of heresy,
they had determined to make a vigorous onslaught
upon all apostles of culture.   But, seeing that the
ban was directed only against these four poor men,
and that they dared not attack the wealthy, respected Mises, who openly poured ridicule upon Talmudical Judaism, their cowardice rendered their
zeal ineffectual.   The sentence of excommunication
did not have the expected result, and Orenstein was
compelled by the Austrian authorities to withdraw

it. It hardly affected Rapoport, who had a fairly independent, if somewhat inferior position, and who had instructed the young gratuitously. In the eyes of the common people, however, he was a heretic; but this did not hinder him from becoming district rabbi of Tarnopol and afterwards chief rabbi of Prague.

Poor Erter, however, was severely affected, because he had to support himself and his family by teaching. Although the rabbi was obliged to recall the ban, Erter found that many parents did not care to entrust their sons to him, and he had to take up his staff and journey to Brody. But he had his revenge upon Orenstein and the zealots: he immortalized their bigotry and pettiness by his poetry. Indignation and anger at being persecuted by such tormentors forced the pen into his hand, and gave rise to his masterpieces of delineation. Erter harmed Orenstein with his poetical thunders of excommunication more severely than he himself had been made to suffer, and completely crushed him. In a poem he represented a court of justice which determined the value of objects from a stand-point dissimilar to that of the actual world. Books of immense size shrink to nothing, because their contents prove to have been stolen from various quarters, and the plagiarism is discovered; only the title-page remaining the property of the author. This satire was aimed at Orenstein, who had published a Rabbinical work in many volumes, which he was said to have adorned with borrowed plumes.

Börne and Heine would certainly never have credited it, had they heard that, hidden away in Poland, among the bearded Jews, there lived a brother artist "as capable of making filigree-work of finest words, of weaving a wire-net for the souls of gnats, or pointing a satire so sharp that it could penetrate through the pores of glass." As they had improved, refined, and polished the German language, so Erter improved the Hebrew tongue. He breathed youthful vigor and freshness into "the old woman with silvery hair and wrinkled brow, who showed only traces of her former beauty" (as he says), made her susceptible to the prevailing influences of the day, and docile to express new thoughts. Was Erter a poet? In his prose he was a perfect poet. In his faithful and touching descriptions, there is a store of magic poetry and humor, which, like the offspring of Heine's wit, attracts and enchains our minds.

Two thousand years after the prophets had ceased, there arose a voice which sounded at once familiar and new. And in this intermingling of the old and the new in Erter's style, which recalls Isaiah and Heine, there lies an extraordinary charm. Faithfully translated, Erter's poems would still be interesting; but the peculiar, indescribable fragrance of his work would have passed away. In their original form and color, in the contrast of solemnity and childlike simplicity, of sublimity and detailed description, these poetical productions make an inexpressibly pleasant impression upon minds susceptible to delicate shades of thought. In perusing these masterly delineations, one only regrets that they are not longer, and that this profound artist left no more than six of these delightful pictures, and only a few equally beautiful letters.

Like a true poet, Erter had come too late at the distribution of the world's goods, and had to contend with poverty. In his thirty-third year, when he already had marriageable daughters, he began to study medicine, in order to earn his daily bread therewith. The time spent in efforts to rejuvenate the Hebrew language had to be snatched from sleep, and death hurried him away in the full maturity of his poetical powers. Erter performed great services for Judaism. Through his proofs of the flexibility of the Hebrew language he awakened fresh love for it, and created a comparatively new medium for disseminating the young science of Judaism. His influence upon his contemporaries is unmistakable. Whilst the Hebrew style of Nachman Krochmal was rugged, awkward, almost as stiff as that of the Tibbonides, and reads like a translation from a foreign language, Rapoport, Natkes, Jacob Solomon Byk, the Goldbergs, father and son, and the younger men of the Galician school, displayed flow of language, fluency, and ease, which were afterwards misused in rendering French novels and conceits into Hebrew.

Rapoport accordingly did not stand alone in Lemberg; he found friends who participated in his ideas and efforts. It was especially favorable to the development of his mental powers that Krochmal served him as a living book, which contained all worth knowing. From the days of his youth until far into manhood, for nearly thirty years, Rapoport made it a practice, at least once a month, to take a journey from Lemberg to Zolkiew, to visit the bold, and at the same time timid, philosophical inquirer, Krochmal, and to enter into intellectual conversation with him. This intercourse with his gifted young friend became such a necessity to Krochmal, that whenever he was engaged in a subject of research, he sought out Rapoport in Lemberg to reach clearness by an interchange of ideas. Rapoport needed only suggestion; he had inborn taste and love for Jewish history, and as he possessed both scholarship and keen perceptions, he made prolific discoveries. In the interchange of thought between master and disciple, they in company arrived at important results, and in the end they did not know from whose mind they had emanated, or rather they worked together at the solution of problems. It is therefore perplexing to know exactly which of the many results of their common investigations are to be ascribed to the master and which to the disciple. These fruitful conversations between Krochmal and Rapoport marked the birth of the science of Judaism on the historical side.

However, despite their combined discoveries, as soon as both grew to full maturity of intellect, the respective territories of their research became distinct. Krochmal had more liking for general and encyclopædic studies; details served him only as a confirmation of his theory. Rapoport, on the other hand, was more interested in minute, especially in biographical, research; and general studies did not attract him. In his youth, Krochmal had planned a survey of the development of thought in Judaism, bearing upon the varying phases of enlightenment and obscuration. Rapoport also commenced a work in his youth, but it was to be a biography of the most noted representatives of Judaism and its ideas.

As this laborious task demanded a great amount of time and attention, and as Rapoport was not master of his own time, the fruits of his researches ripened but slowly. When, however, he published in succession five biographies (1829-31), with great fullness of luminous detail and suggestion, the pathway for a thorough knowledge of the internal history of Judaism and the Jewish race was opened up. Rapoport proved indisputably and upon strictly scientific grounds that the great representatives of Judaism, its leaders, in the Middle Ages, instead of shunning the light of knowledge, actually kindled and fed it. He showed that, at a time when European nations were still steeped in the darkness of the Middle Ages, the Jews cultivated general science. Chronology, historical geography, the history of literature, and other branches important for the critical investigation of history, which had hitherto been altogether neglected, or only superficially treated, were by him first proved necessary and applied. The acute intelligence with which he united disjointed facts, and separated others apparently connected; the critical touchstone which he applied to distinguish the true from the false, and facts from legends, produced such suggestive results that, after Krochmal, he must be considered the father of Jewish science.   All that had been achieved by Jost and other predecessors vanished before these researches like superficial talk before a well digested, well constructed, clearly conceived oration. What gave these investigations an especial value, and distinguished them from the productions of pedantry was the fervor and love with which they were undertaken. They must, therefore, be regarded as national performances, not as the products of idle scholarship.   So far as the Jews took an interest in these labors, they saw themselves reflected in them, and considered the history of their mental development as laid down in them as their own work, or the guiding-line to be followed in future. Rapoport achieved more in this direction than Krochmal, because he did not allow himself to be intimidated by heretic-hunters, and displayed more manly courage openly to defend the truth recognized by him as such.   The scientific movement within Judaism, which since his time has continually grown in force, must be entirely attributed to him.   The spring which pours forth water from its bosom, and allows it to trickle down among the bushes unseen is of no significance compared with the broad stream revealed to every eye, bearing upon its surface large ships, and with its overflow fertilizing the adjoining fields.   His greatness was recognized, for he was elected district rabbi of Tarnopol, and shortly afterwards chief rabbi of Prague.   Once again was a Pole called to Germany, but under what altered circumstances !

The effects of Rapoport's system of research soon manifested themselves.   A scholar of the first rank, who slowly piled brick upon brick for the construction of the inner history of the Jews, one of the triumvirate of the Berlin Society for Culture, finding consolation in investigation for the disappointment met with on another field, utilized Rapoport's results and system of inquiry, to shed light upon another side of Jewish history. Zunz, in his "Homilies of the Jews in Divine Worship," reviewed them in their origin, their growth, their sublimity, and their degeneration (1832). They portrayed Judaism from another point of view, and brought conclusive proofs that the Jews in the Middle Ages had not been a rough, half-savage horde, as was asserted by their bitter enemies, in order to calumniate them and deprive them of their rights of equality; that they were not a barbarous fraternity without morals and decency, but an intelligent community with a culture peculiar to themselves, yet actively promoting general culture.

"From the earliest times we find in the constitution of the Jewish nation measures for upraising men steeped in the trials and errors of life, or chained down by sensuality and coarse lusts. Sabbath and festivals, sacrifices and holy convocations, public worship and instruction in the law, were to afford comfort to the sinner, support to the weak, and teaching to all, and to preserve a holy flame of faith and patriotism in the midst of the nation, as in the breast of the individual. Centuries have since then passed away, the Jews have lost their independence and their country; but on the downfall of every institution the synagogue remained as the sole representative of their nationality. Towards this center their faith was directed, and from it they obtained instruction for their daily conduct, strength to endure unheard-of sufferings, and hope for a future dawn of freedom. The public worship of the synagogue became the standard of Jewish nationality, the miraculous shield of the Jewish faith."

The form of prayers and sermons was traced in this peculiar work in their manifold shapes from the boundary line of the Bible period and that of the Soferim till the time of their perfection, their decline, and their regeneration. This book was the first solid, sober, and convincing work, by a Jewish author, conceived in the spirit of the German scholars' guild. It displayed an array of facts which either had been wholly unknown, or inaccurately known. It therefore made a lasting impression, and in turn was fruitful in suggestions. It occupies a place of high importance in the edifice of Jewish science. The "Homilies of the Jews" was devoted also to the furtherance of two side issues—the emancipation of the Jews and the promotion of reform. In supporting these aims it was carefully pointed out and emphasized that up to the last century, in Portuguese and Italian congregations, sermons were delivered in the vernacular. But these two movements, emancipation and reform, were not much advanced, and whatever was accomplished in these two directions, is in no way due to the "Homilies of the Jews." But they made scientific accuracy in the German sense the indispensable quality of future investigations, and removed the reproach of superficiality from Jewish authors.

Newly-fledged Jewish science soon created new organs wherein to express itself. The oldest and most noteworthy was carried on in Hebrew: it was called the "desirable vineyard" (Kerem Chemed), and was founded by Samuel Löb Goldberg of Tarnopol, and during ten years was of great use in offering the different views of Judaism the opportunity of expression. The chief topic was Jewish history; the greatest care was bestowed upon this subject. In accordance with their ability, knowledge, or ripeness of intelligence, the contributors to the "Vineyard" brought great or small offerings, without expecting any reward or tangible honor. What university or academy was there to repay their laborious researches by the bestowal of a professor's chair or post of distinction? There was not even a prospect of situations as rabbis for men engaged in subjects utterly dissimilar, often opposed, to rabbinical studies. On the contrary, their zeal for science rendered them unworthy of rabbinical honor in the eyes of the strictly orthodox. The chief contributors to the new journal were the leaders of the Galician school, among whom Rapoport held the first place, although he incurred opposition by his candid utterances. Encouraged by Rapoport's example, Krochmal also consented to publish over his own name single chapters from his encyclopædic work. The German Jews supplied only two representatives, both of whom were talented men, viz., the author of the "Homilies of the Jews" and the high-minded Michael Sachs, to whom, however much they differed in their conception of Judaism, Jewish science is deeply indebted for rich increase.

The little band of Jewish inquirers received reinforcement from Italy, a country which for a long time had been buried in slumber, and had taken but little part in Jewish history. Besides old Reggio, Rabbi Ghirondi of Padua, Almanzi, a wealthy layman, and Samuel Vita della Volta, a physician of Mantua, special prominence is due to Samuel David Luzzatto (born in Trieste, 1800; died in Padua, 1865).

The self-sacrifice of Jewish inquirers in the Middle Ages, who in the midst of unspeakable privations and sufferings had occupied themselves in the cultivation of their minds, Luzzatto also manifested as a model for the younger generation. During his whole life, and although he enjoyed European fame, Luzzatto and his family suffered through poverty. Privations, however, did not hinder him from increasing his knowledge with endurance all the more heroic because not publicly displayed. To be poor in Poland, as was the case with Rapoport and Erter, was not so distressing as to be poor in Italy, because in the former, requirements were slight, and contentment on the smallest means was almost universal; besides, generous, wealthy men saved the men of science from starvation. But in Italy, where even the middle class craved comfortable living, and where indifference to knowledge among the Jews had reached a high pitch, it is matter for great surprise that Luzzatto could find, amidst his struggles for daily bread, the peace and cheerfulness necessary to accomplish so much for the promotion of Jewish science. At every discovery, however trifling, Luzzatto felt childlike pleasure, which appears strange to an onlooker: it was the self-created recreation of the martyr, which for a moment causes gnawing pain to be forgotten.

Luzzatto was not naturally gifted with aptitude for historical studies. His most conspicuous trait was enthusiastic love of poetry, Judaism, and Hebrew literature, and this threefold love became one within him. But lofty enthusiasm, united with extraordinarily delicate taste for poetical beauty, could not compensate for lack of creative power; it could do no more than make of him a more talented Wessely. His Hebrew verses, by which he hoped to re-animate biblical poetry, are blameless in form, rhythmical, and of Hebraic coloring; but like Wessely's verses, they lack soul, true poetry. Luzzatto's Hebrew prose, polished and elegant though it be, cannot be compared with Erter's magical language. This he felt, and he was sufficiently just to award the palm to his Galician fellow-artist. His deep comprehension of the true art of poetry, especially of the delicacy of biblical literature, and his extremely refined taste, opened to Luzzatto another field of labor, viz., the exposition of Holy Writ. To purify this treasure from the rust of thousands of years had hitherto been the task of strangers, who did not bring to this work proper appreciation, still less the needful devotion. Christian Bible exegetes, such as Eichhorn, De Wette, Gesenius, and others, had pursued the work of purification in a clumsy manner, and for want of critical ability had flung away the true ore as dross. Luzzatto was one of the first Jews in modern days to devote himself to biblical exegesis. He possessed a sure instinct for recognizing the true spirit and beautiful form of biblical literature, and he called

attention to the disturbing elements whilst restoring
the original ones.   No one better than he understood the construction of the Hebrew language,
even to its most delicate points and grammatical
minutiæ.

In the new Rabbinical College of Padua (the
Collegio Rabbinico) Luzzatto found opportunities
of engaging zealously in the study of the Bible, and
of ascertaining the correct meaning of the words of
the prophets and inspired writers.   If Luzzatto
with his happy feeling for language and his Jewish
fervor had remained true to this branch of research,
he would have produced splendid results, and he
might have performed a substantial service to Jewish science, for he would have invited many disciples, inasmuch as his orthodoxy was unimpeach-
able.   But he was suddenly frightened by his own
boldness, or rather feared that he might misuse it.
If the walls of the Massorah are torn down, he
feared, the sacred text will become the prey of
incompetence and unending revolution, causing
direst confusion.   He did not trust criticism to heal
the wounds it inflicted, or rather he did not believe
that it effected a cure by administering poison.
He therefore took up an equivocal position, and
re-erected the outworks of the Massorah, which he
himself had undermined.

Roused by the achievements of Rapoport in history, he plunged into that study, and produced
important results.   Owing to the dispersion of the
Jews and their tragic fate, the fairest pages of their
history during the Franco-Spanish epoch had been
lost.   Luzzatto's zeal was kindled to discover these
pages, and in Italy his efforts were crowned with
success.   The persecuted Jews from Spain and
France had mostly passed through Italy in their
flight.   Here, therefore, the greater part of Jewish
literary treasures had been deposited, but they were
buried from fear of the Argus-eye of the bloody

Inquisition. Luzzatto unearthed them, published them in scientific organs or as separate works, and so made them available. Through him the Jewish history of the Middle Ages received its authentication, its firm basis, its coloring, and exposition. If Krochmal and Rapoport are the fathers of Jewish history, then Luzzatto was its mother.

Through him it became possible to obtain a clear understanding of facts hitherto only vaguely depicted, to arrange them in proper groups, and discern their original splendor. The beginnings of neo-Hebraic poetry, its flourishing period in the time of Jehuda Halevi, and in general the prolific mental activity of the Jews of Spain, were first set forth by him. And to his last breath Luzzatto was untiring in his researches and investigations. He collected a number of valuable works, and stimulated other friends of Jewish science to do the same. Unstintingly he permitted the use of his discoveries, and was happy when he could benefit the public by his newly found treasures. He was a priest in the service of Jewish science, and his memory will never be forgotten in the House of Israel.

Next to the Hebrew organ of Jewish science (Kerem Chemed), various German journals were started, which, besides dealing with the topics of the day, treated of Jewish scientific studies, and popularized them. One of these organs, "The Scientific Journal," from its very commencement assumed an over-confident tone, as if desirous of setting itself up as the highest tribunal, before which all efforts should await final judgment. And yet, most of its contributors, unless proved in other ways, learned by teaching. Those still among us must confess, if they are sincere, that on beginning their undertaking, instead of being at the head of Jewish science, they were mere tyros, possessing only a superficial smattering, and that the Galician school was their guide.

The soul of the periodical was its founder,
Abraham Geiger (born 1810; died 1874), a man of
considerable talents, of clear intellect, penetrating
sagacity, comprehensive knowledge, and stern character, bordering almost upon obstinacy and defiance.
He was also of a weak disposition, and was easily
led, and this quality helped to change what had
hitherto caused only differences of opinion concerning Judaism, into the harsh extreme of a split
amongst various sects.   Although born and bred in
a family schooled in the Talmud, Geiger became
filled with burning hatred towards it, and seeing
that the religious life of the Jews had been hitherto
regulated by the Talmudical standard, he regarded
it as the aim of his existence to bring about its
deposition and to introduce reforms of a radical
nature, outstripping those of his predecessors.   The
reform of Judaism was Geiger's chief desire; and to
further it, he used his influence as a preacher and
his scientific researches.   He felt no respect for
antiquity or for religious practices, and never spared
those co-religionists who adhered to traditional
customs.   He did not shrink from effecting the
most thorough-going schism and disunion.   Geiger's
scientific labors did not produce lasting results, as
he cared less for inquiries after truth than for plans
of reform.   His journal, however, succeeded in
inculcating self-reliance and self-knowledge.   It
courageously attacked the shameless presumption
of sciolist Jew-haters like Hartmann, and inveighed
against weak-minded Jews who attributed all ideals
to Christianity.   It may be reckoned to the credit
of this periodical or this school, that it recalled
neglected, because despised, personages, the Karaites, those talented sceptics and hypocrites.
    Through the impetuosity of the new school, life
and action were brought into Jewish circles, and the
results of research were diluted and made popular.
Who can say now whether the gain or the loss to

Judaism was greater? For instance, it gave currency to grave errors, by making Judaism a theologic system, and its representatives, the rabbis and teachers of the law, mere clergymen and pastors. This tendency narrowed Judaism, and degraded the achievements bidding defiance to the centuries by coupling them with contemporary phenomena. In hot haste it desired to apply practically the results of scientific investigation but recently made, or, according to its shibboleth, to "establish harmony between law and life"—sacrificing the half understood law to life, *i. e.*, to the promptings of convenience, to civil equality. Science was not in itself an end, only the means whereby to deprive Judaism of its characteristic peculiarities, and remodel it into something entirely new. It desired to invest the arbitrariness with which Friedländer, Jacobson, and their companions had introduced reforms with the appearance of necessity, and justify it on scientific grounds. By its violent, dogmatic attitude, fierce opposition was aroused, and thus the seeds of dissension were scattered in the vineyard of Jacob.

But even this phenomenon had its favorable side. It was a challenge to the orthodox party, which had hitherto met innovations with silence, or impotent rage, but always awkwardly, or, as in the person of Bernays, had made sphinx-like utterances. They altogether denied the justification of the reform which the advanced party so confidently urged. The "Nineteen Letters on Judaism," by Ben Usiel, a disciple of Bernays (1836), were the first tones of a powerful opposition against the leveling of Judaism to a commonplace religion, to consist of sermons, German hymns, and confirmation, so forcing its generous proportions to adapt themselves to the narrow limits of the synagogue. This was the commencement of a contest between two different sets of views, a strife which has not yet ceased. The struggle was confined to Germany. The Jews of the other European countries were not cognizant thereof. In Germany it was so difficult to destroy the old state of ignominy, so toilsome to obtain the new freedom, that educated Jews, imagining the peculiarities of their belief to be one of the obstacles in the way of securing equal privileges, were ready to sacrifice these, trying to persuade themselves that it was not surrender, merely a shedding of the outer skin. Christian society refused to recognize them as Germans, and, therefore, they desired to show, by stripping off their original garb, that they were Germans, naught but Germans, and kept up only a distant connection with Judaism. The spirit of subtle inquiry which had been awakened to a high degree, chiefly in Germany, furthered the habit of fault-finding, not alone with details, but with the whole structure of Judaism; of considering it as a work rotten with age, which, with the exception of a few foundation-stones, ought to be destroyed.

It was strange that thoughtful Christians admired the tents of Jacob in their simplicity, whilst the adherents of Judaism felt confined in them, and desired to exchange the Tabernacle and the Ark of the Covenant for the pomp and parade of the Church, or wished to surround them with disfiguring adornments. Two poetically-gifted Christian scholars, astounded by the wonderful fact that the persecuted Jewish people even in modern days produced neo-Hebraic poetry—spring blossoms in the midst of the violence of winter—strove to spread understanding and love of it in Christian circles. The "History of Neo-Hebraic Poetry" (1836), by Franz Delitzsch, and the "Hebrew Chrestomathy" (1837), by Adam Martinet, are tokens of the homage brought by Christians to the Jewish mind. The authors were astounded at its creative faculty, and at the capacity for development existing in the Hebrew language, although they knew only fragments, and were unacquainted with the most modern and the fairest specimens of neo-Hebraic poetry. This side of Jewish ability convinced them of the immortality of the race. "No one can deny," remarked the former, "that the Jewish people is the most remarkable of all nations, and next to those of the Church, its history and literature deserve the deepest and most devoted attention. Poetry forms a large part of this colossal mass of literature, and is the truest image of the inner history of this people. The elegiac poetry of the synagogue reveals to us the constant recurrence of suffering which God imposed on the exiles, and the impressions which these sufferings have left upon the heart of the nation. The Orient is an exile in the midst of the West, and from the tears of its home-sickness springs forth Jewish poetry."

Martinet desired "to ascertain the height, depth, and breadth of the Jewish spirit of our times as shown in the treasures of its own literature," and was fortunate in having found a noble, deeply interesting, in every way fine fragment. His "Chrestomathy" was intended as a vindication of neo-Hebraic literature—beauteous Eastern flowers reared upon Western soil, which he arranged in an odorous bouquet, in order to gain admirers for them, and induce them to cull radiant garlands of still fairer flowers from the magic garden.

The new school of reform felt little of the enthusiasm of appreciative Christians. They regretted that doubts, conflict, and dissension had sprung up in the place of confidence, peace, and perfect unity and sincerity; that all minds were filled with uncertainty and discomfort, creating a state of irritability which enervated all will-power. But they themselves had contributed, if not actually to call this ill-humor into existence, at least to nurse it, and so infect healthy minds. They imagined that the decomposition of Judaism had already commenced until they became convinced of it, and like romantic dreamers indulged in artificial grief, until it became real. In Germany, on account of the contest for the removal of disabilities, the awakening of self-consciousness and the dawn of knowledge were purchased at a heavy price, at the cost of internal disruption and self-torment.

The somber views of those who, whilst admiring Judaism in its ancient and venerable form, yet entertained doubts as to its continuance, were truthfully represented in "The Plaints of a Jew" (1837). The Prussian Jews at this time were placed in a situation both comic and tragical by an ordinance worthy of the Byzantine court promulgated by King Frederick William III. Instead of a partial grant of the liberty guaranteed to them, they were no longer to be officially called "members of the Mosaic faith," but curtly "Jews," and were not allowed to bear Christian names. The police were directed to insist that this law be carried into effect. This method was expected to bring waverers over to baptism. The self-respect of the Jews was not yet sufficiently strengthened for them to endure the intended humiliation with dignity. Many Jews in the large cities, especially in Berlin, who were nearer to the church than to the synagogue, considered it a slight, and implored the king to protect them against such undeserved contempt. They mourned as if they were to be again thrust into exile. This comic sadness was depicted after the manner of the Psalms in "The Plaints of a Jew."

"The children of my people came to me complaining and weeping. The old men and the mothers drew near, and anxious suffering was depicted on their countenances. I asked the little ones, 'Why are you weeping so early in life?' and to the elders I said, 'Why are you complaining so late in life?' The children lisped, 'Alas! we may no longer bear the bright, beautiful names of the Christians, but have to use the dull, hateful ones of the Jews. We are meant to be branded at our very games.' And the old men said, 'The quiver of anger is again emptied, and threatens our children with misery and danger.' Then I replied, ... 'Comfort yourselves, be quiet, and bear proudly the proud names of your fathers. They are the names of heroes, of martyrs crowned with fame, of an ancient nobility, of an ancient knighthood. . . . . When the West was still sunk in utter barbarism, your names flourished in immortal splendor, ruling the world, and enlightening and delivering it.   For I say unto you, that before the hand of the clock of history turns round, many empty names of the West will be swept off the face of the earth like stubble by the sharp scythe.   But as long as time endures there will always remain royally enthroned the names of Abraham, Moses, and Isaiah.'"

Joel Jacoby, the son of a strictly orthodox father, introduced into his "Plaints of a Jew" many untrue outpourings of fantastic sentimentality and a feigned sense of pain; but some of his elegies are ardent and beautifully constructed.

CHAPTER XVII.

THE YEAR 1840 AND THE BLOOD ACCUSATION AT DAMASCUS.

Mehmet Ali—Ratti Menton—Damascus—Father Tomaso—His Disappearance—Blood Accusation against the Jews of Damascus—Imprisonment of Accused—Their Tortures and Martyrdom—Blood Accusation in Rhodes—In Prussia—Adolf Crémieux—Meeting of English Jews—Moses Montefiore — Nathaniel de Rothschild—Merlato, the Austrian Consul—Plots—Thiers—Steps taken by the Jews in Paris and London—Bernard van Oven—Mansion House Meeting—Montefiore, Crémieux, and others sent to Egypt—Solomon Munk.

1840 C. E.

If Joel Jacoby wavering between faith and apostasy thus addressed Judaism, "Feeble is thy body, my people, and thy spirit weary: therefore do I bring thee a coffin and dedicate to thee a tomb"; and if Geiger's paper, half in pain, half in spite, testified that "the bond which used to keep together the congregations is torn asunder, and now they are only externally united, the will-power of the community is broken," the wish was father to the thought, or the writers greatly deceived themselves. Superficial observers, self-willed opinionists, they thought the symptoms of rapid growth signs of swift consumption, and praised their own quack medicines, which would surely have brought about dissolution.

An unforeseen event, insignificant at the beginning, but of vast importance in its results, gave the lie to the false prophets and quacks, and showed how wondrous the force which holds the members of the Jewish race in an indissoluble union; how strong the invisible bond which without their knowledge embraces them; and how a serious menace to Judaism arouses the patriotism of the reformer and the orthodox, of the politician who appears to have forsaken his faith and the recluse engrossed only in the Kabbala or the Talmud, of the Jew in frivolous France and of him in serious Asia. Strangely enough, the despised " Jewish Question " became interwoven in the complicated threads of European and Asiatic politics, and the Russian despot Nicholas as also the American Republic had to take up the cause of the Jews in Damascus. He who remembers this time, and can appreciate the marvels of history, cannot misunderstand the wonderful intermingling of events. Ratti Menton, an Italian naturalized in France, a reckless, unconscientious fortune-hunter; Hanna Bachari Bey, a renegade, who had passed from Christianity to Islam, a thorough knave and bitter Jew-hater; Mohammed El-Telli, a man of like caliber, who threatened a rich Jew in Damascus with a blood accusation unless he advanced money to relieve him of his difficulties; and finally a Christian Arab, Shibli Ajub, a worthless wretch panting for revenge, because he had been imprisoned on the charge of embezzlement preferred by a Jew; this is the list of fiends who originated a bloody drama, in which the part of martyrs was once more played by the Jews. But their sufferings induced courage, exaltation, and proud self-reliance.

Political events, as intimated, served as the background for this drama. The cunning Mehmet Ali, Pasha of Egypt, by splendid victories had wrested all Syria and Palestine from the Turkish sultan, his feudal lord. He oppressed the inhabitants of these countries more severely even than those of his own pashalic, in order to fill his coffers. The so-called Citizen King, Louis Philippe, equally cunning, in order to disarm the resentment of the legitimate princes of Europe, supported Mehmet Ali's plans of conquest, and French agents aided the Egyptian robbery system. These intrigues increased when the

strong-minded but unfortunate Sultan Mohammed
was dead, and his weak, pampered son, Abdul
Meg'id, only seventeen years old, ascended the
throne (July, 1839). Then the Eastern Question
commenced to wax warm. Russia supported feeble
Turkey that it might not fall into the arms of
Mehmet Ali. France, on the other hand, supported the Egyptian robber, in order to checkmate
Russia. Austria and England were unsettled in
their policy, and Prussia was the fifth wheel on the
van of the European Pentarchy. Owing to the
close union between Louis Philippe and Mehmet
Ali, the Christians in Palestine and Syria, hitherto
oppressed, could now raise their heads; for France
delighted to pose as the protector of Christianity in
the East in order to gain title and power, as she
coquetted with the clerical party at home in order
to suppress the friends of liberty. The clergy and
monks of many orders in the East, especially the
Catholics or Latins, until lately the oppressed, now,
relying upon French protection, became the
oppressors.

In Damascus, which at that time contained five
thousand Jewish families, or about twenty thousand
souls, the guardian of a Capuchin cloister, Father
Tomaso (Thomas), of Sardinia, together with his
servant, disappeared one day (February 5, 1840).
He was no saint in the Catholic sense of the word,
but a man of the world, more ready to take than to
give money. He pottered in medicine, especially
occupying himself with inoculation for small-pox,
and as often visited in Jewish and Mahometan as in
Christian quarters. What had become of the
Father so well known to the whole population of
Damascus? No one knew exactly. There was a
rumor that Tomaso had some days before quarreled
with a Turkish mule-driver, who was said to have
sworn, "This Christian dog shall die by no other
hand than mine." It was said that insults and vio-

lence followed.   As soon as it was known that the Father had disappeared, and had probably met with a violent death, the monks besieged the unscrupulous Ratti Menton, the French consul in Damascus, with entreaties to search for the murderer.   Attention was immediately directed to the Jews, some of them having innocently testified that they had seen Tomaso and his servant in the Jewish quarter, on the evening before they disappeared.   The monks, chief among them a fanatical Jew-hater, Father Tusti, quickly caught up the suspicion against the Jews, hoping thereby to gain several ends.   They could satiate their hatred against the Jews, suppress the inquiry as to whether Father Tomaso had indeed quarreled with Mussulmans and reviled them, and finally a new martyr, slain by the Jews, would be added to their list of saints, which was always a source of profit.   Ratti Menton, in turn, from interested motives, quickly endorsed the suspicion against the Jews, and relinquished every other theory, although a clue had been given by the fact that the Turkish merchant, who had been present at the quarrel with the Father, had hanged himself.   Sherif Pasha, the governor of Damascus, was readily induced to permit or carry on the persecution of the Jews from a desire to be on friendly terms with the French consul, and hoping to obtain profit for himself from a blood accusation against the Jews.   To save appearances, the accusers quoted the evidence of a pious fraud, who assured them that Tomaso and his servant had been murdered in the Jewish quarter in such and such a house.   This trick was probably perpetrated by Bachari Bey.   The Turkish rascal, Mohammed El-Telli, offered his services as a spy to Ratti Menton, if he would free him from prison and debt.   He willingly consented ; the two scoundrels were worthy of each other.

Proofs soon accumulated.   Christians testified

that they had heard Jews say, "Let us shut the gates, and not go out, because danger is imminent," or that they had seen the monk in the house of a Jew shortly before his disappearance. The bill of accusation was quickly prepared: "The Jews have murdered Tomaso and his servant to use the blood for their Passover Festival,"—as though they would be so ridiculous as to keep it for six weeks! Efforts were made to arouse the Christians and the Turkish populace. Several Jews were arrested, brought before Ratti Menton, and examined. A poor Jewish barber from inborn fear showed great confusion during the examination in the presence of the spies. But he firmly denied participation in, or knowledge of, the murder of the missing monk. Nevertheless the French consul handed him over for trial to Sherif Pasha, as a man under strong suspicion. The latter ordered him to receive the bastinado, five hundred blows with a stick upon the soles of his feet. This torture, however, appeared too mild to Ratti Menton. The poor barber was subjected to the cruellest tortures, but he remained steadfast. He was then visited by Mohammed El-Telli, who was in prison for debt. Induced by deceitful speeches, the barber, afraid of fresh torture, agreed to name the guilty persons. He named, upon suggestion, seven distinguished and wealthy Jews, David Arari (Harari), with his son and brothers, then Moses Abulafia, Moses Saloniki, and Joseph Laniado, an old man of eighty years. When arrested and examined they denied their guilt. The bastinado was resorted to, but the executioners, fearing that the old men would sink under the blows, and that their confessions would be of no use, employed another method of torture. The accused, guarded by soldiers, were compelled to stand erect for thirty-six hours, without food or drink, and without being allowed to go to sleep. As this torture bore no result, the bloodthirsty villains proceeded at Ratti Menton's orders to inflict a violent beating with switches; at the twentieth blow the unhappy victims fell to the ground unconscious. The French consul nevertheless ordered the scourging to be continued when they revived.

All this, however, did not extort a confession. Sherif Pasha invented a new species of torment, or employed one suggested to him. More than sixty children between the ages of three and ten were torn from their parents, shut up in a room, and deprived of food, so that the mothers, agonized by the piteous cries of the children, might be driven to make confessions, even though untrue ones. This means also failed. In spite of compassion for their children, the Jewish mothers in no way confirmed the horrible accusation. Only one woman and her daughter were driven by grief and love of their children into the arms of Islam. Sherif Pasha became enraged, and threatened that if the Father were not found, many Jewish heads should fall. With a band of soldiers (February 18) he marched into the Jewish quarter, and commanded the magnificent house of David Arari to be destroyed, in order to find the corpse of the monk or suspicious traces. The houses of the other accused were also ruined. Distressed by so much cruelty, a Jewish youth ventured to go to the Pasha and give evidence that he had seen Father Tomaso enter the shop of a Turk shortly before his disappearance. Instead of following this clue, Ratti Menton and his private secretary, Baudin, tried to hush up the evidence. The youth was unmercifully flogged, and in the same night died, the first martyr in this tragedy.

Ratti Menton was inexhaustible in devices for extorting a confession from the Jews. He ordered an experiment to be tried upon David Arari's Turkish servant, Murad el Fallat. He had nothing to confess, and permitted himself to be scourged till his body was almost lacerated. Mohammed El-

Telli then interviewed him, and by mingling friendly overtures and threats obtained some information from him. The servant accused himself of having murdered Tomaso at the command of David Arari in the presence of the other prisoners; and the Jewish barber was persuaded to confirm this statement. Ratti Menton then caused the two mutilated men to be led to a place where the bones and skulls were supposed to have been thrown into a canal. He found a piece of bone and a fragment of cloth; Christian doctors declared that this bone belonged to a human body, and the patch was judged to be part of the monk's cowl. Positive proof of the murder having been thus found in the Jewish quarter, the seven accused were again examined, and subjected to cruel tortures. They were ordered to produce the flask of blood taken from the murdered men for the Passover Festival. The tortures killed the old man Joseph Laniado. Moses Abulafia, to escape further torture, assumed the turban. The others, worn out by suffering, said all that was demanded of them; they had become dull, and only desired a speedy death. Their confession, however, did not help them. The French consul wanted tangible evidence, such as the flask of blood and other proofs. But the poor prisoners, however willing, were unable to produce them.

New tortures were applied, the only result being that the wretched victims retracted their former confessions. As Ratti Menton needed new victims, Arari's servant was required to assist in supplying them early in March. Suspicion fell upon other distinguished Jewish families: upon the wealthy family of Farchi (Parchi), upon a young man named Isaac Levi Picciotto (Peixotto), and upon Aaron Stambuli. Three rabbis of Damascus, Jacob Anteri, Solomon and Azaria Halfen, had been arrested earlier, and tortured, but the desired evidence was not obtained. Of the distinguished

Jews said to be implicated in the charge of murder, only two could be found: Raphael Murad Farchi who, owing to his high position as consul, thought himself safe, and Picciotto, the nephew of the consul-general of Aleppo, who had been knighted for his services by the Austrian emperor. Picciotto alone remained steadfast, and boldly upbraided Ratti Menton and the Pasha with the inhumanity of their conduct. He was protected by the Austrian consul, an Italian named Merlato, who despite all threats and arguments refused to allow an Austrian subject to be tortured without substantial proofs of his guilt. This new complication produced a change in the horrifying drama. Merlato had long looked on calmly at the inhuman acts, like the other European consuls, especially the English consul named Werry, who was Ratti Menton's accomplice. But at length Merlato's patience was exhausted; he openly attacked the barbarous, horrible proceedings. Consequently he had to endure a good deal of abuse. The Christian populace heaped curses upon him, because he defended the Jews, and would not surrender his protégé Picciotto into the hands of the cannibals. His house was surrounded by spies, and the Mahometan mob was also inflamed against the Jews by foul means.

Ratti Menton was indefatigable in inventing new charges and sham proofs. He ordered a contemptible book against the Jews, by Lucio Ferrajo, which had been shown him by the monks, to be translated into Arabic. This book proved from the Talmud that the Jews used blood, that they slew Christian children, and outraged the Host, which afterwards worked miracles. The Arabic translation was given by Ratti Menton to Sherif Pasha, and he circulated it among the Mahometan populace. To set on foot a thorough-going persecution, Franciscus of Sardinia, a venomous Capuchin monk, was brought from Beyrout, being well known for his ability to give an appearance of truth to perversions and falsehoods. The Pasha then commanded that the three imprisoned rabbis be separated, and directed to translate into Arabic certain suspicious passages in the Talmud, with the threat of death if they were caught in a deception. Thoughtful Turks shook their heads at this systematic persecution of the Jews; but they held their peace. Ratti Menton closed the proceedings, and pronounced judgment, as if it had been incontrovertibly proved, that the arrested and tortured Jews were the murderers of Father Tomaso. Those still alive were sentenced to be beheaded. Sherif Pasha obtained the assent of his lord, Mehmet Ali, to this deed.

As if to give verisimilitude to the blood-accusation against the Jews, and justify their destruction as bloodthirsty cannibals, a similar incident occurred at about the same time on the island of Rhodes, which belonged to Turkey. A boy of ten years of age, the son of a Greek peasant, had hanged himself, and the Christians hastened to charge the Jews with his murder. The European consuls took the matter in hand, and demanded of the governor, Jussuf Pasha, a strict investigation against the Jews. Upon the evidence of two Greek women that the boy had followed a Jew of Rhodes, the man was arrested, tried, imprisoned, and, because of his denial, inhumanly tortured. His nostrils were pierced by an iron wire, red-hot coals placed upon his head, and a heavy stone upon his breast. This was done or approved by Europeans and Christians, consuls of the European powers, of England, France, and Sweden. Here, too, the Austrian consul took no part in the barbarous persecution. The torture was applied to the accused Jew by his officers without the knowledge of the Pasha. The confession which they desired to obtain was that he had killed the Greek boy to send his blood to the chief rabbi at Constantinople. It was a sort of conspiracy of the Christians in Turkey against the Jews, to bring them to the edge of the precipice, perhaps due to envy, because the young Sultan, Abdul Meg'id, on ascending the throne, in his congratulatory address (Hatti-Sherif of Gulhane) had conceded equal privileges to all subjects of his kingdom, Jews included.   The Greeks and Latins in Turkey thought but little of their freedom, because they had to share it with the hated Jews.

Induced by the cruel torture, the half lifeless Jew in Rhodes made a confession.   He incriminated several Jews in the murder of the boy, hoping that they had already fled from fear of persecution.   But some of them were still in Rhodes.   As in Damascus, they were incarcerated, tortured, and brought near to death's door.   Nevertheless they remained firm.   The consuls then ordered the Ghetto to be closed, so that no one might pass in and out, and the Jews might be unable to lay their complaints before the Pasha, or even before the Sultan.   For three days the Jews received no food from outside. Greeks were constantly prowling around the Ghetto to throw in bones, to be able to say afterwards that they were the bones of a murdered Christian.   The Austrian consul, who at first had taken the part of the Jews, was ultimately induced to join their enemies.

In consequence of this double accusation, a perfect storm arose against the Jews in Syria and Turkey.   In Djabar, near Damascus, the mob broke into the synagogue, pillaged and destroyed it, and tore the scrolls of the Law to shreds.   In Beyrout the Jews were protected from ill-treatment by the interposition of Laurilla, the Dutch consul, and Sason, the Prussian consul.   The spirit of enmity spread as far as Smyrna, and was attended by many attacks upon the Jews.

Was it a mere accident that at the same time (beginning of March, 1840) a blood accusation was

raised against a Jew in Rhenish Prussia, in Jülich?
A Christian girl, nine years of age, asserted that a
Jew had stabbed her.   Her little brother, six years
old, confirmed her statement.   A Jew and his wife,
who happened to be journeying through Jülich, were
identified by the children as the criminals, and the
girl added that the Jew at the same time had killed
an old Christian with a knife.   If truth speaks from
the mouth of children, this Jew would have had to
be sentenced as a murderer of Christians, a vampire.
If the torture had been applied, an avowal of the
crime would probably have been extorted from the
Jew and his wife.   But a strict judicial inquiry
elicited that the statements of the children were idle
falsehoods and deception.   The Christian supposed
to have been murdered was alive.   The pretended
wound on the girl's body was only a smudge of
blood.   The accused Jew was acquitted, and a
rumor, referred to by the state attorney himself,
charged two Christians from Düsseldorf with having
drummed these horrible accusations into the
children's heads.

In Rhenish Prussia the truth and the innocence
of the Jews were brought to light quickly.   In
Damascus and Rhodes, on the other hand, the
struggle was prolonged, because fiendish European
Christians had intentionally woven such a network
of lies, that even guileless persons were deceived.
In vain the ill-treated Jews wrung their hands, and
entreated their European brethren to aid them by
means of their more favorable circumstances.   They
found it exceedingly difficult to bring the truth to
light and to unmask villainy.   Religious fanaticism,
Judæophobia, and political party passions, all combined to assist the triumph of falsehood.   The
underhand plotters employed the art of Guttenberg
—whose four hundredth jubilee was then being
celebrated—to circulate accusations throughout the
world that Jews were eager drinkers of Christian
blood.

Ratti Menton arranged that a report from Damascus presenting the events from his point of view be inserted in the French journals to inform the European world that the Jews had murdered a priest and his servant, and had collected the blood for their unleavened bread for the Passover. One corpse had been thrown into the canal in their quarter, and the other into a Jew's cellar. They had confessed, acknowledging that they had committed the crime in order to celebrate the mysteries of their religion. Without Ratti Menton's zeal the culprits would not have been discovered, and without his interposition the Jewish quarter and all its inhabitants would have been destroyed. Not only the newspapers controlled by the Catholic clergy zealously spread this charge against the Jews, but also the liberal journals, in order to glorify the power of France in the East, published as facts all the distorted statements from Damascus. The eyes of Europe being at this time directed towards the entanglements in Turkey, the false reports rapidly spread through the veins of European journalism. The hatred of the Middle Ages against the Jews might have been easily re-awakened, and might have caused scenes of blood to be re-enacted. The Jews of Europe were filled with horror that in the broad daylight of the nineteenth century they had still to contend against the dark specter of the blood accusation, that it might not drag them down into the grave.

The press, which had been used by their adversaries, was now employed to greater advantage in the cause of the Jews. Calumnies and lying accusations against them could no longer be concealed under the veil of secrecy. There were courageous Jews who tore off the mask of virtue from falsehood and hypocrisy. Such a man was Adolf Crémieux (born 1796, died 1880), who shortly before this time had celebrated triumphs of eloquence. This extraordinary man was destined, as will be shown, to become the bold and powerful advocate of the Jews in their tribulation. The false charges brought against them in Damascus made him their advocate, and induced him to take an active part in the history of his co-religionists. Crémieux, who, among the many talented orators of France, was considered an exceptionally fine speaker, employed his great gifts in the defense of innocent prisoners, without distinction of creed, position, or party. Although Crémieux was at this time a member of the Franco-Jewish consistory, he had not hitherto troubled himself much about Jewish affairs; his soul was filled with patriotism for France. The blood accusation at Damascus, which had been spread far and wide by the opponents of the Jews, first reminded him of his Jewish origin, and inspired him with courage and zeal to take up the cause of his brethren in religion and race, and developed in him a glowing patriotism for Judaism. At the first news of the dark proceedings in Damascus, thoroughly convinced that the Eastern like the European Jews were innocent of blood, Crémieux hastened to the French minister to ask him whether the government had more precise information on the matter. The minister replied that he had not received the slightest information on the subject from the consul or any other source. Thus it was made evident how this game was played. With all the glowing fire of his eloquence and the courage instilled by a righteous cause, Crémieux opposed the wide-spread slanders which echoed through France (April 7), and became the center of a patriotic movement of the French communities. Crémieux was then vice-president of the central consistory; and the Jews of France looked to him, their appointed representative, to rend asunder the network of lies which extended from Damascus to France.

Like the French Jews, those of England also

aroused themselves suddenly. By their wealth and
honorable conduct they stood very high in public
opinion. Some had been elected to fill the honorable post of sheriff; and it was to be expected that
they would soon be admitted into Parliament. The
most distinguished Jews of England, among them
Baron Nathaniel Rothschild, Sir Moses Montefiore
(who from a pious sentiment had undertaken a pilgrimage to the Holy Land), Salomons, and the
highly-esteemed brothers Goldsmid, held a meeting
(April 21), and resolved to appeal to the governments of England, France, and Austria, to use their
influence to put a stop to the inhuman proceedings
in Damascus. Crémieux came to London, and was
present at the meeting, in order to consider a common course of action. The unanimity was noteworthy with which prominent Jews took up the
cause of their persecuted brethren, and defended
the purity of Judaism, of its Law, and the Talmud.
On the same day (May 1), Crémieux presented himself before Louis Philippe, king of France, and a
Jewish deputation waited on the English minister,
Lord Palmerston, in order to obtain the protection
of these two countries for the victims in Damascus.

Louis Philippe replied with much feeling:

"I do not know anything about the occurrence; but if anywhere
there are unfortunate Jews who appeal to the protection of my government, and if anything can be effected by its means, I will conform
with your wishes."

Whether the asseveration was seriously meant
by this diplomatic monarch cannot be known. A
vice-consul was, however, appointed to visit Damascus, investigate the matter, and draw up a report.
But he was only a subordinate, whom, as might
have been imagined, Ratti Menton could easily
deceive, or venture to oppose. The answer of
Lord Palmerston was more straightforward. He
promised the Jewish deputation, who laid before
him full proofs of the innocence of the accused at

Damascus and Rhodes, that he would empower the English ambassador at Constantinople, as also the consul at Alexandria, to use every effort to check the continuance of such cruelties. In another quarter, less public, but more effective, steps were taken to obtain the support of Vienna and the Austrian cabinet. The Austrian consul in Damascus, Merlato, was the only one who had seen through the wickedness of Ratti Menton, his assistants, and the monks, and with true soldierly courage had offered firm resistance. In return, he was abused by his opponents both in the East and the West; they decried him as a Jew, to throw suspicion upon his defense of the Jews, and thus destroy its effects. But Merlato felt himself morally pledged to plead the innocence of the Jews as a personal matter. He issued a faithful and comprehensive report of the groundless attacks of the mob upon the victims at Damascus. This narrative, a defense of his conduct in protecting Picciotto, he despatched to his superior, the consul-general of Egypt, and it was sent by the latter as a correct account to Metternich, the Austrian minister. Although adverse to publicity, Metternich had allowed all writings favorable to the Jews to be circulated in the newspapers. In this report Ratti Menton, whom the clerical intriguers had glorified as an angel of light, was shown to be an evil demon. A revolution ensued in public opinion which filled the Jews with courage, and foreshadowed the triumph of justice. It is difficult to say whether Metternich's intervention in this matter arose from his own impulse, from displeasure at the cruelty practiced, or from political hostility to France and a desire to break her power in the East, or, perhaps, from complaisance to the house of Rothschild, whose members were extraordinarily zealous on behalf of their co-religionists in this affair. At any rate, Metternich encouraged the Austrian agents in Egypt and Syria to stand up boldly in defense of the Jews.

In Constantinople, at the divan of the Sultan, the representatives of European governments friendly to the Jews, obtained a revision of the trial for blood accusation in the island of Rhodes. Jewish deputies from Rhodes had at length succeeded in reaching Constantinople. Nathaniel de Rothschild also betook himself thither, and as a result Abdul Meg'id issued a Firman (July 27) that the Greek population should send to the capital three primates as accusers, and the Jews as many elders as defendants. A tribunal, under the presidency of Risaat Bey, was appointed to inquire into the matter, the result being that Jussuf Pasha was dismissed from his post of governor of Rhodes, and the Jews charged with child-murder were acquitted. Further, they were instructed to demand compensation for the losses sustained from those who had unjustly accused them, viz., some of the European consuls. In three months—from the beginning of May till towards the end of July—the affair was settled.

With Mehmet Ali there were greater difficulties to be encountered. He had, indeed, as early as the beginning of April, promised the Austrian consul-general Laurin to put an end to the atrocities; but this was prevented by the French consul-general, Cochelet, and, foolishly trusting in France, he could not quarrel with the agents of the French government. But Laurin, acting on the instructions of Metternich, was untiring in his efforts to withdraw the Pasha of Egypt from the net of the French intriguers. At his instigation the Jews of Alexandria presented an eloquent and spirited address to Mehmet Ali. It was remarkable that the Egyptian Jews did not receive the bastinado for speaking the truth; Mehmet Ali well knew who supported them. A letter of Metternich to the Pasha produced a wonderfully favorable effect. In the settlement of the Eastern Question, the latter could not afford to break with Austria, from which country the Sultan could obtain reinforcements more quickly than from France.

Mehmet Ali therefore resolved to form a court of justice, consisting of the consuls of Austria, England, Russia, and Prussia, to carry on the trial according to European usages. The tribunal was empowered to dispatch a commission to Damascus, and institute an impartial examination of witnesses on the spot. An order was sent to Damascus to Sherif Pasha, commanding him to discontinue the torture of the prisoners, and in general to stop the persecution of the Jews. To suppress any riotous outbreak of the Christians, whose courage had increased, eight hundred soldiers were sent thither. The matter began to look as if the truth would be vindicated. The four consuls nominated as chief judges, diffident of their ability to conduct so complicated a trial, turned for aid to Vienna, and asked that four German judges, well versed in criminal law, investigate the matter, but a political interlude interrupted the proceedings.

A secret war was waged between the overwise king, Louis Philippe, and the cunning statesman Thiers, who was trifling with the minister's portfolio, and whose little person and big phrases so thwarted the king that he kept him as much as possible at arm's length. Just at this time (in May) Thiers played a trick on the king, and forced him to make him president of the cabinet. The little "fly," as he was called, began to hum and buzz, behaving as if he could acquire the Rhine as French property, and settle the Eastern Question according to the views of France. To secure a majority in the Chamber, Thiers was forced to gain the good graces of the clerical party, which was especially strong in the Chamber of Peers. Thus it happened that no strict investigation into the Damascus affair could be permitted, in order that the brutal behavior of Ratti Menton and the monks might not be brought to light.   At any rate, it had been a slight upon France that its consul had been excluded from the new court of justice.   Besides this, Thiers was not on friendly terms with the financial world, that is, with the Rothschilds, and he desired to strike a blow to make them yield.   The French consul-general Cochelet, in Alexandria, received instructions from Thiers to stay the hand of Mehmet Ali, and prevent the misdeeds in Damascus from being brought to light.   The Egyptian Pasha, misled by Thiers' plotting, obeyed his orders, and withdrew the promise made to the four consuls.   Thus the drama which had seemed to be approaching a conclusion was again prolonged, but its end was not favorable to Thiers and his protégés.

Jews of every shade of opinion had become possessed of sufficient independence to defy the prevarications of a minister or of a consul.   Achille Fould, who was bound to Judaism by only a slender tie, as well as the strictly orthodox Hirsch Lehren in Amsterdam, both regarded it as their duty to take a bold part in the defense of their persecuted co-religionists in Syria.   In the French Chamber of Deputies (July 2) Fould questioned Thiers so sharply that the latter was forced to make excuses.

"The French consul had ordered the torture, and after the French nation had set the example of obedience to the rule of 'equality before the law' as well as in religious matters, a Frenchman countenanced this exception to the rule, employed torture, and thus supported the executioners of the Pasha.   This behavior was so deeply resented by the other European agents that the French ambassador was excluded from the council which had been established, because he was the accuser, whilst the others were the defending advocates."

To this statement Thiers was compelled to reply, but each word he uttered sounded like a falsehood. Two Christian deputies took the part of the Jews in this discussion.   Count Delaborde, who had traveled in the East, highly praised the Jews of Turkey, and stated that well-deserved respect was accorded to them, and that, like Lamartine, he had received the most hearty and generous hospitality from their wealthy members. Thiers' positive assertion that he was in possession of papers which proved the innocence of Ratti Menton, was met by another deputy, Isambert; he produced a report drawn up by the apostolical missionary, the successor of Father Tomaso, which stated "that the exertions and zeal of the French consul in torturing the Jews of Damascus surpassed all comprehension." The Chamber of Deputies, however, did not pass a vote of censure upon the minister, who so belied the courteous character of the French nation, but the looks of the deputies condemned him. Thiers felt such discomfort that he made a petty attack upon the Jews, "who had stirred up a storm throughout Europe, asking the assistance of the ministers of every state, and had thus shown that they possessed more influence than was asserted."

The Jews, to be sure, had to unite and develop especial activity, seeing that the Catholic party in France, Italy, and Belgium had formally conspired, or received a hint from headquarters to enshroud in darkness the events in Damascus, and to represent the Jews in the East and in Europe as murderers and cannibals. Throughout Italy the documents in favor of the Damascus victims or against Ratti Menton were not allowed to be printed: the censorship, which was under the care of the clergy, forbade it. A French journal had called on baptized Jews to state upon oath and to the best of their knowledge, whether they had ever found among their former co-religionists or in Jewish writings, the slightest trace or precept concerning the abominable crime imputed to the unhappy people in Damascus. Several Jews who had been converted to Protestantism, and even held ecclesiastical positions, asserted the innocence of the Jews of this crime— amongst them, Augustus Neander, known as Church historian and a man of tender conscience.

No Catholics, with the exception of one man, came forward to do so. Perhaps they were compelled to remain silent. The clerical enemies of the Jews now published a fresh accusation, that the Talmud which the European Jews knew and studied might indeed be free from passages hostile to Christians and advising the shedding of blood, which may have been expunged from the copies out of fear, but the Jews of the Orient, under Turkish rule, still possessed the Talmud in its original form, which was full of hatred against all men, especially against Christians.

Thus the Jews were forced to establish a bond of truth against the untrue, to make public the innocence of the martyrs in Damascus, and at the same time attest the purity of their own doctrines; in short, they had to help themselves. The French central consistory, which had received solemn promises from Louis Philippe, saw itself deceived in its hopes. Crémieux was compelled to make the painful statement to his brethren, "France is against us." The urgent cries of the Jews from Damascus, Beyrout, Alexandria, and Constantinople, in letters to the Rothschilds, to Moses Montefiore, Crémieux, and to Hirsch Lehren in Amsterdam, made it apparent that it was necessary for prominent European Jews to repair to the scene of action, in order to obtain more effective results. The central consistory therefore determined to send an emissary, with an escort, to Alexandria, whose burning eloquence might gain the favor of Mehmet Ali. Entrusted with this dangerous and honorable mission, Crémieux entered into communication with the heads of the Jewish community in London.

Here a committee of the noblest and most distinguished Jews, including Montefiore and Rothschild, had been formed, who, in a meeting held in the vestibule of a synagogue (June 15), passed the following important resolution, that Montefiore, accompanied by a friend chosen by himself, should undertake the journey to Egypt together with Crémieux, "to represent the Jews of England at the court of the Pasha, and to defend their persecuted brethren in the East by means of his weighty influence and his zeal." It was also determined at this meeting to collect large sums of money, because it was seen that they would be wanted, not indeed as bribes in the pending trial at Damascus, but that large rewards might be offered to discover the murderer of Father Tomaso. A thousand pounds sterling were offered as a reward for the discovery of the criminal. The readiness of the Jews to contribute was on this occasion again manifested in a most conspicuous manner. Poor men as well as millionaires contributed to the just cause. The committee also caused unfalsified public opinion, as it exists in England, to make itself heard in Parliament on behalf of the Jews, and Sir Robert Peel, who exercised great influence, undertook this task.

The session of the House of Commons (June 22) affords an interesting contrast to the sitting of the French Chamber of Deputies at the same time and upon the same subject. Peel rightly introduced the questions to the ministers with the words, "that it was merely necessary to mention the matter in the Lower House, to reach the great ends of justice and humanity." Lord Palmerston answered in a totally different manner to Thiers :

"I have already directed the English consul-general Hodges to represent to Mehmet Ali what effect the news of such atrocities must produce in Europe, and that it was in his own interest to inquire into the matter, and hand over to punishment the guilty parties, if they were discovered, whilst the innocent victims should be indemnified, if this were still possible. I have also sent instructions to Her Majesty's consul in Damascus to make a thorough investigation into all that has taken place, and to send home an exact report as to the part which the European consuls had taken in the matter."

The air of England rendered susceptible to feelings of liberty even those who were accustomed to elevate the enslavement of bodies and minds to the rank of a dogma. O'Connell, the fiery Irish agitator for the emancipation of the Catholics in England, advocated in Parliament that a similar privilege be granted to the Jews.

"Observations upon this subject would have been stronger, if a member of this House belonging to the creed of the accused had been able to make them. The Government ought to introduce a bill for the complete emancipation of the Jews."

Thus spake England by the mouths of its worthiest representatives.

Next day (June 23) a numerous assembly of the most distinguished Jews in London was held in the Great Synagogue to make final arrangements for sending Montefiore to Egypt. It was proved on this occasion what a noble circle of Jews England harbored, and that their minds were filled by lofty sentiments of attachment to Judaism and its adherents. Hitherto the English Jews had taken but little part in Jewish history, they had remained passive owing to their insignificant numbers. But when for the first time they asserted themselves, they displayed their independence, and gave a brilliant example to others. Montefiore, De Castro, Rothschild, Van Oven, Salomons, and many others, spoke and acted like Jews conscious of their dignity, who were ready to make the greatest sacrifices, in order to secure the triumph of their impugned belief. Crémieux had come over from Paris to be present. The meeting first acknowledged its gratitude to those men, Christians as well as Jews, who had zealously defended the unhappy people of Damascus, viz., James de Rothschild, who had largely contributed towards the support of the impoverished Jews in Damascus, Metternich and his agents, Laurin and Merlato, and also Hodges, the English consul. Bernard van Oven delivered a glowing speech, which, however, was to the point, and was received with much applause.

Many words were not required at this meeting.
All were firmly resolved to make every effort and
every sacrifice to obtain satisfaction for those falsely
accused of shedding blood. This high-minded Jewish assembly in London was somewhat similar to
that held in Alexandria exactly eighteen centuries
before, when Judaism, in the time of the Emperor
Caligula, was branded with disgrace by shameless,
diabolical enemies. At that time, also, the most
prominent Jews, famed for their culture, nobility of
mind, and wealth, gathered together. But the
Alexandrine assembly, surrounded by foes, had met
with terror and fear, whilst the one in London was
encouraged and supported by the good wishes and
sympathy of the citizens of the capital. In the second Jewish congregation, that of Manchester, a similar meeting was held.

Assured of success by these signs, Montefiore set
out on his important journey, provided with letters
of recommendation from prominent men in the
state, and accompanied by the good wishes of millions of persons, foremost among them Queen
Victoria. On his departure she gave him audience,
and placed at his disposal her vessel in which to
cross the Channel—certainly an extraordinary mark
of favor and sympathy for the misfortunes of the
Jews, but at the time the feeling in their favor was
so strong, that it did not create great surprise.
Montefiore was accompanied by a gentleman of the
legal profession and by his wife Judith, who insisted
upon sharing her husband's hardships on this expedition in the cause of her nation. She was the
ideal of a Jewish woman, cultured, noble-minded,
proud of her confession and devotedly attached to
her race, a brilliant contrast to the women of Berlin,
who had brought disgrace upon Judaism. Before
Montefiore and his escort left England, the two
chief rabbis of the German and Portuguese communities, Solomon Herschel (died 1842), and David

Meldola, deemed it necessary to repeat the solemn oath which Manasseh ben Israel and Moses Mendelssohn had taken: that the blood accusation against the Jews had not a shadow of support in Talmudical writings, or in fact. In view of the baseness of the clerical French party and the venality of German newspapers, this oath was by no means superfluous. Catholic agitators in France and Belgium reviled the Jews, for a contemptible, yet comprehensible reason, and with a definite plan of entrapping the conscience of the free in their nets. But the German writers acted in this way from low motives, in order to utilize the misfortunes of others as a source of wealth. A certain Dr. Philibert had sent a letter to the house of Rothschild in Paris, stating that for a large sum of money he would undertake the defense of the Damascus Jews in every European journal, adding the threat that if this blood-money were refused he would influence public opinion in the opposite direction. Such miserable creatures were repulsed by the Jews with scorn. They felt that they could rely upon their own strength and the power of truth. Foiled in their expectations, the contemptible scribblers attacked the Jews, and increased the number of lies and slanders which had accumulated around the Damascus murder. The chief rabbis had therefore to swallow their pride, and to take an oath on a matter as clear as daylight.

However, if the Jews were attacked in the French and German newspapers, England afforded them sufficient cause to forget all the sufferings of the Jews throughout fifteen centuries. Distinguished merchants, proprietors of large banking-houses, and members of parliament, about two hundred and ten in all, preferred a request to the Lord Mayor of London, Marshall, to call a public meeting and enable them to express their feelings and their sincere sympathy with the persecuted Jews in Damascus. The Lord Mayor, being of their opinion in the matter, cordially assented, and a brilliant meeting was held in London (in the Mansion House, July 3) which was in itself a victory. Many ladies of rank were among the audience. The chairman, Thompson, remarked at the very outset :

" The Jews of Damascus are as worthy of respect as those who dwell among us in England. And of those I permit myself to say that none of our fellow-citizens are more zealous in the spread of humanity, in aiding the poor and oppressed, in protecting the orphan and in promoting literature and knowledge than they are, and that their benevolence is not only extended to the people who belong to their own religion, but also to Christians, equally with members of every creed."

A member of Parliament named Smith, who rose to move the first resolution, said :

"I consider these charges as false as the natures of those who invented them are cruel and evil. I am certain that the whole country with one voice, and one accord, will rise to suppress such atrocities, such barbarities, as have been carried on in Damascus. And what people is it that has been subjected to such pain? A nation connected with us by everything that religion holds dear and sacred ; a nation whose faith is based upon history, that awaits with unfaltering confidence its political and religious restoration ; a nation closely bound up with the progress of trade and civilization throughout the whole world, and in friendly intercourse with the whole world. . . . . In past times they were the men who led the way in educating the human race, and granted to others that very civil and religious freedom which at the present time they demand for themselves. This nation has given the best proof of the value it sets upon freedom, seeing that by its own example it has shown how greatly it was actuated by this principle in its conduct towards others without distinction of creed ; it therefore has a claim to the highest tolerance."

A prominent clergyman, Lord Howdon, added :

" We often find in the mysterious ways of Providence that good arises from evil, and therefore I, together with all the friends of mankind, hope that the Parliament of this country, expressing its opinion of this cruelty, will offer a recompense to the Jews for their sufferings by legislation in their favor."

The motion was carried unanimously :

" That this meeting deeply deplores the fact that in this enlightened age a persecution of our Jewish brethren could be set on foot by ignorance and inflamed by bigotry."

Towards the end of the meeting O'Connell entered.   He thought that his presence would be required to arouse enthusiasm.   But when he saw that the zeal on behalf of the Jews had been raised to a high pitch, he merely added :

"After the testimony given to demonstrate the moral worth of the Jews, could any man be so insane as to believe that they use blood for their rites ? Is not a Jew an example in every relation of life? Is he not a good father, a good son ?   Are they not true friends ? Are they not honest, industrious ? . . . . I appeal to all Englishmen to raise their voices in defense of the victims of that shameful oppression.   May the appeal go from one end of the British Isles to the other, and if the concurrence of an Irishman be wanting, here am I to testify to it."

This three hours' meeting in the Mansion House forms a noteworthy episode in Jewish history.   In the name of the meeting, the Lord Mayor communicated the resolutions which were passed, not only to the English government, but also to the ambassadors of all European powers, requesting them at the same time to obtain expressions of sympathy with the Jews from their respective nations and rulers.   So effective was the result of unbiased public opinion, that the emperor of Russia, Nicholas, as well as the American Republic, felt themselves morally compelled to express their abhorrence at tortures inflicted on Jews.

A few weeks later a similar meeting was held in Manchester, and, although most of the speakers were clergymen, the same sentiments with regard to the Jews were pronounced.   Why had not such views predominated in the fourth and fifth centuries, when Christianity first became paramount ?   What tears and bloodshed would have been avoided ! But the Jewish race was to be tested and strengthened by martyrdom.

Montefiore was enabled to begin his journey filled with courage.   He was not only supported by the government, but was accompanied by the sympathies of the best men in England, and therefore he

felt hope. For Crémieux the matter was not so
easy. In fact, he was hampered by the French
ministry. Thiers wished to show himself firm. Perhaps he was not so much to blame as was generally
supposed; it is possible that Louis Philippe, who
was very cunning, hindered him from yielding. He
was reminded also in the Chamber of Peers (July
10) by honorable men, that by his defense of Ratti
Menton, he was compromising the honor of France,
but he continued in his ambiguous attitude. Events
brought the cunning of Thiers and the king to
naught. Whilst they thought that by petty intrigues,
childish obstinacy, and by deceiving Mehmet Ali
they were strengthening the position of France,
the four remaining European powers—England,
Russia, Austria, and Prussia—formed the Quad-
ruple Alliance (July 15) against France, which
agreed that Syria should be restored to the Sultan.
The downfall of Thiers was imminent, while he was
boasting of his successes.

A day before the conclusion of the alliance,
Montefiore and Crémieux, with their respective
escorts, set out for Egypt. In Crémieux's company
was Solomon Munk, who worthily represented Jewish learning. Thus the Jewish embassy was not
lacking in what is requisite for the success of a great
enterprise—devotion, pure trust in God, eloquence,
and deep scholarship. In their journey through
France these noble-minded, gallant representatives
of Judaism were received with enthusiasm in the
Jewish communities, in Avignon, Nîsmes, Carpentras, and Marseilles, and were followed by good
wishes. In Leghorn, where the royal ship anch-
ored, the Portuguese community solemnly celebrated
the day of their landing. Every distinction among
the Jews disappeared in the unanimous admiration
for men who had undertaken so difficult a task, and
in the hope that they would succeed. All Israel was
once more of one heart and soul. Orthodox rabbis

allowed prayers for Montefiore and Crémieux to be interpolated in the Divine service. Every Jew, even the most humble, was ready to bring some sacrifice in order to lighten the task.

On arriving at Cairo (August 4), they hastened on their mission, without taking any rest. Montefiore, strongly supported by the English consul-general Hodges, who had received instructions from Palmerston to that effect, at once solicited an interview with Mehmet Ali (August 6), by whom he was received, and to whom he handed a petition in the name of the Jewish community requesting permission to go to Damascus and there conduct an inquiry into the circumstances of the case. For this purpose a safe-conduct was required for himself and his friends, and also the privilege of speaking to the prisoners as often as was necessary, and of hearing evidence. Mehmet Ali was sorely perplexed. He would willingly have acceded to this request, because he earnestly wished to pose as a just prince before the eyes of Europe. But the French consul-general Cochelet—instructed by Thiers—checked this inclination, and made every effort to prevent the veil from being lifted. Cochelet, contrary to custom, would not even introduce Crémieux to the Pasha. Crémieux was therefore obliged to seek an audience for himself; but, like Montefiore, he received only evasive answers. The Eastern Question had at that time become extremely perplexing. Every moment Mehmet Ali was expecting the final decision of the European powers, that he should submit to the Sultan, surrender his independence, and give up Syria. He did not wish to break with those powers which took up the cause of the Jews, more especially with England and Austria, nor with Thiers, nor Louis Philippe, who would not forsake Ratti Menton and the monks. Owing to Mehmet Ali's indecision, matters dragged on for three weeks. The Jewish envoys received no definite reply. They were not discouraged, but sought to devise new means by which to attain their aim. Crémieux hit upon the best plan. All the European consuls, or as many as were willing to sign a petition, were to demand the liberation of the prisoners in Damascus. Nine consuls agreed to this, in fact all except the French consul. Mehmet Ali, however, obtained information of the proposed petition, and in order that it might not appear that he had yielded to the pressure of foreign powers, through their representatives, he determined to despatch an order to Damascus (August 28) that the prisoners should forthwith be set at liberty.

The two envoys and their escort were filled with heartfelt joy. The three synagogues in Alexandria resounded with prayers of thanksgiving and blessings for Mehmet Ali, Metternich, and the Austrian consuls Laurin and Merlato, and all who had taken part in the deliverance and who were delighted at the result of their efforts.

Great was the astonishment, however, of the two Jewish representatives, when a Turkish copy of Mehmet Ali's order reached them, and Munk, who was a skilled linguist, read out the words, "Mr. Moses Montefiore and M. Crémieux have besought me to bestow mercy upon the Jews in Damascus and to grant them liberty," which implied that the accused Damascus Jews, though guilty, had been treated by the Pasha with mercy, instead of justice. The hand of Cochelet was visible in this attempt to shield Ratti Menton and the monkish executioners. Crémieux straightway hastened to the Pasha, explained to him how the expression "mercy" cast a slur upon the accused, and with them upon all Jews, because they were thus declared to be guilty. He asked that the words "liberty and peace" be substituted. Mehmet Ali ordered this alteration to be made in the Firman, and thus the last intrigues of Cochelet were destroyed.

As soon as the order arrived at Damascus, Sherif Pasha, who knew Mehmet Ali's severity, was obliged to liberate the nine Jewish prisoners who were still detained in jail (September 6) without consulting Ratti Menton. Seven of the men had been mutilated by the tortures, only two having escaped injury who had suffered persecution, while four victims had died. No sooner did the joyful news of their liberation get abroad in Damascus, than all the Jews and many Turks assembled before the prison, and accompanied the sufferers to the synagogue, to offer up thanks to God for their regained freedom, and to pray for Mehmet Ali and their Jewish protectors.

The joy of the Jews in all parts of the world, on hearing of the triumph of their just cause, may be imagined; it was a national rejoicirg, in which the best men, both in Europe and Asia, participated. All that remained to be effected was to obtain from Mehmet Ali the official statement that the blood accusation was a calumny, and of this there were ample proofs when everyone in Damascus could speak freely about the sad occurrence. The Jewish envoys also made it their duty to induce the Pasha to abolish torture altogether. But political complications prevented the accomplishment of this humane proposal. Mehmet Ali was obliged to surrender Syria as well as Crete to Turkey. Thus punishment overtook him for having complacently witnessed for nearly three months the scenes of blood in Damascus out of deference to France. Sherif Pasha, even before Damascus was captured by the Turks, was dragged in chains to Cairo, and there executed, it is said for treason. François Salins, one of the malicious French persecutors of the Jews in Damascus, was torn to pieces by the mob. The fanatical Catholics of this city, who under Mehmet Ali had been permitted to practice so much cruelty, were humiliated, or felt humiliated, when Raphael Farchi, the distinguished Jew, was again installed

in his position as member of the city council. No
longer able to torture the Jews, they cooled their
hatred by inciting to a crusade against them. The
representative of the Greek Patriarch, the Armenian
bishop Vantabiet, the vicar of the Holy Land, the
Syrian priest Jacob, and the representative of the
Catholic Patriarch, the priest Maruni—in short, the
representatives of three sects who bore deadly hatred
against each other united in fastening a new calumny
on the Jews, who were hated equally by all three.

"The Jews of Damascus allowed themselves grossly to insult the
Christians, to abuse them and subject them to all sorts of indignities.
Several persons made complaints of the disgraceful behavior of the
Jews, abominable behavior, which humiliates all Christians."

The majority of European Christendom were,
however, sufficiently well acquainted with the veracity of the clergy of Damascus to pay no attention
to this hypocritical lament, and the heads of Catholicism felt ashamed of having exposed themselves in
the Damascus affair.

The Jewish envoys did not think their task completed, unless they sought to prevent, as far as lay
in their power, the repetition of events which branded
all Judaism with dishonor. Foreseeing that Syria,
together with Damascus, would be restored to
Turkey, Montefiore made his way to Constantinople,
entered into communications with the Porte, to which
he had influential letters of recommendation, and
together with some distinguished Jews of the Turkish capital obtained an audience of the Sultan, when
he asked for a Firman (November 6), which should
in future secure the Turkish Jews from blood accusations.

Crémieux chose another field for his activity. The
martyrdom of the Damascus Jews had the unexpected effect of strengthening the connection
between the Jews in Europe and those in the East.
The latter saw with astonishment how much their
European brethren could accomplish by means of

culture, influence, and courage, and that they were treated with distinction by princes and the great, whilst they themselves bent their backs, unresistingly, to every blow.   This reverent admiration of the Asiatic Jews for those of Europe, Crémieux utilized in the attempt to emancipate the Egyptian Jews (or at least those in the two capitals of Alexandria and Cairo) from their state of ignorance, and render them susceptible to civilization.   Their ignorance of even Jewish writings, a consequence of the immeasurable oppression under which they had labored, as well as of their indescribable poverty, was the cause of the intense contempt in which they were held by Mahometans and Christians.   From this ignominy Crémieux hoped to free them, and he was powerfully supported by Solomon Munk, who appears to have been destined to be the intermediary between the European and the Egyptian Jews— between the past and the present.   Munk addressed an eloquent Hebrew and Arabic circular letter (Elul 23) to the Jews of Egypt, in which he contrasted the former splendor of the Jews of that country in the time of the Second Temple, in the time of Philo and Maimuni, when they stood at the head of Jewish spiritual activity, with the darkness of their present misery, the consequence of their intellectual decay. He exhorted them to wake from their deathlike torpor and establish schools, where their children might obtain a knowledge of Judaism and of Jewish literature, and at the same time a secular and practical education.   Munk effected for the Egyptian Jews what Wessely had done for those of Europe. But, unlike his predecessor, he was not denounced as a heretic for his efforts.   On the contrary, the rabbi of Alexandria was the first to offer assistance in the work.   A distinguished Jew, named Valensino, placed himself at the head of a society for establishing schools and supervising public education.   Then Crémieux, together with Munk, repaired to Cairo, where there dwelt a large congregation of about 300 families, only about twelve of whom were very wealthy, while about 200 lived on charity. Here also the rabbi, Moses Joseph Algazi, an aged man of seventy-six, and a prominent man named Adda, readily assisted in founding schools. Owing to their exertions and those of other persons, two schools for boys were opened in Cairo (October 4), and one for girls ; these were called the Crémieux schools. Here Munk succeeded in bringing about an important reconciliation. In spite of the fanaticism of the rigidly orthodox, he succeeded in having the children of Karaites admitted to the schools, there being only about a hundred persons of this sect left in Cairo. The rabbi Algazi also supported the innovation, which seemed to be a step tending to restore brotherhood between Rabbanites and Karaites. Stirred by these movements, the grand rabbi of Constantinople (Chacham Bashi), Moses Fresco, issued a circular letter (October 28) to the Turkish congregations, urging that it was the duty of the Jews to learn the language of the country (Turkish), in order to meet the Sultan's wishes, who, by his Firman Hatti-Sherif, had raised them from their abject state. The mixed language in which this circular letter of the Chacham Bashi was written (Old Spanish with Hebrew and Turkish words), proved sufficiently the necessity of a pure language for the Jews.

However, these beginnings were merely seeds scattered in the desert sand, and it was doubtful whether they would take root and grow. The efforts were resumed on a larger scale twenty years later, under the name of "the Universal Alliance of Israelites" (Alliance Israélite Universelle). The mission to Egypt produced practical and lasting fruit for Jewish science, chiefly through Solomon Munk (born at Glogau, 1802 ; died at Paris, 1867). It is doubtful whether the spotless character of this man, or his devoted attachment to science, is to be more admired. He added to the number of great men produced among the Jews during the first half of the nineteenth century. His modesty was a marked feature, which grew in proportion to the increase of his scientific importance. For his patience in misfortune, and cheerfulness in the sufferings which he had incurred in the service of science, he was greatly admired in his native country, Germany, and in France, his adopted country, and he was loved as much as he was revered. Munk possessed all the virtues of the Jews without their faults. In the comprehensive range of Arabic literature he was one of the first masters of the day, and the most profound scholars in the same study recognized his equality, or awarded him the palm. As interpreter to the escort of Crémieux, he spoke and wrote Arabic like one born in an Arab tent. He divined the words and sense of any manuscript passage by a kind of instinct, which only increased in keenness when he lost his sight from poring over manuscripts. His intellectual sight compensated for the loss of his physical power. The darkness which enshrouded him for nearly twenty years before his death did not prevent his vision from being clear and distinct.

The glory of Jewish history during the Middle Ages developed during the rule of the Arabs in the East and West; its dawn began with Saadiah, and it reached its zenith with Maimuni. Munk banished the obscurity in which this epoch had been enwrapped, and illumined it with the full light of his profound studies. The innermost thoughts of Maimuni, the awakener of intellects, to whom the Jewish race is chiefly indebted for its renaissance in modern days, were completely revealed only through the researches of Munk. He renewed in its original form what had been spoilt by continual emendations. The proud boast of Christendom, that even in the

obscurity of the Middle Ages it had disseminated
the bright germs of thought, Munk controverted by
incontestable proofs that without Arabic and Jewish
philosophy, the darkness of the Middle Ages would
have been impenetrable, and that the so-called
Christian schools of philosophy of that period were
fed upon the crumbs which fell from the lips of
Jewish thinkers. Munk so conclusively established
this historical fact that it is scarcely possible to
speak of a Christian philosophy. Another historical
fact, the origin and development of the Karaite sect,
which, notwithstanding the powerful influence it
exercised upon thought in the Jewish Middle Ages,
was known only in rough outlines, was brought to
light by Munk; in a word, Jewish science is deeply
indebted to him. He not only greatly added to it
by his profound knowledge, but he also showed how
to pursue a sound course of investigation. As
Luzzatto opened up new Hebrew sources for Jewish
science, so Munk discovered new Arabic sources,
rendering them comprehensible and accessible, and
thereby greatly adding to the knowledge of Judaism,
which he loved with all his heart. Munk's sojourn
in Alexandria and Cairo was of extraordinary value
in his literary and historical researches. From that
soil, which had lain unproductive as to intellectual
results for many a day, he excavated rich treasures
for Jewish science. Munk fully recognized that the
self-respect of the Jews would be confirmed only by
self-knowledge, reached along the paths of science.

CHAPTER XVIII.

EVENTS PRECEDING THE REVOLUTIONS OF FEBRUARY AND MARCH, 1848, AND THE SUBSEQUENT SOCIAL ADVANCE OF THE JEWS.

Return of Montefiore and Crémieux from the East—Patriotic Suggestions—General Indecision—Gabriel Riesser—Michael Creizenach—Reform Party in Frankfort—Rabbinical Assembly—Holdheim—Reform Association — Zachariah Frankel — The Berlin Reform Temple—Michael Sachs—His Character—His Biblical Exegesis—Holdheim and Sachs—The Jewish German Church—Progress of Jewish Literature—Ewald and his Works—Enfranchisement of English Jews—The Breslau Jewish College—Its Founders—The Mortara Case—Pope Pius IX—The Alliance Israélite—Astruc, Cohn, Caballo, Masuel, Netter—The American Jews—The "Union of American Hebrew Congregations"—The Anglo-Jewish Association—Benisch, Löwy—The "Israelitische Allianz"—Wertheimer, Goldschmidt, Kuranda—Rapid Social Advance of the Jews—Rise of Anti-Semitism.

1840—1870 C. E.

THE return from the East of the Jewish envoys, who not only had saved a few men from death, but had rescued all Judaism from disgrace, was a veritable triumphal procession. From Corfu to Paris and London, and even to the depths of Poland, the Jewish communities were unanimous in expressions of thanksgiving to the rescuers, and sought by visible signs to evince their gratitude, and at the same time show their patriotic sentiments for Judaism. The tributes took the form of public orations, addresses, articles written in every European language, naturally also in Hebrew, and both in prose and verse. Attentions and gifts were freely bestowed upon the two chief representatives of Judaism, to celebrate in a worthy fashion the momentous events which had occurred in Damascus, and transmit the remembrance of these deeds to posterity. Crémieux, who was the first to set out on the return journey, received enthusiastic homage in Corfu, Trieste, Venice, Vienna, Fürth, Nuremberg, Frankfort, and Mayence (November—December, 1840). The large communities through whose cities he could not pass sent deputations and addresses. It was naïvely touching that old-fashioned orthodox rabbis, at a loss how to show their gratitude, bestowed upon him the title of Rabbi (Morenu), as the highest honor in their gift. Only the Jewish community in Paris behaved in a cool fashion, and prepared no fitting reception for their emissary, as if fearing to wound the sensitiveness of King Louis Philippe, whose ambiguous attitude had been striking.

Montefiore, who had remained in Constantinople a long time, in order to obtain a favorable Firman, and who began his return journey later, and traveled mostly by sea, did not come into contact with so many congregations as Crémieux, hence did not receive so much public homage. He was, however, overwhelmed with letters from all sides. By his watchful care, continually directed to the welfare and honor of his brethren, and without any idea of reward, he had in his simplicity put their enemies to shame. He obtained a promise from Cardinal Rivarola, the protector of all Capuchins in Rome, that the tombstone should be removed which had been erected in the Capuchin church at Damascus recording the murder of Father Tomaso by the Jews, and representing him as a martyr. He also compelled King Louis Philippe to appear pleased with what had occurred. At an audience obtained through the English ambassador, Lord Granville (February 22, 1844), Montefiore handed the king a copy of the Sultan's Firman which testified the innocence of the Damascus Jews, and tacitly condemned the French consul. Louis Philippe was compelled to swallow this humiliation, and assume a gracious manner for the sake of appearances, and congratulate Montefiore on the success of his journey and his mission.   Queen Victoria thanked Montefiore all the more sincerely, through Lord Palmerston (who was prime minister at the time, and to whom he was presented on his return), for the succor which he had brought his co-religionists.

The entire body of Jews in Europe were at this time engaged in carrying out three objects : offering to their two rescuers an enduring and striking token of gratitude, perpetuating the memory of the deliverance effected by them, and finally, discovering, through combined action, a means whereby to prevent the recurrence of similar false accusations against Jews and Judaism.   The leaders of the German Jews felt themselves especially moved to put on record their interest in the events, and their admiration for the two noble representatives of their race.   They, the very ones who had hitherto taken the lead in advocating progress, had done little in connection with the sanguinary events of Damascus. A prominent Jewish scholar, Zunz, had completely refuted the alleged proofs, supposed to be drawn from the Talmud, of the use of blood by the Jews. The Jewish newspapers had boldly fought against anti-Jewish attacks and slanders.   But this was all that had been done in Germany towards vindicating the honor of Judaism.   Riesser might easily have joined Montefiore and Crémieux, might have accompanied them to Egypt as the representative of the German Jews, and used his eloquence on behalf of the sufferers ; but no such idea was even suggested.   Geiger, from hatred to the Talmud, had actually admitted that the anti-Semites were right in attributing misanthropical expressions to the Talmud.   Certain high-minded Jews in Germany felt it the more necessary to take public action in the matter.   Riesser, together with a few friends, desired to found societies, through which the Jews of the four chief countries of Europe were to offer some public recognition to their two representatives.

But this plan of acknowledging their indebtedness
fell through.   In fact, the three objects desired by
the people were only imperfectly carried out,
because the right means to attain them were not
pursued.   The services of Montefiore were, however, acknowledged with fervent enthusiasm on his
return to London by a public celebration in the
synagogues, and a piece of plate was presented to
him in remembrance of his success.   A still greater
distinction awaited him at the hands of Queen Victoria.   She rewarded him with an addition to his
armorial bearings (June 24), a great honor both to
his race and himself.   Yet more important than
this toy for adults were the words of Her Majesty
that accompanied the gracious distinction :

"Inasmuch as it was brought to our notice, that in consequence
of tidings from the East, which stated that, on account of the accusation that they had murdered Father Tomaso, Jews in Damascus and
Rhodes had been imprisoned and tortured, that many children had
been thrown into prison and deprived of almost all nourishment, and
that many persons had been so cruelly tortured that death ensued,
. . . . . our trusty and well-beloved Sir Moses Montefiore, accompanied by Lady Montefiore, had quite voluntarily journeyed to Alexandria with the view of proving the falsehood of the charge and
of conducting the affairs of his unhappy and persecuted brethren ;
that he succeeded in obtaining from the Pasha, Mehmet Ali, the honorable liberation of the accused who were incarcerated, and the permission for those who had fled the city to return home ; that for this
purpose he procured a Firman in Constantinople from his Imperial
Majesty the Sultan Abdul Meg'id, which declared the innocence of
the Jews, and assured equal rights with all other subjects to members
of the Jewish religion under Turkish rule—we have taken the above
mentioned facts into our royal consideration, and desire to give to
Montefiore a special mark of our royal favor, in memory of his per-
severing efforts on behalf of his suffering and persecuted brethren in
the East, and of his nation in general."

It was an extract from the history of modern Jews
related by the Queen herself.

In comparison with this distinction, the proposal
of certain French congregations of the Upper Rhine
to strike a medal in honor of Crémieux appears
very trivial.   They shared the general idea, "that it
was important for future generations to perpetuate
the memory of the events of 1840 affecting Israel-

ites." But Crémieux declined the medal. In what manner these joyful, national memories were to be immortalized was a matter concerning which there was general indecision. Crémieux asked the French Jews and others to support the schools that he had established in Alexandria and Cairo by their contributions. Only a small amount, however, was subscribed: the maintenance of the Crémieux schools in Egypt was only accidentally connected with the main question, and was not likely to keep the exaltation of the Jews at a high pitch. One suitable proposition was made, but no notice was taken of it.

"It is not by ostentatious gifts, nor by clamorous celebrations, that we can testify our gratitude. We would offer the finest testimonial to the men who went to the rescue by perpetuating this great historical event in a religious form appropriate to its religious spirit. It should be commemorated by an annual festival equal to the festivals of Chanuka and Purim ; for on those days it may be said that Israel was delivered from bodily suffering, whilst on this day it was delivered from spiritual servitude."

Judaism never knew a more effectual way of commemorating its liberation and victories and arousing a spirit of emulation in posterity than by establishing days of memorial, by means of which, time, the destroyer, is made the protector of historical events. If that most skillful master of the Hebrew language, Isaac Erter, had completed the narrative of the persecution and the deliverance in Damascus, which he had commenced in the simple biblical style, and if the heads of the Jewish communities had resolved to commemorate the most important day in the Damascus affair, and to read this "Scroll" (Megillah) in public, the lasting remembrance of these occurrences would have been assured, and at the same time a means would have been found of cementing afresh the bonds of fellowship. The Jews of Asia and Africa and on the whole globe would joyfully have accepted such a festival as an international memorial. Munk, whose voice carried great weight, remarked:

"Would that the sad Damascus incident might at least serve to make us take cognizance of our disorganized condition, which, though mournful to contemplate, is unfortunately a fact. Would that it might show us that in times of danger we must rely upon ourselves, and that the bond that formerly united us might be renewed."

Instead of unity, however, a rupture took place within German Judaism, which, though caused by a trifling dispute that might easily have been settled in the commencement, grew to great proportions. The consciousness of opposition was present, and by chance it asserted itself on this occasion; but it might equally well have shown itself at any other time, so long as it was not allayed, or had not worn off. The Hamburg Temple, which twenty years before had first stirred up dissensions between the old-fashioned orthodox party and the reformers, again brought about a quarrel, which henceforth assumed a fiercer complexion. The congregation of the Temple had largely increased in numbers since its foundation. The younger members of the old-fashioned community had joined, because in the old synagogue they found no satisfaction for their devotional cravings, and they objected to the continual disorder that prevailed. The new congregation had already grown to nearly eight hundred members, and included a man who in his own person was a great attraction. After the death of Bresselau, the secretary of the congregation, Gabriel Riesser had accepted that post. He became closely connected with the Temple, and was elected to the office of second warden. As his name was in extraordinary repute, owing to his untiring zeal for the political and social emancipation of the Jews in Germany, his adhesion to the Temple shed new luster upon it. When the members of the Temple determined to erect a new and larger house of prayer, the old party by complaining to the senate threw obstacles in the way of the undertaking. The authorities of the Temple had also caused a new prayer-book to be compiled.

The altered liturgy of the Temple was published and announced as a general "Prayer-Book for Israelites," but was so objectionable to the orthodox party as to be utterly rejected. The circumstance that the new prayer-book claimed to be used by all Jews gave rise to great annoyance. Chacham Bernays therefore renewed on a Sabbath, in the three synagogues (Marcheshvan 1, October 16, 1841), the proclamation against heretics which the three rabbis had issued on the foundation of the Temple, forbidding any Israelite to use this prayer-book. In the reasons assigned, harsh expressions were employed charging that this prayer-book, even more than the former, gave wanton and frivolous treatment to the religious convictions contained in the Hebrew prayers. This denunciation naturally excited the Temple congregants, and transported even the cautious Riesser to inordinate lengths. Whilst the preachers regarded the insulting expression of opinion from a religious standpoint, Riesser saw in it an encroachment upon their rights, "because the Chacham had no authority over the Temple." The Temple committee then published a counter-declaration (October 24), in which Bernays was charged not alone with "arrogance, impotent partiality, and malicious ignoring of the contents of the book," but with "ignorance of all theological and liturgical literature." There now arose a violent dispute, conducted with such passion, that the senate was compelled to reprove both parties. The Chacham and the leaders of his congregation, who sided with him, circulated thousands of copies of the sentence of condemnation upon the prayer-book in many communities; whilst the authorities of the Temple (November) requested rabbis and preachers holding the same religious views to give their opinions as to the value or worthlessness of the innovations, expecting that the decisions would be in their favor. On this occasion, the changes which had taken place in the German communities during two decades became evident. Whereas formerly only three rabbis had ambiguously given their assent to the ritual of the Temple, and many others had condemned it, at this second discussion only the rabbi of Altona supported Bernays, whilst twelve or thirteen others pronounced judgment adverse to him ; this was at the close of 1841, or the beginning of 1842. Then began the aggressive stage of the reform movement. Young rabbis or clergymen, pastors (as they preferred to be called), who had mostly drawn their wisdom from academies, and were enthusiastic for the reform which had become the fashion, now were at the head. The old rabbis, on the other hand, no longer ventured to oppose them. Thus it seemed as if all the Jews of Germany were in favor of innovations in the synagogue, and only a few wanting in spirit struggled against this tendency.

The contest concerning the Hamburg Temple bore no results in the city itself, as a terrible conflagration (May, 1842) transformed a great part of the town into a mass of ruins, and distracted attention from party interests. The flame of reform blazed up from another point, and threatened to spread far and wide. In Frankfort-on-the-Main, for some time past, there had been discontented persons who had broken away from the Judaism of the day. These disturbing elements partly originated in a school called the Philanthropin (which from small beginnings had grown into an important institution), partly in the first Jewish Freemasons' lodge. The managers and teachers of the school and the members of the lodge favored a radicalism repugnant to Judaism. For a long time Michael Creizenach (born 1789, died 1842), a teacher at the Philanthropin, formed the center of an invisible society. Creizenach, who was honest, judicious, but uninteresting, had published many pamphlets

combating Rabbinical Talmudical Judaism, but
owing to their temperate tone and want of depth,
these writings made little impression. By his personal influence, however, he filled the circle of his
friends and admirers with a passion for innovation
and a deep aversion to antiquity.

After his death several of his adherents endeavored to form a congregation, and to establish a sect,
even at the risk of separating from Judaism. Their
aim was in a measure to remove the pretext of
anti-Jewish politicians, who withheld equal rights
from the Jews on the score of attachment to their
nationality, to the Talmud, and to old forms, and they
also desired to secure freedom of action for themselves. They were educated laymen, who, owing
to the prevailing confusion, had lost mental balance, or they may have been misled by false
leaders. They constituted themselves a Society of
the Friends of Reform (October, 1842), and drew up
a confession of faith, which clearly proved the perplexity of the times. They refused to recognize the
Talmud as an authority. But the Bible? "They
considered the Mosaic religion capable of continual
development." First of all they wished to throw
off the fetters of the dietary laws, because they "had
originated in the ancient constitution of the state,"
and at the present day had lost their significance as
a religious act or symbol. They definitely gave up
all hope in the Messiah, or a return to Palestine,
"because they regarded their native land as their
sole fatherland."

The Creizenach Friends of Reform did not find
many supporters. They therefore sought to interest Gabriel Riesser, whose importance was already
acknowledged, and who might attract others. He
was at first inclined to join them. He appears not
to have overcome the excitement into which he had
been thrown by Bernays' intervention in the affairs
of the Hamburg Temple. He did not even shrink

from total secession, although he had hitherto constantly desired to have "the shell of Judaism respected on account of its soul." The idea of freedom, which completely filled his mind, destroyed his emotional attachment to existing Judaism. He was therefore eminently in favor of the paragraph in the Creizenach or Frankfort programme which declared that it was optional with every Jewish father to have his sons circumcised, and that in case of the omission of this rite civil disabilities should not be entailed. Riesser wished to combat any presumptive right of forcing conscience. However, others who had been asked to join, took umbrage at this very question of circumcision. The founders of the Society of the Friends of Reform, therefore, saw themselves obliged to relinquish this point as well as the declaration against the dietary laws, and to adhere to only three out of the five resolutions of their original programme : that against the Talmud, that against the Messiah, and that enunciating the possibility of the development of the "Mosaic religion." This abridgment and enfeebling of the original confession, Riesser considered illogical and cowardly, and he withdrew his support. The power of attraction was lacking in the society, and as only a few joined, it perished at its birth. The question of circumcision was shortly afterwards brought forward from another quarter. Several unfortunate accidents at the circumcision of Jewish boys had induced the health officers in Frankfort-on-the-Main to issue an order (February 8, 1843) with the ambiguous wording, "Israelite citizens and inhabitants, if they desire to have their children circumcised, must employ the services of competent persons." From this it appeared that the Frankfort Senate made it optional with Jewish parents to perform the rite or neglect it, and did not regard it as a necessary mark of the Jewish religion. The Senate at the same time explained that they did not mean thereby to give untrammeled liberty to the innovators. But the reformers seized upon the words in order to have a pretext for abolishing the rite of circumcision. In consequence, Rabbi Solomon Trier invited the opinions of his brother rabbis upon the subject (1843-44) in order to dispose of the question forever. However, it caused but a slight sensation, seeing that even young rabbis favorably disposed to reform had decisively asserted the obligation and necessity of circumcision. Therefore, no seceding sect was formed among the Jews of Germany, although the elements existed, and an uneasy state of feeling was the result.

This feeling was especially noticeable among the younger rabbis, who were not very clear about the purpose and extent of the reforms to be instituted, or met with continual opposition on one side or the other in their congregations, and in their isolation were without support. At this time the fashion of assemblies and societies had come into vogue; railways had already been built between the great cities, and had facilitated personal intercourse. Thus the invitation calling a conference of rabbis met with approval. This meeting of rabbis and preachers who were, to some extent, at one upon the subjects under discussion, at first awakened a certain expectancy; it was a novelty, and this always possesses a certain amount of charm. However, at the first session only twenty-two rabbis assembled in Brunswick, the majority coming from southern and western Germany. The remainder waited until the resolutions of the assembly should be made known, and according as they agreed or disagreed with them, they would decide whether to join or to hold aloof. Few rabbis attended who adhered to the Judaism rooted in the Talmud; most of the members had partially, or wholly, severed themselves from the Talmud, although they did not practically manifest this severance in their religious practices.

The first Rabbinical Assembly was dominated by a man possessing all the qualities calculated to widen the breach and bring about a complete separation. This was Samuel Holdheim (born at Kempen, 1806; died at Berlin, 1860). It is a curious yet natural fact that Talmudism, which had acquired its power and extensive range through Polish students, should be attacked by a Pole with unsparing severity. On emerging from boyhood Holdheim displayed not only extraordinary acquaintance with the Talmud and Rabbinical literature, but also such remarkable versatility in dialectics and the art of discussion that he won the admiration of grey-bearded rabbis, and was considered a highly-skilled Talmudist.

Like Solomon Maimon, Holdheim when he already had a son began his secular education in the academy at Prague, skipping the lower grades. All that he heard in the philosophical lecture-rooms in this not very distinguished university was new to him, astounded and dazzled him, and resulted in great perturbation of mind. He quickly assimilated such elements of knowledge as were connected with his previous acquirements, such as Christian theology and the commonplace philosophy tolerated in Austria under Metternich. But he had no appreciation of solid, disciplining branches of learning, and even the subjects which attracted him he had first to reproduce in a Talmudical form. Holdheim's knowledge therefore was only of a fragmentary nature, and contained numerous gaps. He was, however, sufficiently careful and practical to devote himself to useful work, to acquire a good style, which had been neglected in his education, and cultivate pulpit eloquence. Owing to his poverty, he was compelled to devote himself to professional studies, and was thus unable to spend time upon his favorite subjects. The Bible which had hitherto been a closed book to Holdheim, or had only been examined by him through Talmudical glasses, he studied solely

to obtain verses for his sermons. It is not granted
to everyone to possess ideals and regulate his conduct by them. There must also exist dry, calm,
doubting natures, occupied only with the world of
real things, who build themselves huts here below,
and look with contempt on all sublime and ideal sentiments as being froth and folly. Such Mephistophe-
lian temperaments, the incarnation of the spirit of
doubt, are as necessary in the sphere of moral life
as opposition in nature. Holdheim had this tendency,
and his Talmudical culture nourished and developed
it. He knew of no enthusiasm, neither for the calm
light of pale memories, nor for the dim, cloudy
dreams of the future. The firm ground of the
present was more to his taste. Since Judaism consists of memories and hopes, Holdheim was not
heart and soul devoted to it, but sought to remodel
and alter it, so that he might not be inconvenienced.

Mecklenburg-Schwerin, where the typical brutality
of the Middle Ages had been preserved, and where
mere caprice wielded the scepter, was at this time
ruled by a prince, who, instead of making his Jews
free in action, wished them to be Freethinkers.
They were to cast off all old memories and forms
and remodel themselves. A superintendent was
appointed for the disciplining of the congregations,
and Holdheim was made chief rabbi (1840) to assist
in reforms, and stamp innovations with the rabbinical seal. Here he felt untrammeled, and could
abolish whatever was distasteful to him. He who
formerly had had no conception that divine service
must possess dignity, now discovered that disorder
in the synagogue was unseemly, and determined to
remove everything not countenanced by the spirit
of the times. As, however, a desire for changes in
the synagogue did not originate from any impulse
of his own, he looked around for patterns, and introduced the Würtemberg ritual, undisturbed by any
consideration as to whether he was forcing the con-

sciences of the mostly old-fashioned orthodox congregations.

But Holdheim was not to win laurels by introducing innovations into the synagogue. He marked out a wider field for himself. He wished to alter the whole of Judaism in its threefold form, with its Biblical, Talmudical, and Rabbinical components, to confuse all ideas and stultify the consciences. Since Paul of Tarsus, Judaism had not known such an enemy in its midst, who shook the whole edifice to its very foundations. But Holdheim possessed no original ideas to use as a lever for overthrowing Judaism: he had only a certain ingenuity which he had gained from the Talmud. He was therefore obliged to make use of such thoughts of others as had become public property. His acute intellect, however, enabled him to piece together these disjointed, half true premises, and give them a coloring of truth. Judaism, he said, consists of a close combination of religious and moral ideas with national and political elements. Holdheim accepted this definition in order to separate the religious from the national ordinances, the latter having lost all significance since the downfall of the Jewish state. Which laws are national and therefore temporary? Holdheim gave a wide application to the term, calling all observances national and political which are inconvenient, and require a certain amount of self-denial, such as keeping the Sabbath, the Jewish laws of marriage, and even the acquisition of the Hebrew language, which he desired to banish from the midst of the Jewish race, because it is a national bond of union; and still more national is a hope in the Messiah. To this sophistry Holdheim added other quibbles. He considered every state, however constituted, even Russian despotism, an all-devouring Moloch which continually demands victims, and whose lust for sacrifices can be satisfied only by the abnegation of independence, freedom, and every religious sentiment. The culminating point of Holdheim's theory was that Talmudical Judaism itself, in the expression "the law of the state is law for the Jews" (in civil relations), obliges every Jew to subordinate his religious affairs to those of the state; Judaism, in other words, prescribes its own suicide, if the state provides it with a silken halter. Had he lived in the time of the Maccabees, Holdheim would have joined the renegade Menelaus in urging the Jews to worship the Greek Zeus, because the state, which was then called Antiochus Epiphanes, had so commanded. In the time of Hadrian, like a second Acher, he would have lauded the cult of Jupiter of the Capitol, and in the days of Philip of Spain and Emanuel of Portugal he would have advocated the worship of the cross. The millions of Jewish martyrs, according to his theory, were malefactors against the state, inasmuch as they had opposed the laws given to them. Holdheim, the son of the Talmud, struck down Talmudical Judaism with the weapons which it had bestowed upon him. The authority and power which the legislative Synhedrion had formerly possessed, or is said to have possessed, Holdheim wished to see transferred to the Christian state, even the right of interfering with matters of conscience. These ideas he propounded with sophistic casuistry, unmistakably according to the method of the Polish Rabbinical school. It was difficult for Holdheim to decide what Judaism actually was, and what would be left of it, after everything in any way connected with national political life had been excluded, and when supreme authority was besides vested in each state, to change, command, or prohibit religious practices.

The majority of the members of the first assemblage of rabbis in Brunswick looked upon Holdheim with awe as a Talmudical scholar and a reckless reformer, and he obtained distinct influence over the

discussions and resolutions of the meeting. Less
attention was paid to the letter and spirit of Judaism "than to the state, the exalted German governments, and the intangible, whimsical "spirit of the
age." The Talmud was sacrificed by most of the
delegates as a scapegoat. Yet the debates and
conclusions of the Brunswick conference of rabbis
(June, 1844) produced but little effect. The congregations troubled themselves as little about it
as they did about the protest from seventy-seven
rabbis of Germany, Bohemia, Moravia, and Hungary, which, set on foot by an upright, self-sacrificing, disinterested, but bigoted zealot, Hirsch Lehren
of Amsterdam, utterly condemned the assembly of
Brunswick.

Events in the Christian world at about this time
demonstrated more effectually than this laboriously
constructed protest, that Judaism with its ancient
confession had not yet become superfluous. The
exhibition of the pretended holy coat of Jesus in
Treves, to which more than a million Catholics from
all countries made a pilgrimage and bent the knee
(August—October, 1844), showed that the "spirit
of the age" was a deceptive standard. In consequence of this excess of mediæval superstition and
credulity, there arose in Germany what promised to
be an influential anti-Catholic movement. A German Catholic Church was established (January,
1845), and next to it, in the bosom of Protestantism,
"Communities of the Friends of Light" were
formed, who threatened Christianity, its belief in the
Trinity, and the Divine Incarnation, with imminent
dissolution. Every period has its delusions, and
Jews can always be found ready to imitate strange
customs. Here and there voices were raised in
favor of founding a German Jewish Church after the
pattern of the German Catholic. In Breslau the
agitation for this new scheme was only artificially
kept alive, but this movement was somewhat more

energetic in Berlin. In this city a popular preacher, Stern, had been delivering lectures upon Judaism and Jewish history, and had characterized Jewish doctrines as a capricious system. At his suggestion, some twenty men, whose opinions upon these topics were in accord with his own, assembled for the purpose of establishing a sort of Church system of a peculiar type, called the Reform Association (April 2, 1845). They believed that the majority of German Jews had disowned all attachment to ancient Judaism in their hearts, and would gladly adopt a new creed. The founders of the Berlin Reform Association therefore issued a summons to all Israel to attend a synod, in order to establish a new Jewish religion. In their programme they naturally tabulated only negative principles, such as the rejection of the Talmud and of the Messianic doctrine, because they belonged with body and soul to their Berlin home ; they advocated a return to Holy Writ, not to its literal sense, but to its spirit. The affirmative principles were : "We desire faith, positive religion, Judaism." The confusion of ideas at this time was as great as when the Christian communities of old were first originated from semi-Jewish elements, and even clear heads became affected.

The matter did not, however, result in a synod for the discussion of reform, which would indeed have marked the Jews as slavish imitators of the Church and of the "Friends of Light." The speeches in favor of the movement made in various quarters proved full of hollow phrases. The Berlin Society adhered to its programme, and as this found no favor in the eyes of the masses, it was to be ratified by the second Rabbinical Convention held in Frankfort (July, 1845), as being in consonance with Judaism.

This Assembly aroused greater excitement and fiercer passion than the first, because, on the one hand, the Berlin Reform Union participated in it, in order to infuse their own spirit or to effect its downfall, whilst, on the other hand, a skillful leader of the orthodox party temporarily joined it, in order to show how Judaism should be purified, or to throw obstacles in the way, if the Reformers should seem to rush to reckless extremes. The orthodox leader was Zachariah Frankel (born 1801, died 1875). He somewhat resembled Holdheim. Both were profoundly learned in the Talmud, and both acquired their secular education when advanced in years, but their points of dissimilarity were yet more striking. In Holdheim's character the prominent features were his innate or acquired love of scoffing at, and his utter contempt for, the past. In Frankel one is struck by the moral earnestness which, together with his warm-heartedness, rendered him worthy of respect by his true regard for inherited forms, his conscientiousness in every matter, and his firm but somewhat peculiar character. Holdheim loved the present and the practical, Frankel the future and the ideal: the former strove to erase from men's memories all traces of the Talmud and Rabbinical Judaism, if not of Judaism altogether; whilst the latter justified and glorified the Talmud. The main aim of Frankel's scientific activity was to demonstrate that Talmudical tradition was correct, and that another Talmud had been known even before ours. He sought traces of this original tradition in the ancient Greek translation of the Pentateuch, in the compositions of the two Judæo-Greek authors, Philo and Josephus, and especially in non-Talmudical sources. Such comprehensive studies were possible only in a man of his marvelous intellectual power and wonderful constitution.

Although Frankel labored to maintain the glory of the Talmud and to prove that reverence was due to Jewish antiquity, he was not averse to religious

reforms, nor was he blind to the necessities of modern times.   However, although he would not recognize the claim of an individual to institute reforms,
he was ready to appeal to a scientific tribunal and
the voice of the people, the whole Jewish world.
He did not desire to revive obsolete forms into a
semblance of life, even though they had formerly
been of importance, and was willing to abolish such
existing customs as scientific inquiry pronounced to
be unjustified or hurtful.   Frankel wished to see a
conference of rabbis, or, more correctly, of notables
in the foremost rank of Jewish learning, so that the
chasm between the old and the new systems might
be bridged over.   He therefore joined the assembly
of rabbis at Frankfort, hoping to counteract the
eager desire for reform by the weight of his name,
which, owing to his distinguished position as a
writer, was already famous, and to aid in guarding
against imprudent measures, or at least in modifying
them.   Like Holdheim and Geiger, who brought
their programmes of reform with them, he brought
his, and in it he endeavored to reconcile antiquity
with progress.

Harassed by the contending influences of Frankel
and the reformers, the conference grew vacillating.
The first motion brought forward, which was not
wholly unexpected, that the Hebrew language
should, if possible, be eradicated from the minds
and memories of the whole Jewish race, obliged
Frankel to sever his connection with the assembly
publicly, and the applause that his conduct called
forth revealed the fact that the Rabbinical Convention did not represent the entire body of the German
Jews, but only a small, active party.   Unconsciously
the Frankfort Assembly had lost its balance.   Its
members were obliged to dissemble before the
Reform Society.   They had to praise its actions, or
they would have lost its support.   On the other
hand, they did not dare openly to espouse its hollow

views, or they would have lost favor with the congregations. A subterfuge helped them out of this perplexity ; they promised to support the efforts of the Reform Association to the utmost, if the latter would "agree with the principles by which they thought reform in Judaism ought to be guided," which sounded like a hidden reproach.

The Reform Society was not repelled by this partial condemnation ; they knew that the leaders of the conference, especially Holdheim, sided with them, and they deceived themselves with the delusion that they were creating an essentially new form of Judaism. They formed themselves into a congregation of about two hundred members, and celebrated a consecration (April 2, 1846), when Holdheim as high priest offered up clouds of incense. The congregation and their pastor were well fitted for each other, and however much they resisted at first, in the end they had to embrace in friendship. Thus a "German Jewish Church" was established with a temple, a preacher, and a ritual of its own. It seemed as if time had gone back some seventeen centuries, and that they were in some town of Syria, or Asia Minor, or in Rome, when, out of the conflict of ancient Judaism with semi-Christian and semi-pagan elements, new congregations had arisen, retaining only faint traces of Judaism. The new customs prevailed in the Reform Temple in Berlin. Praying with uncovered heads especially marked it as of foreign growth, and repulsed even some who otherwise approved of reform. Hebrew was retained only in a few prayers and in the readings from the Pentateuch. The Reform Temple, in fact, assumed a Germanic tinge, and threw off its Jewish cosmopolitan character. The trace of its Jewish origin was visible only in the divine service ; in their mode of living the members could not be recognized as the descendants of Jews. Perhaps Holdheim was even more fanatically desirous of seeing every Jewish custom abolished than his free-thinking congregants. He disregarded not alone Rabbinical Judaism and the Talmud, but also duties ordained by the Holy Scripture. But even in the reform community it was evident that Jewish self-reliance had progressed greatly since the time of Friedländer. The reform party had completely overcome its inclination towards Christianity. Of its constituents, who number one thousand souls, not one member nor any of their children joined the Christian Church. They do not desire to be considered a separate sect, but as an integral element of the Jewish race.

The Berlin reformers, however, remained isolated, and found no following in Europe. In their own midst, a lukewarm spirit crept in, sooner even than their opponents had anticipated. From want of visitors to the house of prayer, the Sabbath worship had to be transferred to Sunday, the same change that had been made by the Jewish Christians in the first century. The question of Sunday worship cannot be discussed here; it belongs to the immediate present. Such lukewarmness and lack of interest should have convinced the founders, who lived to witness them, that they had committed some mistake. To give an account of this blunder in its entirety cannot be attempted in this history; it would be overstepping the bounds of a record of events. One circumstance, however, must not be forgotten, that the Berlin Society of Reform had an antagonist in its vicinity. This enemy, of whom it had taken no account, was the more dangerous, as he used his incisive eloquence and every fiber of his being to protest against the new sect founded by the Berlin Committee. This opponent was Michael Sachs, who was born at Glogau, 1808, and died at Berlin at the beginning of 1864.

If bountiful nature had determined to create a thorough contrast to Holdheim, she succeeded in Sachs. Externally, mentally, in appearance, speech, attitude, and tendency of mind, in his learning and character, even in habits and fancies—in everything the two men were so totally opposed, that at first sight they could hardly be recognized as members of the same race, devotees of the same calling. If Holdheim represented the Jewish Polish spirit, strung to the highest pitch by Talmudical dialectics, Michael Sachs called to mind the Jewish emigrants from the Pyrenean peninsula, ennobled by classic forms and æsthetic teachings. He resembled the noble Isaac Cardoso, or Isaac de Pinedo, or any one of the numerous poets and scholars of Marrano lineage in Holland and Italy, who combined deep devotion to Judaism with taste for poetical or philological studies.

Owing to his peculiar nature, and the twofold influence exercised upon his mind by Hebrew and Greek literature, Sachs became an ideal personality, like Gebirol and Jehuda Halevi, who could flourish only upon the clear heights of existence, and felt physical disgust at everything of a mean character. There was no equivocation in him ; feeling, thought, and action all flowed from one source. He was, therefore, mercilessly bitter against falsehood, ambiguity, and hypocrisy, against all ostentation and pomposity, against noisy hollowness and vanity ; he scourged them with the lash of his words and with his striking, brilliant wit. Noble-minded and self-sacrificing to a fault, humble before God and before man as bearing the impress of the Divine, Sachs was proudly repellent to all who in religion, art, science, or public life use counterfeit coin, and conceal their own self-seeking petty interests under the veil of a general, large purpose. If Sachs in respect to convictions, character, moral elevation, capacity for self-denial, and devotion to duty and his faith, was thoroughly Jewish, in his deep love of beauty he was Hellenic, and in his person contradicted the alleged impossibility of this dual nature, which had been asserted by Heine. Whatever was ugly, inharmonious, or ungainly, was as repugnant to him as the immoral and the untrue.

Judaism was dearest to his heart, for he considered it a revelation from the God who directs mankind, and the embodiment of all that is exalted and sacred; and he would not allow it to be subtly explained away by the philosophy of the times. Sachs did not fail to observe the objectionable excrescences which had arisen on its surface, but he knew their origin, and believed that time, which had produced, would destroy them. He hesitated, however, to lay hands upon them, for fear of injuring the sound, whilst removing the unsound and decayed parts. He would not trust himself, nor any one, with the task of making innovations. This suspicion of decisive reforms originated partly in his aversion to active measures, which was one of his failings. As he was only human he could not be without faults. Another error, which avenged itself upon him and the party he represented, was his unconquerable dislike to uniting for common action even with those who shared his opinions. Sachs would have joyfully subordinated himself to leaders whose loftiness of mind could have inspired him with respect. But as he found no such characters among his contemporaries, he would not attach himself to men in no way superior to himself, or who did not even attain to his own height. Thus he was equally unfit to be a party-leader and a partisan.

Sachs' great qualities and small failings forced his vocation upon him : he was destined for the pulpit. The easy stream of his eloquence, his depth of feeling, warmth of conviction, grace of gesture, the charm that he exercised when interpreting the prophets and Agadists, the brilliant wit at his command, the beauty of his voice and his smooth diction —all combined to make him unsurpassed by the best preachers of his time, and his only equal was

Mannheimer. When standing in the pulpit, Sachs appeared to be transfigured and oblivious of himself; it seemed as if one of the prophets of God were exhorting the people, or encouraging the despondent by his tidings of an ideal future. Even those of his hearers who did not share his convictions were carried away by his eloquence, and were compelled to yield him a tribute of praise. Sachs, however, was a persuasive speaker not only in the pulpit, but also in ordinary conversation. His speech overflowed with the warmth of the sentiments which filled his heart. His impressive words, which issued from the depths of his being, attracted many faithful adherents to Judaism. Whosoever came into contact with him was drawn into a magic circle, and absorbed somewhat of his convictions. His influence was the greater because he never made an effort to persuade; he simply spoke out what was in him. Nothing was more hateful to him than the display of official dignity, sham devotional fervor, and the pastoral airs copied from Christian clergymen.

In Prague, where he roused the German-speaking inhabitants, both Christians and Jews, to a high pitch of enthusiasm, a happy chance brought him into contact with Rapoport (1840-44), one of the founders of Jewish science. An intimate friendship sprang up between these two men, whose education had been conducted on such different lines, and Sachs was introduced by his friend into the rich domain of Jewish literature, which had hitherto been only in part accessible to him, as his attention had been concentrated on the study of the Holy Scriptures and on classical literature. His talent of vividly perceiving the essential and excellent elements of a subject and storing them in his brain, soon made him master of this new material, and enabled him to impart it to a wide circle in a refined form. But Sachs never became fully acquainted with the dialectics of the Talmud, which was Hold-heim's strong point, and this territory remained foreign to him. Though he deeply lamented this deficiency in his knowledge, it was no real defect, for such studies did not accord with the Hellenic side of his nature, and would have blighted the blossoms of his genius. As though destined to counteract the influence of the Jewish German Church, which was to assume form in Berlin, and to become the opposite pole to Holdheim's endless negations, he was elected by the congregation of Berlin as preacher and rabbi. Here, by instilling into the minds of his congregants the same Jewish confidence with which he was inspired, and a feeling of righteous pride in belonging to so ancient, noble, and cultured a race, he succeeded to some extent in curing them of their inclination to Christianity, and the evil habit of imitation to which they had so long been subject. This change in thought, which affected the most remote circles, weakened the antipathy towards the Jews of Berlin, which since the time of Friedländer had prevailed in other communities. Sachs was included among the most distinguished personages of the Prussian capital; the cultured Christian world lavished attentions on him, although he did not seek them. Had he given vigorous and energetic effect to his words, and created perma-nent institutions—for which plenty of opportunity would have been given him by the liberal Berlin community—perhaps the reform congregation might not have arisen.

He combated the reform tendency with all his strength. In Holdheim and his allies he beheld only perverters of Judaism and false leaders of the people, and he openly expressed this opinion, for, as he often remarked, "Against insult and harsh words I am hardened and indifferent." From the pulpit he wielded the scourge of his annihilating scorn against the Jewish German Church, which had

so limited the development of Judaism, that it could
be contained in a nutshell.   But even his opponents
admitted that he employed only honorable weapons,
the use of others being at variance with his noble
nature.   He did great harm to the Reform Temple.
Persons who had heard Sachs' sermons were wearied by those in the reform synagogue.   A comparison between Sachs and his opposite, Holdheim,
who was a contrast to him in every way, always
resulted in favor of the former. Whilst the Temple
where Holdheim preached became more and more
deserted, the synagogue in which Sachs officiated
became more crowded week after week.

As Sachs performed great services in elevating
and strengthening Jewish self-respect, so also he
promoted Jewish knowledge.   His contributions to
the latter touch the form rather than the essence.
In fact, he merely popularized Jewish subjects, and
rendered them accessible to educated Christians.
Sachs did not indeed promulgate novel, epoch-mak-
ing truths, or discover new facts.   Nor was he a
poetical artist who could create brilliant pictures of
ideal worlds.   There was more poetry in his life
and teachings than in his verses.   His refined perceptions enabled him to recognize and reproduce
the slightest shades in the beauties which other
artists had created, and he idealized what other inquirers had discovered.   The most decided bent of
his intellect was towards the exegetical interpretation of Holy Writ.   His fervent love of Judaism
and its ancient scriptures, his profound knowledge
of Hebrew, which was the language of his heart,
and finally his delicate æsthetic feeling for philology,
were all displayed in his exegetical work.   Early in
life Sachs conceived the idea, to which he ever remained true, of restoring to the Hebrew Scriptures
their pure and original sense, and freeing them
from all accretions and blemishes.   Inspired by the
example of Rückert, " the poet of the East and West,

the learned master in translation and exposition," he commenced with the Psalms, which might have been the outpourings of his own pious heart. Afterwards, assisted by various fellow-workers, Sachs translated several books of Holy Scripture in an admirable style to form a "Bible for Israelites." But as he worked more with his heart than his brain, his biblical exegesis was wanting in a firm basis. The task of opening up new paths in this direction fell to the lot of Christian scholars.

Sachs took an active part in excavating the buried figures of the Jewish past, cleansing them from disfiguring incrustations, and placing them in their proper light. Three periodicals were particularly devoted to this purpose—the "Kerem Chemed" and the "Zion" in Hebrew, and the "Orient" in German. Young and old assisted in erecting a Jewish temple of fame, and contributions flowed in from all parts of Europe. The "forties" were especially prolific in the cultivation of Jewish science. It was not pedantic scholarship, but their heart that urged Jewish authors to bring forward clear proof that Judaism, in all its ramifications, went hand in hand with civilization. The Judæo-Spanish epoch exercised special attraction upon Jewish inquirers. It showed what the Jews had accomplished, and could accomplish in wealth of thought and beauty of form. Jewish science at the same time was to serve as an apology to the detractors of Jews and Judaism, and as an ideal for arousing emulation. The brilliant Spanish epoch was known to Jewish scholars alone, and to them only in rough fragments. Sachs undertook to reconstruct from these fragments an organic, beautiful whole, and by his eloquent language to attract those who had no religious interest in the subject. His "Religious Poetry of the Jews in Spain" (1845) offers more than the title indicates. Sachs attractively describes the series of the products of Jewish genius, from the time "when in terrible agony the limbs were torn from the living body," after the destruction of the Jewish center by the Romans, until the flourishing period of neo-Hebraic poetry in Spain. The attention of the cultured world was directed by Sachs' work to the wealth and beauty of Jewish literature in the Middle Ages, of which hitherto it had had no suspicion; even Heine was seized with admiration, and employed his golden pen in its cause.

At the same time the literature of the mediæval Jews in France and Germany, and of the Jewish poets of Provence was treated with copious detail, but in a style fitted for a learned audience. Zunz, the author of this work, justly rebuked his contemporaries for their contemptuous neglect of this branch of literature, to which Christian students of the sixteenth and seventeenth centuries had devoted so much attention.

Continuous devotion to the literature of the Middle Ages threatened to become too one-sided. That epoch, with its productions, was after all only the offspring of the national activity of bygone days, and the grandchild or great-grandchild of a still more important period. This obscure question, the dual origin of Judaism, from the Bible and the Talmud, was clearly illumined by the light of investigation through Jewish science in the "forties." The Talmud lay under a ban, and was treated with most offensive contempt. It was the scapegoat upon which all the guilt and misery of the Jews were laid. Like a leper it was shunned by respectable investigators. But this did not last; the question was raised whether the very writings which had served as the basis for Christianity had not been interpenetrated with Talmudic elements. The proof of the affirmative answer to this question was boldly undertaken by Frankel. Yet more important was the fact that it was made apparent that the strong side of the Talmud lies in its ideas of justice and their development. The superiority of the Talmudic penal code over the legislation of ancient times was established. The result of a scientific treatment of the Talmud was that Judaism had no cause to be ashamed of it.

But Judaism, together with its followers, remained an undecipherable hieroglyphic, a dark mystery, which one century transmitted to the other unsolved, so long as the "original rock from which it had been hewn, the depths from which it had been hollowed" continued to be unknown. Only a thorough knowledge of its primary sources, its sacred scriptures, could supply the key to this riddle. Centuries had elapsed, and the solution was not yet found. After Holy Writ, the mother of two or three religions, had so long been deified by the masses that it was regarded as "the all in all," and its explanations of life, nature, and history had been eagerly accepted, it had fallen into contempt since the middle of the eighteenth century. It shared the fate of the Jewish race. The rationalistic school indeed paid a good deal of attention to Hebrew sources, but only with the intention of diminishing their value. Eichhorn, Gesenius, Von Bohlen, De Wette, and Tuch were filled with antipathy to the Jews, and were thereby hindered from arriving at a correct understanding of the Old Testament. The clericals Tholuck and Hengstenberg sought vainglory therein, and what they discovered they claimed for Christianity. In Jewish circles there were only three men who occupied themselves in a scientific manner with the exposition of the Scriptures, namely, Krochmal, Luzzatto, and Sachs; but they were timid, they feared pressing too close to the borders of Sinai. A man of childlike mind was the first to raise the veil, to comprehend the language of the Prophets and Psalmists, and to reveal the ancient history of the Jewish people in its true light. With the appearance of "The Prophets of the Old Testament," and "The History of the People of Israel" (1843-1847) by Heinrich Ewald, a new path was opened up for the comprehension of the Hebrew genius and people. The riddle so long obscured approached its solution by the discovery of the key.

"The nations of antiquity, the Babylonians, Indians, Egyptians, Phœnicians, Greeks, and Romans, each under favorable circumstances, pursued only one particular object, till at length they reached an eminence not attained by later generations. . . . . . . The people of Israel, on the other hand, from the beginning of its historical consciousness, has so clearly kept in view its ultimate goal, and so strongly striven to attain it, that it could not lose it from sight for any length of time, and after any momentary pause it pursued it only the more perseveringly. Its goal is perfect religion. . . . . . . The history of this ancient people is the history of true religion showing every stage of development up to perfection."

This new promising school has, as its fundamental idea, that the race which owed its origin to the seed of Abraham is actually and truly a "people of God," that has given the world truths of salvation in abundance. The unfolding of these truths is manifested in the course of the history and in the literature of the Israelites. It is certainly a grave error of this school, the first to unravel the artistic web, to imagine that the last page of the history of God's people was written eighteen centuries ago, and that since that period it has only led a shadowy existence. Great memories bring about resurrections, and what people has a grander or more brilliant past than the Jewish, or Israelite, or Hebrew people? But if this people is still to accomplish work in the world's history, its chains must be removed, not only those which weigh down the limbs, but also those which confine the mind. The nation had to be freed, only then was it possible to find out whether it would continue an independent existence, or whether it would succumb in the conflict of races.

Unexpectedly the hour of freedom for the European Jews dawned with the revolutions of February and March (1848) in Paris, Vienna, Berlin, in Italy, and other countries. An intoxicating desire for liberty came over the nations of Europe, more over-powering and marvelous even than the movement in 1830. With imperious demands the people confronted their princes and rulers. Among the demands was that of the emancipation of the Jews. In all popular assemblies and proclamations, the despised Jews of yesterday were admitted into the bond of "Liberty, Equality, and Fraternity." What the most sanguine had never ventured to hope for suddenly took place. Jews were elected into parliaments with a vote in the reconstruction of states. A member of the Prussian Landtag had expressed aversion to the idea that a Jew should one day sit beside him, and be able to vote. The following day it actually came to pass, for Riesser and Veit took their seats next to this very man, in order to consider the reconstruction of Germany, whilst Mannheimer, together with Meisels, a rabbi of the old school, clad in Polish garb, helped to reorganize Austria. An assembly of Protestant clergymen had declared that the conversion of a Christian to Judaism was a sign of insanity or idiocy, but within a short space of time, the laws were compelled to concede freedom even to that creed.

During the stormy years of the Revolution and those which followed, newly-established constitutions in Germany were plentiful as blackberries. When, however, the first panic of terror had passed away, and the privileges of nations had become greatly restricted, the emancipation of the Jews was nevertheless taken as a matter of course (even in such cases where a constitution had been forced upon the people), as though this unqualified "Vox populi vox dei" should not be in any way infringed.

It is probable that the partisans of the reaction, as also their rulers, did not intend to realize those paragraphs in the conditions, but the written words had unexpectedly worked like a magic rune. On England alone the storm-year had no effect. The disabilities imposed upon the Jews of that country were gradually put aside as occasion offered. Distinguished personages were elected as aldermen and sheriffs. But the last link in the chain, that of opposition to their admission into Parliament, had not yet been removed. When Baron Lionel de Rothschild was elected as representative of the City, in London, a Bill to confirm this election was repeatedly presented (in the years 1847-51), but after passing through the House of Commons with a majority, it was each time thrown out by the Peers. Although their opponents conceded that the Jews were worthy of admission to Parliament, they were excluded by the formulary of the prescribed oath, "on the true faith of a Christian." Great was the sensation created when David Salomons, after having filled the office of Alderman, and on being elected member for Greenwich, was daring enough to enter the House, and on three occasions to take part in the debates. For this conduct he was fined £1,500, being £500 for each breach of the law. The absurdity of such exclusion became the more striking, when the High Court of Appeal confirmed the heavy penalty (1852) as justifiable by law.

From that time the Liberal party determined to effect the abolition of the form of oath. As no prejudice prevailed in England against the descendants of the Patriarchs, but, on the contrary, a tendency existed in their favor, it was to be foreseen that this last limitation would also disappear. In fact, a few years later a resolution was passed in the House of Peers, that Jews should be admitted without taking the prescribed oath, and this vote was immediately approved by Queen Victoria (1858). Since that time several Jews have occupied the post of Lord Mayor, Baron Nathaniel M. de Rothschild has been created a Peer, and the late Sir George Jessel, Master of the Rolls.

Meanwhile Judaism has made marked progress in another direction. A home for Jewish science was founded in Breslau (1854). It was a matter of pressing necessity, although the want was not universally felt. The march of progress surprised Judaism before the needful measures for remodeling its religious life had been determined upon. Talmudical schools, even in Russia and Hungary, had collapsed for want of support. The rabbis were useless in this emergency. Some who adhered to the old forms found that the congregations no longer appreciated their importance; others who visited the universities chiefly studied Christian theology, but were at a loss how to acquire Jewish knowledge. This knowledge existed only in an embryonic state. There certainly were various learned periodicals, both in Hebrew and in modern tongues, which treated of Jewish scientific subjects, but these afforded only fragmentary information. The teachers of Judaism needed first of all to learn, what is Judaism? What justification is there for it in the new phase of the world's history? They did not know, and could only grope about blindly. They were required to teach, and had not yet acquired the rudiments of the subject. Their precious heritage, the Scriptures, was not sufficiently prized, and only a few specialists, Nachman Krochmal, Michael Sachs, and Samuel David Luzzatto, occupied themselves with this study, and even they threw light only upon certain points. Jewish theological students, unable to drink at the pure source of the word, listened to Christian exponents, and were led astray.

Jewish religious philosophy had still fewer representatives, viz., Solomon Steinheim and Solomon Munk. It is true that there existed a species of theological seminary (which was recognized by the state) for French-Jewish students in Metz, and for Italian-Jewish students in Padua, but the instruction given was not based on scientific principles. It was, therefore, an event of no mean importance when a noble donor, Jonas Frankel, determined to supply the necessary funds for establishing a Jewish theological college. Fortunately, the undertaking was organized by men who stood at the summit of scientific knowledge—Zachariah Frankel* (died 1875), Jacob Bernays (died 1882), and Emanuel Joel (died 1890). At first they were undecided as to the plan of study to be pursued, and as to the division of subjects, and the distinction to be made between the chief branches and subsidiary matters, and they realized the saying that "one learns by teaching." In a comparatively short space of time the chief posts in the more important communities in Germany, Austria, and Hungary were occupied by students from the Breslau College. So universally was the necessity recognized of having schools, that institutions for the study of Jewish theology were founded in Buda-Pesth, Berlin (two), Amsterdam, Cincinnati, and, in a modified form, in London.

There is no more striking example of the transformation effected in Judaism itself than by comparing the various institutions, even those conducted in the true orthodox spirit, with the Talmud Torah schools (Beth ha-Midrash) in the Russian, and some in the Hungarian communities. They contrast with each other both internally and externally like an architectural structure with a mud-hut.†

The occasional recurrence of persecutions against the Jews awakened a feeling of brotherhood unexampled in Jewish history since the separation of Israel from Judah. The chief impulse to this feeling arose from the action taken by Pope Pius IX.

---

* The author of this work was, together with Frankel, one of the original founders. (Note by the Author.)

† A Theological-Jewish Faculty, an offshoot of the University, and a Jewish Academy are still needed. (Note by the Author.)

A Christian servant living at Bologna with a Jewish family named Mortara secretly took a sick child to be baptized. Some years later this fact came under the cognizance of the priests. Thereupon the boy Mortara, then six years old, was carried away from his parents, by the officers of the papacy, and placed in a monastery (1858). All steps taken by the father to regain possession of his son were useless. Equally fruitless were the efforts of various governments and even of Emperor Napoleon III, who protested against this act as one likely to injure the papacy, if in the nineteenth century it countenanced so barbarous a proceeding as the abduction of a child. Pius IX at a former time had shown liberal tendencies, but he afterwards revived the narrow-minded course of action which prevailed in the Middle Ages, and even commanded the Roman Jews to be shut up within the dreary walls of the Ghetto. Against all representations Pius IX obstinately maintained his reply of "non-possumus." The boy Mortara was kept hidden away, and brought up in the ways of Catholicism; he eventually learned to curse his parents and his race. But the papacy reaped no advantage. The loss of Rome, or of the so-called Papal States, followed soon.

This event and similar acts of intolerance induced six noble young Frenchmen to establish a sort of brotherhood for bringing help to those of their co-religionists who were oppressed and suffering. By their united efforts they endeavored to ameliorate the condition of Jews who lived under intolerant rulers, and to spread the advantages of education amongst those in need of it. These men were Aristides Astruc, collaborator to the chief rabbi of Paris; Isidore Cohn, professor of the rabbinical college; Jules Caballo, engineer; Narcisse Léven, lawyer; Eugene Masuel, professor at the University of Paris; and Charles Netter, merchant, only two of whom (Astruc and Léven) are still living. They

founded an institution which bears the title of the
"Alliance Israélite Universelle" (1860), having as
its motto, "All Israelites are responsible the one
for the other." This institution met with a cordial
reception, and members joined from all parts of the
globe. The accessions continued to increase, especially after Adolf Crémieux became president, and
in 1873 the number of subscribers had attained the
high figure of 12,526.

In the United States, where in the year 1775-6, after
the War of Independence, the republican form of government was adopted, the equality of the Jews was
established as a matter of course. At first there
were only a few Jewish immigrants in New York
and Newport, but owing to the facilities offered to
all industrial pursuits and every species of commercial activity, the number of American Jews rapidly
increased. They also formed themselves into a
body for the protection of their less favored brethren,
under the title of the "Union of American Hebrew
Congregations." They earnestly desired to promote
the welfare of the Jewish communities, built numerous synagogues, and still continue to take a lively
interest in all that concerns their brethren in Europe.
In the year 1878 the Jewish-American population
numbered about 250,000 souls, and maintained 278
synagogues. In these places of worship the reform
ritual is chiefly followed. There being no communal
traditions to abolish, the changes which in Europe
could be brought about only after severe struggles,
were easily introduced. Even so radical a reform
as that of transferring the divine service from
the Sabbath to Sunday, which had been originated by the insignificant Reform Congregation in
Berlin, was copied in various American congregations. The warm sympathy displayed towards
Judaism and the Jews by the Americans is to be
highly commended, and to such sympathy the Union
owed its origin.

The English Jews, to whom the task of leading their brethren seems to have been allotted, were not backward in uniting for the promotion of the well-being of their race.   At the instigation of two excellent men, Abraham Benisch, editor of the "Jewish Chronicle" (died 1878), and Albert Löwy, one of the ministers of the Reform Congregation in London (whose unassuming character would be wounded were he to be praised according to his deserts), an institution was founded (1871) in connection with the Alliance Israélite, and was called the "Anglo-Jewish Association." Although the number of English Jews is comparatively small (about forty thousand in London and barely thirty thousand in other towns and the Colonies), yet the members of the Association number four thousand.   Active correspondence is maintained through its members between Australia, Canada, India, Gibraltar, and the parent body.

In Vienna, also, through the efforts of Joseph Wertheimer, Ignatz Kuranda, and Moritz Goldschmidt, an association was established under the name of the "Israelitische Allianz." Their main object was to work hand in hand with the "Alliance," but the primary task undertaken by them was to promote an improved condition of affairs amongst the Jews of Galicia.   The Jews living in this province of Austria, who number about one million, are for the greater part in the lowest stage of culture. Owing to poverty and the heavy labor required to cultivate so barren a soil, they hardly made further progress than enables them to learn their prayers. Even those who possess the necessary ability and leisure to acquire European culture are kept back by the perversions of Neo-Chassidism, which possesses many followers amongst them.   To raise them from their degraded condition is the praiseworthy object of the Viennese Alliance.   The Alliance counts about five thousand members.

This union amongst the flower of Judaism for common action, besides its civilizing tendency, has also a defensive purpose, for the prevention of detraction and degradation. It could not, however, have been foreseen at the outset, that so wide a scope would have been presented for the work undertaken.

After the Jews had been emancipated in Western Europe, as they were in America, they labored unceasingly at their own improvement, and could soon point out distinguished co-religionists in the highest ranks in every profession—crown lawyers, councilors of state, members of Parliament, musicians, authors, academicians, and in France even generals.

The Jews of Western Europe became so amalgamated with their surroundings, that timid minds began to fear that Israel might be submerged in the current. But suddenly they were confronted by a bitter enemy who endeavored to exclude and oust them from the positions to which they had attained. This enemy all but challenged them to recall their past, prove their own value in opposition to their detractors, and show that though they are a peculiar people, this peculiarity is as much an agent in the world's history, as a product of it. This enemy, the bitterest Anti-Semitism, the offspring of delusion and falsehood, robs rejuvenated Israel of its peace, plays an active part in the immediate present, and unfortunately cannot as yet be relegated to the domains of History.

THE END.

RETROSPECT.

THE history of a people has here been narrated, which, dating from primæval times, continues to possess all the vitality necessary for its continued existence. Having entered the arena of history more than three thousand years ago, it shows no desire to depart therefrom.

This people, then, is both old and young. In its features the traces of hoary age remain indelibly impressed; and yet these very features are fresh and youthful, as if they were but of recent development. A nation, a relic of ages immemorial, which has witnessed the rise and decay of the most ancient empires, and which still continues to hold its place in the present day, deserves, for this fact alone, the closest attention. It must be borne in mind that the subjects of this History—the Hebrews, Israelites, or Jews—did not spend their existence in seclusion and contemplative isolation. Far from it! During all epochs they were dragged along in the fierce whirl of passing events. They struggled much, and suffered severely. The life of the people during more than three thousand years received many shocks and injuries. It still bears the trace of its many wounds, while no one can deny its right to the crown of martyrdom; and nevertheless it lives to the present day! It has accomplished much useful work, a fact that is gainsaid by none except pessimists and malignant cavilers. Had it only succeeded in disillusioning the cultured portion of mankind from those deceptions of idolatry which end in moral and social corruption, it would deserve special attention for this alone; but it has rendered far greater services to the human race.

Whence came the high culture, on which the enlightened modern nations pride themselves? Surely they themselves have not originated it. They are simply the fortunate heirs of an ancient heritage, which they have turned to good account and have augmented.

There were but two nations of creative mind who originated this culture and raised humanity from the slough of barbarity and savagery. These two were the Hellenic and the Israelite people. There was no third race of coadjutors. The Romans, indeed, introduced and transmitted far-reaching social rules and a high degree of military science; but only when they had attained to a servile stage did they perform services comparable to those of the insect, which carries the fertilizing pollen to the receptive stigma. The Greeks and the Hebrews were the sole originators of a higher culture. If the modern Roman, German, and Sclavonic nations, both on this side and on the other side of the ocean, could be despoiled of what they received from the Greeks and the Israelites, they would be utterly destitute. This idea, however, is a mere fancy; the nations can no longer be deprived of what they once borrowed, and what has since then become welded into their very nature. The participation of the Greeks in the regeneration of civilized races is conceded without a dissenting voice and without a suspicion of envy. It is freely admitted that the Greeks scattered abroad the budding blossoms of art, and the ripe fruits of a higher intelligence; that they opened up the domain of the beautiful, and diffused the brightness of Olympic ideas. It is also acknowledged that their intellectual genius found its embodiment in their whole literature, and that from this literature and the surviving relics of their ideals in the fine arts, there still issues forth new life-giving energy. These classical Greeks are now long dead, and to the departed, after-comers are prone

to be just. Jaundiced malignity and hatred are
silent at the grave of the illustrious man; his merits
as enumerated there are, in fact, as a rule overrated.

Now this aspect differs in the case of the other
creative race. Just because of their continued
existence, the merits and moral attainments of the
Hebrews are not generally acknowledged, or are
subjected to cavil—their qualities are depreciated
under wrong designations, with the view of black-
ening their original character, or of denying altogether the efficacy of that character, and, although
candid thinkers admit that the Hebrews introduced
the monotheistic principle amongst the nations, and
a superior code of morality, yet there are but few
who appreciate the wide bearing of these admis-
sions. Even deep thinkers do not carefully consider how it came to pass that the one nation died
out notwithstanding its dominant master minds and
its rich talents, while the other nation, so often near
unto death, still continues to exist in the world of
man, and has even succeeded in regaining its pristine youthfulness. Notwithstanding the fascination
of the mythology of the Greeks, the loveliness of their
productions in art, and their vivifying wisdom, these
qualities proved of no avail in the troublous days
when the Macedonian phalanxes and the Roman
legions, instead of allowing them to behold the
joyous side of life, caused them to experience the
seamy side. Then they despaired of their bright
Olympus, and at best only retained sufficient courage
to resort to suicide. In misfortune a nation displays characteristics similar to those of the individual. The Greeks were not gifted with the power
of living down their evil fortune, or of remaining
true to themselves when dispossessed of their territories; and whether in a foreign country or in their
own land they lost their mental balance, and became
merged in the medley of barbaric nations. What
caused this total collapse? There was a potent

reason for the extinction of the Romans, the mightiest nation of the ancient world, and likewise a reason for the extinction of their various powerful predecessors, for all of them relied too much on the sword. Even among nations this law of retribution holds good, "He who relies on the sword becomes the prey of the sword." But how was it that the Greeks succumbed to an analogous fate? The answer is, that they had no decided and clearly defined mission. The Hebrew people, on the other hand, had to fulfill the life-task by which it was held together, and by which in direst misfortune it was comforted and preserved. A nation cognizant of its mission, becomes strong and consolidated, and forbears to spend its existence in futile dreaming and scheming. From a national standpoint it was the mission of the Israelites to work out their self-discipline, to overcome or regulate their selfish desires, to gain the full force of resignation, or, to use the words of the prophet, "to circumcise the heart." Abstinence, regarded from a religious standpoint, induced them to exercise self-restraint, and was combined with duties which sustained the health of body and soul. The history of humanity bears evidence to this. All the nations that polluted themselves by profligacy, and grew callous through violence, were doomed to destruction. Not so with the Israelite race. In the midst of a debauched and sinful world and amid vices with which, in its beginnings, the Jews were also infected, they yet freed themselves, they raised on high an exalted standard of moral purity, and thus formed a striking contrast to other nations.

The practical theory of life amongst ancient nations was intimately connected with their conception of the Divine; the one implied the other. Was their perverted morality the result of perverted theology, or its original cause? Whatever may have been the relationship between cause and effect, the injurious consequences remained the same. Polytheism, however poetically described, produces discord, passion, and hate. In a council of gods, there must be strife. Even when the objects of worship are of a dual nature, the result is an inimical contrast—one god of creation and one of destruction, one god of light and one of darkness. -The creative divinity is usually divided into two sexes, and is endowed with all the frailties of sex. Although it has been said that man formed his gods according to his own image, yet when theology was once systematized, morality was demanded from the worshipers of the gods, who nevertheless became as sinful as the images which they adored. The people of Israel proclaimed a God at one with Himself, and unchangeable; a holy God, who requires holiness from mankind, the Creator of heaven and earth, of light and darkness. He, though mighty and exalted, is yet near to humanity, especially protecting the poor and the oppressed, a jealous but not a vengeful God, to whom the moral conduct of man is not a matter of indifference, although he is a God of mercy, and regards all mankind with love as the work of His hands. To this God evil is an abomination, for He is a God of justice, a Father to the orphan, and a Defender of the widow. These words of world-wide import penetrated deep into the heart of man, and, at a later period, were the means of hurling the beautiful gods of the heathen into the dust.

The thought and desire that men should be equal before the law as before God, that the stranger should have equal rights with the native, also grew from the idea of man's resemblance to the divine image, and became established amongst the Israelites as a fundamental law of the state. This was the first recognition of the rights of man, for, among the nations of old, even the leaders of civilization never conceded that right which has now become an established rule. If a stranger, wrecked on a foreign shore, was no longer offered up as a sacrifice, as in the earliest times, he was nevertheless placed under exceptional laws, and only considered to be a degree higher than a slave. This harshness towards the stranger, to the disgrace of nations, actually survived the destruction of the ancient world.

Israel's dominant idea became of far-reaching importance in its ethical tendency. It is by no means a matter of indifference in the moral conduct of man, as regards both great and small things, whether the earth, the scene of action, is governed by one Power or by several mutually antagonistic forces. The one conception ensures unity and peace, the other unveils a picture of dissension and discord, and leads to barbarism. The likeness of man to God—in opposition to the blasphemous idea of God's likeness to man—and the train of thought arising from monotheism impresses man with self-respect and with a regard for his fellow-man. Thereby the life of even the humblest of men is placed under religious and moral protection.

Is the abandonment of the new-born infant by its parents a crime? Amongst the ancients, even amongst the Greeks, it was not so regarded. The mountains resounded with the wailings of female children, and the rivers bore along the corpses of the little creatures, whom their parents (finding it inconvenient to rear them) had cast into the depths of the streams without a pang or regret. The ancients felt no prick of conscience at sighs of a murdered infant, and still less would a tribunal of justice demur at such crime. To kill a slave was of no more consequence than to slay an animal in the chase. Why, then, do cultured persons now shudder at the idea of such misdeeds? Because the people of Israel proclaimed the law, "Thou shalt not kill, for in the image of God has man been created. Thou shalt not take even a young life, nor one whose existence is passed in servitude." It has been asserted that man's intellect has made giant strides, whilst his moral culture has remained far behind, or has progressed but little since primæval times. But it must be remembered that the barbarous state of man declined much later than his ignorance.

Slumbering conscience and a repugnance to crime was aroused only at a later period, and this awakening was due to the people of Israel. Still less did the ancient nations recognize chastity of conduct, for they were sunk in the depths of vice and unchastity. Whilst the nations were still at the pinnacle of their greatness the Jewish Sybilline poets repeatedly uttered warnings that the sinful nations would be given over to death, because of their unnatural vices, their atrocities, and perverted worship, and the abominations which had ensued in consequence.

But they only scoffed at the warning voice, continued to pursue their evil ways, and were destroyed. Their arts and their wisdom could not save them from death. This shows that the Israelite nation alone and solely effected the emancipation of man by proclaiming holiness of life, the equal rights of aliens and home-born, and all that is included in the term humanity. It is not superfluous to point out that the foundation-stone of culture, "Thou shalt love thy neighbor as thyself," was laid by this people. Who prayed that the poor might be raised from the dust; the suffering, the orphan, and the helpless from the dunghill? The Israelite people. Who declared that everlasting peace was the holy ideal of the future, "when one nation should no longer draw sword against the other, and should no longer learn the art of war"? Israel's prophets. That people has been called a wandering mystery, but it should rather be called a wandering revela-

tion.   It has revealed the secret of life, and the art
of all arts—how a nation may guard itself against
being given up to destruction.

This people cannot be charged with having introduced self-mortification, self-torture, and a gloomy
view of life, and as having thus paved the way for
that monkish asceticism which covers the brightness of life with the pall of death.   Quite the contrary ; all the nations of antiquity except the Israelites laid especial importance on death, made
immolations at the graves of the departed, and
gave themselves up to pious melancholy.   These
were the mysteries which, like all exaggerations,
passed to an opposite extreme, and ended in the
excesses of orgies.   The gods themselves did not
escape contact with death ; they had to make a
death-journey, and here and there might be seen
the grave, or the Calvary, of some god.   The
Israelite conception, which revered in God "the
source of life," places so much value on life, that it
seeks to banish from the circle of holiness all that
recalls death.   So little is thought of what lies
within and beyond the grave, that the Israelites
have been reproached with having indulged in the
enjoyments of life.   And this is true.

The prophets knew no higher ideal than that the
earth should be filled with the knowledge of God as
the sea covers its bed.   Life is highly prized, but it
must be a pure and holy life.   Only after a long
and unhappy course of history did a gloomy and
ascetic theory of life creep in, and produce a sad
and misanthropic order, which stamped out pure
gladness as a sin, and regarded the earth as a val-
ley of tears, and to this condition it actually became,
to some extent, reduced.

The Israelite people have nothing in common with
their kindred, who are called Semites, whether in
their self-torturing madness in honor of one god,
or in their dissipated excesses in honor of another

god. The Israelites were severed from the Semitic tribes by hard discipline, and they weaned themselves from the perversions of their alien kinsmen. It is likewise erroneous to endeavor sophistically to attribute the peculiarities of Israel to the Semitic character, or to consider the relationship of the two nations as that of two descendants from one stock. The Israelites and other Orientals, through divergent causes, are the result of a mixed union, and both have lost many traits of their inherited nature.

The Israelites decidedly have great faults; they have greatly erred, and have been severely punished for their shortcomings. History describes and reveals these errors, their origin, their eventful results, and the consequences which resulted from them. Many of these faults were acquired, and were to some extent the effect of their surroundings; but there were also peculiar and original features in the character of this people. Why should they be more perfect than all other nationalities, not one of which has ever attained to perfection in all directions?

Those who eagerly endeavor to show the failings and shortcomings of the Israelite people as through a magnifying glass unconsciously pay them high honor by making greater demands upon them than upon other nations. It is a decided defect on the part of the Israelites that they left behind neither colossal buildings nor architectural memorials. Possibly the race did not possess any talent for architecture; or perhaps, owing to its ideals of equality, the kings and warriors were not so highly esteemed that it was considered necessary to erect in their memory stupendous palaces, pyramids, or marble monuments. The hovels of the poor ranked higher. The Israelites did not even erect a temple to God (Solomon's Temple being built by the Phœnicians), for the heart was God's temple. The Israelites neither sculptured nor painted gods, for they did not consider the Deity a subject for pleasant pastime, but gave Him pious and earnest devotion. Nor did the Israelites excel in artistic epics, and still less in drama or comedy. This may have been a want in their idiosyncrasy, and is also connected with their strong distaste for mythological births and scandals. They evinced a similar dislike to all dramas, public games, and theatrical displays. However, in compensation, they had poetical conceptions which adequately reflect the ideals of life, as these are described in the Psalms and in the poetically fashioned eloquence of the prophets. Both possess this trait in common, that their fundamental quality is truth and not fiction, whereby poetry instead of being a mere toy and plaything for the imagination, became the instrument for attaining ethical culture.

Their literature, though it does not treat of the drama, is yet full of dramatic vigor; and, if not actually humorous, is nevertheless replete with irony, and from its ideal pedestal proudly contemplates all delusions. The Israelite prophets and psalmists, whilst developing a beautiful poetic form, never sacrificed the truth of the subject for the sake of style. The Israelites also introduced a historical style of their own, which pictured events according to the canons of truth, and without any endeavor to excuse or hide the shortcomings of heroes, kings, or nations. This peculiar Hebrew literature, of which no other nation on earth can show the like (at best only an imitation), through its excellence has achieved many moral conquests. The nations capable of culture could not withstand the warmth and truth which pervade these writings. If Greek literature elevated the dominion of art and its perceptions, Hebrew literature idealized the domain of holiness and morality. The history of a nation which has achieved so much has a decided right to full appreciation.

Judged superficially, the course of history from

the entry of the Israelites into Canaan until far into the times of the kings may easily give rise to misconception, for the most striking events seem to bear a political character. Invasions, battles, and conquests, occupy the foreground of history. We behold on the scene leaders of nations, heroes, kings, and generals, treaties are made and broken, whilst the prevailing intellectual activity is hardly perceptible in the background. The hero-judges who first form the subjects of history—Ehud, Gideon, his son Abimelech, and especially Jephthah and Samson—evince so few of the national characteristics that they might equally well pass for Canaanites, Philistines, or Moabites. Of Samson it has been asserted that he is cast in the mould of the Syrian Hercules. Most of the kings, and also their sons and courtiers, acted as arbitrarily as if there had been no code of law to set limits to their despotic will, and as if they had never even heard of the Ten Commandments of Sinai.

For centuries the people wore the bonds of wild idolatry, and differed only in a slight degree from the heathen world which surrounded it. Was the race in its beginnings actually of no importance? Did the people for a considerable time keep pace with its Semitic kinsmen, and only at a given period become stamped with those peculiarities which caused it to contrast so strongly with its neighbors? Did not Sinai illumine its very cradle? or was this fact stated to have been the case only in after-days and by historians? Sceptics have said as much, but the fragments of Israelite poetry, dating from primæval times, give the lie to this assertion. Several centuries before the inception of kingly rule, and in the first days of the hero-judges, in the days of Deborah, "the mother in Israel," a poet sang of the marvels of the revelation; at Sinai he described the people of God as contrasting strikingly with their environment, and ascribed their lapses to the fact that they had followed "false gods," and thereby fallen away from their widely different origin. Even if one were inclined to doubt the veracity of history, yet credence must be given to poetry as a trustworthy eye-witness. It is not to be denied, that the spiritual birth of the Israelite people was simultaneous with their actual birth, and that Sinai was the scene of the one event, as Egypt was of the other; and that the Ark of the Covenant with the sacred Ten Commandments was its faithful attendant from the earliest days.

The nucleus of the people's faith in God and in their mission, the fundamental doctrine graven on the tablets of stone, were of hoary antiquity, coeval with their representatives. Men especially chosen, and having no connection with the work-a-day actions and turmoil of the people, like the Cherubim at Shiloh, were to shield the sanctuary. This sanctuary only apparently bears a religious stamp, is only apparently theocratic, but its essence is contained in the laws of morality. God is the origin of the doctrine, but not its end, which lies rather in individual and communal life and its legitimate demands

In this law God is the Holy Will, determining whatever is ethical and good. He is the sacred Type which indicates the way, but not the cause for which actions are to be performed, in order that some definite advantage may accrue. The Israelite creed is, therefore, by no means a dogmatic doctrine, but one of duty. Though a law of deliverance, it has no mystic admixture. But this religion or law of redemption was certainly beyond the comprehension of the people while yet in its infantine stage, and the ideal which was intended to endow it with significance and vitality remained for a long time an enigma to the people. This enigma was first solved by the prophets. A considerable period elapsed even after the prophets had spoken their burning words of fire, before the nation became the guardian of the teachings heard at Sinai, and before they erected a temple for it in their own hearts.

But as soon as this maturity was attained, and the "heart of stone had become a heart of flesh," as soon as the prophetic body were able to dispense with the intervention of the priesthood, they could depart from the scene; they had become super-fluous, for the nation itself had attained to a complete comprehension of its own being and its own mission. History shows how this twofold transformation was effected; how the family of a petty sheik became the nucleus of a people; how this small people was humiliated to the condition of a horde; how this horde was trained to become a nation of God through the law of self-sanctification and self-control; and how these teachings, together with a spiritual ideal of God, became breathed into it as its soul.

This national soul likewise grew into the national body, was developed and took the form of laws, which, though they were not subjected to the fluctuations of time, were yet suited to the occurrences of the age. The transformation was effected only amidst severe struggles; obstacles from within and without had to be overcome, and errors and relapses to be amended, before the nation's body could become a fitting organ for the nation's soul. The hidden things had to be revealed, the obscure to be illumined, vague notions to be brought into the light of certainty, before that ideal Israel (as foreshadowed by the prophets in the far distance of time, and which had been expressly distinguished by them from Israel as it then existed with all its defects) might become a "light unto the nations." Assuredly, there is no second people now dwelling upon the globe, or hidden within the stream of time, which, like Israel, has carried with it a pre-ordained law. This people not alone possessed such a law, but also the full conviction that it existed only on account of this law, and in order to be the exponent of this law, and that its sole importance lay in its vocation to announce the truths of salvation. These were to be inculcated not by violence and compulsion, but by example, by action, and by the realization of those ideals which as a people the Israelites were to proclaim.

The profound insight afforded by History has proved that it was the mission of the Greeks to bring to light the ideals of art and science, but the Greeks themselves had no knowledge of this fact.

It was otherwise with the Israelites. Not only was their task apportioned to them, but the revelation was made to them that it was their task, and that without it they were of no more significance than "a drop in the pitcher, or a mote of dust in the balance." Only on this account did the men of God call the Israelites a chosen people. The fact of being chosen imposed on the nation heavier and more important responsibilities, and a greater measure of duty; and when their mission, as the exponents of a special and religious moral conception, became clear to them, the people prized their task beyond all things—more highly than their fatherland and nationality, and even more than life itself. And because they sacrificed themselves, the idea which dominated them attained to enduring existence and to immortality.

The Israelites were the first people who possessed the courage of their own opinions, and who risked all worldly goods for their convictions. They proved that a propaganda-making truth can be sealed only by the blood of its martyrs. The loyalty of their convictions endowed them with steadfastness and endurance. Their inner core cannot have been utterly corrupt, seeing that they were enabled to bid defiance to the destructive force of

nearly four thousand years, and to a host of enemies. The history of the Israelite nation in its
beginnings is of a decidedly changeful character.
Two distinct factors determined its elevation and
decadence, one physical, the other spiritual, one
political, the other ethical. Suddenly, there gushed
forth a spiritual current, strong and foaming like
the mountain spring which has been gradually
gathering whilst hidden from sight, and the existence of which commenced only at the moment when
it issued from its rocky bed.

The appearance of gifted prophets and psalmists
from the days of Amos and Isaiah resembles, in its
force and fertilizing power, the outpouring of a
mountain spring. The prophets and psalmists who
sowed the seed of great and ever true thoughts in
a charming and attractive form, and who constitute
the flower of the Israelite people, could not have
arisen and carried out all that they actually
effected, unless the previous conditions had been
favorable to their purpose. They arose because
the soil had been spiritually fertilized for them,
and they were understood only because their
exalted moral theories of life did not announce anything novel or strange to the people, but they
preached what was already well known, in impassioned and poetically illumined words, and were
impelled by self-abnegation, zeal, and manly
courage.

Even those who do not believe in wonders must
admit and admire the marvelous course of Israel's
history. Is it not marvelous that just during the
untoward conditions of the Babylonian exile, in a
country "full of idols and license," and amongst a
Judæan nobility who, untaught and unconverted by
their . sad experience, continued their evil ways
during exile—that amid such surroundings a spiritual movement could be developed which found vent
in a peculiarly characteristic manner? During the

Babylonian exile the psalmists bewailed in touching
strains, and with poetic brilliance, their own sorrows
and the national misfortunes, and these strains
resound even to-day in the high-places of worship.
During this exile that magnificent didactic poem
in semi-dramatic form between the suffering Job and
his friends was composed, a poem consisting in
dialogues on human destiny and Divine Providence,
which is almost unrivaled. During this exile the
prophets once more addressed their deaf and blind
community in poetic strains. Amongst them was
that divinely-favored man, the second Isaiah, who
was called the "great unknown." His words of fire
pour forth with inimitable power, chastising like a
father, yet comforting like a mother, wounding as
with a lash, yet healing as with balm. This prophet
fully established the fundamental idea for the justification of Israel's continued existence, that, by its
submission of martyrdom, it is destined to be the
servant of God, to become a light to all nations, and
to carry salvation to the ends of the earth. Is it less
marvelous that Cyrus accorded to the Babylonian
exiles the permission to return to their native land,
to cultivate the deserted country, to rebuild Jerusalem and the Temple in honor of their God, and
again to enjoy a certain amount of independence?
Still more wonderful is it that prophets had predicted with unqualified certainty the regeneration of
the nation in a single day, and that the exodus from
Egypt would be succeeded by an exodus from
Babylon. Even their prophecy that the heathen
would join the Judæan people was fulfilled. Thus
the Judæan nationality became resuscitated in their
own land, the people became filled with ancient rec-
ollections and new hopes, and were determined to
realize the exhortations of the prophets. The people preserved their independence in their own
country during six hundred years. The proneness
to idolatry, which, to a great extent, had been found

irresistible in the pre-exilic period, suddenly disappeared, and with it also pagan customs and vices. The Torah, as the law book, was to become the guiding-line of the regenerated nation, whose "heart of stone had been changed into a heart of flesh," and not only of the individual but of the whole community. By periodically reading the Torah in the Synagogue—a custom which was now introduced—and by explaining it at least in one of the school-houses, its teachings became the common property of the higher classes. The Torah was the "Magna Charta" of public life in the same way as the Judæan community developed into a species of "Civitas Dei."

The prophets could now withdraw, for the law-givers—Pharisees (Soferim)—relieved them of their duties, and created a Synhedrion, which also possessed a legislative function. Thus post-exilic history received a form entirely different to that of pre-exilic times. The tribunal of the Synhedrion was filled with painful anxiety as to the rigid execution of pentateuchal ordinances. The teachers of the people desired to avoid the repetition of pre-exilic conditions, of idolatry, intercourse with the heathen, and the imitation of pagan customs. Entire separation from the heathen world and total isolation were the consequences. A similar state of things was also maintained against the Samaritans, who defiantly sought to obtain equal rights of citizenship in the "Civitas Dei." This was denied to them. As, however, they would not be prevented from worshiping the God of Israel, they erected a rival temple on Mount Gerizim. Thus there arose the first semi-Judæan sect, that of the Samaritans, who assumed an inimical bearing towards Jerusalem. This was one result of over-punctiliousness. The other consequence was the result of the maxim, "Make a fence round the law." Thereby everything which had formerly been permissible, and which only touched on the fringe of what was forbidden, was interdicted. The members of the Synhedrion, or authorized teachers of the law, on the ground of this maxim, added fresh decisions to the pentateuchal laws. These new sopheric laws, and the prevailing punctiliousness, did not prevent the establishment of Jewish colonies in Alexandria, Antioch, and other Greek centers which had been founded by Alexander of Macedon and his successors. The Jewish colony in Egypt built a special Temple, that of Onias, which rivaled the sanctuary at Jerusalem. There the law was first translated into Greek, and in this language it was read in all Greek-speaking countries. This was a turning-point in the course of Jewish history, although, owing to the practice of reading the law in Greek, public mourning was instituted in Jerusalem. Judaism from this cause became, to some extent, more closely approximated to the pagan world, and the accession of nations into the community of Abraham was promoted. On the other hand, the Hellenizing of Judaism brought the nation close upon the verge of destruction, and exposed it to the persecution of Antiochus Epiphanes, and also to apostasy. From these troubles it was only delivered through the revolt of the Maccabees, whose rising was the cause of many martyrdoms.

These victories were followed by a retrograde movement. The laws which the Hellenist apostates had daringly broken, and on account of which so many martyrs had fallen, even those laws which had been superadded as a fence, were henceforth yet more zealously and scrupulously practiced. Judaism assumed an altered Pharisaic (*i. e.*, punctilious) character. For a portion of the people, the over-scrupulous (Assidæans), even this was not sufficient. They imagined that only by retirement from the world could the laws be strictly followed, and therefore, under the designation of Essenes, they separated from the rest, and followed their particular mode of thought and peculiar observances. The more worldly, such as the warriors and statesmen, offered sharp opposition to such asceticism, and rejected the additional ordinances which were not justified by the letter of the law. Hence arose the division into Pharisees, Essenes, and Sadducees, which was one of the results of the Maccabæan war. Internal dissensions ensued, and facilitated the subjugation of Judæa by Pompey and the Roman legions, and the political independence of the Judæans under their own king, which had been maintained during a century, now came to an end.

Unfortunately, the Romans appointed their protégé, Herod, to be king, and he instilled his venomous ideas into the hearts of the Patriarchs. In order, to some extent, to shield the populace from the alienation desired by the Herodians, the exclusive laws, more particularly the ritual ordinances, were made more stringent. This was the work of Hillel and Shammai. Further, fanatical zeal was displayed in commemorating the liberty which had been disgracefully forfeited; this was the work of the founder of the zealot party—Judah of Galilee—with whom the Shammaites were to some extent connected. The zealots incited the whole nation to wage fierce war against the Roman conquerors of the world, but their attempt ended in the destruction of the community and of Jerusalem, and the greatly-revered Temple was laid waste. It is, however, a marvelous fact that the nationality and the religion did not perish, but survived the destroyers, Vespasian, Titus, and their successors, as they had survived Nebuchadnezzar and his dynasty. The populace was rescued through the law, which had become its very soul. The Synhedrial school-house now became the center, but the law had totally changed in aspect.

Masses of new religious enactments now overlaid the law; fences, Synhedrial enactments, customs

dating from more ancient or from recent times,
which had been orally delivered, and had accumulated to an immense extent. These oral Halachas,
as they were termed, ranked, if not higher than,
certainly equal with, the written laws.

The Sadducæan opposition to these laws had
ceased; young Christendom, which had sprung
from the lap of Judaism, or, to speak more correctly, from Essenism, enhanced the value of the
highly-prized and overrated laws, and was indifferent to their origin. In contradistinction to the Judæo-
Christians, who thought that they could merge the
old laws with the new faith, the apostle Paul created
the Pagan-Christian idea, which rejected every prescription of the law as entrammeling, and proclaimed
evangelical liberty. This attack on the law, and the
mystic formulas evolved by the Gnostics from the
letters of Holy Writ, caused all that bordered upon
religious precepts to become more precious and to
be more rigidly observed in Judæan circles.

The transmission of Halachic doctrines had been
endangered by the divergence of opinion between
the disciples of Hillel and of Shammai regarding their
scope, limits, justification, and applicability, and in
consequence of the fatal termination of the disastrous war. Those teachers of the law who had survived the catastrophe were the more eager to hand
down such laws, which they claimed to have transmitted faithfully, and to rescue them from oblivion.
Youths and men, now rid of political cares, thronged
to the celebrated colleges in order to impress on
their memories the traditions handed down to them.
They vied with each other in teaching and learning.
But this eagerness did not crush out zealotism and
a desire to take up arms in the cause of freedom.
Fiery youths, especially the disciples of the school
of Akiba, quitted the school-house in order at an
opportune moment to carry on a bloody feud with
the Roman legions—in the first instance this

occurred under Trajan, scarcely half a century after the fall of Jerusalem, and again two decades later under Hadrian. These attempts ended disastrously; Hadrian instituted a system of persecution directed more against Judaism than against the Judæans, and especially against teachers and disciples, in the hope of destroying the Law, the very soul of the nationality, but he did not succeed in his object. The fiery zeal for the traditional law was increased through the activity of Akiba's disciples, who had returned from exile.

The center was, however, transferred to Galilee, as Judæa, the southern portion of the country, had been laid waste, and was chiefly in the possession of pagan colonists. Here was situated the Patriarchate which represented the unity of the people, the post of Patriarch being occupied by a descendant of Hillel, who, as it was alleged, came from the royal house of David, and who, from the tiny territory of Galilee, from Sepphoris and Tiberias, governed the numerous communities of the Diaspora—beyond the land and the sea, in Egypt, Babylon, Asia Minor, and Europe. His encyclicals, which were sent by special messengers, were greeted with respect, and were obeyed like those of a spiritual chief. The Mishnah, the fundamental text of the voluminous Talmud, a collection of Halachic laws, and species of "corpus juris civilis canonici," which was compiled by the Patriarch Judah I, owed its universal recognition to that cause. This spiritual greatness, however, was destroyed through Byzantium, from the time that the Roman Empire worshiped, or was compelled to worship, Jesus instead of Jupiter, and the fanatical persecution practiced mutually amongst the Christian sects was visited upon the Jews.

The Byzantine emperors, Constantine, Theodosius II, and Justinian, treated the sons of Jacob even more mercilessly than their heathen enemies. They deprived them of their Roman rights of citizenship, of their rights as men, and also encroached upon their freedom in religious practices. This example was followed by the rulers in various European countries, more especially in France and Spain.

Fortunately, there had been formed a new center in another quarter, on the banks of the Euphrates and Tigris, where numerous Judæan communities occupied a favorable position, and lived almost in a state of political independence, under their own Judæan prince, the Exilarch. The schools which were here established replaced those which had been destroyed in the Holy Land. These schools exercised authority over the entire Jewish community, with but few interruptions, during seven hundred years. Here there arose the Babylonian Talmud, which was more fortunate than its companion-work, the Palestinian or Jerusalem Talmud, a religious code of a peculiar kind. This work with its phases of light and shade exercised an influence in Jewish circles (which continues to the present day), and it almost over-shadowed Holy Writ. Here also Talmudical dialectics became developed, and endowed the Jews who stood beneath the spell of the Talmud with peculiar characteristics, especially imbuing them with that love of hair-splitting which afterwards deteriorated into sophistic subtlety. The authority of the Talmud, however, was to some extent lessened through events which occurred on the Arabian Peninsula. Mahomet, the son of Abdallah, from Mecca, had established the Islamite religion on the basis of various fragments of Judaism. The Arabs at first lived on friendly terms with the Judæans who dwelt in their land, and who were warlike, lovers of freedom and of song, and superior to the Arabs by reason of their possession of Holy Writ. Mahomet, however, having been derided by them, afterwards waged war against one Judæan tribe after another, and exiled them from

Arabia, which proscription was upheld by Caliph Omar.

The exiles settled in Palestine and Babylon, where they became acquainted with tribesmen and co-religionists, who, having followed the Talmudical precepts, had acquired totally different habits. They found the Talmudical restrictions incompatible with their hereditary and unquenched thirst for liberty. This Judæo-Arabic circle declared war against Talmudism. The contest, which in the first instance was only of a mild character, the needful ability to sustain it being wanting, afterwards became fiercer, when Anan, a connection of the Prince of Captivity, eagerly joined in the fray, asserting Holy Writ to be the sole source of religion, and the Talmud to be only the work of man.

Thus arose a new sect, the Ananites, or Karaites. Although small in numbers, yet by their energy and combativeness they aroused the less active minds, and stimulated the desire for a knowledge of Holy Writ, which had hitherto fallen into neglect. The impulse given to this study was so powerful that Saadiah, the representative of a Talmudical school, devoted his entire attention to it. Through him a philosophical tendency was introduced into Judæan circles. Until this time, as in Christendom and Islam, a belief in existing authorities had caused it to be considered heretical to speculate upon religion.

From Babylon there now emanated a spark of rational thought and scientific inquiry, which traveled as far as the Pyrenean Peninsula. This territory, being under Mahometan rule, was connected in spirit with the East. A long succession of eminent personages had during two centuries fostered and cultivated a spirit of deep research in Spain, whilst in Christendom a fanatical desire for persecution resulted in the destruction of the Jews, or in their banishment from the homes which they had possessed for so long a time. The culminating point of philosophical thought was attained by Moses Maimuni, who for centuries was " the Guide of the Perplexed," and who also, under the sanction of the Church, exercised a powerful influence on Dominican scholasticism. Where there is great light there must also be much shadow. The shadows caused by the light which had proceeded from Maimuni became embodied in the vagaries of the Kabbala, which confused the minds of the multitude by its forgeries, and corrupted the feelings by its excesses.

A deep gulf was created in Spain and Southern France between the Maimunists and anti-Mai-munists, between faith based upon intellectuality, and faith based upon authority. This schism would have given rise to sectarianism, had not the accu-mulated sufferings of the people riveted their atten-tion on what was proximate—the misery of all. Faith in authority proved victorious, under the influence of the Kabbala, and every scientific pursuit, excepting that of medicine, was proscribed in Spain, as if it were intended to undermine the continuance of Judaism. The fourteenth century ignored the tenth century. Solomon ben Adret, who had solemnly pronounced an interdict against philosophy, ranked Saadiah as to some extent a heretic. It seemed as if, with the decay of knowledge, the glory of the Spanish Jews were to be entirely extinguished.

The cup of sorrow, drained by the Jews through-out Central Europe—from the Rhine to the Vistula, and from the Alps to the marsh-lands of the Ger-man Ocean—in consequence of the Black Death, as if they had indeed been poisoners, also reached the Spanish Jews. Their grandees, who had been employed at the court as ministers of finance, diplo-matists, private secretaries, or court physicians, were powerless to protect them, as they had form-erly done.

The horrible massacre in 1391 had driven many Jews, with wild despair in their hearts, into the arms of the Church, and they deceived themselves with the idea that they could outwardly join the Church, whilst remaining inwardly faithful to the God of Israel.

Thus arose the Marranos. Their fanatical persecutors, however, knew no peace until they had succeeded in arousing the thunders of the Inquisition against the Jews, in lighting the stake, in causing them to be banished from Spain by hundreds of thousands, and in enforcing compulsory baptism in Portugal. But the Inquisition and the stake in both of these countries only awoke a deeper love for Judaism in the hearts of the Marranos. Great as was the number of those who perished at the autos-da-fé, or who pined away in prison, yet their offspring, who secretly continued to cherish their own faith at the risk of their lives, after one or two centuries sought to escape from the hell on the Pyrenean Peninsula.

Under the guise of Spanish or Portuguese merchants, they founded large communities in Bordeaux, Amsterdam, London, and in various parts of Italy. From their step-fatherland they brought with them a higher culture and an aristocratic demeanor. Consequently they did not suffer from the contempt with which other Jews were treated in political and social circles. In fact, the Jews of Marrano descent looked down upon their co-religionists as gypsies, on account of their external deterioration. With marvelous rapidity, however, did those who were considered as gypsies regenerate and elevate themselves ; and, what was more marvelous, this change did not proceed from the aristocratic Sephardim. The personage to whom this transformation was due sprang from the midst of those who were so despised and contemned. He bore no trace of culture in his youth, but was deformed, awkward, and shy—this was Moses Mendelssohn, from the petty community of Dessau. Had the call reached him to become the leader of his co-religionists, he would have replied, like the great Prophet in Egypt —"Who am I?" It is remarkable that Mendelssohn, without desiring or intending to do so, paved the way for the emancipation of the Jews and the purification of Judaism. The present age has given the lie to the assertion of Jew-haters (who at the close of the eighteenth century and commencement of the nineteenth century were numberless), that generation after generation must pass away before any improvement could be expected in the debased condition of the Jews.

In two decades there appeared on the canvas of History a series of noble, if not of ennobled Jews, in Germany, France, Holland, and Italy, and these ranked as high as if they had been of equal birth with Christians of the aristocratic class.

The historic course of the Israelite nation not only shows, as with other nations, the stages of growth, bloom, and decay, but it exhibits the extraordinary phenomenon that the decay was succeeded, on three different occasions, by a new budding and blossoming time. The history of the crystallization of the Israelite family group into a nation, and their entry into the land of Canaan, until the establishment of a kingdom, constitutes the growth. The stage of bloom was in the days of the kings David and Solomon, who raised the condition of the Israelite people to that of a state of the first rank. The period of blossoming was short, and was followed by loss of power and by the downfall of the nationality. But again it gradually revived under the rule of the Persians and Greeks, developed under the Maccabees, only to decay away under the Romans. This decay, however, was merely superficial, and was destined to give place to a resuscitation in another form.

One of the prophets has represented the growth of the Israelite nation in Egypt by the picture of a deserted female child left lying in the fields, begrimed with blood and filth, but who, notwithstanding her desertion and misery, develops into a blooming maiden. The development of the race in Babylon is described by another prophet under the image of an unhappy and sorrowing widow, who has been robbed of her children, until, on the unexpected return of her numerous offspring from all ends and corners of the earth, she is comforted, and regains her lost youth with them. For the third rejuvenescence of the Jewish race tradition has likewise found a fitting picture.

At the gates of Rome there lies a human form, clothed in rags, leprous, half dead, an object of horror and pity. Suddenly this abject figure is touched with a staff, on which biblical sentences are inscribed. He rises, his hideous coverings and disfigurements vanish, and he stands erect in the beautiful glow of youth. Similes are but lame, and give no adequate representation of a phenomenon to which there is no equal in every-day existence. In any case, the Jewish nation is an extraordinary phenomenon, dating as it does from hoary antiquity, but possessing youthful vigor, having passed through numberless vicissitudes, yet remaining ever true to itself.

INDEX.